Lecture Notes of the Institute for Computer Sciences, Social Informatics and Telecommunications Engineering 263

More information about this series at http://www.springer.com/series/8197

Victor Sucasas · Georgios Mantas
Saud Althunibat (Eds.)

Broadband Communications, Networks, and Systems

9th International EAI Conference, Broadnets 2018
Faro, Portugal, September 19–20, 2018
Proceedings

 Springer

Editors
Victor Sucasas (iD)
Instituto de Telecomunicações
Lisboa, Portugal

Georgios Mantas (iD)
Instituto de Telecomunicações
Lisboa, Portugal

Saud Althunibat (iD)
Communications Engineering
Al-Hussein Bin Talal University
Ma'an, Jordan

ISSN 1867-8211   ISSN 1867-822X (electronic)
Lecture Notes of the Institute for Computer Sciences, Social Informatics
and Telecommunications Engineering
ISBN 978-3-030-05194-5   ISBN 978-3-030-05195-2 (eBook)
https://doi.org/10.1007/978-3-030-05195-2

Library of Congress Control Number: 2018963823

This Springer imprint is published by the registered company Springer Nature Switzerland AG
The registered company address is: Gewerbestrasse 11, 6330 Cham, Switzerland

Preface

We are delighted to introduce the proceedings of the ninth edition of the 2018 European Alliance for Innovation (EAI) International Conference on Broadband Communications, Networks, and Systems (BROADNETs). This conference brought together researchers, developers, and practitioners from around the world who are leveraging and developing 5G services and IoT applications. The theme of BROADNETs 2018 was "5G Technologies, Applications and Services for the Internet of Everything (IoE)."

The technical program of BROADNETs 2018 consisted of 33 full papers in the main track and 15 workshop papers. The conference included three invited papers in oral presentation sessions at the main conference tracks. The conference sessions in the main track were: Session 1 – Advanced Techniques for IoT and WSNs; Session 2 – SDN and Network Virtualization; Session 3 – eHealth and Telemedicine Mobile Applications; Session 4 – Security and Privacy Preservation; Session 5 – Communication Reliability and Protocols; Session 6 – Spatial Modulation Techniques; Session 7 – Hardware Implementation and Antenna design. Aside from the high-quality technical paper presentations, the technical program also featured three keynote speeches. The three keynote speakers were Prof. Raed Mesleh from German Jordanian University, Jordan, Dr. Constantinos Papadias from Athens Information Technology, Greece, and Prof. Frank Fitzek from Technische Universitat Dresden. The workshop organized was the First ITN-SECRET Workshop on Energy-Efficient Next-Generation Mobile Small Cell Networks. The SECRET workshop aimed to address the new directions and novel applications of network coding on mobile small cells, covering different perspectives such as security, communication reliability, energy efficiency, in addition of innovative design of RF components including antennas and power amplifiers.

Coordination with the steering chairs, Imrich Chlamtac, Krishna Sivalingam, Y. Thomas Hou, and Ioannis Tomkos, was essential for the success of the conference. We sincerely appreciate their constant support and guidance. It was also a great pleasure to work with such an excellent Organizing Committee team for their hard work in organizing and supporting the conference. In particular, the Technical Program Committee, led by our TPC co-chairs, Prof. Noelia Correia, Prof. Jonathan Rodriguez, and Prof. Jose-Fernán Martínez, who completed the peer review of the technical papers and made a high-quality technical program. We are also grateful to conference manager, Radka Pincakova, the local chair, Claudia Barbosa, and the workshop chair, Dr. Ayman Radwan, for their support, and all the authors who submitted their papers to the BROADNETs 2018 conference and workshop.

We strongly believe that BROADNETs 2018 provided a good forum for all researchers, developers, and practitioners to discuss all science and technology aspects that are relevant to 5G services and IoT applications. We also expect that the future BROADNETs editions will be as successful and stimulating, as indicated by the contributions presented in this volume.

November 2018   Victor Sucasas
                                                                          Georgios Mantas
                                                                          Saud Althunibat

Organization

Steering Committee

Imrich Chlamtac	University of Trento, Italy
Krishna Sivalingam	University of Maryland at Baltimore County, USA
Y. Thomas Hou	Virginia Tech, USA
Ioannis Tomkos	Athens Information Technology, Greece

General Co-chairs

Victor Sucasas	Universidade de Aveiro, Portugal
Georgios Mantas	Instituto de Telecomunicações - Aveiro, Portugal
Saud Althunibat	Al-Hussein Bin Talal University, Jordan

Technical Program Committee Chairs

Jonathan Rodriguez	Instituto de Telecomunicações - Aveiro, Portugal
José-Fernán Martínez	Universidad Politécnica de Madrid, Spain
Noélia Correia	CEOT, Universidade do Algarve, Portugal

Web Chair

Cláudia Barbosa	Instituto de Telecomunicações - Aveiro, Portugal

Publicity and Social Media Chairs

Joaquim Bastos	Instituto de Telecomunicações - Aveiro, Portugal
Riccardo Bassoli	University of Trento, Italy
Zoran Vujicic	Instituto de Telecomunicações - Aveiro, Portugal

Workshops Chairs

Felipe Gil Castiñeira	University of Vigo, Spain
Ayman Radwan	Instituto de Telecomunicações - Aveiro, Portugal

Sponsorship and Exhibits Chairs

Cláudia Barbosa	Instituto de Telecomunicações - Aveiro, Portugal
Joaquim Santos	Instituto de Telecomunicações - Aveiro, Portugal

Publications Chair

Georgios Mantas   Instituto de Telecomunicações - Aveiro, Portugal

Panels Chair

Fátima Domingues   Instituto de Telecomunicações - Aveiro, Portugal

Local Co-chairs

Cláudia Barbosa   Instituto de Telecomunicações - Aveiro, Portugal
Noélia Correia   CEOT, Universidade do Algarve, Portugal

Local Staff

Álvaro Barradas   CEOT, Universidade do Algarve, Portugal
Jaime Martins   CEOT, Universidade do Algarve, Portugal

Technical Program Committee

Rossi Kamal   Shanto-Mariam University of Creative Technology
                              Uttara, Bangladesh
Pablo Fondo Ferreiro   University of Vigo, Spain
Pedro Castillejo   Universidad Politécnica de Madrid, Spain
Talha Faizur Rahman   COMSATS Institute of Information Technology,
                              Pakistan
Mahmoud Khasawneh   Concordia University, Canada
Nikos Komninos   City, University of London, UK
Alireza Esfahani   IT-Aveiro, Portugal
Firooz B. Saghezchi   IT-Aveiro, Portugal
Shahid Mumtaz   IT-Aveiro, Portugal
Ayman Radwan   IT-Aveiro, Portugal
Zoran Vujicic   Universidade de Aveiro, Portugal
Sherif Adeshina Busari   IT-Aveiro, Portugal
José Carlos Ribeiro   IT-Aveiro, Portugal
Alvaro Barradas   CEOT, University of Algarve, Portugal
Jaime Martins   CEOT, University of Algarve, Portugal
Faroq AL-Tam   CEOT, University of Algarve, Portugal
Tomás Sanguino   Universidad de Huelva, Spain
Anteneh Atumo   Ericsson, Sweden
Riccardo Bassoli   University of Trento, Italy
Senka Hadzic   University of Cape Town, South Africa
Dimitrios Lymberopoulos   University of Patras, Greece
Satya Shah   University of Greenwich, UK

Contents

eHealth and Telemedicine Mobile Applications

Security and Privacy Preservation

Communication Reliability and Protocols

Spatial Modulation Techniques

Hardware Implementation and Antenna Design

SECRET Workshop

Advanced Techniques for IoT and WSNs

Evaluation of a Robust Fault-Tolerant Mechanism for Resilient IoT Infrastructures

José Manuel Lozano Domínguez$^{(\boxtimes)}$![ORCID],

Tomás de J. Mateo Sanguino![ORCID], and Manuel J. Redondo González![ORCID]

University of Huelva, Dpto. Ing. Electrónica, de Sistemas Informáticos
y Automática, Ctra Huelva - La Rábida S/N, 21819 Palos de la Frontera, Spain
josemanuel.ldominguez@alu.uhu.es

Abstract. Gateways in IoT infrastructures generally represent a single point of failure, thus resulting in a total loss of network operability. This paper presents the design, implementation and experimentation of a fault-tolerant protocol for a critical infrastructure applied to the field of road safety. The proposed mechanism establishes a node hierarchy to prevent loss of communication against AP failures in WLANs based on the IEEE 802.11n standard. This mechanism automates the management of the node roles by means of an election and promotion process between stations in search of designated and backup APs. The convergence times of the protocol obtained suitable values of 3.34 s for the formation of a BSS from zero, as well as 15.20 s and 18.84 s for the failover conditions of the backup and designated APs with a minimum traffic load of 42.76% over the WSN traffic.

Keywords: Failover mechanism · Fault tolerance · IoT · Resilience
WSN

1 Introduction

Typically, IoT infrastructures communicate through a central node or gateway that serves as a connection point between sensors, controllers and the outside [1]. However, this represents a single point of failure that diminishes the availability and reliability required by critical applications such as health monitoring [2], cybersecurity in infrastructures [3, 4] or personal safety [5]. The state of the art on protocols related to IoT and WSN applications have been mainly designed to improve the performance and hierarchy of networks. For instance, the improvements studied in [6] focus on the automation of the management and maintenance of tasks, as well as on increasing robustness under failures (e.g., electrical or communication). Thus, the use of third-party management protocols (e.g., SNMP) was proposed in [7] to monitor the node status and send warning messages. Moreover, a local self-recovery mechanism based on flash memories was proposed in [8] to prevent data transfer and network load. In [9, 10] several ways to avoid the loss of communication between a cluster and the outside were addressed, where the gateway is selected according to battery levels. Also for this purpose, in [11] is described a solution to detect failures (e.g., low energy thresholds) and manage gateways locally to avoid loss of communication of a WSN using virtual cells or groups of

© ICST Institute for Computer Sciences, Social Informatics and Telecommunications Engineering 2019
Published by Springer Nature Switzerland AG 2019. All Rights Reserved
V. Sucasas et al. (Eds.): BROADNETS 2018, LNICST 263, pp. 3–12, 2019.
https://doi.org/10.1007/978-3-030-05195-2_1

nodes. Similarly, a cluster-head structure consisting of cell-head nodes is organized to communicate with a base station depending on the sensors' energy [12]. Moreover, the works described in [13, 14] focus on restoring the communication and retrieving information between a node and its gateway designating new routes through backup clusters. Also, [15] describes a technique that offers fault tolerance in large IEEE 802.11 infrastructures working in an ESS topology. This technique uses an algorithm that structures the network using the coverage and performance criteria in such a way that, when an AP fails, a new route is searched to reach any point of the network through a Spanning Tree Protocol [16].

The protocol presented in this paper has been implemented as part of an intelligent object detection and signaling system applied to road safety [17]. The goal of the system, consisting of a set of autonomous sensing devices, is to interact with the environment to distinguish vehicles, generate visual alerts in the presence of pedestrians on zebra crossings and help reducing road accidents. Each device comprises a unit based on a microcontroller and a wireless communication module responsible for sending and receiving pedestrian detection messages to activate the light signaling units. To this end, a WSN infrastructure of nodes that work in a coordinated way within a BSS has been implemented. One of the sensing devices has the role of AP, whose function is to manage and control the network operation. The rest of the devices are clients in such a way that when one of them detects a pedestrian, it sends a broadcast message to the rest of the devices through the WLAN. Said communication system has the function, therefore, of synchronizing a light signaling barrier over the road. Due to its critical mission, the proposed mechanism has the objective of preventing the loss of communication in the WLAN through a redundancy and high availability strategy based on a hierarchy of nodes that act as APs.

This paper is structured as follows: Sect. 2 describes the protocol as well as its operation; Sect. 3 shows the experimentation carried out and the results. Finally, Sect. 4 presents the conclusions and future work.

2 Protocol Description

The protocol presented in this paper is applied to IoT infrastructures based on WLAN nodes operating through a BSS. More specifically, the communication is based on the IEEE 802.11n standard [18] working at 300 Mbps, which uses WPA/WPA2 encryption [19], IPv4 unicast/broadcast packets at the network layer, and UDP datagrams at the transport layer since it accelerates the message delivery with regard to TCP by dispensing with ACK messages as discussed in [20].

The protocol has been designed in the application layer of the OSI model and its objective is to prevent an IoT infrastructure from running out of communication due to faults in the central AP (e.g., power failures). This is possible thanks to a high availability structure consisting of a designated AP (APd), a backup AP (APb) and client nodes. The APd is responsible for coordinating the delivery of data frames at the MAC level, the APb aims to assume the functions of the APd in case of failure and the clients have the capability to auto reconfigure themselves as APd or APb.

The protocol autonomously manages the node roles and responds to changes in the WLAN structure through an active exchange of messages. In brief, the operation is as follows: (1) initially, the node that acts as AP is designated; (2) secondly, the node that acts as APd or APb is determined based on the existing neighbors; (3) the adjacency between APd and APb is maintained by bidirectional hello messages sent periodically; (4) in case of losing adjacency after n hello messages, a promotion process is initiated between the nodes to assign new roles according to the case (i.e., APd, APb or both). To do this, the protocol also manages the automatic IP addressing via a DHCP server. Thus, the station set as APd takes the first IP address of the network (e.g., 192.168.0.1) and the rest of nodes receive consecutive IP addresses from the available pool. When the APd node changes, all clients have to reconnect to the new APd node and renew their IP addresses.

The protocol establishes a set of phases through which each node must jump until the roles converge. These are divided into a preliminary phase that determines if a node should act in AP or station mode (Fig. 1) along with three subsequent phases called init, stability and maintenance (Fig. 2). Thus, each time a node joins the WLAN, it first checks if there is an AP to which to link and request the network status. In negative case, the node is set to AP mode, waits for new incoming clients and then goes to the init phase.

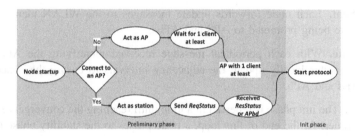

Fig. 1. Description of a node startup process and protocol launching.

2.1   Init Phase

This phase aims to determine which WLAN nodes act as APd and APb as they join the BSS. Each node initiates a competition consisting in exchanging messages with the neighbors considering a priority value—provided under the network administrator's criteria— and the MAC address fields as follows: (1) the node with lowest priority will have the highest probability of being APd; (2) the node with the next lowest priority will be candidate for APb; (3) in case of tie, the minor MAC address is taken as criteria; (4) when the information converges, the rest of the WLAN is informed by identifying the APb and APd nodes. In detail, the different tasks that each node can carry out in this phase are the following.

First Message. When a node initiates the protocol and has no information received from the network yet, it sends a first message including its own MAC address, the priority values to be candidate for APd and APb, and the default interval to exchange the adjacency messages, among other fields.

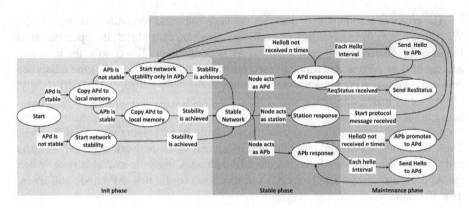

Fig. 2. Operating states of the protocol.

Message Received. When a node receives a message, it processes the data and compares the information received with the information locally stored.

Selection Mechanism. For each message received, a node inspects the priority values and MAC addresses to learn or replace their values in the APd or APb fields if better.

Message Sent. Each node forwards update messages to the WLAN identifying the nodes that are being promoted to APd and APb.

Hello Update. With each periodical message received identifying the APd of the WLAN, the nodes locally update the adjacency intervals to ensure the concordance between APd and APb.

Wait Time. The init phase is repeated in a loop until reaching the convergence or until expiring a timer. At the end of this loop, a node passes to the stability phase (Fig. 3).

2.2 Stability and Maintenance Phases

The stability phase remains idle all the time when the roles of the APd, APb or the clients are assigned, but the nodes leave it to enter the maintenance phase if a network event occurs. The possible events consist in receiving messages to request the network status, exchange protocol information or maintain adjacencies, as well as managing the expiration of the waiting times. In the latter case, the nodes return to the init phase to search for new APb or APd nodes according to the case.

2.3 Message Structure

The protocol establishes four different messages: (*a*) status request, (*b*) status response, (*c*) exchange of protocol information, and (*d*) adjacency.

The status request message (*ReqStatus*) consists of 9 bytes, where the first 8 bytes include the identification tag and the last one indicates the protocol version (Fig. 4a). This message is sent by a client node connected to the AP that remains in station mode during the init phase. The status response message (*ResStatus*) and the exchange of

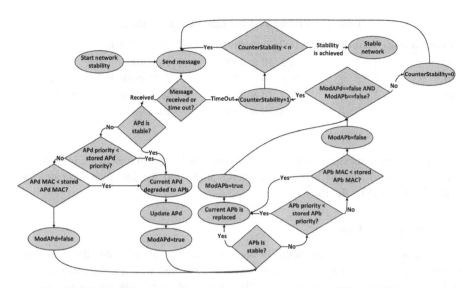

Fig. 3. Diagram of the init phase designed to determine the APd and APb nodes.

protocol information messages (*APdb*) consist of 23 bytes and 19 bytes respectively, matching the same fields except for the first field to differentiate the type of request (Fig. 4b). While the *ResStatus* message can only be sent from the APd node to the unicast address of the client that requested the information on the network state, the *APdb* message can be sent from all the network nodes to a broadcast address to determine which node will act as APd and APb. The rest of the fields contain the following labels: *APdID* and *APbID* include the MAC address of the APd and APb nodes, *APd Priority* and *APb Priority* establish the precedence of the APd and APb nodes, *WLAN Area* identifies the community to which the message belong, *Hello Interval* codifies the time gap in seconds (Table 1), *Network Status* indicates the state of the network (Table 1) and *Version* stands for the form of protocol used.

8 bytes	1 byte
ReqStatus	Version

(a)

6 bytes	1 byte
HelloD	Version

(c)

6 bytes	1 byte
HelloB	Version

(d)

4 / 8 bytes	6 bytes	6 bytes	1 byte			1 byte		1 byte
32 / 64 bits	48 bits	48 bits	4 bits	4 bits	4 bits	2 bits	2 bits	8 bits
APdb / ResStatus	APd ID	APb ID	APd priority	APb priority	WLAN area	Hello interval	Network status	Version

(b)

Fig. 4. Protocol message formats: (a) status request (*ReqStatus*), (b) exchange of protocol information (*APdb*) or status response (*ResStatus*), (c) and (d) adjacency maintenance (*Hello*).

Table 1. Hello interval and network status coding.

Binary coding	Decimal coding	Hello intervals by default	Network status
00	0	3, 5, 10 & 20 s	Network no stable
01	1	3, 5, 10 & 20 s	APd stable & APb no stable
10	2	3, 5, 10 & 20 s	APd stable & APb stable
11	3	3, 5, 10 & 20 s	Reserved

The adjacency message consists of 7 bytes, where the first 6 bytes include the *HelloD* or *HelloB* tags to identify the source node and the last byte indicates the protocol version (Fig. 4c and d).

2.4 Message Exchange

The APd node alternates the stability and maintenance phases after the following events: (*i*) a *ReqStatus* message arrives, which is answered with a *ResStatus* message; (*ii*) the *HelloD* interval expires, initiating the delivery of a new adjacency message; (*iii*) a *HelloB* message arrives from the APb, indicating adjacency; (*iv*) the timer expires after *n* consecutive intervals with no *HelloB* messages, thus indicating loss of adjacency with the APb node. In this case, a procedure to send an *APdb* message is initiated to start the search for a new node that acts as backup AP.

Moreover, the APb node leaves the idle state and enters the maintenance phase after the following cases: (*i*) a *HelloD* message arrives from the APd, indicating adjacency; (*ii*) the *HelloB* interval expires, initiating the delivery of a new adjacency message; (*iii*) the timer expires after *n* consecutive intervals with no *HelloD* messages, thus indicating loss of adjacency with the APd node. In this case, the APb node promotes itself to APd and initiates a procedure by sending an *APdb* message to start the search for a new node that acts as backup AP.

Finally, the nodes acting as stations remain in the stability phase until receiving an *APdb* message. Then, a contention process between the WLAN nodes is initiated to designate a new backup AP.

3 Experimentation

The experimentation carried out consisted in measuring the convergence time and traffic load of the WSN in three representative case studies: (*i*) establishing the BSS from zero, (*ii*) after APb failover, and (*iii*) after APd failover. To this end, a WSN with 6 nodes was deployed in a real working scenario. The network stability was perturbed to trigger the contention mechanism and promote the nodes to APd, APb or remain as stations. We used the ESP8266 microcontroller from Espressif Systems Ltd. The code size required to store the developed protocol occupied 261 KB, standing for the 26.1% of the flash memory.

The protocol was configured to establish the network convergence after receiving $m = 3$ APdb messages and to lose the adjacency after mislaying $n = 5$ consecutive hello messages (i.e., *HelloD* or *HelloB*). An analysis performed with Acrilyc® WiFi Home showed 41 neighboring APs coexisting in the working environment, of which 24 APs were in adjacent Wi-Fi channels with a separation less than 30 MHz. The RSSI of the AP deployed was -49.05 ± 6.28 dB, while the average RSSI of the inferring channels was -63.18 ± 7.20 dB. As a result, the air quality of the BSS obtained an equivalent score of 3 out of 10.

Establishing the BSS from Zero In this case, there was no APd or APb operating previously in the network. The condition to achieve the stability by the AP and the rest of the nodes was measured considering a series of 10 samples, counting the total time (t_z) from the first *ReqStatus* message received in the network until the end of the *APdb* message exchange (Fig. 5a). The standard deviation observed in Table 2 indicates the co-channel interference level due to other APs in the area. This caused collisions between the frames and therefore the forwarding of new messages.

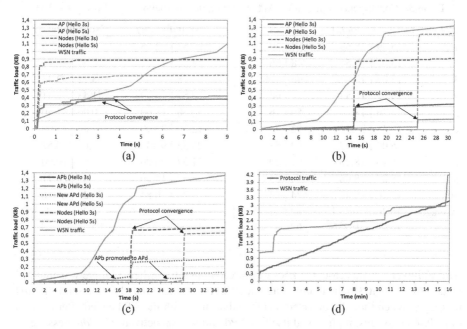

Fig. 5. Accumulative traffic load in short and long terms: (a) establishing the BSS from zero, (b) APb failover, (c) APd failover, and (d) protocol traffic *vs* background traffic.

APb Failover. In this scenario, the BSS was already operative when the APb was induced to fail, so it stopped issuing *HelloB* messages. Subsequently, the APd sent an *APdb* message to activate the mechanism once the loss of adjacency with the APb was detected and the rest of the nodes competed for being the following APb. The convergence time (t_b) was measured from the last hello message successfully received from the APb until the end of the *APdb* message exchange (Fig. 5b). The time resulted in the expression $t_b = n \times t$, where the hello interval was set to $t = 3$ s (Table 3).

Table 2. Convergence values stablishing the BSS from zero.

Test	Time (s) for t_z	Frames	AP traffic (%)	Node traffic (%)
1	3.19	60	26.67	73.33
2	4.81	53	28.30	71.70
3	3.19	49	26.53	73.47
4	3.28	45	33.33	66.67
5	3.11	65	24.62	75.38
6	3.12	58	28.81	71.19
7	3.14	59	28.81	71.19
8	3.22	81	19.75	80.25
9	3.18	63	26.98	73.02
10	3.15	82	14.63	85.37
Average	3.34 ± 0.52	61.50 ± 12.19	24.72 ± 5.13	75.28 ± 5.13

Table 3. Convergence values after APb & APd failovers (hello interval every $t = 3$ s).

Test	Time (s) for $t_b \mid t_d$	Frames	AP traffic (%)	Node traffic (%)
1	15.09 | 18.68	54 | 49	29.63 | 22.45	70.37 | 77.55
2	15.06 | 18.54	48 | 66	37.50 | 21.21	62.50 | 78.79
3	15.06 | 18.72	46 | 106	34.78 | 7.55	65.22 | 92.45
4	15.27 | 18.55	70 | 68	28.57 | 20.59	71.43 | 79.41
5	15.26 | 18.56	50 | 86	30.00 | 18.60	70.00 | 81.40
6	15.48 | 21.52	82 | 76	12.20 | 25.00	87.80 | 75.00
7	15.09 | 18.47	60 | 53	23.33 | 9.43	76.67 | 90.57
8	15.16 | 18.26	51 | 20	31.37 | 30.00	68.63 | 70.00
9	15.27 | 18.68	70 | 85	28.57 | 15.29	71.43 | 84.71
10	15.26 | 18.42	74 | 83	29.73 | 10.84	70.27 | 89.16
Average	15.20 ± 0.13 | 18.84 ± 0.95	60.5 ± 12.62 | 69.2 ± 24.10	27.60 ± 6.88 | 16.62 ± 7.24	72.40 ± 6.88 | 83.38 ± 7.24

APd Failover. In this case, the BSS was already operative when a failure was induced in the APd, so it stopped providing the WLAN service and did not send *HelloD* messages. When the APb detected that the adjacency with the APd ended after the loss of *HelloD* messages, it promoted itself as APd and sent an activation *APdb* message so that the rest of nodes would compete for being the following APb. The convergence time (t_d) was measured from the last hello message successfully received from the APd until the end of the *APdb* message exchange (Fig. 5c). The convergence time resulted in the combination of $t_d = t_z + t_b$ as shown in Table 3.

Figures 5a-5d show the cumulative traffic load of the protocol with respect to time considering a set of hello messages sent every $t = 3$ s and 5 s. The typical traffic generated by the WSN under normal operating conditions, as described in [17], has been included with the goal of evaluating the impact of the APdb protocol on the network. The behavior was measured in short and long term. From the traffic response

(Fig. 5a–c), it is observed that the hello interval (t) does not modifies the protocol pattern except that the sequence of messages exchanged between the nodes is simply shifted in time. As shown in Fig. 5d, the WSN traffic *vs* APdb protocol traffic required 4311 bytes and 3220 bytes respectively after 16 min of operation. This represents a 42.76% of traffic load with respect to the total traffic generated, thus presenting an assumable impact on the WSN operation.

4 Conclusions

Typically, IoT infrastructures communicate through a central node that serves as a connection point between sensors, actuators and the outside. When said node fails, it compromises reliability, endangering the entire network. To avoid it, protocols must automate the network management and provide high tolerance to failures (e.g., electrical, communication, etc.).

With this aim, this paper proposes a protocol that autonomously manages a high availability node-based structure for critical WSN applications based on microcontroller. For this purpose, a promotion and adjacency maintenance process between neighbors has been designed using bidirectional control and hello messages whose goal is to designate a main AP (APd) and a backup AP (APb) from the WSN. This voting process combines MAC addresses and priority values configurable for each node to gain flexibility. The experimentation carried out has shown that the protocol is robust in a real scenario with co-channel interferences (i.e., 3/10 air quality) and consistent to changes in the hello messages and intervals (n, m, t). With the proposed default values, the tests showed that the protocol generates a lower traffic load (42.76%) than the WSN background traffic with acceptable convergence times to establish a BSS from zero ($t_z = 3.34 \pm 0.52$ s), to detect and re-establish the backup AP ($t_b = 15.20 \pm 0.13$ s), as well as to detect and restore the main AP ($t_d = t_z + t_b = 18.84 \pm 0.95$ s).

Future works will be focused on optimizing the delivery of adjacency messages between the designated and backup APs according to battery power levels. In this way, the higher the available energy the larger will be the intervals between messages (i.e., less likely to suffer a power failure) and vice versa, being able to increase the WSN life cycle based on the energy as criteria. Other future works are oriented to validate the protocol scalability in large and populated WSNs (i.e., more than 50 nodes) by means of simulations based on the analysis with intelligent agents.

References

1. Zanella, A., Bui, N., Castellani, A., Vangelista, L., Zorzi, M.: Internet of things for smart cities. IEEE Internet Things J. **1**(1), 22–32 (2014)
2. Ortiz, K.J.P., et al.: IoT: Electrocardiogram (ECG) monitoring system. Indonesian J. Electr. Eng. Comput. Sci. **10**(2), 480–489 (2018)
3. Alonso, L., Barbarán, J., Chen, J., Díaz, M., Llopis, L., Rubio, B.: Middleware and communication technologies for structural health monitoring of critical infrastructures: a survey. Comput. Standars Interfaces **56**, 83–100 (2018)

4. Samboni, F., et al.: MEC IoT: monitorización de estructuras civiles en el contexto IoT. In: Colombian Conference on Communications and Computing, pp. 1–6, Cartagena (2017)
5. Helen, A., Fathila, F., Rijwana, R., Kalaiselvi, V.K.G. A smart watch for women security based on IoT concept 'watch me'. In: International Conference on Computing and Communications Technologies, pp. 190–194, Chennai (2017)
6. Ray, P.P., Mukherjee, M., Shu, L.: Internet of things for disaster management: state-of-art and prospects. IEEE Access **5**, 18818–18835 (2017)
7. Gautam, B.P., Wasaki, K., Sharma, N. A Novel Approach of Fault Management and Restoration of Network Services in IoT Cluster to Ensure Disaster Readiness. In: Networking and Network Applications, pp. 423–428, Hakodate (2016)
8. Pan, W.M.: Dynamic update mechanism in wireless sensor Networks. Appl. Mech. Mater. **526**, 267–272 (2014)
9. Din, S., et al.: Energy efficient topology management scheme based on clustering technique for software define wireless sensor network. In: Peer-to-Peer. Springer US (2017). https://doi.org/10.1007/s12083-017-0607-z
10. Xian, T.: A modified energy efficient backup hierarchical clustering algorithm for WSN. In: Information Security and Control, pp. 45–48, Taiwan (2012)
11. Asim, M., Mokhtar, H., Merabti, M.: A Cellular approach to fault detection and recovery in wireless sensor networks. In: Sensor Technologies and Applications, pp. 352–357, Glyfada, Athens (2009)
12. Yektaparast, A., Nabavi, F.H., Sarmast, A.: An improvement on LEACH protocol (Cell-LEACH). In: International Conference on Advanced Communication Technology, pp. 992–996, Pyeong Chang (2012)
13. Goratti, L., Kato, S.N.A.C.R.P., et al.: A connectivity protocol for start topology wireless sensor network. IEEE Wirel. Commun. Lett. **5**, 12–123 (2016)
14. Induja, K., Deva Kupra, A.J.: A connectivity protocol for star topology using wireless sensor network. In: Nextgen Electronic Technologies: Silicon to Software, pp. 50–56, Chennai (2017)
15. Bhoi, S.K., Panda, S.K., Khilar, P.M.: A network survivability approach to resist access point failure in IEEE 802.11 WLAN. In: Sathiakumar, S., Awasthi, L., Masillamani, M., Sridhar, S. (eds.) Proceedings of International Conference on Internet Computing and Information Communications. Advances in Intelligent Systems and Computing, vol. 216. Springer, New Delhi (2014). https://doi.org/10.1007/978-81-322-1299-7_28
16. Sfeir, E., Pasquahi, S., Schwabe, T., Iselt, A.: Performance evaluation of ethernet resilience mechanisms. In: Workshop on High Performance Switching and Routing, pp. 356–360, Hong Kong, China (2005)
17. Lozano Domínguez, J.M., Mateo Sanguino, T.J.: Design, modelling and implementation of a fuzzy controller for an intelligent road signaling system. Complexity, 2018, Article ID 1849527 (2018)
18. IEEE Computer Society: IEEE Standard for Information Technology–Telecommunications and Information Exchange Between Systems Local and Metropolitan Area Networks–Specific requirements - Part 11: Wireless LAN Medium Access Control (MAC) and Physical Layer (PHY) Specifications. Technical Report (2016)
19. Adnan, A.H., et al.: A comparative study of WLAN security protocols: WPA, WPA2. In: Advances in Electrical Engineering, pp. 165–169, Dhaka (2015)
20. Masirap, M., et al: Evaluation of reliable UDP-based transport protocols for internet of things (IoT). In: IEEE Symposium Computer Applications & Industrial Electronics, pp. 200–205, Penang (2016)

Indoor Positioning Using Adaptive KNN Algorithm Based Fingerprint Technique

Mahmood F. Mosleh[1(✉)], Raed A. Abd-Alhameed[1,2],
and Osama A. Qasim[1]

[1] Electrical Engineering Technical College, Middle Technical University,
Baghdad, Iraq
drmahmoodfarhan@gmail.com, os.sh54@gmail.com,
R.A.A.Abd@bradford.ac.uk
[2] School of Engineering and Informatics, University of Bradford, Bradford, UK

Abstract. In this paper, an experiment of the indoor position location is applied to one floor of the selected building which is chosen as a case study. Four Access Points (APs) of 2.4 GHz are mounted on the experimented area. Their locations are determined using Ekahau Site Survey software to ensure the building is fully covered. A fingerprinting method is utilized as a localization algorithm to estimate the coordinate of the user. This method consists of two stages, namely disconnected data preparing stage and the on-line situating stage. The first one is applied by creating a Radio Map (RM) with 58 Reference Point (RP) in the tested area. A database included the Received Signal Strength (RSS) from all directions of each RP is recorded using Net Surveyor 0.2 Package. In the second phase, K-Nearest Neighbor (KNN) method with fix value of K is applied to estimate the position location. The results show that the average absolute error between actual and estimated coordination equal to 1.796044 m and average elapsed time equal 0.030439 s, which is unacceptable in our opinion because the localization system must be more accurate. To address this problem, a proposed improvement on KNN algorithm with a variable K is presented in this paper. The idea is to vary the value of K according to the difference between the measured signals and the corresponding value of the stored database. The results show that the adapted algorithm led to a significant decrease of 46% and 52% for absolute error and elapsed time respectively.

Keywords: Indoor Positioning System · K-Nearest neighbors
Fingerprint

1 Introduction

The location-based service alludes to the applications that rely upon a client's position to give services such as structure real-time locating and safety [1]. The Global Positioning System (GPS) is broadly utilized in outdoor environments around the plant and can give an accuracy around 10 m [2] but it does not work well in the indoor environments due to multi-path problems.

© ICST Institute for Computer Sciences, Social Informatics and Telecommunications Engineering 2019
Published by Springer Nature Switzerland AG 2019. All Rights Reserved
V. Sucasas et al. (Eds.): BROADNETS 2018, LNICST 263, pp. 13–21, 2019.
https://doi.org/10.1007/978-3-030-05195-2_2

An Indoor Positioning System (IPS) is a way to locate objects or individuals inside a building using radio waves, acoustic signals, magnetic fields, or other tactile information gathered by cell phones. IPS may be integrated with other technologies such as Wi-Fi access points and Magnetic locations to measure the distance from RPs nodes that have known positions. The IPS inside buildings is done either effectively determine cell phones or give surrounding area or environmental context for devices to discover the sensed signal. Position information is an important side of a cell phone context [3]. Wi-Fi network infrastructure is found in many public facilities and can be utilized for indoor situating. In addition, the pervasiveness of Wi-Fi capable devices made this approach, particularly cost-effective.

IPS has been addressed by many researchers for indoor position applications like in [4], the researcher proposed an alternative and novel path to indoor positioning, that signals are combined from multiple sensors. By focusing on visible and inertial sensors that are ubiquitously found in mobile devices. The results confirm that it can be solved the multi-path and unpredictable signal absorption problems. In [5], the researchers got the solution to the complexity of the indoor environment to get a low-cost and accurate situating system remains open by using the Wi-Fi-based technique that can enhance the position performance from the bottleneck in ToA/AoA. The outcomes demonstrated that the Wi-Fi-based location can accomplish 1 m exactness with no equipment change in commercial Wi-Fi products. Such method appears to be superior to the regular solutions to both academia and industry concerning and the trade-off between the cost and complexity of the system. Also, in [6], the researcher proposed an algorithm to implement an IPS relying on the Bluetooth and to merge it into the Global Positioning Module (GPM) which used to uphold the education in the Institute of services science at the University of Geneva. The work compares the signal strengths of surrounding Bluetooth devices to a database of measurements taken over the indoor territory, in order to assess the client's position. Through an assessment of the system, an exactness about 1.5 m has been gotten. Finally, in [7], it has been proposed an accurate fingerprinting based indoor positioning algorithm with three methods or technologies such as triangulation method, fingerprinting technique and Cell-ID technique. The results showed that the accuracy of the proposed method is 86%, which is better than the accuracy of fingerprinting method 72.58%, and triangulation method 45.63%.

This paper attempt to develop an indoor position sensing system using fingerprint methodology and integrated environment. A special KNN algorithm is adopted for position prediction by collecting the RSSs for multiple RPs, each one with two levels to improve the accuracy of location estimation as compared with a conventional KNN algorithm.

The rest of this paper is structured as follows. Section 1 explains the fingerprinting technique. In Sect. 2 explains our suggested a special KNN algorithm with higher accuracy. Finally, Sect. 3 concludes the conclusion.

2 Proposed Algorithm

2.1 The Disconnected Data Preparing Stage

In this research, the second floor of Communication Engineering/Mosul University building is used as a case study. Smart Drawn software is applied to draw the building was allocated to the experiment as shown in (Fig. 1).

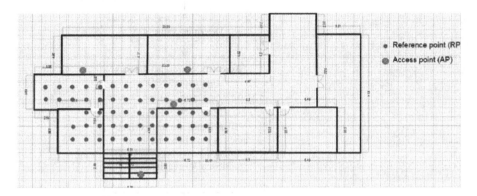

Fig. 1. The selected building covered by the grid.

To determine the best locations of APs in the study area, an Ekahau Site Survey was used to ensure the building was covered. Note that only four APs are chosen which decorated as a green point in Fig. 2. Each one having two antennas and operated by 2.4 GHZ frequency. To build the RM to the targeted area, 58 RPs have been chosen from the total study area. Net Surveyor 0.2 Package is used to measure and record signal strength named S_1, S_2, S_3 and S_4 received from the APs and arrangement those recorded values as a row in a database for each reading to create RSSs$_{(train)}$ array as.

$$RSS_{(Train)} = \begin{pmatrix} S_{1,1} & S_{1,2} & S_{1,3} & S_{1,4} \\ \vdots & \vdots & \vdots & \vdots \\ S_{N,1} & S_{N,2} & S_{N,3} & S_{N,4} \end{pmatrix}_{Nx4} \qquad (1)$$

Where RSSs$_{(train)}$ represent all stored values of signal strength and N is the number of recorded signals in a database. An AutoCAD package version 2011 is used to calculate the coordinates of each RP and store those coordinates (x_i, y_i) corresponded to its values of signals stored in advance where $i = 1, 2, 3, 4 \ldots N$ as.

$$RSS_{(Train)} = \begin{pmatrix} S_{1,1} & S_{1,2} & S_{1,3} & S_{1,4} \\ \vdots & \vdots & \vdots & \vdots \\ S_{N,1} & S_{N,2} & S_{N,3} & S_{N,4} \end{pmatrix}_{Nx4} \begin{pmatrix} X_{1,1} & Y_{1,2} \\ \vdots & \vdots \\ X_{N,1} & Y_{N,2} \end{pmatrix}_{Nx2} \qquad (2)$$

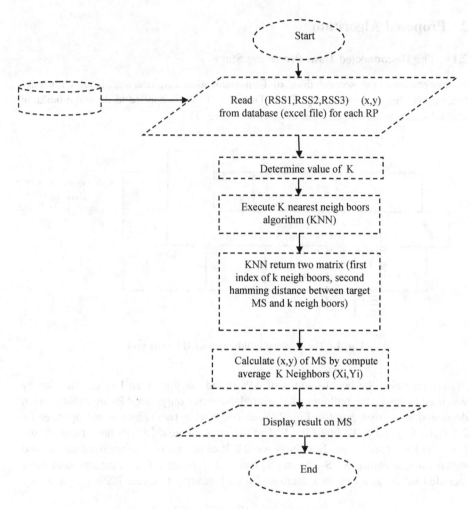

Fig. 2. Conventional KNN algorithm with K constant.

To build enough strong database, 32 readings have been gathered at each RP with four directions (8 readings for each orientation) and two levels for each trend (4 readings for each level). To make ensure that most values of signals strength are recorded and the sample can represent as a matrix as.

$$Sample_j = \begin{pmatrix} S_{1,1} & S_{1,2} & S_{1,3} & S_{1,4} & X_j & Y_j \\ \vdots & \vdots & \vdots & \vdots & \vdots & \vdots \\ S_{32,1} & S_{32,2} & S_{32,3} & S_{32,4} & X_j & Y_j \end{pmatrix}_{32x4} \tag{3}$$

Where samples represent the number of readings for each RP and j is the number of RPs $j = 1, 2, 3, 4 \ldots 58$.

Conventional KNN algorithm with constant K = 3 is applied to estimate the location of MS as shown in (Fig. 2).

The on-Line Situating Stage. In this phase, Wi-Fi has been used to interface an MS carrying by a person with a Base Station (BS) to estimate his unknown location. The RSSs values will be measured by an MS from four APs and send these values to the BS to apply the conventional KNN algorithm and calculate the user's location. The BS will evaluate (x, y) position and sends back to MS. To calculate the time required to find k neighbours (elapsed time) and absolute error of such algorithm, 18 Test Points (TPs) in different places in the targeted area are chosen and got the results shown in Table 1.

Table 1. Evaluate absolute error and elapsed time for conventional KNN algorithm.

Test Points	Actual coordinate (X)	Actual coordinate (Y)	Estimate coordinate (X)	Estimate coordinate (Y)	Elapsed time (sec)	Absolute error (m)
1	8.3500	4.0027	9.2500	4.0027	0.396455	0.9000
2	9.2500	7.6027	8.6500	7.6027	0.008957	0.6000
3	12.8500	8.5027	12.8500	8.2027	0.008887	0.3000
4	18.2500	8.5027	18.2500	7.6027	0.008387	0.9000
5	2.0500	3.1027	2.6500	2.8027	0.009404	0.6708
6	5.6500	3.1027	5.6500	4.6027	0.009236	1.5000
7	5.6500	5.8027	9.2500	4.6027	0.009544	3.7947
8	16.4500	4.9027	15.2500	4.6027	0.008896	1.2369
9	16.4500	3.1027	16.4500	7.6027	0.009109	4.5000
10	18.2500	5.8027	17.0500	7.6027	0.007968	2.1633
11	18.2500	6.7027	17.0500	5.2027	0.008903	1.9209
12	20.0500	5.8027	20.0500	4.0027	0.009129	1.8000
13	20.0500	6.7027	18.8500	7.6027	0.008164	1.5000
14	18.2500	2.2027	18.8500	4.6027	0.009287	2.4739
15	20.500	8.5027	18.8500	5.2027	0.009249	3.6895
16	16.4500	9.4027	17.6500	7.6027	0.009234	2.1633
17	20.0500	7.6027	19.4500	7.6027	0.008122	0.6000
18	14.6500	8.5027	14.0500	7.0027	0.008963	1.6155

Such an algorithm has an average absolute error equal to 1.796044 m and average elapsed time equal 0.030439 s. (Figure 3) Shows the schemes of absolute error and elapsed time.

The results show there are large differences between actual coordinates and estimated coordinates, which lead inaccuracy in locating the targeted person due to signal fluctuation in the testing area and the value of k neighbour is constant.

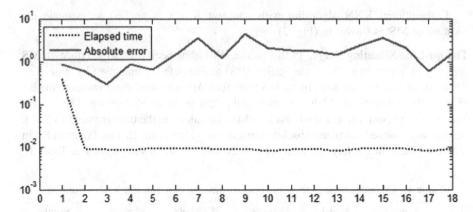

Fig. 3. The absolute error and the elapsed time of conventional KNN (x-axis represents the test point number).

Adaptive KNN Algorithm. Due to the large error in locating MS according to the results that shown in Table 1, an adaptive KNN is proposed by varying the value of K according to the Euclidean distance between the measured signals and the previously stored entries. Where the similarity distance has been exploited to make it adaptable by adding new neighbour or removing existing neighbour according to a threshold (threshold is an acceptable distance between the measured and pre-stored signal strength) especially for this building.

The results of the modified algorithm show that the time required to find K nearest neighbours is long due the large numbers of entries into the database and there was a fluctuation in the received signal due to the movement towards people in the tested area. To solve this problem, the tested area is divided into sub-regions as shown in (Fig. 4) that illustrates each sub-region with a different symbol. This will lead to a reduction in the time required to determine the location of the user as well as control the pulse of the signal fluctuation.

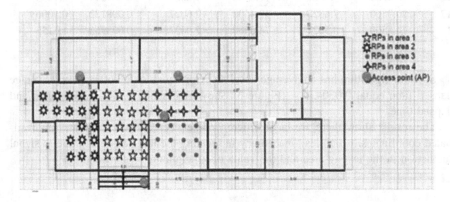

Fig. 4. The targeted area is divided into four sub-regions.

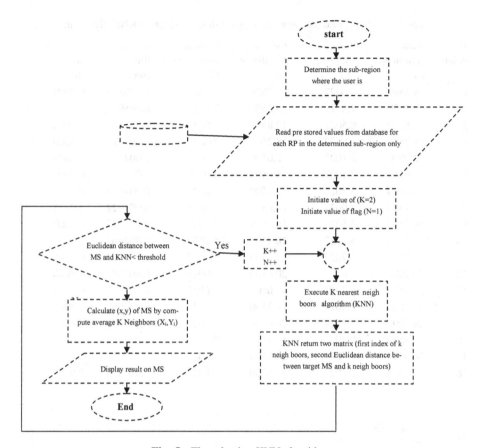

Fig. 5. The adaptive KNN algorithm.

The new adaptive KNN algorithm as shown in (Fig. 5) was tested by choosing the same previous TPs in the targeted area. The results are listed in Table 2.

The results show that the average absolute error of the proposed algorithm is equal to 0.817706 m. In addition, an average elapsed time equal to 0.015885 s. (Figure 6) shows the schemes for absolute error and elapsed time for each TP as compared with a conventional KNN algorithm, where a black colour represents the results of conventional KNN and red colour represent the results of adaptive KNN algorithm.

The results show there is a slight difference between actual and estimated coordinates of MS that lead to decrease average absolute error from 1.796044 m to 0.817706 m and average elapsed time from 0.030439 s to 0.015885 s. So, the new adaptive algorithm can optimize the MS localization by reducing average absolute error and elapsed time in half.

Table 2. Evaluate absolute error and elapsed time of adaptive KNN algorithm.

Test Points	Actual coordinate (X)	Actual coordinate (Y)	Estimate coordinate (X)	Estimate coordinate (Y)	Elapsed time (sec)	Absolute error (m)
1	8.3500	4.0027	9.2500	4.0027	0.196819	0.9000
2	9.2500	7.6027	9.2500	7.6027	0.005987	0
3	12.8500	8.5027	12.8500	7.6027	0.005565	0.9000
4	18.2500	8.5027	18.2500	7.6027	0.005511	0.9000
5	2.0500	3.1027	2.0500	2.2027	0.004687	0.9000
6	5.6500	3.1027	5.6500	4.0027	0.004915	0.9000
7	5.6500	5.8027	5.6500	5.8027	0.004654	0
8	16.4500	4.9027	14.6500	4.0027	0.005222	2.0125
9	16.4500	3.1027	16.4500	4.0027	0.004675	0.9000
10	18.2500	5.8027	18.2500	5.8027	0.004902	0
11	18.2500	6.7027	18.2500	5.8027	0.005164	0.9000
12	20.0500	5.8027	20.0500	4.0027	0.004887	1.8000
13	20.0500	6.7027	20.0500	7.6027	0.005797	0.9000
14	18.2500	2.2027	18.2500	4.0027	0.004957	1.8000
15	20.500	8.5027	20.0500	7.6027	0.005804	1.0062
16	16.4500	9.4027	16.4500	9.4027	0.004792	0
17	20.0500	7.6027	20.0500	7.6027	0.005782	0
18	14.6500	8.5027	14.6500	7.6027	0.005813	0.9000

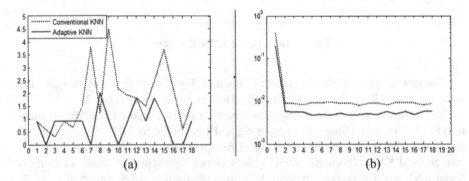

(a)   (b)

Fig. 6. Comparison of the results, (a) absolute error and (b); elapsed time (x-axis represents the test point number). (Color figure online)

3 Conclusions

In this paper, an experimenter fingerprint algorithm based on KNN method has been presented to estimate the unknown position of MS. The results show that an unacceptable error is achieved by applying KNN with fixed K number. It was noted that the variable K was varied according to the distance between the measured signals and the previously stored entries in the database. The results confirm that the proposed algorithm achieved reasonable results by reducing the average absolute error from 1.796044 m to 0.817706 m and average elapsed time from 0.030439 s to 0.015885 s.

References

1. Katsuhiro, T., Jianhua, M., Bernady, O.A.: A dangerous location aware system for assisting kids safety care. In: Proceedings of the 20th International Conference on Advanced Information Networking and Applications, Vienna, Austria, pp. 657–662 (2006)
2. Per, K.E.: The global positioning system: signals, measurements, and performance. Int. J. Wireless Inf. Networks 1, 83–105 (1994)
3. Dmitry, N.: On indoor positioning. Int. J. Open Inf. Technol. 2307–8162 vol, 3 (2015)
4. Ashish, G., Alper, Y..: Indoor positioning using visual and inertial sensors. In: Proceedings of the IEEE Sensors, Orlando, FL, USA, pp. 1–3 (2016)
5. Chouchang, Y., Huai-Rong, S.: Wi-Fi-based indoor positioning. IEEE Commun. Mag. (2015)
6. Anja, B.: Bluetooth Indoor Positioning. University of Geneva, Geneva (2012)
7. Min-Seok, C., Beakcheol, J.: An accurate fingerprinting based indoor positioning algorithm. Int. J. Appl. Eng. Res. 12, 86–90 (2017)
8. Ahmed, A.K., Saba, Q.J., Mohammed, Q.S., Desheng, W.: Wireless indoor localization systems and techniques: survey and comparative study. Indonesian J. Electr. Eng. Comput. Sci. 3, 392–409 (2016)

Modeling of Sensor Clouds Under the Sensing as a Service Paradigm

J. Guerreiro$^{(\boxtimes)}$ (ID), L. Rodrigues (ID), and N. Correia (ID)

CEOT, FCT, University of Algarve, 8005-139 Faro, Portugal
{jdguerreiro,lrodrig,ncorreia}@ualg.pt

Abstract. 5G technologies will facilitate the emergence of applications integrating multiple physical Things. In such scenarios, Cloud-integrated platforms end up having a key role due to their storage and processing capabilities. Therefore, a clear understanding of Sensor Clouds, and on how Cloud mechanisms can be orchestrated to better face requests, becomes a very relevant issue as Sensing as a Service models emerge. This article presents a model for Sensor Clouds, suitable for emerging IoT related Sensing as a Service business models. Such a model is used to assess the impact of resource allocation approaches and unveil the trade-off between scalability, elasticity and quality of experience. Results show that the best resource allocation approach is highly dependent on the suppliers/consumers scenario.

1 Introduction

With the *Internet of Things* (IoT), devices/Things can easily exchange data over the Internet. Resources can be easily discovered, accessed and managed, making Things accessible to a large pool of developers. The 5th generation wireless technology will have a key role in such scenarios and 5G IoT is already called the Internet of everyone and everything [1]. 5G technologies meet the requirements of mobile communications and needs for Thing data transmission, facilitating the emergence of applications integrating multiple physical Things with virtual resources available at the Internet/Web. The *Sensing as a Service* (Se-aaS) model emerges from this reality, allowing everyone to benefit from such an IoT eco-system, and Cloud-integrated platforms are usually used due to their storage and processing capabilities [2,3].

The most relevant "as a service" models under the Cloud Computing paradigm are: (*i*) *Infrastructure as a Service* (IaaS), providing computing resources (e.g., virtual machines); (*ii*) *Platform as a Service* (PaaS), providing computing platforms that may include an operating system, database, Web server, and others; (*iii*) *Software as a Service* (SaaS), where the Cloud takes over the infrastructure and platform while scaling automatically [4]. The Se-aaS model emerged more recently for sensors/data to be shared. This means that there is a multi-supplier deployment of sensors, and multi-client access to resources [5]. Cloud service providers should find some incentive mechanism for device owners to participate [6,7].

© ICST Institute for Computer Sciences, Social Informatics and Telecommunications Engineering 2019
Published by Springer Nature Switzerland AG 2019. All Rights Reserved
V. Sucasas et al. (Eds.): BROADNETS 2018, LNICST 263, pp. 22–30, 2019.
https://doi.org/10.1007/978-3-030-05195-2_3

In this article, the modeling of Sensor Clouds is addressed. Although a first attempt was done in [5], their focus is on *Wireless Mesh Networks* (WSNs) and on how these can move to Sensor Clouds, not being adequate for other IoT Se-aaS business models. More specifically, in [5] sensors are allocated to a single application and mashups are not addressed. Therefore, it can be seen as a WSN virtualization. Here we propose a model that is suitable for emerging IoT related Se-aaS business models, including the one in [5]. This model considers sensors/data sharing by multiple applications and mashups, allowing one to assess the impact of resource allocation approaches (both Cloud and physical Things), and better understanding of trade-offs, so that mechanisms can be orchestrated to face future requests.

The remainder of this article is organized as follows. In Sect. 2, previous research on Se-aaS paradigm is discussed. Section 3 presents the mathematical model, while Sect. 4 analyses it and discusses trade-offs. Finally, Sect. 5 draws conclusions.

2 Related Work

The Se-aaS was initially discussed in [6] for Cloud-based sensing services using mobile phones. Such work analyses its design and implementation challenges. In the context of smart cities, Se-aaS is discussed in [2,8]. The first addresses technological, economical and social perspectives, while the last proposes the abstraction of physical objects through semantics, so that devices can be integrated by neglecting their underlying architecture. In [9,10], the semantic selection of sensors is also addressed.

Multimedia Se-aaS is explored in [11–13]. These focus on real-type communication requirements, and [13] explores Cloud edges and fogs. For a survey on mobile multimedia Cloud computing see [14].

In [5,15,16], the integration of WSNs with the Cloud is investigated. Their concerns are mainly data storage and/or device assignment to tasks. In [5], a WSN virtualization model is discussed.

This article, contrarily to previous works, addresses a multi-supplier and multi-client modeling of Sensor Clouds, allowing client applications to request for available devices and build mashups. The focus is not on crowd sensing making data from mobile phones available to multiple clients, but instead on how applications can share devices and build mashups, which is not considered in [5,15,16]. Mashups may lead to internal data flows in the Cloud, if data is used by different mashups (each integrating it differently with other Internet/Web resources), and this has not been accounted for by previous approaches.

3 Theoretical Modeling of Sensor Cloud

3.1 Definitions

Definition 1 (Physical Thing). *A sensor detecting events/changes, or an actuator receiving commands for the control of a mechanism/system. The model of a physical Thing i includes all properties necessary to describe it, denoted by*

$\mathcal{P}_i$, and all its functionalities, denoted by $\mathcal{F}_i$. That is, $\mathcal{P}_i = \{p : p \in \mathcal{P}\}$, where $\mathcal{P}$ is the overall set of properties (e.g., sensing range, communication facility, location), and $\mathcal{F}_i = \{f : f \in \mathcal{F}\}$, where $\mathcal{F}$ is the overall set of functionalities (e.g., image sensor), considering all devices registered at the Cloud.

It is assumed that properties and functionalities, at $\mathcal{P}$ and $\mathcal{F}$ respectively, result from a semantic description of physical Things registered at the Cloud. That is, specific vocabularies are used when naming properties and functionalities (see [17], for example). Each property $p_i \in \mathcal{P}_i$ has a "subject/predicate/object" description[1] denoted by $spo(p_i)$ (e.g., temperature hasValue 30 °C). The set of all physical Things is denoted by $\mathcal{T}^P$, and sensor owners voluntarily register/deregister physical Things to/from the Cloud.

Definition 2 (Mashup). *Workflow built by wiring together Things and services from various Web sources, on which an application is based.*

That is, applications (at the user side) should be able to access Things at the Cloud and, if necessary, blend them with other services and data sources on the Web, as shown in Fig. 1. However, for resources to be used efficiently, applications should not pick physical Things directly. Instead, a functionality requirement and minimum/maximum property requirements should be specified for each element n included in a mashup, denoted by $\bar{f}_n$ and $\bar{\mathcal{P}}_n$, allowing then an optimized allocation of physical Things to mashup elements. Each $p_n \in \bar{\mathcal{P}}_n$ can have a "subject/predicate/object" description of the condition/requirement that is being defined (e.g., cameraResolution greaterThan 12.1MP; frequencySampling equalTo 10 s), denoted by $spo(p_n)$. The overall population of mashup elements (from all applications) at the Cloud will be denoted by $\mathcal{N}$.

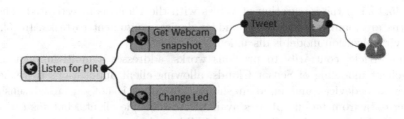

Fig. 1. Thing mashup.

For devices/data to be consumed by multiple applications, virtual Things will be created at the Cloud. Then, each mashup element is binded to a single virtual Thing, while a virtual Thing can be binded to multiple mashup elements (with same functionality and compatible property requirements). Basically, virtual Things represent multiple mashup elements, from multiple applications,

---

[1] A Resource Description Framework (RDF) triple.

and these are the ones to be materialized into physical Things. Such an approach allows data generated by a virtual Thing to be consumed by multiple applications, while reducing data collection/storage and increasing data utility. Mashup elements are, however, application dependent.

Definition 3 (Virtual Thing). *Thing at the Cloud to which mashup elements are binded to. A virtual Thing j is materialized through one or more concerted physical Things, denoted by $\mathcal{M}_j$, $\mathcal{M}_j \subset \mathcal{T}^P$, able to provide the requirements associated with the virtual Thing (requirements from all mashup elements binded to it). Therefore, $f_j \triangleq \cup_{i \in \mathcal{M}_j} \mathcal{F}_i$ and $\mathcal{P}_j = \cup_{i \in \mathcal{M}_j} \mathcal{P}_i$.*

That is, a virtual Thing can have one or multiple physical Things in the background working together. The set of all virtual Things is denoted by $\mathcal{T}^V$.

   With virtualization users remain unaware of the physical devices used, allowing these to be dynamically allocated to virtual Things. The client ends up having no deployment and maintenance costs, while having an on-demand fault tolerant service because virtual Things can always use other available physical Things.

3.2   The Model

Assumptions: A *Cloud Service Provider* (CSP), denoted by $\mathcal{S}$, includes a set of distributed computing resources, each set serving a certain region or having a certain role. Therefore, $\mathcal{S} = \{\mathcal{S}_1, ... \mathcal{S}_{|\mathcal{S}|}\}$. The set of applications (outside the Cloud), requesting for sensors with certain properties, is denoted by $\mathcal{A} = \{\mathcal{A}_1, ..., \mathcal{A}_{|\mathcal{A}|}\}$. An application $\mathcal{A}_i$ can have one or more independent components, denoted by $\mathcal{C}(\mathcal{A}_i) = \{\mathcal{C}_1^i, ... \mathcal{C}_{|\mathcal{C}(\mathcal{A}_i)|}^i\}$, and each component $\mathcal{C}_j^i$ is binded to a mashup (at the Cloud) of δ_j^i steps, $\mathcal{C}_j^i \triangleq \{1, ..., \delta_j^i\}$. The following is also assumed:

- Web templates are used to draw the mashup associated with each component, where minimum/maximum property and functionality requirements are specified for each mashup element. Elements can be connected, and $succ(n)$ denotes the successors of element n at the mashup workflow (elements to which n sends data to).
- Final mashups' data is sent to the corresponding application components through bindings.
- Virtual Things are created, and binded to mashup elements, by the Cloud.

Formalization: One or more physical Things materialize one virtual Thing. Assuming $\tau^i = \{\mathcal{T}_1^{P,i}, \mathcal{T}_2^{P,i}, ...\}$ to be a partition of $\mathcal{T}^P$, function $g_1 : \tau^i \to \mathcal{T}^V$ is defined for virtual Thing materialization:

$$g_1(\mathcal{T}_j^{P,i}) = \{\exists! k \in \mathcal{T}^V : f_k \triangleq \cup_{l \in \mathcal{T}_j^{P,i}} \mathcal{F}_l\}. \tag{1}$$

This states that a virtual Thing $k \in \mathcal{T}^V$ is mapped to $\mathcal{T}_j^{P,i}$ if they are functionally similar. Assuming now $\eta^i = \{\mathcal{N}_1^i, \mathcal{N}_2^i, ...\}$ to be a partition of $\mathcal{N}$ (all elements in $\mathcal{N}_j^i$ with the same functionality requirement), function $g_2 : \eta \to \mathcal{T}^V$ is defined to bind $\mathcal{N}_j^i$ to a virtual Thing:

$$g_2(\mathcal{N}_j^i) = \{\exists! k \in \mathcal{T}^V : \bar{f}_n = \mathcal{F}_k \wedge \bar{\mathcal{P}}_n \subseteq \mathcal{P}_k \wedge \Delta(spo(p_n), spo(p_k)) = true,$$
$$, \forall n \in \mathcal{N}_j^i, \forall p_n \in \bar{\mathcal{P}}_n, \forall p_k \in \mathcal{P}_k\}. \quad (2)$$

where Δ specifies whether p_n is compatible with p_k, or not. This states that a virtual Thing $k \in \mathcal{T}^V$ mapped to $\mathcal{N}_j^i$ must: (i) provide the functionality being requested by elements in $\mathcal{N}_j^i$; (ii) fulfill the property requirements of all elements in $\mathcal{N}_j^i$.

Different resource allocation approaches (partitions and allocations done by g_1 and g_2) can be adopted by sensor Clouds, each with an impact on scalability, elasticity and *Quality of Experience* (QoE). Let us assume that η^U is the universe set of all feasible partitions of mashup elements, $\eta^U = \{\eta^1, \eta^2, ..., \eta^{|\eta^U|}\}$ and $\eta^i = \{\mathcal{N}_1^i, \mathcal{N}_2^i, ..., \mathcal{N}_{|\mathcal{T}^V|}^i\}$, $\forall i \in \{1, ..., |\eta^U|\}$. Also, τ^U is the universe set of all feasible partitions of physical Things, $\tau^U = \{\tau^1, \tau^2, ..., \tau^{|\tau^U|}\}$ and $\tau^i = \{\mathcal{T}_1^{P,i}, \mathcal{T}_2^{P,i}, ..., \mathcal{T}_{|\mathcal{T}^V|}^{P,i}\}$, $\forall i \in \{1, ..., |\tau^U|\}$. Thus, each element in τ^U is a feasible materialization of virtual Things. For such universe sets, the most scalable resource allocation approach (system can accommodate more load/clients in the future) would select the following solution:

$$(\eta^i, \tau^j)^{SCA} = argmin_{\eta^i \in \eta^U} \{|\eta^i|\}. \quad (3)$$

That is, since each element of partition η^i will be associated with a virtual Thing, fewer virtual Things not only means less virtual workspaces but also more productive virtual Things, as data flowing from them serves more mashups/applications.

Elasticity is the ability to adapt resources to loads. That is, resources should become available when the load increases, but when the load decreases then unneeded resources should be released. Thus, the most elastic resource allocation approach would select the following solution:

$$(\eta^i, \tau^j)^{ELA} = argmin_{\eta^i \in \eta^U} \{max_{\mathcal{S}_l \in \mathcal{S}} \{\sum_{k \in \mathcal{T}^V} \xi(k, \mathcal{S}_l)\}\} \quad (4)$$

where $\xi(k, \mathcal{S}_l)$ is the amount of computational resources allocated to virtual Thing k at $\mathcal{S}_l$. Therefore, virtual Things are evenly distributed by CSPs.

Regarding the resource allocation approach with a better impact on the QoE perceived by users, this would be the one selecting the following solution:

$$(\eta^i, \tau^j)^{QoE} = argmin_{\eta^i \in \eta^U, \tau^j \in \tau^U} \{h(\eta^i, \tau^j)\} \quad (5)$$

where $h : \eta^U \times \tau^U \to \Re^+$ is a cost function defined as:

$$h(\eta^i, \tau^j) = \sum_{k \in \mathcal{T}^V} \sum_{k' \in \chi(k)} TF^{V2V}(k, k') + \sum_{\mathcal{A}_i \in \mathcal{A}} \sum_{k \in \Phi(\mathcal{A}_i)} TF^{V2A}(k, \mathcal{A}_i) +$$

$$+ \sum_{k \in \mathcal{T}^V} \sum_{k' \in \Psi(k)} TF^{P2V}(k', k). \quad (6)$$

The $TF^{V2V}(k, k')$ is a transfer cost associated with the data flow between the workspaces of virtual Things k and k' at the Cloud (Virtual-to-Virtual cost), because mashup elements can be connected. The $\chi(k)$ must provide all virtual Things requiring data flow from virtual Thing k. That is,

$$\chi(k) = \{k'' \in \mathcal{T}^V : k = g_2(\mathcal{N}_l^i), k'' = g_2(\mathcal{N}_m^i) \wedge n' = succ(n), n \in \mathcal{N}_l^i,$$

$$, n' \in \mathcal{N}_m^i, \mathcal{N}_l^i, \mathcal{N}_m^i \in \eta^i\}. \quad (7)$$

The $TF^{V2A}(k, \mathcal{A}_i)$ is a transfer cost associated with the data flow between the workspace of virtual Thing k and the user application $\mathcal{A}_i$. The $\Phi(\mathcal{A}_i)$ provides all virtual Things consumed by application $\mathcal{A}_i$,

$$\Phi(\mathcal{A}_i) = \{k' \in \mathcal{T}^V : k' = g_2(\mathcal{N}_l^i) \wedge succ(n) = \emptyset \wedge n \in \mathcal{C}_j^i, \mathcal{N}_l^i \in \eta^i, n \in \mathcal{N}_l^i,$$

$$, \mathcal{C}_j^i \in \mathcal{C}(\mathcal{A}_i)\}. \quad (8)$$

Finally, the $TF^{P2V}(k', k)$ is a transfer cost associated with the data flow between the physical Thing k' (or its corresponding proxy/gateway) and the workspace of virtual Thing k, which depends on the materialization of k. Therefore, $\Psi(k)$ will be

$$\Psi(k) = \{k'' \in \mathcal{T}^P : k = g_1(\mathcal{T}_j^{P,i}) \wedge k'' \in \mathcal{M}_k, \mathcal{T}_j^{P,i} \in \tau^j\}. \quad (9)$$

Regarding the transfer cost itself, this may include the number of hops, processing required at the destination, etc, or any combination of these.

4   Analysis of Results

4.1   Scenario Setup

A set of random graphs, using the algorithm in [18], were used to apply the model described. These graphs, each with 10 nodes, represent the location of CSP's resources, $\mathcal{S}_1, ... \mathcal{S}_{|\mathcal{S}|}$. There are $|\mathcal{A}| = \kappa_1 \times |\mathcal{S}|$ applications and $|\mathcal{T}^P| = \kappa_2 \times |\mathcal{S}|$ physical Things registered at the Sensor Cloud, where κ_1 and κ_2 are integers. Each $\mathcal{S}_i \in \mathcal{S}$ connects, on average, $\frac{|\mathcal{A}|}{|\mathcal{S}|}$ applications and $\frac{|\mathcal{T}^P|}{|\mathcal{S}|}$ physical Things to the Cloud.

The virtual Things to be built depend on physical Things, application requirements and aggregation level when allocating mashup elements to virtual Things. Therefore, tests were done for different amounts of virtual Things,

$\frac{|\mathcal{A}| \times \kappa_3 \times \kappa_4}{10} \leq |\mathcal{T}^V| \leq \frac{|\mathcal{A}| \times \kappa_3 \times \kappa_4}{2}$, where κ_3 is the average number of components per application and κ_4 is the average number of elements at mashups. For transfer costs in Eq. (6), the following is assumed:

- TF^{V2A}: Since there will be κ_3 bindings of data flow from the Cloud to an application, a virtual Thing k will send its data towards application $\mathcal{A}_i$ with probability $prob(k, \mathcal{A}_i) = \frac{\kappa_3}{|\mathcal{T}^V|}$.
- TF^{V2V}: Since each mashup has $\kappa_4 - 1$ flow links[2], a virtual Thing k has a data flow towards k' with probability $prob(k, k') = \frac{(\kappa_4 - 1) \times \kappa_3 \times |\mathcal{A}|}{|\mathcal{T}^V| \times (|\mathcal{T}^V| - 1)} \times \alpha$, where α is the virtual Thing sharing factor or ratio $\frac{\kappa_4 \times \kappa_3 \times |\mathcal{A}|}{|\mathcal{T}^V|}$.
- TF^{P2V}: A physical Thing k' has a data flow towards virtual Thing k with probability $prob(k', k) = \frac{\kappa_5}{|\mathcal{T}^P|}$, where κ_5 is the average number of physical Things in a virtual Thing materialization.
- The number of hops is assumed to be the transfer cost in TF^{V2A}, TF^{V2V} and TF^{P2V}.

Table 1 shows the parameter values assumed.

Table 1. Simulation parameters.

Parameter	Value
Number of nodes at CSP graph ($|\mathcal{S}|$)	10
Number of applications ($|\mathcal{A}|$)	30
Number of physical Things ($|\mathcal{T}^P|$)	30
Avg number of components per app (κ_3)	3
Avg number of elements at each mashup (κ_4)	3
Virtual Thing materialization factor (κ_5)	1
Lowest number of virtual Things	$\frac{|\mathcal{A}| \times \kappa_3 \times \kappa_4}{10}$
Highest number of virtual Things	$\frac{|\mathcal{A}| \times \kappa_3 \times \kappa_4}{2}$

4.2 Discussion

Figure 2 shows[3] the impact of $|\eta^i|$ (or number of virtual Things), which is a consequence of the aggregation level used by resource allocation approaches. Less virtual Things means that solutions are more scalable.

A relevant observation regarding the impact of making more or less scalable choices (virtual Things serving more or less applications), is that in general the QoE and elasticity improve as Sensor Clouds choose for less scalable solutions. In this case, virtual Things are serving less applications and, therefore, less data transfers between virtual Things occurs and data takes less hops to flow towards

---

[2] A flow tree is assumed.
[3] Average of results obtained for all generated graphs.

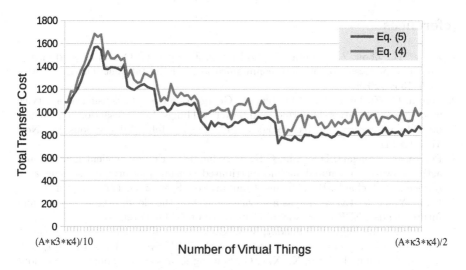

Fig. 2. Impact of $|\eta^i|$ (or number of virtual Things).

applications. Also, for each virtual Thing there will be less load. However, this does not happen for a small number of virtual Things. In this case, increasing the number of virtual Things leads to a higher transfer cost, with a negative impact on QoE, and worse elasticity. This happens because virtual Things are already highly dependent, and flow from physical Things towards the Cloud takes over the previously mentioned benefit of using more virtual Things. Thus, scalability can have a positive or negative impact on QoE and elasticity depending on the scenario (mashups, etc), which will determine possible allocations of mashup elements to virtual Things, and the best resource allocation approach to use.

5   Conclusions

In this article, a model for Sensor Clouds is presented allowing the impact of resource allocation approaches to be assessed, and trade-off between scalability and QoE/elasticity to be unveiled. Results also show that the best resource allocation approach to use will depend on mashups, etc, influencing possible allocations of mashup elements to virtual Things. This awareness allows Sensor Cloud providers to choose the best approach according to their case.

Acknowledgment. This work was supported by FCT (Foundation for Science and Technology) from Portugal within CEOT (Center for Electronic, Optoelectronic and Telecommunications) and UID/MULTI/00631/2013 project.

References

1. Zhang, D., Zhou, Z., Mumtaz, S., Rodriguez, J., Sato, T.: One integrated energy efficiency proposal for 5G IoT communications. IEEE Internet Things J. **3**(6), 1346–1354 (2016)
2. Perera, C., Zaslavsky, A., Christen, P., Georgakopoulos, D.: Sensing as a service model for smart cities supported by Internet of Things. In: Transactions on Emerging Telecommunications Technologies, vol. 25, No. 1. John Wiley & Sons, Inc. New York (2014)
3. Perera, C., Talagala, D.S., Liu, C.H., Estrella, J.C.: Energy-efficient location and activity-aware on-demand mobile distributed sensing platform for sensing as a service in IoT clouds. IEEE Trans. Comput. Soc. Syst. **2**(4), 171–181 (2015)
4. Duan, Y., et al.: Everything as a service (XaaS) on the cloud: origins, current and future trends. IEEE International Conference on CLOUD (2015)
5. Misra, S., Chatterjee, S., Obaidat, M.S.: On theoretical modeling of sensor cloud: a paradigm shift from wireless sensor network. IEEE Syst. J. **PP**(99) (2014)
6. Sheng, X., Tang, J., Xiao, X., Xue, G.: Sensing as a service: challenges, solutions and future directions. IEEE Sens. J. **13**(10), 3733–3741 (2013)
7. Pouryazdan, M., Kantarci, B., Soyata, T., Foschini, L., Song, H.: Quantifying user reputation scores, data trustworthiness, and user incentives in mobile crowd-sensing. IEEE Access **PP**(99) (2017)
8. Petrolo, R., Loscrì, V., Mitton, N.: Towards a smart city based on cloud of things, a survey on the smart city vision and paradigms. Transactions on Emerging Telecommunications Technologies, Wiley Online (2015)
9. Misra, S., Bera, S., Mondal, A., Tirkey, R., Chao, H.-C., Chattopadhyay, S.: Optimal gateway selection in sensor-cloud framework for health monitoring. IET Wireless Sens. Syst. **4**(2), 61–68 (2014)
10. Hsu, Y.-C., Lin, C.-H., Chen, W.-T.: Design of a sensing service architecture for internet of things with semantic sensor selection. In: International Conference on UTC-ATC-ScalCom (2014)
11. Lai, C.-F., Chao, H.-C., Lai, Y.-X., Wan, J.: Cloud-assisted real-time transrating for HTTP live streaming. IEEE Wireless Commun. **20**(3), 62–70 (2013)
12. Lai, C.-F., Wang, H., Chao, H.-C., Nan, G.: A network and device aware QoS approach for cloud-based mobile streaming. IEEE Trans. Multimedia **15**(4), 747–757 (2013)
13. Wang, W., Wang, Q., Sohraby, K.: Multimedia sensing as a service (MSaaS): exploring resource saving potentials of at cloud-edge IoTs and fogs. IEEE Internet Things J. **PP**(99) (2016)
14. Xu, Y., Mao, S.: A survey of mobile cloud computing for rich media applications. IEEE Wireless Commun. **20**(3), 46–53 (2013)
15. Zhu, C., Li, X., Ji, H., Leung, V.C.M.: Towards integration of wireless sensor networks and cloud computing. IEEE International Conference on CloudCom (2015)
16. Dinesh Kumar, L.P., et al.: Data filtering in wireless sensor networks using neural networks for storage in cloud. In: International Conference on ICRTIT (2012)
17. Compton, M., et al.: The SSN ontology of the W3C semantic sensor network incubator group. In: Web Semantics: Science, Services and Agents on the World Wide Web, Science Direct, Vol. 17. Elsevier (2012)
18. Onat, F.A., Stojmenovic, I.: Generating random graphs for wireless actuator networks. IEEE International Symposium WoWMoM (2007)

Resource Redesign in RELOAD/CoAP Overlays for the Federation of Sensor Networks

L. Rodrigues$^{(\boxtimes)}$ ⓘ, J. Guerreiro ⓘ, and N. Correia ⓘ

CEOT, FCT, University of Algarve, 8005-139 Faro, Portugal
{lrodrig,jdguerreiro,ncorreia}@ualg.pt

Abstract. With 5G technologies new platforms for global connectivity of sensing devices are expected, many of them relying on federated sensor networks. Such federation can be done through P2P overlays where proxy nodes, of constrained environments, announce device resources or data. However, P2P resources may end up including similar device resource entries, if these can be announced under different P2P resource umbrellas, posing consistency and efficiency problems. Changes in a device resource (or data) will require the update of multiple P2P resources. To avoid this, a two-layer overlay architecture is used in this article so that P2P resources can include references to P2P anonymous resources, specifically created to avoid duplicate entries. In this article, procedures to keep P2P resources (anonymous or not) updated over time are proposed. Results show that these are effective in avoiding duplicate entries.

Keywords: Federated networks · Wireless sensor networks
RELOAD · CoAP · CoAP usage

1 Introduction

The Internet of Things (IoT) brings the opportunity for Things to connect globally and exchange data within the existing Internet infrastructure [1]. This means that sensing devices may interconnect for wide-area coverage, eventually cooperating to accomplish certain tasks, allowing for wide-area complex applications to be developed (e.g., environmental monitoring, earthquake/tsunami early-warning systems, correlation of health data, ...). Since 5G technologies meet the requirements of mobile communications and needs for Thing data transmission, these are expected to have a key role in such scenarios, enabling new platforms for global connectivity to emerge [2]. Such platforms may rely on the federation of multiple sensor networks.

In federation scenarios two standards end up having a significant role: (*i*) REsource LOcation And Discovery (RELOAD) base protocol, providing a generic self-organizing Peer-to-Peer (P2P) overlay network service supporting

© ICST Institute for Computer Sciences, Social Informatics and Telecommunications Engineering 2019
Published by Springer Nature Switzerland AG 2019. All Rights Reserved
V. Sucasas et al. (Eds.): BROADNETS 2018, LNICST 263, pp. 31–40, 2019.
https://doi.org/10.1007/978-3-030-05195-2_4

different applications through the use of *Usages* [3]; (*ii*) Constrained Application Protocol (CoAP), a Web application transfer protocol for RESTful services to be provided in constrained nodes and networks, similarly to Hypertext Transfer Protocol (HTTP) [4]. A Usage in RELOAD defines how data is mapped into something (data object) that can be stored in the P2P overlay, how resources stored at the overlay are identified, how to retrieve data, and how to secure data. Since CoAP is expected to be a common application layer transfer protocol at constrained devices, a CoAP Usage for RELOAD has been proposed in [5]. This allows proxy nodes, of constrained environments, to form a P2P overlay to announce available resources and sensor data, so that any client can discover them. This is illustrated in Fig. 1. P2P models have the advantage of being decentralized, scalable and resilient.

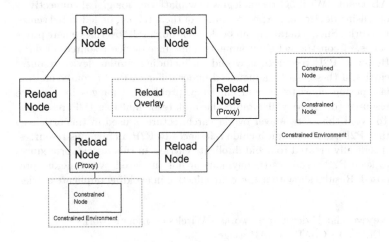

Fig. 1. RELOAD/CoAP overlay network.

A RELOAD/CoAP overlay may announce device resources or sensor data. When announcing device resources (e.g., temperature sensor), the P2P data object (called P2P resource) includes entries (linking information) for physical device resources to be reached using the CoAP protocol. When announcing sensor data, P2P resources include sensor information directly (value, timestamp, lifetime). Furthermore, device resources managed by different proxies/RELOAD nodes can be announced under a unique P2P resource umbrella, allowing for the aggregation of a set of device resources of the same type or with similar characteristics. For example, a P2P temperature resource may include temperature sensors from multiple places. This means, however, that P2P resources may end up including similar device resource entries (or similar sensor data in the caching case) because multiple combinations of device resources may give rise to independent P2P resources. This poses consistency/efficiency problems since multiple P2P resources must be updated when device resource entries change (for each device resource, suppliers also would have to keep track of which P2P resources to update). This becomes critical as more and more objects integrate in the IoT (possible combinations of resources will increase exponentially).

To overcome the previously mentioned consistency problem, a two-layer overlay architecture, relying on P2P anonymous resources, is used in this article. P2P anonymous resources can then serve as entries in other P2P resources, similarly to device resources. Procedures are proposed to keep the population of P2P anonymous resources, and any reference to them, updated over time as new P2P resources are announced or existing ones are updated/removed.

The remainder of this article is organized as follows. In Sect. 2, work related with RELOAD/CoAP architectures is discussed. Section 3 analyses the two-layer approach and required resource redesign procedures, and results are discussed in Sect. 5. Section 6 concludes the article.

2 Related Work

The RELOAD/CoAP architecture for wide area sensor and actuator networking, using the previously mentioned CoAP application usage for RELOAD, was initially proposed in [1]. The advantages of such architecture are discussed, which include integration with the Web, self-organization, scalability, robustness, and simulations are performed to compare its performance against a traditional client/server architecture. Federation of autonomous sensor networks, that have to collaborate for achieving a common task, is also discussed in [6]. However, such discussion does not focus on a distributed system, like the P2P-based architecture, and just 2-vertex distinct paths between every pair of WSNs is ensured, while minimizing the number of deployed relay nodes and having average node degree concerns.

Having the RELOAD/CoAP architecture proposed in [1] as a basis, P2P overlays for network coding based constrained environments are discussed in [7]. The goal is for encoding vectors and encoded data to be stored, and a decoding service to be used in case of packet loss. A work more closer to the one discussed in this article, also based on RELOAD/CoAP architecture proposed in [1], is the one in [8]. The focus is also on an effective announcement of P2P resources, for consistency purposes, but no P2P anonymous resources are created. That is, device resource entries can only be replaced by references to existing P2P resources but no extra P2P anonymous resources can be created for consistency purposes.

3 RELOAD/CoAP Overlay Networks

CoAP is a Web application transfer protocol designed for the special requirements of constrained environments [4]. CoAP provides a request/response interaction model between application endpoints and `coap(s)` URI scheme is used to identify CoAP resources. CoAP URI supports the path prefix `/.well-known` so that clients can discover resources available at the host, or discover any policy/information about the host, before making a request [9]. Since CoAP is expected to be a common application layer transfer protocol, a CoAP Usage for RELOAD was proposed in [5].

RELOAD/CoAP nodes, usually proxies, can announce/store NodeID to resource link mappings in the overlay. As an example, if a node participating in overlay overlay1.com, with NodeID 9996172, wants to register a structure with its sensors, a mapping similar to the following would be used:

```
Resource-ID=h("coap://overlay-1.com/proxy-1/.well-known/")
KEY=9996172
VALUE=[
</sensors/temp-1>; rt="temperature-c"; if="sensor",
...
]
```

The hash over the URI, h(...), is used for indexing. The KEY is the Node-ID of the RELOAD/CoAP node responsible for device resources at the VALUE section, which follow the CoRE Link Format specified in [10]. After P2P resource fetching, an AppAttach request can be sent to a specific Node-ID (direct connection for CoAP message exchange).

A P2P resource may also announce device resources managed by different nodes. The following example shows a temperature related P2P resource involving multiple RELOAD nodes:

```
Resource-ID = h("coap://overlay-1.com/temperature/.well-known/")

KEY =  9996172,
VALUE = [
   </sensors/temp-1>;rt="temperature-c";if="sensor",
   </sensors/temp-2>;rt="temperature-c";if="sensor"
]

KEY = 9996173,
VALUE = [
   </sensors/temp-a>;rt="temperature-c";if="sensor",
   </sensors/temp-b>;rt="temperature-c";if="sensor"
]
```

Therefore, different combinations of device resources can be made available under different P2P resource umbrellas, allowing for the aggregation of a set of device resources of the same type or with similar characteristics.

3.1 Motivation

The proliferation of similar entries at multiple P2P resources has disadvantages: (i) keeping all P2P resources up-to-date becomes difficult; (ii) tracking which P2P resources have which device resource entries becomes difficult (new P2P resources can emerge at any time, if devices are available to the public). To overcome this problem, a two-layer overlay approach is used. More specifically, extra P2P anonymous resources are created, and content of announced P2P resources is changed in order to point to such anonymous resources leading to device resource entries of interest. A P2P resource will, therefore, have one of the following content formats:

- *Anonymous* - Includes references to P2P anonymous resources, each following the CoRE Link Format.
- *KeyValue* - Includes (KEY,VALUE) entries following the CoAP Usage format.

As an example, assuming that `coap://overlay-1.com/ heat-related-illness` includes temperature device resource entries similar to `coap://overlay-1.com/temperature`, plus extra CO2 entries, its content would be:

```
Resource-ID = h(coap://overlay-1.com/heat-related-illness/.well-
                                                          known)
[
    <coap://overlay-1.com/10001/>;rt="temperature
                            heat-related-illness";if="leaf",
    <coap://overlay-1.com/10002/>;rt="heat-related-illness";
                            if="leaf"
}
```

and the content of `coap://overlay-1.com/temperature` would be:

```
Resource-ID = h(coap://overlay-1.com/temperature/.well-known)
[
    <coap://overlay-1.com/10001/>;rt="temperature
                            heat-related-illness";if="leaf"
]
```

While these have an Anonymous content format, the P2P anonymous resources `coap://overlay-1.com/10001/` and `coap://overlay-1.com/10002/` would follow the CoAP Usage format, storing (KEY,VALUE) entries with temperature and CO2 device resource links, respectively. Note that the if specifies how to deal with the endpoint, and "leaf" means that its content follows the KeyValue format (otherwise the Anonymous format is assumed). Basically, a graph exists where P2P resources are nodes and references are links, and multiple hops may exist until (KEY,VALUE) entries are reached. The rt indicates resource types for such entry, which end up being the parent P2P resources at the graph. An overlay service would ensure that the client, performing a fetch to a P2P resource, receives just the (KEY,VALUE) entries and would not be aware of P2P anonymous resources.

The previously discussed two-layer overlay approach is able to avoid duplicate entries. However, existing P2P resources may have to be redesigned whenever new ones are created or existing ones are removed/modified. Procedures for this purpose are discusses next.

4   Two-Layer Overlay Approach

4.1   Assumptions and Operation

Let us assume a set of original RELOAD/CoAP P2P resources, $\mathcal{R}$, where each $r \in \mathcal{R}$ includes a set of (KEY,VALUE) entries denoted by $\mathcal{P}_r$, where each $p_r \in \mathcal{P}_r$ includes a set of device resource entries denoted by $\mathcal{E}_{p_r}$. Let us assume also that

P2P resources in $\mathcal{R}$ were redesigned according to the previously mentioned two-layer overlay approach, giving rise to $\mathcal{R}'$. That is, its content has changed so that references to P2P anonymous resources are used to avoid duplicates. The set of created P2P anonymous resources is denoted by $\mathcal{A}$. Such redesign should be done having the following assumptions as a basis.

Assumption 1 (P2P Resource Content). *The content of a P2P resource $r \in \mathcal{R}' \cup \mathcal{A}$ will be of type $T(r)$, where $T(r) \in \{$ "Anonymous", "KeyValue" $\}$. More specifically, if $r \in \mathcal{R}'$ then $T(r) = \{Anonymous\}$, meaning that an entry, denoted by $p_r \in \mathcal{P}_r$, will be a reference to a P2P anonymous resource following the CoRE Link Format. If $r \in \mathcal{A}$, then $T(r) = \{Anonymous\}$ if r is not a leaf and $T(r) = \{KeyValue\}$ if r is a leaf.*

This means that a resource in $\mathcal{R}'$ will always have links to P2P anonymous resources, while P2P anonymous resources in $\mathcal{A}$ will have either links to leaf P2P resources with (KEY, VALUE) entries or links to other P2P anonymous resources.

Assumption 2 (Number of Entries). *A device resource entry can not be included in more than one P2P resource. That is, for any $e \in \mathcal{E}_{p_r}$, $p_r \in \mathcal{P}_r$ and $r \in \mathcal{R}$, the following must hold: $|\{a \in \mathcal{A} : e_{p_a} = e, e_{p_a} \in \mathcal{E}_{p_a}, p_a \in \mathcal{P}_a\}| = 1$. A P2P anonymous resource entry can be included in multiple P2P resources.*

Assumption 3 (Strict Coverage). *P2P resources must be redesigned while not changing the content to be returned. That is, $\bigcup\limits_{p_r \in \mathcal{P}_r} \mathcal{E}_{p_r} = \bigcup\limits_{p_{r'} \in \mathcal{P}_{r'}} \mathcal{E}_{p_{r'}}, \forall r \in \mathcal{R}, \forall r' \in \mathcal{R}'.*

Upon a P2P resource fetch, an overlay service[1] would have to fetch the referenced P2P anonymous resources recursively, so that device resource entries are reached and returned to the client following the CoAP Usage format. This information is the one used by clients to perform AppAttachs.

To keep assumptions valid, P2P resources (anonymous included) will have to be updated when P2P resources are created/modified/removed. A set of merge/split procedures, for this purpose, are discussed next. These procedures assume the existence of a P2P resource per proxy (e.g., `coap://overlay-1.com/KEY=9996172`) containing references to the P2P anonymous resources including proxy's (`KEY,VALUE`) entries. These are referred to as proxy P2P resources.

4.2   Resource Redesign Procedures

P2P Resource Creation: When a new P2P resource r is to be created, initially with (KEY, VALUE) entries in its content, the procedure CREATE shown below must be performed. At line 3, the P2P anonymous resources, whose entries are

---

[1] A service discovery mechanism like ReDiR can be used to distribute load among RELOAD/CoAP nodes able to provide such service, ensuring scalability.

fully included in r, are obtained. A call to these should replace corresponding entries in r. Line 7 fetches P2P anonymous resources sharing content with r. These should be analyzed by SPLIT procedure. At this procedure, the splitting is performed at lines 2–4. This is recursive so that parent nodes are analyzed for splitting too (call at line 10).

CREATE(r)

1: **for** $p_r \in \mathcal{P}_r$ **do**
2:    Extract p_r's KEY and fetch corresponding proxy P2P resources, r'
3:    $\mathcal{I} = \{p_{r'} \in \mathcal{P}_{r'} : p_{r'} \subseteq p_r\}$
4:    **for** $p_i \in \mathcal{I}$ **do**
5:       Replace $p_i \cap p_r$ content in r by reference p_i
6:    **end for**
7:    $\mathcal{I}' = \{p_{r'} \in \mathcal{P}_{r'} \setminus \mathcal{I} : p_{r'} \cap p_r \neq \emptyset\}$
8:    SPLIT($\mathcal{I}', p_r$)
9:    **for** $p_i \in \mathcal{I}'$ **do**
10:      Replace $p_i \cap p_r$ content in r by reference p_i
11:   **end for**
12:   Create P2P anonymous resource if intact p_r content exists, and replace it by reference.
13: **end for**

SPLIT($\mathcal{I}', p_r$)

1: **for** $p_i \in \mathcal{I}'$ **do**
2:    Create resource with content $p_i \cap p_r$
3:    Create resource with content $p_r \setminus \{p_i \cap p_r\}$
4:    Update references at resources in $rt(p_i)$
5: **end for**
6: **if** no changes exist **then**
7:    Return
8: **end if**
9: **for** $p_i \in \mathcal{I}'$ **do**
10:   SPLIT($rt(p_i), p_r$)
11:   Delete p_i
12: **end for**

P2P Resource Removal: When a P2P resource $r \in \mathcal{R}'$ is to be removed, the procedure REMOVE shown below must be performed. Lines 2–5 will remove references to the resource being deleted. The MERGE procedure analyses common content, for possible joins. At this procedure, the $\mathbb{P}()$ is the powerset. Merges will be performed at children nodes recursively. It is assumed that the corresponding rt information is updated accordingly.

REMOVE(r)

1: **for** $p_r \in \mathcal{P}_r$ **do**
2:    **for** $i \in rt(p_r)$ **do**
3:       Fetch i
4:       Remove r from $rt(\{p_i \in \mathcal{P}_i : p_i = p_r\})$
5:    **end for**
6:    MERGE($rt(p_r)$)
7: **end for**
8: Delete r

MERGE($resources$)

1: $\mathcal{U} = \bigcup\limits_{i \in resources} \mathcal{P}_i$
2: $\mathcal{I} = \underset{S \in \mathbb{P}(\mathcal{U})}{\arg\max}(|\{i \in \mathcal{S} : rt(i) = \bigcap\limits_{j \in \mathcal{S}} rt(j)\}|)$
3: **if** $|\mathcal{I}| = 1$ **then**
4:    Replace content $\mathcal{I}$, at every $r' \in resources$, by $i \in \mathcal{I}$
5:    Delete $i \in \mathcal{I}$
6:    MERGE($resources$)
7: **else**
8:    **if** $|\mathcal{I}| > 1$ **then**
9:       Create new resource r with content of every $i \in \mathcal{I}$
10:     Replace content $\mathcal{I}$, at every $r' \in resources$, by r
11:     Delete every $i \in \mathcal{I}$
12:     **if** r is not of leaf **then**
13:        MERGE(r)
14:     **end if**
15:    **end if**
16: **end if**

P2P Resource Update: It is assumed that a P2P resource removal is performed, followed by a P2P resource creation.

5   Scenario Analysis

To evaluate the advantages of having P2P anonymous resources, different scenarios were tested. In such scenarios there are public P2P resources (URIs known to the public), each having a set of P2P anonymous resource entries (i.e., of Anonymous content type). The P2P anonymous resources being referenced can then be of Anonymous or KeyValue content type. In the first case another calling level is being built, which may reference any existing P2P anonymous resources. A maximum of two levels exists. Table 1 shows the ranges used to define the number of P2P resources or resource/sensor entries (a random number is picked to run a test). The following plots show the average of 20 tests performed for each scenario.

Table 1. Scenarios under test.

Scenario	Public P2P resources	Anonymous resources per level	Refs for anonymous content	Refs for KeyValue content
A	[1–10]	[5–10]	[1–5]	[1–5]
B	[1–20]	[10–20]	[1–10]	[1–10]
C	[1–30]	[15–30]	[1–15]	[1–15]
D	[1–40]	[20–40]	[1–20]	[1–20]
E	[1–50]	[25–50]	[1–25]	[1–25]
F	[1–60]	[30–60]	[1–30]	[1–30]

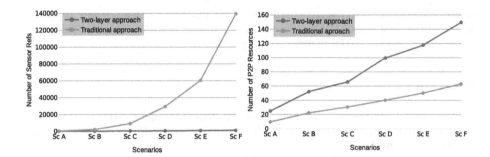

Fig. 2. Number of sensor references and P2P resources.

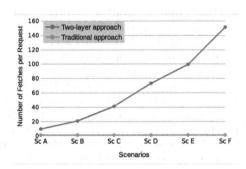

Fig. 3. Number of fetches per public P2P resource.

As shown in Fig. 2, if P2P anonymous resources are not created then the total number of sensor entries will grow exponentially due to duplicate entries. The proposed solution is able to keep a single reference to sensor entries, resulting into very low values for the total number of entries. Duplicate entries are avoided, however, at the expense of additional fetches. Figure 3 shows the number of required fetches per public P2P resource. Note, however, that fetching in parallel will reduce latency (i.e., for two levels the overall delay converges to the time of two fetches in series).

6   Conclusions and Further Work

Resource redesign procedures were proposed to keep P2P resources in RELOAD/CoAP architectures updated over time, while ensuring that sensor resource entries are unique. This ensures data consistency, better coordination of cooperating systems, and timeliness of notifications. Future work includes comparing this approach with other optimization approaches.

Acknowledgment. Work supported by FCT (Foundation for Science and Technology) from Portugal within CEOT (Center for Electronic, Optoelectronic and Telecommunications) and UID/MULTI/00631/2013 project.

References

1. Mäenpää, J., Bolonio, J.J., Loreto, S.: Using RELOAD and CoAP for wide area sensor and actuator networking. EURASIP J. Wireless Commun. Networking **2012**, 121 (2012)
2. Zhang, D., et al.: One integrated energy efficiency proposal for 5G IoT communications. IEEE Internet Things J. **3**(6), 1346–1354 (2016)
3. Jennings, C., et al.: REsource LOcation And Discovery (RELOAD) Base Protocol. RFC 6940 (2014)
4. Shelby, Z., et al.: The Constrained Application Protocol (CoAP). RFC 7252 (2014)
5. Jimenez, J., et al.: A Constrained Application Protocol (CoAP) Usage for REsource LOcation And Discovery (RELOAD). RFC 7650 (2015)
6. Lee, S., Younis, M., Lee, M.: Optimized bi-connected federation of multiple sensor network segments. Ad Hoc Networks **38**, 1–18 (2016)
7. Al-Hawri, E., Correia, N., Barradas, A.: RELOAD/CoAP P2P overlays for network coding based constrained environments. In: Camarinha-Matos, L.M., Parreira-Rocha, M., Ramezani, J. (eds.) DoCEIS 2017. IAICT, vol. 499, pp. 307–315. Springer, Cham (2017). https://doi.org/10.1007/978-3-319-56077-9_30
8. Rodrigues, L., Guerreiro, J., Correia, N.: RELOAD/CoAP architecture with resource aggregation/disaggregation service. IEEE PIMRC, IoT Workshop, Valencia 4–7 September 2016 Spain (2016)
9. Nottingham, M., Hammer-Lahav, E.: Defining Well-Known Uniform Resource Identifiers (URIs). RFC 5785 (2010)
10. Shelby, Z.: Constrained RESTful Environments (CoRE) Link Format. RFC 6690 (2012)

SDN and Network Virtualization

A Practical Approach
for Small Cell Sharing
Using a Time-Multiplexing Scheme

David Candal-Ventureira[1], Felipe Gil-Castiñeira[1(✉)], Jorge Muñoz-Castañer[1,2],
and Francisco J. González-Castaño[1]

[1] atlanTTic Research Center for Telecommunication Technologies,
University of Vigo, Campus Lagoas-Marcosende, 36310 Vigo, Spain
{dcandal,xil,jorgem,javier}@gti.uvigo.es
[2] Gradiant, Galician R and D Centre in Advanced Telecommunications,
Campus Lagoas-Marcosende, 36310 Vigo, Spain

Abstract. The new requirements for 5G, in terms of latency and band-width, demand new technologies such as millimeter-wave small cells, requiring dense deployments to achieve good coverage. Even before the arrival of 5G, small cells were already being deployed to avoid congestion and achieve a good Quality of Service (QoS) in areas with high densities of potential users. These infrastructures require large investments, forcing operators to share them or to use the services of a neutral host, responsible of installation and maintenance. In this paper we present a practical approach for different operators to share a small cell infrastructure, while allowing them to use their respective dedicated frequencies, adjust any parameter, or even deploy any particular radio access technology. This way, each operator can provide a differentiated service that may represent a competitive advantage even on the same physical infrastructure.

Keywords: Small cells · Multi-tenancy · Time-sharing · 5G

1 Introduction

The exponential growth of mobile traffic and the incessant subscriber demand for a better QoS force operators to look for alternatives to increase their network capacity. Furthermore, ITU-R has defined a set of requirements related to technical performance for IMT-2020 networks (5G) including very low latency communications (1 ms) and lower energy consumption [1]. Ultra-dense small cell architectures have proven to be a good choice to address such requirements, as demonstrated in [2–4]. By increasing the density of base stations in an area it is possible to provide higher bandwidths to more users at less power with lower latencies. This holds in areas with high user densities, such as malls, downtown shopping areas, stadiums, factories and enterprise facilities.

© ICST Institute for Computer Sciences, Social Informatics and Telecommunications Engineering 2019
Published by Springer Nature Switzerland AG 2019. All Rights Reserved
V. Sucasas et al. (Eds.): BROADNETS 2018, LNICST 263, pp. 43–51, 2019.
https://doi.org/10.1007/978-3-030-05195-2_5

However, although the installation of low power nodes (such as small cells) entails significant lower costs than the installation of macrocells (thanks to their small form factor and simpler power sources), these nodes still require substantial investments. Indeed, "mobile-first" "bring-your-own-device" (BYOD) businesses require very good coverages regardless of the operators providing service to employees, customers or visitors [5]. In such scenarios there are market incentives for multi-operator infrastructure sharing or neutral hosts. Distributed Antenna Systems (DAS) or Wi-Fi hotspots are typical neutral host approaches. Nevertheless, both systems have drawbacks, such as the high cost of DAS deployments and the QoS challenges in Wi-Fi installations.

Nonetheless, there are non-technical issues that slow down the adoption of sharing strategies. For example, some regulators do not permit spectrum sharing because they perceive it as a risk against healthy competition (in Spain this was the case prior to March 2017), and some operators may perceive risks in sharing their infrastructure with their competitors. In this regard, according to [5], a good approach is to combine dedicated and shared cells. Also, recent research projects have considered the "Small Cells as a Service" concept [6], where different operators share a cloud-enabled small cell.

In this paper we present a practical implementation that makes it possible to assign small cells on demand to particular operators in environments with dynamic, high user densities. In this scenario different operators may require more or less resources (small cells) from some moment on. Therefore, a mechanism for fast cell reallocation is necessary. We also present our work-in-progress and the future research lines.

In Sect. 2 we discuss related work in small cell sharing. In Sect. 3 we explain our practical approach. Finally, in Sect. 4 we provide some conclusions and describe our future work.

2   Related Work

In their traditional business model, operators own a network and leverage it to provide better services (in terms of coverage, bandwidth, etc.) than their competitors. Nevertheless, the introduction of new wireless technologies (such as 4G or 5G) is increasingly complex and requires frequent updates. Telecommunications equipment is a commodity and the mere provision of a new technology does not provide a competitive advantage. Operators try to differentiate themselves with specialized services. In this context Radio Access Network (RAN) sharing is a common strategy to increase coverage while keeping costs at bay [7].

3GPP has considered this problem and has provided specifications to share the network [8]. There exist different technical architectures for RAN sharing, ranging from mere location and "tower" sharing (passive RAN sharing) to using exactly the same infrastructure (for example when an operator signs an agreement with another for the users of the first to roam over the infrastructure of the second). Multi-Operator RAN (MORAN) [9] is an interesting intermediate architecture in which operators retain a great level of control over their traffic and capacity because, even though they share the same physical eNodeB, several virtual instances with independent parameters are generated. For example, each operator keeps using its own dedicated frequency bands and controlling its QoS levels. However, at least one independent radio head is required for each operator.

RAN sharing becomes especially relevant for deployments that require the installation of a large number of base stations, for example small cell deployments to increase network capacity in very dense areas [2–4]. The number of subscribers per cell decreases with the coverage area, reducing eNodeB congestion. Millimeter bands (30 GHz–300 GHz) have raised a lot of interest for 5G small cells because they are uncongested and allow allocating large channel bandwidths (and thus increasing transmission rates). In fact, as they are subject to higher propagation losses, they are only adequate for dense infrastructures [10].

Although a MORAN architecture provides several advantages, it has been less extended in the small cell ecosystem because of its higher complexity and deployment effort [5] than other architectures such as Multiple Operator Core Network (MOCN) [8], where all RAN elements are shared (including the spectrum). Our solution is similar to MORAN, in the sense that we make it possible to dynamically assign small cells to operators respecting their particular frequencies and configurations. This way, it is possible to cover an area with small cells and dynamically assign them to different operators according to their needs at every moment.

Other authors have also studied solutions for radio resource sharing among operators. The typical approach is based on a Cloud-RAN architecture [11,12] that distributes the implementation of the cellular base stations. Baseband processing is centralized on a cloud server, leaving only the radio frequency functionality in the base stations and, thus, simplifying radio resource sharing. This method reduces the complexity (and therefore, the cost) of radio access network equipment and, at the same time, increases flexibility and efficiency. Cloud-RAN is usually combined with Software Defined Radio (SDR), so that baseband signal processing is performed purely on a general purpose computer (implementing by software elements such as modulators, filters and mixers, which traditionally were implemented by hardware) [13]. Only conversion, channelization and amplification are implemented by hardware at the transmission site.

Most RAN sharing proposals take advantage of OFDMA spectrum division, introduced in cellular communications by the Long Term Evolution (LTE) standard. OFDMA splits spectrum into time and frequency slots (Physical Resource Blocks, PRBs), which are dynamically allocated to the subscribers. In [14] the authors introduce the Network Virtualization Substrate (NVS) concept, which applies a two-step scheduling process for enabling "network slicing" [15] up to the eNodeBs. In this way, the entire physical network is divided into several logical networks specially adapted to provide services with different QoS requirements. On each transmission opportunity, PRBs are firstly distributed among the slices according to their requirements, and then each slice decides how to allocate the received resources among their subscribers. In [16] the authors analyze an extension of NVS that enables partial resource reservation. Each slice is guaranteed a minimum amount of PRBs, but it may also use idle resources of the other slices.

The NVS concept can be extended to enable sharing a RAN infrastructure by multiple Mobile Virtual Network Operators (MVNOs) through the allocation of a set of slices to each operator, as considered in [17]. The authors propose a new scheduler that assigns PRBs to different operators based on the decisions taken by a SDN controller, so that different slices may share a common pool of frequencies according to their requirements.

Considering dense deployments, a finer and more efficient use of the RAN elements can be achieved by centralizing the control plane of the base stations, as proposed in [18,19]. Thus, the interference from adjacent cells can be reduced by considering their location and the interference perceived from other nodes [18] or taking into account the PRBs allocated by the adjacent cells [19].

Although RAN sharing based on a shared scheduler enables efficient spectrum utilization, since MVNOs can use those PRBs that are not assigned to other operators, the control over radio resources is coarse. The operators must agree on parameters such as transmission and reception gains of the radio devices. The radio access technology (RAT) must also be the same for each operator on each radio. In addition, operators have less control over the scheduled PRBs, which limits their choices of slots to improve channel conditions for their subscribers. This fact also hinders the adoption of this approach for multiple independent Mobile Network Operators (MNOs), as control signaling and management is performed in specific PRBs and times in LTE. Finally, spectrum sharing is still forbidden or has been only recently allowed (for example, in Spain), making alternative solutions interesting.

Our proposal provides a simple solution for several independent operators to share a small cell infrastructure, while allowing them to use their respective dedicated frequencies, adjust any parameter, or even deploy any particular radio access technology. To the best of our knowledge, this is an original approach.

3   Implementation

We assume an scenario with a high user density (mall, downtown, stadium, etc.). In it, in order to ensure good QoS, it is necessary to deploy a dense small cell network covering the whole area.

A multi-operator "neutral host" or "infrastructure provider" is in charge of the small cell network, which is shared by different operators. A "neutral host" orchestrator distributes the radio devices among the operators, based on algorithms that seek to maximize the aggregate operator performance and user QoS, under certain Service Level Agreements. Due to the dynamic user location and densities, small cell radios must be configured in the shortest time possible.

With this scenario in mind we have implemented a LTE small cell sharing proof-of-concept using OpenAirInterface (OAI) [20]. OAI is an open source platform developed by the OpenAirInterface Software Alliance (OSA), which allows running a 3GPP-compliant LTE testbed on a general purpose computer and an SDR device. It provides all the necessary network entities in an LTE architecture (eNodeB, MME, HSS, SGW and UEs). The OAI front radio is compatible with some popular SDR devices, such as Ettus Research USRPs and Lime Microsystem's LimeSDRs. Specifically, in our proof-of-concept we have used a LimeSDR device, a low cost software defined radio which is able to operate in frequencies ranging from 100 kHz up to 3.8 GHz, and handle up to 61.44 MHz channels [21].

3.1   Initial Tests

Each small cell would be implemented on an embedded computer running the basebands selected by each operator (in our experiment OAI's eNodeB). The small cell would be connected to an operator Core Network (CN) by decision of the neutral orchestrator. However, OAI is not designed to be "plugged" and "unplugged" from the SDR device, so our first step was a procedure for disabling the eNodeB that is using the radio up to a certain moment and launching a new eNodeB for the new operator. This procedure takes setup times of approximately 16.3 s with a USRP SDR device and 10.2 s when using a LimeSDR.

  These times may be quite large for highly dynamic scenarios, so we analyzed the different stages completed during the setup of an OAI eNodeB in order to decrease them. Successively, the eNodeB:

1. starts the set up for each protocol stack layer on independent threads,
2. requests the SDR device,
3. configures the SDR device with the appropriate radio parameters,
4. starts the transmission.

As all the stack processes are independent of the radio, a first possibility to reduce this delay is forcing those processes to be ready before the radio is allocated to the eNodeB. Therefore, we modified the eNodeB to complete all internal start up tasks and then keep waiting for a grant message to use the radio device. Thereby, the transition delay is reduced to the time it takes to configure the SDR device. We estimated this delay running multiple independent executions, and the results show that, on average, it was reduced to 2.81 s.

3.2   Abstracting the Radio from the eNodeBs

We then analyzed other possibilities. We found that by introducing a new element, exclusively in charge of all the transceiver tasks, we are able to keep the previous transceiver configuration state. This way, on each radio reallocation, it is only necessary to modify the parameters that differ from those in the previous session, so the transition time is reduced. We called this new element "transceiver coordinator".

  Figure 1 shows the proposed system architecture. The transceiver coordinator and operator's base station processes run on an embedded computer on which the SDR device is connected. In our experiment, both processes are connected

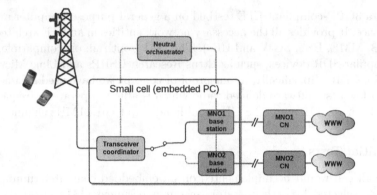

Fig. 1. High-level system architecture.

through UNIX sockets. All the operator's core networks are reachable from this computer. The base station processes susceptible to take the radio are kept ready for being deployed and to inform the neutral orchestrator about the radio parameters they need. When a radio reallocation takes place, the orchestrator informs the transceiver coordinator and notifies the new radio parameters, which are compared with the previous configuration and set only if they are different. Then, the transceiver coordinator notifies the radio availability to the implied base station processes. From that moment on, the new base station process may begin transmitting and receiving IQ samples.

The non-deterministic communication delay between the base stations and the transceiver coordination processes does not affect the radio frequency transmission. Most of the commercial SDRs exchange signals by blocks labeled with

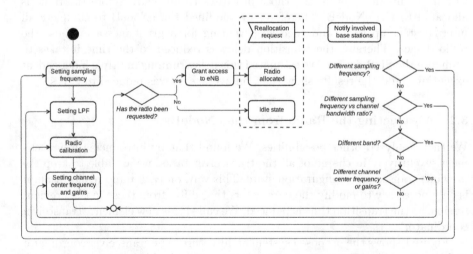

Fig. 2. Flow diagram of transceiver coordination processes.

time stamps, identifying the instants in which they must be transmitted or were received, according to the radio clock. The margin between the moments when the samples are generated and when they must be transmitted is large enough to allow the transceiver coordinator to receive them on time.

Figure 2 shows the flow diagram of the transceiver coordination process. Specifically, for reallocating the radio to another operator, it:

1. is notified to allocate the radio to a new operator,
2. notifies both base station processes involved in the reallocation procedure,
3. sets those radio parameters which must be modified from the current session,
4. starts using the new base station sockets for exchanging the IQ samples with the radio.

3.3   Results

Some minor tasks performed during the radio initialization (which take up to 710 ms) can be avoided, as they only need to be run once. The exact time to reassign a small cell to a new operator will depend on the parameters that must be modified given the ones used by the previous operator:

− Changing the sampling frequency takes only 225 ms on average, but it requires reestablishing the baseband low pass filter.
− Setting the baseband low pass filter consumes about 1.10 s. Once established, the filter may not need to be modified until the bandwidth/sampling frequency ratio changes.
− The radio calibration task introduces a delay of about 0.73 s. This task should be performed when the channel central frequency, the channel bandwidth or the sampling frequency are modified. However, the calibration may be reused for adjacent channels without noticeable signal degradation. Within LTE band 7, we were able to keep signal quality by calibrating the radio once at the band center frequency and then using different channels along the band (sharing the rest of the parameters).
− Finally, modifying the reception and transmission RF frequencies and gains takes 43 ms on average.

If both operators share the same parameters, the transition delay will only be the time to grant the communication to the new operator and the time to synchronize the base station with the radio clock (which in our tests was always 1 ms). If it is necessary to change the channel frequencies and gains, this delay increases by about 43 ms.

A new sampling frequency or channel bandwidth leads the transition to slow down for up to 0.96 s. However, setting the low pass filter and the sampling frequency could be avoided by digitally resampling and filtering the baseband signals at the transceiver coordinator, so that the sampling frequency and filter on the radio remain unchanged.

Considering all the aforementioned optimizations, it would be possible to switch operators in just 44 ms in the worst case, and in less than 1 ms when both radio services use the same parameters. This is a great improvement from the 10.2 s we achieve when we do not preserve the radio configuration state. Therefore, it should be possible to deploy a small cell infrastructure in which an "infrastructure provider" would assign small cells dynamically to the different operators according to their instant needs in up to 44 ms.

4   Conclusions and Future Work

In this paper we have presented a practical approach for different operators to share a small cell deployment. Each small cell is assigned exclusively to one operator at a time. Thus, such operator may keep a tight control of traffic and capacity, as it continues using its own dedicated frequency bands and controlling its QoS levels. It may even use a different RAT. If one operator requires more resources at some moment, it may be granted more small cells that were initially assigned to other operators. According to our analysis, this reallocation can be performed in less than 1 ms in optimum circumstances and up to 44 ms in the worst case.

An LTE proof-of-concept has confirmed the viability of our approach, which is akin to the MORAN concept. We are currently exploring other mechanisms to share small cells. For example, how to transmit different waveforms in different frequencies of a small cell at the same time, even when they use different RATs.

References

1. ITU-R: MT Vision - Framework and overall objectives of the future development of IMT for 2020 and beyond. Recommendation ITU-R M.2083-0, September 2015
2. Bhushan, N., et al.: Network densification: the dominant theme for wireless evolution into 5G. IEEE Commun. Mag. **52**(2), 82–89 (2014)
3. Andrews, J.G., et al.: What will 5G Be? IEEE J. Sel. Areas Commun. **32**(6), 1065–1082 (2014)
4. Nakamura, T., et al.: Trends in small cell enhancements in LTE advanced. IEEE Commun. Mag. **51**(2), 98–105 (2013)
5. 5G Americas, Small Cell Forum. Multi-operator and neutral host small cells. Technical Report (2016)
6. Giannoulakis, I., et al.: Enabling technologies and benefits of multi-tenant multi-service 5G small cells. In: 2016 European Conference on Networks and Communications (EuCNC 2016), Athens, pp. 42–46 (2016)
7. Frisanco, T., Tafertshofer, P., Lurin, P., Ang, R.: Infrastructure sharing and shared operations for mobile network operators from a deployment and operations view. In: NOMS 2008 - 2008 IEEE Network Operations and Management Symposium, Salvador, Bahia, pp. 129–136 (2008)
8. 3GPP, TS 23.251: Network Sharing: Architecture and Functional Description. version 14.1.0 Release 14 (2017)
9. Wang, X., Granberg, O.A.: Multiple operator radio access network (MORAN) in a telecommunications system. U.S. Patent No. 9,667,478, 30 May 2017

10. Dehos, C., et al.: Millimeter-wave access and backhauling: the solution to the exponential data traffic increase in 5G mobile communications systems? IEEE Commun. Mag. **52**(9), 88–95 (2014)
11. China Mobile Research Institute: C-RAN the road towards green RAN (2013)
12. Checko, A., et al.: Cloud RAN for mobile networks – a technology overview. IEEE Commun. Surv. Tutor. **17**(1), 405–426 (2015)
13. Jondral, F.K.: Software-defined radio–basics and evolution to cognitive radio. EURASIP J. Wirel. Commun. Netw. **2005**(3), 275–283 (2005)
14. Kokku, R., Mahindra, R., Zhang, H., Rangarajan, S.: NVS: a substrate for virtualizing wireless resources in cellular networks. IEEE/ACM Trans. Netw. **20**(5), 1333–1346 (2012)
15. Zhang, H., Liu, N., Chu, X., Long, K., Aghvami, A.H., Leung, V.C.M.: Network slicing based 5G and future mobile networks: mobility, resource management, and challenges. IEEE Commun. Mag. **55**(8), 138–145 (2017)
16. Guo, T., Arnott, R.: Active LTE RAN sharing with partial resource reservation. In: IEEE 78th Vehicular Technology Conference (VTC Fall), Las Vegas, USA (2013)
17. Costanzo, S., Fajjari, I., Aitsaadi, N., Langar, R.: A network slicing prototype for a flexible cloud radio access network. In: 2018 15th IEEE Annual Consumer Communications & Networking Conference (CCNC), Las Vegas, USA (2018)
18. Gudipati, A., Perry, D., Erran, L., Katti, S.: SoftRAN: software defined radio access network. In: HotSDN 2013 - Proceedings of the Second ACM SIGCOMM Workshop on Hot Topics in Software Defined Networking, pp. 25–30, Hong Kong, China (2013)
19. Gudipati, A., Erran, L., Katti, S.: RadioVisor: a slicing plane for radio access networks. In: HotSDN 2014 - Proceedings of the Third Workshop on Hot Topics in Software Defined Networking, pp. 237–238, New York, USA (2014)
20. Nikaein, N., et al.: OpenAirInterface: an open LTE network in a PC. In: Mobicom, pp. 305–308, USA, Maui (2014)
21. Software Defined Radio - Lime Micro. http://www.limemicro.com/products/software-defined-radio/

On Controllers' Utilization
in Software-defined Networking
by Switch Migration

Faroq AL-Tam$^{(\boxtimes)}$ ⓘ, Mohammad Ashrafi ⓘ, and Noélia Correia ⓘ

Center for Electronic, Optoelectronic and Telecommunications (CEOT),
Faculty of Science and Technology - University of Algarve, 8005-139 Faro, Portugal
{ftam,a41301,ncorreia}@ualg.pt

Abstract. This work presents a model to solve the switch migration problem in software-defined networking. This model is formulated as a mixed-integer linear programming, and compared against the static mapping approach. Two scenarios of homogeneous and heterogeneous controllers are evaluated. The experimental results show that the dynamic mapping enabled by the proposed model can enhance the controllers' utilization by ≈63% for homogeneous scenario and ≈47% for heterogeneous scenario, while maintaining a low control plane overhead.

Keywords: Software-defined networking · Multi-controller SDN
Switch migration · Load balancing

1 Introduction

Software-defined Networking (SDN) is an emergent technology that offers a promising software oriented design to manage IP networks [11], Internet of Things (IoT) [3] and 5G networks [5]. In SDN, the data and control planes are decoupled to make the forwarding devices programmable and to promote network scalability and evolution [4]. Network policies are defined in the management plane, materialized by software modules in controllers in the control plane, and carried out by switches in the data plane [11,13]. From a layer perspective, the communication between the data and control planes is made available via standardized **southbound** interfaces (e.g., OpenFlow [7]), while the communication between the management and control plane is usually done through non-standardized **northbound** interfaces [9].

Control plane can be centralized or distributed. In the former, a single controller is responsible for managing all flow requests from the switches, while in the latter, multiple controllers are used. A single controller ensures a unified

This work was developed within the Centre for Electronic, Optoelectronic and Telecommunications (CEOT), and supported by the UID/MULTI/00631/2013 project of the Portuguese Science and Technology Foundation (FCT).

V. Sucasas et al. (Eds.): BROADNETS 2018, LNICST 263, pp. 52–61, 2019.
https://doi.org/10.1007/978-3-030-05195-2_6

knowledge about the network, however, it represents a possible single point of failure [11,21]. Additionally, a centralized control plane does not scale well [21], is susceptible to overloading [19], and can hinder the Quality of Service (QoS) [10]. On the other hand, in multi-controller SDN [7] each controller is responsible for a set of switches (domain). A controller can be master, equal, or slave, where the first two types can process the flow requests from the switches and install the forwarding rules in the switches. A slave controller can only read the switch flow table, but can not update it. Each switch can have multiple equal and slave controllers, but only one master controller. Furthermore, a master controller for a specific switch can be slave controller for another one, and whenever a master controller fails, a slave or local controller can request (via OpenFlow `role-request` message) to become the new master of the affected switches.

The multi-controller paradigm is shown to improve many aspects of SDN [22], but it presents many challenges, especially for controllers' utilization when switch-controller assignments are static. The load of a controller is mainly caused by the processing of the `packet-in` messages sent from the switches [19], and due to network dynamics, the number of these messages vary both regionally and temporally [2]. As a result of these variations, some controllers will be overcommitted (hot spot), while some others will be underutilized (cold spot). This leads to domain failure (and multi-domain failure [18]), or network underutilization. Therefore, switch migration (SM) [6] can be used as a key-enabler for dynamic switch-controller mappings in order to adaptively shift the load of controllers. Whenever overloading is detected in a master controller, it selects a switch from its domain and asks a slave controller to become the new master of this switch.

This work presents a simple and concise modeling of the SM problem as a mixed integer linear programming (MILP), which considers the load balancing of the controllers, and the overhead created by the migrated switches. Two scenarios of homogeneous and heterogeneous controllers are considered.

This work is organized as follows: Related work is described in Sect. 2, and the proposed model is presented in Sect. 3, the experimental results and the conclusions are presented in Sects. 4 and 5, respectively.

2   Related Work

SM problem is clearly addressed for the first time in ElastiCon [6]. Since then some approaches have been proposed [22]. SM is not only used for balancing load [12], but also for improving resource utilization [20] and security [17]. SM is usually treated and modeled within linear [1,8] or nonlinear [14,16] models of dynamic switch-controller assignments. In these models, the mappings are calculated for all switches and controllers. However, in SM only a subset of controllers and a subset of switches require reassignments. Therefor, it is more appropriate to model the SM separately. The most recent works that model SM separately are presented in [15,23], but aspects like heterogeneous controllers' utilization are not investigated. In [15], the overloading is detected based on the load diversity matrix of the controllers. A user-defined threshold is used to decide which controller is overloaded. A switch is migrated based on a probabilistic measure. In [23], SM is modeled within the earth mover distance (EMD), which is a histogram matcher that calculates the cost of "morphing" one histogram into another.

3 The Proposed Model

The proposed model considers various factors in SM, some of them are not already considered in the literature, like switch importance in its original domain and the ratio between the remaining capacity in the controller and the number of flow requests in the migrated switches. These are two important factors in order to reduce the control plane overhead when exchanging information of the migrated switches.

3.1 System Model

The network scenario for switch migration problem is depicted in Fig. 1, and the notation used is described in Table 1. A set $\mathcal{C}$ of controllers is managing a set $\mathcal{S}$ of switches. Each switch is connected to exactly one master controller (thin solid lines) and one or more slave controllers (thin dashed lines). Therefore, each controller is managing a subset (domain) $\mathcal{S}_i \subset \mathcal{S}$ of switches. The latency between controller c_i and switch s_j is known and denoted by d_{ij}, and the latency between controllers c_i and $c_{i'}$ is known and denoted by $v_{ii'}$.

At each switch s_j, a number of `packet-in` messages per second r_j is generated (usually following Poisson distribution). Each controller has a limited processing capability γ_i to process a certain number of `packet-in` messages per second. In addition, each switch has a relative-importance θ_j, which is related to the size of its flow table and the number of neighbor switches in the same domain.

Given a scenario where loads at the controllers are imbalanced, the objective is to find a set of switches to be migrated between controllers, in order to reestablish the load balance, while minimizing the control plane overhead.

3.2 Controller Load

The load ω_i of controller c_i is the aggregation of the flow requests from the switches in its domain $\mathcal{S}_i$:

$$\omega_i = \sum_{s_j \in \mathcal{S}_i} r_j, \quad \forall c_i \in \mathcal{C}, \tag{1}$$

and after switch migration, the load of controller c_i, denoted by $\tilde{\omega}_i$, can be calculated as [23]:

$$\tilde{\omega}_i = \omega_i - \sum_{c_{i'} \in \mathcal{C}: c_i \neq c_{i'}} \sum_{s_j \in \mathcal{S}} r_j x_j^{ii'} + \sum_{c_{i'} \in \mathcal{C}: c_i \neq c_{i'}} \sum_{s_j \in \mathcal{S}} r_j x_j^{i'i}, \quad \forall c_i \in \mathcal{C} \tag{2}$$

where $x_j^{ii'}$ is the migration decision variable to be calculated.

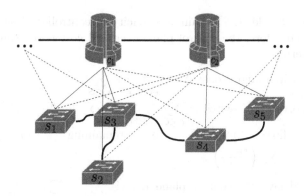

Fig. 1. The SDN model. Thick solid lines are the physical inter-plane links, thin solid lines are the switch-controller master mappings, and thin dashed lines are the switch-controller slave mappings.

Table 1. Notation used through out this paper.

Term	Description
$\mathcal{C}$	Set of controllers
$\mathcal{S}$	Set of switches
r_j	Number of packet-in messages generated by switch s_j
θ_j	Switch importance (weight) in its domain
γ_i	Capacity of controller c_i
d_{ij}	Latency between controller c_i and switch s_j
$v_{ii'}$	Latency between controller c_i and controller $c_{i'}$
ω_i	Load at controller c_i
l	Minimum load-to-capacity ratio
u	Maximum load-to-capacity ratio
$x_j^{ii'}$	Migration decision variable, $x_j^{ii'} = 1$ if switch s_j is to be migrated from controller c_i to $c_{i'}$, zero otherwise

3.3   Cost Function

The cost function is a linear combination of the load balancing and the control plane overhead costs. The load balancing cost is defined as the difference between the maximum and minimum load-to-capacity ratios, denoted by the real-valued variables u and l, respectively. The control plane overhead cost, caused by migrating switch s_j from controller c_i to controller $c_{i'}$, is denoted by $\vartheta_j^{ii'}$. Therefore, for two user-defined weights α_1 and $\alpha_2 = 1 - \alpha_1$, the cost function is defined as:

$$f = \alpha_1(u - l) + \alpha_2 \sum_{c_i \in \mathcal{C}} \sum_{c_{i'} \in \mathcal{C}: c_i \neq c_{i'}} \sum_{s_j \in \mathcal{S}} \vartheta_j^{ii'} x_j^{ii'} \qquad (3)$$

To calculate $\vartheta_j^{ii'}$, let the remaining capacity in controller c_i be denoted by $\hat{\gamma}_i = \gamma_i - \omega_i$. Therefore, the control plane overhead cost is the composition of the following terms:

1. Number of switch migrations: $\sum\limits_{c_i \in \mathcal{C}} \sum\limits_{c_{i'} \in \mathcal{C}: c_i \neq c_{i'}} \sum\limits_{s_j \in \mathcal{S}} x_j^{ii'}$

2. Overall importance of switches: $\sum\limits_{c_i \in \mathcal{C}} \sum\limits_{c_{i'} \in \mathcal{C}: c_i \neq c_{i'}} \sum\limits_{s_j \in \mathcal{S}} \theta_j x_j^{ii'}$

3. Migrated flow requests to remaining capacity ratio: $\sum\limits_{c_i \in \mathcal{C}} \sum\limits_{c_{i'} \in \mathcal{C}: c_i \neq c_{i'}} \sum\limits_{s_j \in \mathcal{S}} \left(\frac{r_j x_j^{ii'}}{\hat{\gamma}_{i'}} \right)$

4. Inter-plane delay and control plane delay: $\sum\limits_{c_i \in \mathcal{C}} \sum\limits_{c_{i'} \in \mathcal{C}: c_i \neq c_{i'}} \sum\limits_{s_j \in \mathcal{S}} r_j d_{i'j} x_j^{ii'} +$
$\sum\limits_{c_i \in \mathcal{C}} \sum\limits_{c_{i'} \in \mathcal{C}: c_i \neq c_{i'}} \sum\limits_{s_j \in \mathcal{S}} \theta_j v_{ii'} x_j^{ii'}$

Combing these sub-costs, $\vartheta_j^{ii'}$ can be calculated as:

$$\vartheta_j^{ii'} = \left\{ \left(\frac{r_j}{\hat{\gamma}_{i'}} (d_{i'j}\hat{\gamma}_{i'} + 1) + \theta_j(v_{ii'} + 1) + 1 \right) \right\} \tag{4}$$

3.4 Overall Formalization

The switch migration problem that handles the load balancing and minimizes the control plane overhead, can be now formulated as a mixed-integer linear programming as:

$$\text{Minimize } f \tag{5}$$

subject to:

$$0 \leq \sum\limits_{c_i \in \mathcal{C}} \sum\limits_{c_{i'} \in \mathcal{C}: c_i \neq c_{i'}} x_j^{ii'} \leq 1, \qquad \forall s_j \in \mathcal{S} \tag{6}$$

$$0 \leq l \leq \frac{\tilde{\omega}_i}{\gamma_i} \leq u < 1 \qquad \forall i \in \mathcal{C} \tag{7}$$

$$x_j^{ii'} \in \{0, 1\}, \qquad \forall c_i, c_{i'} \in \mathcal{C}, s_j \in \mathcal{S} \text{ and } l, u \in [0, 1) \tag{8}$$

The first constraint (6) ensures that when a switch is chosen for migration it can be only migrated to one controller. The controller capacity limitation and the upper and lower bounds, l and u, are determined by the second constraint (7). The last constraint (8) defines the domains of the binary and real-valued variables.

4 Experimental Results

To evaluate the proposed model, a comparison against the static mapping model is performed. A random topology of 4 controllers and 16 switches is created (Fig. 2). The number of flow requests for each switch is generated randomly

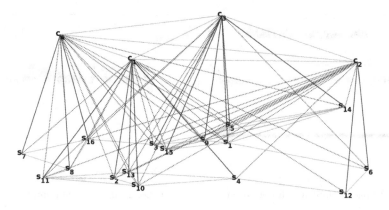

Fig. 2. A random SDN topology with 4 controllers and 16 switches used for simulation. Blue lines are intra-plane connections; red solid lines are the master assignments; and red dashed lines are the slave assignments. (Color figure online)

in the range [100, 400] `packet-in` messages per second, the latency is chosen from the range [0.1 1] milliseconds, and the simulation time is set to 1000 s. The weights in (3) are empirically set to $\alpha_1 = 0.7$ and $\alpha_2 = 0.3$. For the controllers capacity, two scenarios are considered: homogeneous and heterogeneous.

4.1   Homogeneous Controllers

In this scenario, the capacity γ of each controller is set to 2000 `packet-in` messages per second. In order to create a realistic network fluctuation, a hotspot is generated by stressing controller c_3, in Fig. 2, from time 100 to 150 s. The simulation results of this scenario are shown in Fig. 3.

In Fig. 3a, the load of this controller increases until it eventually exceeds its limited capacity, which will cause in a real case scenario a failure in the domain managed by c_3. However, when applying the proposed switch migration model, in Fig. 3b, the loads of all controllers are shifted under the limited capacity, with remaining capacity $\hat{\gamma} \approx 500$ `packet-in` messages per second in all time slots after the stressing period (i.e., >150 s).

In order to assess the controllers' utilization, the min-max ratio is used. The range of this ratio is between 0 and 1. When it is 1, it means all controllers have the same load, i.e., a perfect utilization. On the other hand, values close to 0 mean very low utilizations. Figure 3c shows this measure for the static and proposed models. In average, the static model produced ≈21%, while the proposed model produced ≈84%, i.e., with enhancement of 63%. However, when calculating this measure after the stressing period, the static model produced ≈20%, while the proposed model produced ≈92%, with improvement of ≈72%.

When considering the number of migrated switches in the proposed model, and as shown in Fig. 3d, before the stressing period (i.e., ≤100 s) no migration has occurred, and during the stressing period, only 9 switches were migrated

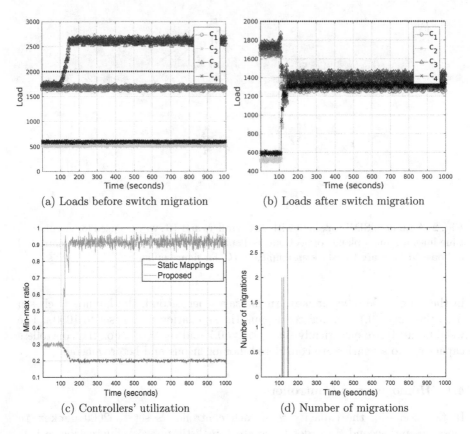

(a) Loads before switch migration

(b) Loads after switch migration

(c) Controllers' utilization

(d) Number of migrations

Fig. 3. Simulated results of 4 homogeneous controllers and 16 switches.

(with maximum of 3 switches at time 143 s) in order to cope with the traffic change. After the stressing period, no switch migration was required. Therefore the proposed model is able to maintain high utilization with low control plane overhead.

4.2 Heterogeneous Controllers

As shown in Fig. 4a, in this scenario the controllers have different capacities, but the total capacity is the same as in the previous test (i.e., 8000): $\gamma_1 = 2250$, $\gamma_2 = 1500$, $\gamma_3 = 2500$, and $\gamma_4 = 1750$. The simulation results of this scenario are shown in Fig. 4.

Comparing Figs. 4a and b, it is easy to see that the proposed switch migration model was successfully able to shift the loads of all controllers under their limited capacities, leading to a better controllers' utilization.

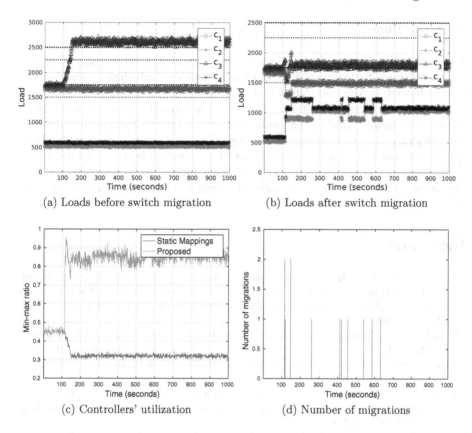

Fig. 4. Simulated results of 4 heterogeneous controllers and 16 switches.

When considering the min-max ratio in Fig. 4c. The static model produced in average ≈34%, while the proposed model produced ≈81%, with improvement of ≈47%. When considering only the time horizon after the stressing period, the static model in average produced ≈32%, and the proposed model produced ≈85%, with improvement of ≈53%.

Considering the number of migrated switches in Fig. 4d, no switch is migrated before the stressing period, 5 switches are migrated during the stressing period, with a maximum of 2 switches at two instances of time. After the stressing period, 7 (with maximum of 1 switch) switches are migrated, which might slightly increase the control plane overhead when compared to the homogeneous scenario. In fact, these 7 migrations has happened in a large time horizon (i.e., $1000 - 151 = 849$ time slots).

When comparing the results of the static model in both homogeneous and heterogeneous schemes, the latter produced better min-max ratio because controllers with small capacities can be easily utilized. The proposed model, however, produced better min-max ratio in the homogeneous scheme. In what concerns to the number of migrated switches, it is possible to experience slightly more switch migrations in the heterogeneous scenario.

5   Conclusions

This article has presented a model for solving the switch migration problem in software-defined networking. The problem is modeled such that it considers the load balancing of the controllers and minimizes the controller plane overhead created by the migrated switches. The model is formulated as a mixed integer linear programming, and the experimental results show that the proposed model can efficiently solve this problem for homogeneous and heterogeneous controllers. The results show that homogeneous controllers produce better utilizations and a slightly lower control plane overhead. As a future work, a robust and fast algorithm will be developed to solve the switch migration problem for large SDN networks.

References

1. Bari, M.F., et al.: Dynamic controller provisioning in software defined networks. In: Proceedings of the 9th International Conference on Network and Service Management (CNSM 2013), pp. 18–25, October 2013. https://doi.org/10.1109/CNSM.2013.6727805

2. Benson, T., Akella, A., Maltz, D.A.: Network traffic characteristics of data centers in the wild. In: Proceedings of the 10th ACM SIGCOMM Conference on Internet Measurement, IMC 2010, pp. 267–280. ACM, New York (2010). https://doi.org/10.1145/1879141.1879175

3. Bizanis, N., Kuipers, F.A.: SDN and virtualization solutions for the Internet of Things: a survey. IEEE Access **4**, 5591–5606 (2016). https://doi.org/10.1109/ACCESS.2016.2607786

4. Casado, M., Freedman, M.J., Pettit, J., Luo, J., McKeown, N., Shenker, S.: Ethane: taking control of the enterprise. In: Proceedings of the 2007 Conference on Applications, Technologies, Architectures, and Protocols for Computer Communications, SIGCOMM 2007, pp. 1–12. ACM, New York (2007). https://doi.org/10.1145/1282380.1282382

5. Chen, T., Matinmikko, M., Chen, X., Zhou, X., Ahokangas, P.: Software defined mobile networks: concept, survey, and research directions. IEEE Commun. Mag. **53**(11), 126–133 (2015). https://doi.org/10.1109/MCOM.2015.7321981

6. Dixit, A., Hao, F., Mukherjee, S., Lakshman, T.V., Kompella, R.: Towards an elastic distributed SDN controller. ACM SIGCOMM Comput. Commun. Rev. **43**(4), 7–12 (2013). https://doi.org/10.1145/2534169.2491193

7. Open Networking Foundation: OpenFlow Switch Specification. Technical report (2011)

8. Gao, X., Kong, L., Li, W., Liang, W., Chen, Y., Chen, G.: Traffic load balancing schemes for devolved controllers in mega data centers. IEEE Trans. Parallel Distrib. Syst. **28**(2), 572–585 (2017). https://doi.org/10.1109/tpds.2016.2579622

9. Hakiri, A., Gokhale, A., Berthou, P., Schmidt, D.C., Gayraud, T.: Software-defined networking: challenges and research opportunities for future internet. Comput. Netw. **75**(A), 453–471 (2014). https://doi.org/10.1016/j.comnet.2014.10.015

10. Karakus, M., Durresi, A.: A survey: control plane scalability issues and approaches in Software-Defined Networking (SDN). Comput. Netw. **112**, 279–293 (2017). https://doi.org/10.1016/j.comnet.2016.11.017

11. Kreutz, D., Ramos, F.M.V., Verissimo, P.E., Rothenberg, C.E., Azodolmolky, S., Uhlig, S.: Software-defined networking: a comprehensive survey. Proc. IEEE **103**(1), 14–76 (2015). https://doi.org/10.1109/JPROC.2014.2371999

12. Liang, C., Kawashima, R., Matsuo, H.: Scalable and crash-tolerant load balancing based on switch migration for multiple OpenFlow controllers. In: 2014 Second International Symposium on Computing and Networking (CANDAR), Shizuoka, People's Republic of China, 10–12 December 2014, pp. 171–177 (2014). https://doi.org/10.1109/CANDAR.2014.108

13. McKeown, N., et al.: OpenFlow: enabling innovation in campus networks. ACM SIGCOMM Comput. Commun. Rev. **38**(2), 69–74 (2008). https://doi.org/10.1145/1355734.1355746

14. Sridharan, V., Gurusamy, M., Truong-Huu, T.: On multiple controller mapping in software defined networks with resilience constraints. IEEE Commun. Lett. **21**(8), 1763–1766 (2017). https://doi.org/10.1109/LCOMM.2017.2696006

15. Wang, C., Hu, B., Chen, S., Li, D., Liu, B.: A switch migration-based decision-making scheme for balancing load in SDN. IEEE Access **5**, 4537–4544 (2017). https://doi.org/10.1109/ACCESS.2017.2684188

16. Wang, T., Liu, F., Xu, H.: An efficient online algorithm for dynamic SDN controller assignment in data center networks. IEEE/ACM Trans. Netw. **25**(5), 2788–2801 (2017). https://doi.org/10.1109/TNET.2017.2711641

17. Wu, P., Yao, L., Lin, C., Wu, G., Obaidat, M.S.: FMD: a DoS mitigation scheme based on flow migration in software-defined networking. Int. J. Commun. Syst. **31**(9), e3543 (2018). https://doi.org/10.1002/dac.3543

18. Yao, G., Bi, J., Guo, L.: On the cascading failures of multi-controllers in software defined networks. In: Fu, X., Hilt, V., Wolf, T., Zhang, L., Zhang, Z.L. (eds.) 2013 21st IEEE International Conference on Network Protocols (ICNP). IEEE International Conference on Network Protocols Proceedings, Gottingen, Germany, 7–10 October 2013. IEEE; IEEE Computer Society; VDE, Information Technology Society; Gesell Informatik (2013)

19. Yao, G., Bi, J., Li, Y., Guo, L.: On the capacitated controller placement problem in software defined networks. IEEE Commun. Lett. **18**(8), 1339–1342 (2014). https://doi.org/10.1109/LCOMM.2014.2332341

20. Ye, X., Cheng, G., Luo, X.: Maximizing SDN control resource utilization via switch migration. Comput. Netw. **126**, 69–80 (2017). https://doi.org/10.1016/j.comnet.2017.06.022

21. Yeganeh, S.H., Tootoonchian, A., Ganjali, Y.: On scalability of software-defined networking. IEEE Commun. Mag. **51**(2), 136–141 (2013)

22. Zhang, Y., Cui, L., Wang, W., Zhang, Y.: A survey on software defined networking with multiple controllers. J. Netw. Comput. Appl. **103**, 101–118 (2018). https://doi.org/10.1016/j.jnca.2017.11.015

23. Zhou, Y., Zheng, K., Ni, W., Liu, R.P.: Elastic switch migration for control plane load balancing in SDN. IEEE Access **6**, 3909–3919 (2018). https://doi.org/10.1109/ACCESS.2018.2795576

ONAP Architectures for Network Function Virtualization

Abel Fernández-Nandín, Felipe Gil-Castiñeira[(⊠)],
and Francisco J. González-Castaño

atlanTTic Research Center for Telecommunication Technologies,
Universidade de Vigo, Campus Universitario, 36310 Vigo, Spain
{abel,xil,javier}@gti.uvigo.es

Abstract. The Network Function Virtualization paradigm is changing the telecommunications industry. Network applications in general purpose telco infrastructures will be instantiated on demand or deployed in the most appropriate location for each use case. Nevertheless, these virtualized scenarios are complex and require tools to manage the different components flexibly and reliably. ONAP is one of the projects that are implementing such tools. It provides a rich set of elements that can be executed in virtual machines or containers, following different architectures. In this paper we present the different possibilities for that and analyze their advantages and disadvantages.

Keywords: Network Function Virtualization · Containers · ONAP

1 Introduction

In the last years, cloud computing has become a key enabler in the IT field. Infrastructure virtualization has been crucial to optimize resource usage [1], and has brought unparalleled management flexibility. The continuous search for improvements has spawned several solutions that continue to shape the cloud computing world.

One of the most relevant technologies in the last years is containers [2], which provide means to encapsulate applications without using virtual machines. Since there is no virtual kernel between the host machine and the containerized application, this technology is lighter, but also less secure: a vulnerable application that compromises the host kernel also compromises the rest of the containers [3]. This is challenging for multi-tenancy scenarios. The most frequent solution is to launch these containers on top of virtual machines [4] that are already running, which does not involve extra boot time.

Containers technology has had such an impact that not only new associated solutions like Kubernetes [5] have appeared, but also traditional cloud computing software like OpenStack has been adapted to support them [6]. There also exist implementations of orchestration engines to automate application deployment, scaling, and management [7].

© ICST Institute for Computer Sciences, Social Informatics and Telecommunications Engineering 2019
Published by Springer Nature Switzerland AG 2019. All Rights Reserved
V. Sucasas et al. (Eds.): BROADNETS 2018, LNICST 263, pp. 62–71, 2019.
https://doi.org/10.1007/978-3-030-05195-2_7

The telco sector has not been indifferent to this revolution. Initially, telecommunications were just commodities that provided connectivity to the cloud (for the users or to interconnect data centers). Since then many telcos have become cloud computing service providers themselves trying to leverage their intrinsic advantages (such as large network bandwidth) to reach a new market [8]. Nevertheless, the real impact in the telco sector started with network "softwarization". Typical network functions started to migrate from proprietary hardware to Commercial-Off-The-Shelf (COTS) computers, simplifying tasks such as feature upgrades, fixing bugs, or scaling the service [9]. The next logical step is the virtualization of these network functions, by turning network equipment into virtual entities. This is the driving force behind the Network Function Virtualization (NFV) concept [10]. The new virtual appliances that satisfy the NFV paradigm can be instantiated on demand or deployed in any cloud location with enough available resources, and scaled with the number of requests. Furthermore, the same hardware can perform different functions at a time (by executing different virtual network functions or VNFs in the same hardware) or at different times (e.g. different services over the same physical platform for different customers).

Software Defined Networking (SDN) is another related technology that decouples the control and data planes and centralizes the decisions in a controller [11]. These planes are separated through a well defined API between the switches and the controller. The most popular API nowadays is OpenFlow. SDN allows controlling traffic flows from a centralized location, simplifying the creation of new NFV instances and relocating of existing ones, without interrupting service for end users.

A NFV infrastructure supported by a SDN enabled network is a complex environment that also requires an architecture for management and orchestration. For this purpose, the ETSI NFV group defined the management and orchestration (MANO) framework [12]. It standardizes the functionalities for the provisioning of VNFs, their configuration, and the configuration of the supporting infrastructure. It also includes the orchestration and management of the physical and virtual resources that the VNFs require.

The ONAP (Open Network Automation Platform) project provides a unified operating framework that comprises the orchestration and automation of VNFs, SDNs and the services combining both. Thus, ONAP is a superset of ETSI MANO with extra capabilities. It evolved from the merge of ECOMP (Enhanced Control, Orchestration, Management and Policy) and Open-O, and is under the umbrella of the Linux Foundation. Nowadays it has strong momentum with the participation of vendors that cover over 60% of mobile customers worldwide [13]. This makes ONAP an interesting platform to analyze how containers can help build an NFV infrastructure.

This paper reviews different ways to stack technologies to support VNFs with the ONAP platform, which is discussed in depth in Sect. 3. Section 2 presents the related work. Section 4 describes different architectures for ONAP deployment. Finally, Sect. 5 presents our conclusions and plans for future work.

2   Related Work

The NFV paradigm appeared with the maturity of virtualization techniques. Previous work has addressed how to combine different virtualization technologies to deploy NFV in a telco environment [14,15], including containers [16,17]. Nevertheless, we are not aware of any other work analyzing the different possibilities to use ONAP for this task.

OpenStack is a platform that allows managing the networking, computing, and storage resources in a cloud. It is very popular in the virtualization field and is one of the main components in ONAP. In [18] the authors studied its suitability for provisioning and deploying NFV services. The paper also discussed future challenges for OpenStack to be adopted to implement an NFV infrastructure. For example, the authors state that OpenStack should not affect service performance, and that its configuration options should cover VNF services from different vendors. Some limitations were identified regarding networking capabilities, traceability, the assignment of VNFs to specific hardware resources and security. Finally, the paper also described the different options to deploy VNFs (on virtual machines, containers, or bare metal) and the interest of such flexibility.

In [19] the authors describe a resource allocation strategy based on ONAP for deploying Virtualized Network Functions (VNFs) on distributed data centers. They also describe the different ONAP components, how they are integrated, and the mechanism for resource allocation (basically, it is the heuristic algorithm implemented in OpenStack's scheduler), but they do not discuss the different options to deploy ONAP.

In [20] the authors describe the existing interest in using containers for NFV and other telecom infrastructures, but they also present several issues that make them not ready for a production state. One of the main concerns is related to the security of the deployments with containers. In [21] the authors discuss the Docker environment's security implications. Docker security relies on three factors: isolation of processes at the userspace level, the enforcement of the isolation by the kernel, and security in the networks operation. If an attacker compromises a container, it should not be possible to affect another. To conclude the paper, the authors state that an orchestrator could solve some of the security issues with mechanisms implemented at higher levels of abstraction, and by using automation to provide an automated way to audit the security and to patch the system. Therefore, if such measures are implemented in ONAP, containers should be a valuable alternative to deploy NFV services (and even the ONAP infrastructure).

Summing up, although there exists significant work on NFV requirements and base technologies (such as OpenStack), we are not aware of any publication on the suitability of different virtualization architectures to deploy ONAP.

3 ONAP and Its Supporting Technologies

ONAP's architecture is divided into its Design-Time and Run-Time frameworks.

The Design-Time framework features the Service Design and Creation (SDC) and the Policy subsystems, which enables developers to define, simulate, and certify assets and their associated processes and policies.

The Run-Time framework comprises the Active and Available Inventory (AAI), which allows visualizing and managing the assets' inventory; controllers for managing the state of a resource; the Data Collection, Analytics and Events (DCAE) subsystem, which gathers performance and usage metrics of the resources to find anomalies; the Master Service Orchestrator (MSO), which arranges, sequences, and implements tasks based on rules and policies to coordinate the creation, modification, or removal of resources in the managed environment; and the Security Framework, which aims at providing security by design in a variety of ways.

ONAP relies on OpenStack to allocate resources. Let us mention some key components for ONAP. OpenStack Heat plugin implements an orchestration engine. The infrastructure for a cloud application can be described in a text file, which simplifies version control. The Magnum plugin brings several container orchestration engines into OpenStack. It uses Heat to build virtual machine clusters, on top of which an orchestration engine deploys containerized services. The alternatives for orchestration engines are Docker Swarm, Apache Mesos and Kubernetes. The latter has become the de facto standard for deploying, scaling, and managing containerized applications. Its architecture follows a master/slave hierarchy, in which the master nodes that belong to the control plane manage the worker nodes. Kolla allows deploying Openstack clouds by containerizing its services. This simplifies the configuration and scalability of clouds, since they may run on top of Kubernetes for lifecycle management. Ironic is useful to employ bare metal machines instead of virtual instances, for those cases where a virtualization layer could hinder the performance of the system. By combining this plugin with Magnum container execution reaches peak performance.

4 Possible ONAP Architectures

By combining previous technologies it is possible to build different architectures for ONAP, which may have advantages and disadvantages in particular scenarios.

The following sections discuss different alternatives for the deployment of ONAP and VNFs. The diagrams in this section represent the different elements of the architectures with the following color code:

- ☐ Operating System
- ☐ Bare-metal machine
- ☐ Virtual Machine
- ☐ Container

Finally, Table 1 summarizes the main features of the alternative architectures. It describes the cloud computing software used to deploy ONAP's services, the VIM (Virtual Infrastructure Manager) used by said services to launch the VNFs, the ease of integration between the proposed architecture and an existing Open-Stack cloud, the ease of managing the system according to how independent the different technologies are from each other, the qualitative estimation of the resources it uses, and the degree of security it provides according to the existence of a virtualization layer between the host machine and both the VNFs and ONAP's services.

4.1   ONAP on OpenStack

Figure 1 shows an architecture where a vanilla OpenStack installation runs bare-metal on top of Ubuntu (or any other Linux distribution). In this scenario, ONAP services are deployed as several virtual machines orchestrated by OpenStack Heat.

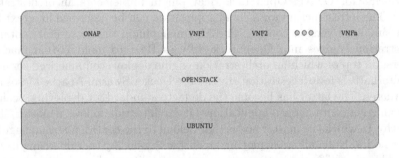

Fig. 1. ONAP on OpenStack

The OpenStack infrastructure that hosts ONAP services also acts as its own VIM. Therefore, VNFs are launched as virtual machines on top of the same OpenStack infrastructure.

The high hardware costs make this choice unattractive in principle. However, it may be useful in a scenario where a tenant with an OpenStack cloud wants to adopt ONAP without any changes in its architecture.

4.2   ONAP on Kubernetes on OpenStack

The architecture depicted in Fig. 2 shows a bare-metal OpenStack installation on top of which a virtualized Kubernetes cluster runs.

ONAP services now run as containerized applications managed by Kubernetes, which simplifies management, scaling, and auto-healing. Kubernetes may be installed manually inside virtual machines or by using the Magnum plugin.

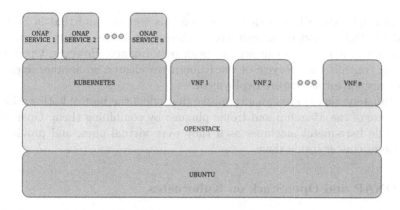

Fig. 2. ONAP on Kubernetes on OpenStack

Since containers, unlike virtual machines, do not need to secure resources before they run, their resource usage is more efficient. Moreover, the fact that ONAP services still run on top of OpenStack makes integration almost as easy. However, if a tight integration between Kubernetes and OpenStack is desired, it would be necessary to install the Magnum plugin. This would presumably require some cloud architecture changes and, therefore, adoption is not as straightforward as in Sect. 4.1.

4.3 ONAP on Kubernetes and Openstack

The architecture in Fig. 3 has two independent components, Kubernetes and OpenStack, which run bare-metal.

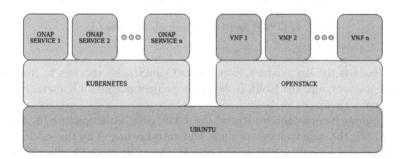

Fig. 3. ONAP on Kubernetes and Openstack

OpenStack no longer serves as the infrastructure for ONAP. It just acts as a virtual infrastructure manager to launch the VNFs. Kubernetes, however, allows managing the containerized ONAP services. This scenario behaves as that in Sect. 4.2, but ONAP services are more efficient because there is no virtualization layer between them and the host machine.

In principle, there is a trade-off between this scenario and that in Sect. 4.2 related to ONAP services infrastructure. Since Kubernetes is now bare-metal, the containers it manages can achieve peak performance. However, OpenStack no longer controls the lifecycle of the Kubernetes cluster, so another approach is necessary for infrastructure deployment.

Fortunately, there exists an alternative that offers the best of both worlds by making use of the Magnum and Ironic plugins: by combining them, OpenStack can handle bare-metal machines as if they were virtual ones, and provision a Kubernetes cluster inside them.

4.4　ONAP and OpenStack on Kubernetes

The architecture in Fig. 4 corresponds to a scenario in which a bare-metal Kubernetes containerizes and manages services from both ONAP and OpenStack.

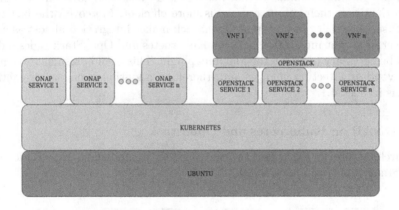

Fig. 4. ONAP and OpenStack on Kubernetes

Here Kolla is the key enabler, as it allows OpenStack's services to run inside Docker containers, and the Kolla-Kubernetes project permits a Kubernetes cluster to manage them.

This approach containerizes the whole underlying infrastructure of the platform, enabling the management, scaling, and auto-healing of all the services both from ONAP and OpenStack. It would also be the most resource-efficient due to the lack of virtualization. However, it no longer takes advantage of an existing OpenStack deployment, so it would not integrate well with a cloud where ONAP and an existing platform must coexist.

The VNFs, however, are not free of a virtualization layer, since they run on virtual machines on top of OpenStack. The transition from VNFs to cVNFs (containerized VNFs) will be discussed in Sect. 5.

Table 1. Comparison of architectures

Architecture	ONAP infrastructure	VIM	Integration	Management	Resource usage	Security environment
Architecture 4.1	OpenStack	OpenStack	Easy	Easy	High	Virtualized infrastructure + VNFs
Architecture 4.2	Virtualized Kubernetes	OpenStack	Easy	Medium difficulty	Medium	Virtualized infrastructure + VNFs
Architecture 4.3	Kubernetes	OpenStack	Medium difficulty	Hard	Medium	VNFs
Architecture 4.3	Kubernetes	Containerized OpenStack	Hard	Medium difficulty	Low	VNFs

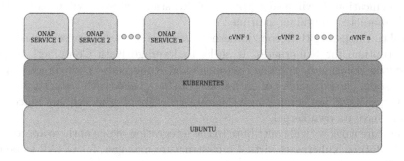

Fig. 5. ONAP on Kubernetes

5 Conclusions and Future Work

From the discussion of the different architectures, one might infer a development trend of cloud computing platforms for NFV towards containerization. However, the support for containerized VNFs is not fully extended or developed. For this reason, ONAP has been taking steps into integrating Kubernetes as a virtual infrastructure manager, which would enable containerized VNFs to reside adjacently to containerized ONAP services. This would result in a flat architecture as shown in Fig. 5. One important benefit derived from this flat architecture would be that the way of enforcing security and load balancing policies would be shared between the ONAP services and the cVNFs, since Kubernetes provides those capabilities. Because the current solutions make use of both Kubernetes and OpenStack, the configuration of these policies is split among the two platforms and, therefore, more cumbersome to implement.

It is apparent that containerizing platforms as much as possible would greatly benefit the infrastructure, but there is some concern that this approach would not be valid for multi-tenancy scenarios. As a consequence, there is a trade-off between virtual machines and containers. The former are secure but slow, and the latter are fast but insecure. This is caused by sharing the kernel between the host machine and the guest applications. There are some solutions that bring the best of both approaches.

For example, Hyper (https://hypercontainer.io/) aims at providing a suitable environment for multi-tenancy by implementing hardware-enforced isolation, which is achieved by containing applications within separate kernel spaces. Since the kernel is really streamlined, it does not affect the performance of the container heavily, so sub-second boot times are still feasible.

Clear Containers has a similar goal (https://clearlinux.org/containers), since it implements lightweight virtual machines by placing an optimized kernel between the host machine and the guest application.

Kata Containers (https://katacontainers.io/) is an upcoming project by the OpenStack Foundation. It will combine underlying technologies of the previous projects, Hyper's runV and Clear Containers' runtime. The goal is an architecture-agnostic system to be run on multiple hypervisors, supporting the OCI specification. It will also support the CRI standard, so it will be compatible with Kubernetes' container runtime.

Frakti (https://github.com/kubernetes/frakti) is a hypervisor-based container runtime for Kubernetes. It seeks to leverage Kata Containers to provide strong isolation by running containers and Kubernetes' pods directly inside hypervisors. The containers of each pod will share the kernel, reducing burden. However, this will not compromise the infrastructure of other tenants, since each pod will have its own kernel.

As future work we will contribute to the integration of one of these approaches with the future Kubernetes virtual infrastructure manager, for ONAP to be not only fully containerized but also multi-tenant.

References

1. Armbrust, M., et al.: Above the clouds: a Berkeley view of cloud computing. Technical report UCB/EECS-2009-28, vol. 4, pp. 506–522. EECS Department, University of California, Berkeley (2009)
2. Vaughan-Nichols, S.J.: New approach to virtualization is a lightweight. Computer **39**(11), 12–14 (2006)
3. Gao, X., Gu, Z., Kayaalp, M., Pendarakis, D., Wang, H.: ContainerLeaks: emerging security threats of information leakages in container clouds. In: 47th Annual IEEE/IFIP International Conference on Dependable Systems and Networks (DSN), pp. 237–248. IEEE (2017)
4. Manco, F., et al.: My VM is lighter (and safer) than your container. In: Proceedings of the 26th Symposium on Operating Systems Principles, pp. 218–233. ACM (2017)
5. Brewer, E.A.: Kubernetes and the path to cloud native. In: Proceedings of the Sixth ACM Symposium on Cloud Computing, pp. 167–167. ACM (2015)
6. Cacciatore, K., et al.: Exploring Opportunities: Containers and OpenStack. OpenStack White Paper, 19 (2015)
7. Vaquero, L.M., Rodero-Merino, L., Buyya, R.: Dynamically scaling applications in the cloud. ACM SIGCOMM Comput. Commun. Rev. **41**(1), 45–52 (2011)
8. Lei, X., Zhe, X., Shaowu, M., Xiongyan, T.: Cloud computing and services platform construction of telecom operator. In: 2nd IEEE International Conference on Broadband Network & Multimedia Technology, IC-BNMT 2009, pp. 864–867. IEEE (2009)

9. Afolabi, I., Taleb, T., Samdanis, K., Ksentini, A., Flinck, H.: Network slicing & softwarization: a survey on principles, enabling technologies & solutions. IEEE Commun. Surv. Tutor. (2018)
10. Chiosi, M., et al.: Network functions virtualisation: an introduction, benefits, enablers, challenges and call for action. In: SDN and OpenFlow World Congress, pp. 22–24 (2012)
11. Kreutz, D., Ramos, F.M., Verissimo, P.E., Rothenberg, C.E., Azodolmolky, S., Uhlig, S.: Software-defined networking: a comprehensive survey. Proc. IEEE **103**(1), 14–76 (2015)
12. ISG, N.: Network Functions Virtualisation (NFV): Management and Orchestration. European Telecommunications Standards Institute, Technical report (2014)
13. Parker-Johnson, P., Doiron, T.: Succeeding on an open field: the impact of open source technologies on the communication service provider ecosystem. ACG Research Report (2018)
14. Duan, Q., Ansari, N., Toy, M.: Software-defined network virtualization: an architectural framework for integrating SDN and NFV for service provisioning in future networks. IEEE Netw. **30**(5), 10–16 (2016)
15. Kourtis, M.A., et al.: T-NOVA: an open-source MANO stack for NFV infrastructures. IEEE Trans. Netw. Serv. Manag. **14**(3), 586–602 (2017)
16. Cziva, R., Jouet, S., White, K.J., Pezaros, D.P.: Container-based network function virtualization for software-defined networks. In: 2015 IEEE Symposium on Computers and Communication (ISCC), pp. 415–420. IEEE (2015)
17. Cziva, R., Pezaros, D.P.: Container network functions: bringing NFV to the network edge. IEEE Commun. Mag. **55**(6), 24–31 (2017)
18. Kavanagh, A.: OpenStack as the API framework for NFV: the benefits, and the extensions needed. Ericsson Rev. **2** (2015)
19. Slim, F., Guillemin, F., Gravey, A., Hadjadj-Aoul, Y.: Towards a dynamic adaptive placement of virtual network functions under ONAP. In: Third International NFV-SDN 2017-O4SDI-Workshop on Orchestration for Software-Defined Infrastructures (2017)
20. Rotter, C., Farkas, L., Nyíri, G., Csatári, G., Jánosi, L., Springer, R.: Using Linux containers in telecom applications. In: 19th International ICIN Conference - Innovations in Clouds, Internet and Networks, pp. 234–241 (2016)
21. Combe, T., Martin, A., Di Pietro, R.: To Docker or not to Docker: a security perspective. IEEE Cloud Comput. **3**(5), 54–62 (2016)

A Scalable and Reliable Model for the Placement of Controllers in SDN Networks

Mohammad Ashrafi$^{(\boxtimes)}$, Noélia Correia, and Faroq AL-Tam

Center for Electronic, Optoelectronic and Telecommunications (CEOT), Faculty of Science and Technology, University of Algarve, 8005-139 Faro, Portugal
mohammad.ashrafi@gmail.com, {ncorreia,ftam}@ualg.pt

Abstract. In this article, a mathematical model is developed to place controllers in multi-controller software-defined networking (SDN), while considering: resilience, scalability, and inter-plane latency. The model proved to be effective since it is able to provide resilient solutions under different fail-over scenarios, while at the same time avoid working close to the capacity limits of controllers, which offers a scalable model for multi-controller SDN.

Keywords: Control placement · Software Defined Networking Reliability · Scalability

1 Introduction

Software Defined Networking (SDN) is an emergent paradigm that offers a software-oriented network design, simplifying network management by decoupling the control logic from forwarding devices [10]. The SDN is composed of three planes: management, control, and data. The management plane is responsible for defining the network policies, and it is connected to the control plane via northbound interfaces. The brain of SDN is the control plane, which interacts with the data plane using southbound interfaces like OpenFlow [5].

Most of the current available controllers, like NOX [6] and Beacon [4], are physically centralized. Although a single controller offers a complete network-wide view, it represents a single point of failure and lacks both reliability and scalability [19]. For this reason multi-controller SDNs were developed [5], allowing the control plane to be physically distributed, but maintaining it logically centralized by synchronizing the network state among controllers [20]. Controllers of this type include OpenDaylight [11] and Kandoo [7]. Multi-controller SDNs

---

This work was developed within the Centre for Electronic, Optoelectronic and Telecommunications (CEOT), and supported by the D/MULTI/00631/2013 project of the Portuguese Science and Technology Foundation (FCT).

V. Sucasas et al. (Eds.): BROADNETS 2018, LNICST 263, pp. 72–82, 2019.
https://doi.org/10.1007/978-3-030-05195-2_8

are able to solve the main problems found in the centralized SDN, but new challenges are introduced, like network state synchronization and switch-controller mappings. Another main problem in multi-controller SDNs is the Controller Placement Problem (CPP) [15]. The problem is proved to be NP-hard [17], and is one of the hottest topics in multi-controller SDNs [8,12,13,17].

When a switch receives a new packet, it consults its forwarding rules in the flow table in order to determine how to handle the packet. If there is no match in the flow table, the packet is buffered temporarily and the switch initiates a `packet-in` message to the responsible controller. Reactively, the controller calculates the path for this packet and installs a new rule in the affected switches. Two major factors that influence the effectiveness of this process are: (*i*) load at the controller; (*ii*) propagation delay between the switch and the controller. These two constitute a single efficiency measure: the flow setup time, which will be twice the propagation delay between switch and controller plus the queuing and processing time of the packet in the controllers.

The CPP aims at deciding the number of required controllers and where to place them [8], partitioning the network into subregions (domains), while considering some quality criteria and cost constraints [1,12]. The CPP model discussed in this article incorporates the previously mentioned flow setup time, while presenting reliable and scalable solutions.

The remaining part of this paper is organized as follows. Section 2 discusses work related with CPP in SDNs. Section 3 discusses the mathematical model, whose results are discussed in Sect. 4. Finally, some conclusions are drawn in Sect. 5, together with future work.

2 Related Work

The placement problem was mentioned for the first time in [8]. In fact, this problem is similar to the popular facility location problem, and is solved in the aftermentioned article as K-center problem, to minimize the inter-plane propagation delay. In [17] the problem is extended to incorporate the capacity of the controllers. A new metric called expected percentage of control path loss is proposed in [16] to guarantee a reliable model. Cost, controller type, bandwidth, and other factors are considered in [12], and the expansion problem is considered in [13]. The problem is usually modeled in these articles as integer programming.

Heuristic methods that incorporate switch migration can be found in [18]. In [2] a game model is also proposed. A comprehensive review of heuristic methods can be found in [9]. QoS-aware CPP is presented in [3] and solved using greedy and network partitioning algorithms. Recently, scalability and reliability issues in large-scale networks are considered in [1]. Clustering and genetic approaches are proposed, but these approaches are prune to sub-optimality.

When comparing our model with other in the literature, our model determines the optimal placement considering different failure scenarios and latency to reduce latency and overload of controllers while ensuring scalability, leading to reduced overload at controllers.

Table 1. Known information.

Term	Description
$\mathcal{C}$	Set of controllers
$\mathcal{N}_c$	Possible places for $c \in \mathcal{C}$, $\mathcal{N}_c \subset \mathcal{N}$
h_c	Number of requests per second that can be handled by controller $c \in \mathcal{C}$
$\mathcal{S}$	Set of switches
p_s	Number of requests not matching the lookup table of $s \in \mathcal{S}$
$\mathcal{F}$	Set of physical link failure scenarios. Includes a scenario where all links are up
$\mathcal{L}_f$	Set of physical links failing when scenario $f \in \mathcal{F}$ occurs

Table 2. Required variables.

Variable	Description
σ_n^c	One if controller $c \in \mathcal{C}$ is placed at location $n \in \mathcal{N}_c$
$\mu_{n_i,n_j,f,l}^{c_i,c_j}$	One if link $l \in \mathcal{L} \backslash \mathcal{L}_f$ is used for inter-controller $c_i - c_j$ communication, located at nodes n_i and n_j respectively, when failure $f \in \mathcal{F}$ occurs
β_f^l	One if link $l \in \mathcal{L} \backslash \mathcal{L}_f$ is used for inter-controller communication when failure $f \in \mathcal{F}$ occurs
$\gamma_f^{s,c}$	One if switch $s \in \mathcal{S}$ is assigned to controller $c \in \mathcal{C}$ when failure $f \in \mathcal{F}$ occur
$\lambda_{n,f}^{s,c}$	One if switch $s \in \mathcal{S}$ is assigned to controller $c \in \mathcal{C}$ when failure $f \in \mathcal{F}$ occurs, and the controller is placed at location $n \in \mathcal{N}_c$
$\phi_{f,l}^{s,c,ni}$	One if switch $s \in \mathcal{S}$ is assigned to controller $c \in \mathcal{C}$ located at nodes $n_i \in \mathcal{N}_c$ when failure $f \in \mathcal{F}$, and uses link $l \in \mathcal{L} \backslash \mathcal{L}_f$ in its path
δ	Scalability factor, $0 \le \delta \le 1$
Θ^{TOTAL}	Total latency, under any failure scenario
Π^{TOTAL}	Total number of links used, under any failure scenario

3 Mathematical Model

In the following discussion the physical topology graph is assumed to be defined by $\mathcal{G}(\mathcal{N}, \mathcal{L})$, where $\mathcal{N}$ is a set of physical nodes/locations and $\mathcal{L}$ is a set of physical links. The remaining notation for known information and variables, used through this paper, is presented in Tables 1 and 2.

Objective Function: To ensure the linear scale up of the SDN network the goal will be:

$$\text{Minimize } \delta + K_1 \frac{\Theta^{\text{TOTAL}}}{\Delta} + K_2 \frac{\Pi^{\text{TOTAL}}}{\Delta} \tag{1}$$

where Δ is a big value. The primary goal is to minimize δ, and then to reduce latency. The factors K_1 and K_2 should be adapted according to inter-controller and switch-controller latency relevance. The motivation behind giving δ more importance is that the provided solution for controller placement will be used for a relatively long period of time, during which traffic conditions may change. Therefore, the scalability of the solution is considered to be critical.

Constraints: The following additional constraints must be fulfilled.
- Placement of controllers:

$$\sum_{\{n \in \mathcal{N}_c\}} \sigma_n^c = 1, \forall c \in \mathcal{C} \tag{2}$$

$$\sum_{\{l \in \mathcal{L} \setminus \mathcal{L}_f : src(l) = n\}} \mu_{n_i, n_j, f, l}^{c_i, c_j} - \sum_{\{l \in \mathcal{L} \setminus \mathcal{L}_f : dst(l) = n\}} \mu_{n_i, n_j, f, l}^{c_i, c_j} =$$

$$= \begin{cases} \sigma_{n_i}^{c_i}, & if \ n = n_i \\ -\sigma_{n_j}^{c_j}, & if \ n = n_j, \forall c_i, c_j \in \mathcal{C}, \forall f \in \mathcal{F}, \forall n_i \in \mathcal{N}_{c_i}, \forall n_j \in \mathcal{N}_{c_j}, \forall n \in \mathcal{N} \\ 0, & otherwise \end{cases} \tag{3}$$

Constraints (2) ensure a single location for each controller $c \in \mathcal{C}$, while constraints (3) ensure that there will be a path between every pair of controllers, under any failure scenario, while considering their location. These paths are used for state synchronization.

In [14] it is stated that the controller load can be reduced, achieving load balance among neighboring controllers, if controller needs to communicate only with its local neighbors. Therefore, the paths from any controller, towards all the other controllers, should share as many links as possible (leads to a bus logical topology). This is ensured by the following constraints.

$$\beta_f^l \geq \mu_{n_i, n_j, f, l}^{c_i, c_j}, \forall c_i, c_j \in \mathcal{C}, \forall n_i, n_j \in \mathcal{N}_c, \forall f \in \mathcal{F}, \forall l \in \mathcal{L} \tag{4}$$

$$\Pi^{\text{TOTAL}} = \sum_{\forall f \in \mathcal{F}} \sum_{\forall l \in \mathcal{L}} \beta_f^l \times 1/2 \tag{5}$$

where Π^{TOTAL}, counting for the highest number of end-to-end hops in inter-controller communication, is to be included in the objective function.
- Switch to controller mapping:

$$\sum_{\{c \in \mathcal{C}\}} \gamma_f^{s,c} = 1, \forall s \in \mathcal{S}, \forall f \in \mathcal{F} \tag{6}$$

$$\sum_{\{s \in \mathcal{S}\}} \gamma_f^{s,c} \times p_s \leq h_c \times \delta, \forall c \in \mathcal{C}, \forall f \in \mathcal{F} \tag{7}$$

Constraints (6) ensure single mapping, and constraints (7) avoid the overload of controllers, while ensuring scalability regarding future switch migrations (triggered to deal with load fluctuations) due to the use of δ, which is, be included in the objective function too. Again, the multiple failure scenarios are taken into consideration.

– Switch-controller latency:

$$\lambda_{n,f}^{s,c} \geq \gamma_f^{s,c} + \sigma_n^c - 1, \forall c \in \mathcal{C}, \forall n \in \mathcal{N}_c, \forall f \in \mathcal{F}, \forall s \in \mathcal{S} \tag{8}$$

$$\sum_{\{l \in \mathcal{L} \setminus \mathcal{L}_f : src(l) = n\}} \phi_{f,l}^{s,c,ni} - \sum_{\{l \in \mathcal{L} \setminus \mathcal{L}_f : dst(l) = n\}} \phi_{f,l}^{s,c,ni} =$$

$$= \begin{cases} \lambda_{n,f}^{s,c}, & if \ n = loc(s) \\ -\lambda_{n,f}^{s,c}, & if \ n = n_i, \quad \forall s \in \mathcal{S}, \forall c \in \mathcal{C}, \forall f \in \mathcal{F}, \forall n_i \in \mathcal{N}_c, \forall n \in \mathcal{N} \\ 0, & otherwise \end{cases} \tag{9}$$

where $loc(s)$ is the location of switch s. The total latency is obtained by:

$$\Theta^{\text{TOTAL}} = \sum_{\{s \in \mathcal{S}\}} \sum_{\{c \in \mathcal{C}\}} \sum_{\{f \in \mathcal{F}\}} \sum_{\{l \in \mathcal{L}\}} \sum_{\{n \in \mathcal{N}_c\}} \phi_{f,l}^{s,c,n} \tag{10}$$

Θ^{TOTAL} is included in the objective function for latency minimization.

– Non-negativity assignment to variables:

$$0 \leq \delta \leq 1; \sigma_n^c, \mu_{n_i,n_j,f,l}^{c_i,c_j}, \beta_f^l, \gamma_f^{s,c}, \lambda_{n,f}^{s,c}, \phi_{f,l}^{s,c,ni} \in \{0,1\}; \Theta^{\text{TOTAL}}, \Pi^{\text{TOTAL}} \in \Re^+. \tag{11}$$

This model assumes that the physical layer is not disconnectable under a single physical link failure. The CPLEX[1] optimizer has been used to solve the problem instances discussed in the following section.

4   Results

The values for input parameters, used by the optimizer, are displayed in Table 3. Different failure cases were used to evaluate the model under three different topologies (Fig. 1). A case relates to single link failure (no two links fail at the same time in each scenario), while the other relates to multiple link failure scenarios. Two percentages for affected links were tested. More specifically:

Case I: Single link failure scenarios, where $\cup_{f \in \mathcal{F}} \mathcal{L}_f$ affects a total of 5% (a) or 15% (b) of all the links;

Case II: Two or more links failing simultaneously, in each failure scenario, where $\cup_{f \in \mathcal{F}} \mathcal{L}_f$ affects a total of 5% (a) or 15% (b) of all the links.

---

[1] IBM ILOG CPLEX Optimizer version 12.8.

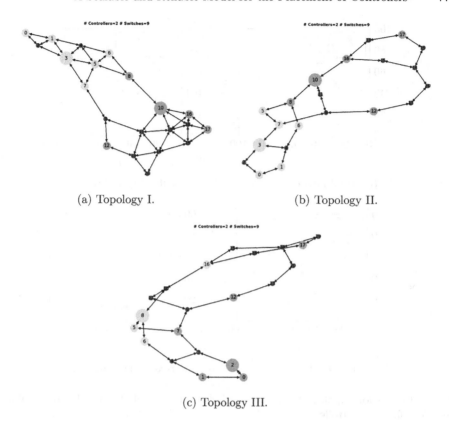

(a) Topology I.

(b) Topology II.

(c) Topology III.

Fig. 1. Physical topologies used for analysis of results. Large nodes are controllers, medium are switches, and small are non-used locations.

Table 3. Input parameters.

Parameter	Value
K_1	0.5
K_2	0.5
p_s	[40, 100]
h_s	[500, 600]

That is, in case Ia 5% of the links may fail, but no two links fail at the same time, while in case IIa there is a 0.5 probability for any pair of links to go down at the same time, which may lead to failure scenarios where two or more links fail simultaneously. In cases Ib and IIb, 15% of the links may fail.

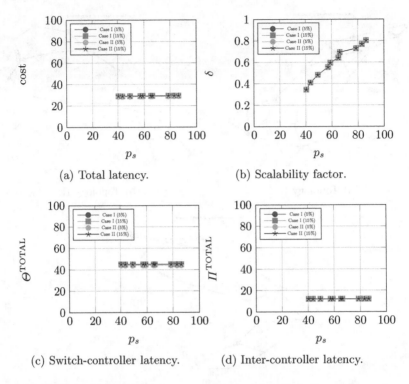

(a) Total latency.

(b) Scalability factor.

(c) Switch-controller latency.

(d) Inter-controller latency.

Fig. 2. Results for Topology I: high connectivity and relatively low number of possible locations for the controllers.

Table 4. Physical topology details.

Topology	# Nodes	# Links	# Possible controller locations
Topology I	21	40	4
Topology II	21	25	4
Topology III	21	25	9

Topology I: Results for this topology are shown in Fig. 2. This is the most dense topology, with relatively small number of possible locations for controllers. The scalability factor δ increases linearly as the number of `packet-in` messages increases.

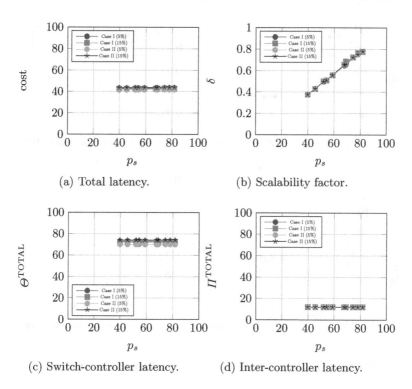

Fig. 3. Results for Topology II: low connectivity and relatively low number of possible locations for the controllers.

Topology II: Results for this topology are depicted in Fig. 3. This topology presents less links than Topology I, but the number of possible locations are kept similar. The main difference regarding these results is that the switch-controller latency has increased.

Topology III: Results for this topology are shown in Fig. 4. This topology also presents less links than Topology I, but the number of possible locations for each controller is increased. In this case it is possible to observe that the total latency significantly decreases. Therefore, the model was able compensate the reduced number of links, finding adequate places for controllers that lead to lower latency.

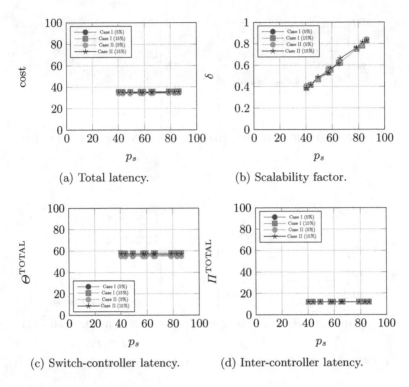

(a) Total latency.   (b) Scalability factor.

(c) Switch-controller latency.   (d) Inter-controller latency.

Fig. 4. Results for Topology III: low connectivity and relatively high number of possible locations for the controllers.

5 Conclusions

In this paper, a scalable and reliable model for controller placement is introduced. This model is mathematically formulated and optimal solutions for controller placement, under different failure scenarios, are obtained. Results show that scalability is ensured under different failure scenarios, while latency increase can be compensated through more freedom in controller's locations. The model also serves adequately multiple failure scenarios, presenting similar results for more critical failure scenarios and less critical ones.

In general, results show that the model is able to keep scalability (δ) while considering failure scenarios, ensuring load balancing among controllers. The latency may increase when less network connectivity decreases, but this might be avoided if more possible locations for controllers are allowed. Results are similar for Cases Ia, Ib, IIa and IIb, meaning that the model makes a controller placement that serves adequately multiple failure scenarios.

References

1. Bannour, F., Souihi, S., Mellouk, A.: Scalability and reliability aware SDN controller placement strategies. In: 13th International Conference on Network and Service Management (CNSM), pp. 1–4, November 2017
2. Cheng, G., Chen, H.: Game model for switch migrations in software-defined network. Electron. Lett. **50**(23), 1699–1700 (2014)
3. Cheng, T.Y., Wang, M., Jia, X.: QoS-guaranteed controller placement in SDN. In: IEEE Global Communications Conference (GLOBECOM) (2015)
4. Erickson, D.: The beacon OpenFlow controller. In: Proceedings of the Second ACM SIGCOMM Workshop on Hot Topics in Software Defined Networking, HotSDN 2013, pp. 13–18. ACM, New York (2013)
5. Open Networking Foundation: OpenFlow switch specification. Technical report ONF TS-025 (2015)
6. Gude, N., et al.: NOX: towards an operating system for networks. SIGCOMM Comput. Commun. Rev. **38**(3), 105–110 (2008)
7. Hassas Yeganeh, S., Ganjali, Y.: Kandoo: a framework for efficient and scalable offloading of control applications. In: Proceedings of the First Workshop on Hot Topics in Software Defined Networks, HotSDN 2012, pp. 19–24. ACM, New York (2012)
8. Heller, B., Sherwood, R., McKeown, N.: The controller placement problem. ACM SIGCOMM Comput. Commun. Rev. **42**(4), 473–478 (2012). https://doi.org/10.1145/2377677.2377767
9. Lange, S., et al.: Heuristic approaches to the controller placement problem in large scale SDN networks. IEEE Trans. Netw. Serv. Manag. **12**(1), 4–17 (2015)
10. McKeown, N., et al.: OpenFlow: enabling innovation in campus networks. ACM SIGCOMM Comput. Commun. Rev. **38**(2), 69–74 (2008)
11. Medved, J., Tkacik, A., Varga, R., Gray, K.: OpenDaylight: towards a model-driven SDN controller architecture. In: IEEE 15th International Symposium on a World of Wireless, Mobile and Multimedia Networks (WOWMOM). IEEE (2014)
12. Sallahi, A., St-Hilaire, M.: Optimal model for the controller placement problem in software defined networks. IEEE Commun. Lett. **19**(1), 30–33 (2015)
13. Sallahi, A., St-Hilaire, M.: Expansion model for the controller placement problem in software defined networks. IEEE Commun. Lett. **21**(2), 274–277 (2017)
14. Schmid, S., Suomela, J.: Exploiting locality in distributed SDN control. In: Proceedings of the Second ACM SIGCOMM Workshop on Hot Topics in Software Defined Networking, HotSDN 2013, pp. 121–126. ACM, New York (2013)
15. Vizarreta, P., Machuca, C.M., Kellerer, W.: Controller placement strategies for a resilient SDN control plane. In: Jonsson, M., Rak, J., Somani, A., Papadimitriou, D., Vinel, A. (eds.) Proceedings of 2016 8th International Workshop on Resilient Networks Design and Modeling (RNDM), pp. 253–259 (2016)
16. Yannan, H., Wendong, W., Xiangyang, G., Xirong, Q., Shiduan, C.: On reliability-optimized controller placement for software-defined networks. China Commun. **11**(2), 38–54 (2014)
17. Yao, G., Bi, J., Li, Y., Guo, L.: On the capacitated controller placement problem in software defined networks. IEEE Commun. Lett. **18**(8), 1339–1342 (2014)

18. Yao, L., Hong, P., Zhang, W., Li, J., Ni, D.: Controller placement and flow based dynamic management problem towards SDN. In: IEEE International Conference on Communication Workshop (ICCW), pp. 363–368. IEEE (2015)
19. Yeganeh, S.H., Tootoonchian, A., Ganjali, Y.: On scalability of software-defined networking. IEEE Commun. Mag. **51**(2), 136–141 (2013)
20. Zhang, Y., Cui, L., Wang, W., Zhang, Y.: A survey on software defined networking with multiple controllers. J. Netw. Comput. Appl. **103**, 101–118 (2018)

eHealth and Telemedicine Mobile Applications

Handling ECG Vital Signs in Personalized Ubiquitous Telemedicine Services

Maria Papaioannou[1], George Mandellos[1],
Theodor Panagiotakopoulos[2], and Dimitrios Lymperopoulos[1(✉)]

[1] Wired Communication Laboratory, Department of Electrical and Computer
Engineering, University of Patras, Patras, Greece
ece7887@upnet.gr, {mandello, dlympero}@upatras.gr
[2] Mobile and Pervasive Computing, Quality and Ambient Intelligence
Laboratory, School of Science and Technology, Hellenic Open University,
26335 Patras, Greece
tepanag@gmail.com

Abstract. Nowadays, telemedicine services are based on real time acquisition and processing of several types of in vitro patient data, especially vital signs. In this context, the storage, transmission, and management of digital ECG signals are major topics of debate and research nowadays as ECG is one of the most commonly performed examinations all over the world. Hence, many efforts have been already spent in constructing low power and small size ECG biosensors as well as in developing the adequate protocols for organizing and assessing the collected data. Despite SCP-ECG is the common accepted protocol, an excessive amount of ECG formats has been proposed and implemented by a plethora of researchers. This paper presents the SCP-ECG protocol and surveys the current state of medical frameworks and systems for collecting and organizing ECG data and other biosignals' data that are commonly used for the provision of personalized and ubiquitous telemedicine services.

Keywords: SCP-ECG protocol · Telemedicine services

1 Introduction

The electrocardiogram (ECG) helps the health-care providers to provide healthcare services to patients with heart problems. The analysis of the patients' electrocardiograms can exclude the problems of heart rotation, rhythmic and conduction problems, and some symptoms of specific diseases. More precisely, ECG signal is the process of recording the electrical activity of the heart over a time period using surface electrodes placed on the skin. These electrodes detect the tiny electrical changes on the skin that arise from the heart muscle's electrophysiologic pattern of depolarizing and repolarizing during each heartbeat. The final signal passes through various types of human tissues, that add a certain amount of electrical noises. Many external sources also account to this noise.

© ICST Institute for Computer Sciences, Social Informatics and Telecommunications Engineering 2019
Published by Springer Nature Switzerland AG 2019. All Rights Reserved
V. Sucasas et al. (Eds.): BROADNETS 2018, LNICST 263, pp. 85–94, 2019.
https://doi.org/10.1007/978-3-030-05195-2_9

ECG is the most commonly performed examination all over the world. So, its transmission, the storage and the management are major topics of discussion and research nowadays. An excessive amount of ECG formats has been proposed and implemented by a plethora of researchers. For transmission and remote management of ECG signals, the most well-known and commonly used is the Standard Communication Protocol for Computer assisted Electrocardiography (SCP-ECG) established by the European Standard Committee (CEN) for ECG recordings.

SCP-ECG is a standard that defines the data structure and format for a patient's ECG signal and demographic data, as well as rules for the above data interchange between digital ECGs and remote computer systems. More specifically, it introduces specific ECG traces, annotations, and metadata that define the interchange format and the messaging procedure. It stores also compressed data by known algorithms. It is recommended as an alternate to ECG databases.

Despite the advanced functionality of SCP-ECG, there is a need for adding extra patient's medical information except the required by the physicians during various telemedicine projects earlier [1]. The e-SCP-ECG$^+$ [2] is a remarkable extension of SCP-ECG that introduces new tags for extra demographic related data and data reference to the medical equipment [1]. It also defines additional sections for handling extra vital signals: noninvasive blood pressure (NiBP), body temperature (Temp), Carbon dioxide (CO2), blood oxygen saturation (SPO2), and pulse rate, and allergies, which are required for an integrated remote health monitoring.

Structuring of Personalized Ubiquitous Telemedicine Services (PUTS) is a key factor for providing high quality remote health monitoring. This paper, firstly surveys the structural, operational and performance attributes of the most expanded ECG and daughter protocols that could be exploited within the PUTS context. Section 2 examines the fundamentals of SCP-ECG. Section 3 discusses the current proposed frameworks and systems for handling ECG vital signs. Finally, Sect. 4 proposes specific expansions of SCP-ESC guided by PUTS context.

2   The Fundamentals of SCP-ECG Protocol

2.1   SCP-ECG Scope

With the increasing user acceptance and commercialization of digital electrocardiography and ICT technologies, the SCP-ECG came to allow the storage and the exchange of ECGs between medical ECG devices and user systems. Nowadays, it is integrated in the ISO/IEEE 11073 family of standards and the goal is to interoperate with other medical devices and not only ECG specific.

For this reason, SCP-ECG structures a binary encoded format of data and mechanisms for the signal's compression and the final reduction of the file's size. So, the ECGs are transmitted with low transmission ratios and the resulting disk space is used for the storage of the signal. This standard also handles ECG measurements, ECG feature extraction, pattern recognition, ECG interpretation and diagnostic classification.

Regarding SCP-ECG compliant software, there are many freely available programs including viewers, writers, parsers, format and content checkers. There are also methods for the harmonization of this ECG standard with others, such as the DICOM Waveform Supplement 30 [3], HL7 aECG [4] and MFER (Part 2.6 of the protocol).

2.2   SCP-ECG Structure and Data Content

As mentioned before, SCP-ECG integrates a patient's ECG data structure, an elementary demographics format, and also, the rules for interchanging data between digital ECG carts and hosts that, respectively, obtain and store the ECG data. An SCP-ECG formatted file divided in twelve (12) sections -dedicated per information category- includes all this information referred above. Finally, it includes several sections for the handling of manufacturer-specific content that can adequately handle various types of information through continuous health monitoring applications, and there are also some free sections for future use.

Each one of the 12 sections is defined by its own specific encoding rules and preceded by a common header. Regarding their contents, they may be divided in the following six different groups of information:

Group 1 (including entire Section 0): it stores the pointers to the start of the remaining sections in the record. This section is considered as public.

Group 2 (including tags 0–3, 5, 14–26, 31 of Section 1): these fields include the identification of the patient and the physicians, institutions and all the devices used for the acquisition, analysis and diagnosis of the ECG. This information is considered as highly confidential since it can identify the patient in a file full of health data.

Group 3 (including tags 4, 6–13, 27–30, 32–35, 255 of Section 1): these fields incorporate general information about the patient (e.g. age, weigh), his health condition (e.g. medical history, drugs) and data for the correct interpretation of the ECG (type of filtering applied). In terms of privacy, these data itself do not identify the patient.

Group 4 (including Sections 2–6): these sections identify the present leads in the record (Section 3) and store the ECG signal data (Section 6), which may be stored as uncompressed raw data or alternatively compressed using different algorithms. The compression ratio which can be accomplished ranges from less than 2–4:1, when only using Huffman tables (Section 2), or up to 6–20:1 when combining second-order differences (using Sections 4 and 5) with Huffman encoding and downsampling, at the cost of lower signal quality.

Group 5 (including Sections 7–11): these sections can be optionally added to incorporate: (a) global measurements (Section 7) and measurements from each lead independently (Section 10), to help the physician's work, and (b) the diagnostic interpretation of the ECG record (Section 8), which must be consistent with the manufacturer interpretive statements (Section 9) and the universal ECG interpretive statement codes and coding rules (Section 11). These data help to interpret the patient's ECG, so if he is identified, this information must be considered as highly confidential.

Group 6 (including Sections numbered 12 to 127 and those above 1023): these sections are reserved for future use.

3 Current Proposed Frameworks and Systems for Handling ECG Vital Signs

This section describes the main existing frameworks and systems for collection, management, processing, and transmission of ECG data.

3.1 ECG Data Collection by Biosensors

Biosensors are the devices that capture the biological signal and convert it into a detectable electrical signal. There are several classifications of biosensors employed in this scientific field. For instance, based on the application site, biosensors are distinguished in wearable, mobile, implanted, ingestible and ambient.

In some studies, ambient sensor networks for environmental monitoring are employed in conjunction with WBANs, to augment medical data with patient's context data (e.g. temperature, humidity, luminosity and movement). Along this context, for the remote monitoring of patients, the typical mobile system is a three-tier network architecture [5], especially in situations of elderly or chronic patients in their residence. The lower tier incorporates two systems: an integration of suitable medical sensors equipped with a Bluetooth transceiver; and the ambient wireless sensors deployed in the patient's surroundings. In the middle tier, an ad hoc network of powerful mobile computing devices (e.g., laptops, PDAs) collects the demographics, medical and ambient sensory data and forwards them to the higher tier. The middle-tier devices must be equipped with several network interfaces in order to communicate with the lower tier and WLAN or cellular capabilities for the higher layer. Finally, the higher tier is structured on the Internet and incorporates all the application databases and servers accessed by the healthcare providers. The proposed framework provides a flexible and secure solution that can be applied to several scenarios, including home, hospital and nursing home environments for the monitoring of multiple patients.

Moreover, for the monitoring and location tracking of patients within hospital environments a group of researchers proposed a system architecture based on two independent subsystems [6, 18]. The healthcare monitoring subsystem consists of smart shirts with integrated medical sensors. The location subsystem has two components: IEEE 802.15.4 end devices, on the patients, that gather signal strength information from the received beacons, and a deployment of wireless IEEE 802.15.4 nodes that are installed in known locations within the hospital infrastructure and broadcast periodic beacon frames. Both subsystems forward their acquired data to a gateway through an IEEE 802.15.4-based ad hoc distribution network. The gateway has wired Internet connectivity and forwards the data to the management server and the monitoring mHealth application, that the healthcare providers have easily access. The proposed system achieves real-time data reconstruction, high reliability, and sufficient battery lifetime of the sensors used.

It is well-known that low power wireless sensors, personal wireless hub (PWH) and receivers can reduce the workload of the paramedic staff in a hospital. In this context, Naeem et al. [7] used several PWHs to transmit sensory data to the main central controller. A well designed multiple PWH assignment and power control scheme can decrease the electromagnetic and in-band interference induced to the other medical devices in the hospital. They proposed a framework and an algorithm with low complexity for interference aware joint power control and multiple PWH assignment (IAJPCPA) in a hospital building with cognitive radio capability. They presented an efficient PWH assignment and power control scheme for IAJPCPA.

Later, the same researchers [8] extended their work presenting an advanced study about Wireless Resource Allocation in Next Generation Healthcare Facilities. Healthcare facilities with intelligent wireless devices can decrease the workload of the paramedic staff. These devices incorporate low-power wireless sensors, personal wireless hub (PWH), and receivers. The PWH acts as a relay in the hospital network. To help the wireless sensor devices, they used multiple PWHs to forward sensory data to the main central controller. It also enhances reliability to the coverage of the wireless network. In the proposed framework (IAJPCPA), any wireless sensor device can send and receive data from multiple PWHs. The main objective of IAJPCPA is to maximize the total transmission data rate by assigning PWHs to the wireless sensor devices under the constraint of acceptable interference to the licensed wireless devices.

3.2 Transmission of ECG

A large-scale study was carried out about the characteristics of transmission media in the healthcare system, and design various telemedicine systems by using advanced wireless communication technique, while Telemedicine performed by employing a highspeed and robust advanced wireless communication system, such as the healthcare system can provide ubiquitous medical services at any time.

Researchers are endeavoring along this promising path. Lin and Yi-Li [9], proposed a direct-sequence ultra-wideband (DS UWB) transmission system for wireless telemedicine system. An essential feature of this system is that it provides larger power and schemes offering significant error protection for the transmission of medical information that requires higher quality of service. To achieve maximum resource utilization, or minimum total transmission power, they also incorporated an M-ary Binary Offset Keying (MBOK) strategy into the system. Thus, in their proposed medical system, high power, a long length MBOK code, and scheme providing significant error protection schemes are employed for the transmission of medical messages that require a stringent Bit-Error Rate (BER). In contrast, low power, short length MBOK codes, and less capable error protection schemes are provided for messages that can tolerate a high BER. The resulting model is being verified by a simulation carrying out the proper functioning of the proposed system in a practical wireless telemedicine scenario.

Later, Lin and Yi-Li [10], expanded their research work proposing a power assignment mechanism for direct-sequence ultra-wideband (DS UWB) wireless telemedicine system with unequal error protection. Their analysis was followed up by a simulation to validate the proper functionality of the proposed DS UWB wireless healthcare system.

In other work, the multiple transmitter relay pairs desire forwards their gathered information to a main data center. This relay-aided hospital wireless systems in cognitive radio environment was investigated in [18]. For that system, the proposed transmission framework follows IEEE 802.22 WRAN and adopts the listen before talk and geolocation/database methods to achieve the protection of the primary users. Regarding the proposed transmission strategy, in each subsystem, the wireless sensor device (WSD) with the highest signal to noise ratio (SNR) is selected to transmit signals at each time and then, a two-hop half duplex decode and forward (DF) relaying transmission is launched among the selected WSD, the corresponding personal wireless hub (PWH) and the data center. As a result, an optimization problem is formulated to maximize the system sum rate via power allocation. They then solved it by using convex optimization theory and KKT condition method and derive a closed form solution of the optimal power allocation. By finishing their work, the validity of their proposed scheme is proved by their Simulation results, showing also the effects of the total power, the interference thresholds and the scale of the network on the system performance, which offer some insights for practical hospital wireless system design.

3.3   Management and Processing of ECG

A plethora of researchers work on automatic pattern recognizers using Artificial Neural Networks (ANN) and compound neural network (CNN). Nowadays, the development of independent processor-based structures with sufficient processing capabilities is an emerging technology in order to make early and accurate diagnosis so as to provide early treatments [11–13]. Today, we tend to rely a great deal on the application of pattern recognition methods to help us achieve such a goal. In this line, several studies of automatic recognition of ECG data have been proposed.

Meghriche et al. [14] developed two approaches. In the first one the Compound Neural Network (CNN) is structured in three different multilayer neural networks of the feed forward type, and the second one based on only a multi-layer perceptron (MLP). The result is that in both approaches there is the capability to classify ECGs as carrying atrioventricular blocks (AVB) or not. Finally, they concluded confirming that neural networks can be reliably used to improve automated ECG interpretation process for AVB and also that this kind of networks can be used as an accurate decision-making support by even an experienced healthcare provider.

De facto, digital medical examinations are one of the pillars for the expansion of e-health, a new medical paradigm which enables the implementation of new ICT-based services and the decrease of the patients' and healthcare systems' costs. Personal patient data and health status, ECG measures or the diagnosis are mainly stored as metadata in a digital ECG file. As a result, there are several governmental regulations that protect these examinations both at the storage point and during transmission. Reliability and privacy are the two general requisites must be guaranteed.

In this line, Rubio et al. [15] proposed a SCP-ECG security extension. Their work offers SCP-ECG files to be stored safely and proper access to be granted (or denied) to users. The access privileges are scaled by means of role-based profiles supported by cryptographic elements (ciphering, digital certificates and digital signatures). These elements are considered as metadata into a new section. The application's capacity to authenticate users and to protect the integrity of files and the privacy of sensitive data, with a low impact on file size and access time, has been extensively tested. The main advantage of this solution is its combability with any version of the SCP-ECG, so as can be easily integrated into e-health platforms.

3.4 Machine to Machine Systems

Kartsakli et al. [16], presented a comprehensive survey on Machine-to-Machine (M2M) systems. In the new era marked by the increasing number of wireless electronic devices, (M2M) communications are an emerging technology in order to achieve an interconnection between the devices without the human interaction. The use of mHealth applications based on M2M technology provides considerable benefits for both patients and healthcare providers. Hence, at first, they presented an advanced methodological study of Wireless Body Area Networks (WBANs), which establish the enabling technology at the patient's side, and then discuss end-to-end approaches that comprise the design and implementation of applied mHealth applications.

Regarding the mHealth, the M2M approach supports the use of suitable sensor devices on the patients. The medical sensors form a Wireless Body Area Network (WBAN), and mostly they are organized through short-range wireless networks. In the next step, an M2M-enabled gateway node gathers all the sensory data collected from the WBAN and forwards them to a remote online server, where processing and integration with medical-related software applications take place. At that time, they are used long-range communication access technologies for Wireless Local/Metropolitan Area Networks (WLANs/WMANs). The collection of significant amount of data and their timely delivery to the healthcare providers in an unobtrusive way for the patient and autonomously- without needing the human interaction, can significantly facilitate the management of chronic diseases and speed up the early and accurate diagnosis. So, in this context this technology paves the way for new possibilities for mHealth applications, by enabling the telemonitoring of vital signals [17], the early detection of critical conditions and the telecontrol of certain healthcare treatments [18].

There is no doubt that the area of M2M communications for mHealth enjoys a rapidly growing. Despite that, there are still many challenges in the variety of aspects of the mHealth systems. Although, there is the need to standardize the activities and methods, that will enable the market exploitation of the scientific contributions in this field of healthcare services by paving the road for the development of interoperable M2M mHealth solutions and approaches.

Another noteworthy trend is that people all over the world are getting older and this fact has created the need for designing new, ubiquitous and cost-effective healthcare systems. In this respect, distributed and networked embedded systems seem the most attractive technology to achieve continuous telemonitoring of aged people. Along these lines, Tennina et al. [19] proposed recent advancements by introducing WSN4QoL. The project involves the implementation and design of wireless sensor networks (WSNs) specifically structured to meet the existing healthcare application requirements. In particular, the system architecture is presented to deal with the challenges imposed by the specific application scenario. This incorporates a network coding (NC) algorithm and a distributed localization approach that have been implemented on WSN testbeds to achieve efficiency in the communications and to enable indoor people tracking.

4 Discussion

Nowadays, we are already on the transition from the traditional desktop-based computing technologies towards ubiquitous computing environments that will enfold us in almost all our daily situations and activities. Simultaneously, there is an amplified tendency of creating a patient-centric service delivery. As a result, the services in the ubiquitous environments should be adapted to the current context, the needs and the preferences of users. As a result, mobile and pervasive health systems encompass complex mechanisms to collect and process an increasing range of data, instead of simply acquiring, analyzing and interpreting purely medical data.

For instance, the majority of contemporary health systems that rely on ECG measurements to deliver healthcare services are increasingly taking into account accelerometer data to distinguish abnormal ECG measurements due to pathological reasons from abnormal ECG measurements caused by certain activities (e.g. running). In addition, location information is deemed a prerequisite to deliver appropriate care in case of a critical cardiac episode. Apart from context data, preferences of patients (e.g. who to be informed when care provision is required), play an important role in personalizing service functionality and achieving higher degrees of user acceptance and market diffusion.

The above and many other cases suggest that protocols, frameworks, and systems for ECG data transmission and management should also consider data referring to non-medical aspects of a patient, such as location, activity and temporal information, or, in other words, the context of a measured ECG and a reasoned health status. Nevertheless, while infrastructural capabilities of pervasive health systems, in terms of sensing devices, middleware architectures, as well as service logic approaches (i.e. data analysis technologies), have addressed this need, it is also essential traditional ECG oriented protocols to incorporate contextual information by integrating additional sections in the protocols' structure.

5 Conclusions

After decades of continuous work in information systems dedicated to the healthcare domain, there is a growing demand not only for hospital-based care but also for personalized and ubiquitous healthcare delivery. For example, an especially critical healthcare domain is cardiology; almost two third of cardiac deaths occur out of hospital, and patients do not survive long enough to benefit from in-hospital treatments. For this reason, it is needed to adopt new healthcare models that enable continuous patient monitoring without spatiotemporal restrictions and orchestrate timely care provision moving the point of care beyond traditional healthcare settings. The ECG is only immediate diagnostic test to prevent a cardiac event. The early detection of cardiac events requires advanced decision-making techniques guided by reliable alarm messages and involving care provider only if necessary. Above all, there is the need the patient to control its own health status by being able to perform related tests at the early stage of the onset of the symptoms without involving skilled personnel and healthcare providers. The solution should be a combination of medical protocols, frameworks and systems for collecting, transmitting, managing, and organizing ECG data and other biosignals' data that are commonly used for the provision of personalized and ubiquitous telemedicine services.

References

1. Trigo, J.D., Alesanco, Á., Martínez, I., García, J.: A review on digital ECG formats and the relationships between them. IEEE Trans. Inf. Technol. Biomed. 16(3), 432–444 (2012)
2. Mandellos, G.J., Koukias, M.N., Lymberopoulos, D.K.: Structuring the e-SCP-ECG+ protocol for multi vital-sign handling. In: Proceedings of the 8th IEEE International Conference on BioInformatics and BioEngineering (BIBE 2008), Athens, Greece (2008)
3. Sakkalis, V., Chiarugi, F., Kostomanolakis, S., Chronaki, C., Tsiknakis, M., Orphanoudakis, S.: A gateway between the SCP-ECG and the DICOM supplement 30 waveform standard. In: Computers in Cardiology, pp. 25–28 (2003)
4. Schloegl, A., Chiarugi, F., Cervesato, E., Apostolopoulos, E., Chronaki, C.: Two-way converter between the HL7 aECG and SCP-ECG data formats using BioSig. In: Computers in Cardiology, pp. 253–256 (2007)
5. Mandellos, G., Koukias, M., Styliadis, I., Lymberopoulos, D.: e-SCP-ECG+ protocol: an expansion on SCP-ECG protocol for health telemonitoring – pilot implementation. Int. J. Telemed. Appl. (2010). https://doi.org/10.1155/2010/137201
6. Liu, J., Xiong, K., Zhang, Y., Zhong, Z.: Resource allocation for relay-aided cooperative hospital wireless networks. In: Zhou, Y., Kunz, T. (eds.) Ad Hoc Networks. LNICST, vol. 184, pp. 192–204. Springer, Cham (2017). https://doi.org/10.1007/978-3-319-51204-4_16
7. Naeem, M., Pareek, U., Lee, D.C., Khwaja, A.S., Anpalagan, A.: Efficient multiple personal wireless hub assignment in next generation healthcare facilities. In: Wireless Communications and Networking Conference. IEEE (2015)
8. Naeem, M., Pareek, U., Lee, D.C., Khwaja, A.S., Anpalagan, A.: Wireless resource allocation in next generation healthcare facilities. IEEE Sens. J. 15(3), 1463–1474 (2015)
9. Lin, C.-F., Yi-Li, C.: A DS UWB transmission system for wireless telemedicine. WSEAS Trans. Syst. 7(7), 578–588 (2008)
10. Lin, C.-F., Yi-Li, C.: A power assignment mechanism for DS UWB wireless telemedicine system with unequal error protection. In: 12th WSEAS International Conference on SYSTEMS, Heraklion, Greece (2008)
11. Bobbie, P.O., Chaudhari, H., Arif, C.-Z., Pujari, S.: Electrocardiogram (EKG) data acquisition and wireless transmission. WSEAS Trans. Comput. 3(8), 2665–2672 (2004)
12. Kumar, A., Dewan, L., Singh, M.: Real time monitoring system for ECG signal using virtual instrumentation. WSEAS Trans. Biol. Biomed. 3(11), 638–643 (2006)
13. Renumadhavi, Ch., Madhava Kumar, S., Ananth, A.G., Srinivasan, N.: Algorithms for filtering and finding SNR of ECG signals with powerline interference. WSEAS Trans. Signal Process. 2(9), 1320–1325 (2006)
14. Meghriche, S., Boulemden, M., Draa, A.: Agreement between multi-layer perceptron and a compound neural network on ECG diagnosis of aatrioventricular blocks. WSEAS Trans. Biol. Biomed. 5(1), 12–22 (2008)
15. Rubio, Ó.J., Alesanco, Á., García, J.: A robust and simple security extension for the medical standard SCP-ECG. J. Biomed. Inform. 46(1), 142–151 (2013)

16. Kartsakli, E., et al.: A survey on M2M systems for mHealth: a wireless communications perspective. Sensors **14**(10), 18009–18052 (2014)
17. Lalos, A.S., Alonso, L., Verikoukis, C.: Model based compressed sensing reconstruction algorithms for ECG telemonitoring in WBANs. Digit. Signal Process. **35**, 105–116 (2014)
18. ETSI. Machine to Machine Communications (M2M): Use Cases of M2M Applications for eHealth. http://www.etsi.org/deliver/etsi_tr/102700_102799/102732/01.01.01_60/tr_10273 2v010101p.pdf. Accessed 23 Sept 2014
19. Tennina, S., et al.: WSN4QoL: a WSN-oriented healthcare system architecture. J. Distrib. Sens. Netw. **10**(5), 503417 (2014)

Software-Defined Networking for Ubiquitous Healthcare Service Delivery

Foteini Andriopoulou[1](✉), Konstantinos Birkos[1], Georgios Mantas[2,3],
and Dimitrios Lymberopoulos[1](✉)

[1] Department of Electrical and Computer Engineering,
University of Patras, 26500 Patras, Greece
{fandriop,dlymbero}@upatras.gr,
kmpirkos@ece.upatras.gr
[2] Faculty of Engineering and Science, University of Greenwich, London, UK
G.Mantas@greenwich.ac.uk
[3] Instituto de Telecomunicações, Aveiro, Portugal

Abstract. The growth of the mobile, portable devices and the server-to-server communication through cloud computing increase the network traffic. The dependence of the ubiquitous healthcare service delivery on the network connectivity creates failures that may interrupt or delay the treatment plan with adverse effects in patients' quality of life even leading to mortality. In the present work, we propose the incorporation of Software Defined Networking (SDN) features in the healthcare domain in order to provide the appropriate bandwidth and guarantee the accurate real time medical data transmission independently of the connectivity of the ISP provider. The SDN controller monitors the network traffic and specifies how traffic should be routed providing load balancing, lower delays and better performance. Finally, the proposed healthcare architecture addresses the SDN scalability challenge by incorporating the logically centralized control plane using multiple distributed controllers. A 2-tier hierarchical overlay is formed among SDN controllers following the principles of peer-to-peer networking.

Keywords: Software defined network · Body area networks
Ubiquitous healthcare service delivery

1 Introduction

The explosion of internet and mobile applications with the evolution of the pervasive environment, during the last few years, have dramatically changed the way that healthcare is delivered. Wireless and mobile technologies have enabled real time data transmission through numerous portable devices, sensors and other computing entities in order to access care remotely and receive fast treatment in emergency cases. This explosive growth of data transmission introduces many challenges in terms of data storage, interoperability and availability of resources. Cloud computing approach was adopted to address the aforementioned issues [5].

© ICST Institute for Computer Sciences, Social Informatics and Telecommunications Engineering 2019
Published by Springer Nature Switzerland AG 2019. All Rights Reserved
V. Sucasas et al. (Eds.): BROADNETS 2018, LNICST 263, pp. 95–104, 2019.
https://doi.org/10.1007/978-3-030-05195-2_10

However, the rapid growth of storage resources in the cloud platforms and the need for efficient access to these resources has increased the requirements for fast underlying networks. While healthcare services become more dependent on the network connectivity, network failures may interrupt or delay the healthcare service delivery with adverse effects in patients' quality of life even leading to mortality. In this context, more than ever is required a flexible, scalable and agile network that simplifies the network configuration and management. Software Defined Networking (SDN) [17] is the most promising solution for increasing network utilization and reducing hardware complexity and costs. SDN is a networking architecture that provides network intelligence out of the switching devices by abstracting the logical part of the computer networks and placing it on the controllers [9, 16, 17].

In large scale networks such as ubiquitous healthcare network, the controller could become a bottleneck with negative effects on network maintenance and data forwarding. Multiple solutions have been proposed for avoiding the increased traffic in the controller. Some of them propose the insertion of multiple controllers into the network architecture for replacing the disconnected controllers, while some other propose two levels of hierarchy in order to share responsibilities among cotrollers [18]. DevoFlow [2] seperates the flows in two classes, the short-lived flows and the long-lived for reducing the tasks executed by the controller. Only the long lived flows were forwarded to the controller where the short lived flows are handled in the data plane. HotSwap [14] proposed a mechanism through which a controller is able to be replaced by another new controller on-the fly without any disruption of the network. However, the error possibilities are many as well as this process introduces further delays. Koponen et al. [6] proposed Onix platform, a distributed control platform on top of which a network control plane can be implemented. It provides flexible distribution components that enable software designers to implement control applications without re-inventing distribution mechanisms [6]. Tootoonchain et Ganjali proposed HyperFlow [13], a logically centralized but physically distributed event-based control plane. It allows deployment of any number of controllers which share the same broad network view. They serve requests without active contact of any remote node that decrease the delays and the flow installation time. Kandoo [4], provides a distributed control plane with two levels of hierarchy for the controllers, the local controllers and the root controllers. The local controllers are located closer to the data path in order to receive requests from the switches while the root controllers control the local switches and handles applications that require network wide knowledge.

In the present work, we propose the incorporation of the SDN in both the access and core network of the ubiquitous healthcare system architecture in order to achieve network intelligence. Incorporating the SDN in the access network, the network devices of the end users (patients) provide access to the core network where the SDN controller classifies the packets. These packets are prioritized over the network. Then, the SDN controller which has broader knowledge of the network status is able to take decisions for routing or redirecting the vital bio-signals and other essential medical data over neighbor paths providing the appropriate bandwidth for the accurate real time data transmission. The proposed healthcare network architecture incorporates a logically centralized control plane using multiple distributed controllers. These controllers constitute a large-scale distributed system following the principles of peer-to-peer networking [11]. The maintenance of the distributed multiple controllers based on the peer-to-peer paradigm provides scalability, robustness and low response time. A 2-tier hierarchical overlay is proposed. It enables efficient cooperation and ensures the dynamic communication and information exchange through the ISP and healthcare providers.

The rest of the paper is organized as follows: Sect. 3 presents the basic architecture of the healthcare network enhanced with the SDN principles. It provides the basic use cases for the mobile and wireless networks or access the network and how the MPLS functionality is implementing for these purposes. Finally, Sect. 3 concludes the present work.

2 Healthcare Network Architecture Over SDN

2.1 Overview

Wireless sensor networks and BANs are considered fundamental for supporting ambient living and providing high-quality healthcare service delivery [7, 10]. Figure 1 presents an overview of the healthcare environment with the involved entities.

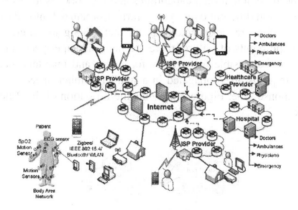

Fig. 1. An overview of the ubiquitous healthcare environment.

The patient uses wearable and mobile sensors that acquire bio-signal information and transmit it to a control device. The control device aggregates all the signals from the sensors and forwards them via an ISP [15] for further processing to healthcare providers. Healthcare providers provide services for ubiquitous patient monitoring and have their own network that can be a legacy network or based on SDN/OpenFLow principles. Figure 2 presents the system overview of the ubiquitous healthcare network based on SDN.

The multiple controllers of the ISPs and healthcare providers are organized into a 2-tier hierarchical overlay network following the peer-to-peer paradigm [11]. Each ISP and healthcare provider organizes its controllers *peers* in an over-lay. Peers in the same overlay establish and maintain logical connections with other peers, perform overlay

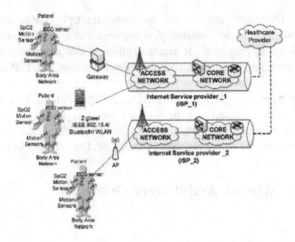

Fig. 2. The overview of the healthcare network.

routing, store and retrieve information such as available resources, network traffic, etc. Peers with enhanced computational capabilities and network resources become *super-peers*. Super-peers from different overlays are further organized into an overlay and are responsible for handling requests among peers that belong to different overlays. In order to avoid single points of failure, there are multiple super-peers in each overlay. Bootstrap peers are responsible for overlay formation and maintenance. In this hierarchical scheme, requests are propagated in a smaller number of ISPs and controllers, achieving low response time. Figure 3 presents the formation of the 2-tier hierarchical overlay network.

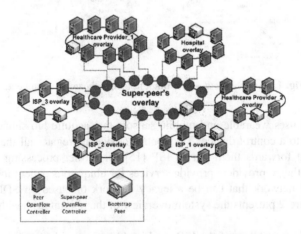

Fig. 3. The 2-tier hierarchical overlay formation

2.2   Basic Architecture

Each healthcare provider is responsible to check periodically the reception of vital bio-signals from the subscribed patients. If no bio-signals have been received within a predefined threshold duration or if the received data rate is below an expected value, the healthcare provider contacts the Bootstrap peer and sends a request with information related to the required QoS level (minimum bitrate, delay, packet loss) for the acceptable provisioning of the healthcare services. Bootstrap peer forwards the request to the ISP providers in order in order to find to which ISP the patient is subscribed. The ISP providers forward further the request to their overlay and a success or failure response is sent to the Bootstrap. The ISP is informed about the healthcare requirements and initiates a set of actions towards the restoration of network access.

However, a patient may not have an Internet connection or his connectivity may be intermittent due to mobility. If limited or no connectivity is observed, the ISP executes a set of actions to recover its network connectivity or may request to cooperate with another ISP in order to support the patient. In the following section, we analyze two possible ways that an ISP may execute for network access restoration based on the SDN functionality: the wireless network restoration through WiFi access points and the enhancement of LTE mobile access.

Wireless Network Access In this section, we propose how the ISP can provide enhanced wireless network access to the patients. In this context, patients carry WiFi-enabled devices while their ISP operates a set of OpenFlow-compatible WiFi APs controlled by one or multiple controllers. The controller interacts with specialized applications for network management. The healthcare provider may also have a set of public APs which can be used to assist patients for medical data transmission. A special interface provides communication with the ISPs of the registered users.

The network management application that runs on top of the controller of the ISP tries to find the patient's location based on his recent activity, global positioning information from his device or geo-location information from the cellular network. Then it selects a set of candidate APs that can be used for connecting the user to the network. The controller of the ISP has global knowledge of the network connections and their status. Therefore, it can assess the status of the connection between each AP and the healthcare provider. Based on this information, the AP that meets the constraints better is selected. The controller installs a rule inside this AP that permits connectivity to the MAC address of the device of the patient. At this point, the device can access the network and transmit data to the healthcare provider. Figure 4 depicts the proposed setup.

However, public APs or APs connected to other ISPs may also be available within the area of the patient. In order to support cooperation for medical data transmission, the healthcare providers and the ISPs are interconnecting through the aforementioned super-peer's overlay as presented in Fig. 5. In this cooperative scheme, if the patient's ISP cannot provide any active APs appropriate for the bio-signal transmission, it informs the Bootstrap peer which broadcasts a request through the super-peer's overlay to other ISPs for requesting access. Each ISP's super-peer forward the request to its internal overlay in order to search for available network resources. The controllers (peers) of each ISP overlay check the available APs and report back to the ISP's

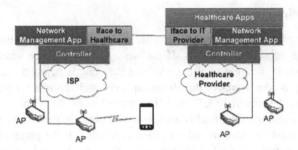

Fig. 4. SDN-based wireless network access for healthcare data flows.

super-peer. The ISPs' super-peers response to the Bootstrap with a message that contains the active and available APs. Bootstrap peer compares the candidate APs, selects the one that meets the QoS constraints better and sends a request to the corresponding ISP. Then the controller instructs the AP to accept connection of the patient's device and permit traffic flows towards the IP of the healthcare provider.

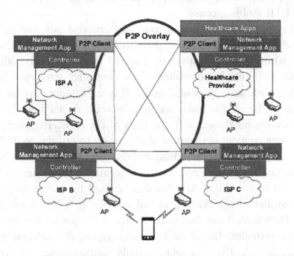

Fig. 5. Peer-to-peer overlay for wireless network access across multiple ISPs.

Mobile Network Access. In this section, the proposed solution for enhanced mobile network access for healthcare purposes is presented. In this case, bio-signals are sent to the healthcare provider via an OpenFlow-enabled LTE cellular network [1, 8, 12].

In the proposed system, the Serving Gateways (S-GWs) consist of two distinct parts: a data-plane part and a control-plane part. The control plane is actually removed from S-GW and it is implemented by the controller of the Mo-bile Network Operator (MNO). In the same manner, the control plane of the Packet Data Network (PDN) Gateway (P-GW) may also be realized by means of a controller. In this case, the necessary interaction between S-GW and P-GW occurs through the communication of the corresponding controllers. On top of the controllers, specialized applications perform network monitoring, control, radio resource management and mobility management. Therefore, the Mobility Management Entity (MME) is also part of the software on top of the controller. Figure 6 shows how mobile network access for healthcare data flows is provided through an SDN-enabled LTE network.

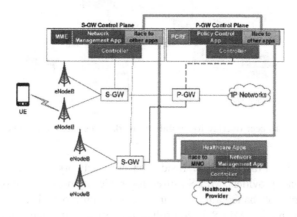

Fig. 6. SDN-based mobile network access for healthcare data flows.

In order to provide specialized access policies to healthcare users, the MNO must be aware of the set of these users and the related QoS requirements. This information is provided by the healthcare provider via the super-peer's overlay (P2P overlay) described in the previous section. The network management application executed on top of the controller of an S-GW has complete knowledge of the devices producing healthcare data flows that are connected to the eNodeBs of its jurisdiction. This global visibility enables MNOs to favor healthcare applications more easily and more efficiently.

If the users experience poor signal strength, the serving eNodeBs are dictated by the controller to selectively increase the power allocated to the corresponding sub-channels. In addition, the network management application can protect devices running healthcare applications from interference and treat them differently. When performing Inter-Cell Interference Coordination (ICIC), the sub-channels allocated to these specific devices can be excluded from power reduction. Under increased user density, enhanced ICIC (eICIC) can create pico-cells in certain overloaded areas to cover the devices that communicate with the healthcare provider.

It is also possible that in certain rural areas the user has too poor coverage from its own operator. In this case, it can be served by alternative MNOs that may provide better coverage. This scenario requires cooperation among multiple operators and/or the healthcare provider. Cooperation and coordination is realized by means of the peer-to-peer overlay of providers. When poor or no coverage at all is observed, the current MNO broadcasts a request to the peer-to-peer overlay. After a negotiation among candidate MNOs, the best MNO in terms of coverage and traffic load is selected to serve the user. Figure 7 depicts the peer-to-peer overlay for mobile network access across multiple MNOs.

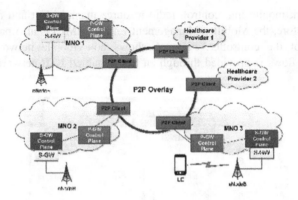

Fig. 7. Peer-to-peer overlay for mobile network access across multiple MNOs.

SDN-based MPLS Functionality. Inside the core network of each provider (ISP, MNO or healthcare provider), MPLS is used for traffic engineering purposes in order to provide the appropriate bandwidth, QoS and access control to the healthcare data flows. However, in our model, MPLS is controlled by software modules, according to the SDN paradigm. The introduction of SDN control in MPLS networks has significant advantages. A major advantage is that SDN-based MPLS provides better control over the formation and maintenance of Label-Switched Paths (LSPs). In addition, network dynamics induce churn effects which are difficult to be handled by conventional MPLS which lacks global knowledge and centralized control [3].

In the proposed system, the MPLS control plane resides on top of centralized controllers. It has a holistic view of the active flows of healthcare data which may enter the network via different ingress routers. Each time a healthcare data flow is initialized, the MPLS control plane selects or forms an MPLS tunnel that meets certain bandwidth, delay and packet loss constraints. The global network view offered by the controller enables the MPLS control plane to create routes that meet multiple criteria efficiently. Any change in the network topology or the status of the links is resolved by the MPLS control plane with minimal messaging overhead.

Due to auto-route and auto-bandwidth features of MPLS, flows may need to migrate to different LSPs or existing LSPs may need to be reconstructed. The MPLS control plane protects the healthcare data flows from frequent changes and prioritizes them in the bandwidth reservation inside the MPLS tunnels. Moreover, the network access of multiple concurrent healthcare data flows is globally optimized. QoS requirements of individual flows as well as fairness among competing flows are the objectives of the optimization process.

3 Conclusion

In the present work, we proposed the use of the SDN in both the access and core network of the ubiquitous healthcare system architecture in order to achieve network intelligence in favor of healthcare service provisioning. In the proposed architecture, multiple distributed controllers constitute a large-scale hierarchical peer-to-peer overlay which enables efficient cooperation and information exchange among ISPs and healthcare providers. We have shown how this interaction can lead in proper transmission of the medical data by enhancing admission control, prioritization, network resource management and traffic shaping.

It is our strong belief that the proposed ubiquitous healthcare network enhanced with SDN features and strengthened with the peer-to-peer paradigm is able to: (a) help the end-users to overcome some network restrictions in order to transfer their vital measurements and (b) support the communication and collaboration of the ISP and healthcare providers in an efficient and scalable manner. As a future work the proposed network platform will be emulated using Mininet and open source controllers in order to study the opportunistic behavior of the system in real time conditions.

References

1. Brief, O.S.: Openflow-enabled mobile and wireless networks (2013)
2. Curtis, A.R., Mogul, J.C., Tourrilhes, J., Yalagandula, P., Sharma, P., Banerjee, S.: Devoflow: scaling flow management for high-performance networks. In: ACM SIGCOMM Computer Communication Review, vol. 41, pp. 254–265. ACM (2011)
3. Das, S., Sharafat, A., Parulkar, G., McKeown, N.: Mpls with a simple open control plane. In: Optical Fiber Communication Conference, p. OWP2. Optical Society of America (2011)
4. Hassas Yeganeh, S., Ganjali, Y.: Kandoo: a framework for efficient and scalable offloading of control applications. In: Proceedings of the First Workshop on Hot Topics in Software Defined Networks, pp. 19–24. ACM (2012)
5. Hogan, M., Liu, F., Sokol, A., Tong, J.: NIST Cloud Computing Standards Roadmap. NIST Special Publication 35 (2011)
6. Koponen, T., et al.: Onix: a distributed control platform for large-scale production networks. OSDI 10, 1–6 (2010)
7. Lee, Y.D., Chung, W.Y.: Wireless sensor network based wearable smart shirt for ubiquitous health and activity monitoring. Sens. Actuators B Chem. 140(2), 390–395 (2009)
8. Li, L.E., Mao, Z.M., Rexford, J.: Toward software-defined cellular networks. In: 2012 European Workshop on Software Defined Networking (EWSDN), pp. 7–12. IEEE (2012)
9. McKeown, N., et al.: Openflow: enabling innovation in campus networks. ACM SIGCOMM Computer Communication Review 38(2), 69–74 (2008)
10. Pandian, P., et al.: Smart vest: Wearable multi-parameter remote physiological monitoring system. Med. Eng. Phys. 30(4), 466–477 (2008)
11. Risson, J., Moors, T.: Survey of research towards robust peer-to-peer networks: search methods. Comput. Netw. 50(17), 3485–3521 (2006)
12. Said, S.B.H., et al.: New control plane in 3GPP LTE/EPC architecture for on-demand connectivity service. In: 2013 IEEE 2nd International Conference on Cloud Networking (CloudNet), pp. 205–209. IEEE (2013)

13. Tootoonchian, A., Ganjali, Y.: HyperFlow: a distributed control plane for openflow. In: Proceedings of the 2010 Internet Network Management Conference on Research on Enterprise Networking, p. 3. USENIX Association (2010)
14. Vanbever, L., Reich, J., Benson, T., Foster, N., Rexford, J.: HotSwap: correct and efficient controller upgrades for software-defined networks. In: Proceedings of the Second ACM SIGCOMM Workshop on Hot Topics in Software Defined Networking, pp. 133–138. ACM (2013)
15. Vouyioukas, D., Maglogiannis, I.: Communication issues in pervasive healthcare systems and applications. In: Pervasive and Smart Technologies for Healthcare: Ubiq-uitous Methodologies and Tools, pp. 197–227 (2010)
16. Wang, W., Haas, R., Salim, J.H., Doria, A., Khosravi, H.M.: Forwarding and control element separation (forces) protocol specification (2010)
17. Xia, W., Wen, Y., Foh, C.H., Niyato, D., Xie, H.: A survey on software-defined networking (2014)
18. Yeganeh, S.H., Tootoonchian, A., Ganjali, Y.: On scalability of software-defined networking. IEEE Commun. Mag. 51(2), 136–141 (2013)

Profile Management System in Ubiquitous Healthcare Cloud Computing Environment

Evy Karavatselou[1], Maria-Anna Fengou[2], Georgios Mantas[3,4], and Dimitrios Lymberopoulos[1(✉)]

[1] Electrical and Computer Engineering Department,
University of Patras, Patras, Greece
{karavats, dlympero}@upatras.gr
[2] Intrasoft International, Athens, Greece
[3] Faculty of Engineering and Science, University of Greenwich, London, UK
G.Mantas@greenwich.ac.uk
[4] Instituto de Telecomunicações – Aveiro, Aveiro, Portugal

Abstract. A shift from the doctor-centric model to a patient-centric model is required to face the challenges of the healthcare sector. The vision of patient-centric model can be materialized integrating ubiquitous healthcare and the notion of personalization in services. Cloud computing can be the underlying technology for ubiquitous healthcare. The use of profiles enables the personalization in healthcare services and the use of profile management systems facilitates the deployment of these services. In this paper, we propose a profile management system in ubiquitous healthcare cloud computing environment. The proposed system exploits the cloud computing technology and the smart card technology to increase the efficiency and the quality of the provided healthcare services in the context of the patient-centric model. Furthermore, we propose generic healthcare profile structures corresponding to the main classes of the participating entities in a ubiquitous healthcare cloud computing environment.

Keywords: Ubiquitous healthcare · Cloud computing
Profile management system · Smart card technology

1 Introduction

Advances in healthcare sector show that a shift from the established doctor-centric model to a patient-centric model to meet the rising demand for healthcare services of different population groups and at the same time to reduce the costs of delivering healthcare services is required. The vision of patient-centric model can be achieved integrating Ubiquitous Healthcare (UH) and the notion of personalization in healthcare services.

In the patient-centric model, UH is essential in order to provide effective treatment, disease prevention, proactive actions and life quality improvement at the right time, right place and right manner without limitations on time and location. The adoption of cloud computing technology can be the underlying technology for achieving UH in patient-centric model. Cloud computing, according to the National Institute of

© ICST Institute for Computer Sciences, Social Informatics and Telecommunications Engineering 2019
Published by Springer Nature Switzerland AG 2019. All Rights Reserved
V. Sucasas et al. (Eds.): BROADNETS 2018, LNICST 263, pp. 105–114, 2019.
https://doi.org/10.1007/978-3-030-05195-2_11

Standards and Technology (NIST) is defined as a model for enabling ubiquitous, convenient, on-demand network access to a shared pool of configurable computing resources (e.g., networks, servers, storage, applications, and services) that can be rapidly provisioned and released with minimal management effort or service provider interaction [1]. Thus, cloud computing technology can enable the creation of the appropriate environment where efficient ubiquitous healthcare systems to be deployed.

The personalization of healthcare services plays a very important role to make the patient-centric model a reality. Personalization can be enabled making use of user profiles that store the preferences and the interests of the user as well as contextual and bio information related to the user. Recently, a number of personalized healthcare systems based on user profiles have been deployed. The deployment of personalized healthcare systems is based on profile management [2].

In this paper, we propose a profile management system in UH cloud computing environment. The main objective of the proposed profile management system is to increase the efficiency and the quality of the provided UH services exploiting the advantages of the cloud computing technology and the smart card technology. Furthermore, we propose generic healthcare profile structures that correspond to the main classes of the participating entities in a UH cloud computing environment. The profiles of the participating entities, which are based on the proposed five generic structures, are created and managed dynamically by the proposed profile management system [3, 4].

2   Related Work

Several platforms have been proposed that focus on cloud computing implemented in the healthcare domain. MoCAsH [5] is an infrastructure for assistive healthcare. It inherits the advantages of cloud computing and embraces concepts of mobile sensing, active sensor records, and collaborative planning.

In [6], McGregor presents Artemis Cloud, a cloud computing based Software-as-a-Service and Data-as-a-Service approach for the provision of remote real-time patient monitoring and support for clinical research. This research is demonstrated using a neonatal intensive care unit case study supporting clinical research for earlier onset detection of late onset neonatal sepsis. In [7] the active monitoring scheme is integrated with the cloud-based healthcare platform to provide the UH monitoring service. It investigates the approaches of patient monitoring and care under the cloud-based telecare system. By considering the scenarios for fixed and mobile users, the cost-effective health promoting methods are proposed and simple experiments are conducted to verify the effectiveness of the methods. Finally, in [8] Balboni et al. make analysis and recommendations in order the mobile cloud computing technologies to help the growth of the European eHealth Sector.

Personalization and user profile management holds the promise of improving the uptake of new technologies and allowing greater access to their benefits [2]. In a typical profile management scenario, there are multiple profile storage locations. Many of these locations will not store the total profile but only components that apply to a device, an application or a network/service function. Different locations may have different persistence and priority levels. Although the user profile data are distributed amongst a range of devices, applications and services, ideally, all profile data should always be available, overall networks, from all supported devices and services, including fixed and mobile services allowing service continuity and optimal user experience [2]. In [9], Sutterer et al. introduce a user profile management approach that provides means for managing and delivering context-dependent user profiles for several applications, decouples the application development from context processing taking into account the re-use and sharing of application-related user data between different applications in ubiquitous computing environments. In [10] a user profile management framework is proposed, in which the user's desires, needs and preferences for services are managed through a wearable personal station, a terminal device worn by users. Finally, [11] presents a wider view of personalization and user profiles, making the preferences available to a range of services and devices. More specifically, this paper focuses on the architecture work within the standardization activities in the personalization and user profile management area performed at ETSI by the Specialist Task Force 342.

In [12], a smart card based healthcare information system is developed. The system uses smart card for personal identification and transfer of health data as well as provides data communication via a distributed protocol which is particularly developed for this study. Two smart card software modules are implemented that run on patient and healthcare professional smart cards, respectively. In addition to personal information, general health information about the patient is also loaded to patient smartcard. Healthcare providers use their own smart cards to be authenticated on the system and to access data on patient cards. System is developed on Java platform by using object oriented architecture and design patterns.

Finally, [13] combines benefits of Open Services Gateway Initiative (OSGi) and Smart card technologies in embedded devices for developing middleware application for home appliances. More specifically, it describes an electronic-prescription system currently under development for home-based telemedicine. It also notes aspects or bundles in OSGi, which is used, XML as a means of data storage format, smart card technology for storing and accessing patient prescription and personal information, and a wireless PDA interface for remote access to the home gateway (set-top box).

3   UH Domain

As Fengou et al. presented analytically in [15, 16], a UH domain (*UH-domain*) should be composed, at least, by the following classes of UH entities (*UH-entities*):

- *Patient*, i.e. the receiver of healthcare personalized services. The health status of the patient is continuously monitored using real time collected contextual and bio information, which is gathered by wearable or implanted biosensors as well as by environmental arrays of sensors. Patient is considered as a user in the UH domain.
- *Healthcare Provider,* can belong to one of the two main categories; Medical Professionals and Caregivers. The category of Medical Professionals includes medical doctors, nurses and other medical personnel that provide medical services in a systematic way to patient. The category of Caregivers consists of trainee persons (e.g. relatives, volunteers, etc.) with discrete roles at the healthcare provision to patients. Healthcare Provider is considered as a user in the UH domain.

- *Living Environment:* The residence of patients that guarantees safe and qualified living conditions.
- *Working Environment:* A place that allows patients to work safely through the control of critical environmental conditions.
- *Outdoor Environment:* The city of residence or the country surrounding the patients.
- *Hospitalization Environment:* The unit where the patients are hospitalized whenever they are in critical situation.
- *Vehicle:* The transport means of the patients.
- *Alarm Center:* A computerized office that collects alarm messages and activates health monitoring services, whenever the patients are in critical situation.

Based on the above, the UH-domain is modelled as following described.

The entity "patient" is the core UH-entity. The UH-domain should ensure continuous care to patients, through UH services (*UH-services*). A healthcare service is characterized as UH-service, if it is provided everywhere and always. Additionally, it is characterized as personalized if it is tailored upon patient's therapeutic and monitoring medical protocols as well as patient's preferences.

The health status of any patient is characterized by discrete states, such as normal, crisis, etc. Each state refers to a different range of bio-signal values and poses determinative considerations upon the type and the way of UH-service provision (global or personalized).

The daily activities of the patients take place in specific environments, such as mentioned above (living, working, outdoor, hospitalization and vehicle). Patients move between environments and perceive each environment through the collecting contextual information. The perception and sense of contextual information differs among patients, due to their different health status. For example, the same contextual parameters (humidity, noise, temperature, etc.) of an office may have different influence in the health status of two workers performing the same activities.

The "Alarm Centre" handles a pool of patients. It holds extended archives (case records) of them, and it is always aware about their health status, position and activities. An evaluation mechanism, inside the Alarm Centre, processes the acquired data per patient and estimates his/her health status. If the status is stable, no action is required. If the status changes towards a more precarious state, an alarm is set and a UH-service is activated. Providing of this UH-service must be continuous and independent of patient's environmental conditions and activities.

The main aim of the Alarm Centre is to ensure the continuous and uninterrupted provision of UH-services. This is powerfully tied up with the "healthcare provider". For this reason, beyond the serving patients, the Alarm Centre handles also a pool of healthcare providers. A subset of the them is always alert and hastens to help, whenever it is called by the Alarm Centre. Whenever an alarm is set, the Alarm Centre assess first properly the health state of the patient and then activates the appropriate sum of healthcare providers. During the provision of the UH-service, each healthcare provider plays a predetermined role. In this way, during the provision of a UH-service, different healthcare providers may be involved, each one playing a different role.

It is obvious that the provision of a UH-service is an application dependent task. By default, UH-service balances between the need for fast estimation of the patient's situation, on one hand, and the fast selection and the high performance of the healthcare providers, on the other hand. Per case, the Alarm Centre must be flexible for:

- assessing the collected information (bio/context);
- monitoring the patient's health status;
- choosing, in each case, of the best healthcare providers;
- accurate description of the healthcare providers' attributes, such as skills, roles, preferences;
- controlling and synchronizing of all entities involved in the provision of UH;

Traditionally in E-Health domain, the healthcare provision was based upon the medical information (e.g. symptoms, examinations, etc.) that was included in the electronic Medical Health Record (e-MHR). In the UH-domain however, the UH-service provision requires the dynamic manipulation of attributes of all UH-entities being involved. Therefore, we have set the following fundamentals:

- each class of UH-entities is characterized by a dedicated profile's structure;
- each UH-entity is the occupant of a profile that contains a personalized group of attributes, such as identifiers (e.g. capabilities, skills, infrastructure, etc.), contextual information, groupware rules (e.g. costs, responsibilities, performance roles, etc.), behavioral descriptors (e.g. preferences, time scheduling, etc.), etc.;
- common management tools are used for the creation, modification, and deletion of all classes of profiles;
- common delivering facilities are used for communicating of profiles within the UH-domain;

3.1 Profile Management System in UH Cloud Computing Environment

The proposed profile management system is applied in a UH cloud computing environment for providing personalized healthcare services to patients. The UH cloud computing environment integrates a wide spectrum of the participating UH-entities of the UH-domain, such as patients, doctors, nurses, family members, hospitals, smart homes, offices and vehicles. The UH cloud computing environment, where the proposed profile management system is applied, is depicted in Fig. 1.

Each participating UH-entity has its own profile that follows the structure corresponding to one of the proposed generic healthcare profile structures according to the main category to which the participating UH-entity belongs. Hence, the proposed profile management system makes use of the *User Healthcare Profiles, Hospitalization Environment Profiles, Living Environment Profiles, Vehicle Profiles, Working Environment Profiles, Outdoor Environment Profiles* and *Alarm Center Profiles* [35]. The data of each profile are stored in distributed databases in the UH cloud computing environment.

The infrastructure of the proposed profile management system, depicted in Fig. 2, includes a Profile Provider, a number of Service Providers and a Broker.

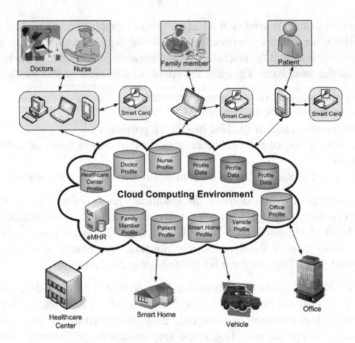

Fig. 1. UH cloud computing environment.

Profile Provider: is the main entity of the proposed profile management system. It receives the profile data and dynamically integrates them in order to generate the user profile. When the user profile is created, it is stored in a User Profile Registry.

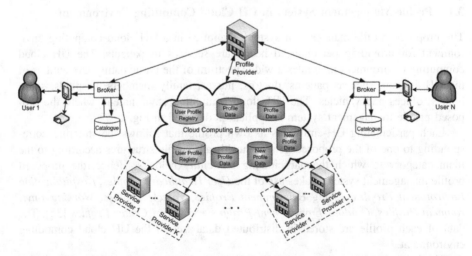

Fig. 2. Infrastructure of the proposed profile management system in UH cloud computing environment.

Service Provider: incorporates databases in the cloud computing environment containing profile data that are used for the creation of the user healthcare profile.

Broker: is the intermediate component between the user and the Service Provider as well as the user and the Profile Provider. The Broker possesses a catalogue with the URLs of all the Service Providers that have profile data that may be included in the profile. It also communicates with the Profile Provider who possesses the User Healthcare Profile Registry where the user profiles are formed and stored before sent to the user who has requested them. The Broker is part of the Profile Provider and its main objectives are to (a) manage the user's requests, (b) gather the corresponding data from the Service Providers and (c) send them to the Profile Provider.

Each user makes use of their personal device (e.g. PDA) to communicate, to process their profile data and request a profile. In the personal device, an Agent is incorporated that communicates with the Broker in order to send the user's requests and receive notifications. The personal device also includes a smart card. The smart card contains all the URL information pointing to the locations where the user's profile data are hosted.

The proposed profile management system is deployed within the Service Providers and the Profile Provider. It manages three different cases: *the creation of profile*, *the update of the profile (modification, deletion)* and *the profile extension*. The key components of the proposed profile management system are:

Profile Editor: through the Profile Editor the user can make changes (insertion, modification and deletion) to his profile and alert the Personal Assistant Agent for these.

Context Information Agent: its function is related with the context of the user. For example, the Context Information Agent can collect the biosignals of the patient and alerts the Personal Assistant Agent when deterioration in the patient's health condition is detected. Furthermore, the Context Information Agent can send the user's current location.

Service Provider's Agents: Each Service Provider contains the following agents: Processing Agent, Query Agent, Repository Agent, and Database Creation Agent.

Profile Provider: The Profile Provider contains the following agents: Processing Agent, Query Agent and Repository Agent.

The operation of the Agents as well as all the processes for the management of the profiles (creation, modification, deletion and extension) are analytically presented in [16].

4   Implementation

After comparing open source cloud computing platforms in order to select the most suitable platform for the deployment of the UH cloud computing environment, where the profile management system is applied., the Eucalyptus platform [14] was selected as the most appropriate platform to deploy our profile management system [16].

Figure 3 presents the proposed profile management system based on Eucalyptus architecture. The adopted hierarchical approach on the control and management is more reliable and reduces human intervention.

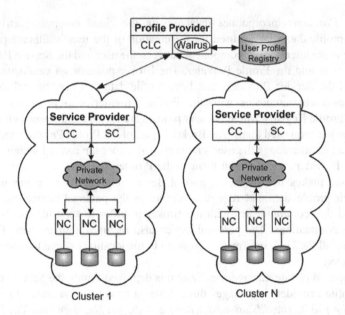

Fig. 3. The proposed profile management system based on the eucalyptus architecture.

The main components within which profile management system is deployed are the Profile Provider and a number of Service Providers.

The Profile Provider has the Cloud Controller (CLC) and the Walrus as it is responsible to create the user profile and store it in a User Profile Registry respectively. CLC provides high-level management of the cloud resources, user accounts and client requests. It also provides a web interface for cloud management.

Walrus is the storage service which allows storing persistent data. It provides a bucket-based object store. It shares a Java-based database holding user account information with the CLC, and accesses metadata of buckets and objects similarly stored in databases. The storage space for buckets and objects is mapped to a single, non-shared file system directory mounted on the machine on which Walrus runs. In this file system the user profiles are stored. Both users outside the cloud and user applications running on compute nodes in the cloud upload and download data through the REST interface of Walrus.

The Cluster Network consists of many cloud nodes; in each cloud node there is the Service Provider containing specialized nodes to provide storage and management services. Each cloud node runs one or more virtual machine images, each equipped with at least one local disk to store the host OS and hypervisor software.

Each Service Provider has the Cluster Controller (CC) and the Storage Controller (SC) as it has databases in the cloud containing profile data that are used for the creation of the user profile.

CC is the front-end for each cluster defined in the cloud and is responsible for managing the entire virtual instance network controlling specific VM instances. The CC maintains all the information about the NC that is grouped in the cluster.

It performs per cluster scheduling and networking. It gathers information from each NC and schedules client requests to individual NCs. The CC is in the same Ethernet broadcast domain as the nodes it manages.

SC provides block storage services. The data storage service, is responsible to manipulate VM images delivering them to NCs when a client instantiates a VM. It is particularly suited as it supplies database, file system, or access to raw block level storage.

The Private Network of each Service Provider contains a pool of physical computers that provide generic computation resources to the cluster and a number of NCs in each of these machines.

NC is responsible for fetching VM images, starting and terminating their execution and managing the virtual network endpoint. NC communicates with the OS and the hypervisor running on the node on one side and the CC on the other side. NC requests the Operating System running on the node to find out the node's physical resources, the size of memory, the number of cores, the disk space available. It also learns about the state of VM instances running on the node and broadcasts this data up to the CC. It controls the hypervisor on each compute node configuring it, sets up VMs on it and hosts OS as directed by the CC. It executes in the host domain (in KVM) or driver domain (in Xen).

5 Conclusions

In this paper, we have proposed a profile management system in a UH cloud computing environment. It aims to increase the quality and the efficiency of the provided UH services exploiting the advantages of the cloud computing technology, the smart card technology and the notion of user profile in the context of the patient-centric model. Furthermore, we have proposed generic profile structures corresponding to the main classes of the participating entities in the UH cloud computing environment.

The profile management system that we propose in this paper is focused only on User Healthcare Profiles (i.e. Patients and Healthcare providers). We intend to continue our research in this direction in order to deploy a profile management system incorporating the profiles of all possible participating entities in a UH cloud computing environment. Thus, as future work, we plan to implement a profile management system integrating the creation and management of User Healthcare Profiles, Hospitalization Environment Profiles, Living Environment Profiles, Vehicle Profiles, Working Environment Profiles, Outdoor Environment Profiles and Alarm Center Profiles.

References

1. Mell, P., Grance, T.: The NIST definition of Cloud Computing. National Institute of Standards and Technology (NIST) (2011)
2. ETSI ES 202 746 V1.1.1, Human Factors (HF); Personalization and User Profile Management; User Profile Preferences and Information (2010)
3. Fengou, M.A., Mantas, G., Lymberopoulos, D., Komninos, N.: Ubiquitous healthcare profile management applying smart card technology. In: Proceedings of 2nd International ICST Conference on Wireless Mobile Communication and Healthcare (Mobihealth), Kos, pp. 248–255 (2011)

4. Fengou, M.A., Mantas, G., Lymberopoulos, D., Komninos, N.: Healthcare profile management system in smart cards. In: Proceedings of International Conference on Advances of Information and Communication Technology in Health Care, Jakarta, pp. 182–185 (2011)
5. Hoang, D.B., Lingfeng, C.: Mobile cloud for assistive healthcare (MoCAsH). In: Proceedings of IEEE Conference Asia-Pacific Services Computing, pp. 325–332 (2010)
6. McGrecor, C.: A cloud computing framework for real-time rural and remote service of critical care. In: Proceedings of 24th International Symposium on Computer-Based Medical Systems (CBMS), Bristol (2011)
7. Ho, C.-S., Chiang, K.-C.: Towards the ubiquitous healthcare by integrating active monitoring and intelligent cloud. In: Proceedings of 5th International Conference on Computer Science and Convergence Information Technology (ICCIT), Seoul, pp. 840–843 (2010)
8. Balboni, P., Iafecine, B.: Mobile cloud for enabling the EU eHealth sector regulatory issues and opportunities. In: Technical Symposium at ITU Telecom World (ITU WT), Geneva, pp. 51–56 (2011)
9. Sutterer, M., Droegehorn, O., David, K.: User profile management on service platforms for ubiquitous computing environments. In: 65th Vehicular Technology Conference, Dublin, pp. 287–291 (2007)
10. Suh, Y., Dongoh, D., Woo, W.: Context-based user profile management for personalized services. In: Proceedings UbiComp Workshop (ubiPCMM), pp. 64–73 (2005)
11. Kovacikova, T., et al.: Personalization and user profile standardization. In: Proceedings of 7th IASTED International Conference on Communication Systems and Networks, Spain (2008)
12. Kardas, G., Tunali, E.T.: Design and implementation of a smart card based healthcare information system. Comput. Methods Programs Biomed. 81(1), 66–78 (2006)
13. Bobbie, P., Ramisetty, S., Yussiff, A.-L., Pujari, S.: Designing an embedded electronic-prescription application for home-based telemedicine using OSGi framework. In: Arabnia,H. R., Yang, L.T. (Eds.) Proceedings of International Conference on Embedded Systems and Applications, pp. 16–21. CSREA Press, Las Vegas (2003)
14. Nurmi, D., et al.: The eucalyptus open-source cloud computing system. In: Proceedings 9th IEEE/ACM International Symposium on Cluster Computing and the Grid (CCGrid), Shanghai, China, pp. 124–131, May 2009
15. Fengou, M.-A., Athanasiou, G., Mantas, G., Griva, I., Lymberopoulos, D.: Towards personalized services in the healthcare domain. In: Furht, B., Agarwal, A. (eds.) Handbook of Medical and Healthcare Technologies, pp. 417–433. Springer, New York (2013). https://doi.org/10.1007/978-1-4614-8495-0_19
16. Fengou, M.-A., Mantas, G., Lymberopoulos, D., Komninos, N., Fengos, S., Lazarou, N.: A new framework architecture for next generation e-health services. IEEE J. Biomed. Health Inform. 17(1), 9–18 (2013). Author, F.: Article title. Journal 2(5), 99–110 (2016)

A Telemedicine Application for Remote Diagnosis and Assessment of Mood Disorders

Georgia Konstantopoulou[1], Theodor Panagiotakopoulos[2],
George J. Mandellos[3], Konstantinos Asimakopoulos[4],
and Dimitrios K. Lymberopoulos[3(✉)]

[1] Special Office for Health Consulting Services, University of Patras,
Patras, Greece
gkonstantop@upatras.gr
[2] Mobile and Pervasive Computing, Quality and Ambient Intelligence
Laboratory, School of Science and Technology, Hellenic Open University,
26335 Patras, Greece
tepanag@upatras.gr
[3] Wire Communication Laboratory, Electrical and Computer Engineering
Department, University of Patras, 26504 Rion, Greece
{mandello, dlympero}@upatras.gr
[4] Department of Psychiatry, School of Medicine, University of Patras,
Patras, Greece
kassima@upatras.gr

Abstract. Depression in its various forms is a widespread phenomenon in modern societies. Its high prevalence, associated costs, the chronic nature it develops and the challenges in diagnosing it put a lot of pressure on public healthcare systems. In response to these challenges, ICT-based approaches are increasingly implemented to support effective patient management and discovery. This paper presents a web application named "feeldistress", which is based on a novel distress evaluation framework to enable remote diagnosis of anxiety and depression, facilitate continuous evaluation of patients and assist prevention of suicide. The developed application was used and evaluated from a qualitative perspective by 117 students (47% women) who had visited the Special Office for Health Consulting Services of the University of Patras between 2014 and 2017. The majority of the users were very satisfied by the functionality, usability and appearance of the application showing it can be extremely useful tool for someone before hitting the door of a mental health specialist.

Keywords: Telemedicine · Mood disorders · Remote diagnosis

1 Introduction

Depression in its various forms (major depression, dysthymia, depressive phase of bipolar disorder) is a widespread phenomenon in modern societies that causes significant level of disability. Depressive people experience various emotional, physical, cognitive and mobility problems, including negative beliefs about themselves and intense pessimism about the present and the future, diminished mood, unwillingness to

V. Sucasas et al. (Eds.): BROADNETS 2018, LNICST 263, pp. 115–124, 2019.
https://doi.org/10.1007/978-3-030-05195-2_12

take any deliberate action and suicidal ideation or suicidal behavior. They often report that their mind is confused and their thoughts are slow, and that they have difficulty restraining information or solving problems [1]. Apart from the negative impact depression has on a personal level, it also affects society as a whole (e.g. job withdrawal and low productivity) and accounts for significantly increased financial cost to all involved stakeholders (i.e. patients, health systems, social security, etc.), mainly because of its intense and persistent consequences, the recurrent characteristics and its under-treatment in all walks of life [2, 3]. Studying eight countries that differ in cultural characteristics and GDP, researchers from the London School of Economics and Political Science (LSE) reported that depression costs a total of more than 220 billion euros a year to Brazil, Canada, China, Japan, Korea, Mexico, South Africa and US [4]. The results of their investigation carried out among 8000 officials working in these countries, showed that the US (EUR 75.5 billion) and Brazil (EUR 56 billion) have the highest rates of loss of productivity due to the systematic presence of employees suffering from depressive symptoms. Concerning European citizens, approximately 5% of them have clinical depression, and it is estimated that 17% will experience significant depression at some point in their lives [1].

It is widely known that timely diagnosis of depression enables early treatment, which could be critical in terms of its scaling and intensity [5]. However, diagnosis of this severe mental illness and its forms is hindered by several subjective (e.g. inability to reach an experienced health provider) and objective (e.g. lack of quantified clinical tests) problems. Unfortunately, depression is significantly underdiagnosed or misdiagnosed and subsequently undertreated, particularly in the primary care environment. Although more patients are seeking help and utilization of antidepressants is on the rise, the level of treatment is inadequate [6]. An indicative research resulted that in the primary care setting, people with depression received a correct diagnosis less than 50% of time [7]. Likewise, African Americans who suffer from depression experience frequent underdiagnosis and inadequate management in primary care [8]. In general, a wide range of subjective factors is acknowledged by the literature to account for this diagnosis and treatment shortfall, which is even bigger in rural areas, such as stigma, distance between people living in remote locations (e.g. islands) and medical experts, limited resources, lack of adequate mental health professionals and services. In addition, depression often co-exists with other mental problems such as anxiety disorders, a situation that also puts barriers to early diagnoses of depression [9].

The above and other data show the high prevalence of depression, its associated costs, the chronic nature it develops and the challenges concerning the critical task of diagnosis. As a result, a lot of pressure is been put on public healthcare systems highlighting the need of new models to offer adequate support to depressive patients. Assisting depression diagnosis and management in primary care could induce faster and more accurate diagnoses, enabling a timely and more precise intervention to great advantage of both patients and health systems. To this end, various researches and initiatives in the field of Health and Education for integration, social inclusion and support for people with mental illness have shown a growing interest in exploring the use of Information and Communication Technologies (ICT) to support effective patient management and discovery. ICT-based solutions are indeed showing great potential in supporting all the stages of care provision to patients with depression improving access to healthcare services, delivering faster and better care to patients, enabling continuous patient monitoring and automatic assessment, providing risk prediction and delivering personalized feedback provisioning services among others.

In this context, this paper presents the preliminary validation data of an online tool that enables remote diagnosis of anxiety and depression, facilitates continuous evaluation of patients to assess illness progress and response to followed treatment and assists prevention of suicide. The developed web application named "feeldistress" incorporates a novel distress evaluation framework that integrates a combination of weighted questionnaires provided in a specific sequence according to users' replies. As the users fill the questionnaires, the application provides feedback based on the scores of their replies in each questionnaire, in order to inform them of their health status and suggest appropriate actions.

2 Related Work

The use of ICT and, more specifically, the role of telemedicine in psychiatry has been subject of research for many years. Telepsychiatry mainly employs synchronous video consultation and is an increasingly common method of providing psychiatric care at a distance in response of various major limitations in care delivery (e.g. distance, transportation cost, lack of local expertise, etc.). Ruskin et al. [10] examined 119 depressed veterans referred for outpatient treatment in three US clinics, who were randomly assigned to either remote treatment by means of video-based telepsychiatry or in-person treatment to compare treatment outcomes of the two approaches over a 6-month psychiatric treatment. Patient evaluation using the Hamilton Depression Rating Scale (HDRS) and the Beck Depression Inventory (BDI) showed that telepsychiatric therapy was as effective as facial treatment in terms of symptom improvement.

A major category of ICT solutions consists of mobile, wearable and pervasive health systems. These systems are more sophisticated, complex and agile than conventional telemedicine systems enabling constant patient monitoring through various sensing devices and employing real-time data analysis, in order to assist diagnosis, patient management and treatment support. Joshi et al. [11] developed a multimodal framework to fuse audio and video data for depression diagnosis, which could analyze intra-facial muscle movements and movements of head and shoulders, in conjunction with audio signals through various fusion methods. Other systems, such as the ICT4D [12] utilize wearable biosensors for activity monitoring and measurement of various electrophysiological indicators and apply data analysis algorithms to reason about the state of depressive patients and the risk of a potential relapse. Based on the induced information ICT4D provides appropriate feedback via mobile phone and the web.

Another important category of ICT-enabled approaches exploit the Internet to deliver various eHealth and telemedicine services through web-based applications. Adriana Mira et al. [13] developed an Internet-based program to teach adaptive ways to cope with depressive symptoms and daily problems. 124 participants who were experiencing at least one stressful event that caused interference in their lives, many of whom had clinically significant depressive symptoms, were randomly assigned into one of the following three groups: (1) intervention group with ICT support (automated mobile phone messages, automated emails, and continued feedback), (2) intervention group with ICT support plus human support (brief weekly support phone call without clinical content) and (3) a waiting-list control group. The constructed treatment protocol was adapted to a completely self-help Internet-based, multimedia (video, image, etc.), interactive application designed for optimal use on a personal computer. Analysis of a 12-month usage of the Internet-based program showed that it was effective and well accepted, with and without human support, resulting in a significant improvement pre- to posttreatment, compared with the control group.

Farvolden et al. [14] developed Web-Based Depression and Anxiety Test (WB-DAT), a freely-available, web-based, self-report screener for major depressive disorder and anxiety disorders. This web-based diagnostic tool was administered to 193 subjects who presented for assessment and/or treatment in research projects that were conducted at the Mood and Anxiety Program and Clinical Research Department at the Centre for Addiction and Mental Health in Toronto, Ontario, Canada. Preliminary data from the comparison between WB-DAT and conventional clinical assessment tools suggested that WB-DAT was reliable for identifying patients with major depressive disorder and various anxiety disorders.

In our study, we focus on the development and implementation of a web application for remote diagnosis and assessment of individuals that feel distress, anxiety and/or depression symptoms. This tool is based on an innovative distress evaluation framework that considers a specific sequence of multiple scales, in contrast to existing approaches that use individual scales, which are mainly applied to assess a medical process than provide a diagnosis. Thus, it considers multidimensional data to create a more integrated clinical view and achieve a more accurate and multifaceted diagnosis while recommending the most appropriate actions to be taken.

3 Tools and Methods

3.1 Distress Evaluation Framework

As described in the previous sections, our approach integrates a combination of questionnaires, which consist of the Hospital Anxiety and Depression Scale (HADS), the State Trait Anxiety Inventory form Y (STAIY), the Beck Depression Inventory (BECK) and the Risk Assessment Suicidality Scale (RASS). HADS was developed by Zigmond and Snaith in 1983 [15] and is commonly used by physicians to determine the levels of anxiety and depression of a person. The HADS is a fourteen item scale that generates ordinal data. Seven of the items relate to anxiety and the other seven relate to depression. Each item on the questionnaire is scored from 0-3 and this means that a person can score between 0 and 21 for either anxiety or depression. Bjelland et al. [16] identified a cut-off point of 8/21 for anxiety or depression. For anxiety (HADS-A) this gave a specificity of 0.78 and a sensitivity of 0.9. For depression (HADS-D) this gave a specificity of 0.79 and a sensitivity of 0.83. We used the Greek version of HADS [17], which shows a high internal consistency and validity, as well as good psychometric properties and can be proven in practice as a useful tool for clinicians to identify symptoms of anxiety and depression in primary healthcare.

The STAIY scale [18] was published in 1985 and consists of two strands, which calculate the State and Trait anxieties. State Anxiety (S-Anxiety) is the subjective and transient feeling of pressure, nervousness and anxiety at a given time, which can be is accompanied by activation of the autonomic nervous system. The Trait Anxiety (T-Anxiety) refers to the relatively constant individual differences with regard to the anxiety proneness, which they constitute personality trait. The scale for S-Anxiety consists of twenty statements that assess how the subject feels at the time the scaled is filled. The scale for T-Anxiety is also composed of twenty statements, but assesses how the subject feels generally. Ratings for both S-Anxiety and T-Anxiety range between 20 and 80 and studies in the Greek population showed that scores above 40 indicate potential mental health problems [19].

The Beck Depression Inventory (BDI) [20] is a multiple-choice self-report inventory, one of the most widely used psychometric tests for measuring the severity of depression. It contains 21 questions, each answer being scored on a scale value of 0 to 3. Higher total scores indicate more severe depressive symptoms. The standardized cutoffs are: 1–10 = normal fluctuation, 11–16 = mild mood disorder, 17–20 = marginal clinical depression, 21–30 = moderate depression, 31–40 = severe depression and >40 extreme depression. The Greek version of BDI has very good internal consistency and test-retest reliability, as well as high validity. The scale's good psychometric properties were confirmed for the Greek population, suggesting that its translation and adaptation to the Greek language yield a valid and reliable tool [21].

Risk Assessment Suicidality Scale (RASS) [22] was constructed as a self-report instrument with emphasis on the items that describe suicide-related behavior targeting assessment of suicidal risk in the general population as well as in mental patients. RASS consists of 12 items (with 4 possible answers – not at all, a little, quite enough very much) that estimate different views of suicidal behavior, by looking at intention and attitude towards life among others. The RASS is a reliable and valid instrument which might prove valuable in the assessment of suicidal risk in the general population as well as in mental patients.

By using and stepping through the sequential activation of the aforementioned questionnaires, someone feeling distress can quickly evaluate the symptoms of depression and/or the levels of anxiety, the suicidal ideation, or even check if there is a relapse of the disease in the past. The first step in our methodology is to fill the HADS scale (including HADS-A and HADS-D). Questions refer to marketing issues rather than physical problems (e.g. I feel anxious or terrified; I lost interest in my appearance). If the user scores more than 8 in the HADS-A scale (high level of anxiety) he/she is driven to the STAIY scale. STAIY evaluates the emotional state of the subject (transient stress as a result of the current situation). We want to know how the user feels right now, by answering questions such as "I feel calm," "I'm upset", which score range from 1 (not at all) to 4 (very much). Stress is proportional to the score on the scale, meaning that the higher the score on the scale, the greater the temporary anxiety, according to the aforementioned classification of STAIY (e.g. if the score is higher than 40, we have severe anxiety or panic attack).

If the score is more than 8 on the HADS-D scale (high level of depression) the user is driven to the BDI scale, a reliable tool for psychological assessment of depression and accurate measurement of its severity. The user is called to provide answers that best describe how he/she feels over the past few days. Depending on the overall score in the BDI scale, the user should receive feedback suggesting actions to be performed. For instance, if the BDI score is above 17 for at least 2 weeks the user should seek specialist help. Special attention should be given to a BDI's question concerning suicidal tendencies, specific replies to which might suggest risk of suicide requiring immediate psychiatric help. In this case, as well as if the total score in the BDI scale is 17 or more, the user is driven to the RASS questionnaire that consists of 12 questions, such as "Do you fear that you will die?" and "Do you enjoy life?. RASS aims at identifying suicidal risks to inform users to immediately seek for psychiatric help.

3.2 Feeldistress Application

The "feeldistress" application (available at www.feeldistress.gr) was developed through a set of contemporary web technologies, such as PHP7, HTML5, Javascript and Ajax. For the needs of data storage a MySQL v10.2.12 was built. Initially, the user is required to register and during registration the user is called to provide several demographic data. These data include age, gender, family and occupational status, lifestyle, education, socio-economic status and some information about chronic illnesses, dealing with difficulties in everyday life (functionality), drug use or other substances. After registration and login, the user is able to start filling the scales based on the framework described in the previous section.

The first scale is the HADS and depending on the accumulative individual scores of HADS-A and HADS-D the application provides the STAIY and BDI scales respectively. If both STAIY and BDI are to be provided, STAIY is provided first and BDI is given after BDI is filled. Finally, based on the answers of the BDI scale, the application provides the RASS scale, which is shown in Fig. 1. Depending on the users' replies,

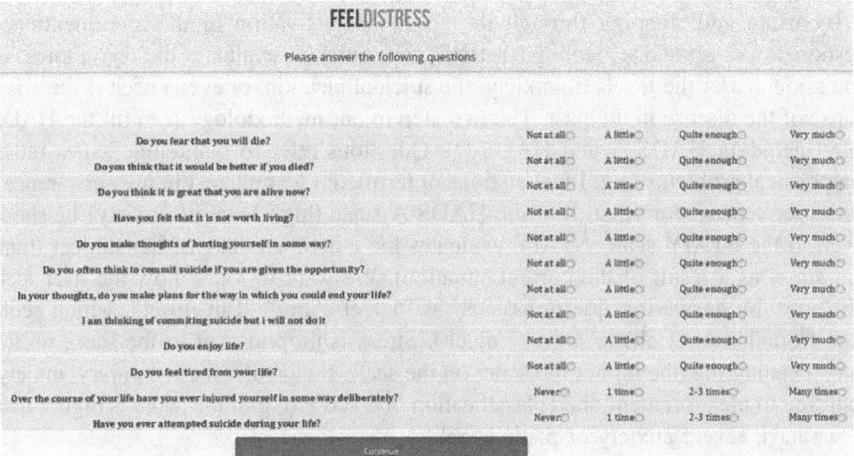

Fig. 1. The RASS scale in the feeldistress application.

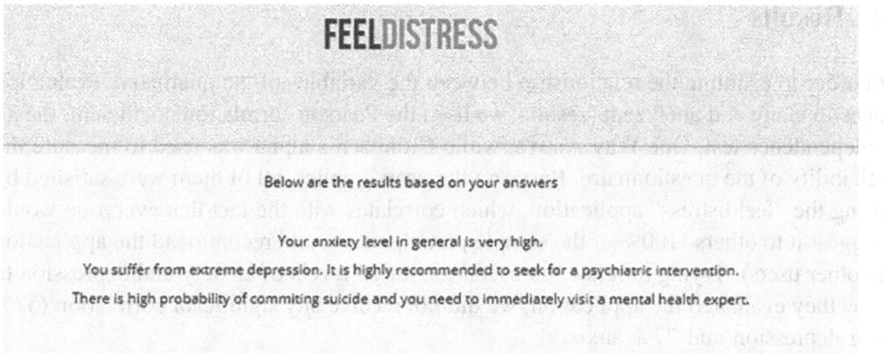

FEELDISTRESS

Below are the results based on your answers

Your anxiety level in general is very high.

You suffer from extreme depression. It is highly recommended to seek for a psychiatric intervention.

There is high probability of commiting suicide and you need to immediately visit a mental health expert.

Fig. 2. Example feedback provided by the feeldistress application.

the application diagnoses and evaluates the level of depression they are experiencing and provides feedback by recommending appropriate actions (Fig. 2).

3.3 Experimental Setup

The developed application was used by 117 students (47% women) who had visited the Special Office for Health Consulting Services of the University of Patras between 2014 and 2017, because they felt distress due to anxiety or depression symptoms. The scope of the Special Office for Health Consulting Services is to diagnose mental disorders, manage interventions (psychiatric and psychotherapeutic) and provide psychosocial support to the students of the University of Patras.

These students had already filled the HADS, the BDI and the Beck Anxiety Inventory (BAI) in the academic years 2014 - 2017. Results of the HADS showed that 57% and 77% of the test sample suffered from depression and anxiety respectively. Based on the BAI results, 31.6% was experiencing moderate anxiety 32.5% mild to moderate anxiety and 29.1% severe anxiety. The BDI test revealed that 16.2% was suffering from extreme depression, 19.7% from moderate depression, 13.7% from severe depression and 14.5% from clinical depression.

Prior to using the application, all the test subjects had "psycho-diagnostic" interview by phone, to talk about their lives at that period and get informed of the feeldistress application. Subsequently, the students were invited to use this application via email, which included a short user guide and a consent form (requested to be signed and sent back to us before using the application) describing that their participation was for research purposes and they would not have any kind of gain by using it. In addition, the test subjects were given a questionnaire to qualitatively evaluate the application that was anonymously filled and sent back to us. This questionnaire consisted of 11 questions, 4 of which referring to demographics and 4 to the application in terms of ease of use, functionality, aesthetic and content reliability and utility. Potential answers were excellent, very good, adequate and poor. The final three were open questions: Which improvements would you suggest?; Would you recommend feeldistress to other users?; How often do you visit mental health related web pages and applications and for which reasons?

4 Results

In order to examine the relationship between the variables of the qualitative evaluation questionnaire and analyze its results, we used the Pearson correlation coefficient, the x2 independence test, One Way Anova, while Cronbach's alpha was used to measure the reliability of the questionnaire. Bases on the users' replies, all of them were satisfied by using the "feeldistress" application, which correlates with the fact that everyone would suggest it to others (100% of the sample participants would recommend the application to other users). Trying to relate the users' identified levels of anxiety and depression to how they evaluated the application, we did not receive any significant correlation (57% had depression and 77% anxiety).

Regarding ease of use, 82% of the participants (96 out of 117) consider "feeldistress" app as excellent and 12% very good. Combining these percentages with the answers to the open question "What improvements would you suggest", we've seen that some participants found difficult to locate unanswered questions at the point they have reached at the end of each questionnaire. Concerning functionality, 83.7% (98 out of 117) found "feeldistress" excellent and 13,6% very good, while aesthetic was largely considered as excellent (93%). Finally, in the case of content reliability and utility, 63% of the participants (74 out of 117) found them excellent, 27% stated they were very good and 8.5% adequate.

5 Discussion and Concluding Remarks

ICTs are increasingly explored and implemented in health and, more specifically, in mental health to support clinical practice and offer new capabilities in care provision and healthcare service delivery. The web application "feeldistress" aims at assisting depression diagnosis and treatment of depression mainly by enabling an initial remote health status assessment. Based on a multidimensional evaluation framework it creates an integrated health and mood profile to accurately evaluate anxiety and depression status and motivate users to contact a specialist if required. The developed application attempts a structured diagnosis of psychometric-treated therapy. The goal of psychometric techniques is to provide the specialist with the ability to develop a structured psychiatric assessment, i.e. to provide a skeleton, which helps him get the basic information required for diagnosis. Also with the psychometric tools there are concrete results, which classify the patients to specific norms, thus obviously facilitating the final diagnosis, the observance of objective statistical data and the research.

Results of the "feeldistress" app evaluation by people who had experienced anxiety discomfort or depression symptoms in the past showed that it can be an extremely useful tool for someone before hitting the door of a mental health specialist. The majority of the users were very satisfied by the functionality, usability and appearance of the application. This even more important if we take into account the fact that all of the users that frequently use mental health web pages and apps (31.6% of the users) were very positive with "feeldistress". As indicated by the users, a major improvement would be to utilize pop up messages to indicate unanswered questions more precisely.

This was the most frequent problem participants faced, which is completely rational considering the multitude of questions they are call to answer.

As this paper presented some preliminary results of the qualitative evaluation of the developed application, we plan to validate its usefulness through specific application scenarios (e.g. applied treatment assessment) and reveal meaningful hidden relationships among patient data elicited by the questionnaire filling. We also plan to use "feeldistress" as the basis to a more sophisticated portal that will include instructions and advice, online chat and teleconference capabilities to facilitate both synchronous and asynchronous communication between patients and physicians. We intend to add more features, such as mood recording and automatic mood chart creation and display to support a regular monitoring of patients and provide physicians with additional patient information.

References

1. Jonsson, U., Bohman, H., Hjern, A., von Knorring, L., Olsson, G., von Knorring, A.L.: Subsequent higher education after adolescent depression: a 15-year follow-up register study. Eur. Psychiatry **25**, 396–401 (2010)
2. Hirschfeld, R.M.A., Keller, M.B., Panico, S., et al.: The national depressive and manic-depressive association consensus statement on the undertreatment of depression. J. Am. Med. Assoc. **277**, 333–340 (1997)
3. Simos, G. (eds.): Cognitive - Behavioral Therapy. A Guide to Clinical Practice, Ed. Pataki (2010)
4. Evans-Lacko, S., Knapp, M.: Global patterns of workplace productivity for people with depression: absenteeism and presenteeism costs across eight diverse countries. Soc. Psychiatry Psychiatr. Epidemiol. **51**(11), 1525–1537 (2016)
5. Kupfer, D.J., Frank, E., Perel, J.M.: The advantage of early treatment intervention in recurrent depression. Arch. Gen. Psychiatry **46**(9), 771–775 (1989)
6. Sheeran, D.V.: Depression: underdiagnosed, undertreated, underappreciated. Manag. Care. **13**(6Suppl Depression), 6–8 (2004)
7. Mitchell, A.J.: Are one or two simple questions sufficient to detect depression in cancer and palliative care? a Bayesian meta-analysis. Br. J. Cancer. **98**(12), 1934–1943 (2008)
8. Bailey, R.K., Patel, M., Barker, N.C., Ali, S., Jabeen, S.: Major depressive disorder in the African American population. J. Natl Med. Assoc. **103**(7), 548–559 (2011)
9. Balazs, J., Miklósi, M., Keresztény, Á., Hoven, C.W., et al.: Adolescent subthreshold depression and anxiety: psychopathology, functional impairment and increased suicide risk. J. Child Psychol. Psychiatry **54**(6), 670–677 (2013)
10. Ruskin, P., et al.: Treatment outcomes in depression: comparison of remote treatment through telepsychiatry to in-person treatment. Am. J. Psychiatry Publ. **161**(8), 1471–1601, August 2004. https://doi.org/10.1176/appi.ajp.161.8.1471
11. Joshi, J., et al.: Multimodal assistive technologies for depression diagnosis and monitoring. J. Multimodal User Interfaces **7**(3), 217–228 (2013)
12. Warmerdam, L., et al.: Innovative ICT solutions to improve treatment outcomes for depression: the ICT4 Depression project. Ann. Rev. Cybertherapy Telemedicine **181**(1), 339–343 (2012)

13. Mira, A., Bretón-López, J., García-Palacios, A., Quero, S., Baños, R.M., Botella, C.: An Internet-based program for depressive symptoms using human and automated support: a randomized controlled trial. Neuropsychiatric Dis. Treat. **13**, 987–1006 (2017)
14. Farvolden, P., McBride, C., Bagby, R.M., Ravitz, P.: A web-based screening instrument for depression and anxiety disorders in primary care. J. Med. Internet Res. **5**(3), e23 (2003)
15. Zigmond, A.S., Snaith, R.P.: The hospital anxiety and depression scale. Acta Psychiatr. Scand. **67**(6), 361–370 (1983)
16. Bjelland, I., Dahl, A., Haug T., Neckelmann, D.: The validity of the hospital anxiety and depression scale an updated literature review. J. Psychosom. Res. **52**(2), 69–77 (2002)
17. Michopoulos, I., et al.: Hospital anxiety and depression scale (HADS): validation in a Greek general hospital sample. Ann. Gen. Psychiatry **7**(1), 4 (2008)
18. Spielberger, C.: Manual for the State Trait Anxiety Inventory (Self Evaluation Questionnaire). Consulting Psychologists press, Palo Alto (1970)
19. Fountoulakis, K.N., et al.: Reliability and psychometric properties of the Greek translation of the state-trait anxiety inventory form Y: preliminary data. Ann. Gen. Psychiatry **5**(1), 2 (2006)
20. Beck, A.T., Steer, R.A., Brown, G.K.: Manual for the Beck Depression Inventory-II. Psychological Corp, San Antonio (1996)
21. Giannakou, M., Roussi, P., Kosmides, M.E., Kiosseoglou, G., Adamopoulou, A., Garyfallos, G.: Adaptation of the beck depression inventory-II to greek population. Hellenic J. Psychol. **10**(2), 120–146 (2013)
22. Fountoulakis, K.N., et al.: Development of the risk assessment suicidality scale (RASS): a population-based study. J. Affect. Disord. **138**(3), 449–457 (2012)

e-SCP-ECG⁺v2 Protocol: Expanding the e-SCP-ECG⁺ Protocol

George J. Mandellos[1], Maria Papaioannou[1],
Theodor Panagiotakopoulos[2], and Dimitrios K. Lymberopoulos[1(✉)]

[1] Wire Communication Laboratory, Electrical and Computer Engineering
Department, University of Patras, 26504 Rion, Greece
{mandello,dlympero}@upatras.gr, ece7887@upnet.gr
[2] Mobile and Pervasive Computing, Quality and Ambient Intelligence
Laboratory, School of Science and Technology, Hellenic Open University,
26335 Patras, Greece
tepanag@upatras.gr

Abstract. Nowadays, the fast-growing technology market for sensors and smart devices allows anyone to constantly monitor important vital parameters, like electrocardiogram (ECG). Mobile health systems typically employ data transmission to the premises of the health service provider via appropriate telecommunication protocols, which often consider only vital parameters. However, these parameters are likely to vary, depending on each person's exercise, psychological condition, habits, environmental conditions and many other factors. Thus, it is necessary to utilize a protocol that is able to carry additional data concerning factors that are tightly connected with the quality of vital sign measurements. This paper proposes an extended version of the e-SCP-ECG⁺ protocol, mainly used for ECG data transmission, in order to include several types of information that affect the quality of the obtained signal, as well as the diagnosis process. The aim is to offer medical experts with an enriched clinical view of the patients so as to diagnose a medical incident more accurately.

Keywords: e-SCP-ECG⁺ · Vital signs · Health communication protocol

1 Introduction

Recent advancements in several areas of consumer electronics and computer science, such as wearable and mobile networked devices, wireless sensors and sensor networks, pervasive computing and artificial intelligence have massively benefited mobile health and Ambient Assisted Living (AAL) systems. Such systems include a wide range of applications that span from health monitoring and medication compliance to cognitive assistance and activities of daily living facilitation, as well as location tracking and social inclusion. Health monitoring of individuals is the most prevalent application category aggregating numerous research prototypes as well as commercial systems and applications. Being able to wirelessly monitor health status without spatiotemporal restrictions is a significant factor for an increased quality of life. Especially, older adults and people with chronic health problems require constant monitoring and care

V. Sucasas et al. (Eds.): BROADNETS 2018, LNICST 263, pp. 125–135, 2019.
https://doi.org/10.1007/978-3-030-05195-2_13

provision driving the need of technology enabled solutions that provide adequate support to allow them to stay in their domestic environment for longer while retaining their safety, independence and autonomy.

Health monitoring mainly concerns continuous measurement of human physiological parameters, in order to visualize measured data, evaluate the medical status of an individual, perform specific medical care actions (e.g. produce an alert to a physician or relative) based on the identified medical status, or store data for further analysis (e.g. recognition of abnormalities in heart function through a 24–48 h electrocardiogram (ECG) analysis). A specific group of physiological parameters called vital signs consists of the most important signs that indicate proper human body function (i.e. ECG, pulse oximetry, heart rate, blood pressure and body temperature), which are the most commonly monitored health parameters.

The last decades various Health Telemonitoring Systems (HTS) have been proposed in the literature. The first step in these systems is to acquire a number of relevant data (based on each system's objectives and requirements) using appropriate sensing devices. Conventional telemedicine systems enable live or asynchronous transmission and display of measured data from a remote place to centrally located physicians primarily for diagnostic purposes. More sophisticated mobile and pervasive health systems employ signal processing techniques and data analysis algorithms in order to autonomously assess one's health status. The next step of the latter systems is to employ decision support functions to reason over the services to be delivered. In the majority of these systems, sensed data usually have to be transmitted in a central location for storage, management and visualization.

However, capturing purely health data in many cases is not enough. There are many other factors that interfere with the measured values and have a direct relation to health status assessment and treatment provision processes. For instance, acceleration data is also used to identify whether an individual is doing some exercise affecting ECG measurements. On the other hand, context information is equally important either for delivering appropriate healthcare services (e.g. location data for on-point care), or getting to understand influencers of several disorders (e.g. anxiety and mood disorders), while other types of information such as lifestyle and habits (e.g. sleep patterns, exercise, etc.) may also contribute to an enhanced clinical view of an individual. Continuous development of sensors market and smart devices, offers the ability to collect easily more and more useful information concerning health, context and personal data. The increased emergence of commercial off-the-shelf eHealth devices and HTS facilitate collection and transmission of various types of data previously hard to acquire, such as emotional state, habits and environmental coefficients, data which are either directly or indirectly relate to one's overall health status (i.e. physiological, psychological, mobility, etc.).

Many protocols have been proposed for biosignal collection and transmission, especially concerning ECG. A widely used protocol is the Standard Communication Protocol for Computer-assisted Electrocardiography (SCP-ECG) [1, 2], which is used for the ECG data communication and handling. As mentioned above, there is a significant amount of occasions that an expert needs more information about an individual than sole ECG recordings to make a more accurate diagnosis. Moreover, there are many factors that are tightly connected with the quality of ECG measurements, which in some cases may completely alter the acquired signals' characteristics and lead to imprecise diagnosis.

A previous research led to the construction of an extended protocol named e-SCP-ECG$^+$ [3], which used the flexible structure of SCP-ECG to augment existing sections for management of additional information. The enriched protocol considered new sections for vital, context aware and patient-centric data. Vital signs sections comprised of at least six biosignals (ECG, NiBP, SPO$_2$, Temp, CO$_2$ and Pulse Rate), as well as plethysmographic (PLE) data for SPO$_2$ measurement. The context aware sections contain information about geo-location and altitude. Finally, the patient-centric information sections incorporate data about allergies, blood group, environmental elements (residence, work, etc.), and personal constraints (e.g. interdiction of blood-transfusion for religious reasons).

Aiming to address the introduction of all these new types of information in conjunction with the need of obtaining more information on factors interfering with ECG measurements to increase diagnoses' accuracy, in this paper we propose some further extensions to the e-SCP-ECG$^+$ protocol, trying to enrich the patients' available data a medical expert is going to evaluate. The latest version of the protocol has included in its structure new sections for data collected by sensing devices that monitor activity, and also data about patient drug usage, body morphology, life time habits, acts before the test, mental state and other. The extra data could be useful to an expert that is called to evaluate medical data collected by a nonprofessional in an unknown environment.

2   Factors Affecting the Vital Sign Quality and Reliability

When a patient undergoes an examination in a hospital, the medical stuff follows standard procedures in order to have correct tracing quality and reliable results. But when an examination is done outside a hospital setting, at regional medical centers or by a private physician, a series of information may not be taken into consideration resulting in inaccurate medical status assessments. Alike, in wireless health monitoring systems data are collected in real world dynamically changing non-controlled settings and biosignal vital sign transmission has to be coupled with additional information (e.g. location, activity, etc.) in order to reach a valid diagnosis and deliver better healthcare services. In all the aforementioned scenarios, acquisition of various additional data about the examined patient and the ambient environment is a necessity. There exists a variety of researches [4, 5], which mention important factors that can affect vital sign measurements. Sex [6–8], ethnicity, mental state [9, 13] and emotions [10–12], life style [14], food and drink consumption [15, 16], blood analysis indexes [5, 16, 17], medication [16, 18, 19] and environmental interactions [20, 21] are some of these.

In this context, in our current work, we extended the e-SCP-ECG$^+$ protocol inserting new sections for context aware and patient-centric data. The context aware section comprises of data from accelerometers, magnetometers and gyroscope devices that are able to provide information concerning the current activity, specific body movements, potential falls and current location. The patient-centric information incorporates data about patient's anatomy (morphology), pregnancy (if patient is woman), food or drink the patient consumed before the vital sign acquisition, smoking, blood examination results, drugs and mental state among others.

Using the extra information, a medical expert has a more integrated picture of the examined patient resulting in a more reliable diagnosis, especially when artifacts are involved in the collected data.

3 Additions to the e-SCP-ECG⁺ Protocol

The Standard Communication Protocol for Computer-assisted Electrocardiography, version prEN 1064:2002 (SCP-ECG) [1, 2] was defined in order for ECG devices produced by various manufactures to be able to communicate with computers through a common language.

The SCP-ECG covers first the connection establishment between digital electro-cardiographs (ECG carts) and heterogeneous computer systems (hosts) and second the rule definition for the cart to host or cart to cart data exchange (patient data, device's manufacturer data, ECG waveform data, ECG measurements and interpretation results).

The contents in a SCP-ECG formatted file are structured as a set of sections. Each section holds different type of information than the other sections. The SCP-ECG protocol defines section ID numbers 0 through 11 in its structure, reserves section numbers 12 to 127, as well as numbers above 1023, for future use. Section ID numbers 128 through 1023 are left for manufacturer-specific information.

A previous paper presented an extension of the SCP-ECG protocol named e-SCP-ECG⁺. That extension introduced novel sections into SCP-ECG structure for transferring data for positioning, allergies and five additional bio signals: noninvasive blood pressure (NiBP), body temperature (Temp), Carbon dioxide (CO_2), blood oxygen saturation (SPO_2) and pulse rate. It also introduced new tags in existing sections for transferring comprehensive demographic data.

The proposed e-SCP-ECG⁺v2 protocol comes to enrich the e-SCP-ECG⁺ protocol assigning the following new sections:

- Section-208 for accelerometer data,
- Section-209 for gyroscope data,
- Section-210 for magnetometer data,
- Section-211 for drugs data,
- Section-212 for patient status data,

All the sections of the e-SCP-ECG⁺v2 protocol adopt the general sections format of the SCP-ECG protocol which are constituted of two parts, the section Identification Header and the section Data Part. The section Identification Header part is used without any modification. Bellow in Fig. 1 the structure of the Data Part (DP) of the new sections is analyzed. Each field contains a specific number of bytes as indicated in Fig. 1.

The Section-208 DP (**Fig.** 1) handles accelerometer data (triples of x-axes, y-axes and z-axes). The accelerometer data can be acquired either through using a permanent rhythm (mt = 1) or asynchronously (mt = 0). It consists of the "DP Header", the "Data Parameters", and the "Data Block". The "DP Header", contains the measurement type (mt), the units and the range. If mt = 1, "Data Parameters" records Date, Time, time

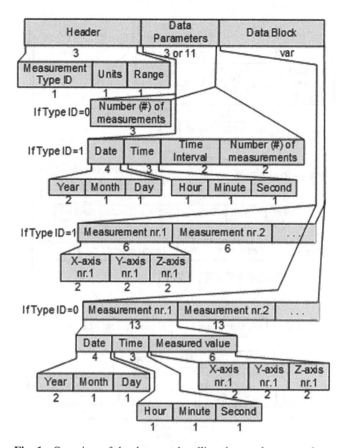

Fig. 1. Overview of the data part handling the accelerometer data.

interval and number (#) of measurements. If mt = 0, "Data Parameters" records only the number (#) of measurements. The "Data Block" records the captured triples of measurements. If mt = 1, "Data Block" keeps the successive recordings of the periodically acquired triples of values. If mt = 0, "Data Block" keeps successive recordings of distinct measurements (Date, Time and triples of values).

The Section-209 DP (**Fig.** 2) handles gyroscope data (triples of x-axes, y-axes and z-axes). The gyroscope data can be acquired either through using a permanent rhythm (mt = 1) or asynchronously (mt = 0). It consists of the "DP Header", the "Data Parameters", and the "Data Block". The "DP Header", contains the measurement type (mt), the units, the sensitivity and the range. If mt = 1, "Data Parameters" records Date, Time, time interval and number (#) of measurements. If mt = 0, "Data Parameters" records only the number of measurements. The "Data Block" records the captured triples of measurements. If mt = 1, "Data Block" keeps the successive recordings of the periodically acquired triples of values. If mt = 0, "Data Block" keeps successive recordings of distinct measurements (Date, Time and triples of values).

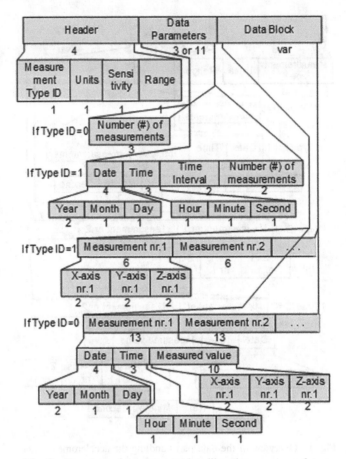

Fig. 2. Overview of the data part handling the gyroscope data.

The Section-210 DP (**Fig.** 3) handles magnetometer data (triples of x-axes, y-axes and z-axes). The magnetometer data can be acquired either through using a permanent rhythm (mt = 1) or asynchronously (mt = 0). It consists of the "DP Header", the "Data Parameters", and the "Data Block". The "DP Header", contains the measurement type (mt), the units and the accuracy. If mt = 1, "Data Parameters" records Date, Time, time interval and number (#) of measurements. If mt = 0, "Data Parameters" records only the number (#) of measurements. The "Data Block" records the captured triples of measurements. If mt = 1, "Data Block" keeps the successive recordings of the periodically acquired triples of values. If mt = 0, "Data Block" keeps successive recordings of distinct measurements (Date, Time and triples of values).

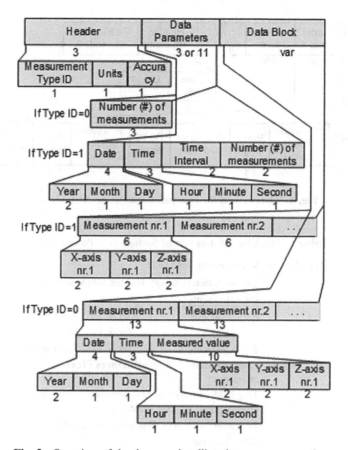

Fig. 3. Overview of the data part handling the magnetometer data.

The Section-211 DP (**Fig.** 4) handles data about drugs which the patient takes. It registers one record per each drug containing: Active substance code, commercial drug name, dosage, usage duration, comments on reactions.

The Section-212 DP (**Table** 1) handles data about patient status. This section includes information related with factors affecting the measured values of the collected biosignals and should be considered when determining patients' health status. This information concerns potential pregnancy (if patient is woman), the weight distribution on a patient's body, foods, drinks or smoking before the biosignal acquisition, usage of abused substances, hematology indexes (especially Potassium, Calcium, Sodium and Magnesium), acts before the measurement acquisition and comments on the person's psychological state.

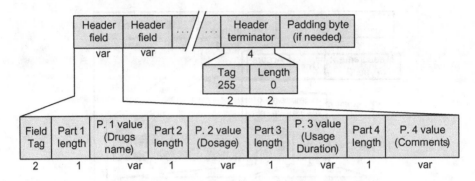

Fig. 4. Overview of the data part handling the drugs data.

Table 1. Definition of data part of Section-212 (Patient status)

Tag	Length	Value (Parameter Data)			
1	1	**Consumption** (Binary). Has the following format:			
		Bit	Contents		
		0	Alcohol	Set = Yes	Reset = No
		1	Coffee	Set = Yes	Reset = No
		2	Smoking	Set = Yes	Reset = No
2	**length**	**Consumption – other substances** (Text characters) This field permits free text comments about the consumption of other substances			
3	1	**Pregnancy** (Binary). Has the following format:			
		Bit	Contents		
		0	pregnant	Set = Yes	Reset = No
		1	1 fetus	Set = Yes	Reset = No
		2	2 fetus	Set = Yes	Reset = No
		3	3 fetus	Set = Yes	Reset = No
4	1	**Acts before examination** (Binary). Has the following format:			
		Bit	Contents		
		0	running	Set = Yes	Reset = No
		1	climbing stairs	Set = Yes	Reset = No
		2	quick stepping	Set = Yes	Reset = No
5	1	**Weight distribution** (Binary). Has the following format:			
		Bit	Contents		
		0	Physiological	Set = Yes	Reset = No
		1	Chest region	Set = Yes	Reset = No
		2	Belly region	Set = Yes	Reset = No

(*continued*)

Table 1. (*continued*)

Tag	Length	Value (Parameter Data)			
6	1	**Hematology indexes** (Binary). Has the following format:			
		Bit	Contents		
		0	Potassium	Set = Yes	Reset = No
		1	Magnesium	Set = Yes	Reset = No
		2	Calcium	Set = Yes	Reset = No
		3	Sodium	Set = Yes	Reset = No
7	2	**Emotions** (Binary). Has the following format:			
		Byte	Contents		
		1	Bit 0 Fear	Set = Yes	Reset = No
			Bit 1 Anger	Set = Yes	Reset = No
			Bit 2 Sadness	Set = Yes	Reset = No
			Bit 3 Joy	Set = Yes	Reset = No
			Bit 4 Disgust	Set = Yes	Reset = No
			Bit 5 Surprise	Set = Yes	Reset = No
			Bit 6 Trust	Set = Yes	Reset = No
			Bit 7 Anticipation	Set = Yes	Reset = No
		2	Bit 0 Shame	Set = Yes	Reset = No
			Bit 1 Kindness	Set = Yes	Reset = No
			Bit 2 Pity	Set = Yes	Reset = No
			Bit 3 Indignation	Set = Yes	Reset = No
			Bit 4 Envy	Set = Yes	Reset = No
			Bit 5 Love	Set = Yes	Reset = No
8	length	**Mental state** (Text characters) This field permits free text comments about the psychological state of the patient.			

4 Discussion and Concluding Remarks

The biosignal waveforms collected from a subject are sometimes influenced by physiological, technical pathophysiological, emotional and environmental factors. Many studies from different researchers have tried to prove the role of each factor and its impact on vital sign acquisition and accurate diagnosis. For example, changes in a person's mental state can be reflected on the quality of ECG. There are inner emotions such as joy, fear, anger, hope, etc., and outer emotions such as crying, laughing, sweating, etc., which differently affect the output signal of ECG. Environmental factors such as magnetic fields from electrical wires or machines, location and physical conditions (e.g. humidity, temperature, etc.) also play a crucial role in the quality of the obtained ECG. Other factors interfering with ECG recordings include consumption of food or drink, smoking, body's fatigue immediately before the measurements acquisition, while many drugs and substances influence the ECG waveforms. Morphology of the torso, body mass index and pregnancy, as well as changes of the body position and posture can also have significant effects on the collected data.

So, complementing ECG measurements with a group of other relevant information about a patient is deemed essential for a referring doctor to better evaluate collected data, especially in cases where the data are acquired by devices operated by non-technical stuff. Towards this direction, the e-SCP-ECG$^+$v2 protocol integrates different types of information about a person along with his medical data in a single file. As a result, the newly defined protocol can be used in a big variety of medical oriented applications, providing medical experts with a wider dataset to base their diagnosis and choose upon the treatment to be followed.

References

1. Health Informatics – Standard Communication Protocol – Computer assisted electrocardiography, CEN/TC251, prEN 1064 (2002)
2. OpenECG Portal, Internet address. www.OpenECG.net
3. Mandellos, G., Koukias, M., Styliadis, J., Lymberopoulos, D.: e-SCP-ECG + Protocol: an expansion on SCP-ECG protocol for health telemonitoring — pilot implementation Hindawi publishing corporation. Int. J. Telemed. Appl. **2010**(137201), 17 (2010)
4. Adams-Hamoda, M., Caldwell, M., Stotts, N., Drew, B.: Factors to consider when analyzing 12-lead electrocardiograms for evidence of acute myocardial ischemia. J. Crit. Care **12**(1), 9–18 (2003)
5. Zhang, X., Wang, X., Li, L., Zhang, G., Gao, Y., Cui, J.: An analysis of factors influencing electrocardiogram stress test for detecting coronary heart disease. Chin. Med. J. (Engl.) **112**(7), 590–592 (1999)
6. Rautaharju, P.M., Zhou, S.H., Wong, S., et al.: Sex differences in the evolution of the electrocardiographic QT interval with age. Can. J. Cardiol. **8**, 690–695 (1992)
7. Dellborg, M., Herlitz, J., Emanuelsson, H., Swedberg, K.: ECG changes during myocardial ischemia: differences between men and women. J. Electrocardiol. **27**(suppl), 42–45 (1994)
8. Goloba, M., Nelson, S., Macfarlane, P.: The Electrocardiogram in Pregnancy, Computing in Cardiology, pp. 693 − 696, Belfast (2010). ISSN 0276-6574
9. Singh Dhillon, H., Singh Rekhi, N.: The effect of emotions on electrocardiogram. Acad. Res. Int. **1**(1), 280–283 (2011). ISSN: 2223-9553
10. Selvaraj, J., Murugarran, M., Wan, K., Yaacod, S.: Classification of emotional states from ECG signals: a non-linear approach based on hurst. Biomed. Eng. Online **12** (2013)
11. Emotion detection in human beings using ECH signals. Int. J. Eng. Trends Technol. **4**(5), 1337–1342 (2013)
12. Agrafioti, F., Hatzinakos, D.: ECG pattern analysis for emotion detection. Proc. IEEE Trans. Affect. Comput. **3**(31), 102–115 (2012)
13. Iwanga, K., Saito, S., Shimomura, Y., Harada, H., Katsuura, T.: The effect of mental loads on muscle tension, blood pressure and blink rate. J. Physiol. Anthropol. Appl. Hum. Sci. **19**(3), 135–141 (2000)
14. Frank, S., Colliver, J.A., Frank, A.: The electrocardiogram in obesity: statistical analysis of 1,029 patients. J. Am. Coll. Cardiol. **7**, 295–299 (1986)

15. https://www.quora.com/Does-taking-coffee-before-an-ECG-test-affect-the-results-If-so-how-and-in-which-direction
16. https://www.sharecare.com/health/circulatory-system-health/what-affect-exercise-electrocardiogram-results
17. Atsushi Kotera, A., et al.: Electrocardiogram findings of patients with serum potassium levels of nearly 10.0 mmol/L: a report of two cases. Acute Med. Surg. **1,** 234–237 (2014)
18. Cairo, J.M.: PILBEAM's Mechanical Ventilation - Physiological and Clinical Applications, 5th edn. Elsevier Mosby, Missouri (2012)
19. https://www.nurseslearning.com/courses/nrp/nrp1619/section1/p01.html (DRUGS)
20. http://multimedia.3m.com/mws/media/128344O/factors-affecting-ecg-trace-quality.pdf
21. Hazari, M., Haykal-Coates, N., Winsett, D., Costa, D., Farraj, A.: Continuous electrocardiogram reveals differences in the short-term cardiotoxic response of wistar-kyoto and spontaneously hypertensive rats to doxorubicin. Toxicol. Sci. **110**(1), 224–234 (2009)

Security and Privacy Preservation

Towards an Autonomous Host-Based Intrusion Detection System for Android Mobile Devices

José Ribeiro[1,2(✉)], Georgios Mantas[1,3], Firooz B. Saghezchi[1],
Jonathan Rodriguez[1], Simon J. Shepherd[2],
and Raed A. Abd-Alhameed[2]

[1] Instituto de Telecomunicações, Aveiro, Portugal
{jcarlosvgr, gimantas, firooz, jonathan}@av.it.pt
[2] Engineering and Informatics, University of Bradford, Bradford, UK
{s.j.shepherd, R.A.A.Abd}@bradford.ac.uk
[3] Faculty of Engineering and Science, University of Greenwich, London, UK

Abstract. In the 5G era, mobile devices are expected to play a pivotal role in our daily life. They will provide a wide range of appealing features to enable users to access a rich set of high quality personalized services. However, at the same time, mobile devices (e.g., smartphones) will be one of the most attractive targets for future attackers in the upcoming 5G communications systems. Therefore, security mechanisms such as mobile Intrusion Detection Systems (IDSs) are essential to protect mobile devices from a plethora of known and unknown security breaches and to ensure user privacy. However, despite the fact that a lot of research effort has been placed on IDSs for mobile devices during the last decade, autonomous host-based IDS solutions for 5G mobile devices are still required to protect them in a more efficient and effective manner. Towards this direction, we propose an autonomous host-based IDS for Android mobile devices applying Machine Learning (ML) methods to inspect different features representing how the device's resources (e.g., CPU, memory, etc.) are being used. The simulation results demonstrate a promising detection accuracy of above 85%, reaching up to 99.99%.

Keywords: Mobile Intrusion Detection System · Android · Security
5G communications · Machine Learning · Malware detection · Host-based IDS

1 Introduction

Nowadays, the growing popularity of mobile devices (e.g., smartphones) along with the increased data transmission capabilities of future 5G networks, the wide adoption of open operating systems and the fact that mobile devices support a large variety of connectivity options (e.g., 3G/4G, Bluetooth) are factors that render the mobile devices a prime target for cyber-criminals. Apart from the traditional SMS/MMS-based Denial of Service (DoS) attacks, the future mobile devices will also be exposed to more sophisticated attacks originated from mobile malwares (e.g., viruses) that target both the device itself and the 5G network. Moreover, the open operating systems will allow users to install applications on their devices, not only from trusted, but also from

© ICST Institute for Computer Sciences, Social Informatics and Telecommunications Engineering 2019
Published by Springer Nature Switzerland AG 2019. All Rights Reserved
V. Sucasas et al. (Eds.): BROADNETS 2018, LNICST 263, pp. 139–148, 2019.
https://doi.org/10.1007/978-3-030-05195-2_14

untrusted sources (i.e., third-party markets). Consequently, mobile malwares can be included in applications looking like innocent free software packages (e.g., games), that can be downloaded and installed on users' mobile devices (e.g., smartphones), exposing them to many threats. In particular, mobile malwares can be designed to enable attackers to exploit the stored personal data on the device or to launch attacks (e.g., DoS attacks) against other entities, such as other user mobile devices, the mobile access networks, the mobile operator's core network and other external networks connected to the mobile core network [1–4]. Thus, security mechanisms such as mobile Intrusion Detection Systems (IDSs) are essential to protect mobile devices from many known and unknown security threats and to ensure user privacy.

During the last decade, a lot of research effort has been placed on IDSs for Android mobile devices, as Android is the most popular mobile device OS in the market, so it remains the main target for mobile threat actors [5–7]. Additionally, the emergence of cloud computing has led a lot of IDS solutions to be cloud-based, since they take advantage of the effectiveness that the centralized data collection and processing provide [8–10]. However, this trend is characterized by two main constrains. First, it needs a continuous connectivity of the mobile device (e.g., smartphone) to a remote central server. Although 5G aims to provide ubiquitous coverage and full connectivity, it is yet possible, even in the 5G era, for the mobile devices to suffer from the channel fading or the network outage. In addition, the second constraint is the risk of sensitive information leakage that can occur (e.g., via IDS alerts sent out from the device) and lead to compromising user privacy. Hence, it is fundamental to investigate the design and development of more autonomous host-based IDSs to protect future Android mobile devices from a plethora of known and unknown security threats and to ensure user privacy in a more efficient and effective manner.

Therefore, in this paper, we propose an autonomous host-based IDS for Android mobile devices (e.g., smartphones) that overcomes the limitation of continuous connectivity to a central server and addresses the risk of data leakage due to communication of the IDS with the remote central server. The proposed IDS is based on dynamic analysis of device behaviour for detecting suspicious behaviour on Android mobile devices. In other words, the detection takes place through analysis of deviations in device's behaviour which is described through a vector of features. The proposed IDS continuously monitors a specific set of features of the mobile device at the device level to define its run-time behaviour and apply Machine Learning (ML) algorithms to classify it as benign or malicious. It is worthwhile to mention that the monitoring process (i.e., real-time data acquisition) does not require root access, and thus the proposed IDS is able to run directly on un-rooted Android devices. In particular, the proposed IDS was implemented as a regular Android application running on an un-rooted Samsung Galaxy (J1 model: SM-J100H) smartphone running Android KitKat (version 4.4.4). Finally, to the best of our knowledge, publicly available datasets including benign and abnormal behaviour of Android mobile devices do not exist. Thus, in order to evaluate the proposed IDS, we generated our own two datasets: (a) benign activity dataset; and (b) abnormal activity dataset. The evaluation results demonstrate that the proposed IDS has a low impact on the data collection process in terms of CPU consumption, memory and battery usage.

Following the introduction, this paper is organized as follows. In Sect. 2, we describe the architecture of our proposed IDS and its different components. In Sect. 3, we introduce different features that we use for building ML models. In Sect. 4, we discuss how we construct our own datasets and present the evaluation results. Finally, Sect. 5 concludes the paper and provides some hints for the future work.

2 Proposed Host-Based IDS for Android Mobile Devices

The proposed Host-based Intrusion Detection System (HIDS) employs ML algorithms including One Rule (OneR), Decision Tree (DT), Naïve Bayes (NB), Bayesian Network (BN), Logistic Regression (LR), Support Vector Machine (SVM) or k-Nearest Neighbour (k-NN) to identify suspicious behaviour on the Android device by analysing the system log files and then it calculates the probability of intrusion. To this end, we identified the features that effectively characterize the impact of mobile malware on the Android device and maximize the effectiveness of ML techniques for detection of suspicious activity. These features are monitored in real-time by the IDS in order to collect the required data for suspicious behaviour detection.

2.1 Overall Architecture of the Proposed Host-Based IDS

The architecture of our proposed host-based IDS is composed of the following components as shown in Fig. 1: (a) real-time data acquisition, (b) real-time dataset generation, (c) feature normalization, (d) classifier, (e) intrusion probability assessment, and (f) alert manager. In the following, we briefly explain these components.

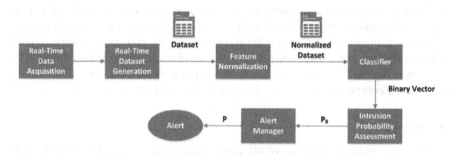

Fig. 1. Architecture of the proposed HIDS

2.2 Real-Time Data Acquisition

The *Real-Time Data Acquisition* component is responsible for collecting real-time information about the following features: total CPU usage, memory consumption, outgoing/incoming network traffic, battery level/voltage/temperature, number or running processes/services, and a binary indicator representing whether the screen is on or off during a data acquisition period.

2.3   Real-Time Dataset Generation

The *Real-Time Dataset Generation* module is responsible for constructing the training and/or testing datasets in real-time. The collected real-time information is saved in csv (comma-separated values) files. Each file contains the data collected during a *data acquisition interval*, which can be adjusted from several minutes up to one hour (see Fig. 2). Each entry (row) represents a sample (training example) and each column represents a feature. Data collection can be performed periodically every hour, every two hours, or so during a day. The data collected during each *data acquisition period* is saved in a separate csv file.

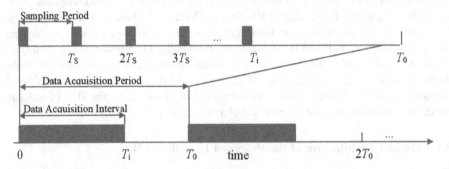

Fig. 2. Data acquisition period, data acquisition interval, and sampling period for dataset generation.

2.4   Feature Normalisation

The *Feature Normalisation* component receives the raw data from the *Real-Time Dataset Generation* component and normalises it as follows: for each column (representing one feature), it first subtracts the mean value of the column from each element of the column and then divides the result by the standard deviation of the column. This operation is repeated for all columns and the output is again saved in a new csv file. That is, each column of the new csv file has mean 0 and standard deviation 1.

2.5   Classifier

The *Classifier* module makes use of ML algorithms, namely OneR, DT, NB, BN, LR, SVM (with the polynomial kernel with exponent equal to 1) or k-NN in order to classify each entry of the normalized dataset. It is worth mentioning that OneR is a classifier which simply has only one rule for classification; it checks the feature that yields the best classification performance. For DT algorithm, we consider at least ten objects per each leaf, and for k-NN, we consider $k = 1$; that is, each new example is assigned to the class of its nearest neighbour example amongst all previously classified examples. Particularly, the output for each entry is classified as either benign (represented by the binary value 0) or malicious (represented by 1). Therefore, the output of the Classifier is a binary vector whose length is equal to the number of the entries in the normalized dataset. This binary vector is the input to the *Intrusion Probability Assessment* component.

2.6   Intrusion Probability Assessment

The *Intrusion Probability Assessment* calculates the probability of intrusion for a given *data acquisition period*. Denoting the output (binary) vector of the *Classifier* in Fig. 1 as $y \in \mathbb{R}^{m \times 1}$, the probability of intrusion in data acquisition period k is calculated as follows:

$$P_0(k) = \frac{\sum_{i=1}^{m} y_i}{m} A \tag{1}$$

where A denotes the accuracy of the Classifier, which is defined as follows:

$$A = \frac{TP + TN}{TP + TN + FP + FN} \tag{2}$$

where:

- TP (True Positives): the number of positive entries (malicious behaviour) that are correctly classified,
- TN (True Negatives): the number of negative entries (normal behaviour) that are correctly classified,
- FP (False Positives): the number of negative entries (normal behaviour) that are wrongly classified as positive (malicious behaviour), and
- FN (False Negatives): the number of positive entries (malicious behaviour) that are wrongly classified as negative (normal behaviour).

Furthermore, we define additional three metrics that later on in Subsect. 4.2 will be used for evaluating the performance of the ML algorithms that we consider for the Classifier in Fig. 1, namely Precision, Recall and F-Measure, as follows.

Precision: the ratio of the total generated alerts by the IDS, either correct or false, that are really originated from malicious incidents:

$$P = \frac{TP}{TP + FP} \tag{3}$$

Recall: the ratio of the total positive incidents that are successfully detected by the IDS:

$$R = \frac{TP}{TP + FN} \tag{4}$$

F-Measure: a combination of precision and recall defined specifically as their harmonic mean.

$$F = 2\frac{P \times R}{P + R} \tag{5}$$

2.7 Alert Manager

The overall probability of intrusion given the probability of intrusion for the current and the past monitoring periods is calculated by the *Alert Manager* component. We assume that the incident of intrusion is independent from one monitoring period to another and calculate the overall probability of intrusion as follows:

$$P(k) = 1 - \prod_{i=1}^{\alpha-1} (1 - P_0(k - i)), \tag{6}$$

where α is the number of consecutive alerts that the alert manager receives up to k^{th} *data acquisition period*. For instance, if the *Alert Manager* receives three consecutive alerts and the probability of intrusion for each alert is 0.87, then the overall probability of intrusion would be $P = 0.998$. In case the overall probability exceeds a threshold, the HIDS sends an alert to the user (i.e., notification message).

3 Feature Extraction

To detect suspicious behaviour on Android mobile devices (e.g., smartphones), the proposed IDS needs to analyse different kinds of features. For this reason, the proposed IDS continuously monitors the following features of the mobile phone at the device level: the total CPU usage, memory consumption, outgoing/incoming network traffic, battery level/voltage/temperature, number or running processes/services, and a binary indicator representing whether the screen is on or off during each data acquisition period. The complete list of the monitored features is reported in Table 1.

4 Evaluation

To evaluate the performance of the proposed IDS, we implemented it as a regular Android application on an un-rooted Samsung Galaxy (J1 model: SM-J100H) smartphone running Android KitKat (version 4.4.4). In particular, we used the Android Studio platform to develop the proposed IDS, as it contains specific tools for developing mobile Android applications [10]. However, to the best of our knowledge, publicly available datasets representing benign and abnormal behaviour of Android mobile devices do not exist. Thus, we generated our own two datasets: (a) the benign activity dataset; and (b) the abnormal activity dataset to evaluate the proposed IDS.

Table 1. Monitored features for malware detection.

Feature	Description
Total CPU usage	Overall CPU consumption
Memory usage	Overall memory usage
Memory available	Mem Free + Cached
Memory Free	Memory not used
Cached	Memory used as cache
Total Rx bytes	Received bytes
Total packets Rx	Received packets
Total Tx bytes	Transmitted bytes
Total packets Tx	Transmitted packets
Batt Level	Battery level percentage
Batt Voltage	Battery voltage
Batt temp	Battery temperature (°C)
Running Processes	Total number of running processes
Running Services	Total number of running services
Time Display On	Total seconds of the display is on
Display On/Off	Display is: on = 1; off = 0

4.1 Dataset Generation

We defined the *data acquisition period, the data acquisition interval* and the *sampling period*, as illustrated in Fig. 2, for the purpose of dataset generation.

To create our datasets, we set these parameters as follows:

(a) *Data Acquisition Period, $T_0 = 1$ h*
(b) *Data Acquisition Interval, $T_i = 20$ min*
(c) *Sampling Period, $T_s = 2$ s*

The process starts by collecting data from the device for the benign behaviour dataset. To generate the benign behaviour dataset, we run a game (Mind games) while listening an online radio station (radioonline.com.pt). Then, the device was infected with a malware and we run the same game as before while listening the online station in order to generate the malicious behaviour dataset. The process was repeated for each of the five malwares listed in Table 2; the table also provides additional information about the type of misbehaviour that each malware manifests. The device was cleaned after each operation so that only one malware was running at a time.

The collected data is saved in csv files. Each file contains the data collected during a *data acquisition interval*. Each entry (row) represents a training example and each column represents a training feature. For the *data acquisition interval* which is equal to 20 min, the csv file contains 600 samples, as the sampling period is set to 2 s. Thus, since the *data acquisition period* was equal to 1 h, 24 csv files were created for the benign behaviour during one day. On the other hand, as we infected our smartphone with five different malwares, each at a time, 120 (24x5) csv files were created for the malicious behaviour during a day.

Table 2. Android Malwares used for testing the proposed IDS.

Malware	Type of misbehaviour	Package name
Adobe Flash Player	CPU consumption, Admin. rights, Activate Wifi, Fake Google store	com.paranbijuv. aijuy
Adobe Flash Player	CPU consumption, Admin. rights, Activate Wifi, Fake Google store, lock the screen	com.android. locker
Secrettalk_Device	Admin. rights, CPU consumption	com.android. secrettalk
Google Installer	AndroidXbot, Admin. rights, CPU consumption	org.luckybird.core
Radardroid2Map	Used to mine and generate bit coins	com.ventel. android. radardroid2

4.2   Evaluation Results

For performance evaluation, we construct two datasets using the data collected from both benign and infected versions of a mobile device discussed in the previous section. We refer to these new datasets as dataset 1 and dataset 2. Each dataset contains 12000 training examples, 6000 benign and 6000 malicious, uniformly and independently chosen from the collected benign and malicious data. In particular, the 6000 malicious examples in each dataset is uniformly and randomly selected from five malwares listed in Table 2. That is, each dataset contains 1200 examples from each malware.

For numeric evaluation, we conduct two experiments. In the first experiment, we train and test over the same dataset, namely dataset 1, using 10-fold cross validation, whereas in the second experiment, we train the algorithm using dataset 1 and test it on examples from dataset 2. The main rational behind the second experiment was to inspect the generalisation capability of the constructed ML model for the IDS. Table 3 summarises the results for the first experiment. As can be seen in the table, all algorithms show impressive performance, leading to over 99% accuracy, precisions, recall, and F-measure. This shows that the ML algorithm correctly classifies most of the training instances except few FPs or FNs. Furthermore, surprisingly, the simple k-NN algorithm yields the best performance. However, it is worth mentioning that unlike other learning algorithms where the training is the most computationally intensive part and the testing is just a simple calculation, the k-NN algorithm essentially has no training phase and testing a new example is computationally expensive, as we have to search for the nearest neighbour amongst all previously classified examples.

On the other hand, Table 4 summarizes the results for the second experiment, i.e., training on dataset 1 and testing against dataset 2. Although the results of the first experiment were impressive, the results of the second experiment show that the ML method for IDS still has limitations in terms of generalisation. Noticeably, all algorithms lead to above 99% of recall, while showing lower values for the precision. This implies that most of the detection errors are due to FPs, and there are occasional FNs. Furthermore, the SVM algorithm demonstrates the best generalization performance among all applied classification algorithms, where its accuracy reaches up to 84%.

Table 3. Evaluation results for 10-fold cross validation over training dataset 1.

Algorithm	Accuracy	Precision	Recall	F-Measure
OneR	0.9895	0.9913	0.9877	0.9895
DT	0.9992	0.9993	0.9990	0.9992
NB	0.9987	0.9973	1	0.9987
BN	0.9993	0.9987	1	0.9993
LR	0.9988	0.9992	0.9985	0.9988
SVM	0.9994	0.9993	0.9995	0.9994
k-NN	**0.9999**	**1**	**0.9998**	**0.9999**

Finally, similar to the first experiment, the k-NN algorithm demonstrates an impressive generalisation performance. As seen in Table 4, its performance is comparable with the one of the SVM algorithm, with 84 per cent of detection accuracy.

Table 4. Evaluation results for training on dataset 1 and testing against dataset 2.

Algorithm	Accuracy	Precision	Recall	F-Measure
OneR	0.5563	0.5301	0.9893	0.6904
DT	0.5903	0.5496	0.9992	0.7092
NB	0.7152	0.6371	1	0.7783
BN	0.5483	0.5254	1	0.6889
LR	0.5608	0.5324	0.9983	0.6945
SVM	**0.8447**	**0.7632**	**0.9995**	**0.8655**
k-NN	0.8406	0.7582	1	0.8625

The results reveal that ML methods for IDS achieve a satisfactory performance, but they still lead to a high number of FPs, which can render the IDS into an inefficient and troublesome tool since when receiving an intrusion alert, the user has no idea if it is originated from an intrusive event or it is just a false alarm. Therefore, additional mechanisms are needed to further inspect the alerts before notifying the user. This is what is done by the post detection processing modules (i.e., Intrusion Probability Assessment and Alert Analysis modules) of our proposed IDS architecture in Fig. 1. These modules essentially generate an alert when the overall probability of intrusion exceeds a predefined threshold, relying on how many consecutive positive outcomes (indicating a malicious incident) are observed in a row.

5 Conclusion and Future Work

In this paper, we proposed an autonomous host-based IDS for Android mobile devices. The proposed IDS is based on dynamic analysis of the device's behaviour for detecting suspicious behaviour on Android mobile devices. In other words, the detection takes place through analysis of the deviations in device's behaviour described through a vector of features. The proposed IDS continuously monitors a specific set of features of the mobile device at the device level, i.e., without individually inspecting the behaviour of each application, in order to define its run-time behaviour and apply machine learning techniques to classify it as benign or malicious. The simulation results demonstrate a promising detection accuracy of above 85%, reaching up to 99.99%. For future work, we plan to incorporate statistical algorithms for malware detection in Android mobile devices. An interesting aspect of this approach is that it relies primarily on the benign data, for building a normal profile, and requires only few malicious examples for tuning the IDS. This is crucially important for an IDS design since constructing a training dataset with an equal number of benign and malicious examples is tedious in practice.

Acknowledgments. José Ribeiro would like to acknowledge his PhD grant funded by the Fundação para a Ciência e Tecnologia (FCT-Portugal) with reference SFRH/BD/112755/2015. This work is supported by the European Regional Development Fund (FEDER), through the Regional Operational Programme of Centre (CENTRO 2020) of the Portugal 2020 framework [Project MOBITRUST with Nr. 003343 (CENTRO-01-0247-FEDER-003343)].

References

1. Polla, L., Martinelli, F., Sgandurra, D.: A survey on security for mobile devices. IEEE Commun. Surv. Tutor. **15**(1), 446–471 (2013)
2. Becher, M., Freiling, F.C., Hoffmann, J., Holtz, T., Uellenbeck, S., Wolf, C.: Mobile security catching up? Revealing the nuts and bolts of the security of mobile devices. In: Security and Privacy (SP), pp. 96–111. IEEE (2011)
3. Mantas, G., Komninos, N., Rodriguez, J., Logota, E., Marques, H.: Security for 5G Communications, pp. 207–220. Wiley, Chichester (2015)
4. Arabo, A., Pranggono, B.: Mobile malware and smart devices security: trends, challenges and solutions. In: Control Systems and Computer (CSCS), 2013 19th International Conference, pp. 526–531. IEEE (2013)
5. Shabtai, A., Kanonov, U., Elovici, Y., Glezer, C., Weiss, Y.: "Andromaly": a behavioral malware detection framework for android devices. J. Intell. Inf. Syst. **38**(1), 161–190 (2012)
6. Burguera, I., Zurutuza, U., Nadjm-Tehrani, S.: Crowdroid: behavior-based malware detection system for android. In: Proceedings of the 1st ACM Workshop on Security and Privacy in Smartphones and Mobile Devices, pp. 15–26. ACM, October 2011
7. Xu, R., Saïdi, H., Anderson, R.: Aurasium: practical policy enforcement for Android applications. In: Proceedings of 21st USENIX Conference on Security Symposium. USENIX Association (2012)
8. Borges, P., et al.: Towards a hybrid intrusion detection system for android-based PPDR terminals. In: 2017 IFIP/IEEE Symposium on Integrated Network and Service Management (IM), Lisbon, pp. 1034–1039 (2017)
9. Ulltveit-Moe, N., Oleshchuk, V.A., Koien, G.M.: Location-aware mobile intrusion detection with enhanced privacy in 5G context. Wireless Pers. Commun. **57**(3), 317–338 (2011)
10. Huang, D., Zhang, X., Kang, M., Luo, J.: MobiCloud: building secure cloud framework for mobile computing and communication. In: 2010 Fifth IEEE International Symposium in Service Oriented System Engineering (SOSE), pp. 27–34 (2010)

Machine Learning to Automate Network Segregation for Enhanced Security in Industry 4.0

Firooz B. Saghezchi[1](✉), Georgios Mantas[2], José Ribeiro[2],
Alireza Esfahani[2], Hassan Alizadeh[1], Joaquim Bastos[2],
and Jonathan Rodriguez[1]

[1] University of Aveiro,
Campus Universitário de Santiago, 3810-193 Aveiro, Portugal
{firooz,hassan.alizadeh,jonathan}@ua.pt
[2] Instituto de Telecomunicações,
Campus Universitário de Santiago, 3810-193 Aveiro, Portugal
{gimantas,jcarlosvgr,alireza,jbastos}@av.it.pt

Abstract. The heavy reliance of Industry 4.0 on emerging communication technologies, notably Industrial Internet-of-Things (IIoT) and Machine-Type Communications (MTC), and the increasing exposure of these traditionally isolated infrastructures to the Internet, are tremendously increasing the attack surface. Network segregation is a viable solution to address this problem. It essentially splits the network into several logical groups (subnetworks) and enforces adequate security policy on each segment, e.g., restricting unnecessary intergroup communications or controlling the access. However, existing segregation techniques primarily depend on manual configurations, which renders them inefficient for cyber-physical production systems because they are highly complex and heterogeneous environments with massive number of communicating machines. In this paper, we incorporate machine learning to automate network segregation, by efficiently classifying network end-devices into several groups through examining the traffic patterns that they generate. For performance evaluation, we analysed the data collected from a large segment of Infineon's network in the context of the EU funded ECSEL-JU project "SemI40". In particular, we applied feature selection and trained several supervised learning algorithms. Test results, using 10-fold cross validation, revealed that the algorithms generalise very well and achieve an accuracy up to 99.4%.

Keywords: Industry 4.0 · Cyber-Physical Production Systems
Security · Machine learning · Network segregation · IIoT · MTC
Traffic classification

V. Sucasas et al. (Eds.): BROADNETS 2018, LNICST 263, pp. 149–158, 2019.
https://doi.org/10.1007/978-3-030-05195-2_15

1 Introduction

Recent advancements in information and communications technologies and the emergence of Industrial Internet of Things (IIoT) and Machine-to-Machine (M2M) communications bring about the fourth industrial revolution (Industry 4.0), where product, man and machine are fully interconnected across the whole supply chain from supplying raw material to providing the final product to the market. This allows more efficient, flexible and customized production as well as remote operation and control. However, connecting previously isolated production facilities to the Internet tremendously increases the attack surface, for most of the equipment is still legacy, primarily designed for reliable operation, with certain limited interfaces between the legacy equipment and the modern infrastructure [1]. Therefore, there is an urgent need to address cyber-physical security in these key infrastructures.

Network segregation is considered as an effective access control mechanism for information security management in ISO/IEC 17799:2005. It essentially divides the network into subnetworks, each called a network segment. Such splitting helps boost not only the network performance, by minimizing the local traffic, but also the network security through: (i) limiting the broadcast domain to the local segment; (ii) reducing the attack surface, in case of compromise in the machines hosted by a network segment; and (iii) allowing the access privileges be independently controlled for each network segment. Furthermore, network segregation can also limit the effect of local failures on other network segments. Security Group Tagging (SGT) and Access Control List are common practices for implementation of network segregation at different layers. However, in an industrial network there are tremendously huge number of heterogeneous machines, mostly legacy, communicating with each other. There is limited or no documentation at all about their communication profiles. Therefore, it is impractical to manually define rules for identifying the communication patterns in order to group the end devices. As illustrated by Fig. 1, a viable approach is to use Machine Learning (ML) to group network devices by learning their communication patterns as there exist considerable regularities in the way machines communicate or interact in an industrial network.

In this paper, we employ supervised ML algorithms to identify communication patterns in an Industry 4.0 Cyber-Physical Production Systems (CPPS) by classifying the traffic flows crossing the network. The data that we analyse has recently been collected from a large segment of Infineon's network, which is around 5 GB network trace files, in PCAP format, containing only the packet headers plus the initial 20 bytes of each payload. The independence of our flow processing algorithms from the packets' payload is crucially important to ensure the preservation of user privacy as well as the protection of industry's intellectual property. We construct labelled datasets using a Deep Packet Inspection (DPI) tool and apply following supervised ML algorithms: One Rule (OneR), Decision Tree (DT), Naïve Bayes (NB), Bayesian Network (BN), Support Vector Machine (SVM), and k-Nearest Neighbour (k-NN). The results show that among them, DT and k-NN outperform the others, with an accuracy reaching up to 99.4%. To the best of our knowledge, this is the first attempt on applying ML for network segregation and traffic analysis in industrial networks.

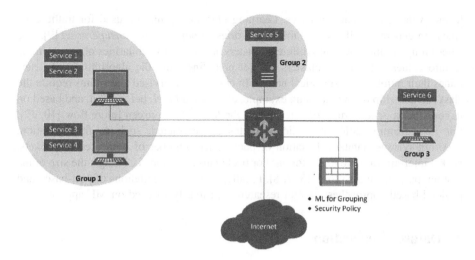

Fig. 1. Machine learning for automatic grouping of network endpoints to apply proper security policy on each network segment.

The rest of this paper is organized as follows. Section 2 reviews the related work. Section 3 describes how we construct datasets from the raw data (which is in PCAP format) collected from Infineon's network. Section 4 defines the metrics that we use for performance evaluation. Section 5 presents the supervised ML algorithms that we use for traffic classification. Section 6 presents and discusses the results. Finally, Sect. 7 concludes the paper and draws some guidelines for the future work.

2 Related Work

There are three main approaches for network traffic classification: *port-based*, *payload-based* and *flow features-based* [2–12]. In the early days of the Internet, traffic classification relied on transport layer port numbers, typically registered with the Internet Assigned Numbers Authority (IANA) to designate well-known applications. Nonetheless, more recently, growing number of applications, notably those for Peer-to-Peer (P2P) file sharing, hide their identity, by using a random port number or the well-known port of other applications, which renders port-based approach inefficient [7].

On the other hand, traffic classification based on payload analysis is more reliable and is mostly incorporated by commercial solutions, e.g., *Bro*, *Prelude*, and *Snort*, where packet payloads are inspected for specific string patterns (also called *signatures*) of known applications. Although this approach is more accurate, it suffers from concerns for protecting intellectual property – which is especially sensitive in industrial networks – and violating user's privacy. Furthermore, it scales poorly for high bandwidths, is computationally expensive, and is inefficient for encrypted packets [7, 8].

Finally, flow features-based approach adopts ML or statistical algorithms to build a model for each traffic type, by feeding a training set containing flow examples. The model is then able to predict class membership for new instances by examining the feature values for unknown flows. Learning algorithms that are used for traffic classification generally fall into two main categories: *supervised* and *unsupervised* [9]. The latter groups traffic flows into different clusters according to similarities observed in the feature values [11]. These clusters are not predefined and the algorithm itself determines their number and statistical nature. In contrast, supervised algorithms require the class membership of each training example, also called *label*, beforehand, and based on it, construct a general rule for determining the label of an unseen future flow [10, 12]. For flow feature, different traffic attributes are extracted, such as flow duration, max/min/average/standard deviation of packet size, number of sent/received packets, packet inter-arrival time in the forward or backward direction, TCP flags, the size of the first ten packets, and so forth [3, 7, 8]. Finally, due to the limitations of port-based and payload-based approaches, current research is primarily focused on ML approach.

3 Dataset Generation

We use *libprotoident 2.0.12*[1] DPI to construct a labelled dataset. The output file is in a Comma Separated Values (CSV) format (see Table 2), where, for each row, the first element indicates the label, i.e., the Application protocol and the next elements indicate flow attributes, representing training features in the order listed by Table 1.

4 Evaluation Metrics

For numerical evaluation, we perform k-fold cross validation, with k = 10. That is, we divide the whole data into k subsets and repeat the test k times. In each trial, we use one of the k subsets as the test set and the rest k-1 subsets as the training set. We then calculate the average performance over all k trials. This in fact provides a good indication of algorithm's generalisation capability when classifying an unseen data point [8]. Finally, we use the following standard evaluation metrics [9]:

- *Accuracy*: the percentage of correctly classified instances over the total number of instances;
- *Precision*: the number of class members classified correctly over the total number of instances classified as class members;
- *Recall* (or *true positive rate*): the number of class members classified correctly over the total number of class members.
- *F-Measure*: a combination of precision and recall defined specifically as their harmonic mean. The traditional F-measure, also called balanced F-score or F_1 measure, is calculated as follows:

$$F = 2\frac{Precision \times Recall}{Precision + Recall},\tag{1}$$

---

[1] https://github.com/wanduow/libprotoident.

Table 1. List of training features, representing different columns of the dataset.

Column	Feature
1	*Application layer protocol (label)*
2	Transport protocol (e.g., 6 stands for TCP and 17 stands for UDP)
3	Total number of packets sent in the forward direction
4	Total number of bytes sent in the forward direction
5	Total number of packets sent in the backward direction
6	Total number of bytes sent in the backward direction
7	Minimum payload size sent in the forward direction
8	Mean payload size sent in the forward direction
9	Maximum payload size sent in the forward direction
10	Standard deviation of payload size sent in the forward direction
11	Minimum payload size sent in the backward direction
12	Mean payload size sent in the backward direction
13	Maximum payload size sent in the backward direction
14	Standard deviation of payload size sent in the backward direction
15	Minimum packet inter-arrival time in the forward direction
16	Mean packet inter-arrival time for packets sent in the forward direction
17	Maximum packet inter-arrival time in the forward direction
18	Standard deviation of packet inter-arrival time in the forward direction
19	Minimum packet inter-arrival time in the backward direction
20	Mean packet inter-arrival time in the backward direction
21	Maximum packet inter-arrival time in the backward direction
22	Standard deviation of packet inter-arrival time in the backward direction
23	Flow duration (in microseconds)

Table 2. Few training examples from the constructed dataset.

Label	Training examples
HTTP	,6,3,19,5,85,0,6,19,9,0,17,85,34,81,386,982,421,0,0,1,0,1163,1499110420.978695
DHCP	,17,23,2254,0,0,98,98,98,0,0,0,0,0,0,0,1,0,0,0,0,0,11,1499110681.654235
DNS	,17,23,4002,0,0,174,174,174,0,0,0,0,0,0,0,1,0,0,0,0,0,11,1499110482.156615
RTP	,17,0,0,2,344,0,0,0,0,172,172,172,0,0,0,0,0,0,1,2,1,2,1501080810.070283

which is a special case of the general F_β measure $(\beta \geq 0)$.

$$F_\beta = \left(1 + \beta^2\right) \frac{Precision \times Recall}{\beta^2 Precision + Recall} \qquad (2)$$

Two other commonly used F measures are the F_2 measure, which weights recall more than precision, and the $F_{0.5}$ measure, which puts more emphasis on precision than recall.

5   Classification Algorithms

In the following, we briefly elaborate ML algorithms that we use for traffic classification in an Industrial Network, which have widely been employed for Internet traffic classification [7, 8] as well. Note that all of these algorithms are supervised, i.e., requiring labels for training.

One Rule (OneR): is a simple yet effective classification algorithm based on only one rule. During the training phase, it creates one rule for each feature and picks the one that leads to the minimum classification error as the general classification rule.

Decision Tree (DT): creates a model based on a tree structure where each node represents a test on a feature and the resulting braches represent possible outcomes of this test, and each leaf node represents a class label. Determining the label of a test instance is the matter of tracking the path of nodes and branches to a terminating leaf.

Naïve Bayes (NB): is based on Bayes rule for inferring the posterior probability using prior class probabilities and the conditional probabilities (likelihood). It is literally called Naïve because it makes a naïve assumption that all features are independent from each other. However, despite this unrealistic assumption, the algorithm works well in most of the cases even if this assumption is violated.

Bayesian Network (BN): is a directed acyclic graph whose nodes represent features and edges represent their probabilistic relations. Each node contains a table for the conditional probabilities of its representing feature given the outcomes of the parent node. Every node is assumed to be dependent only on its immediate parent node. BN may outperform the NB algorithm if the conditional independence assumption between the features in the NB algorithm is violated.

Support Vector Machine (SVM): constructs the optimal separating hyperplane, which maximises its distance to the closest example, from any class. It leads to a maximum-margin separation between the classes. In two-dimensional space, the hyperplane is reduced to a line dividing the plane in two parts where the examples of each class lay in either side.

k-Nearest Neighbour (k-NN): computes the Euclidian distance between a new test example and the k nearest examples from previously classified examples, in the n-dimensional feature space, and assigns the test tuple the majority label of these k nearest neighbours. We use k = 1, which means that we assign a new test example to the class of its nearest neighbour example amongst the previously classified examples. Unlike other training examples which normally include a computationally expensive training phase and simple calculation for the test phase, the k-NN algorithm essentially requires no training phase and the test phase is computationally expensive.

6   Performance Evaluation

For performance evaluation, we conduct three experiments. The first one studies the performance of different learning algorithms using all 22 original raw features. The second experiment, examines the performance of the same algorithms when we apply the Principal Component Analysis (PCA) technique with 95% variance coverage, which reduces the number of features down to 13. Finally, the last experiment investigates the impact of the variance retained by the PCA algorithm on the accuracy of a learning algorithm.

6.1   Experiment 1: Training and Testing with All Original Features

Our training dataset contains 448,724 examples from network traffic generated by 39 applications, including HTTP, DHCP, DNS, NTP, Skype, SNMP, etc. Each example is composed of 23 traffic attributes listed above in Table 1. Note that, in this table, the first attribute, in fact, indicates the output label, which is the application protocol. Hence, the training set actually contains 22 training features. For the purpose of simulations, we conduct several experiments. For the first experiment, we train the six abovementioned classification algorithms (OneR, DT, NB, BN, SVM, k-NN with k = 1) and test them using 10-fold cross validation method. In this experiment, we do not apply any feature selection algorithm and perform the training phase using all 22 original features. Table 3 summarizes the results. Here, Accuracy means the ratio of test examples that are correctly classified. We observe that DT and k-NN algorithms outperform the others, achieving an accuracy of up to 0.994, which means that among 448,724 test examples, these algorithms successfully classify 99.4% of them and commit mistakes in only 6% of them.

6.2   Experiment 2: Applying PCA with 95% Variance Retain

Applying PCA, with 95% variance retain, considerably reduces the number of features from 22 down to 13. In order to assess the impact of this remarkable dimensionality reduction on the classification performance, we conducted the second experiment, where we first applied PCA algorithm and then again trained and tested the same ML algorithms employed in the first experiment. Table 4 summarizes the results. We observe that applying PCA algorithm with 95% variance retain, surprisingly boosts the overall performance of learning algorithms. This is due to the fact that some learning algorithms such as NB are quite sensitive to the violation of the underlying assumption about the independence of all training features one from another. Applying PCA, provided that the variance retain is high enough, can help extract a set of independent but informative features out of the original ones. In particular, DT and k-NN still outperformed other algorithms and applying PCA has no impact on their performance. Furthermore, the PCA algorithm considerably improves the performance of OneR and the Bayesian classifiers (NB and BN) and only slightly deteriorates the performance of SVM algorithm. It is worthwhile to stress that the combination of OneR and PCA algorithms results in a quite promising performance, considering its pretty simple decision rule for classification.

6.3   Experiment 3: Feature Selection with PCA

In this experiment, we apply PCA algorithm choosing different values for the covered variance, ranging from 95% down to 10%. As summarized by Table 5, the number of remaining attributes after applying PCA algorithms is 13 for 95% variance retaining and only one attribute for 10% variance coverage. We also incorporated DT algorithm for classifying the output instances of the PCA algorithm. The results are presented by the last column of this table. An interesting finding is that reducing the variance retain down to 70% reduces the number of remaining attributes considerably, resulting in

Table 3. Results for Experiment 1, training with all 22 original features.

Algorithm	Accuracy	Precision	Recall	F-Measure
OneR	0.904	0.914	0.904	0.896
DT	**0.994**	**0.993**	**0.994**	**0.993**
NB	0.391	0.535	0.391	0.404
BN	0.969	0.976	0.969	0.972
SVM	0.890	0.881	0.890	0.878
k-NN	**0.994**	**0.994**	**0.994**	**0.994**

Table 4. Results for experiment 2, employing PCA with 95% variance retain and training with 13 selected features.

Algorithm	Accuracy	Precision	Recall	F-Measure
OneR	0.972	0.971	0.972	0.972
DT	**0.993**	**0.992**	**0.993**	**0.993**
NB	0.446	0.511	0.447	0.442
BN	0.974	0.989	0.974	0.980
SVM	0.795	0.771	0.795	0.755
k-NN	**0.994**	**0.994**	**0.994**	**0.994**

only 6 attributes, out of 22 original ones, yet the sacrifice in the accuracy of the learning algorithm is negligible, only 0.01%. Furthermore, choosing variance retain of 50% leads to elimination of two additional features while reducing the accuracy marginally, 0.16% comparing to the case with 70% variance retain. Finally, applying PCA with only 10% variance coverage results in only one remaining feature while witnessing a minor reduction in the classification accuracy, only 3.65% additional sacrifice relative to the case with 50% variance coverage. This highlights the importance of performing feature selection before implementing any ML algorithm for traffic classification. For example, the output of PCA algorithm with 10% variance retain is the following feature, where the parameters are the abbreviations of attributes listed by Table 1: maximum forward packet length (*maxfpktl*), maximum backward packet length (*maxbpktl*), standard deviation of backward packet length (*stdbpktl*), standard *deviation* of forward packet length (*stdfpktl*), average backward packet length (*meanbpktl*).

$$0437 maxfpktl + 0.43 maxbpktl + 0.425 stdbpktl + 0.413 stdfpktl$$
$$+ 0.292 meanbpkt \dots$$

Table 5. Results for experiment 3, feature selection with PCA with different variance retains.

Variance retain	Number of remaining attributes	Accuracy of DT algorithm (%)
0.95	13	99.36
0.90	11	99.35
0.80	8	99.35
0.70	**6**	**99.35**
0.50	4	99.19
0.20	2	98.97
0.10	1	95.56

7 Conclusion

Security of CPPSs is a mounting concern in Industry 4.0, where IIoT and MTC technologies are massively employed to connect all stakeholder, including man, product, and machine, across the whole supply chain. In spite of this revolution, still, there is considerable legacy equipment in factories that cannot be replaced immediately, all at once, due to excessive capital expenditure and typically long lifespan of the machineries. To address this concern, network segregation seems essential to divide the network into different segments, based on the communications needs, to control the access to machines sitting in each segment, and to restrict unnecessary inter-segment communications. To this end, machine learning is a promising tool to classify network endpoints based on their communication patterns. In this paper we applied ML and traffic classification to group network endpoint in Industry 4.0 networks. We analysed the data collected from a large segment of Infineon's network, within the realization of ECSEL research project SemI40. Using DPI tools, we constructed labelled datasets with 22 traffic features and applied several supervised algorithms. The results reveal that DT and k-NN demonstrate outstanding performance, with an accuracy reaching up to 99.4%. Moreover, applying PCA algorithm can reduce the number of feature remarkably from 22 features down to only six features, with a negligible loss of 0.05% in the accuracy of the learning algorithm. This work can be extended in the following directions. First, determining different groups of network endpoint in a CPPS, based on the traffic flows that they generate, is an important research topic. Second, integrating the proposed grouping intelligence into a conventional network device, e.g., Firewall, is another critical research problem.

Acknowledgment. The authors would like to thank Infineon Technologies, especially Christian Zechner and Stephan Spittaler for their great support in data acquisition and identifying the addressed challenges. It is also acknowledged that this work has been developed within Power Semiconductor and Electronics Manufacturing 4.0 (SemI40) project, under grant agreement No. 692466, co-funded by grants from Austria, Germany, Italy, France, Portugal (through Fundação para a Ciência e Tecnologia ECSEL/0009/2015) and Electronic Component Systems for European Leadership Joint Undertaking (ECSEL JU).

References

1. Esfahani, A., et al.: A lightweight authentication mechanism for M2M communications in industrial IoT environment. IEEE Internet Things J. (2017). https://doi.org/10.1109/JIOT.2017.2737630
2. Finsterbusch, M., Richter, C., Rocha, E., Muller, J.A., Hanssgen, K.: A survey of payload-based traffic classification approaches. IEEE Commun. Surv. Tutor. **16**(2), 1135–1156 (2014)
3. Shi, H., Li, H., Zhang, D., Cheng, C., Cao, X.: An efficient feature generation approach based on deep learning and feature selection techniques for traffic classification. Comput. Netw. **132**, 81–98 (2018)
4. Zhang, J., Chen, C., Xiang, Y., Zhou, W., Xiang, Y.: Internet traffic classification by aggregating correlated naive Bayes predictions. IEEE Trans. Inf. Forensics Secur. **8**(1), 5–15 (2013)
5. Valenti, S., Rossi, D., Dainotti, A., Pescapè, A., Finamore, A., Mellia, M.: Reviewing traffic classification. In: Biersack, E., Callegari, C., Matijasevic, M. (eds.) Data Traffic Monitoring and Analysis. LNCS, vol. 7754, pp. 123–147. Springer, Heidelberg (2013). https://doi.org/10.1007/978-3-642-36784-7_6
6. Zhang, J., Chen, X., Xiang, Y., Zhou, W., Wu, J.: Robust network traffic classification. IEEE/ACM Trans. Netw. (TON) **23**(4), 1257–1270 (2015)
7. Kim, H., Claffy, K.C., Fomenkov, M., Barman, D., Faloutsos, M., Lee, K.: Internet traffic classification demystified: myths, caveats, and the best practices. In: Proceedings of the 2008 ACM CoNEXT Conference, pp. 11:1–11:12. ACM (2008)
8. Williams, N., Zander, S., Armitage, G.: A preliminary performance comparison of five machine learning algorithms for practical IP traffic flow classification. ACM SIGCOMM Comput. Commun. Rev. **36**(5), 7–15 (2006)
9. Nguyen, T.T., Armitage, G.: A survey of techniques for internet traffic classification using machine learning. IEEE Commun. Surv. Tutor. **10**(4), 56–76 (2008)
10. McGregor, A., Hall, M., Lorier, P., Brunskill, J.: Flow clustering using machine learning techniques. In: Barakat, C., Pratt, I. (eds.) PAM 2004. LNCS, vol. 3015, pp. 205–214. Springer, Heidelberg (2004). https://doi.org/10.1007/978-3-540-24668-8_21
11. Erman, J., Arlitt, M., Mahanti, A.: Traffic classification using clustering algorithms. In: Proceedings of the SIGCOMM Workshop on Mining network data, pp. 281–286. ACM (2006)
12. Moore, A.W., Zuev, D.: Internet traffic classification using Bayesian analysis techniques. ACM SIGMETRICS Perform. Eval. Rev. **33**(1), 50–60 (2005)

Security Framework for the Semiconductor Supply Chain Environment

Alireza Esfahani[1(✉)], Georgios Mantas[1], Mariana Barcelos[1],
Firooz B. Saghezchi[2], Victor Sucasas[2], Joaquim Bastos[1],
and Jonathan Rodriguez[2]

[1] Instituto de Telecomunicações (IT), 3810-193 Aveiro, Portugal
{alireza,gimantas,m.aleixo,jbastos}@av.it.pt
[2] University of Aveiro, Aveiro, Portugal
{firooz,vsucasas,jonathan}@ua.pt

Abstract. This paper proposes a security framework for secure data communications across the partners in the Semiconductor Supply Chain Environment. The security mechanisms of the proposed framework will be based on the SSL/TLS and OAuth 2.0 protocols, which are two standard security protocols. However, both protocols are vulnerable to a number of attacks, and thus more sophisticated security mechanisms based on these protocols should be designed and implemented in order to address the specific security challenges of the Semiconductor Supply Chain in a more effective and efficient manner.

Keywords: Industry 4.0 · Semiconductor Supply Chain
Network secure communications · SSL/TLS · OAuth2

1 Introduction

Nowadays, data communication across the partners in the Semiconductor Supply Chain can be the target of many known and unknown security threats exploiting many security breaches in the internal/external environment of the partners due to its heterogeneous and dynamic nature as well as the fact that non-professional users in security issues usually operate their information systems. Particularly, these vulnerabilities in the Semiconductor Supply Chain Environment can be exploited by attackers with a wide spectrum of motivations ranging from criminal intents aimed at financial gain to industrial espionage and cyber-sabotage. Attackers can compromise the data communication between legitimate parties in the Semiconductor Supply Chain and thus can jeopardize the delivery of services across the partners as well as the continuity of the service provision. As a result, Semiconductor Supply Chain partners will suffer from damaging repercussions, which can cause significant revenue loss, destroy their brand and eventually hinder their advancement. Consequently, a security framework for secure data communications across the partners in the Semiconductor Supply Chain Environment is of utmost importance.

Therefore, the main objective of this paper is to provide a security framework for secure data communications across the partners in the Semiconductor Supply Chain. Towards this direction, in this paper, we firstly consider representative examples of

V. Sucasas et al. (Eds.): BROADNETS 2018, LNICST 263, pp. 159–168, 2019.
https://doi.org/10.1007/978-3-030-05195-2_16

various attacks that have been seen in the wild and can cause potential security issues and challenges in the Semiconductor Supply Chain Environment. The range of the attacks shows how vital is a security framework for secure data communications for the partners in the Supply Chain of the Semiconductor Industry. Moreover, we provide a categorization of the various attack examples based on the intrusion method that they use to compromise the target and gain a persistent foothold in the target's environment. Furthermore, we propose a security framework for secure data communication across the partners in the Supply Chain. The security mechanisms of the proposed framework will be based on the SSL/TLS and OAuth 2.0 protocols, which are two standard security protocols. The SSL/TLS protocol is the de facto standard for secure Internet communications [1]. On the other hand, the OAuth 2.0 protocol is the industry-standard protocol for authorization [2]. However, both the SSL/TLS protocol and the OAuth 2.0 protocol are vulnerable to a number of attacks, and thus more sophisticated security mechanisms based on these protocols should be designed and implemented in order to address the specific security challenges of the Semiconductor Supply Chain in a more effective and efficient manner.

2   Cybersecurity Issues and Challenges in the Semiconductor Supply Chain Environment

In this section, we consider representative examples of various attacks in industrial and enterprise domains that have been seen in the wild and can cause potential security issues and challenges in the Semiconductor Supply Chain Environment. We categorize these attack examples into 5 main categories based on the intrusion method that they use to compromise the target and gain a persistent foothold in the target's environment. The 5 main categories that we identified are the following: (a) spear phishing attacks, (b) watering hole attacks, (c) attacks based on "trojanized" third-party software, (d) attacks based on malicious code and counterfeit certificates, and (e) attacks based on tampered devices.

2.1   Spear Phishing Attacks

Phishing is a kind of social-engineering attack where adversaries use spoofed emails to trick people into sharing sensitive information or installing malware on their computers. Indeed, victims perceive these spoofed emails as being associated with a trusted brand. In other words, phishing attacks target the people using the systems instead of targeting directly the systems that people use. Thus, phishing attacks are able to circumvent the majority of an organization's or individual's security measures. Moreover, it is worthwhile to mention that phishing has spread beyond email to include VOIP, SMS, instant messaging, social networking sites, and even massively multiplayer games. Moreover, cyber-criminals have shifted from sending mass-emails, hoping to trick anyone, to more sophisticated but also more selective "spear-phishing" attacks that use relevant contextual information to trick specific groups of people. In principle, "spear-phishing" attacks are more dangerous than typical phishing attacks [3]. Here are a few examples of "spear-phishing" attacks from the wild.

Icefog. In 2011, Kaspersky Lab started to investigate a threat actor called 'Icefog' that attacked many different groups, such as government institutions, military contractors, telecom operators, satellite operators, among others, through their supply chain. This campaign targeted organizations mostly in South Korea and Japan, but it was suspected that it also targeted the United States and Europe [4]. The intrusion method of this attack was phishing e-mails with a malicious attachment or a link to an infected web page. The attacker could compromise the victim's machine either by tricking the victim to install the attached malware or by tricking the victim to visit the malicious web page [5]. Afterwards, the attacker could steal files from the victim's machine, run commands to locate and steal specific information from the victim's machine, and also communicate with local database servers in order to steal information from them. In addition, Icefog was capable of uploading special tools to extend the capabilities of the installed malware, such as tools for stealing cached browser passwords in the infected machine. In 2012, a Mac OS version of Icefog (Macfog) was created [4], but Kaspersky suspected that it was a beta-testing phase to be used in targeted victims later. Finally, it is worth mentioning the "hit and run" nature of Icefog, since the Icefog attackers appeared to know very well what they need from the victims and thus, once the information was obtained, the victim was abandoned.

Target. At the end of 2013, Target suffered a cyber-attack that exposed approximately 40 million debit and credit card accounts [6] and 70 million e-mail addresses, phone numbers and other personal information. The hackers started their attack by sending phishing e-mails, including malware, to employees of a third-party vendor, but it was not known if only one vendor was targeted. In addition, it was suspected that the malware in question was Citadel, a password-stealing bot that was a derivative of the ZeuS banking trojan and allowed the attackers to access Target's network by using stolen credentials. It was estimated that the phishing campaign had started at least two months before the main attack carried out. Brian Krebs was the first to break the news about this attack on his security blog followed by Target's Statement, released a day after.

Home Depot. In April 2014, just four months after the Target attack, Home Depot was the victim of a data breach. However, they only started investigations on 2nd September, 2014 and released a statement on 8th September, 2014 [7]. It was found that the attackers, similar to the attackers of Target attack, used third party vendor's credentials to access Home Depot's network. After being inside the retailer's network, the attackers exploited a known vulnerability in Windows XP called "zero-days" in order to escape detection [7]. Finally, this attack resulted in the theft of 53 million e-mail addresses and 56 million credit card accounts.

German Steel Mill. In late 2014 (no specific date was provided), Germany's Federal Office for Information Security (BSI) released a report communicating that a German steel mill had been attacked. The attackers' point of entry was the plant's business network and the infiltration was made possible with a spear phishing attack [8]. The phishing emails could have had a malicious attachment or a link to a website from where malware could be downloaded. Once the malware was installed, the attackers were able to take control of the production software. SANS Institute provided the BSI's report, translated to English, where it is mentioned that the attack resulted in an incident where the furnace could not be shut down properly, and as a result, it led to a "massive damage" to the German steel mill.

Dragonfly - 1st Tactic. A cyber-espionage group, known as Dragonfly or Energetic Bear, began a campaign in late 2010 [9] with the intention of targeting the energy sector and industrial control systems (ICS) through their Supply Chain. In other words, the Dragonfly group attacked the suppliers of the target instead of attacking the target directly.

The Dragonfly group applied at least three different infection tactics against victims in the energy sector. The first one was an email spear-phishing campaign and is examined in this section. However, the Dragonfly group used two main pieces of malware in its attacks. Both are Remote Access Tool (RAT) type malware enabling the attackers to access and control the compromised computers.

The favoured malware tool of the Dragonfly group was Backdoor.Oldrea, which was also known as Havex or the Energetic Bear RAT. Symantec reported that Oldrea was used in around 95% of infections. This malware acted as a back door for the attackers onto the victim's computer, enabling them to extract information and install further malware. In particular, Oldrea, gathered system information such as operating system, computer and user name, country, language, Internet adapter configuration information, available drives, default browser, running processes, desktop file list, My Documents, Internet history, program files, and root of available drives. In addition, Oldrea collected data from Outlook (address book) and ICS related software config-uration files [10]. All this data was collected and written to a temporary file in an encrypted form before it was POSTed to the remote C&C (command-and-control) server controlled by the Dragonfly attackers. Moreover, the second main malware tool used by the Dragonfly group was Trojan.Karagany. It was a back door programmed in C/C++ and used mainly for reconnaissance operations. Specifically, it was designed to download and install additional files and exfiltrate data. Moreover, it had plugin capability and its payload was approximately 72 KBs in size. Finally, Trojan.Karagany contained a small embedded DLL file, which monitored WSASend and send APIs for capturing "Basic Authentication" credentials [10].

According to the first approach (i.e., email spear-phishing campaign), selected executives and senior employees in target companies received emails with a malicious PDF attachment. Symantec states that the infected emails had two possible subject lines: "The account" and "Settlement of delivery problem". In addition, all the emails were from a single Gmail address. The email spear-phishing campaign was conducted from February 2013 to June 2013 [10].

2.2   Watering Hole Attacks

To attack an organization, cyber criminals "trojanize" a legitimate website often visited by the target company's employees. RSA Advanced Threat Intelligence Team corre-lated this behaviour with the one of a lion waiting for its prey at a watering hole, hence the name. RSA was the first to use the term "watering hole", in late July 2012 [11]. Here are a few examples of watering hole attacks from the wild.

VOHO. According to [11], "VOHO" campaign targeted Financial Services or Technology Services in Massachusetts and Washington, DC. This campaign worked by inserting JavaScript element in the legitimate website that would redirect the victim (i.e., website visitor) unknowingly to an exploit website. Then, the exploit website would check if the user was running a Windows machine and Internet Explorer browser, and then it would install a version of "gh0st RAT". "gh0st RAT" was a Remote Access Trojan that allowed attackers to control the infected endpoints, log keystrokes, provide live feeds of webcam and microphone as well as download and upload files.

Dragonfly - 2nd Tactic. As described before in "Dragonfly - 1st tactic" section, the Dragonfly group has used at least three infection tactics against targets in the energy sector. After the earliest tactic (i.e., email spear-phishing campaign) that was described in "Dragonfly - 1st tactic" section, the Dragonfly attackers shifted their focus to watering hole attacks. It was noticed that this shift happened in June 2013 [10]. The Dragonfly attackers compromised a number of energy-related websites and injected an iframe into each of them. Then, this iframe would redirect users to another legitimate, but also compromised, website hosting the Lightsout exploit kit, as shown in Fig. 1. This in turn would exploit either Java or Internet Explorer to download Oldrea or Karagny on the target's machine. Besides, in September 2013, the Dragonfly group started using a new version of this exploit kit, known as the Hello exploit kit. The main web page for this kit contained JavaScript that was able to identify installed browser plugins. Then, the victim was redirected to a URL which in turn determined the best exploit to use according to the collected information [10].

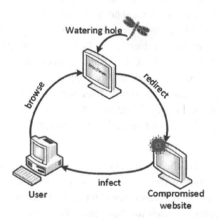

Fig. 1. Watering hole attack.

Shylock. In November 2013, BAE Systems Applied Intelligence announced that a series of legitimate websites had been infected with the Shylock malware [12]. The cyber-criminals infected a legitimate website by inserting a JavaScript file that initially identified when the browser was used and then this JavaScript file was responsible to show a message, in the browser's style, prompting the user to download the malware that, however, was presented as innocent software. BAE Systems gave the following message example: "Additional plugins are required to display all the media on this page", with a button saying "Install Missing Plugins…". In case that the user decided to proceed and install the "missing plugins", the Shylock malware was installed on his/her machine.

2.3 Attacks Based on "trojanized" Third-Party Software

This section includes a real-life example of attacks based on "trojanized" software of ICS equipment providers.

Dragonfly - 3rd Tactic. The third tactic of the Dragonfly group was the infection of a number of legitimate software packages. Particularly, three different ICS equipment providers were targeted and the Dragonfly attackers inserted malware into the software bundles that these providers had made available online for download from their websites [10]. The first provider discovered that it was compromised shortly after infection, but the malware had already been downloaded 250 times. The second provider had infected software available for download for at least 6 weeks and the third provider had infected software available online for 10 days, approximately.

2.4 Attacks Based on Malicious Code and Counterfeit Certificates

This section includes two examples of attacks based on malicious code and counterfeit certificates in industrial environment.

Stuxnet. The German Steel Mill attack described earlier is not the first attack that caused physical damage of equipment. The first one was the Stuxnet attack [13] that was designed to target SCADA systems and was responsible for attacking an Iranian nuclear facility. Stuxnet exploited four zero-days vulnerabilities, compromised two digital certificates, injected code into ICS and hid the code from the operator [14]. After implementing the code (process that probably took a long time), the attackers had to steal digital certificates, in order to avoid detection [14]. Stuxnet compromised the system via USB and infected every Windows PC it could find. However, in terms of controllers, it was much pickier. It targeted only controllers from one specific manufacturer (Siemens).

Meltdown and Spectre. In the early 2018, researchers revealed that almost every computer chip manufactured in the last 20 years contains fundamental security flaws, with specific variations on those flaws being named Meltdown [15] and Spectre [16]. The flaws arise from features which are built into chips and enable them to run faster. These vulnerabilities allow attackers to use malicious programs to get access to data previously completely protected. It is accomplished by exploiting two important techniques used to speed up computer chips, called speculative execution and caching.

2.5   Attacks Based on Tampered Devices

This section includes a real-life example of attacks based on tampered devices in business environment.

Michaels Stores Attack. In May 2011, Michaels Stores reported an attack that allowed criminals to steal credit and debit cards and the associated PIN codes. To steal this information, attackers tampered at least 70 point of sale (POS) terminals [17]. In a blog entry from Krebs on Security, Krebs explained that there are few ways to tamper with POS terminals. One way is to have pre-compromised terminals ready to be installed at the cash register. In addition, fake POS terminals can also be used to record data from swipe cards and PIN entry. For precaution, Michaels Stores replaced 7,200 PIN pads and trained employees to check regularly if the equipment had been compromised.

3   Security Framework for the Semiconductor Supply Chain Environment

3.1   Definition of the Security Framework

The security framework for the Semiconductor Supply Chain environment should provide appropriate security mechanisms to address the specific security challenges of the Semiconductor Supply Chain in a more effective and efficient manner. As it is shown in Fig. 2, the security mechanisms of the proposed framework will be based on the SSL/TLS and OAuth 2.0 protocols, which are two standard security protocols. The SSL/TLS protocol is the de facto standard for secure Internet communications and the OAuth 2.0 protocol is the industry-standard protocol for authorization. However, both the SSL/TLS protocol and the OAuth 2.0 protocol are vulnerable to a number of attacks, and thus more sophisticated security mechanisms based on these protocols should be designed and implemented in order to address the specific security challenges of the Semiconductor Supply Chain in a more effective and efficient manner. Specifically, as it is shown in Fig. 2, the proposed framework is focused on security mechanisms for the following two types of communication in the Semiconductor Supply Chain Environment: (i) Client-to-Server communication, and (ii) Server-to-Server communication. Thus, the security framework should include appropriate security mechanisms ensuring secure data communication between the partners' clients and partners' servers, and appropriate security mechanisms ensuring secure data communication between the servers of the Semiconductor Supply Chain partners. The security mechanisms for the Client-to-Server communication will be based on the SSL/TLS and OAuth 2.0 protocols, and the security mechanisms for the Server-to-Server communication will be based only on SSL/TLS protocol.

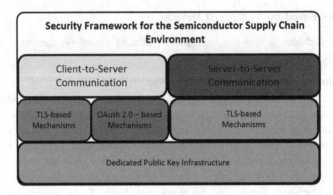

Fig. 2.   Security framework.

3.2   Dedicated Public Key Infrastructure (PKI) for the Semiconductor Supply Chain Environment

In this section, we provide the description of the dedicated Public Key Infrastructure (PKI) that is an essential component of the Security Framework of the Semiconductor Supply Chain Environment. The dedicated PKI is responsible for issuing and managing all the required digital certificates that will be used by the security mechanisms.

Public Key Infrastructure. In principle, a public key infrastructure (PKI) is based on digital certificates. Digital certificates are sometimes also referred to as X.509 certificates or simply as certificates. PKI is defined by RFC 2822 (Internet Security Glossary) as a set of software, hardware, encryption technologies, people and procedures that allow a trusted third party to establish the integrity and ownership of a public key. Furthermore, the trusted third party, called Certification Authority (CA), typically issues the certificates. The CA signs the certificate by using its private key. Moreover, it generates the corresponding public key to all eligible participating parties.

Dedicated PKI Trust Model. The dedicated PKI trust model for the Semiconductor Supply Chain Environment follows the traditional hierarchical PKI trust model which is based on the establishment of superior-subordinate CA relationships (See Fig. 3). It can be represented as a tree with the root at the top and the branches extending towards the bottom. The elements of the inverted tree are nodes and leaves. The nodes represent the CAs and the leaves represent the end entities. The root (i.e., CA) is the node located at the top of the inverted tree and below the root CA there are zero or more layers of subordinate CAs. The root CA is the starting point for trust and issues a self-signed certificate as well as certificates to subordinate CAs that are immediately below it but not to the end entities. Subordinate CAs, in turn, issue certificates to the next lower level subordinate CAs or end entities, respectively.

According to the dedicated PKI trust model, each of the retailers, distributors, front-end components, back-end components, inventories, and suppliers hosts its own CA that issues the certificates of its registered end-users (i.e., servers). In addition, there is a CA (i.e., Retailer CA) that issues the CA certificates of all the CAs which are set up into the retailers of the specific Semiconductor Supply Chain environment. Moreover,

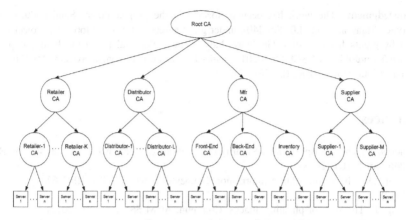

Fig. 3. Dedicated PKI trust model.

there is a CA (i.e., Distributor CA) that issues the CA certificates of all the CAs which are set up into the distributors' premises. Furthermore, there is a CA (Manufacturing (Mfr) CA) that issues the CA certificates of the CAs which are set up into the front-end component's premises, back-end component's premises and inventory. Similarly, there is a CA (i.e., Supplier CA) that issues the CA certificates of all the CAs which are set up into the suppliers' premises. Finally, there is a CA (i.e., Root CA) that issues the CA certificates of the Retailer CA, Distributor CA, Manufacturing (Mfr) CA, and Supplier CA. It is supposed that the Root CA, Retailer CA, Distributor CA, Manufacturing (Mfr) CA, and Supplier CA are controlled by the main entity (e.g., Infineon) of the specific Semiconductor Supply Chain environment in order to avoid trust concerns associated with subordination between the participating entities belonging to different domains.

4   Conclusion and Future Work

In this paper, we provided a number of representative examples of various attacks that have been witnessed in the wild and can cause potential security issues and challenges in the Semiconductor Supply Chain Environment. Furthermore, Moreover, we provided a categorization of the various attack examples based on the intrusion method that they use to compromise the target and gain a persistent foothold in the target's environment. Furthermore, we proposed a security framework for secure data communication across the partners in the supply chain. The security mechanisms of the proposed framework will be based on the SSL/TLS and OAuth 2.0 protocols, which are two standard security protocols. However, both protocols are vulnerable to a number of attacks. Thus, as future work, we plan to design and implement more sophisticated TLS – based mechanisms and OAuth 2.0 – based mechanisms for the proposed security framework in order to address the specific security challenges of the Semiconductor Supply Chain in a more effective and efficient manner.

Acknowledgment. The work has been performed in the project Power Semiconductor and Electronics Manufacturing 4.0 (SemI40), under grant agreement No 692466. The project is co-funded by grants from Austria, Germany, Italy, France, Portugal (from the fundação para a ciência e Tecnologia - ECSEL/0009/2015) and - Electronic Component Systems for European Leadership Joint Undertaking (ECSEL JU).

References

1. Dierks, T.: The Transport Layer Security (TLS) Protocol Version 1.2, RFC 5246, vol. RFC 5246, pp. 1–104 (2008)
2. Hardt, D.: The OAuth 2.0 Authorization Framework [RFC 6749], RFC 6749, pp. 1–76 (2012)
3. Hong, J.: The state of phishing attacks. Commun. ACM **55**(1), 74–81 (2012)
4. GReAT, The Icefog APT: A Tale of Cloak and Three Daggers, Kaspersky Labs (2013)
5. Mantas, G., Komninos, N., Rodriuez, J., Logota, E., Marques, H.: Security for 5G communications, Fundamentals of 5G Mobile Networks, pp. 207–220 (2015)
6. Krebs, B.: Target Hackers Broke in Via HVAC Company, Krebs on Security (2014)
7. Hawkings, B.: Case Study: The Home Depot Data Breach, SANS Institute (2015)
8. Krebs, B.: Sources: Target Investigating Data Breach, Krebs on Security (2013)
9. Nelson, N.: The impact of Dragonfly malware on industrial control systems (2016)
10. Symantec, Dragonfly: Cyberespionage Attacks Against Energy Suppliers (2014)
11. Gragido, W.: Lions at the Watering Hole – The 'VOHO' Affair, RSA (2012)
12. BAE Systems Applied Intelligence, Shylock. Banking malware. Evolution or revolution? (2014)
13. Zetter, K.: A cyberattack has caused confirmed physical damage for the second time ever, Wired, pp. 1–19 (2017)
14. Falliere, N., Murchu, L.O., Chien, E.: W32.Stuxnet Dossier, vol. 4, February 2011
15. Lipp, M., et al.: Meltdown (2018). no. ArXiv eprints: arXiv:1801.01207
16. Kocher, P., et al.: Spectre Attacks: Exploiting Speculative Execution * (2018). no. ArXiv eprints: arXiv:1801.01203
17. Krebs, B.: Breach at Michaels Stores Extends Nationwide, Krebs on Security (2011)

A Study on Data Dissemination Techniques in Heterogeneous Cellular Networks

Roberto Torre[(⊠)] and Frank H. P. Fitzek

Deutsche Telekom Chair of Communication Networks, Dresden, Germany
{roberto.torre,frank.fitzek}@tu-dresden.de
https://cn.ifn.et.tu-dresden.de/

Abstract. Cellular networks are undergoing a major shift in their deployment and optimization. Regardless the deployment of LTE led to an overall performance increase in cellular networks, disseminating data to multiple users inside a cell is still under development. This dissemination is currently achieved via unicast connections, which is inefficient in terms of throughput and power consumption because the antenna is sending duplicated data to co-located users. The 3rd Generation Partnership Project (3GPP) proposed a new standard to be able to multicast and broadcast information over cellular networks. However, different studies stated that this solution might have problems related to the spectrum, and new multicasting alternatives which provide better performance have appeared. Since these new alternatives came up, a race for the control of cellular multicast/broadcast has started. In this paper, we collect, analyze and compare the leading technologies that enable the system to efficiently disseminate data over cellular networks, and conclude by indicating which ones are the most likely to succeed.

Keywords: Survey · Cellular networks
Random Linear Network Coding (RLNC) · Multicast
Cooperative networks · 5G · Traffic offload

1 Introduction

Over the last years, the amount of traffic over cellular networks has greatly increased year by year. In the Technical Report of Cisco 2011 [1] it was reported that the global Mobile Traffic was going to increase from 1 exabyte (eB) per month to more than 10, and the traffic of mobile video will reach the 70% of this traffic. Credit Suisse reported that 23% of base stations globally had utilization rates of more than 80 to 85% in busy hours during the deployment of LTE [2]. In the end, 11 eB was reached in 2017, and the trend is to continue growing up to 49 eB in 2021 [3], where 78% of the traffic will be video streaming. The amount of wireless traffic will increase as well, comprising a 63% of total IP

© ICST Institute for Computer Sciences, Social Informatics and Telecommunications Engineering 2019
Published by Springer Nature Switzerland AG 2019. All Rights Reserved
V. Sucasas et al. (Eds.): BROADNETS 2018, LNICST 263, pp. 169–179, 2019.
https://doi.org/10.1007/978-3-030-05195-2_17

traffic by 2021. Moreover, the number of devices will massively increase up to three times the global population in 2021. New infrastructure elements, such as femto/pico base stations, fixed/mobile relays, cognitive radios, and distributed antennae are being massively deployed, thus making future 5G cellular systems and networks more heterogeneous [4]. With all these information above exposed it can be concluded that, during the next years, the actual infrastructure and protocols will not be able to support the amount of traffic between devices due to mobile video.

Nowadays, each user requesting data from a broadband connection will be connected to a unicast link from the cellular base station to the user equipment. In the case these users are requesting the same video file, a replicated scenario appears for each of user who is downloading the same data. Hence, an efficient way of disseminating data over cellular networks must be developed. Several lines of research have appeared with different principles and different results. Even though all these novel technologies have appeared, there is still no study that compares all of them and gives an idea of where each technology could stand out.

The aim of this paper is to gather the current leading technologies that enable multicast/broadcast over cellular networks, analyze and provide a holistic comprehensive comparison of them in terms of throughput, latency, energy consumption, packet resilience, protocols used and assumptions made. We discuss which problems have been tackled, which challenges are still on the plate and what are the potential research directions in the field. We also summarize which ones would stand out in a near future and which impact they will have in this field.

The remainder of the paper is organized as follows. In Sect. 2 we give a detailed information about the current leading technologies studied. In Sect. 3 the key enablers of these technologies can be found. Section 4 gathers the possible comparison approaches in disseminating data over cellular networks. In Sect. 5 a summary table with the main technologies named in the paper and its major properties is depicted. Section 6 collects the correlation between the studied publications, differences, and similarities. In Sect. 7 the conclusion of our work is presented.

2   Data Dissemination in Cellular Networks

The simplest dissemination scenario studied in standards consists on a communication where one source is sending to multiple sinks simultaneously and only one single transmission is used. The first approach to provide data dissemination in cellular networks was done by the Conventional Multicast Scheme (CMS) [5] in 2000, which describes an optimal allocation algorithm for an OFDM broadband system in comparison with TDMA. An alternative approach is the Optimized Opportunistic Multicast Scheduling (OMS) [6], where not all User Equipments (UEs) are served in a given time slot but maximizes the system throughput according to the channel quality, as it is studied in [7]. In a similar line of research, the 3GPP group developed the Multimedia Broadcast/Multicast

Service (MBMS) [8], who transforms an LTE network into a single frequency network (SFN) from a device perspective, to enable broadcast or multicast of any type of content to interested users, such as live sports events, live concerts or a news service; and the enhanced version of it [9,10]. In this approach, a basic WiFi multicast scenario is replicated in the cellular network, with similar discovery, initiation, transfer, and termination protocols. The deployment of MBMS would have been unquestionable, however, diverse research studies [7,11,12] found some technical constraints that stalled its expansion, mainly in terms of spectrum.

Parallel studies [13,14] have developed new methods in order to provide an efficient data dissemination in mobile networks. The principles these methods use are based on the creation of small subgroups inside the cell. New applications [15–18] that use this approach have recently appeared. These small subgroups often behave as cloudlets [19] with intermediate nodes acting as relays in order to offload traffic from the cellular network. The work in [20] shows that relaying inside cells increases network performance. In these scenarios, the cellular base station has to make sure the information is sent at least once to the whole subgroup via unicast links, and then a short range (SR) communication protocol, e.g. WiFi, is used to distribute the data over the nodes inside the group. Since the speed of WiFi is higher and energy consumption is lower [21–23] than LTE, systems that use this architecture argument that by offloading the LTE traffic from cellular networks onto WiFi they will increase network throughput and devices battery lifetime.

The last approach to be studied in this survey is the content sharing in cellular networks through device-to-device (D2D) systems [24,25]. In this approach all nodes in the cellular network behave as if they were in a mesh network, being able to talk to their respective neighbors and share their information with their peers via unicast connections. It can be studied as a particular example of a subgrouping architecture where the cell behaves as the subgroup and nodes cannot multicast among themselves.

3   Background

Broadband Communication in Heterogeneous Networks. Cellular networks are undergoing through massive changes in the last years. New elements have recently appeared making the environment heterogeneous [26,27]. The size of cells is diminishing year by year. Currently, femtocells are the type of cell which is most likely to succeed in small cell networking [28]. These cells are small, which is important because it may allow a short-range communication between the nodes in the cell using different communication protocols with lower ranges.

Cooperative Mobile Wireless Systems. Nowadays, in the cellular environment, a massive amount of users are coexisting in a cellular network, and the trend is to continue increasing [3]. In the case those devices are downloading the same content and they are close enough to communicate among themselves, gathering nodes in groups may reduce the overall data to be transmitted over the cellular network [29–31] as well as the energy consumption per UE. Thus, the base station will be able to offer a better Quality of Service to the user or to have access to a bigger number of nodes. This cooperative architecture is known as mobile Clouds (MC) or Cooperative Mobile Clouds (CMC) in [32–34]. A mobile cloud is a cooperative architecture that shares distributed resources in efficient and novel ways [35].

Traffic Offload from Cellular to Short Range Networks. The amount of traffic in cellular networks will increase 700% in the next five years [3]. This increase in the amount of traffic is unaffordable for the current cellular architectures, therefore several solutions such as offloading traffic [18,36] from the cellular network to short-range networks have appeared. In [37,38], opportunistic device-to-device communication, and cellular communication are used to disseminate the content taking into account social ties and geographical proximity.

Raptor Codes. Rapid Tornado Codes [39] are a class of erasure correction codes that improve the first practical approach of fountain codes, called LT codes [40]. They were first introduced in 2004, but the first dedicated publication was [41]. It was very successful in its early stages, where the 3rd Generation Partnership Project (3GPP) [42] defined the Raptor Codes as the main codes to be used in mobile cellular wireless, defined in IETF RFC 5053 [43]. These codes were also used for future 3GPP protocols in cellular wireless communications for multicasting, as in [8].

Random Linear Network Coding. In this emerging heterogeneous networking environment where cellular networks are continuously adapting to new user requirements, it was demonstrated that the use of Network Coding can increase wireless network throughput [44]. A high-performance improvement used to overcome those errors is Random Linear Network Coding (RLNC), which was first introduced in [45]. Some studies also stated that the interplay of Random Linear Network Coding along with different technologies (such as Cooperative Networking [46,47] or other correction techniques [17]) can substantially increase network throughput and packet resilience in comparison with its predecessors and have created an innovative communication paradigm known as Network-Coded Cooperative (NCC) networks [48,49]. This tool has been as well a great way of designing broadcast/multicast applications [50,51]. Since users will be close to each other, middle nodes in cooperative clouds can work as relays and take advantage of the interplay between RLNC and cooperation [52].

4   Classification Schemes

There are two well-differentiated lines of research in this field. On one hand, some researches are trying to adapt the multicast technology of WiFi to broadband communications. On the other hand, researches opt for the creation of small subgroups inside the cell, unicasting information to the group only once, and then spread the data inside the subgroups. Figure 1 shows the two possible approaches. In the first one, there is a single frequency communication from the base station where each UE is able to subscribe to. In the subgroup-based scheme part, the content is delivered to each UE that requests it via a unicast connection, and each node of the subgroup shares its data to the rest via P2P or Wifi multicast. The impact of different error correction techniques, the amount of throughput or latency in the output, the power consumed in each device or in the base station, the different communication protocols used, are some of the features that will be important for this survey.

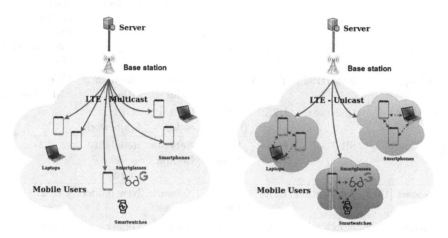

Fig. 1. Conventional Multicast Scheme (Left) versus Subgroup-based Scheme (Right).

5   System Comparison

In Table 1 the main technologies to multicast data in cellular networks are gathered. Some are enablers to other models, they have different approaches, or their assumptions are different, but all of them have the same objective, the possibility to multicast over cells.

eMBMS is the most robust one since it has been developed by the 3GPP group. It was the first one developed, taking the model of IP multicast and [5,6]. However, EBU technical Report [11] showed that multicasting over 3G and later over LTE had several technical issues that needed to be improved before deploying eMBMS to the world. Multiple use cases in different platforms were studied and the main drawbacks found were:

- Signal attenuation, requirement of LoS (Line of Sight)
- Location of the UE and the nodeB
- Eco-system development
- Spectral inefficiency
- Disagreements with LTE network operators

Table 1. Comparison of current leading technologies. 1. Model presented. 2. Nature of the model. 3. Cellular communication notes. 4. Short Range communication notes. 5. Error correction techniques. 6. Results obtained. 7. Asumptions made for the protocol.

Arch.[1]	Approach[2]	Cell.[3]	SR Comm.[4]	Error Corr.[5]	Results[6]	Asumptions[7]
CMS [5]	Analytical	OFDM	-	-	Capacity Increase	Quasi-static channel, Full information of channel
OMS [6]	Analytical	TDMA	-	Raptor codes	Minimum Delay	Channel SNR known
eMBMS [9]	Holistic	LTE	-	Raptor codes	3GPP Framework	-
NCVCS [15]	SR Tool	None	WiFi Mcast	Network Coding	Reliability in lossy channels	-
Microcast [16]	Application	LTE	Wifi Ucast	Network Coding	New model	UE: 2 Ifaces
AL-RLNC [17]	Application	LTE	Wifi Ucast	RLNC + HARQ	Higher Through-put	Small testbed
CoopStream [18]	Application	LTE	Wifi Ucast	RLNC	Cell Offload	UE: 2 Ifaces
NCC Netw. [49]	Application	LTE	Wifi Mcast	RLNC	Energy Gain	UE: 2 Ifaces
Coop. D2D [25]	Application	LTE	Various	-	Cell Offload	No error communi-cation

Since eMBMS is the technology to beat, most of the alternatives presented are using these drawbacks to state that their solutions can compete with eMBMS. However, most of the studies focus only on one specific part of the development process (Analysis, Application) or the testbeds they are doing are too small. These subgroup-based schemes are right now taking the lead in the main mobile conferences and multiple institutions are researching on it. In Table 1, it can be observed these new approaches, using similar technologies and, in the end, obtaining different results depending on what they are focusing on. It would be easy for somebody who values throughput over latency to select [17] instead of [16]. The main problem these approaches have is that UEs are required to have 2 interfaces. However, it is expected that next generation phones can use both LTE and Wifi interfaces at the same time to download data.

Another topic discussed in this paper is about the short-range communication protocol used in the subgroup-based scheme technologies. Some of them consider Bluetooth, but it is rapidly discarded due to its short range. WiFi is the selected technology. However, there is still not clear if WiFi unicast should be used or if WiFi multicast is better. Unicast provides better reliability, but wifi multicast spreads out the data in a more efficient way since it is designed for that. Further researches should be done on this aspect. Regarding the error correction techniques, RLNC is taking the lead over other NC codes or raptor codes. RLNC is performing better and it is the most likely to succeed in the near future.

6   Publication Correlations

Since there are different approaches to solve the same problem, correlations between the publications are also separated into two groups. On one hand, the eMBMS group, which comprises CMS, OMS, and eMBMS. On the other, the sub-grouping scheme group, formed by NCVCS, Microcast, NCC Networks and D2D Cooperative Networks. The technology to beat is eMBMS since it is the one proposed by the 3GPP Partnership Project. That is the reason why all the subgrouping publications work around eMBMS and its troubles encountered to multicast, so they give another possible solution with better performance.

Another form of grouping can be the differentiation between the enablers [5,6,15], and the applications [9,16,25,49]. [5] and [6] are two ground technologies looking for the same purpose, adapt the unicast to OFDM/TDMA in order to be able to multicast. This is the starting point of eMBMS, however, different studies [7,11,12] showed that this technology had complications. Hence, novel approaches appeared, such as [16] or [49], who had [15] as an enabler, or [25] using a different approach.

7   Conclusion

Cellular networks are undergoing a major shift in their deployment and optimization. Even though the deployment of LTE led to an overall performance increase in cellular networks, disseminating data to multiple users inside a cell is still under development. The Third Generation Partnership (3GPP) proposed a solution, eMBMS, to deal with the increasing amount of traffic. However, it was reported that this solution had troubles in several aspects which stalled this technology from its deployment. Hence, alternative approaches appeared based on a subgrouping scheme where the cellular base station send data to some nodes in the cell, which will work as relays. The new approaches proposed got better results in terms of throughput, latency and power consumption. However, these technologies have not been tested in real scenarios, and further researches must be carried out following this line of research.

There are several problems that need to be overcome in both approaches (IP multicast adaptation and subgrouping schemes) in order to deploy LTE multicast in the near future. On one hand, the 3GPP group needs to find the optimal solutions to the problems explained in this paper. On the other hand, the subgrouping scheme technologies should move their testbeds to a bigger scale, within a whole cell in a real heterogeneous environment. Moreover, most of them are developing applications, but equations supporting the results and models of the protocols are missing.

Even though eMBMS looks like the strongest technology nowadays, alternative technologies are obtaining better results in terms of throughput, latency, and energy consumption, and the spectrum issues of eMBMS do not seem to disappear. Hence, we rely on the subgroup-based technologies to take the lead and end up being the multicast alternative for 5G.

Acknowledgements. This project has received funding from the European Union's H2020 research and innovation program under grant agreement H2020-MCSA-ITN-2016-SECRET 722424 [53].

References

1. Cisco: Cisco Visual Networking Index: Forecast and Methodology, 2011 to 2016. Technical report, Cisco Technologies (2012)
2. Goldstein, P.: Credit Suisse Report: U.S. Wireless Networks Running at 80% of Total Capacity, July 2011
3. Cisco: Cisco Visual Networking Index: Forecast and Methodology, 2016 to 2021. Technical report, Cisco Technologies, 28 March 2017
4. Heath, R.W., Kountouris, M.: Modeling heterogeneous network interference. IEEE Inf. Theory Appl, Workshop (Feb (2012)
5. Rhee, W., Cioffi, J.M.: Increase in capacity of multiuser OFDM system using dynamic subchannel allocation. In: IEEE 51st Vehicular Technology Conference Proceedings, pp. 1085–1089 (2000)
6. Low, T.P., Pun, M.O., Hong, Y.W.P., Kuo, C.C.J.: Optimized opportunistic multicast scheduling (OMS) over wireless cellular networks. IEEE Trans. Wirel. Commun. **9**, 791–801 (2010)
7. Militano, L., Condoluci, M., Araniti, G., Iera, A.: Multicast service delivery solutions in LTE-Advanced systems. In: IEEE International Conference on Communications (ICC), pp. 5954–5958, June 2013
8. 3GPP: Multimedia broadcast/multicast service (MBMS). Technical report, December 2017
9. Viavi Solutions: LTE multimedia broadcast multicast services (MBMS). White paper (2015)
10. Lecompte, D., Gabin, F.: Evolved multimedia broadcast/multicast service (eMBMS) in LTE-Advanced: overview and rel-11 enhancements. IEEE Commun. Mag. **50**(11), 68–74 (2012)
11. EBU: Delivery of broadcast content over LTE networks. Technical report, July 2014

12. Afolabi, R.O., Dadlani, A., Kim, K.: Multicast scheduling and resource allocation algorithms for OFDMA-based systems: a survey. IEEE Commun. Surv. Tutor. **15**(1), 240–254 (2013)

13. Araniti, G., Condoluci, M., Iera, A.: Adaptive multicast scheduling for HSDPA networks in mobile scenarios. In: IEEE International Symposium on Broadband Multimedia Systems and Broadcasting, June 2012

14. Araniti, G., et al.: Efficient frequency domain packet scheduler for point-to-multipoint transmissions in LTE networks. In: IEEE International Conference on Communications (ICC), June 2012

15. Wang, L., Yang, Z., Xu, L., Yang, Y.: NCVCS: Network-coding-based video conference system for mobile devices in multicast networks. Ad Hoc Netw. **45**, 13–21 (2016)

16. Keller, L., et al.: Microcast: Cooperative video streaming on smartphones. In: MobiSys 2012, 25-29 June 2012, Low Wood Bay, Lake District, UK (2012)

17. Assefa, T.D., Kralevska, K., Jiang, Y.: Performance analysis of LTE networks with random linear network coding. In: International Convention on Information and Communication Technology, Electronics and Microelectronics, May 2016

18. Aymen, L., Ye, B., Nguyen, T.M.T.: Offloading performance evaluation for network coding-based cooperative mobile video streaming. In: Proceedings of the International Conference on the Network of the Future (NOF) (2016)

19. Satyanarayanan, M., Bahl, P., Caceres, R., Davies, N.: The case for VM-based cloudlets in mobile computing. IEEE Pervasive Computing, October 2009

20. Laneman, J.N., Tse, D.N.C., Wornell, G.W.: Cooperative diversity in wireless networks: efficient protocols and outage behavior. IEEE Trans. Inf. Theory **50**(12), 3062–3080 (2004)

21. Huang, J., Qian, F., Gerber, A., Mao, Z.M., Sen, S., Spatscheck, O.: A close examination of performance and power characteristics of 4G LTE networks. In: Proceedings of the 10th International Conference on Mobile Systems, Applications, and Services, pp. 225-238 (2012)

22. Agilent Technologies: Power-consumption measurements for LTE user equipment. Application note from Agilent Technologies, June 2014

23. Sun, L., Sheshadri, R.K., Zheng, W., Koutsonikolas, D.: Modeling WiFi active power/energy consumption in smartphones. In: 2014 IEEE 34th International Conference on Distributed Computing Systems, June 2014

24. Chen, X., Proulx, B., Gong, X., Zhang, J.: Exploiting social ties for cooperative D2D communications: a mobile social networking case. IEEE/ACM Trans. Netw. **23**(5), 1471–1484 (2015)

25. Wang, X., Zhang, Y., Leung, V.C.M., Guizani, N., Jiang, T.: D2d big data: Content deliveries over wireless device-to-device sharing in large-scale mobile networks. IEEE Wirel. Commun. **25**(1), 32–38 (2018)

26. Radwan, A., et al.: Low-cost on-demand c-ran based mobile small-cells. IEEE Access **4**, 2331–2339 (2016)

27. Radwan, A., et al.: Mobile caching-enabled small-cells for delay-tolerant e-health apps. IEEE International Conference on Communications, May 2017

28. Andrews, J.G., Claussen, H., Dohler, M., Rangan, S., Reed, M.C.: Femtocells: Past, present, and future. IEEE J. Sel. Areas Commun. **30**(3), 497–508 (2012)

29. Albiero, F., Fitzek, F., Katz, M.: Cooperative power saving strategies in wireless networks: an agent-based model. In: Symposium on Wireless Communication Systems, October 2007

30. Pedersen, M.V., Fitzek, F.H.P.: Mobile clouds: The new content distribution platform. Proceedings of the IEEE (2012)
31. Albiero, F., Katz, M., Fitzek, F.H.P.: Energy-efficient cooperative techniques for multimedia services over future wireless networks. In: IEEE International Conference on Communications, pp. 2006–2011, May 2008
32. Fitzek, F., Katz, M., Zhang, Q.: Cellular controlled short-range communication for cooperative P2P networking. Wireless World Research Forum (WWRF) 17 (2006)
33. Fitzek, F.H., Katz, M.D.: Mobile Clouds. Exploiting Distributed Resources in Wireless, Mobile and Social Networks. Wiley, UK (2014)
34. Militano, L., Condoluci, M., Araniti, G., Molinaro, A., Iera, A., Fitzek, F.H.P.: Wi-Fi cooperation or D2D-based multicast content distribution in LTE-A: a comparative analysis. In: IEEE International Conference on Communications Workshops (ICC), pp. 296–301, June 2014
35. Bagheri, H., Salehi, M.J., Khalaj, B.H., Katz, M.: An energy-efficient leader selection algorithm for cooperative mobile clouds. In: IEEE Wireless Days, 2013 IFIP, January 2014
36. Saghezchi, F.B., et al.: A novel relay selection game in cooperative wireless networks based on combinatorial optimization. In: VTC Spring, May 2011
37. Han, B., Hui, P., Kumar, V.A., Pei, M.V.M.G., Srinivasan, A.: Cellular traffic offloading through opportunistic communications: a case study. In: Proceedings of the 5th ACM Workshop on Challenged Networks (CHANTS), pp. 31-38 (2010)
38. Ioannidis, S., Chaintreau, A., Massoulie, L.: Optimal and scalable distribution of content updates over a mobile social network. In: IEEE INFOCOM 2009, April 2009
39. Shokrollahi, A., Luby, M.: Raptor codes. Found. Trends®Commun. Information Theory 6(3–4), 213–322 (2011)
40. Luby, M.: LT codes. In: The 43rd Annual IEEE Symposium on Foundations of Computer Science, 2002. Proceedings (2002)
41. Shokrollahi, A.: Raptor codes. IEEE Trans. Inf. Theory, June 2006
42. 3GPP: Third generation partnership project, March 2018
43. IETF: Raptor forward error correction scheme for object delivery, March 2018
44. Ahlswede, R., Cai, N., Li, S.Y.R., Yeung, R.W.: Network information flow. IEEE Trans. Inf. Theory 46(4), 1204–1216 (2000)
45. Ho, T., Medard, M., Shi, J., Efiros, M., Karger, D.R.: On randomized network coding. Proc. 41st Annual Allerton Conference on Communication Control and Computing, Vol. 1, No. 1, pp. 11–20 (2003)
46. Rossetto, F., Zorzi, M.: Mixing network coding and cooperation for reliable wireless communications. IEEE Wirel. Commun., February 2011
47. Fitzek, F.H.P., Heide, J., Pedersen, M.V., Katz, M.: Implementation of network coding for social mobile clouds [applications corner]. IEEE Signal Process. Mag. 30(1), 159–164 (2013)
48. Renzo, M.D., Iezzi, M., Graziosi, F.: On diversity order and coding gain of multisource multirelay cooperative wireless networks with binary network coding. IEEE Trans. Veh. Technol. 62(3), 1138–1157 (2013)
49. Pandi, S., Arranz, R.T., Nguyen, G.T., Fitzek, F.H.P.: Massive video multicasting in cellular networks using network coded cooperative communication. In: 15th IEEE Annual Consumer Communications Networking Conference (CCNC), pp. 1–2, January 2018

50. Swapna, B.T., Eryilmaz, A., Shroff, N.B.: Throughput-delay analysis of random linear network coding for wireless broadcasting. IEEE Trans. Inf. Theory **59**(10), 6328–6341 (2013)
51. Ho, T., et al.: A random linear network coding approach to multicast. IEEE Trans. Inf. Theory **52**(10), 4413–4430 (2006)
52. Toemoeskoezi, M., et al.: On the packet delay characteristics for serially-connected links using random linear network coding with and without recoding. In: Proceedings of European Wireless 2015; 21st European Wireless Conference, May 2015
53. Rodriguez, J., et al.: Secret-secure network coding for reduced energy next generation mobile small cells. In: ITA Conference (2017)

Towards Reliable Computation Offloading in Mobile Ad-Hoc Clouds Using Blockchain

Saqib Rasool[1,2(✉)], Muddesar Iqbal[1,3], Tasos Dagiuklas[3], Zia ul Qayyum[1], and Adnan Noor Mian[2]

[1] University of Gujrat, Gujrat, Pakistan
saqibrasool@gmail.com
[2] Information Technology University, Lahore, Pakistan
[3] London South Bank University, London, UK

Abstract. Mobile Ad-hoc Cloud (MAC) refers to the computation offloading of a mobile device among the multiple co-located mobile devices. However, it is difficult to convince the randomly participating mobile devices to offer their resources for performing the computation offloading of other mobile devices. These devices can be convinced for resource sharing by limiting the compute shedding of a device nearly equal to the computation that same device has already performed for other mobile devices. However, this cannot be achieved without establishing the trust among the randomly co-located mobile devices.

Blockchain has been already proven for the trust-establishment between multiple independent stakeholders. However, to the best of our knowledge, no one has used blockchain for reliable computation offloading among the independently operating co-located mobile devices of MAC. In this position paper, we proposed the mapping of blockchain concepts for the realization of reliable computation offloading in MAC. We have also identified the future research directions that can be focused for improving the proposed integration of blockchain and MAC.

Keywords: Mobile Ad-hoc Cloud · Mobile Cloud Computing
Mobile edge computing · Multi-access Edge Computing · Blockchain

1 Introduction

Mobile Cloud Computing (MCC) refers to the computation offloading from mobile devices to the nearby fog computing layer or the cloud computing layer for reducing the resource consumption of mobile devices [19]. It not only helps in preserving the battery of mobile devices for longer time intervals but also ensures the quick execution of CPU intensive tasks by the dedicated resources of fog/cloud computing layer [5]. Multi-access Edge Computing (MEC), in contrary to MCC, shifts the computation from cloud towards edge devices [15]. Increasing capabilities of mobile devices are encouraging researchers and practitioners to exploit the resources of edge devices for performing the tasks that were

© ICST Institute for Computer Sciences, Social Informatics and Telecommunications Engineering 2019
Published by Springer Nature Switzerland AG 2019. All Rights Reserved
V. Sucasas et al. (Eds.): BROADNETS 2018, LNICST 263, pp. 180–188, 2019.
https://doi.org/10.1007/978-3-030-05195-2_18

previously confined to the dedicated resources of fog/cloud only. MEC not only reduces the response time but also minimizes the cost of operating the dedicated resources that are required for MCC.

Mobile Ad-hoc Cloud (MAC) [20] is formed by the collaborative computation offloading among the multiple co-located mobile devices and it supports some of the features of both MCC and MEC. Participants of MAC observe the MCC features when they offload their computation to the neighbouring mobile devices and these neighbouring mobile devices are supporting the MEC by performing the computation at the edge of the network. Mobile devices of MAC are voluntarily working in collaboration for supporting each other. However, there must be some motivation for encouraging the random mobile devices for joining the MAC.

In this position paper, we have proposed the initial offering of idle resources by the volunteer mobile devices, for supporting the computation offloading for other co-located mobile devices, and nearly the equal amount of resources will be offered to the same devices for sharing their computational load in future. This is achieved by metering the consumed resources of a mobile device for supporting the computation offloading for neighbouring peer devices and earning the nearly equal amount of resources so that the device can use the earned resources for offloading its computation in future. However, it is the reliability of the metering and awarding system that motivates the volunteer devices for joining the MAC and in this paper, we have presented the blockchain for the reliable computation offloading in MAC.

Blockchain is already there for tackling the trust management issue among the independently operating entities [4]. However, to the best of our knowledge, no one has used the blockchain for establishing trust among the voluntarily collaborating mobile devices of MAC. We have not only mapped the blockchain concepts for managing trust among the random mobile devices of MAC but also identified new research directions that can be focused for improving the proposed integration of blockchain and MAC.

Upcoming section two elaborates the importance of MAC and the challenge of trust establishment associated with it. Section three explains the features of blockchain that can be employed for tackling the trust establishment challenge of of MAC. Section four elaborates some of the related work and last section concludes this paper along with some future research directions.

2   Importance of Mobile Ad-hoc Cloud and Its Challenge of Trust Establishment

With the exponential growth in the capabilities of mobile devices in last decade, efforts have been made to exploit the under-utilized resources of powerful mobile devices. MAC is an effective way of collecting the resources of multiple independently operating co-located mobile devices and capitalize the collected resources for distributing the computational load of few of the neighbouring mobile devices. This section explains the importance of MAC by differentiating the horizontal resource sharing in MAC and the vertical resource sharing of fog/cloud. It also

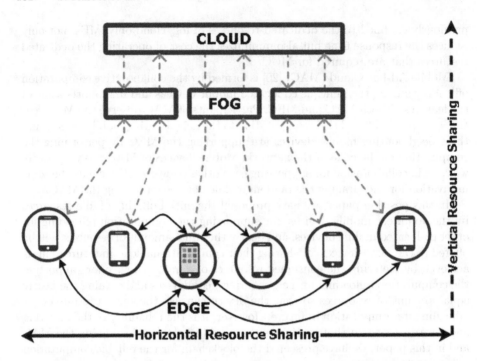

Fig. 1. Horizontal resource sharing in MAC vs vertical resource sharing

elaborates the need for trust establishment among the independently operating
co-located mobile devices of MAC.

Figure 1 contains a mobile device running multiple applications and is interested in reducing its resource consumption along with the reduction in response
time of CPU intensive tasks. Mentioned mobile device has two options available
to offload computation by vertical resource sharing or horizontal resource sharing. Dotted lines in Fig. 1 are referring to the option of vertical resource sharing
while solid lines are representing the horizontal resource sharing option. In case
of vertical resource sharing, mobile device will first offload the computation to
the nearby fog node. If the fog node has enough resources available for performing the required computation then it will not involve the cloud computing layer.
However, if more computational resources are required then the computation
will be further offloaded to the cloud computing layer.

In case of horizontal resource sharing, the mentioned mobile device will not
involve the fog computing layer and will only consider the neighbouring mobile
devices for offloading its computation. Hence, all the participating mobile devices
formulate another computing layer at the edge of the network, known as the
Mobile Ad-hoc Cloud (MAC) computing layer. Following is the comparison of
horizontal resource sharing in MAC with the vertical resource sharing option.

Operational Cost of vertical resource sharing is greater than the cost of horizontal resource sharing because fog/cloud computing layers are based on
dedicated resources while co-located mobile devices of MAC only offer their
idle resources for horizontal resource sharing.

Scalability of horizontal resource sharing is more than the vertical resource sharing because the number of machines in cloud can rarely reach up to few hundred-thousands, number of fog nodes can reach up to few millions while billions of edge nodes are currently operating [1]. Moreover, in case of MAC, every new coming mobile device also serves as an addition to the overall MAC resources and it ensures the scalability of horizontal resource sharing.

Response Time will be less for horizontal resource sharing as compare to the vertical resource sharing because for vertical resource sharing, both fog and cloud nodes are not hosted closer to the mobile devices whereas for the horizontal resource sharing, neighbouring mobile devices are co-located to the device device interested in offloading and it results in the reduction of response time.

.Trust establishment is not very crucial for the dedicated resources based vertical resource sharing in fog/cloud computing layers. However, it is required for the horizontal resource sharing because of the high churn rate of participating devices. Churn rate [9] can be defined as the rate of mobile devices leaving the MAC. High churn rate results in the higher number of stranger devices participating in the MAC. Blockchain ensures the reliable collaboration among the strange devices and its integration with MAC is discussed in next section.

3 Blockchain: An Enabler for Trust Establishment in Mobile Ad-hoc Cloud

Blockchain [18] has already been proven as the perfect solution for removing dependency on a central entity and distributing the authority among multiple independently distributed entities. Bitcoin is the first and most popular application of blockchain [12]. There are many important features in blockchain that makes it unique and effective in comparison to other application development techniques. In this section, we have elaborated the strengths of blockchain that can be used for tackling the trust establishment challenge of MAC.

3.1 Blockchain and Its Integration with MAC

Blockchain is a tamper proof distributed ledger and following are some of its important features that can be integrated within MAC to ensures the reliable computation offloading within independently operating mobile devices of MAC.

Transparency through shared ledger. Shared ledger is the main feature of blockchain and it is also important for supporting transparent coordination among multiple participating devices of MAC. Miners are the devices that ensure the propagation of updated ledger among all the participants of MAC. This shared ledger will contain the metering and awarding details against each participant which not only gain the trust of participants but also ensures the transparency. This will also incentivize the more devices to join the MAC equipped with proposed computation offloading scheme.

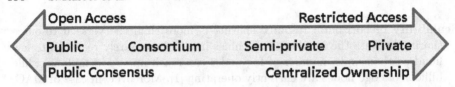

Fig. 2. Classification of blockchain networks based on the ownership and access

Public blockchain network. Miners are the devices that control the growth of blockchain using consensus [14]. Based on the assignment of mining rights, blockchain networks can be classified into four different categories [13], of public, private, consortium and semi-private (compared in Fig. 2). We are proposing the public blockchain for integration with MAC so that any mobile device can join or leave the network and it will help in establishing a transparent and open system.

Proof of Existence (PoE) ensures the data integrity without sacrificing its privacy [3]. This is achieved by passing the original data to a one-way hashing algorithm and using its output for representing the original data. Many blockchain projects [8,17] are already using it for various use cases especially for storing the sensitive information on blockchain.

Trust through consensus algorithm. It is really important to establish the trust among the mutually cooperating mobile devices of MAC. Miners of blockchain uses the consensus algorithm [23] for automatically establishing the consensus against any conflicting situation, without involving any central authority. Thus consensus algorithms help in making system more reliable and temper-proof. Proof of Work (PoW) [7] is the first consensus algorithm which has been used in the first application of blockchain known as bitcoin. However, it consumes a lot of energy and therefore, many other variants of consensus algorithms (like proof-of-stake [10], proof-of-reputation [6] etc. [16]) have been successfully adopted in the industry.

3.2   Three Generations of Blockchain for Each of the Three Phases of Data Value Chain

Data value chain helps in making decisions from the data and it is categorized into three broader phases of data discovery, data integration and data exploitation [11]. Different blockchain protocols and platforms are targeting each of these phases and existing blockchain tools can be categorized into three generations, targeting each of the phases of data value chain. However, most of the existing blockchain platforms belong to the first two generations and thus the blockchain community is mostly focused on the first two phases of the data value chain. Next is the description of three phases of data value chain along with the blockchain solutions targeting each of these phases. This discussion will help in understanding the proposed integration of blockchain and MAC with reference to the existing blockchain solutions (Fig. 3).

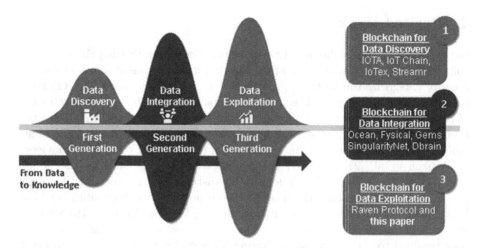

Fig. 3. Three generations of blockchain tools for three phases of data value chain

Data Discovery is the first phase of data value chain and is only concerned with the data. First generation of blockchain tools focuses on this phase by efficiently collecting the data from different devices or sources. IOTA[1], IoTChain[2], IoTex[3] and Streamr[4] are some of the blockchain projects that are targeting the first phase of data value chain.

Data integration is the second phase of data value chain and it covers the curation of data by integrating it from different data streams or sources. Second generation of blockchain solutions are targeting this phase of data value chain. Ocean Protocol[5], SingularityNet[6], Fysical[7], Gems[8] and Dbrain[9] are few of the blockchain solutions that provides that integration and supports this second phase of data value chain.

Data Exploitation is the third phase of data value chain and is focused on the analysis of data. Currently a protocol named as Raven[10] is targeting this third phase of data value chain. However, it is just in a proposal yet and no operational details are available. Moreover, Raven is only confined to the collaborative computation for deep learning. However, our proposed integration of blockchain and MAC can be used for any type of CPU intensive tasks including the computation for deep learning.

---

[1] https://iota.org/.
[2] https://iotchain.io/.
[3] https://iotex.io/.
[4] https://streamr.com/.
[5] https://oceanprotocol.com/.
[6] https://singularitynet.io/.
[7] https://fysical.org/.
[8] https://gems.org/.
[9] https://dbrain.io/.
[10] https://ravenprotocol.com/.

4   Related Work

Incentive based approaches are already in practice for motivating the mutually collaborating participants. Most of the existing incentive based solutions can be broadly categorized in to three groups viz. (1) reputation based [22], (2) reciprocity based [2] and credit based [24]. This paper also falls under the category of credit based incentive solutions as we are proposing to award the computation in return to the resource consumption that was previously done by the same mobile device for supporting the computation offloading of other MAC devices.

Ashkan et al. [21] proposed the computation sharing between the nodes of fog layer. However, it was done without distributing the authority through blockchain. There is a blockchain based Raven protocol(See Footnote 10) which is trying to accomplish the computation sharing for deep learning. However, it is just a proposal yet and no operational details are available. Moreover, it is only confined to the computation sharing for deep learning while our proposed integration of blockchain and MAC can be used for sharing computation for any type of tasks.

5   Conclusion and Future Work

This paper is focused on incentivizing the co-located mobile devices to share their resources for supporting the computation offloading for each other. Transparent metering and auditing is required for gaining the trust of the participating mobile devices and therefore, we have proposed the integration of blockchain and MAC for establishing the trust among the participating devices of MAC. Following are some of the research areas that can be focused for improving the proposed integration of blockchain and MAC.

Consensus algorithm. Proof of Work (PoW) is the consensus algorithm used in bitcoin, the most popular application of blockchain. However, the PoW consumes alot of energy and there are many alternative consensus algorithms available that offers different set of features along with less energy consumption. Therefore, extensive experiments must be conducted for finding the most appropriate consensus algorithm for MAC.

Miner selection. Miner is a machine that runs the consensus algorithm and controls the growth of blockchain. In order to establish a fully distributed global network of blockchain enabled MAC, few of the mobile devices should also serve as miners. A scheduling algorithm must be implemented for ensuring the optimal selection of miner based on the peer ranking algorithm.

Peer ranking algorithm. A peer ranking algorithm must be developed to rank the participating mobile devices based on their available resources. This algorithm will help in deciding how much computation load can be shifted to any particular device.

SLOs for awarding computation. Proper SLOs (Service Level Objectives) must be defined to ensure the transparent awarding of computation against the shared resources of a mobile device.

ACL instead of PoE. Our proposed integration of MAC and blockchain is based on a public blockchain network which works similar to the bitcoin network and allows anyone to join or leave the network at any time. Considering the open nature of public blockchain network, PoE is proposed for preserving the privacy of data of participating devices. However, ACL (Access Control List) [25] can also be applied for securing data within the members of the blockchain network. Hence, PoE can also be replaced with ACL to provide the fine-grained control of data stored in distributed ledger of blockchain.

Reliable data analytics. A validating system must be incorporated within the blockchain based MAC for confirming the accuracy of results submitted by the participating mobile devices. It will help in accomplishing the reliable data analytics through MAC.

Acknowledgment. The present work was undertaken in the context of the "Self-OrganizatioN towards reduced cost and eNergy per bit for future Emerging radio Technologies" with contract number 734545. The project has received research funding from the H2020-MSCA-RISE-2016 European Framework Program.

References

1. Afonso, J.: Edge computing: learn to delegate—octo talks! January 2018. https:// blog.octo.com/en/edge-computing-learn-to-delegate/). Accessed 8 Apr 2018
2. Cohen, B.: Incentives build robustness in bittorrent. In: Workshop on Economics of Peer-to-Peer systems, vol. 6, pp. 68–72 (2003)
3. Dasu, T., Kanza, Y., Srivastava, D.: Unchain your blockchain. In: Proceedings of Symposium on Foundations and Applications of Blockchain, vol. 1, pp. 16–23 (2018)
4. Dorri, A., Steger, M., Kanhere, S.S., Jurdak, R.: Blockchain: a distributed solution to automotive security and privacy. IEEE Commun. Mag. **55**(12), 119–125 (2017)
5. Fernando, N., Loke, S.W., Rahayu, W.: Mobile cloud computing: a survey. Future Gener. Comput. Syst. **29**(1), 84–106 (2013)
6. Gai, F., Wang, B., Deng, W., Peng, W.: Proof of reputation: a reputation-based consensus protocol for peer-to-peer network. In: Pei, J., Manolopoulos, Y., Sadiq, S., Li, J. (eds.) DASFAA 2018, Part II. LNCS, vol. 10828, pp. 666–681. Springer, Cham (2018). https://doi.org/10.1007/978-3-319-91458-9_41
7. Gervais, A., Karame, G.O., Wüst, K., Glykantzis, V., Ritzdorf, H., Capkun, S.: On the security and performance of proof of work blockchains. In: Proceedings of the 2016 ACM SIGSAC Conference on Computer and Communications Security, pp. 3–16. ACM (2016)
8. Gipp, B., Meuschke, N., Gernandt, A.: Decentralized trusted timestamping using the crypto currency bitcoin (2015). arXiv preprint: arXiv:1502.04015
9. Kang, X., Wu, Y.: Incentive mechanism design for heterogeneous peer-to-peer networks: a stackelberg game approach. IEEE Trans. Mob. Comput. **14**(5), 1018–1030 (2015)
10. Kiayias, A., Russell, A., David, B., Oliynykov, R.: Ouroboros: a provably secure proof-of-stake blockchain protocol. In: Katz, J., Shacham, H. (eds.) CRYPTO 2017, Part I. LNCS, vol. 10401, pp. 357–388. Springer, Cham (2017). https://doi.org/ 10.1007/978-3-319-63688-7_12

11. Miller, H.G., Mork, P.: From data to decisions: a value chain for big data. IT Prof. **15**(1), 57–59 (2013)
12. Nakamoto, S.: Bitcoin: a peer-to-peer electronic cash system (2008)
13. Neisse, R., Steri, G., Nai-Fovino, I.: A blockchain-based approach for data account-ability and provenance tracking. In: Proceedings of the 12th International Conference on Availability, Reliability and Security, p. 14. ACM (2017)
14. Pilkington, M.: 11 blockchain technology: principles and applications. In: Research Handbook on Digital Transformations, p. 225 (2016)
15. Porambage, P., Okwuibe, J., Liyanage, M., Ylianttila, M., Taleb, T.: Survey on multi-access edge computing for internet of things realization (2018). arXiv preprint: arXiv:1805.06695
16. Sankar, L.S., Sindhu, M., Sethumadhavan, M.: Survey of consensus protocols on blockchain applications. In: 2017 4th International Conference on Advanced Computing and Communication Systems (ICACCS), pp. 1–5. IEEE (2017)
17. Snow, P., Deery, B., Lu, J., Johnston, D., Kirby, P.: Factom business processes secured by immutable audit trails on the blockchain. Whitepaper, Factom, November 2014
18. Underwood, S.: Blockchain beyond bitcoin. Commun. ACM **59**(11), 15–17 (2016)
19. Yannuzzi, M., Milito, R., Serral-Gracià, R., Montero, D., Nemirovsky, M.: Key ingredients in an IoT recipe: fog computing, cloud computing, and more fog computing. In: 2014 IEEE 19th International Workshop on Computer Aided Modeling and Design of Communication Links and Networks (CAMAD), pp. 325–329. IEEE (2014)
20. Yaqoob, I., Ahmed, E., Gani, A., Mokhtar, S., Imran, M., Guizani, S.: Mobile ad hoc cloud: a survey. Wirel. Commun. Mob. Comput. **16**(16), 2572–2589 (2016)
21. Yousefpour, A., Ishigaki, G., Gour, R., Jue, J.P.: On reducing IoT service delay via fog offloading. IEEE Internet of Things J. (2018)
22. Zhang, Y., van der Schaar, M.: Reputation-based incentive protocols in crowdsourc-ing applications. In: 2012 Proceedings IEEE INFOCOM, pp. 2140–2148. IEEE (2012)
23. Zheng, Z., Xie, S., Dai, H., Chen, X., Wang, H.: An overview of blockchain technology: architecture, consensus, and future trends. In: 2017 IEEE International Congress on Big Data (BigData Congress), pp. 557–564. IEEE (2017)
24. Zhong, S., Chen, J., Yang, Y.R.: Sprite: a simple, cheat-proof, credit-based system for mobile ad-hoc networks. In: Twenty-Second Annual Joint Conference of the IEEE Computer and Communications, INFOCOM 2003. IEEE Societies, vol. 3, pp. 1987–1997. IEEE (2003)
25. Zhu, Y., Qin, Y., Gan, G., Shuai, Y., Chu, W.C.C.: TBAC: transaction-based access control on blockchain for resource sharing with cryptographically decentralized authorization. In: 2018 IEEE 42nd Annual Computer Software and Applications Conference (COMPSAC), pp. 535–544. IEEE (2018)

Communication Reliability and Protocols

CFDAMA-IS: MAC Protocol
for Underwater Acoustic Sensor Networks

Wael Gorma$^{(\boxtimes)}$ ⓘ, Paul Mitchell ⓘ, and Yuriy Zakharov ⓘ

Department of Electronic Engineering, University of York,
Heslington, York YO10 5DD, UK
{wmg503,wmg,paul.mitchell,yury.zakharov}@york.ac.uk
www.york.ac.uk/electronic-engineering/research/communication-technologies/

Abstract. This paper is concerned with coordinating underwater transmissions of acoustic sensor nodes. The use of acoustic waves to communicate underwater poses challenges to the functionality of Medium Access Control protocols. Long propagation delay and limited channel bandwidth are some of these challenges, which place severe constraints on the trade-off between end-to-end delay and achievable channel utilisation. The Combined Free and Demand Assignment Multiple Access (CFDAMA) protocol is known to significantly enhance the delay/utilisation performance. However, CFDAMA will suffer from long round trip delays and inefficient utilisation of its frames if it is implemented in medium and deep water. The major contribution of this paper is a new approach, namely CFDAMA with Intermediate Scheduler (CFDAMA-IS), to efficiently use CFDAMA in underwater environments. The paper compares these two protocols in typical underwater scenarios. It is shown that the proposed approach significantly reduces mean end-to-end delay and enhances channel utilisation.

Keywords: Underwater Acoustic Networks · Medium Access Control

1 Introduction

Underwater Acoustic Networks (UANs) are the enabling technology for a wide range of applications. Monitoring of the underwater environment using sensor nodes is an example of particular interest in this paper. Figure 1 illustrates a typical example of a centralised UAN. The node placed near the sea surface is called a surface node, or gateway. It provides a high-speed connection to the terrestrial world. Sensor nodes are deployed at depth and called seabed nodes. Seabed nodes are designed to communicate acoustically with the gateway. Use of acoustic waves in underwater networks poses extreme challenges to the functionality of Medium Access Control (MAC) protocols. Long propagation delay

The work of P. Mitchell and Y. Zakharov is partly supported by the UK Engineering and Physical Sciences Research Council (EPSRC) through the Grants EP/P017975/1 and EP/R003297/1.

V. Sucasas et al. (Eds.): BROADNETS 2018, LNICST 263, pp. 191–200, 2019.
https://doi.org/10.1007/978-3-030-05195-2_19

and limited channel bandwidth are some of these challenges, which place constraints on striking a balance between network end-to-end delay and channel utilisation [3]. Contention-based MAC protocols are inefficient underwater [1]. Reservation-based protocols, for example, exhibit poor channel utilisation due to the long waiting time needed to establish an acoustic link underwater. Carrier Sense Multiple Access (CSMA) techniques also have poor delay/utilisation performance in UANs due to substantial guard intervals required to accurately sense channels with long and variable propagation delays [5]. Frequency Division Multiple Access (FDMA) [14] and Code Division Multiple Access (CDMA) [11] are less common compared with Time Division Multiple Access (TDMA). FDMA was tested in the Seaweb project [13]. The results were that inefficient use of the bandwidth and high vulnerability to multipath fading were reported. CDMA has some advantages over FDMA. It is not as susceptible to frequency-selective fading because each node can use the entire available bandwidth. However, in practice, the cost associated with these advantages is a decline in the data rate. Achieving low cross-correlation between codes in the underwater environment requires long codes. This would extensively reduce the effective data rates of UAN modems, typically operating at low data rates [15]. TDMA and TDMA-based protocols can easily adjust the number of orthogonal channels, and allocate variable data rates by just changing the number of time slots assigned to a particular node [5]. To improve deterministic schedule-based TDMA methods, contention-based and TDMA-based MAC protocols are combined [1]. They are classified as Adaptive TDMA where capacity is usually assigned on demand. In [3], the following three capacity assignment strategies were examined underwater. Demand Assignment is shown to have much greater tolerance to increasing channel load, but with longer delay. Free Assignment offers close to its theoretical minimum end-to-end delay, but only at only low channel loads. The Combined Free and Demand Assignment Multiple Access (CFDAMA) protocol combines the two latter protocols. CFDAMA is shown to minimise end-to-end delay and maximise channel utilisation, especially for densely populated long-range networks. However, CFDAMA suffers from long round trip delays due to the position of the surface node (the scheduler) that is placed almost site-depth above the seabed nodes. In other words, the distance between the scheduler and the seabed nodes is almost equal to the distance between the surface and the bottom of the underwater site where the network is deployed. This approach to implementing CFDAMA is to deterministically emulate the implementation of CFDAMA in geostationary satellite systems, for which CFDAMA is originally designed [8]. Moreover, the CFDAMA frames [3] are not utilised efficiently underwater. In the satellite scenario data packets need to be transmitted on the downlink frame [6]. This is not the case in the underwater scenario where all data packets are transmitted to the gateway.

The major contribution of this paper is a modification of CFDAMA, exploiting its advantages and overcoming its disadvantages in underwater scenarios. The new protocol is named CFDAMA with Intermediate Scheduler (CFDAMA-IS). The scheduler does not need to be at the surface node as it could operate at

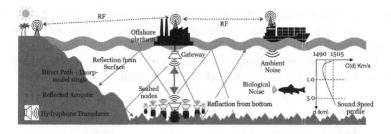

Fig. 1. Underwater acoustic network example

an additional intermediate node that can be placed anywhere near the seabed nodes to reduce round trip delays. This requires a change to the structure of the CFDAMA frames. The proposed approach significantly reduces the average round trip time required for making requests and receiving their acknowledgements and as a result, enhances overall delay/utilisation performance. Riverbed Modeller [4] was used in this paper to investigate CFDAMA-IS.

2   CFDAMA-IS Protocol

Detailed discussion on CFDAMA can be found in [3, 7, 9]. CFDAMA combines two capacity assignment strategies: free assignment and demand assignment. The major advantage of the CFDAMA protocol is that it exploits the contention-less nature of free assignment and the effectiveness of demand assignment in achieving high channel utilisation with a minimum end-to-end delay of only 1.5 surface hops. A surface hop is equivalent to a round trip from seabed nodes to the surface node. This combination can optimise the balance between the end-to-end delay and channel utilisation. However, when applied underwater, CFDAMA has two drawbacks:

- It will suffer from long round trip delays, proportional to the 1.5 surface hops, between the seabed nodes and their transmission coordinator since the scheduler operates at the surface node. Hence, locating the scheduler surface-to-bottom apart from its sensor nodes will extensively reduce CFDAMA performance in coordinating their transmissions.
- Utilising the CFDAMA downlink frame [6] without any adaptation to the underwater scenario will cause significant waste in the slots assigned to transmit data on the downlink frames.

The CFDAMA-IS scheme works in a more efficient way by minimising the round trip delay. The centralised scheduler, required by CFDAMA, does not need to be at the surface node to establish the communication links and coordinate transmissions of seabed nodes. In CFDAMA-IS, a node close to seabed nodes works as both a scheduler and a handover station to relay data packets to the gateway, used to act as the scheduler in the original CFDAMA [3]. CFDAMA-IS requires a change in the structure and use of the two CFDAMA frames to a more efficient exploitation as it is explained in the next section. As shown in Fig. 2 the time of a round trip was reduced significantly, and hence, the time needed to request capacity, receive its acknowledgement and transmit a packet is much less than one surface hop and a half. Other than that, CFDAMA-IS is implemented in a similar way as CFDAMA as explained in [3].

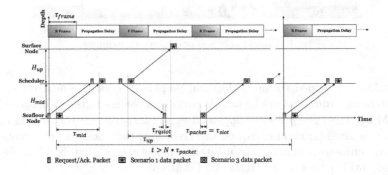

Fig. 2. CFDAMA-IS frame timing

2.1 CFDAMA-IS Frames Structure

Two frames are needed to implement CFDAMA-IS. As shown in Fig. 3, the forward frame (from the scheduler to the seabed nodes and to the surface node) and the return frame (from seabed nodes to the scheduler). Both frames are made up of two segments; a data slot segment plus either a segment of request slots in the case of return frame or a corresponding acknowledgement slot segment in the case of the forward frame. Date slots are allocated to nodes either as free assigned slots (F) or demand assigned slots (D). An appropriate request segment is inserted into the return frame for nodes to make capacity requests if needed. The forward frame is delayed with respect to the return frame by a period named the Forward Frame Delay to allow the request packets received in the return frame to be immediately processed and acknowledged with assignments in the forward frame. During the forward frame, the intermediate scheduler essentially does two jobs: sending acknowledgements of allocated slots to seabed nodes and successively relaying data packets to the gateway.

2.2 CFDAMA-IS Delay Analysis

The approach here is not to develop an exact CFDAMA-IS end-to-end delay model, but to develop a model that will incorporate those dominant factors which contribute significantly in determining the average end-to-end delay of packets. The delay caused by queuing was not involved here not only for simplicity but because of the fact that in scenarios with Poisson traffic and a relatively large number of nodes, queuing is not significant. Each successfully received packet

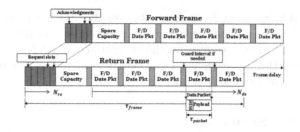

Fig. 3. CFDAMA-IS frame structures

must have gone through one of three possible scenarios. Scenario 1, in which packets get through by the use of free assigned slots. Scenario 2, in which a packet succeeds via a slot requested for a previous packet from the same node, and Scenario 3 in which a packet succeeds via a slot requested and granted for itself. Therefore, a packet's average end-to-end delay will depend on the scenario it experiences. Looking at the frames' timing depicted in Fig. 2 and considering the behaviour in Scenario 1, the mean end-to-end delay $E[D_{eted}]$ experienced by a packet arriving at an empty seabed node's queue is the combination of three terms:

$$E[D_{eted}] \approx \frac{N\tau_{slot}}{2} + 2\tau_{packet} + (\tau_{up} + \tau_{mid}) \tag{1}$$

The first term represents the average time a packet needs to wait until the next transmission slot, where N is the number of seabed nodes and τ_{slot} is the data slot duration. The second term is related to the time needed for the packet transmission at the seabed node and the reception at the surface node which is dependent on the packet duration τ_{packet}. The third term accounts for the aggregate propagation delay which comprises τ_{mid} (the time needed for a seabed packet to travel to/from the mid scheduler), and τ_{up} (the time needed to travel to the surface node). At high channel load values, nodes demand more capacity and therefore have to make a larger number of capacity requests more frequently. The protocol then will run with a much higher proportion of demand assigned slots (Scenario 3) causing an increase in the delay for packet transmissions. Incorporating the frame duration τ_{frame}, the mean end-to-end delay of Scenario 3 can be expressed as follows:

$$E[D_{eted}] \approx \frac{\tau_{frame}}{2} + 3\tau_{packet} + \tau_p$$
$$\tau_{frame} = N_{ds}\tau_{slot} + N_{rs}\tau_{rqt.slot} \tag{2}$$

$$\tau_p = \begin{cases} 3\tau_{mid} + \tau_{up}, & \text{CFDAMA-IS} \\ 3(\tau_{mid} + \tau_{up}), & \text{CFDAMA} \end{cases}$$

It is clear from Eq. (2) that the aggregate propagation delay τ_p that CFDAMA-IS experiences is $2\tau_{up}$ less than that of CFDAMA. This means that the demand assignment in CFDAMA-IS can handle capacity requests faster than it does in CFDAMA. Scenario 2 will dominate over the other two scenarios. Based on the state of the seabed nodes' queues, the average end-to-end delay will be gradually moving from its two extremes, i.e. the low extreme, which is experienced during Scenario 1 and the high extreme, which experienced during Scenario 3. Table 1 identifies the remainder of the parameters.

3   Simulation Scenarios

3.1   Underwater Acoustic Channel Using Riverbed Modeller

Riverbed Modeller (RM) [4] is a network protocol design and simulation tool, which has been used in this study to model the underwater acoustic channel. A number of its pipeline stages, shown in Fig. 4, have been modified to reflect underwater propagation mechanisms. The pipeline stages are primarily designed for the radio channel, but they can be customised to implement other types of wireless communication links. At least four stages, the shaded blocks in Fig. 4, had to be modified. For a large number of applications, the average speed of sound in water has been considered to be 1500 m/s [18]. The Thorp model [17] is commonly used to work out the absorption coefficient from which the total transmission loss is estimated as well as the received power. The undersea ambient noise is very often predicted using a set of empirical equations [16]. In this work, the modified pipeline stages are the propagation delay (stage 5), the background noise (stage 9), and the received power (stage 7) with accordance to the average speed of sound underwater, predicted underwater ambient noise using equations in [16], and estimated underwater received power using the Throp model. Based on these models RM calculates signal to noise ratio (SNR) and Bit Error Rate (BER) values. Depending on these BER values the receiver decides whether to accept or ignore a received packet.

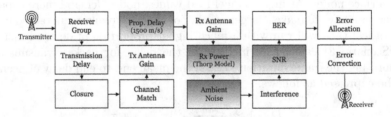

Fig. 4. Riverbed-based underwater acoustic channel

3.2   Network Topology and Data Traffic Model

The CFDAMA-IS specification does not need to assume any predefined information about the network topology or the number of nodes. The scheduling in CFDAMA is mainly based on the number of active nodes and propagation delays. Sensor nodes in the simulated network topology are distributed randomly, to cover an area of $500\,\text{m} \times 500\,\text{m}$. They are placed at two different depths $4\,\text{km}$ and $500\,\text{m}$ centrally below the IS node which is positioned above them at $500\,\text{m}$ and $100\,\text{m}$ depth respectively. The surface node is centralised above the coverage area. These two different depths are selected to reflect on the performance of CFDAMA-IS in two different underwater environments.

The Poisson model [2] is the traditional data traffic model in UANs. At every seabed node, packets are generated independently based on an exponentially distributed inter-arrival time. The mean inter-arrival time λ for each traffic source is worked out with regard to the data carrying capacity of the channel using $\lambda = \frac{T_{frame}}{N_{ds}} \times \frac{N}{G}$. Offered load G is measured in Erlangs [12]. The maximum channel utilisation is determined by observing when the end-to-end delay values reach a specific limit. The simulation parameters are listed in Table 1. These parameters are chosen to be within the range of operating parameters of current commercial modems, for example, the EvoLogics S2CR 15/27 modem [10].

Table 1. Simulation parameters

Attribute	Value	Attribute	Value
H_{up} (see Fig. 2)	3.5 km and 400 m	τ_{slot} (date slot duration)	6.6 ms (64 bit)
H_{mid} (see Fig. 2)	500 m and 100 m	τ_{rqslot} (req. slot duration)	0.83 ms (8 bit)
N (number of nodes)	300 and 20	N_{ds} (number of data slots)	32
Bandwidth	30 kHz	N_{rs} (number of request slots)	32
Data rate	9600 bps	G in Erlangs	0.1–1

4   Results

Figure 5 (a)(b)(c)(d) shows the mean end-to-end delay against a variety of channel load ranging from 0.1 to 1 Erlangs. The graphs are for the four capacity assignment strategies: free assignment, demand assignment, CFDAMA and CFDAMA-IS, with a network of 20 and 300 nodes (sparse and dense networks). To reflect on two scenarios (deep and medium depths), Fig. 5(a)(b) show simulation results for the 4000 m-depth scenario whereas Fig. 5(c)(d) show the 500 m-depth scenario. With a large number of nodes - Fig. 5(b)(d) - it can be seen that the mean end-to-end delay of the Free assignment strategy grows significantly, for example, from 3.8 s at 1% channel load to 7.35 s at 95% channel load in the scenario with 4000 m sea depth. The reason behind this is the long period between successive transmission slots allocated to each node due to the large number of nodes. On the other hand, at low channel loads, the results indicate that the free assignment strategy can provide small end-to-end delay values, approaching the minimum delay limit optioned from Eq. (1). These results show that under the condition of Poisson traffic and a sparse network (low traffic), the free assignment scheme can perform reasonably well. The results in all the cases indicate that the delay performance of demand assignment scheme is generally dominated by the

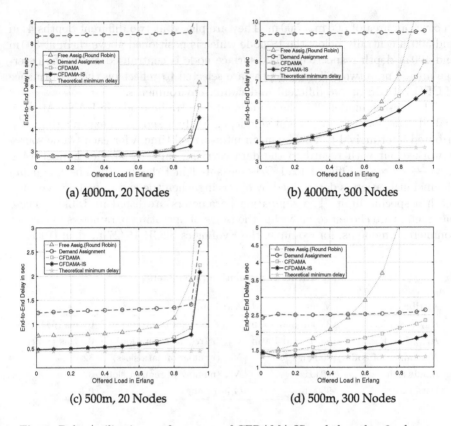

Fig. 5. Delay/utilisation performances of CFDAMA-IS and the other 3 schemes

fundamental lower boundary of 1.5 surface hops (7.860 s for 4000 m depth and 0.93 s for 500 m depth). Interestingly, the scheme shows a much slower increase in the mean end-to-end delay values over virtually the entire channel loads than free assignment. This proves the ability of the demand assignment scheme to support much higher channel load levels owing to the dynamic allocation of the available capacity based on instantaneous node requirements. The results, nevertheless, show a significant difference in the mean end-to-end delay compared to the free assignment strategy in all cases. In the 300-node scenario, for example in Fig. 5(b), the mean end-to-end delay of demand assignment ranges from 9.3 s at 1% channel load to 9.5 s at 95% channel load, which is on average greater than the mean end-to-end delay of free assignment.

The results also show that the CFDAMA algorithm consistently outperforms its two constituent schemes in both mean end-to-end delay and channel utilisation. CFDAMA is inherently adaptive to the variation in channel conditions; it exploits the contention-less nature of free assignment and the effectiveness of demand assignment in achieving high channel utilisation efficiency. More importantly, the results indicate that the CFDAMA-IS protocol has a significant advantage over the other three strategies in terms of both end-to-end delay and channel utilisation. Comparing with the other three schemes, CFDAMA-IS experiences the lowest mean end-to-end delay throughout almost all channel loads and number of nodes shown in the figures in all scenarios. The minimum end-to-end delay that CFDAMA-IS experiences in each scenario is at very low traffic loads when the majority of the slots are freely assigned. At high channel loads, the end-to-end delay increases steadily, but still less than the minimum delay limit of the CFDAMA scheme and its two constituent schemes. For example, as shown in Fig. 5(b), at a channel utilisation of 1% of the channel capacity, the minimum end-to-end delay is only 3.8 s, which is less than the minimum delay of demand assignment. At the highest channel load of 95%, the mean end-to-end delay is still the lowest at 6.4 s.

5 Conclusion

This paper proposes a new form of the CFDAMA protocol underwater. Two major changes have been made to CFDAMA as follows: Firstly, the CFDAMA scheduling node was repositioned from being near the sea surface to just above the seabed nodes. This leads to minimisation of round trip delays between seabed nodes and the scheduler. Secondly, the CFDAMA forward frame is exploited not only for transmitting acknowledgements from the surface node to seabed nodes, but also for relaying data packets to the gateway. Simulation results have shown that the CFDAMA-IS protocol offers excellent performance in dealing with the trade-off between end-to-end delay and channel utilisation for Poisson data traffic through water. The major advantage of the CFDAMA-IS protocol is the fact that it efficiently combines the contention-less nature of free assignment and the effectiveness of demand assignment in achieving high channel utilisation. In CFDAMA-IS, the minimum demand assignment delay bound of 1.5 surface hops is overcome, which results in a significant enhancement in the overall delay/utilisation performance. For a vertical channel with data rate of 9600 bit/s and up to a 4000 m depth/range with Poisson traffic offered by 20 and 300 nodes, CFDAMA-IS makes it possible to load the channel up to 95% of its capacity with a delay performance that is better than that of CFDAMA and far superior to the demand assignment scheme and more bounded than the free assignment scheme.

References

1. Akyildiz, I.F., Pompili, D., Melodia, T.: Underwater acoustic sensor networks: research challenges. Ad Hoc Netw. **3**(3), 257–279 (2005)
2. Frost, V.S., Melamed, B.: Traffic modeling for telecommunications networks. IEEE Commun. Mag. **32**(3), 70–81 (1994)
3. Gorma, W.M., Mitchell, P.D.: Performance of the combined free/demand assignment multiple access protocol via underwater networks. In: Proceedings of the International Conference on Underwater Networks and Systems, WUWNET 2017, pp. 5:1–5:2. ACM, New York (2017)

4. Hammoodi, I., Stewart, B., Kocian, A., McMeekin, S.: A comprehensive performance study of OPNET modeler for ZigBee wireless sensor networks. In: 3rd International Conference on Next Generation Mobile Applications, NGMAST 2009, pp. 357–362 (2009)

5. Heidemann, J., Stojanovic, M., Zorzi, M.: Underwater sensor networks: applications, advances and challenges. Phil. Trans. R. Soc. A **370**(1958), 158–175 (2012)

6. Mitchell, P.D., Grace, D., Tozer, T.C.: Comparative performance of the CFDAMA protocol via satellite with various terminal request strategies. In: Global Telecommunications Conference, GLOBECOM 2001, vol. 4, pp. 2720–2724. IEEE (2001)

7. Mitchell, P.D., Grace, D., Tozer, T.C.: Performance of the combined free/demand assignment multiple access protocol with combined request strategies via satellite. In: 12th IEEE International Symposium on PIMRC 2001, vol. 2, pp. F-90–F-94. IEEE (2001)

8. Mitchell, P.D.: Effective medium access control for geostationary satellite systems. Ph.D. thesis, University of York (2003)

9. Mohammed, J.I., Le-Ngoc, T.: Performance analysis of combined free/demand assignment multiple access (CFDAMA) protocol for packet satellite communications. In: IEEE International Conference on Communications, ICC 1994, SUPERCOMM/ICC 1994 Conference Record, Serving Humanity Through Communications, pp. 869–873. IEEE (1994)

10. Petrioli, C., Petroccia, R., Shusta, J., Freitag, L.: From underwater simulation to at-sea testing using the ns-2 network simulator. In: IEEE OCEANS 2011, pp. 1–9. IEEE (2011)

11. Pompili, D., Melodia, T., Akyildiz, I.F.: A cdma-based medium access control for underwater acoustic sensor networks. Trans. Wirel. Comm. **8**(4), 1899–1909 (2009)

12. Rappaport, T.S., et al.: Wireless Communications: Principles and Practice, vol. 2. Prentice Hall PTR, Upper Saddle River (1996)

13. Rice, J., et al.: Evolution of seaweb underwater acoustic networking. In: Oceans 2000 MTS/IEEE Conference and Exhibition, vol. 3, pp. 2007–2017 (2000)

14. Sozer, E.M., Stojanovic, M., Proakis, J.G.: Underwater acoustic networks. IEEE JOE **25**(1), 72–83 (2000)

15. Stojanovic, M., Freitag, L.: Multichannel detection for wideband underwater acoustic CDMA communications. IEEE J. Oceanic Eng. **31**(3), 685–695 (2006)

16. Stojanovic, M., Preisig, J.: Underwater acoustic communication channels: propagation models and statistical characterization. IEEE Commun. Mag. **47**(1), 84–89 (2009)

17. Thorp, W.H.: Deep-ocean sound attenuation in the sub-and low-kilocycle-per-second region. J. Acoust. Soc. Am. **38**(4), 648–654 (1965)

18. Wilson, W.D.: Speed of sound in sea water as a function of temperature, pressure, and salinity. J. Acoust. Soc. Am. **32**(6), 641–644 (1960)

Location-Aware MAC Scheduling in Industrial-Like Environment

Maurizio Rea[1,2]([⊠]), Domenico Garlisi[3], Héctor Cordobés[1],
and Domenico Giustiniano[1]

[1] IMDEA Networks Institute, Madrid, Spain
maurizio.rea@imdea.org
[2] University Carlos III of Madrid, Madrid, Spain
[3] CNIT and University of Palermo, Palermo, Italy

Abstract. We consider an environment strongly affected by the presence of metallic objects, that can be considered representative of an indoor industrial environment with metal obstacles. This scenario is a very harsh environment where radio communication has notorious difficulties, as metallic objects create a strong blockage component and surfaces are highly reflective. In this environment, we investigate how to dynamically allocate MAC resources in time to static and mobile users based on context awareness extracted from a legacy WiFi positioning system. In order to address this problem, we integrate our WiFi ranging and positioning system in the WiSHFUL architecture and then define a hypothesis test to declare if the link is in line-of-sight (LOS) or non-line-of-sight (NLOS) based on angular information derived from ranging and position information. We show that context information can help increase the network throughput in the above industrial-like scenario.

Keywords: MAC scheduler · Indoor localization system
Context awareness

1 Introduction

Pervasive positioning is a cornerstone to enable several data analytics and applications. While Location-Based Service (LBS) providers are ready to exploit new and better position information for data analytics for personalized services, the potential for networks applications of positioning data remains largely unleashed. Position could provide a much greater benefit to network applications than what done so far. In fact, localization may be exploited not only as a service offered to customers, but also in the network core to support anticipatory networking, enabling reliable mobile communications via advanced resource management policies and adaptive traffic engineering strategies. Last but not least, experimental evaluation in this research field is still in its early stage, as it is requires

V. Sucasas et al. (Eds.): BROADNETS 2018, LNICST 263, pp. 201–211, 2019.
https://doi.org/10.1007/978-3-030-05195-2_20

the integration of several network and positioning software and hardware components involving a large scientific and engineering effort. As a result, there is limited experimental understanding of what is possible to do coupling position and communication. Of particular interest for this paper is the medium access control (MAC) protocol, that serves a vital role in every network. It is directly responsible for controlling access to the shared communication resources. In most cases, the network designer does not know about the network conditions and has to assume that they may change during operation. The usual approach in most MAC protocols to handle unknown or changing conditions is to include some adaptation mechanism in order to adjust the operation to the actual network load and signal-to-noise ratio (for instance, using a different modulation scheme), and recover from failures in data transmission (for instance, detecting collisions). The objective of this work is to investigate how to dynamically allocate MAC resources in time to both static and mobile users based on context awareness extracted from a legacy WiFi positioning system. For our study, we consider an environment strongly affected by the presence of metallic objects, that can be considered representative of an industrial indoor environment with open spaces with metal obstacles. The scenario under study is a very harsh environment where radio communication has notorious difficulties. One of the key aspects is the fact that metallic objects create a strong blockage component, which must be taken into account for the MAC adaptation strategies. These types of environments are of particular interest with the advent of Industry 4.0 solutions to automate manufacturing technologies [3].

In order to address this problem, we first integrate our legacy ranging and positioning system [4] in the WiSHFUL architecture [6], which fully supports hybrid (centralized and distributed) control and network intelligence. We then define a hypothesis test to declare if the link is in line-of-sight (LOS) or non-line-of-sight (NLOS), and thus take effective actions in the allocation of MAC resources. Our preliminary experimental results show that this statistical angular information can help increase the network throughput in the above industrial-like scenario for static and mobile (robots) devices.

2 Motivation

This work targets the investigation and analysis of MAC scheduling strategies with static and mobile users operating in an industrial-like scenario (w.iLab.2 testbed[1] [1]). The environment under study is full of metal objects which block RF signals and cause strong reflections (impacting on the quality of the measurements). The problem we want to address in this work is whether location information can be used to optimize MAC scheduling decisions. The fundamental questions we want to investigate are:

– Can we improve network performance integrating positioning data in the MAC scheduler in mobile contexts?
– How well experiments can help us designing better MAC schedulers?

---

[1] http://doc.ilabt.imec.be/ilabt-documentation/.

– What gain is expected with respect to a classical approach without location and context knowledge, given that location information is far from perfect and it is subjected to position error?

In addition, there is very limited experimental work on MAC scheduling strategies that exploit a prototype location system. While this work does not provide a full answer to a vast topic, yet we believe it explores new directions of investigation.

3   System Architecture

As we aim to investigate how location information can help MAC protocols, we integrate our WiFi positioning system in the WiSHFUL architecture [6], which fully supports hybrid (centralized/distributed) control and network intelligence. The WiSHFUL control framework is provided as an open-source solution and it fully supports several type of devices, sensors and nodes wireless. The WiSH-FUL control framework is based on a two-tier architecture which enables local, global and hierarchical control programs, thus supporting dynamic aggregation of radio monitoring by different nodes and configuration parameters. Nodes can be monitored and controlled individually or in clusters, by exploiting control services devised to coordinate through Unified Program Interface (UPI) calls, a very convenient programming interface that abstracts from the physical device an thus allows to make controlling programs independent from the device brand, model or even technology. Another significant aspect of WiSHFUL is the aim in reproducibility of results, as every experiment is programatically controlled in its entirety, even robot paths. As such, by integrating the positioning system, we can create reproducible location-based experiments for MAC scheduling. WiSH-FUL integrates multiple experimentation platforms for which a software architecture devised to simplify MAC or PHY protocol prototyping was already available. In this work we use the provided Wireless MAC Processor (WMP) platform [7]. The WMP platform was developed exposing an API for controlling the driver, by enabling the possibility to specify the configuration parameters of the WiFi chipset in a declarative language. The API also supports a time-based channel access scheme based on functionality developed under the API to enable a Time-Division-Multiple Access (TDMA)-based scheme. This is performed by specifying the time intervals (slots) in which nodes, specifically packet flows, are allowed to transmit running the usual DCF scheme. The TDMA mechanism has been enhanced in this work to allow for finer scheduling decisions, as we will show next. **Control of TDMA resources allocation.** In order to dynamically allocate MAC resources based on context awareness, we implement both global and local control programs which make use of the WMP platform. The WMP implementation covers both the standard 802.11 CSMA/CA as well as TDMA access protocol or radio programs. For both protocols, communication occurs in the unlicensed 2.4 GHz band to unmodified target devices. In the TDMA radio program, the channel access is divided in periodic frames and each frame is divided in time slots. TDMA is a proven mechanism that can provide high throughput in high-dense environments. Each radio program can be activated after an explicit

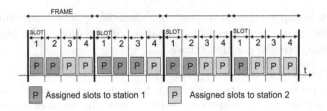

Fig. 1. WMP TDMA access scheme with pattern slots definition.

signaling from the control program and it receives parameters to configure channel access scheme. The TDMA radio program has three main parameters:

- TDMA_SUPER_FRAME_SIZE - Duration of periodic frames used for slot allocations in μs;
- TDMA_NUMBER_OF_SYNC_SLOT - Number of slots included in a super frame;
- TDMA_ALLOCATED_MASK_SLOT - Pattern of used slots in frame;

Figure 1 shows an example of 4 TDMA frames where two stations are active and each frame has 4 slots (pattern: "xxxx"). For instance, in the first frame, the TDMA_ALLOCATED_MASK_SLOT parameter of the station 1 is configured to use the slots 1 and 2 (pattern: "1100"), while the station 2 is configured to use the slots 3 and 4 (pattern: "0011"). The logic for activating the TDMA protocol and setting the relative mask pattern is embedded into the experiment control program.

4 Integration of Location System

In the following sections, we first review our legacy WiFi positioning system and then present our effort to integrate it in the WiSHFUL architecture. **Mobile Tracking System.** For the positioning system to help MAC-level decisions, we integrate our Time-of-Flight (ToF) based positioning system [4,5]. Our ToF-based positioning system uses COTS APs with customized firmware operating in the core of the 802.11 MAC state machine of a low-cost WiFi chipset. It can estimate the position of WiFi legacy devices. The distance from each AP to mobile targets is estimated with ToF two-way ranging measurements, taking advantage of DATA/ACK traffic exchange. Position estimates are then performed based on multi-lateration principle. The system is orchestrated by the Central Location Unit (CLU), which issues measurement rounds to the APs and generates traffic towards target devices. In our system, the APs are equipped with Broadcom WiFi chipsets that run our customized version of the 802.11 OpenFWWF firmware. ToF measurements are passed from the firmware to the open-source b43 driver running in the AP, and subsequently sent in a batch to the CLU. Details of the ranging technique and the overall system can be found in [4,5]. With these ToF ranges, the CLU estimates the distances to the

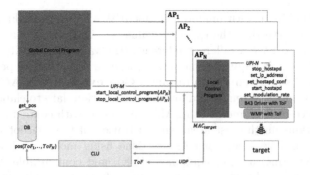

Fig. 2. System architecture: Positioning system integrated in the WiSHFUL framework

APs and the mobile position, and connects to a database where the results are stored, making the data available to location-based applications. **Details of the integration.** We integrate the positioning system to the WiSHFUL testbed (cf. Fig. 2):

- The CLU is our main process, which runs, separate from the APs, on a server. It computes position estimates based on the ToF ranging information obtained from the APs and stores it on a Database (DB), so that it can be exploited by third parties.
- Upon a command from the CLU, the APs send probe packets to the target and measures the response time, which is sent back to the CLU. These APs run the WMP firmware, which enables them to obtain this information and pre-filters out invalid measurements. This is a mandatory step as this system makes use of standard 802.11 messages, so it is needed to identify and process only those messages used for positioning.
- The target is associated to any of the ranging APs by means of a specific SSID common to the whole set of APs. Being connected to one of the APs does not keep the device from responding on the probes from the rest of APs.
- Once the CLU receives all the measurements, it runs a series of algorithms to generate position estimates for that target and instant, and stores it on the DB so it can be retrieved later on by any other entity. In our case, the context-aware MAC resource mechanism.
- We control the whole system by a Global Control Program (GCP) deployed in the same server as the CLU, and we run a Local Control Program (LCP) in each of the APs to handle the elements through Unified Programming Interface (UPI) calls [2].

Evaluation of Ranging Technique. We study the distribution of the raw ToF samples, considering the original OpenFWWF firmware used in past works [4], and the modified WMP firmware used in this work. In Fig. 3(a), we show the results for the original OpenFWWF firmware used in the AP. In Fig. 3(b), we show the results for the modified WMP firmware. For both tests, the target is a B43 WiFi chipset with unmodified OpenFWWF firmware. From Fig. 3(a) and 3(b), we observe that the expected value is shifted. This is a minor issue, as it just needs to have a different reference (the value we identify as distance zero). Nevertheless, it requires some recalibration actions that we perform making multiple tests at given known distance. **Context-aware MAC protocol.** Once the positioning system is laid out, we use location data to elaborate different performance measurements using MAC protocols with context awareness at different positions on the test area. An illustration of the concept is presented in Fig. 4. The mobile measurements are done using mobile nodes (Turtlebot II Robotic platforms) as user equipment (UE), and configurable AP that use Alixes boards. Here, the MAC resources are configured to make measurements in different scenarios. All the control is performed from a controlling function running on the server. On the map in Fig. 5, we depict the area of interest for the experiments, of about 11×22 m. We use AP_1 and AP_4 as context-aware MAC APs, and all five APs for positioning. AP_1 and AP_4 run a program which can adapt the MAC resources. **Metallic obstacle management.** We consider a system where the network has access to the estimated UE location. We also consider that the location of metallic objects in the environment is known and so each AP should avoid to transmit to a UE if it can anticipate that the UE is going behind a metallic blockage. The reason is that the link would be totally disrupted in these conditions. In order to make such as decision, in the ideal case of perfect location position, the AP should "draw a line" between the AP and the UE, and verify if the metallic blockage is in-between. Since noise and obstacles affect the positioning system, the only line between the AP and the estimated UE location does not ensure that the UE is affected by blockage. For this reason, it is convenient to *map position information, including the error, into angular information.* We consider a scenario with a fixed AP and a mobile UE. We assume a two dimensional Cartesian coordinate system. The AP position is known and equal to $\mathbf{p}^{AP} \in \mathbb{R}^{2 \times 1}$. The UE real and estimated positions are $\mathbf{p}^{UE} = P(x, y) \in \mathbb{R}^{2 \times 1}$ and $\hat{\mathbf{p}}^{UE} = \hat{P}(\hat{x}, \hat{y}) \in \mathbb{R}^{2 \times 1}$, respectively, where $\hat{x} = x + e_x$ and $\hat{y} = y + e_y$. The terms e_x and e_y represent the location errors on the x- and y-axis, respectively. We model the error as a bi-variate normal distribution, where the statistical processes e_x and e_y have no correlation, and that e_x and e_y have zero mean. We can compute the *unit vector of the direction* between the AP transmitting data and the estimated UE position as:

$$(\mathbf{p}^{AP} - \hat{\mathbf{p}}^{UE})^T / \|\mathbf{p}^{AP} - \hat{\mathbf{p}}^{UE}\|, \tag{1}$$

with the UE within the angular error of width 2θ based on trigonometric considerations, with

$$\theta = \sin^{-1}\left(\frac{\sqrt{e_x^2 + e_y^2}}{\|\mathbf{p}^{AP} - \hat{\mathbf{p}}^{UE}\|}\right). \tag{2}$$

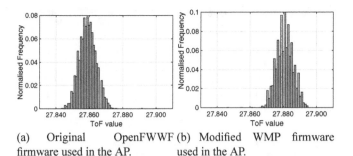

(a)   Original   OpenFWWF (b) Modified WMP firmware
firmware used in the AP.   used in the AP.

Fig. 3. Histogram of ToF values.

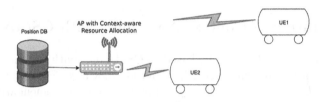

Fig. 4. High-level illustration to exploit context-aware decisions in the allocation of MAC resources.

We then introduce a simple criterion to infer the link state. Knowing the real position of the metallic obstacles, let us define the hypotheses H_1 and H_2 as:

$$\begin{cases} H_1 : \text{"LOS"} \\ H_2 : \text{"NLOS"} \end{cases}$$

The test is as follows. Accept H_2 if both conditions below are fulfilled:

- The position of an obstacle falls within the angular portion 2θ;
- The estimated distance $\hat{d} = \|\mathbf{p}^{AP} - \hat{\mathbf{p}}^{UE}\|$ is higher than the radius from the AP to the metallic object.

Stay with H_1 otherwise. Given the strong link quality degradation in presence of metallic blockage, we allocate the MAC resources only for those links that satisfies the hypothesis H_1 only. In this work, we consider a preset error of 3 m for our positioning system on the x and y axis, which represents fairly well the typical performance of our system observed in several scenarios [4]. The presence of more APs used for positioning guarantees that some of them is in LOS to the UE, which would guarantee fairly good location accuracy also in industrial-like scenario. This benefit would not be present directly computing angular information with phased array antennas with the AP communicating.

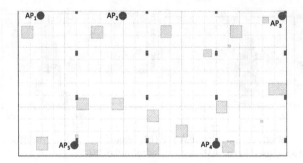

Fig. 5. Map of the testbed.

5 Exploitation of Context Awareness with CSMA/CA

The first scenario considers a MAC based on CSMA/CA with two mobile robots. We focus our attention on a specific scenario, shown in Fig. 6(a), where the positions of UE_1 (robot 15) and UE_2 (robot 13) are in movement with respect to the AP (alix02). The robots are initially positioned on the spots marked with a green cross. From this position, each robot requests access to the 802.11 network and a reliable link is established. The robots move along their given trajectories, and due to the environment (mainly metallic obstacles, marked on the map as yellow rectangles), from a given position and onwards the link quality decreases, drastically reducing the network throughput. To avoid this degradation we apply the method presented in Sect. 4 to allocate traffic only for links accepting the hypothesis H_1. Figure 6(b) shows the results in terms of network throughput, normalized with the respect to the maximum achieved throughput, along the 40-second UE_1 and UE_2 trajectories. Throughput is measured with the tool Iperf. Some time-aggregation effects may appear in the figure as the

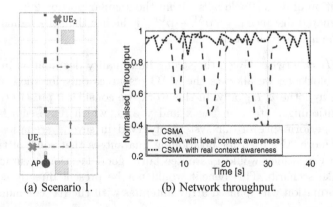

(a) Scenario 1.   (b) Network throughput.

Fig. 6. Allocation of MAC CSMA/CA resources in presence of blockage with different resources allocation strategies in Scenario 1. (Color figure online)

measurement cycles may not match each other. When using simple CSMA/CA, the performance presents a degradation in accordance with the radio link blockage. As we know the real position of the user along its trajectory (this is possible thanks to the knowledge of the actual position as provided by the high accurate Localization and Positioning Engine, LPE, engine in WiSHFUL), we can verify the performance of the algorithm in the ideal condition where the direct link for UE_2 and the AP is subject to blockage and without any error in the position estimation. In case the link is in a NLOS state, we stop allocating traffic for the target, so other UEs may use the AP capacity, therefore maintaining the network throughput constant (red solid line, TDMA with ideal context awareness). Next, we use the positioning system as a source of context awareness information to compare a real-world scenario against the previous ideal scenario. In this case, we use the angular estimation as input to decide whether the UE is in a zone of low network coverage. The overall performance (dotted black line, CSMA with real context awareness) in our experiment shows no difference between real and ideal results, suggesting that the positioning error is low enough for the link decision. In fact, pointing at the estimated position of the user and taking its angular error, we have that the real position is inside the angular error (UE_2 in Fig. 6(a)), and so we cluster the links as NLOS as the real case. **Exploitation of context awareness with TDMA allocation.** We then study a MAC-based on TDMA allocation in two different scenarios. Implementation-wise, in the latter cases we do not stop the traffic, but we allocate different time slots, using the implementation presented in Sect. 3. In particular, the control program configures the TDMA assigned slot based on context awareness extracted from the positioning system itself.

Two Target Devices. The second scenario is illustrated in Fig. 7(a) and it considers a MAC-based on TDMA allocation with one static and one mobile node. Specifically, UE_1 (robot 15) is fixed, while UE_2 (robot 13) is in movement with respect to the AP (alix02). We analyze the normalized network throughput along a 30-second trajectory. From Fig. 7(b), we observe that using simple TDMA with a fair (equality-wise) allocation of the resources (50%–50% with 2 nodes, blue dashed line), the performance presents a degradation in accordance with the radio link blockage. As stated before, if we are aware of the provided context information, we are able to avoid the overall degradation, therefore maintaining an optimal network throughput. The overall performance (dotted black line, TDMA with real context awareness) shows the throughput improvement compared to the simple-TDMA setting, but this time it shows some performance loss compared to the ideal case due to estimation error in the positioning. Yet, the gain with respect to a simple TDMA allocation of 50%–50% is evident from the figure.

Four Target Devices. The third and last scenario is illustrated in Fig. 8(a) and it considers a MAC-based on TDMA allocation with four mobile nodes. We analyze the normalized network throughput along 130-second trajectories.

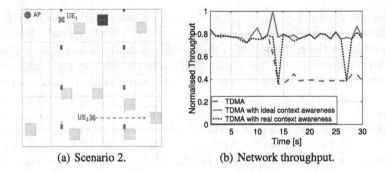

(a) Scenario 2.   (b) Network throughput.

Fig. 7. Allocation of MAC TDMA resources in presence of blockage with different resources allocation strategies in Scenario 2. (Color figure online)

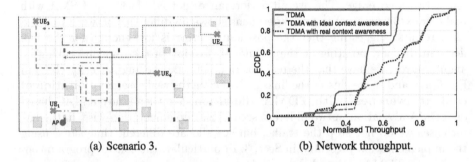

(a) Scenario 3.   (b) Network throughput.

Fig. 8. ECDF of the normalized network throughput for Scenario 3 with different MAC TDMA resources allocation strategies for scenario 3. (Color figure online)

We plot the Empirical Cumulative Distribution Function (ECDF) of the normalized network throughput in Fig. 8(b). We observe that using simple TDMA with a fair (equality-wise) allocation of the resources (25% for each node, blue line), the ECDF presents a maximum normalized throughput close to 0.7, which corresponds to the median value of TDMA with ideal context awareness. Also this time the dotted black line (TDMA with real context awareness) shows the throughput improvement compared to the simple-TDMA setting, and at the same time it shows some performance loss compared to the ideal case due to estimation error in the positioning.

6   Conclusion

The goal of this work was experimenting context-awareness capable MACs in industrial-like scenarios. Our WiFi positioning system has been integrated in the WiSHFUL testbed and we have elaborated simple MAC resource allocation strategies based on position estimations that effectively improve the performance of a network with high-load from stations at different positions and deployed in a harsh environment full of metallic objects and walls. The AP allocates the MAC resources depending on the estimated position of the mobile targets. We have shown the higher network performance of a context-aware strategy in presence of signal blockage from metals. While our results are encouraging, we stress that more studies should be conducted to understand how to exploit context information in diverse scenarios. Our metric is conservative and should be also improved to consider false positive detection of blockage. Yet we have proven that positioning mobile targets can already be beneficial in harsh environments and context data should be integrated in network protocol stack to optimize the overall network performance.

Acknowledgments. This work has been funded in part by the European Commission in the framework of the H2020 project WiSHFUL (Grant agreement no. 645274), and in part by the Madrid Regional Government through the TIGRE5-CM program (S2013/ICE-2919).

References

1. H2020 WiSHFUL project. http://www.wishful-project.eu
2. Kaminski, N.J., Moerman, I., Giannoulis, S., Zubow, A., Seskar, I., Choi, S.: Unified radio and network control across heterogeneous hardware platforms. In: ETSI Workshop on Future Radio Technologies: Air Interfaces, pp. 1–10 (2016)
3. Lee, J., Kao, H.A., Yang, S.: Service innovation and smart analytics for industry 4.0 and big data environment. Procedia Cirp **16**, 3–8 (2014)
4. Rea, M., Fakhreddine, A., Giustiniano, D., Lenders, V.: Filtering noisy 802.11 time-of-flight ranging measurements from commoditized wifi radios. IEEE/ACM Trans. Netw. **25**(4), 2514–2527 (2017). https://doi.org/10.1109/TNET.2017.2700430
5. Rea, M., Cordobés, H., Giustiniano, D.: Twins: Time-of-flight based wireless indoor navigation system. In: Microsoft Indoor Localization Competition – ACM/IEEE IPSN 2018 (2018)
6. Ruckebusch, P., et al.: A unified radio control architecture for prototyping adaptive wireless protocols. In: European Conference on Networks and Communications (EuCNC), pp. 58–63, June 2016. https://doi.org/10.1109/EuCNC.2016.7561005
7. Tinnirello, I., Bianchi, G., Gallo, P., Garlisi, D., Giuliano, F., Gringoli, F.: Wireless mac processors: programming mac protocols on commodity hardware. In: Proceedings IEEE INFOCOM, pp. 1269–1277, March 2012. https://doi.org/10.1109/INFCOM.2012.6195488

Distributed Fault-Tolerant Backup-Placement in Overloaded Wireless Sensor Networks

Gal Oren[1,2]([✉]), Leonid Barenboim[3], and Harel Levin[2,3]

[1] Department of Computer Science, Ben-Gurion University of the Negev,
P.O. Box 653, Be'er Sheva, Israel
orenw@post.bgu.ac.il
[2] Department of Physics, Nuclear Research Center-Negev,
P.O. Box 9001, Be'er-Sheva, Israel
harellevin@gmail.com
[3] Department of Mathematics and Computer Science,
The Open University of Israel, P.O. Box 808, Ra'anana, Israel
leonidb@openu.ac.il

Abstract. Wireless Sensor Networks (WSNs) frequently have distinguished amount of data loss, causing data integrity issues. Sensor nodes are inherently a cheap piece of hardware - due to the common need to use many of them over a large area - and usually contain a small amount of RAM and flash memory, which are insufficient in case of high degree of data sampling. An overloaded sensor can harm the data integrity, or even completely reject incoming messages. The problem gets even worse when data should be received from many nodes, as missing data becomes a more common phenomenon as deployed WSNs grow in scale. In cases of an overflow, our Distributed Adaptive Clustering algorithm (D-ACR) reconfigures the network, by adaptively and hierarchically re-clustering parts of it, based on the rate of incoming data packages in order to minimize the energy-consumption, and prevent premature death of nodes. However, the re-clustering cannot prevent data loss caused by the nature of the sensors. We suggest to address this problem by an efficient distributed backup-placement algorithm named DBP-ACR, performed on the D-ACR refined clusters. The DBP-ACR algorithm re-directs packages from overloaded sensors to more efficient placements outside of the overloaded areas in the WSN cluster, thus increasing the fault-tolerance of the network and reducing the data loss.

Keywords: Wireless sensor networks
Distributed backup-placement · Data loss · Networks connectivity

This work was supported by the Lynn and William Frankel Center for Computer Science, the Open University of Israel's Research Fund, and ISF grant 724/15.

V. Sucasas et al. (Eds.): BROADNETS 2018, LNICST 263, pp. 212–224, 2019.
https://doi.org/10.1007/978-3-030-05195-2_21

1 Introduction

1.1 Fault-Tolerance and Data Loss in WSNs

Considering their independent and environmentally-varied work-fashion, one of the most important factors in WSN applications is fault-tolerance. Due to the fact that the possibilities of an absent sensor node, damaged communication link or missing data are unavoidable in wireless sensor networks, fault-tolerance becomes a key-issue. Among the causes of these constant failures are environmental factors, battery exhaustion, damaged communications links, data collision, wear-out of memory and storage units and overloaded sensors [1]. WSN can be in use for a variety of purposes, nevertheless its fault-tolerance needs to depend mostly on the application type. Wireless video sensor networks, for example, tends to rely on accurate and precise massive amount of sensed data, thus demanding WSNs to support high degree of data sampling [2], which consequently means high quality of recording, processing and transmitting of the data from the captured environment, which sometimes might be unstable. The data storage capacity on the sensors is crucial because whereas some applications [3] require instantaneous transmission to another node or directly to the base station, others demand intervallic or interrupted transmissions. Thus, if the amount of data is large - as a derivative of the data precision needed by the application [4] - WSN nodes are required to store those amounts of data in a rapid and effective fashion till the transmission stage [5].

However, since those requirements are mostly depend on the hardware and the wireless settings, WSNs frequently have distinguished amount of data loss, causing data integrity issues [6]. Sensor nodes are inherently a cheap piece of hardware, due to the common need to use many of them over a large area, sometimes in a non-retrievable environment - a restriction that does not allow a usage of a pricey tampering or overflow resistant hardware, and a damaged or overflowed sensor can harm the data integrity, or even completely reject incoming messages [6]. The problem gets even worse when there is a need for high-rate sampling or when data should be received from many nodes since missing data becomes a more common phenomenon as deployed WSNs grow in scale [7]. Therefore, high-rate sampling WSNs applications require fault-tolerant data storage, even though this requirement is not realistic.

1.2 Data Storage in WSNs

WSNs usually consist of sensor devices that are able to sense or receive data, process it fully or partially, and finally transmit it to another node - either a cluster-head or a base-station. At the receiving-sensing state, in most cases, the data is placed in the memory in a serial fashion, processed minimally or not at all, then transmitted in a First-In-First-Out mode, and then deleted from the sensor device memory [8]. This technique has obvious disadvantages from the energy-efficiency point of view. As a common bypass, a well-known approach to reduce energy-consumption is to place as many data as possible in the RAM, and only when reaching to the full capacity to send it in a batch fashion forward. Another option is to process it minimally and send less data than originally received (e.g. minimum function), as transmitting the data is a very costly operation. Moreover, the relatively recent introduction of flash memory into sensor devices also expanded their capability to store data locally [9]. However, one of the critical problems with this storage is the dramatic disproportionate write-erase granularity. Specifically, erasing one block (64 to 128 pages) while writing only one page (512 B to 8 KB). This means that continuous high-rate data acquisition applications cannot rely on it, since the device will reach its memory limit eventually. Also, because the RAM acts as a buffer towards the flash memory, the pages amount is limited by the RAM capacity, which is usually about an order of magnitude smaller than the flash capacity. Another known problem of the flash memory is its sensitivity to constant write-erase cycles which characterizes high-rate applications, causing a premature fatigue of the hardware, thus to data loss [8].

In order to overcome those flash technology limitations new and enhanced storage technologies were introduced, including the NVSRAM, FRAM and MRAM - which managed to push write-erase granularity performances to the limit [10]. Nonetheless, physical limitation derived by the sensor device shape and budget are not enabling an embedding of more than a 1-megabyte storage per unit. Therefore, for continuous high-rate data acquisition applications, this is not a realistic solution. In the following sections we will devise a solution relying on the reconfigurable nature of the whole network, which eventually would be able to balance the load in an overloaded network properly between the different nodes.

2   The Backup-Placement Problem in WSNs

The backup-placement problem in general graphs was introduced by [11]. This problem turned out to be very challenging in general networks. An approximate solution with a polynomial number of rounds was presented in [11].

In the current work, however, we focus on WSNs, and we are interested in significantly better than polynomial (and even than linear) solution. To illustrate the backup-placement problem in WSNs consider the following scenario: several nodes (sensors) in a WSN have packages (sensed or received data) whose backups (or the package itself) need to find a placement elsewhere in the network, due to overload on the area of the network which those nodes belongs to, in order to improve fault-tolerance and data integrity. Because of the lack of capacity to store or process the data on the node itself or in neighbor nodes - which also might be burdened by an overflow of data - it is mandatory, when the local memory is full, to find a backup-placement to the data outside of the overloaded area. The backup-placement problem is defined as follows. (1) How to place the data only once in a safe and stable node in order to assure with a high degree of certainty the data integrity and minimization of the WSN load, and (2) how to do so without creating an additional data overflow on other areas of the network.

In terms of graph theory, the problem in its simplest form is defined for a network graph $G = (V, E)$ as follows. Each vertex in V must select a neighbor, such that the maximum number of vertices that made the same selection is minimized [11].

In order to demonstrate this problem, we can examine two test cases. Let $G = (V, E)$ be a graph representing a network. If, for example, G is a cycle graph, the optimal solution to the backup-placement problem would be if each node selects its succeeding neighbor to be its backup node, and by that the maximal backup burden for each node would be of only one unit (Fig. 1, right). However, if, for example, G is a star graph, the optimal solution will force all the nodes to choose the center node (beside the center node itself) to be its backup node, and by that the maximal backup burden would be of $|V| - 1$ (Fig. 1, left) - a very problematic solution due to the overload on a single node, which, as previously explained, we specifically wish to avoid. While this is unavoidable in a star graph, it becomes possible in wireless-network topologies.

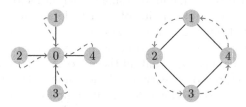

Fig. 1. Optimal backup placement in star graph (left) and cycle graph (right)

Next, we examine a WSN which can be represented as a unit disk graph (UDG) on which a spanning tree has been computed, in order to demonstrate the considerations that must be taken while designing a distributed backup-placement algorithm. We choose UDG because it tends to represent the immanent behavior of wireless communications [8].

Let $G = (V, E)$ be a spanning tree of a UDG representing a sensor network. Let v_0 be the root of G. Now, even if the number of nodes inside v_0's transmission area is large, most of them are interconnected, and form at most 6 different cliques, as the UDG definition forces. It means that v_0 children form at most 6 cliques. Assuming that nodes IDs are consecutively numbered, in each clique each node selects a node with ID greater by 1 than its own to be its backup node, assuming the existence of such a node. If such a node is absent, but some neighbors have greater IDs, then the selection is the neighbor with the closest ID to the backed-up node ID, out of these neighbors. Consequently, only one node in each clique - the one with the highest ID - will be left without a backup node. In total there will be 6 nodes without backup-placement within their clique. Each such node v will set its parent node $\pi(v)$ as its backup node.

Using this algorithm, the maximum extra-load per node is $12 = O(1)$. This is because each node in V is selected by at most 6 of its children, and by at most

---

Algorithm 1. The 1-hop Back-Placement Algorithm

1: **procedure** 1-HOP-BP(NODE v, GRAPH G)
2:    **Find** a node u in the list of sibling nodes connected with v in G such that $ID(u) = ID(v) + k$, where k is the smallest positive integer for which a node u exists in the list
3:    **if** found **then**
4:        **Select** u to be v backup node
5:    **else**
6:        **Select** $\pi(v)$ to be v backup node

---

6 additional sibling nodes. Indeed, two siblings of the same clique cannot select the same sibling neighbor. This is because in this case the latter sibling ID is greater than both IDs of siblings that selected it. But then, one of the selecting siblings does not select an ID that is closest to its own, which contradicts step 3 of the algorithm.

Therefore, the load is optimal up to a small constant factor. The computation is performed within a constant radius of each node and requires $O(1)$ rounds, and so the distributed running time complexity is $O(1)$. Furthermore, instead of representing the original graph as a spanning tree, it is possible to decompose the graph into a set of trees in a way that all those trees will form a spanning forest (See, e.g., [12]). The time complexity of this action is $O(1)$, which consequently turns the total distributed backup-placement complexity of this algorithm to be $O(1)$. However, the 1-hop backup-placement algorithm is not practical for real-world WSNs. One of the reasons is that the distribution of the load on the network is almost never focused on one node, but on an area, which several nodes belong to. Therefore, a backup-placement of one node in this area to its neighbor - which also belongs to this overloaded area - is counterproductive [13]. In this state, all the nodes in the area are overloaded, but nevertheless try to place their incoming packages to other nodes which are also overloaded, and by that create an even greater pressure on this area of the network, subsequently causing a data loss and energy-waste.

Hence, it is clear that the solution to the backup problem with overloaded areas is by transferring the packages outside of the area dynamically, to a non-overloaded area. In order to do so we need to address three main difficulties: (1) How is the distributed algorithm supposed to detect which nodes under which area are not overloaded? (2) How is the distributed algorithm supposed to choose the backup nodes and transfer the packages to it in an optimal fashion? (3) How during this selection process are the parent nodes in the tree will not be overloaded?

It is a necessity to address those difficulties, mainly because (1) the detection of the overloaded areas is an expensive task, (2) the selection of the backup nodes outside of the overloaded areas and the packages transfer to it should be based on an optimal routing scheme as the communication and energy consumption are the top priorities, and (3) the structure of the tree does not insure that many nodes will not transfer their backup packages through small amount of parent nodes, which will consequently cause to their premature death due to energy consumption, and thus to the reduce of connectivity of the whole network [14]. In order to tackle those problems, we first use our distributed Adaptive Clustering Refinement algorithm (or D-ACR) [15] in order to re-cluster the network in a way which will reduce the burden on specific nodes of the WSN as possible, and afterwards we will take advantage of the hierarchical fashion of the D-ACR refinement algorithm tree in order to find a placement for data from overloaded nodes using the DBP-ACR algorithm. These two algorithms are complementary as we will present in the next sections.

3   The DBP-ACR Algorithm

3.1   Problem Formulation

In order to formulate the problem, we first need to define the setting of the network. We assume a WSN with an array of n nodes - including the base station (BS), the cluster-heads (CH) and the non-cluster-heads (NCH) - in a confine $Latitude \times Longtitude(m^2)$ quadrate, while the position of each node in this area is represented by the coordinates (x_i, y_i). We assume a communication model in which the transmission energy is calculated using the d^2 power-loss model. The optimization problem is to find a backup-placement for sensed data packages that could not be stored on their sensing node due to data stream overload and physical constraints, thus creating a data loss. By doing so it is possible to keep data integrity while consuming the minimum energy possible from the WSN as a whole, and also keep a load-balanced WSN structure that will not burden heavily on some parts of the network - resulting premature death of nodes and damage the WSN lifetime and connectivity at once. It is worthwhile mentioning that we take for granted all the general presumptions regarding the network structure as presented in [15].

3.2   D-ACR Algorithm

Unlike other WSN clustering algorithms, that do not re-cluster the network after deployment (except in nodes join/leave), our hypothesis is that it is advisable, in terms of prolonging the network lifetime, to adaptively re-cluster specific regions that are triggered significantly more than other regions in the network. By doing so, it is possible to minimize or even prevent the premature death of CHs, which are heavily burdened with sensing and transmitting actions - much more than other parts of the WSN. In order to do so we introduced the centralized and distributed Adaptive Clustering Refinement (ACR) algorithms [15].

In general (Fig. 2), the D-ACR load-balancing-based algorithm tries to locate the load burdened areas. The amount of the revealed areas establishes the regions amount that will need to re-cluster themselves. Because the load factor determines the refinement action, the D-ACR algorithm can recursively identify the load burdened areas and re-cluster them in a hierarchical tree assembly in which the deeper the nodes are in the tree depth, the more burden they are.

Algorithm 2. The Distributed Adaptive Clustering Refinement Algorithm

---

1: **procedure** D-ACR(NODE v, THRESHOLD t)
2:     **if** v is a leaf and $energy\_use(v) \geq 3t$ **then**
3:         **Refine**(v)
4:         **Add** new CHs as children of v
5:     **if** all children of v are leafs and $average\_energy(children(v)) < (t/5)$ **then**
6:         **Coarsen**(v)
7:         **Remove** the children of v from the tree and mark v as a leaf

---

The D-ACR algorithm is executed by all CHs in parallel. Initially, each CH is provided with a threshold value t of a plausible energy use. If these values are unknown in the beginning of the execution, they can be computed using a single execution of the centralized ACR algorithm (C-ACR). This combination of an initial global execution with numerous local executions following it, is still more efficient than performing several executions of the C-ACR. In the initial configuration, all these values t are the same, and represent a balanced environment. The algorithm can start from any cluster-hierarchy tree, where the simplest configuration is a single CH, which is the root (equivalently, a single leaf). Once an energy use of a leaf v reaches $3t$, we perform a local refinement in the cluster of v [15]. This results in adding new CHs to the tree as leafs that become the children of v. These new leafs correspond to the newly formed clusters. This refinement results in a better energy use in each such newly formed cluster, specifically, bounded by $\frac{3}{10} \cdot 3t < t$ instead of $3t$ [15]. In other words, we balance clusters of excess energy-use by decomposing them into smaller clusters that require less energy.

Once the average energy consumption in the children of a CH node u whose all children are leafs becomes less than $(t/5)$, a coarsening operation is performed (this operation is the opposite of refinement). Specifically, the clusters represented by u and its children are merged into a single cluster. Then u becomes its CH, and former children of u become NCHs. Consequently, the energy use of the newly-formed larger cluster grows, but the tree-distance between the root to some leafs decreases. This completes the description of the algorithm. The algorithm provided below is executed periodically by each CHs.

3.3   DBP-ACR Algorithm and Analysis

In order to present the DBP-ACR algorithm we will first explain its synergy to the D-ACR algorithm. In Fig. 3 there is a WSN with 4 CHs which each has several NCH. We assume that at certain time the load on the leftmost CH sub-network increased dramatically, and that the reconfiguration of the network is based on D-ACR algorithm. Therefore, the network will immediately start re-cluster itself in order to create a load-balanced network.

In [15] it was proven that the maximum depth of a refined tree is bounded by $O(\log(L/t))$, and the maximum tree size is bounded by $2^{O(\log(L/t))}$, where L is the maximum load, t is the threshold value of a plausible energy use, and $k = 2$

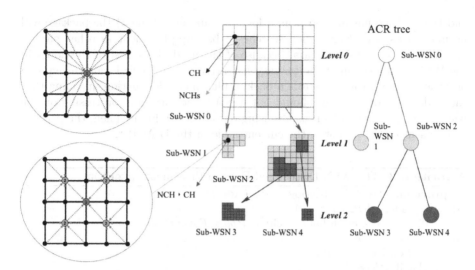

Fig. 2. An ACR WSN-Graph Tree formation example with 2 levels of refinement (right). A finer resolution WSN-Graph is applied each time a sub-WSN is created (middle); A magnification of the square which represent a 5×5 WSN grid with one CH to 24 NCHs before refinement (upper left), and the same grid after refinement with 4 NCHs turned into CHs (lower left).

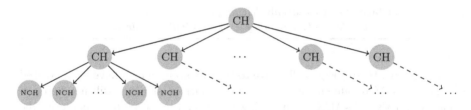

Fig. 3. A WSN with 4 CHs which each has several NCH.

(i.e. each refined CH creates $k^2 = 4$ child-CHs). At each D-ACR refinement, the new CHs know their refinement level in the tree by getting the refinement level from their parent. This requires only one additional message per new CH, each message of size $O(\log \log(L/t))$ bits to represent the depth in the D-ACR tree. The total number of CH nodes in the generated D-ACR tree is bounded by $O(n^2)$, where n is the number of CHs in the input D-ACR tree [15]. Additionally, each package which is needed to be transferred to a backup node will need an additional bit to reference that this package is not a sensed data package, but rather a package that routes to its final destination. We next provide the psudocode of the algorithm and then explain it.

The DBP-ACR algorithm is executed by all nodes in parallel once a package has received. Initially, each node checks its memory vacant capacity (we suppose that the sensor provides this datum). If there is no vacancy in the memory system and the package has arrived from a local sensing area (line 3) the package will be marked as a package which searches a backup-placement in other part of the WSN. This step is essential because of the need of the rest of the nodes in the WSN to figure out if the package has arrived from their local sensing area or either it's in a route towards a backup-placement destination, meaning that the node will not need (or should not need) to perform any processing on the package, or rather handle it as a sensing data of its children. Then, the package will be sent to the parent of the current node in the D-ACR tree.

Algorithm 3. The WSN Distributed Backup-Placement Algorithm

1: **procedure** DBP-ACR(NODE v, PACKAGE P)
2:     Initially, $v.RR\_index \leftarrow 0$
3:     **if** $v.memory$ reach full capacity $\land$ $P.bp = False$ **then**
4:         $P.bp \leftarrow True$
5:         **Send** $P \rightarrow v.father$
6:     **else if** $P.bp = True$ **then**
7:         **if** $v.ACR\_depth \neq NULL$ **then**
8:             **Send** $P \rightarrow v.father$
9:         **else**
10:            $P.bp \leftarrow False$
11:            **if** $v.RR\_index = P.send\_ad$ **then**
12:                $v.RR\_index \leftarrow (v.RR\_index + 1) \bmod len(v.children)$
13:            **Place** $P \rightarrow v.children[v.RR\_index]$
14:            $v.RR\_index \leftarrow (v.RR\_index + 1) \bmod len(v.children)$

Afterwards, the package will arrive to the CH nodes which have been created during the D-ACR refinement stage. Those nodes most likely will not be over-loaded due to the D-ACR re-clustering which creates a load-balancing at the WSN refined zones. At those CHs the package is already marked as a backup-placement package which searches a placement in other part of the WSN (line 6). The algorithm will transfer the package directly all the way through the D-ACR tree newly formed CHs (the depth of the D-ACR tree) until reaching the root node from which the D-ACR refinement process has started (lines 7, 8). The sibling nodes of this root node are most likely have not been overloaded, and not been refined by the D-ACR algorithm (otherwise, most likely they would have been part of the current D-ACR tree). Those nodes, and their sub-trees nodes, are suitable to store or process the package. When the package reached this point (line 9) it stops marking itself as a package searching for backup-placement (line 10) and the root node send it to its final destination by a counter index of its sons (line 13), which distribute the incoming packages evenly between its other children (except the one from which the package has arrived which is stored in $P.send\_ad$ lines 11 and 12) in a round-robin fashion controlled by $v.RR\_index$ (line 14) in order to balance the load on those nodes. It is important to notice that although there is no massive load on those backup nodes at the beginning, as time goes by more and more packages will try to find a backup-placement outside of their D-ACR tree, it means that those other nodes will initiate eventually a D-ACR in order to ease the burden of those packages on the CHs, and eventually start the DBP-ACR algorithm too in order to find placement for the excessive packages arrival. This means that the two distributed algorithms, the DBP-ACR and the D-ACR work in a strong collaboration in order to create a load-balanced WSN, even though the two are completely independent in their work fashion.

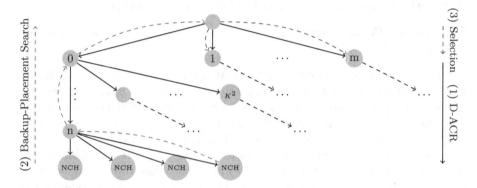

Fig. 4. The DBP-ACR algorithm stages: (1) The D-ACR refinement (2) The backup-placement search (3) The selection of a node as a backup-placement node outside of the overloaded area.

An exemplification of the algorithm action is presented in Fig. 4. As previously explained, the algorithm is based on the refinement re-clustering of the D-ACR algorithm, and the tree in Fig. 4 is based on such refinement of the tree in Fig. 3 (stage 1). Afterwards, one of the leaf nodes of the tree (i.e. NCH) reach the top of its memory capacity and forced to mark the incoming package as a package which need to find a backup-placement. The package is then transferred to the parent node - which is a newly formed CH by D-ACR actions. Then, the package is directly traversed through the n levels of refinement CHs (stage 2) until it reaches the root node - i.e. the father of the node from which the D-ACR initiated at the beginning (node 0). The package then finds his placement among the other descendants of the root node, which are not burdened. Those action are performed locally at each node through the whole process.

The running time of the algorithm is presented in Theorem 1, and the memory consumption of the algorithm in Theorem 2. The energy consumption of the algorithm package transmission is provided by Theorem 3.

Theorem 1. *The running time of the algorithm is bounded by* $O(\log(L/t))$

Proof. Suppose we have maximum load L. The load may be divided to subclusters. Every D-ACR refinement step will decrease the load, allowing no more then $L/3$ load. The D-ACR refinement will repeat this division q times, until the load will be less than $3t$. Thus, we obtain the following formula describing the number of rounds until the necessary refinement is achieved: $L(1/3)^q \geq 3t \Rightarrow q \leq O(\log(L/t))$, while q is the average ratio of graph sizes between two levels of graphs. The DBP-ACR algorithm can initiate at any NCHs under the D-ACR refinement tree, which only adds 1 hop between this node and the immediate parent CH. Also, when the packet reaches the top of the D-ACR tree it finds a backup node in a round-robin fashion at one of the m child nodes of the root node, which means a complexity of $O(1)$. Therefore, the total time complexity of the DBP-ACR algorithm is $1 + O(\log(L/t)) + 1 = O(\log(L/t))$.

Theorem 2. *The extra-memory consumption of the algorithm is bounded by* $O(\log \log(L/t))$

Proof. As previously explained, at each D-ACR refinement, the new CHs knows it refinement level in the tree by getting the refinement level from their parents. Because we proved that the maximum depth of the D-ACR tree is bounded by $O(\log(L/t))$, it means that the number of bits we will need in order to represent this information is $O(\log \log(L/t))$. The additional bit for $P.bp$ and the additional locally allocated argument at the root CH $v.RR\_index$ will result that the extra memory consumption of the algorithm is bounded by $O(\log \log(L/t) + 1 + \log(m)) = O(\log \log(L/t))$, as the m child nodes of the root node are must be small [15].

Theorem 3. *The energy consumption of the algorithm package transmission is bounded by* $O(\log(L/t)E_{elec} + \epsilon_{fs}(\log(L/t)d_{ref})^2)$

Proof. Based on the D-ACR refinement, we can assume the maximum distance between a NCH at the lowest refinement level and its CH in a D-ACR refinement tree to be the distance between any CH in this tree and its parent, which is also a CH. This equality is kept all the way through the distance between the CH at the first refinement level and the root CH node, from which the D-ACR refinement started. We denote the maximum distance between any two nodes in a consecutive hierarchy level (i.e. level i and level $i + 1$) which transfer package for backup-placement purpose to be d_{ref}. Thus, the energy consumption needed to transmit a bit from one node to its parent in the D-ACR tree would be:

$$E_{ACR\_Node} = E_{elec} + \epsilon_{fs}d_{ref}^2 \tag{1}$$

As previously proven (Theorem 1), the maximum depth of a D-ACR tree is bounded by $O(\log(L/t))$. Therefore, the maximum amount of energy that would be spent on this transmission will be:

$$E_{ACR\_BP} = \log(L/t)E_{ACR\_Node} = \log(L/t)(E_{elec} + \epsilon_{fs}d_{ref}^2) \tag{2}$$

As shown in the DBP-ACR algorithm, the last step, of actually placing the package in a backup-placement node, take place outside of the D-ACR tree - meaning that the maximum distance between the D-ACR root node and its parent, and the distance between the D-ACR root node parent and one of its children - where the package will be placed - is at most $\log(L/t)d_{ref}$ each, as this multiplication equals the maximum distance between a node and its child in the original non-refined network (the original maximum distance at is $d = \log(L/t)d_{ref}$). Therefore, the maximum total energy consumption needed in order to find a backup-placement node and place the package in it is:

$$E_{BP\_TOT} = E_{ACR\_BP} + 2E_t = \tag{3}$$
$$\log(L/t)(E_{elec} + \epsilon_{fs}d_{ref}^2) + 2(E_{elec} + \epsilon_{fs}(\log(L/t)d_{ref})^2)$$

Therefore, the energy consumption of the algorithm package transmission is bounded by $O(\log(L/t)E_{elec} + \epsilon_{fs}(\log(L/t)d_{ref})^2)$.

4   Conclusions

In this paper we introduced the Distributed Fault-Tolerant Backup-Placement in Overloaded Wireless Sensor Networks algorithm, named the DBP-ACR. We first surveyed the main fault-tolerance issues that WSNs facing, specifically the data integrity and loss phenomenon and the sensor nodes storage advantages and disadvantages. Afterwards, we defined the Backup-Placement Problem in WSNs and defined the considerations needed in order to actually manage to perform an optimal backup-placement in WSNs. Finally, we showed the complementary fashion of the D-ACR algorithm and the DBP-ACR algorithm, and proved its energy, memory and running time complexities to be close to optimal.

References

1. Kakamanshadi, G., et al.: A survey on fault tolerance techniques in wireless sensor networks. In: International Conference on Green Computing and Internet of Things (ICGCIoT). IEEE (2015)
2. Seema, A., et al.: Towards efficient wireless video sensor networks: a survey of existing node architectures and proposal for a Flexi-WVSNP design. IEEE Commun. Surv. Tutor. 13(3), 462–486 (2011)
3. Mottola, L., et al.: Programming wireless sensor networks: fundamental concepts and state of the art. ACM Comput. Surv. (CSUR) 43(3), 19 (2011)
4. Oren, G., et al.: Adaptive distributed hierarchical sensing algorithm for reduction of wireless sensor network cluster-heads energy consumption. In: Proceedings of the 13th International Wireless Communications and Mobile Computing Conference (IWCMC), pp. 980-986. IEEE (2017)
5. Balazinska, M., et al.: Data management in the worldwide sensor web. IEEE Pervasive Comput. 6(2), 30–40 (2007)
6. Kong, L., et al.: Data loss and reconstruction in sensor networks. In: INFOCOM, 2013 Proceedings. IEEE (2013)
7. Luo, C., et al.: Compressive data gathering for large-scale wireless sensor networks. In: Proceedings of the 15th Annual International Conference on Mobile Computing and Networking. ACM (2009)
8. Wagner, D., et al.: Algorithms for Sensor and Ad Hoc Networks: Advanced Lectures. Springer, Heidelberg (2007). https://doi.org/10.1007/978-3-540-74991-2

9. Vieira, M.A.M., et al.: Survey on wireless sensor network devices. emerging technologies and factory automation, In: Proceedings of ETFA 2003. IEEE Conference. vol. 1. IEEE (2003)
10. Nuns, T., et al.: Evaluation of recent technologies of non-volatile RAM. radiation and its effects on components and systems. In: 9th European Conference on RADECS 2007. IEEE (2007)
11. Halldórsson, M.M., et al.: Distributed backup placement in networks. In: Proceedings of the 27th ACM symposium on Parallelism in Algorithms and Architectures. ACM (2015)
12. Barenboim, L., et al.: Distributed graph coloring: fundamentals and recent developments. Synth. Lect. Distrib. Comput. Theory 4(1), 1–171 (2013)
13. Wajgi, D., et al.: Load balancing based approach to improve lifetime of wireless sensor network. Int. J. Wirel. Mob. Netw. 4(4), 155 (2012)
14. Kakiuchi, H.: Dynamic Load Balancing in Sensor Networks. Stanford (2004)
15. Oren, G., Barenboim, L., Levin, H.: Load-Balancing adaptive clustering refinement algorithm for wireless sensor network clusters. In: Koucheryavy, Y., Mamatas, L., Matta, I., Ometov, A., Papadimitriou, P. (eds.) WWIC 2017. LNCS, vol. 10372, pp. 157–173. Springer, Cham (2017). https://doi.org/10.1007/978-3-319-61382-6_13

Spatial Modulation Techniques

Hybrid Spatial Modulation Scheme with Arbitrary Number of Transmit Antennas

Saud Althunibat$^{(\boxtimes)}$, Mohanad Al-Hasanat, and Abdullah Al-Hasanat

Al-Hussein Bin Talal University, Ma'an, Jordan
saud.althunibat@ahu.edu.jo

Abstract. Spatial Modulation (SM) is a single RF chain Multi-Input-Multi-Output (MIMO) scheme that has significantly improved the spectral efficiency. A major limitation of SM is the constraint on the number of transmit antennas, where the number of transmit antennas must be a power of two. Generalized SM (GSM) is proposed to further improve the spectral efficiency of SM by activating multiple transmit antennas simultaneously. However, activating multiple antennas increases the energy consumption at the transmitter. To this end, a hybrid scheme is proposed in this paper that allows for arbitrary number of transmit antennas to be installed. For a given number of transmit antennas, the proposed scheme achieves higher spectral efficiency than SM. Also, for a given spectral efficiency, the proposed scheme consumes energy less than GSM, and causes a negligible loss in the error performance compared to SM and GSM.

Keywords: MIMO · Space modulation · Spatial modulation

1 Introduction

The growing demand for high data rates and the crowded spectrum bands motivate the research towards promising spectral efficient systems. One of these systems is Multiple-Input-Multiple-Output (MIMO) systems that enhance the overall spectral efficiency as they permit the simultaneous use of multiple antennas at transmitter and receiver [1]. However, a major problem of MIMO systems is the Inter-Channel Interference (ICI) between the transmit antennas [2]. To this end, Spatial Modulation (SM) has been proposed in order to overcome the ICI problem in MIMO systems [3].

In SM, only a single transmit antenna is activated at each transmission time. The index of the activated transmit antenna is selected based on a part of the transmitted block. For a system with N_t transmit antennas, and a signal modulation of order M, SM can transmit $\log_2 N_t M$ bits at each transmission time [4,5]. In each transmitted block, the first $\log_2 M$ bits are modulated and transmitted using a single transmit antenna that is selected based on the last $\log_2 N_t$

This work is funded by Abdul Hameed Shoman Foundation (grant no. 5/2016).

V. Sucasas et al. (Eds.): BROADNETS 2018, LNICST 263, pp. 227–236, 2019.
https://doi.org/10.1007/978-3-030-05195-2_22

bits. As such, ICI is totally avoided as only one transmit antenna is activated. Moreover, compared to other MIMO schemes, using a single RF chain reduces the energy consumption at the transmitter [6,7].

It is clear that N_t must be a power of two in order to have an integer value of the transmitted block length [8]. Thus, in the case that N_t is not a power of two, some transmit antennas will not be used. Generalized SM (GSM) has been proposed to release the constraint, and improve the attainable spectral efficiency [9]. GSM allows for activating multiple transmit antennas at each time. Although GSM can significantly enhance the spectral efficiency and allows for arbitrary number of transmit antennas to be installed, it magnifies the energy consumption at the transmitter since multiple antennas must be activated [10,11]. Energy consumption is a major concern in wireless systems especially for mobile users with limited power resources [12].

In the literature, several works have addressed the problem, and proposed solutions to solve the limitation on the number of transmit antennas in SM systems. In [13], a simple scheme is proposed to overcome the problem and enhance the performance under low Signal-to-Noise Ratio (SNR) conditions. Specifically, in case that N_t is not a power of two, it will be rounded to the nearest power of two value larger than N_t. Consequently, the data will be transmitted in blocks, each of $\lceil \log_2 N_t M \rceil$ bits. Each block is mapped to the antenna with minimum hamming distance in order to minimize the impact on the bit error rate (BER) performance. However, the proposed scheme shows a poor performance in high SNR range. Another solution using Fractional Bit Encoding (FBE) is reported in [14]. It is based on the modulus conversion method in order to allow for the usage of any arbitrary number of transmit antennas. FBE scheme achieves a fractional bit rate larger than that achieved by the conventional SM. However, its complexity cost and the high vulnerability to the propagation errors are the main drawbacks of [14]. Alternatively, an efficient scheme is proposed in [15], where different transmit antennas use different modulation orders. Specifically, the modulation order of the symbols emitted from each antenna and the length of the antenna index are adapted such that the block length is fixed for all symbols.

In this paper, a hybrid scheme of SM and GSM is proposed in order to improve the achievable spectral efficiency compared to SM, and to reduce energy consumption compared to GSM. The proposed scheme implies that if the number of transmit antennas is not a power of two, combinations of two antennas can be used in order to increase the achievable spectral efficiency with a slight increase in the BER. For example, if a transmitter has only 3 antennas, the proposed scheme implies that one combination of two different antennas can act as a fourth antenna. This way, the system will be able to provide one more bit to the spectral efficiency achieved by the conventional SM. The proposed scheme can be seen as a switching process between conventional SM and GSM. For a given number of transmit antennas, the proposed scheme achieves higher spectral efficiency than SM. Also, for a given spectral efficiency, the proposed scheme consumes energy less than GSM, and causes a negligible loss in the BER performance compared to

SM and GSM. The contributions of this works extend to include mathematical analysis of the achievable error performance and the saved energy as compared to the GSM scheme.

2   System Model

A MIMO communication system between two users (a transmitter and a receiver) is considered. The transmitter is equipped with N_t transmit antennas, while the receiver is equipped with N_r receive antennas. The channel matrix between the transmitter and the receiver is denoted by $\mathbf{H}$. The entries of $\mathbf{H}$ (i.e, h_{ji}, $j = 1, 2, ...N_r$, $i = 1, 2, ...N_t$) are assumed independently and identically distributed complex Gaussian random variables with zero mean and unity variance (i.e, $h_{ji} \sim \mathcal{CN}(0, 1)$). Also, we assume that the additive white Gaussian noise to the received signal at a specific receive antenna has zero mean and N_o variance. As such, the SNR at the receiver, denoted by γ is equal to $\gamma = \frac{1}{N_o}$.

Without loss of generality, we consider that the channel response matrix $\mathbf{H}$ is perfectly available at the receiver before each transmission time. This can be attained by a channel estimation process accomplished prior to data transmission between the communicating users. At the transmitter, the transmitted symbol can be conveyed by two different modulation schemes, namely, SM and GSM. In what follows, we give a brief description of both schemes.

2.1   Conventional SM Scheme

In the conventional SM scheme, the length of the transmitted block in bits (k_{SM}) is determined based on the number of transmit antennas N_t and the modulation order M. Specifically, k_{SM} is expressed as follows

$$k_{SM} = \begin{cases} \log_2 N_t + \log_2 M & \text{if } N_t = 2^i \\ \lfloor \log_2 N_t \rfloor + \log_2 M & \text{if } N_t \neq 2^i. \end{cases} \qquad (1)$$

where $i = 1, 2, 3, ...$, and $\lfloor . \rfloor$ represents the flooring operator.

In SM, the first $\log_2 M$ bits of each block is modulated using the adopted modulation scheme, and transmitted through a single transmit antenna selected based on the last $\lfloor \log_2 N_t \rfloor$ bits of the transmitted block. Thus, the transmission vector $\mathbf{X}$ can be modeled as an $N_t \times 1$ vector with all-zero elements except one element which is set to the modulated signal. The index of the nonzero element of $\mathbf{X}$ corresponds to the index of the active transmit antenna.

A special case of SM is called Space Shift Keying (SSK) [16]. In SSK schemes, $M = 1$, and hence, no signal modulation is performed at the transmitter. Consequently, in SSK, data are transmitted by sending a fixed signal from a single transmit antenna whose index is determined based on the transmitted data block.

As k_{SM} must be an integer, (1) states that the conventional SM can only use a number of transmit antennas that is a power of two. Otherwise (i.e. if the number of transmit antennas is not a power of two), the largest power of two that is less than N_t should be used. Therefore, the conventional SM scheme cannot benefit from all the available transmit antennas when their number is not a power of two. Therefore, in such a case, an attainable spectral efficiency will be lost since a subset of the transmit antennas cannot be used.

2.2   GSM Scheme

Aiming at increasing the spectral efficiency of SM systems, GSM has been proposed in [9]. In GSM, the transmitter allows more than one transmit antenna to be activated at each transmission round. The core idea is to transmit through a combination of multiple transmit antennas. Assuming that the number of active antennas is N_a, the number of combinations of N_a is equal to $\binom{N_t}{N_a}$ possible combinations.

The length of transmitted block in GSM (k_{GSM}) is given as follows:

$$k_{GSM} = \begin{cases} \log_2 \binom{N_t}{N_a} + \log_2 M & \text{if } \binom{N_t}{N_a} = 2^i \\ \left\lfloor \log_2 \binom{N_t}{N_a} \right\rfloor + \log_2 M & \text{if } \binom{N_t}{N_a} \neq 2^i. \end{cases} \tag{2}$$

where $i = 1, 2, 3, \ldots$.

Similar to SM schemes, in GSM, the first $\log_2 M$ bits of each block is modulated using the signal modulation scheme, while the the last $\left\lfloor \log_2 \binom{N_t}{N_a} \right\rfloor$ bits determine the N_a transmit antennas (among the N_t antennas) to send the modulated signal. Therefore, the transmission vector $\mathbf{X}$ in GSM includes N_a nonzero elements whose values are set to the modulated signal.

Compared to SM, GSM is able to achieve higher data rate as a longer data block can be delivered at every transmission round. However, the cost is paid by the need to activate N_a transmit antennas. Moreover, activating multiple transmit antennas will definitely increase the energy consumption at the transmitter [17].

3   The Proposed Scheme

The motivation behind the proposed scheme is to overcome the constraint on the number of the transmit antennas in SM. The proposed scheme grants the system designer more freedom to install any number of transmit antennas as long as the overall size of the transmitter is acceptable. It is assumed that the transmitter can switch between SM to GSM modes and via versa in order to convey longer symbols than the conventional SM.

The proposed scheme implies that the transmitted data are divided into blocks, each block contains k_{HSM} bits. Thus, the block length k_{HSM} can be expressed as follows:

$$k_{HSM} = \begin{cases} \log_2 N_t + \log_2 M & \text{if } N_t = 2^i \\ \lceil \log_2 N_t \rceil + \log_2 M & \text{if } N_t \neq 2^i. \end{cases} \tag{3}$$

where $i = 1, 2, 3, \ldots$, and $\lceil . \rceil$ represents the ceiling operator.

Notice that in the case $N_t = 2^i$ (i.e., a power of two), the proposed scheme works exactly as the conventional SM scheme. However, in the case of $N_t \neq 2^i$ (i.e., not a power of two), the transmitter will apply a hybrid mode between SM and GSM schemes. In other words, if N_t is not a power of two, the number of possible data block $2^{k_{HSM}}$ is grouped into two groups of blocks. The first group contains $N_t M$ blocks, and each of them is transmitted using a single transmit antenna as in conventional SM scheme. On the other hand, the second group contain $2^{k_{HSM}} - N_t M$ blocks, where each of them is transmitted using a combination of two antennas as in GSM scheme. The following example explains how the proposed scheme works.

3.1 Numerical Example

Assume that a transmitter is equipped with $N_t = 5$ transmit antennas: $\{A_1, A_2, ..., A_5\}$. Also, assume that M is equal to one (SSK scheme). Conventionally, since 5 is not a power of two, the number of exploited transmit antennas is the largest power of two that is less than 5. Hence, only 4 antennas will be used. Using (1), the block length in the conventional SM is $k_{SM} = 2$ bits. Thus, the transmitted data will be divided into 2-bit blocks, and each block will be mapped to a different antenna, as shown in Table 1. It is worth noting that the fifth antenna (A_5) is not used in the conventional SM scheme.

If we consider GSM with $N_a = 2$ active antennas, the block length is $k_{GSM} = 3$ bits which is computed using (2). Thus, we have $2^3 = 8$ different possible data blocks, where each block is transmitted to a different combination of two transmit antennas, as shown in Table 1.

Following the proposed scheme, based on (3), the block length is $k_{HSM} = 3$ bits. Thus, the number of the possible different data blocks is $2^3 = 8$ blocks. As such, 5 (out of 8) blocks will be transmitted using a single transmit antenna, while the rest of the blocks (3 out of 8) will be transmitted using two transmit antennas for each. Notice that the three two-antennas combinations listed in Table 1 are randomly selected. Although an opportunistic combination selection can enhance the overall performance, such an enhancement is very marginal given the extra complexity accompanied by the selection procedure.

Comparing the three schemes, it is clear that the conventional SM is the most energy efficient among others, since it always uses a single transmit antenna. However, the conventional SM achieves the lowest spectral efficiency where it transmits only 2 bits at each transmission round. On the other hand, the spectral efficiency of the GSM scheme achieves the highest spectral efficiency (3 bits), while its energy efficiency is the worst since it always activates two transmit antennas. However, the proposed scheme is able to attain the best spectral efficiency (3 bits, as in GSM), with an improved energy efficiency compared to GSM systems. The improvement in energy efficiency stems from the fact that the proposed scheme does not always require two active transmit antennas.

For the seek of elaborating, let us assume that the energy consumed in SM is denoted by E_{SM}, and the energy consumed in GSM systems is denoted by E_{GSM}. Both values can be related to each other as follows

$$E_{GSM} = (1 + \rho)E_{SM}, \tag{4}$$

where ρ is a coefficient related to the extra energy consumption due to activating multiple transmit antennas in GSM schemes. Notice that $0 < \rho < 1$ in order to ensure that the extra energy consumption in GSM is less than using another RF chain. As such, the energy consumed in the proposed hybrid scheme, denoted by E_{HSM}, can be represented as follows

$$E_{HSM} = \alpha E_{SM} + (1 - \alpha)E_{GSM}, \tag{5}$$

where α is the probability that the proposed scheme uses a single transmit antenna. The probability α is related to the number of available transmit antennas N_t as follows

$$\alpha = \frac{N_t}{N_t^*}, \tag{6}$$

where N_t^* is the nearest power-of-two number equal or larger than N_t. Notice that if N_t is a power of two, the probability α is equal to 1, and hence, the proposed scheme will completely act like the conventional SM scheme.

Substituting (4) and (6) in (5), the energy consumption of the proposed scheme can be given as follows

$$\begin{aligned} E_{HSM} &= \frac{N_t}{N_t^*}E_{SM} + \frac{N_t^* - N_t}{N_t^*}(1 + \rho)E_{SM} \\ &= \frac{1}{N_t^*}E_{SM}\left(N_t + (N_t^* - N_t)(1 + \rho)\right) \\ &= \frac{1}{N_t^*}E_{SM}\left((1 + \rho)N_t^* - \rho N_t\right) \end{aligned} \tag{7}$$

The percentage of saved energy due to the proposed scheme as compared to the GSM scheme, denoted by E_s, is defined as follows

$$E_s\% = \frac{E_{GSM} - E_{HSM}}{E_{GSM}} \times 100\% = \frac{\rho N_t}{(1 + \rho)N_t^*} \times 100\%, \tag{8}$$

3.2 BER Performance

The average error probability for the proposed SM scheme can be formulated using the union bound technique [18] as follows

$$\text{BER} \leq \frac{1}{k_{HSM}2^{k_{HSM}}} \sum_{i=1}^{2^{k_{HSM}}} \sum_{j \neq i} D_{\mathbf{x}_i, \mathbf{x}_j} \text{PEP}_{\mathbf{x}_i, \mathbf{x}_j} \tag{9}$$

where $D_{\mathbf{X}_i,\mathbf{X}_j}$ is hamming distance (the number of different bits) between the transmission vectors $\mathbf{X}_i$ and $\mathbf{X}_j$, and $\text{PEP}_{\mathbf{X}_i,\mathbf{X}_j}$ is the pairwise error probability between the two vectors $\mathbf{X}_i$ and $\mathbf{X}_j$. The pairwise error probability is defined as the probability that $\mathbf{X}_i$ is detected given that $\mathbf{X}_j$ is transmitted.

For Rayleigh fading channel, the pairwise error probability is also upper bounded as follows [19]

$$\text{PEP}_{\mathbf{X}_i,\mathbf{X}_j} \leq \frac{1}{2\det(\mathbf{I}_{N_r N_t} + \frac{1}{2\sigma_n^2}\boldsymbol{\Psi})} \tag{10}$$

where $\mathbf{I}_{N_r N_t}$ is the identity square matrix, $\boldsymbol{\Psi} = \mathbf{I}_{N_r} \otimes \boldsymbol{\Delta}\boldsymbol{\Delta}^H$, $\boldsymbol{\Delta} = \mathbf{X}_i - \mathbf{X}_j$, the superscript ^{H} denotes the complex conjugate operator, $\otimes$ denotes the Kronecker product, and $det(\cdot)$ denotes the determinant operator. Therefore, the average BER of the proposed scheme over Rayleigh fading channels can be expressed by substituting (10) in (9) as follows

$$\text{BER} \leq \frac{1}{k_{HSM}2^{k_{HSM}}} \sum_{i=1}^{2^{k_{HSM}}} \sum_{j\neq i} \frac{D_{\mathbf{X}_i,\mathbf{X}_j}}{2\det(\mathbf{I}_{N_r N_t} + \frac{1}{2\sigma_n^2}\boldsymbol{\Psi})} \tag{11}$$

Notice that the above upper bound can be used for SM and GSM scheme with careful substitution of the transmission vectors $\mathbf{X}$'s. Also, the average power of each transmission vector should be normalized to one.

Table 1. Symbol-Antenna mapping in the three schemes ($N_t = 5$)

SM		GSM ($N_a = 2$)		Proposed	
Symb.	Ant.	Symb.	Ants	Symb.	Ants
00	A_1	000	A_1 & A_2	000	A_1
01	A_2	001	A_2 & A_3	001	A_2
10	A_3	010	A_3 & A_4	010	A_3
11	A_4	011	A_4 & A_5	011	A_4
		100	A_5 & A_1	100	A_5
		101	A_2 & A_4	101	A_1 & A_2
		110	A_3 & A_5	110	A_3 & A_4
		111	A_1 & A_4	111	A_5 & A_1

4   Simulation Results

In this section we present Monte Carlo simulations in order to show the performance of the proposed hybrid SM scheme compared to the conventional SM and GSM schemes. The comparison metrics are the spectral efficiency, and the average BER.

The spectral efficiency versus the number of transmit antennas (N_t) for the three schemes are shown in Fig. 1. The number of active antennas in GSM is assumed $N_a = 2$. Compared to SM, the proposed scheme provides higher spectral efficiency when N_t is not a power of two, while in the case that N_t is a power of two (see at $N_t = 2, 4, 8$), both schemes achieve the same spectral efficiency. On the other hand, the proposed scheme achieves less spectral efficiency than GSM for a given number of transmit antennas. However, the performance improvement of GSM will be in the cost of the energy consumption.

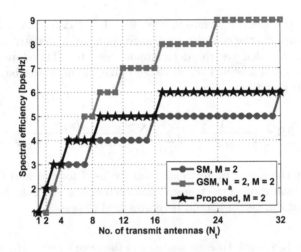

Fig. 1. The achievable spectral efficiency versus the number of available transmit antenna (N_t) for SM, GSM (with $N_a = 2$) and the proposed scheme.

The average BER for the proposed scheme versus the average SNR is shown in Fig. 2. $N_t = 3$, $M = 4$ and different values of N_r have been assumed. The analytical results obtained using the upper bound derived in (11) are added as well. At moderate and high SNR values, both the analytical and simulation curves match each other, which validates the derived formula in (11).

The average BER versus the average SNR for the three considered schemes is shown in Fig. 3. Specifically, SM with $N_t = 8$ and QPSK, GSM with $N_t = 5$, $N_a = 2$ and QPSK, and the proposed scheme with $N_t = 5, 6, 7$, and QPSK. The spectral efficiency of all schemes is 5 bps/Hz. The number of receive antennas is assumed $N_r = 3$. The performance of all schemes are almost equal. However, we zoomed in the average BER at $SNR = 9$ dB in the square shown in Fig. 3. As expected the conventional SM scheme achieves the best performance among all the considered schemes. For the proposed scheme, the achieved BER approaches the one achieved by the conventional SM as N_t approaches the power of two (i.e., 8). Moreover, the proposed scheme records better average BER values compared to GSM scheme.

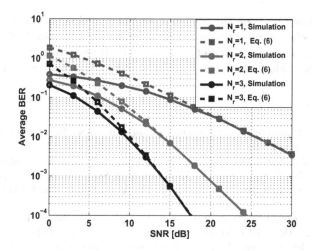

Fig. 2. Simulation and analytic results of the average BER versus the SNR for the proposed scheme. ($N_t = 3$, $M = 4$ (QPSK)).

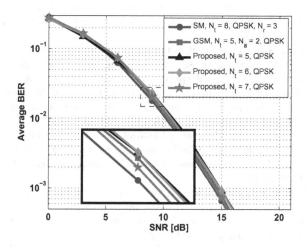

Fig. 3. The average BER versus the SNR for the three considered schemes. ($N_r = 3$).

5   Conclusions

In this paper, a hybrid SM scheme is proposed that allows for an arbitrary number of transmit antennas to be installed. The core idea of the proposed scheme is based on using a combination of two antennas in the case that the number of transmit antennas is not a power of two. The proposed scheme can be viewed as a combination between the conventional SM and GSM schemes. For a given number of transmit antennas, the proposed scheme achieves a moderate spectral efficiency between the conventional SM and GSM schemes. In addition, the proposed scheme consumes less energy compared to the GSM scheme. On the other hand, for a given spectral efficiency, the BER performance of the proposed scheme is almost identical to the BER achieved by the conventional scheme.

References

1. Telatar, E.: Capacity of multi-antenna gaussian channels. Eur. Trans. Telecommun. **10**(6), 585–595 (1999)
2. Mietzner, J., et al.: Multiple-antenna techniques for wireless communications-a comprehensive literature survey. IEEE Commun. Surv. Tutor. **11**(2), 87–105 (2009)
3. Mesleh, R., et al.: Spatial modulation. IEEE Trans. Veh. Technol. **57**(4), 2228–2241 (2008)
4. Maleki, M., et al.: Space modulation with CSI: Constellation design and performance evaluation. IEEE Trans. Veh. Technol. **62**(4), 1623–1634 (2013)
5. Wang, J., Jia, S., Song, J.: Generalised spatial modulation system with multiple active transmit antennas and low complexity detection scheme. IEEE Trans. Wirel. Commun. **11**(4), 1605–1615 (2012)
6. Di Renzo, M., et al.: Spatial modulation for generalized MIMO: challenges, opportunities, and implementation. Proc. IEEE **102**(1), 56–103 (2014)
7. Stavridis, A., et al.: Energy evaluation of spatial modulation at a multi-antenna base station. In: IEEE 78th Vehicular Technology Conference (VTC Fall), pp. 1–5. NV, Las Vegas (2013)
8. Xiao, Y., et al.: Spatial modulaiton for 5G mimo communications. In: 19th International Conference on Digital Signal Processing, pp. 847–851, August 2014
9. Younis, A., et al.: Generalised spatial modulation. In: Asilomar Conference on Signals, Systems, and Computers, Pacific Grove, CA, USA, November 2010
10. Datta, T., Chockalingam, A.: On generalized spatial modulation. In: IEEE Wireless Communications and Networking Conference (WCNC) (2013)
11. Narasimhan, T.L., et al.: Generalized spatial modulation in large-scale multiuser MIMO systems. IEEE Trans. Wirel. Commun. **14**(7), 3764–3779 (2015)
12. Yang, P., et al.: Design guidelines for spatial modulation. IEEE Commun. Surv. Tutor. **17**(1), 6–26 (2015)
13. Althunibat, S.: A mapping technique for space shift keying with arbitrary number of transmit antennas. In: IEEE CAMAD, pp. 1–6 (2017)
14. Serafimovski, N., et al.: Fractional bit encoded spatial modulation (FBE-SM). IEEE Commun. Lett. **14**(5), 429–431 (2010)
15. Yang, Y., Aissa, S.: Information guided channel hopping with an arbitrary number of transmit antennas. IEEE Commun. Lett. **16**(10), 1552–1555 (2012)
16. Jeganathan, J., et al.: Space shift keying modulation for MIMO channels. IEEE Transa. Wirel. Commun. **8**(7), 3692–3703 (2009)
17. Ntontin, K., et al.: Towards the performance and energy efficiency comparison of spatial modulation with conventional single-antenna transmission over generalized fading channels, pp. 120–124. IEEE CAMAD, Barcelona (2012)
18. Simon, M.K., Alouini, M.: Digital communication over fading channels. Wiley series in telecommunications and signal processing, 2nd edn. Wiley, Hoboken (2005). ISBN 978-0-471-64953-3
19. Handte, T., et al.: BER analysis and optimization of generalized spatial modulation in correlated fading channels. In: IEEE 70th Vehicular Technology Conference Fall, Anchorage, AK, pp. 1–5 (2009)

Spatial Modulation or Spatial Multiplexing for mmWave Communications?

Salma Elkawafi[1], Abdelhamid Younis[1], Raed Mesleh[2]([✉]), Abdulla Abouda[3], Ahmed Elbarsha[1], and Mohammed Elmusrati[4]

[1] Electrical and Electronics Engineering Department, Faculty of Engineering, University of Benghazi, P.O. Box 7051, Benghazi, Libya
{salma.elkawafi,a.alhassi,ahmed.elbarsha}@uob.edu.ly
[2] Electrical and Communications Engineering Department, School of Electrical Engineering and Information Technology, German Jordanian University, P.O. Box 35247, Amman 11180, Jordan
raed.mesleh@gju.edu.jo
[3] Almadar Research and Development Office, Almadar Aljadid Company, Tripoli, Libya
a.abouda@almadar.ly
[4] The Department of Computer Science, University of Vaasa, Vaasa, Finland
moel@uwasa.fi

Abstract. In this paper, two large scale (LS)–multiple–input multiple–output (MIMO) systems and their performance over 3D statistical outdoor millimeter wave (mmWave) channel model are considered and thoroughly analyzed. Namely, spatial multiplexing (SMX) and spatial modulation (SM) systems are considered. The performance of both systems in terms of average bit error ratio (ABER) and channel capacity are derived and studied. Obtained results divulge that SM can achieve higher theoretical capacity than SMX system. Further, SMX system is shown to offer better ABER and mutual information performance as compared to SM system for the same system configuration. Yet, SM demonstrate significant energy efficiency (EE) enhancement for large scale number of transmit antennas.

Keywords: Millimeter-wave (mmWave) communication
Spatial modulation (SM) · Spatial Multiplexing (SMX)
Large–scale MIMO (LS–MIMO)

1 Introduction

CISCO anticipated recently [8] that wireless mobile data traffic will witness tremendous growth in the coming few years. Such growth is impelled by the huge spread of IoT applications and video streaming. It is anticipated that data

Granted by Almadar Research and Development Office.

V. Sucasas et al. (Eds.): BROADNETS 2018, LNICST 263, pp. 237–246, 2019.
https://doi.org/10.1007/978-3-030-05195-2_23

Table 1. Spatial Multiplexing and Spatial Modulation

	SMX	SM
Spectral Efficiency	The spectral efficiency increases linearly with the number of transmit antennas	The spectral efficiency increases by base two logarithm of the number of transmit antennas
Computational Complexity (CC)	The CC increases at the receiver since it has to resolve the inter-channel interference (ICI) imposed by transmitting simultaneously from all antennas	It is not affected by ICI and provides the same computational complexity of a single transmit antenna systems
Hardware Complexity	All transmit antennas are active and each antenna requires individual RF chain, which complicate the deployment and increase the cost [12]	Only one transmit antenna is active on each time so only one RF chain is required which reduces the hardware complexity

traffic will reach 30.6 Exabytes per month by 2020. Yet, the existing spectrum is overcrowded and can not accommodate such massive increase in data rates [8]. Therefore, interest in utilizing unregulated wide spectrum has increased in the past few years.

One of the promising technologies for future 5G and beyond wireless systems is millimetre–wave (mmWave) communication [16], which utilizes huge range of unused spectrum and promises significant enhancement is spectral efficiency. Another technique that witness huge research interest is large scale (LS)–multiple–input multiple–output (MIMO) [3] systems, which leads to very high data rates. Combining mmWave with LS–MIMO promises to achieve the needed capacity and to accommodate the demand for high-data rate wireless systems.

mmWave technology provides several gigahertz bandwidths and is a promising solution for the spectrum congestion in current wireless standards. mmWave offers a bountiful spectrum spanning from 24–300 GHz that can be employed to achieve multi-gigabits per second data rates. Hence, it addresses many challenges in future wireless systems including very high data rates, and real-time and reliable communications [6]. Yet, the propagation of mmWave signals require accurate channel modeling that attracted significant research interest in literature [1,16]. Among the many existing models, a 3D channel model is shown in [16] to be the most comprehensive and accurately match measurement data. Therefore, it is considered in this study.

Developing an efficient MIMO technique is an active research topic for the past 20 years aiming to boost the capacity of wireless systems [19]. As such, MIMO systems are the main technology in 4G wireless standard and will play a major role in 5G and beyond standards [13]. Yet, practical implementation of MIMO systems face several challenges and two promising technologies are widely studied. Namely, spatial multiplexing (SMX) [9] and spatial modulation (SM) [2,7,11] MIMO systems promise significant advantages and undergoes intensive research interest. The advantages and disadvantages for each system are tabulated in Table 1. The requirement for massive data rate growth in future systems will rely on LS–MIMO systems [19]. Deploying large number of transmit antennas promises much higher spectral efficiency than conventional MIMO schemes [19]. Combining LS–MIMO and mmWave systems assure significant performance enhancement in terms of spectral efficiency and bandwidth, and are the key technologies for future 5G wireless systems.

This study aims at highlighting the performance of SMX and SM for mmWave system by evaluating their average bit error ratio (ABER), capacity and energy efficiency (EE). Interesting results are reported where it is revealed that SMX is superior to SM in terms of ABER assuming similar MIMO configuration. However, considering LS MIMO system significantly ameliorate SM performance. Even though this enhancement requires large number of antennas, they can be deployed at marginal cost of SM as discussed in [12]. Also, the channel capacity of SM is shown to be higher than that of SMX. Thereby, both MIMO schemes have several pros and cons when combined with mmWave communication. The use of which system depends on the data rate and ABER. For LS–MIMO with hundred of antennas, SM is preferred with its much cheaper energy implementation. Whereas SMX is better scheme for small scale MIMO setup since it promises lower ABER performance.

The rest of the paper is organized as follows: Sect. 2 introduces the system and channel models. The mutual information and theoretical capacity for SMX and SM systems are derived and discussed in Sect. 3. Section 4 summarizes the obtained results. Finally, the paper is concluded in Sect. 5.

2 System and Channel Models

2.1 MIMO Systems

SMX: In SMX, all transmit antennas are activated simultaneously to transmit $\eta = N_t \log_2(M)$ bits, with each antenna transmitting M–quadrature amplitude modulation (QAM) symbol [9]. Activating all antennas simultaneously require that they should be synchronized and the overall transmit power is divided among them.

SM: In SM, only one transmit antenna is activated each time instance. Thus, the spectral efficiency of SM is $\eta = \log_2 N_t + \log_2 M$ bits [5,11]. In SM the incoming η data bits are divided into two parts;

i. The first part, $\log_2(N_t)$, bits determine which transmit antenna l_t is active, where $l_t = 1, 2, .., N_t$.
ii. The second part with $\log_2 M$ bits modulate a symbol driven from M–QAM constellation and then transmitted from the l_t transmit antenna.

The generated SM unique symbol vector, $\mathbf{x}_t$, contains only single nonzero element and the vector is broadcasted over a mmWave MIMO channel matrix with an $N_r \times N_t$ dimension and a transfer function of $\mathbf{H}$. The signal at the input of the receive antennas experiences an N_r-dim additive white Gaussian noise (AWGN) ($\mathbf{n}$), with zero mean and σ_n^2 variance.

The signal at the receiver can be written as

$$\mathbf{y} = \mathbf{H}\mathbf{x}_t + \mathbf{n}. \tag{1}$$

Considering that the transmitted symbol is normalized, i.e., $E_s = \mathrm{E}[\|\mathbf{H}\mathbf{x}\|_\mathrm{F}^2] = N_r$, the signal-to-noise-ratio (SNR) is written as SNR $= E_s/N_0 = 1/\sigma_n^2$, with $\|\cdot\|_\mathrm{F}$ being the Frobenius norm.

2.2 3D Statistical mmWave Channel Model

Assuming that all transmit antennas are omni-directional antennas and operating at a mmWave frequency. The channel between the n_t-th and n_r-th transmit and receive antennas channel, denoted as $h_{n_t,n_r}(t)$, is written as [15],

$$h_{n_t,n_r}(t) = \sum_{l=1}^{L} h_{n_t,n_r}^l \, a_l e^{j\varphi_l} \delta(t - \tau_l) \, \delta\left(\Theta - \Theta_{n_t,l}\right) \delta\left(\Phi - \Phi_{n_r,l}\right), \tag{2}$$

with h_{n_t,n_r}^l denoting the complex channel fading of the l-th sub-path, among the existing L multi-path components, between the n_t-th and n_r-th antennas, and the amplitude, phase and propagation-delay of the same sub-path are denoted by a_l, φ_l and τ_l. Also, the angle of departure (AOD) and angle of arrival (AOA) azimuth/elevation angle vectors are given by $\Theta_{n_t,l}$ and $\Phi_{n_r,l}$ for the n_t-th and n_r-th antennas. Assuming that the antennas at both side are aligned along the z-dimension and separated by equidistant d, the channel in (2) can be simplified to,

$$h_{n_t,n_r}(t) = \sum_{l=1}^{L} h_{n_t,n_r}^l \, a_l e^{j\varphi_l} \delta(t - \tau_l) \, \delta\left(\theta^z - \theta_{n_t,l}^z\right) \delta\left(\phi^z - \phi_{n_t,l}^z\right), \tag{3}$$

with the elevation AOD and AOA for the n_t-th and n_r-th transmit and receive antennas are respectively denoted by $\theta_{n_t,l}^z$ and $\phi_{n_r,l}^z$.

According to [14], the transfer function in (3) is

$$h_{n_t,n_r}(f) = \sum_{l=1}^{L} h_{n_t,n_r}^l a_k e^{j\varphi_l} e^{-j\frac{2\pi}{\lambda} d\left(n_t \sin\left(\theta_{n_t,l}^z\right) + n_r \sin\left(\phi_{n_r,l}^z\right)\right)} e^{-j2\pi f \tau_l}, \tag{4}$$

with λ being the wavelength.

The parameters in this study, a_l, φ_l, $\theta_{n_t,l}^z$, $\phi_{n_r,l}^z$, and τ_l, are generated according to [16] considering outdoor mmWave model.

2.3 Optimum Receiver

The optimum decoder is considered for both SMX and SM in this paper, which can be written as

$$\hat{\mathbf{x}}_t = \underset{\mathbf{x} \in \mathbf{X}}{\arg\min} \left\{ \left\| \mathbf{y} - \tilde{\mathbf{H}}\mathbf{x} \right\|_F^2 \right\} \tag{5}$$

with all possible transmitted vector for each system and grouped in the set $\mathbf{X}$ contains every possible $(N_t \times 1)$ and the estimated vector is denoted by $\hat{\cdot}$.

3 Capacity Analysis

3.1 Mutual Information

To compute the capacity of SM and SMX systems, the mutual information, which represents the number of received and decoded bits without errors, should be computed. For SMX, $I(\mathbf{X}; \mathbf{Y})$, is given by [10],

$$I(\mathbf{X}; \mathbf{Y}) = \mathrm{E}_{\mathbf{H}} \left\{ I\left(\mathbf{X}; \mathbf{Y} \,|\mathbf{H}\right) \right\} = \mathrm{E}_{\mathbf{H}} \left\{ H\left(\mathbf{Y} \,|\mathbf{H}\right) - H\left(\mathbf{Y} \,|\mathbf{X}, \mathbf{H}\right) \right\}, \tag{6}$$

where $H(\cdot)$ denoting the entropy function and all possible $(N_r \times 1)$ receive vectors are grouped in $\mathbf{Y}$. Then, $I(\mathbf{X}; \mathbf{X}|\mathbf{H})$ is written as

$$I\left(\mathbf{X}; \mathbf{Y} \,|\mathbf{H}\right) = \eta - N_r \log_2(e) - \mathrm{E}_{\mathbf{Y}} \left\{ \log_2 \sum_{\mathbf{x} \in \mathbf{X}} e^{\frac{-\|\mathbf{y} - \mathbf{H}\mathbf{x}\|_F^2}{\sigma_n^2}} \right\}. \tag{7}$$

In SM, the channel paths are used as a spatial constellation symbols that are modulated by source data bits and used to convey part of the information data. Hence, the mutual information for SM systems is given by,

$$I\left(\mathcal{H}, \mathcal{S}; \mathbf{Y}\right) = H\left(\mathbf{Y}\right) - H\left(\mathbf{Y}|\mathcal{H}, \mathcal{S}\right) \tag{8}$$

$$= \eta - N_r \log_2(e) - \mathrm{E}_{\mathbf{Y}} \left\{ \log_2 \sum_{\substack{\mathcal{H}_\ell \in \mathcal{H} \\ \mathcal{S}_i \in \mathcal{S}}} e^{\frac{-\|\mathbf{y} - \mathcal{H}_\ell \mathcal{S}_i\|_F^2}{\sigma_n^2}} \right\}, \tag{9}$$

3.2 Capacity

Spatial Multiplexing: By definition, the capacity is [10],

$$C = \max_{p_{\mathbf{X}}} I\left(\mathbf{X}; \mathbf{Y} \,|\mathbf{H}\right), \tag{10}$$

where the theoretical capacity is achieved maximization by selecting proper $p_{\mathbf{X}}$ such that the mutual information is maximized, with $p_{\mathbf{X}}$ being the probability distribution function (PDF) of the transmitted space of vectors $\mathbf{X}$.

Substituting (6) in (10), the capacity for SMX is rewritten as,

$$C = \max_{p_X} \left(H\left(\mathbf{Y}\,|\mathbf{H}\right) - H\left(\mathbf{Y}\,|\mathbf{X},\mathbf{H}\right)\right). \tag{11}$$

A significant conclusion can be drawn from (11) where the entropy $H(\mathbf{Y}\,|\mathbf{X},\mathbf{H})$ is not function of $\mathbf{X}$. Thereby, (11) is maximized if $H\left(\mathbf{Y}\,|\mathbf{H}\right)$ is maximized. Considering that the entropy is maximized if a zero-mean complex Gaussian distribution is considered as derived in [17]. As such, the maximum entropy of $\mathbf{Y}$ is,

$$H\left(\mathbf{Y}\,|\mathbf{H}\right) = N_r \log_2\left(\pi e\left(\frac{1}{N_t}\mathbf{H}\mathbf{H}^H + \sigma_n^2 \mathbf{I}_{N_r}\right)\right) \tag{12}$$

The entropy of $\mathbf{Y}$ knowing $\mathbf{X}$ is,

$$H\left(\mathbf{Y}|\mathbf{X},\mathbf{H}\right) = N_r \log_2\left(\pi \sigma_n^2 e\right). \tag{13}$$

With the help of (11)–(13), the ergodic capacity of SMX is given by,

$$C_{\text{ergodic}} = \mathbf{E_H}\left\{\log_2\left(\left|\mathbf{I}_{N_r} + \frac{1}{\sigma_n^2 N_t}\mathbf{H}\mathbf{H}^H\right|\right)\right\} \tag{14}$$

Spatial Modulation: In SM the information bits are modulated in the different constellations symbols and channel vectors. Therefore, the capacity in (10) can be re-written as,

$$C = \max_{p_{\mathcal{H}},p_{\mathcal{S}}} I\left(\mathcal{H},\mathcal{S};\mathbf{Y}\right) = \max_{p_{\mathcal{H}},p_{\mathcal{S}}} \left\{H\left(\mathbf{Y}\right) - H\left(\mathbf{Y}\,|\mathcal{H},\mathcal{S}\right)\right\} \tag{15}$$

where $p_{\mathcal{H}}$ and $p_{\mathcal{S}}$ are the PDFs of $\mathcal{H}$ and $\mathcal{S}$ respectively.

As in (11), the left hand size of (15) does not depend on $\mathcal{S}$ nor $\mathcal{H}$. Thus, the maximization in (15) is only of $H\left(\mathbf{Y}\right)$. The entropy $H\left(\mathbf{Y}\right)$ is maximized when $\mathbf{Y} \sim \mathcal{CN}\left(\mathbf{0}_{N_r}, \sigma_Y^2 \mathbf{I}_{N_r}\right)$, with σ_Y^2 denoting the variance of $\mathbf{Y}$ and $\mathbf{0}_{N_r}$ is an N_r–length all zeros vector. From (1), the received signal is complex Gaussian distributed only if $\mathcal{H}\mathcal{S} \sim \mathcal{CN}\left(\mathbf{0}_{N_r}, \mathbf{I}_{N_r}\right)$, where $\mathbf{0}_N$ is an N–length all zeros vector, and $\mathbf{I}_N$ is an $N \times N$ identity matrix. By assuming $\mathcal{H}\mathcal{S}$ is complex Gaussian distributed, the entropy of $\mathbf{Y}$ following the same steps as discussed for (13) is,

$$H\left(\mathbf{Y}\right) = N_r \log_2\left(\pi e\left(1 + \sigma_n^2\right)\right). \tag{16}$$

Under these conditions and with the help of (11), (13), and (16), the space modulation techniques (SMT) capacity is given by,

$$C_{\text{ergodic}} = N_r \log_2\left(1 + 1/\sigma_n^2\right) = N_r \log_2\left(1 + \text{SNR}\right). \tag{17}$$

4   Results

Presented results in this section, Figs. 1, 2 and 3, study and compare the performance of SM and SMX over 3D mmWave statistical channel model while varying different system and channel parameters. It is assumed that a base-station with N_t transmit antennas communicates with a single user that has N_r receive antennas.

4.1   ABER Performance Comparison

Figure 1 depicts the ABER while varying N_t for both SMX and SM systems while achieving a spectral efficiency of $\eta = 16$ and considering $N_r = 2$. Reported results reveal that SMX outperforms SM by about 3 dB in SNR. This can be attributed to the fact that SMX requires smaller constellation diagram than SM to achieve the target spectral efficiency.

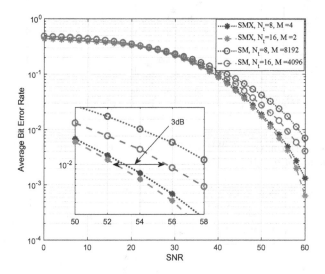

Fig. 1. ABER performance of SM and SMX assuming $N_t = 8$, and 16, $N_r = 2$ and a spectral efficiency of $\eta = 16$ bps/Hz.

Considering the case where $N_t = 16$ while varying N_r for the same $\eta = 16$ is studied and results are illustrated in Fig. 2. Increasing the number of receive antennas enhances the performance of SMX and SM systems. Yet, SMX still outperforms SM by about 6, and 11 dB respectively for $N_r = 2$ and 4. This behavior can be attributed to the same reason as discussed earlier.

4.2   Capacity Results

Mutual information results are depicted in Fig. 3 for $\eta = 8$ and 16 while assuming $N_t = 8$ and $N_r = 4$ antennas. The capacity curves for both systems are also depicted. It is observed that SM and SMX perform nearly the same at a spectral efficiencies of 8. Yet, for $\eta = 16$ bits, SMX offers higher mutual information than SM. It can be seen that at SNR $= 30$ dB, SMX mutual information is 3.32 bits higher than the mutual information of SM. Even though SMX outperforms SM it term of mutual information, SM can achieve higher capacity as can be seen from the figure, where for SMX it is required more 11 dB to achieve the same spectral efficiency, 16 bits.

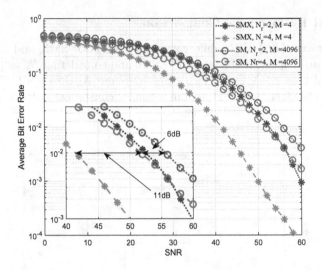

Fig. 2. ABER performance of SM and SMX assuming $N_t = 16$, $N_r = 2$ and 4 and a spectral efficiency of $\eta = 16\,\text{bps/Hz}$.

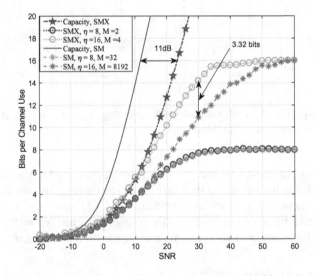

Fig. 3. Mutual information of SM and SMX for variant η while assuming $N_t = 8$ and $N_r = 4$.

4.3 Energy Efficiency

The EE of both systems is studied with respect to the ergodic capacity and for different antenna setups and results are shown in Fig. 4. We define the EE as the ratio between the total number correctly received bits (C) to the total power consumption (P_s) [18], $EE = \frac{C_{\text{ergodic}}}{P_s}$. For comparison analysis, we consider

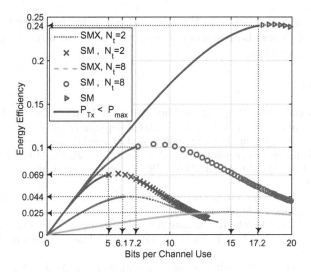

Fig. 4. EE of SM and SMX with $N_r = 4$, (Solid line) when $(P_{Tx} \leqslant P_{max})$.

the EARTH power model, which describes the relation between the total power supplied and the radio frequency (RF) transmit power as [4], $P_s = N_{RF} P_{min} + m P_{Tx}$, where N_{RF} is the required number of RF chains, $N_{RF} = N_t$ for SMX and $N_{RF} = 1$ for SM, P_{min} is the minimum RF chain power consumption, m denotes the slope of the load dependent power consumption, and P_{Tx} is the total RF transmit power. The measurements in [16] were carried in a microcell environment. From [4] for a microcell environment $P_{min} = 53$ w, $m = 3.1$, and the maximum transmit power per RF chain is $P_{max} = 6.3$ w. The figure shows that SM offers better EE than SMX, where SM offers an improvement in the EE by up to 36% and 74% compared to SMX for $N_t = 2$ and $N_t = 8$, respectively. This is because for SM, the total RF transmit power is fixed. However, for SMX it increases by the number of transmit antennas.

5   Conclusions

Two promising MIMO techniques are studied and analyzed in this paper for mmWave communication systems. namely, SM and SMX MIMO systems are evaluated in terms of error probability, capacity and energy efficiency. Reported results reveal that the performance of both systems highly depends on the considered MIMO setup. For the same hardware configuration, SMX is superior to SM since it requires smaller constellation diagram to achieve the same data rate. Yet, SM performance significantly enhances as the number of transmit antennas increase. Considering SM with LS MIMO configuration is very feasible since it can implemented with single RF chain and it does not scale the consumed power. Also, the high frequency of mmWave signals allow for integrating large number of antennas in small dimension without causing significant correlation among them. A clear answer to the raised question in the paper title is shown to be equivocal, where both systems can be traded off in terms of performance and energy consumption.

References

1. 3GPP: Spatial Channel Model for Multiple Input Multiple Output MIMO Simulations. document 3GPP TR 25.996 V12.0.0, September 2014
2. Althunibat, S., Mesleh, R.: Enhancing spatial modulation system performance through signal space diversity. IEEE Commun. Lett. **22**(6), 1136–1139 (2018)
3. Andrews, J., et al.: What will 5G be? IEEE J. Sel. Areas Commun. **32**(6), 1065–1082 (2014)
4. Auer, G., et al.: How much energy is needed to run a wireless network? IEEE Wirel. Commun. **18**(5), 40–49 (2011)
5. Badarneh, O.S., Mesleh, R.: A comprehensive framework for quadrature spatial modulation in generalized fading scenarios. IEEE Trans. Commun. **64**(7), 2961–2970 (2016)
6. Barreto, A., et al.: 5G – wireless communications for 2020. J. Commun. Inf. Syst. **31**, 146–163 (2016)
7. Basar, E.: Index modulation techniques for 5G wireless networks. IEEE Commun. Mag. **54**(7), 168–175 (2016)
8. Cisco Visual Networking Index: Global Mobile Data Traffic Forecast Update, 2016–2021. White Paper, CISCO, February 2017
9. Foschini, G.J.: Layered space-time architecture for wireless communication in a fading environment when using multi-element antennas. Bell Labs Tech. J. **1**(2), 41–59 (1996)
10. Kühn, V.: Wireless Communications over MIMO Channels. Wiley, Chichester (2006)
11. Mesleh, R., Haas, H., Sinanović, S., Ahn, C.W., Yun, S.: Spatial modulation. IEEE Trans. Veh. Tech. **57**(4), 2228–2241 (2008)
12. Mesleh, R., Hiari, O., Younis, A., Alouneh, S.: Transmitter design and hardware considerations for different space modulation techniques. IEEE Trans. Wirel. Commun. **16**(11), 7512–7522 (2017)
13. Mietzner, J., Schober, R., Lampe, L., Gerstacker, W.H., Höeher, P.A.: Multiple-antenna techniques for wireless communications - a comprehensive literature survey. IEEE Commun. Surv. Tutor. **11**(2), 87–105 (2009)
14. Molisch, A.F., Steinbauer, M., Toeltsch, M., Bonek, E., Thoma, R.S.: Capacity of MIMO systems based on measured wireless channels. IEEE J. Sel. Areas Commun. **20**(3), 561–569 (2002)
15. Saleh, A.A.M., Valenzuela, R.: A statistical model for indoor multipath propagation. IEEE J. Sel. Areas Commun. **5**(2), 128–137 (1987)
16. Samimi, M.K., Rappaport, T.S.: 3-D millimeter-wave statistical channel model for 5G wireless system design. IEEE Trans. Microw. Theor. Tech. **64**(7), 2207–2225 (2016)
17. Shannon, C.: A mathematical theory of communication. Bell Syst. Tech. J. **27**, 379–423 & 623–656 (1948)
18. Stavridis, A., Sinanović, S., Renzo, M.D., Haas, H.: Energy evaluation of spatial modulation at a multi-antenna base station. In: Proceedings of the 78th IEEE Vehicular Technology Conference (VTC), Las Vegas, 2–5 September 2013
19. Zheng, K., Zhao, L., Mei, J., Shao, B., Xiang, W., Hanzo, L.: Survey of large-scale MIMO systems. IEEE Commun. Surv. Tutor. **17**(3), 1738–1760 (2015)

Hardware Implementation of Generalized Space Modulation Techniques Using Simulink RF Blockset

Raed Mesleh$^{(\boxtimes)}$, Abdullah Al-Khatib, and Omar Hiari

School of Electrical Engineering and Information Technology, German Jordanian University, Amman-Madaba Street, P.O. Box 35247, Amman 11180, Jordan
{raed.mesleh,a.alkhatib,omar.hiari}@gju.edu.jo

Abstract. Generalized space modulation techniques (GSMTs) are attractive multiple-input multiple-output (MIMO) technologies that promise significant advantages for future wireless systems. Most existing studies of GSMTs in literature tackle several theoretical issues analytically or through Monte Carlo simulations. However, practical implementation and hardware limitations are yet to be studied. In this paper, GSMTs implementations using RF hardware components within the Simulink RF blockset library is considered. The implementation targets minimum hardware components and proposes fundamental baseband models for different GSMTs. The developed models facilitate the investigation of the impact of different parameters on the overall system performance. The accuracy of these models is corroborated through calculating the average BER and compare it to existing curves in literature. In addition, the required hardware components for GSMTs in passband implementation are discussed.

Keywords: MIMO · Space modulation techniques
Simulink–RF blockset

1 Introduction

The number of connected devices to the Internet witnessed tremendous growth in the past few years and the trend is unlikely to cease in the near future. The need for advanced wireless communication systems in terms of spectral and energy efficiencies as well as hardware simplicity are the key elements that drive research in the future 5G standard and beyond. Future systems require devices with marginal cost and energy consumption while achieving fast connectivity, low complexity and very low end-to-end latency [1].

Space modulation techniques (SMTs) [2–4,6] are one of the promising technologies for next generation wireless systems as they promise several advantages in terms of performance, spectral efficiency, hardware complexity and implementation simplicity and cost. In SMTs, multiple transmit antennas exist but

Published by Springer Nature Switzerland AG 2019. All Rights Reserved
V. Sucasas et al. (Eds.): BROADNETS 2018, LNICST 263, pp. 247–256, 2019.
https://doi.org/10.1007/978-3-030-05195-2_24

only certain number of them is active at each time instant. It has been revealed in [6] that these techniques can be implemented with a maximum of a single RF-chain while achieving superior performance as compared to other state-of-the-art MIMO technologies. Yet, in SMTs, the number of transmit antennas must be a power of two integer and the use of arbitrary number of antennas is not feasible. Therefore, a generalization of SMTs is proposed in literature to relax these constraints and allow the use of an arbitrary number of transmit antennas. Such generalization is referred to as generalized space modulation techniques (GSMTs) and include generalized space shift keying (GSSK), generalized quadrature space shift keying (GQSSK), generalized spatial modulation (GSM), and generalized quadrature spatial modulation (GQSM) [5].

In this study, we consider the hardware implementation of different GSMTs using Simulink RF blockset and study the impact of RF-switch insertion loss (IL) on the average bit error probability (BER) of these systems. IL has been shown recently to significantly degrade the BER of different SMTs in [7]. Similar behavior is also noticed here for different GSMTs.

The rest of the paper is organized as follows, Sect. 2 describes GSMTs system and channel models. Section 3 presents the implementation of different GSMTs using Simulink RF blockset. Section 4 discusses the obtained results and elaborates on some of the properties of the proposed models. Finally, the paper is concluded in Sect. 5.

2   System and Channel Models

A MIMO system with N_t transmit and N_r receive antennas is considered in this study. At each time instant, η bits are to be transmitted using one of the existing GSMTs. In all GSMTs, a group of transmit antennas, $1 < N_u < N_t$, is activated at each time instant to transmit an identical symbol. The received signal at the receiver input can be written as

$$y = Hx + n, \tag{1}$$

where H denotes an $N_r \times N_t$ MIMO channel matrix with complex Gaussian i.i.d entries as $h_{ij} \sim \mathcal{CN}(0,1)$, $i \in \{1 : N_r\}$, $j \in \{1 : N_t\}$, x is the transmitted vector of modulated or un-modulated symbols with normalized energy, i.e., $\mathrm{E}\left[xx^H\right] = 1$ and n denotes a vector with additive white Gaussian noise entries each with a zero mean and σ_n^2 variance, $n_i \sim \mathcal{CN}(0, \sigma_n^2)$. As such, the average signal to noise ratio at each receive antenna is $\bar{\gamma} = \frac{1}{\sigma_n^2}$. The received signals are then processed and a maximum likelihood detector is used to retrieve transmitted information bits as

$$\hat{x} = \arg \min_{x_i \in \mathcal{X}} \|y - Hx_i\|_F^2 \tag{2}$$

where $\hat{x}$ denotes the estimated symbol vector indicating modulated symbol and/or active antennas, $\mathcal{X}$ being a set containing all possible transmitted vectors and $\|.\|_F$ being the Frobenius norm. Finally, the average BER is taken by comparing the transmitted word with the received word using an Error Rate calculation block.

The transmitted vector $\mathbf{x}$ is generated based on the considered GSMTs as discussed hereinafter.

2.1 Generalized Space Shift Keying (GSSK)

In a GSSK system [8], $\eta_{\mathrm{GSSK}} = \left\lfloor \log_2 \left(\dfrac{N_t}{N_u} \right) \right\rfloor$ bits are transmitted at each time instant with $\lfloor \cdot \rfloor$ denoting the floor operation. In GSSK, the transmitted bits are incorporated in the location of the activated antennas and the transmitted symbol is un-modulated and only indicating which antennas are active at this time [5].

2.2 Generalized Spatial Modulation (GSM)

GSM is an addition to the GSSK system by transmitting modulated symbols [9]. Hence, the spectral efficiency of a GSM system is $\eta_{\mathrm{GSSK}} = \left\lfloor \log_2 \left(\dfrac{N_t}{N_u} \right) \right\rfloor + \log_2 (M)$. The transmitted symbols can be drawn from arbitrary signal constellations such as quadrature amplitude modulation (QAM) or phase shift keying (PSK).

2.3 Generalized Quadrature Space Shift Keying (GQSSK)

GQSSK is similar to GSSK, where the transmitted symbols are un-modulated and data bits only modulate spatial symbols. However, two groups of antennas are activated in GQSSK, N_u^I and N_u^Q [5]. The first group, N_u^I, transmits the in-phase part of the carrier signal whereas the second group, N_u^Q, transmits the quadrature component of the RF carrier signal as discussed in details in [5]. Hence, the spectral efficiency of GQSSK is $\eta_{\mathrm{GQSSK}} = \left\lfloor 2 * \log_2 \left(\dfrac{N_t}{N_u} \right) \right\rfloor$.

2.4 Generalized Quadrature Spatial Modulation (GQSM)

Modulating the RF carriers in GQSSK results in a GQSM system [5], which achieves spectral efficiency of $\eta_{\mathrm{GQSM}} = \left\lfloor 2 * \log_2 \left(\dfrac{N_t}{N_u} \right) \right\rfloor + \log_2 (M)$.

3 Simulink RF Blockset System Models

In this work, Simulink baseband implementations of GSMTs using the RF Blockset library are introduced. The BER performance of these systems is studied while considering hardware imperfections, namely RF switch IL. The implemented system models for GSSK, GQSSK, GSM and GQSM are respectively shown in Figs. 1, 2, 3, and 4. Each illustrated model consists mainly of four main stages/blocks: The transmitter, the channel, the receiver, and the BER calculation. The depicted models also consider a MIMO setup with arbitrary number of transmit and receive antennas.

It is important to note that practical hardware components suffer from several imperfections other than only IL. Some imperfections include: Frequency offset, weak isolation, return loss, and VSWR. While out of the scope of this work, all of these imperfections need to be studied and their impact on the overall system performance should be analyzed before any practical hardware implementation. However, it would be beneficial to study the imperfections in isolation to better understand the effect on system performance as a whole. Since the RF switch is newly introduced as an active component for the implementation of SMTs in particular, and MIMO in general, it was elected to focus on the switch imperfections first.

In the transmitter blocks, the main function is to handle the input word from the random binary source. The input word, is divided into two parts, the first with $\log_2(M)$ bits (if GSM/GQSK based model) that are routed to a modulator block. The second, are the remainder of the bits that control the RF-switch select lines. Contrary to non-generalized implementations $\log_2(N_t)$ bits cannot be routed directly to the switches since there are different sets of combinations that activate multiple switches. Therefore, a decoder block is utilized to provide a mapping between the received bits and the select line states. In the transmitter blocks, the input signal power is also split through power dividers to the different RF-switch inputs. The number of power dividers needed depends on how many RF-switches are used; two being the minimum.

In the remainder of the model, a channel block exists to generate the **H** matrix, modeling Rayleigh fading, and applying AWGN. The resulting **y** vector and **H** are passed on to the receiver block. Finally, the receiver block applies the maximum likelihood (ML) decoder algorithm where demodulation is applied and the transmitted bits are recovered.

4   Results

The BER of the different GSMTs presented in the previous section is evaluated through Monte Carlo simulations while considering the effect of RF-switch IL. In the results, three different values of IL are considered. Namely, 0 dB IL, which represents the ideal case of no IL, 1.5 dB, and 3 dB IL. The SNR is varied from 0 dB to 30 dB and the average BER is computed for at least 10^6 bits for each depicted SNR value. For fair comparison among different GSMTs, a spectral efficiency of 6 bps/Hz is assumed for all systems while considering $N_r = 4$ receive antennas and varying the number of transmit antennas and/or modulation order. The considered system parameters for different GSMTs to achieve the target spectral efficiency are tabulated in Table 1 (Figs. 5 and 6).

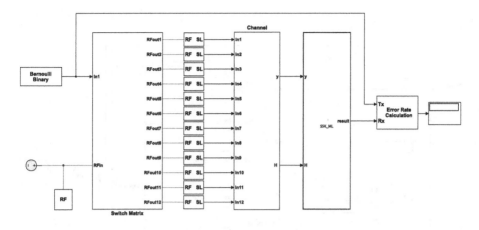

Fig. 1. Simulink model of GSSK with $N_t = 12$, $N_r = 4$, and $N_u = 2$ antennas

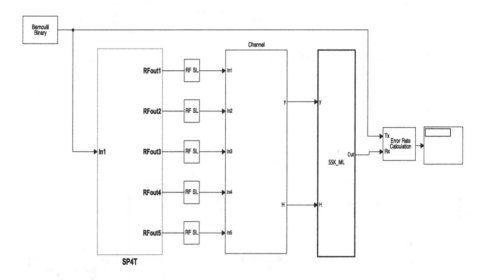

Fig. 2. Simulink model of GQSSK with $N_t = 5$, $N_r = 4$, $N_u = 2$ antennas

Table 1. Simulink GSMTs parameters to achieve a spectral efficiency of $\eta = 6$ bps/Hz.

Model	η (bps/Hz)	$N_t \times N_r$	M	N_u
GSSK	6	12×4	N/A	2
GQSSK	6	5×4	N/A	2
GSM	6	5×4	8	2
GQSM	6	4×4	4	2

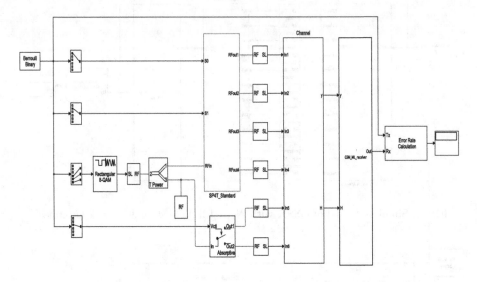

Fig. 3. Simulink model of GSM with $N_t = 5$, $N_r = 4$, $N_u = 2$ antennas

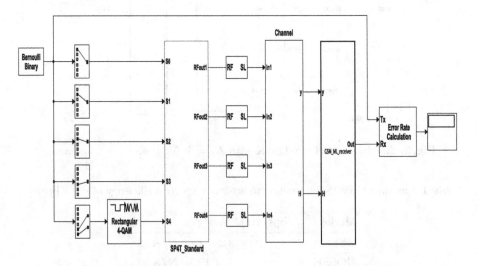

Fig. 4. Simulink model of GQSM with $N_t = 4$, $N_r = 4$, $N_u = 2$ antennas

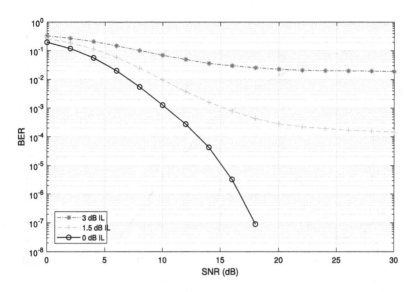

Fig. 5. BER performance of GSSK for different values of IL and with $N_t = 12$, $N_r = 4$, and $N_u = 2$.

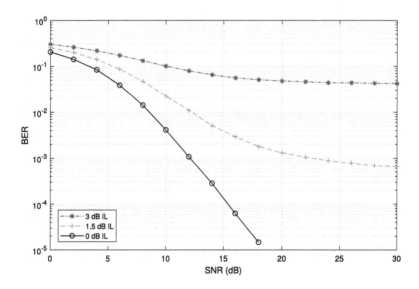

Fig. 6. BER performance of GQSSK for different values of IL and with $N_t = 5$, $N_r = 4$, and $N_u = 2$.

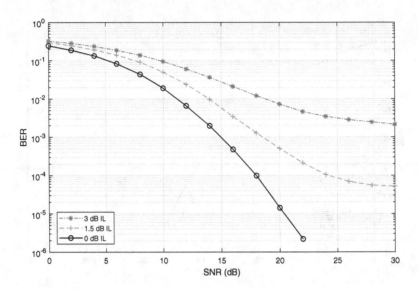

Fig. 7. BER performance of GSM for different values of IL and with $N_t = 5$, $N_r = 4$, $N_u = 2$, and $M = 8$-QAM.

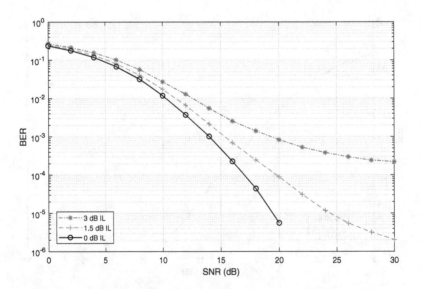

Fig. 8. BER performance of GQSM for different values of IL and with $N_t = 4$, $N_r = 4$, $N_u = 2$, and $M = 4$-QAM.

Depicted results for all systems reveal the negative impact of IL on the average BER performance of all GSMTs. Increasing the IL from 0 dB to 3 dB is shown to significantly deteriorate the system performance and an error floor is noticed for all GSMTs. Comparing the results of the different systems show that GSSK and GQSSK outperform GSM and GQSM in the ideal case of 0 dB IL. However, for large values of IL, GSM and GQSM are shown to be superior over GSSK and GQSSK. This is because IL significantly deteriorates the detection of spatial symbols and increases the BER values of GSSK and GQSSK tremendously (Figs. 7 and 8).

The reported Simulink models in this paper for variant GSMTs can also be used to study the performance of these systems in real time implementations. They are the first step towards practical deployment of these techniques and they can be used to optimize performance and design specific hardware components tailored to the special nature of these techniques.

5 Conclusions

This paper proposes the use of Simulink RF blockset baseband models to implement the different GSMTs and study their performance under practical hardware assumptions and scenarios. To illustrate the effectiveness of the proposed models, the impact of RF switch IL on the overall BER performance of these systems is studied and discussed. Future hardware implementations of GSMTs can be simplified and optimized using the reported models. Future works will address the investigation of different hardware impairments and optimize the design of GSMTs for better and enhanced performance.

Acknowledgments. The authors acknowledge the financial support of the Deanship of Scientific Research at the German Jordanian University under research grant number SIC 41/2016.

References

1. Andrews, J.G., Buzzi, S., Choi, W., Hanly, S.V., Lozano, A., Soong, A.C., Zhang, J.C.: What will 5g be? IEEE J. Sel. Areas Commun. **32**(6), 1065–1082 (2014)
2. Basar, E., Wen, M., Mesleh, R., Renzo, M.D., Xiao, Y., Haas, H.: Index modulation techniques for next-generation wireless networks. IEEE Access **5**, 1–52 (2017)
3. Mesleh, R., Al-Hassi, R.: Space Modulation Techniques, 1st edn. Wiley, 288 pages, 13 June 2018
4. Younis, A., Mesleh, R.: Information-theoretic treatment of space modulation MIMO systems. IEEE Trans. Veh. Technol. **67**, 6960–6969 (2018)
5. Mesleh, R., Hiari, O., Younis, A.: Generalized space modulation techniques: Hardware design and considerations. Phys. Commun. **26**, 87–95 (2018)
6. Mesleh, R., Hiari, O., Younis, A., Alouneh, S.: Transmitter design and hardware considerations for different space modulation techniques. IEEE Trans. Wirel. Commun. **16**(11), 7512–7522 (2017)

7. Hiari, O., Mesleh, R.: Impact of RF switch insertion loss on the performance of space modulation techniques. IEEE Commun. Lett. **22**, 958–961 (2018)
8. Jeganathan, J., Ghrayeb, A., Szczecinski, L.: Generalized space shift keying modulation for MIMO channels. In: IEEE 19th International Symposium on Conference: Personal, Indoor and Mobile Radio Communications, PIMRC 2008, 15–18 September 2008, pp. 1–5 (2008)
9. Younis, A., Serafimovski, N., Mesleh, R., Haas, H.: Generalised spatial modulation. In: Asilomar Conference on Signals, Systems, and Computers, Pacific Grove, CA, USA (2010)

A Half-Full Transmit-Diversity Spatial Modulation Scheme

Sakher AbuTayeh[1], Mohammad Alsalahat[1], Ibrahim Kaddumi[1],
Yahya Alqannas[1], Saud Althunibat[1(✉)], and Raed Mesleh[2]

[1] Department of Communications Engineering, Al-Hussein Bin Talal University,
Maan, Jordan
Saud.althunibat@ahu.edu.jo
[2] School of Electrical Engineering and Information Technology, German Jordanian
University, Amman, Jordan
raed.mesleh@gju.edu.jo

Abstract. One of the main limitations in Spatial Modulation (SM) systems is the lack of transmit diversity, which directly impacts its error rate performance. The lack of the transmit diversity refers to activating only a single transmit antenna in SM systems. In this paper, we propose a novel scheme that aims at improving the performance of SM systems by achieving half-full transmit diversity. The proposed scheme, called *Half-Full Transmit-Diversity SM (HFTD-SM)*, divides the transmit antennas into two-antenna groups. From each group, only a single antenna is activated, and all active transmit antennas emits one modulated symbol. The proposed HFTD-SM scheme is shown to outperform the conventional SM performance in terms of spectral efficiency, error rate, and design flexibility, while maintaining the main property of SM representing by the need of only a single RF chain. Simulation results corroborate the superior performance of the proposed scheme as compared to other SM variants in the literature.

Keywords: MIMO · Space modulation · Spatial modulation
Transmit diversity

1 Introduction

Space modulation systems have been widely investigated in the literature due to their promising features as compared to traditional multi-antenna systems [1,2]. In space modulation, the transmitted bits are not only conveyed by the conventional signal modulation, but also the index of the transmit antenna is exploited to convey additional bits. The earlier version of space modulation is called Spatial Modulation (SM) [3]. SM implies activating only a single transmit antenna to carry a modulated symbol, while other transmit antennas are left silent. As such, SM overcomes a main problem in Multi-Input Multi-Output (MIMO) systems represented by the inter-channel interference. This is attained by avoiding

© ICST Institute for Computer Sciences, Social Informatics and Telecommunications Engineering 2019
Published by Springer Nature Switzerland AG 2019. All Rights Reserved
V. Sucasas et al. (Eds.): BROADNETS 2018, LNICST 263, pp. 257–266, 2019.
https://doi.org/10.1007/978-3-030-05195-2_25

parallel transmissions from different antennas in typical MIMO systems. Moreover, SM is shown to require a single RF chain, which reduces installation and running costs [4].

SM has been extended to the Generalized SM (GSM) [5], where a combination of transmit antennas can be simultaneously used to transmit identical data symbol aiming at improving the spectral efficiency. Another promising advanced SM scheme has been proposed in [6], referred to Quadrature SM (QSM), where the in-phase and the quadrature components of the modulated symbol are emitted over two different transmit antennas. QSM has also been widely investigated in the literature [7–11].

It has been reported that SM encounters several problems and constraints that limit its performance. A first problem is that SM can exploit only a number of transmit antennas that is a power-of-two. Therefore, extra transmit antennas may left unused in the conventional SM scheme. Although GSM scheme releases this constraint by using combinations of transmit antennas, the constraint has been actually moved to the number of antennas' combinations [12]. Other solutions have also been proposed in [13–15]. Another problem is the bit-to-symbol mapping in SM, where it becomes difficult to satisfy the Gray mapping principles in SM due to the dependency on the random channel characteristics [16], and thus, error performance is degraded. In [17,18], efficient bit-to-symbol mapping schemes are proposed aiming at minimizing the hamming distance between adjacent symbols, which consequently, improves the attainable bit error rate. Many other studies investigate SM and QSM from different aspects, including performance under fading channels [19,20], hardware implementation [21], cooperative networks [22–24], spectrum sharing and cognitive radio networks [25,26], wireless sensor networks [27,28], and non-coherent variants [29,30].

Transmit diversity is one of the main features in MIMO systems, which is considered a source of enhanced performance. However, conventional SM does not achieve any transmit diversity due to activating only a single transmit antenna at each transmission time. Improving the transmit diversity should definitely improve the error performance at the receiver. Several works in the literature have attempted to improve the transmit diversity in SM. In [31], the spatial constellation and the diagonal space time block code are combined to improve the transmit diversity. However, it is limited to low modulation orders. Phase alignment is used at the transmitter to improve the diversity of SM schemes in [32]. The impact of several parameters, such as shaping filters and signal constellations, on the transmit diversity has been investigated in [33]. The transmit diversity of QSM is enhanced by using two sets of dispersion matrices in [34]. Recently, the transmit diversity of SM is improved by interleaving the quadrature components of two successive symbols in [35].

In this paper, aiming at improving the transmit diversity in SM, a new SM scheme is proposed. The proposed scheme is referred to Half-Full Transmit-Diversity SM (HFTD-SM) scheme. The proposed HFTD-SM scheme implies dividing the transmit antennas into groups, where each group includes only two transmit antennas. From each group, only a single antenna is activated at each transmit time. All activated antennas at a time instance will emit the same modulated symbol. As such, the proposed scheme still maintains the most important property of SM, which is represented by the need of a single RF chain. On the other hand, the proposed scheme can provide transmit diversity that is equal to the half of the full transmit diversity. Moreover, for the same number of transmit antennas, the proposed HFTD-SM can achieve higher spectral efficiency than the conventional SM. Also, the proposed HFTD-SM scheme does not require a power-of-two number of transmit antennas, whereas an even number of transmit antennas can be fully exploited. Simulation and analytical results demonstrate the high performance of the proposed scheme in terms of the spectral efficiency and the bit error rate as compared to other schemes in the literature.

The rest of the paper is organized as follows. Section 2 presents the system model with a description of the conventional SM scheme. The proposed HFTD-SM is presented and discussed in Sect. 3. The performance of the proposed HFTD-SM scheme in terms of the spectral efficiency and the error rate is analyzed in Sect. 4. Simulation results are presented and discussed in Sect. 5, and conclusions are drawn in Sect. 6.

2   System Model

A MIMO system that includes N_t transmit antennas and N_r receive antennas is considered in this paper. The channel distribution between the ith transmit antenna and the jth receive antenna, denoted by h_{ij}, is modeled as a Rayleigh fading channel with zero mean and unity variance. No correlation is assumed among transmit nor receive antennas.

The transmitted vector is denoted by $\mathbf{x} = [x_1, x_2, \cdots, x_{N_t}]^T$, where x_i represents the transmitted signal from the ith transmit antenna and T denotes the transpose operator. Accordingly, the received signal vector $\mathbf{y}$ is expressed as

$$\mathbf{y} = \mathbf{Hx} + \mathbf{w}, \tag{1}$$

where $\mathbf{H}$ is the $N_r \times N_t$ channel matrix, and $\mathbf{w}$ is the additive white Gaussian noise vector at the receive antennas. The entries of $\mathbf{w}$ are modeled as complex Gaussian random variables with zero mean and σ_w^2 variance.

At the receiver end, Maximum Likelihood (ML) detection is applied to retrieve the transmitted vector as

$$\hat{\mathbf{x}} = \arg \min_{\mathbf{x} \in \mathcal{X}} \|\mathbf{y} - \mathbf{Hx}\|_F^2, \tag{2}$$

where $\hat{\mathbf{x}}$ is the detected vector, $\mathcal{X}$ is a set containing all possible transmission vectors, and $\| \cdot \|_F^2$ is the squared Froeinius norm.

In the conventional SM scheme, only a single antenna is activated which is selected based on $\log_2 N_t$ transmitted bits. Other $\log_2 M$ bits (M is the modulation order) are modulated, and the modulated symbol is sent via the selected transmit antenna. As such, a block of $\log_2 N_t M$ bits is transmitted at each transmission time in the conventional SM. Notice that, as only a single transmit antenna is activated, the transmission vector $\mathbf{x}$ includes only a single nonzero element, which limits the transmit diversity in SM systems. Also, it is clear that N_t should be a power-of-two in order to have an integer number of transmitted bits.

3 Half-Full Transmit Diversity SM (HFTD-SM)

Motivated by the limited transmit diversity in SM systems and the constraint on the number of transmit antennas, a new SM scheme is proposed in this section, aiming to overcome the mentioned limitations. The proposed HFTD-SM scheme is able to achieve to the half of the full transmit diversity, which consequently improves its performance in terms of the error rate at the receiver end.

The proposed HFTD-SM scheme implies that transmit antennas are divided into $\frac{N_t}{2}$ groups, where each group includes only two transmit antennas. A single antenna from each group is activated based on a single transmitted bit. As such, $\frac{N_t}{2}$ bits are used to select the active antennas in all groups. Other $\log_2 M$ bits are modulated and emitted from the selected transmit antennas. As such, the transmitted block includes $\frac{N_t}{2} + \log_2 M$ bits.

It is worth mentioning that the proposed scheme still requires a single RF chain as in the conventional SM, although multiple transmit antennas are simultaneously activated. This is due to the fact that all active antennas will transmit the same modulated symbol at each transmission time, and hence, all active antennas can use the same RF chain. Also, a power-of-two number of the transmit antennas is not anymore a requirement in the proposed HFTD-SM scheme, where an even number of the transmit antennas can be utilized.

3.1 Example

Consider a system with $N_t = 8$ and $M = 4$. Let us denote the transmit antennas by $a_1, a_2, ..., a_8$. HFTD-SM will divide the transmit antennas into 4 groups as follows (a_1, a_2), (a_3, a_4), (a_5, a_6) and (a_7, a_8). Assume the first antenna in each group is labeled by 0, while the second antenna in each group is labeled by 1. The transmitted bit block should include $\frac{N_t}{2} + \log_2 M = 6$ bits. Assume the transmitted block at a specific time is 110101. The first 4 bits are used to determine the active antennas in the four groups, respectively. Therefore, based on the bits and the antennas' labels, the transmit antennas a_2, a_4, a_5 and a_8 will be selected to transmit the modulated symbol. The modulated symbol is generated by modulating the last two bits 01. Using 4-QAM constellation, the modulated symbol is $-1 + j$. Hence, the transmission vector $\mathbf{x}$ is formulated by substituting the value of the modulated symbol in the corresponding elements of the active antennas as follows $\mathbf{x} = [0, -1 + j, 0, -1 + j, -1 + j, 0, 0, -1 + j]$. Notice that to normalize the transmit power to unity, the vector $\mathbf{x}$ is multiplied by $\sqrt{\frac{2}{N_t}}$.

4 Performance Analysis

An analytical discussion on the performance of the proposed HFTD-SM scheme in terms of the spectral efficiency and the average BER is discussed in this section.

4.1 Spectral Efficiency

The spectral efficiency of the proposed HFTD-SM scheme (η_{HF}) is expressed as

$$\eta_{HF} = \frac{N_t}{2} + \log_2 M \tag{3}$$

while the conventional SM can achieve a spectral efficiency given as

$$\eta_{SM} = \log_2 N_t + \log_2 M \tag{4}$$

Clearly, the proposed HFTD-SM can achieve higher spectral efficiency for high values of N_t (i.e., $N_t > 4$). The spectral efficiency difference between the two schemes (Δ) can be expressed as

$$\Delta = \frac{N_t}{2} - \log_2 N_t, \tag{5}$$

which is equal to zero for $N_t = 2$ and 4, while it starts increasing as N_t increases. For example, at $N_t = 16$, the spectral efficiency difference is 4 bps/Hz, which represents a great enhancement in the spectral efficiency as compared to the conventional SM scheme.

4.2 Bit Error Rate

The average BER for the proposed HFTD-SM scheme can be upper-bounded using the well-known union-bound technique [36] given by

$$\zeta = \frac{1}{m2^m} \sum_{k=1}^{m} \sum_{\hat{k}=1}^{m} e_{k\hat{k}} \mathrm{PEP}_{k\hat{k}}, \tag{6}$$

where m is the block length ($m = \frac{N_t}{2} + \log_2 M$), $\mathrm{PEP}_{k\hat{k}}$ is the average pair-wise error probability defined as the probability that $\mathbf{x}_{\hat{k}}$ is detected given that $\mathbf{x}_k$ is actually transmitted, and $e_{k\hat{k}}$ is the hamming distance between the corresponding bit blocks of $\mathbf{x}_{\hat{k}}$ and $\mathbf{x}_k$.

The pair-wise error probability for a given $\mathbf{H}$ can be computed and written with the aid of the Q-function [37] as [20]

$$\mathrm{PEP}_{k\hat{k}/\mathbf{H}} = Q(\mu), \tag{7}$$

where μ is given by

$$\mu = \frac{1}{2\sigma_n^2} \|\mathbf{H}(\mathbf{x} - \hat{\mathbf{x}})\|_F^2 \tag{8}$$

The unconditional pair-wise error probability can be computed by averaging (7) over the pdf of the channel, where it is usually expressed as

$$\text{PEP}_{k\hat{k}} = \frac{2^{N_r-1}\Gamma(N_r + 0.5)}{\sqrt{\pi}(N_r)!} \left(\frac{1}{\overline{\mu}}\right)^{N_r}, \tag{9}$$

where $\overline{\mu}$ is the average value of μ, and $\Gamma(\cdot)$ is the Gamma function [37].

5   Simulation Results

This section provides simulation results of the performance of the proposed HFTD-SM scheme in terms of the spectral efficiency and the average BER. The proposed scheme is compared to two other schemes, namely SM and QSM. The average SNR is defined as the symbol energy per noise power. As the symbol energy is set to unity, the SNR is equal to $\frac{1}{\sigma_n^2}$.

Figure 1 shows the attainable spectral efficiency, η, versus the number of transmit antennas N_t for SM, QSM and HFTD-SM schemes. The modulation order is set to $M = 4$. In both SM and QSM, when N_t is not a power-of-two, the spectral efficiency is equal to the one achieved by the nearest power-of-two lower than N_t. For example, at $N_t = 6$, the spectral efficiency for SM and QSM is 4 and 6 bps/Hz, respectively, which are equal to the spectral efficiency achieved at $N_t = 4$. On the other hand, the proposed HFTD-SM does not require that N_t to be a power-of-two, where it can achieve higher spectral efficiency once N_t becomes an even number. Also, it can be seen that the proposed scheme can achieve higher spectral efficiency than SM for $N_t > 4$, and higher than QSM for $N_t > 8$.

The average BER versus the average SNR for the proposed HFTD-SM and SM schemes is shown in Fig. 2 at a spectral efficiency of 8 bps/Hz. The considered configuration of SM to achieve the desired spectral efficiency is $N_t = 8$ and $M = 32$-PSK, while $N_t = 8$ and $M = 16$-PSK are the considered parameters for the proposed HFTD-SM scheme. The number of receive antennas is set to $N_r = 2$. A clear SNR gain is achieved by the proposed HFTD-SM as compared to the conventional SM scheme, especially at high SNR values. For instance, at a BER of 10^{-4}, the SNR gain is about 4 dB.

Figure 3 confirms the high performance of the proposed HFTD-SM scheme indicated in Fig. 2. The spectral efficiency is set at 10 bps/Hz, which is achieved by $N_t = 8$, $M = 128$-PSK for the SM scheme, and by $N_t = 8$ and $M = 64$-PSK for the proposed HFTD-SM scheme. At a BER of 10^{-4}, the SNR gain is about 6 dB due to the improved transmit diversity provided by the proposed HFTD-SM scheme.

The last result is shown in Fig. 4, where the average BER versus the SNR is plotted for the QSM and the HFTD-SM schemes at a spectral efficiency of 17 bps/Hz. For QSM, $N_t = 32$ and $M = 128$-PSK, while for HFTD-SM, $N_t = 32$ and $M = 2$ (BPSK). In both schemes, $N_r = 2$. At 10^{-4} BER, the proposed scheme can outperform the QSM scheme by about 3 dB SNR gain.

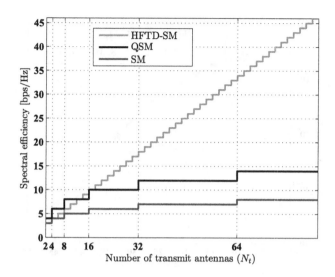

Fig. 1. The spectral efficiency versus the number of transmit antennas for the proposed HFTD-SM, QSM and the conventional SM schemes at a modulation order of 4.

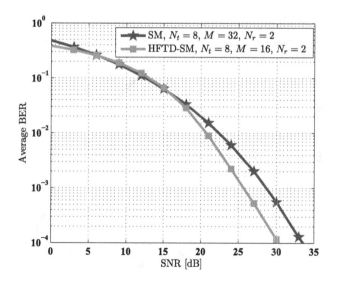

Fig. 2. The average BER versus the SNR for the proposed HFTD-SM and the conventional SM schemes at spectral efficiency of 8 bps/Hz.

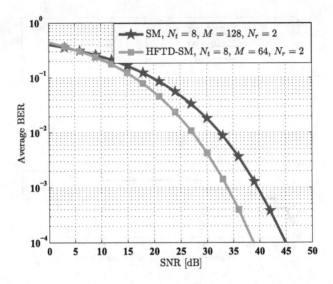

Fig. 3. The average BER versus the SNR for the proposed HFTD-SM and the conventional SM schemes at spectral efficiency of 10 bps/Hz.

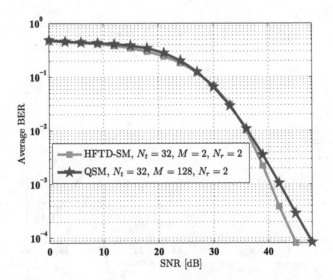

Fig. 4. The average BER versus the SNR for the proposed HFTD-SM and the QSM schemes at spectral efficiency of 17 bps/Hz.

6   Conclusions

A new spatial modulation scheme that is able to achieve half of the full transmit diversity is proposed in this paper. The proposed scheme implies dividing the transmit antennas into two-antenna groups. For each group, a single antenna is activated, and all active antennas will transmit the same modulated symbol. Analytical and simulation results prove the high performance of the proposed scheme in terms of the spectral efficiency and the bit error rate.

References

1. Ishikawa, N., et al.: 50 years of permutation, spatial and index modulation: from classic RF to visible light communications and data storage. IEEE Commun. Surv. Tuts. **20**, 1905–1938 (2018)
2. Basar, E., et al.: Index modulation techniques for next-generation wireless networks. IEEE Access **5**(1), 16693–16746 (2017)
3. Mesleh, R.Y., et al.: Spatial modulation. IEEE Trans. Veh. Technol. **57**(4), 2228–2241 (2008)
4. Yang, P., et al.: Design guidelines for spatial modulation. IEEE Commun. Surv. Tuts. **17**(1), 6–26 (2015)
5. Younis, A., et al.: Generalised spatial modulation. Asilomar Pacific Grove, CA, pp. 1498–1502 (2010)
6. Mesleh, R., et al.: Quadrature spatial modulation. IEEE Trans. Veh. Technol. **64**(6), 2738–2742 (2015)
7. Althunibat, S., Mesleh, R.: Cooperative decode-and-forward quadrature spatial modulation over correlated and imperfect $\eta - \mu$ fading channels. Wireless Networks (2017). https://doi.org/10.1007/s1127
8. Younis, A., et al.: Quadrature spatial modulation performance over nakagami- m fading channels. IEEE Trans. Veh. Technol. **65**(12), 10227–10231 (2016)
9. Afana, A., et al.: Performance of quadrature spatial modulation in amplify-and-forward cooperative relaying. IEEE Commun. Lett. **20**(2), 240–243 (2016)
10. Badarneh, O.S., Mesleh, R.: A comprehensive framework for quadrature spatial modulation in generalized fading scenarios. IEEE Trans. Commun. **64**(7), 2961–2970 (2016)
11. Xiao, L., et al.: Low-complexity signal detection for large-scale quadrature spatial modulation systems. IEEE Commun. Lett. **20**(11), 2173–2176 (2016)
12. Mesleh, R., et al.: Generalized space modulation techniques: Hardware design and considerations. Phys. Commun. **26**, 87–95 (2018)
13. Althunibat, S.: A mapping technique for Space Shift Keying with arbitrary number of transmit antennas. IEEE CAMAD, Lund (2017)
14. Serafimovski, N., et al.: Fractional bit encoded spatial modulation (FBE-SM). IEEE Commun. Lett. **14**(5), 429–431 (2010)
15. Yang, Y., Aissa, S.: Information guided channel hopping with an arbitrary number of transmit antennas. IEEE Commun. Lett. **16**(10), 1552–1555 (2012)
16. Al Sukkar, G., Althunibat, S.: Gray codes for Spatial Modulation systems: an open research issue. IEEE CAMAD, Lund, pp. 1–6 (2017)
17. Yang, P., et al.: Hybrid bit-to-symbol mapping for spatial modulation. IEEE Trans. Veh. Technol. **65**, 5804–5810 (2015)

18. Althunibat, S., Mesleh, R.: A bit-to-symbol mapping scheme for spatial modulation with partial channel state information. IEEE Commun. Lett. **21**(5), 995–998 (2017)

19. Mesleh, R., et al.: Performance analysis of spatial modulation and space-shift keying with imperfect channel estimation over generalized $eta-mu$ fading channels. IEEE Trans. Veh. Technol. **64**(1), 88–96 (2015)

20. Jeganathan, J., et al.: Spatial modulation: optimal detection and performance analysis. IEEE Commun. Lett. **12**(8), 545–547 (2008)

21. Mesleh, R., et al.: Transmitter design and hardware considerations for different space modulation techniques. IEEE Trans. Wirel. Commun. **16**(11), 7512–7522 (2017)

22. Afana, A., et al.: Quadrature Spatial Modulation for Cooperative MIMO 5G Wireless Networks, pp. 1–5. IEEE Globecom Workshops, Washington, DC (2016)

23. Althunibat, S., Mesleh, R.: Performance analysis of quadrature spatial modulation in two-way relaying cooperative networks. IET Commun. **12**(4), 466–472 (2018)

24. Yu, X., et al.: Power allocation and performance analysis of cooperative spatial modulation in wireless relay networks. IEEE Access **6**, 12145–12155 (2018)

25. Ustunbas, S., et al.: Performance analysis of cooperative spectrum sharing for cognitive radio networks using spatial modulation at secondary users. IEEE VTC Spring, Nanjing, pp. 1–5 (2016)

26. Bouida, Z., et al.: Adaptive spatial modulation for spectrum sharing systems with limited feedback. IEEE Trans. Commun. **63**(6), 2001–2014 (2015)

27. Althunibat, S., et al.: On the performance of wireless sensor networks with QSSK modulation in the presence of co-channel interference. Telecommun. Syst. **68**(1), 105–113 (2018)

28. Althunibat, S., Mesleh, R.: Index modulation for cluster-based wireless sensor networks. IEEE Trans. Veh. Technol. **PP**(99), 1. https://doi.org/10.1109/TVT.2018.2820602

29. Bian, Y., et al.: Differential spatial modulation. IEEE Trans. Veh. Technol. **64**(7), 3262–3268 (2015)

30. Mesleh, R., et al.: Differential quadrature spatial modulation. IEEE Trans. Commun. **65**(9), 3810–3817 (2017)

31. Nguyen, T.D., et al.: A spatial modulation scheme with full diversity for four transmit antennas. In: ATC Conference, Ho Chi Minh City, pp. 16–19 (2015)

32. Masouros, C.: Improving the diversity of spatial modulation in MISO channels by phase alignment. IEEE Commun. Lett. **18**(5), 729–732 (2014)

33. Renzo, M.D., Haas, H.: On transmit diversity for spatial modulation MIMO: impact of spatial constellation diagram and shaping filters at the transmitter. IEEE Trans. Veh. Technol. **62**(6), 2507–2531 (2013)

34. Wang, L., et al.: Diversity-achieving quadrature spatial modulation. IEEE Trans. Veh. Technol. **66**(12), 10764–10775 (2017)

35. Althunibat, S., Mesleh, R.: Enhancing spatial modulation system performance through signal space diversity. IEEE Commun. Lett. **22**(6), 1136–1139 (2018). https://doi.org/10.1109/LCOMM.2018.2817621

36. Simon, M.K., et al.: Digital Communication Techniques: Signal Design and Detection. Prentice Hall PTR, Englewood Cliffs (1995)

37. Abramnowitz, M., Stegun, I.A.: Handbook of Mathematical Functions. US Dept. of Commerce, National Bureau of Standards, Washington, DC (1972)

Hardware Implementation of Space Shift Keying on a Xilinx Zynq Platform

Omar Hiari$^{(\boxtimes)}$ (iD), Faris Shahin, Samer Alshaer, and Raed Mesleh (iD)

German Jordanian University, Amman, Jordan
{omar.hiari,f.shahin,s.alshaer,raed.mesleh}@gju.edu.jo

Abstract. The recent definition of hardware system models for space modulation techniques has provided a pathway to physical implementation of such systems. Space Shift Keying (SSK), being at the forefront of all these definitions, implements a pure form of space modulation that does not require a traditional RF chain that generates baseband symbols. On the other hand, compact, SDR-enabled, platforms powered by computationally powerful SoCs, are also becoming increasingly popular in prototyping wireless systems. In this work, we leverage commercially available SDR-enabled platforms, based on the Xilinx Zynq SoC and the Analog Devices AD9361 analog front end, to implement an entry level SSK system.

Keywords: SDR · Space modulation · Zynq

1 Introduction

Trending wireless protocols such as 5G, have introduced an ever increasing demand on wireless systems to increase data rates, spectral efficiency, and reduce power consumption. One of the approaches to address the aforementioned demands was by introducing Multiple Input Multiple Output (MIMO) systems. Through different implementations, the main idea for MIMO systems is to deploy multiple antennas at the transmitter and receiver sides to exploit multipath propagation properties of a channel. Out of the various MIMO techniques, Space Modulation (SM) has emerged as one of the techniques that could address the demands for future systems [9]. Contrary to traditional implementations of MIMO (Ex. Spatial Multiplexing), SM only requires a single RF, or in some cases zero, chain(s). SM achieves that by transmitting a portion of the information bits through the transmit antenna indexes.

As with all new wireless implementations, there still exists a gap in SM between the theoretical and physical (hardware) implementations. As recently introduced in literature, SM is achievable through a family of eight techniques; Space Shift Keying (SSK), Spatial Modulation (SM), Quadrature Space Shift

Supported by the Deanship of Scientific Research at the German Jordanian University under research grant number SIC 41/2016.

V. Sucasas et al. (Eds.): BROADNETS 2018, LNICST 263, pp. 267–275, 2019.
https://doi.org/10.1007/978-3-030-05195-2_26

Keying (QSSK), Quadrature Spatial Modulation (QSM), Generalized Space Shift Keying (GSSK), Generalized Spatial Modulation (GSM), Generalized Quadrature Space Shift Keying (GQSSK), and Generalized Quadrature Spatial Modulation (GQSM) [6,10,11]. Each implementation offering a different complexity, cost, spectral efficiency, and power consumption depending on application demands.

The emergence of heterogeneous computing platforms, such as the Xilinx Zynq, have provided the ability to accelerate the hardware implementation of theoretical wireless systems [3]. These platforms have been used extensively in other works to achieve Software Defined Radio (SDR) implementations as well as proving out wireless models [5,8,14,15]. Being software defined, these platform provide a lot of flexibility to build on and expand to other implementations.

In this work, we provide the details of physically implementing one of the SM family of techniques, namely SSK, utilizing a Zynq platform. SSK was chosen such that it is a foundational technique that all other implementations would need to build on. The rest of the paper is organized as follows, Sect. 2 introduces the SSK system model, Sect. 3 describes the hardware architecture adopted and the implementation of the system, Sect. 4 describe the results obtained, and finally Sect. 5 concludes this paper.

2 System Model

Figure 1 shows the SSK system model definition. At the transmitter side, incoming serial bits are parallelized and connected to the select lines of an RF switch. Through the select lines states, the RF switch controls which antenna is transmitting at each time instance. The RF input of the switch is merely a periodic carrier signal that could be easily generated in various manners. As a result, the spectral efficiency η of the system therefore is defined merely by the number of antennas N_t deployed in an SSK system and is equal to:

$$\eta_{SSK} = \log_2(N_t) \tag{1}$$

The generated RF signal from the transmitter is transmitted over the MIMO channel matrix $\mathbf{H}$. The transmitted signal received by N_r receive antennas in The N_r-dimensional received vector $\mathbf{y}$ is then given by:

$$\mathbf{y} = \sqrt{E_s}\mathbf{H}\mathbf{x} + \mathbf{n}, \tag{2}$$

where E_s denotes the transmitted energy, $\mathbf{n}$ the noise in the channel, and $\mathbf{H}$ being the complex channel matrix with a dimension of $N_r \times N_t$. At the receiver side, the received signals are then demodulated through an IQ demodulator and processed by an optimum ML decoder to retrieve the source bits. The ML decoder is defined as [7,12,13]:

$$\hat{\mathbf{x}} = \arg\min_{\mathbf{x}_i \in \mathcal{X}} \|\mathbf{y} - \mathbf{H}\mathbf{x}_i\|_F^2, \tag{3}$$

where $\hat{\mathbf{x}}$ denotes the estimated transmitted symbol, $\| \cdot \|_F$ is the Frobenius norm, and $\mathbf{x}_i$ is a possible transmitted vector from $\mathcal{X}$, where $\mathcal{X}$ is a set containing all possible transmitted vector combinations.

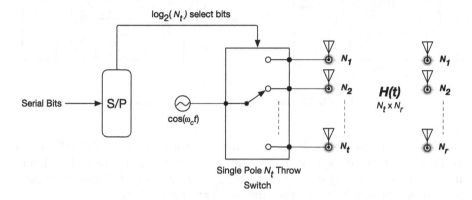

Fig. 1. The SSK system model

3   Hardware System Architecture and Implementation

In order to achieve an SSK realization in hardware, two Xilinx Zynq-based SDR enabled platforms were utilized, one for the transmitter side and another for the receiver [2,3]. The transmitted platform deployed was the Xilinx ZC706 development board with an AD-FMCOMMS5 analog front end attached. The second platform deployed for the receiver was a Zedboard with an AD-FMCOMMS3 analog front end attachment. Both the AD-FMCOMMS3 and AD-FMCOMMS5 incorporate the Analog devices AD9361 [1,4]. The AD-FMCOMMS5 attachment can support four transmit and/or receive chains, on the other hand, the AD-FMCOMMS3 can support only two transmit and/or receive chains. The Zynq device is a heterogeneous System on Chip device that incorporates dual core ARM-A9 cores alongside an FPGA fabric. The platform comes with a base design from Analog Devices providing low level driver support thus providing multiple options to control the low level FPGA and RF front end hardware. The options include; running the hardware with no-OS (i.e. bare metal with low level C drivers), with a Linux image via kernel drivers and GNU radio companion, or a Linux image communicating to MATLAB on a host computer.

The hardware system architecture of the SSK implementation is demonstrated in Fig. 2. On the transmitter side, a Linux image with GNU radio companion is used for creating the transmitter system. Only one of the FMCOMMS5 outputs is activated and is connected to the RF input of an RF switch. The select line of the RF switch is connected to a GPIO output pin coming from the Zynq SoC on the ZC706 board. The RF switch utilized is a SPDT switch with part number ZFSWA2-63DR+ from MiniCircuits, thus allowing for two transmit antenna implementation.

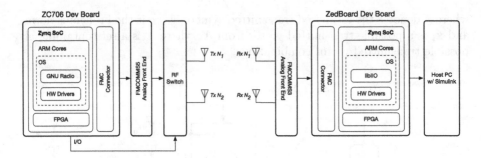

Fig. 2. The hardware system block diagram

The receiver system utilizes both receive chains of the FMCOMMS3 to achieve a 2x2 MIMO system implementation. On the software end, a Linux image with a libIIO object that connects to MATLAB on a PC host is utilized. This allows for simpler post-processing of all the received data.

3.1 Transmitter Implementation

As mentioned earlier, the GNU radio companion was utilized to realize the transmitter implementation. The GNU companion block diagram for the transmitter implementation is shown in Fig. 3. The FMComms5 Sink is a support block provided by Analog Devices to configure and initialize the low level hardware and the AD-FMCOMMS5 RF front-end module. The complex samples required to be transmitted are fed into this sink block. Through the sink block the passband frequency is also determined and it is set to 2.4 GHz. The signal source block generates the desired shape of the transmission signal which the SSK case is a sinusoidal signal. This is the signal utilized to generate the required carrier that connects to the RF switch input.

The TX Frame is a custom block programmed to transmit the required frame. This block contains both bits that are forwarded to the following multiply block and bits that control the switching of the RF switch. The transmit frame consists of 40 bits and is split into three parts as shown in Fig. 4. The first 13 bits contain a barker code sequence to achieve frame synchronization at the receiver side. All of the barker code bits are forwarded to the multiply block to alter the carrier output (enable or disable). During the transmission of the barker code values, the RF switch select line is fixed until the barker code completes transmission. Following the completion of the barker code transmission, a value of 1 is forwarded to the multiply block allowing the carrier output to be enabled for the remainder of the frame transmission. The remainder of the bits in the frame are all transmitted through the antenna indicies by switching the RF switch. Bits 14 and 15 in the transmit frame are pilot bits required for executing channel estimation at the receiver. Finally, the remainder of the frame contains data bits for the message to be transmitted. The switching speed applied to the switch was 20 ms thus achieving a transmission rate of 50 kbps.

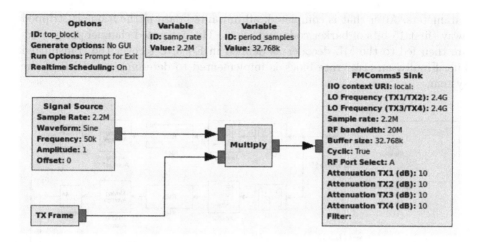

Fig. 3. The GNU radio implementation block diagram at the transmitter

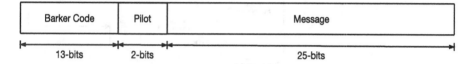

Fig. 4. The transmitted frame

3.2 Receiver Implementation

The receiver system is implemented using Simulink. Simulink provides a hardware interface block that connects and configures the Zedboard platform with the FMCOMMS3. The interface block output is the data received and processed on the low level board hardware. The data format is complex samples that can be further processed in Simulink. The interface block output provides a matrix that combines the samples from the different receive chains.

Figure 5 shows the block diagram implemented in the system on the receiver side. The data received from the board via the interface block is first separated by channel and serialized, such that processing can be performed on each antenna signal separately. Following that, a moving average of the RMS value for the signals is generated to determine the power in the received signals. The signals are then down-sampled for optimized processing. After that the signals are concatenated into a single vector and the frame rebuilt to extract the valid frames through the frame synchronization block. It can be noticed that only one of the channels is connected to the preamble detector for frames. Since frame synchronization is done before any bits are recovered, there isn't a need for information from more than one antenna chain to synchronize frames.

The final block in the receive chain contains the ML decoder and the channel estimator implementations. In this block, the channel estimator leverages the pilot bits and a least squares algorithm in order to determine the channel parameters. After that is completed, all unwanted data in the frame is stripped away (first 15 bits of barker code and pilot). The generated channel parameters are then fed to the ML decoder as defined in Eq. 3 to recover the transmitted bits. Finally, an error rate block is implemented to determine the BER of the system.

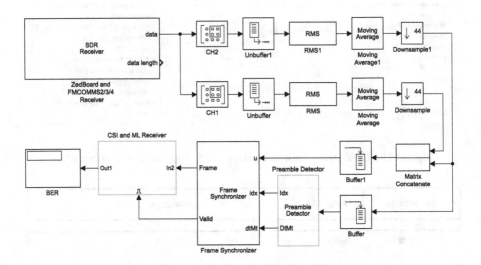

Fig. 5. Simulink model for the SSK receiver

4   Results

A system test run was conducted to determine the correctness of the system implementation. A data file was generated and sent from the transmitter to the receiver in a lab environment. An overall bit error rate of 0.04 was achieved for the transmitted data. Figure 6 shows a plot of the signal received at one antenna at the start of a frame which consists of the 13-bit Barker sequence. For the barker code portion of the transmission, the change in amplitude of the received signal defines whether a zero or a one has been received. Essentially the figure shows that the initial sequence of "1,1,1,1,1,0,0,1,1,0,1,0,1" is being detected.

In Fig. 7, a sample for part of the transmission sequence is shown. The different signal colors indicate the signals on each of the receive channels. The difference in amplitude between the signals is due to the effect of multi-path fading. As a result, comparing the two regions identified on the figure; the switching amplitude levels between signals indicates the antenna that is transmitting. Moreover, it can be noticed in the figure some abnormal transitions appear in between the switching amplitudes. This is due to the effect of switching between antennas on the transmitter side.

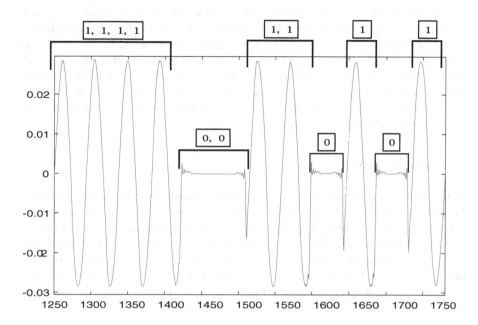

Fig. 6. Barker code signal at the receiver

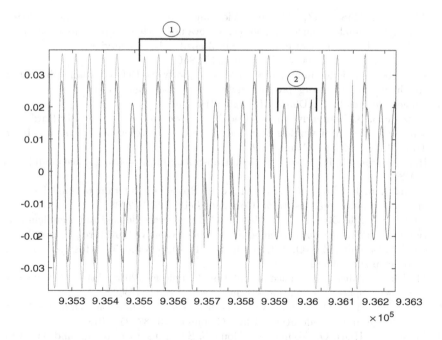

Fig. 7. A sample of the received signal

The results obtained in this work serve as proof of the feasibility of Space Modulation in hardware using an RF switch. However, in the context of future work, this work is still in its preliminary stages as more data, primarily performance data at different antenna configurations and SNRs, needs to be collected. There is also much hardware imperfections impact that need to be studied. Finally, out of the family of space modulation SSK is one of few others presented in literature. This platform would be a good entry level to implement other space modulation techniques.

5   Conclusion

In this work we demonstrate the hardware implementation of one of the Space Modulation Techniques, namely SSK. The implementation is achieved utilizing commercial off the shelf SDR-enabled SoC based platforms. The work shows that the realization of SSK is less complicated than traditional MIMO systems. We also define the architecture of the system, the transmitter, and the receiver implementations. This platform facilitates future research for expanding to other hardware implementations in addition to further studying actual performance of Space Modulation physical implementations.

References

1. AD-FMCOMMS3-EBZ, AD9361 Wideband Software Defined Radio Board. http://www.analog.com/en/design-center/evaluation-hardware-and-software/evaluation-boards-kits/eval-ad-fmcomms3-ebz.html#eb-overview
2. Z7020: Xilinx Zynq-7000 All Programmable SoC
3. Zynq-7000 All Programmable SoC/AD9361 Software-Defined Radio Evaluation Kit. http://zedboard.org/product/zedboard-sdr-ii-evaluation-kit
4. Analog Devices Inc.: AD9361: RF Agile Transceiver
5. Drozdenko, B., Zimmermann, M., Dao, T., Chowdhury, K., Leeser, M.: Hardware-software codesign of wireless transceivers on zynq heterogeneous systems. IEEE Trans. Emerg. Topics Comput. (2017)
6. Hiari, O., Mesleh, R.: Single RF chain transmitter implementing space modulation (2018)
7. Jeganathan, J., Ghrayeb, A., Szczecinski, L.: Spatial modulation: optimal detection and performance analysis. IEEE Commun. Lett. **12**(8) (2008)
8. Junior, S.B., de Oliveira, V.C., Junior, G.B.: Software defined radio implementation of a QPSK modulator/demodulator in an extensive hardware platform based on FPGAs Xilinx ZYNQ. J. Comput. Sci. **11**(4), 598 (2015). https://doi.org/10.3844/jcssp.2015.598.611
9. Mesleh, R., Alhassi, A.: Space Modulation Techniques (2018). https://www.wiley.com/en-us/Space+Modulation+Techniques-p-9781119375692
10. Mesleh, R., Hiari, O., Younis, A.: Generalized space modulation techniques: Hardware design and considerations. Phys. Commun. **26**, 87–95 (2018)
11. Mesleh, R., Hiari, O., Younis, A., Alouneh, S.: Transmitter design and hardware considerations for different space modulation techniques. IEEE Trans. Wirel. Commun. **16**(11), 7512–7522 (2017)

12. Mesleh, R., Ikki, S.S., Aggoune, H.M.: Quadrature spatial modulation. IEEE Trans. Veh. Technol. **64**(6), 2738–2742 (2015)
13. Paulraj, A., Nabar, R., Gore, D.: Introduction to Space-Time Wireless Communications. Cambridge University Press, Cambridge (2003)
14. Pu, D., Cozma, A., Hill, T.: Four quick steps to production: Using model-based design for software-defined radio. Analog Dialogue **49** (2015)
15. Shreejith, S., Banarjee, B., Vipin, K., Fahmy, S.A.: Dynamic cognitive radios on the Xilinx Zynq Hybrid FPGA. In: Weichold, M., Hamdi, M., Shakir, M.Z., Abdallah, M., Karagiannidis, G.K., Ismail, M. (eds.) CrownCom 2015. LNICST, vol. 156, pp. 427–437. Springer, Cham (2015). https://doi.org/10.1007/978-3-319-24540-9_35

Hardware Implementation and Antenna Design

MoM-GEC Analysis
of Fraunhofer-Region Characteristics
over Rectangular Aperture

Imen Khadhraoui[1(✉)] [iD], Taha Ben Salah[2], and Taoufik Aguili[1]

[1] Communications Systems Laboratory (SysCom), National Engineering School
of Tunis (ENIT), University of Tunis El Manar, Tunis, Tunisia
imenk1986@gmail.com, taoufik.aguili@gmail.com
[2] Networked Objects Control and Communication Systems (NOCCS), National
Engineering School of Sousse (ENISo), University of Sousse, Sousse, Tunisia
taha.bensalah@gmail.com

Abstract. In this paper, a determination of radiation characteristics
is performed using rectangular aperture antenna theory and transverse
electric field calculation with method of moments and generalized equivalent circuit MoM-GEC for a rectangular patch antenna contained in
an open-ended waveguide. This study is based on aperture antenna theory and field equivalence principle applied to the two-dimensional Fourier
transform integrals over the aperture. We consider Fraunhofer-zone characteristics in terms of radiation pattern and directivity computed over
an aperture through an assumed perfectly conducting screen. Results
show an acceptable agreement between computed and simulated radiation data in E and H planes.

Keywords: Aperture antenna · Radiation characteristics
MoM-GEC analysis · Planar circuit

1 Introduction

Antenna radiation characteristics are a fundamental key performances in EM
analysis. The determination of radiated properties is based on radiation analysis
over apertures. In this study, we are interested in radiation analysis over a rectangular aperture antenna. Structure analysis is evaluated in terms of radiation
pattern and directivity using rigorous formulation based on MoM-GEC method
(Galerkin implementation in spatial domain of method of moments) and comparing with commercial simulation software CST MWS. Such analysis is intended
to infer full 3D calculation of electromagnetic fields while benefiting of MoM
simplification that helps determination of unknowns at the very discontinuity
plane and hence bringing back 3D spatial problem to 2D spatial problem.

The main aim of this study is to perform radiation characteristics over rectangular aperture. In fact, Fraunhofer zone is closely related to far-zone approx-
imation technique. Hence, this work describes a brief formulation to determine

© ICST Institute for Computer Sciences, Social Informatics and Telecommunications Engineering 2019
Published by Springer Nature Switzerland AG 2019. All Rights Reserved
V. Sucasas et al. (Eds.): BROADNETS 2018, LNICST 263, pp. 279–288, 2019.
https://doi.org/10.1007/978-3-030-05195-2_27

radiation characteristics of a planar circuit based on MoM-GEC method. A set of spatial expressions of Galerkin method are used in this work to investigate electromagnetic performances to conclude thereafter about far-zone characteristics in terms of far field, radiation pattern and directivity.

To outline this paper, our description is organized into four sections. Section 2 is dedicated to introduce few works about radiation approaches over different aperture types. In Sects. 3 and 4, the studied structure and the numerical method analysis is described. In the Sect. 5, an investigation of computed radiation data is presented and discussed.

2   Related Work

There are several types of aperture antennas such as rectangular apertures, circular apertures, open-ended waveguides. Radiation apertures are based on field equivalence principle to express aperture fields by equivalent electric and magnetic surface currents. At Fraunhofer-zone, by the knowledge of the fields over the aperture of the antenna, aperture fields are considered the sources of radiation (Huygens-Fresnel principle).

In [1], a parabolic circular-ended taper is studied to find out maximum power which is computed from circular cophasal aperture based on field equivalence principle formula. A normalized power flux density on the axis of the aperture is also computed in order to enhance factors of different aperture field distributions within various aperture sizes.

Open-ended waveguide is one of radiation aperture types studied in the literature [2]. In [3], field radiated from rectangular open-ended waveguide is determined based on gain correction factor approach of Polk. The open-ended waveguide is excited with TE10 mode and the gain pattern is computed over the open-ended waveguide at Fresnel-zone.

In [4], an approach for calculating the far zone pattern from near field measurements is described. Near field data is utilized to determine far field based on two-dimensional Fourier transform over the aperture of the antenna. A replacement of integrals by a summation over constant increments in X and Y is done to compute far field from a measured near field.

In [5], an integral solution based on vector potentials to determine far field patterns is presented. In, fact, moments method-based is applied to analyze microstrip square patch to evaluate far field results. MoM results are computed in terms of radiation pattern in H and E planes based on Green's functions defined in an assumed infinite substrate to describe a square patch excited with a dipole (coaxial port). A comparison is presented in [5] between results computed with transmission line model, measured data and results obtained by MoM analysis with two types of base functions. Since results are computed with an assumed finite substrate, a negligible effect on radiated fields in H-plane however is investigated and a poor agreement is noted with all compared cases in the E-plane results. In this context, an investigation of finite substrate effect on electric field is studied preceding determination of radiation performances in this work.

3   Studied Structure

The studied structure is a planar circuit: the radiated element is rectangular patch. In this section a description of the studied structure and parameters are given in addition to a concise formulation for radiated properties determination.

3.1   Structure Parameters

The geometry of the structure is shown in Fig. 1 [6]. A microstip rectangular patch antenna acts as radiated element. It is contained in a bounded domain and is placed on short circuited substrate (loss free, 2.2 dielectric constant). The ground plane, the patch and the feed line are designed as PEC. The antenna is contained in an open-ended waveguide (four electric sidewalls EEEE) with short-circuited bottom side (z-axis). Excitation source is considered as constant planar pulse function.

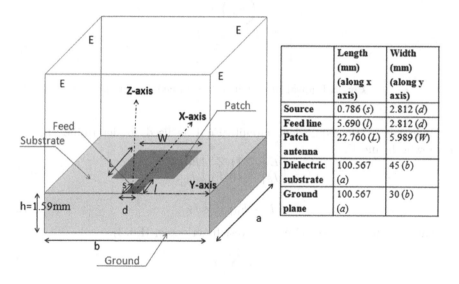

	Length (mm) (along x axis)	Width (mm) (along y axis)
Source	0.786 (s)	2.812 (d)
Feed line	5.690 (l)	2.812 (d)
Patch antenna	22.760 (L)	5.989 (W)
Dielectric substrate	100.567 (a)	45 (b)
Ground plane	100.567 (a)	30 (b)

Fig. 1. Studied structure.

3.2   MoM-GEC Formulation

This paper's approach is based on MoM-GEC formulation as a first step of modeling, so that a characterization of surface E and Js fields are deduced. The second step relies on application of aperture theory to figure out Fraunhofer-zone properties. Numerical formulation is expressed with Galerkin implementation of moments method [7] in spatial domain combined with generalized equivalent circuit MoM-GEC [8]. The equivalent circuit associated to the studied structure is made respecting all electromagnetic boundary conditions (Fig. 2), where:

- E0 is chosen as planar voltage source.
- Js is the surface current (unknown).
- Zsup, Zinf are respectively matched load impedance operator and short circuited impedance operator.
- E is the transverse electric field (unknown).

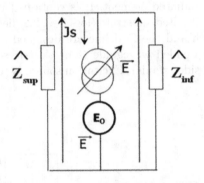

Fig. 2. Equivalent circuit of the studied structure.

Referring to the equivalent circuit, Eq. 1 is used to determine the two unknowns Js and E.

$$\begin{bmatrix} E \\ Js \end{bmatrix} = \begin{bmatrix} 1 & \hat{Z} \\ 0 & 1 \end{bmatrix} \begin{bmatrix} E_0 \\ J_0 \end{bmatrix} \tag{1}$$

$$(E - E_0) = \hat{Z} Js \tag{2}$$

The current J_s is discretized over test functions g_i (Eq. 3).

$$J_s = \sum_i x_i g_i \tag{3}$$

By replacing J_s, the Eq. 2 becomes:

$$\langle g_j, E - E_0 \rangle = \langle g_j, \hat{Z} \sum_i x_i g_i \rangle \tag{4}$$

The second projection on J_s (Galerkin application) gives Eq. 5:

$$\begin{bmatrix} \langle g_1, E_0 \rangle \\ \cdots \\ \langle g_j, E_0 \rangle \\ \cdots \\ \langle g_n, E_0 \rangle \end{bmatrix} = \begin{bmatrix} \langle g_1, \hat{Z} g_1 \rangle & \cdots & \langle g_1, \hat{Z} g_n \rangle \\ & & \\ \cdots & \langle g_j, \hat{Z} g_i \rangle & \cdots \\ & & \\ \langle g_n, \hat{Z} g_1 \rangle & \cdots & \langle g_n, \hat{Z} g_n \rangle \end{bmatrix} \begin{bmatrix} x_1 \\ \cdots \\ x_i \\ \cdots \\ x_n \end{bmatrix} \tag{5}$$

Consequently, the MoM-GEC matrix equation is expressed by:

$$B = AX$$

Where: A: Impedance matrix, B: Excitation column vector and X: Unknown coefficients vector.

So, X is evaluated by matrix inversion. Localized test functions are closely related to the current distribution on the metal. Test functions are set to bi-dimensional overlapping rooftops expressed in two sub-domains: the feed line sub-domain and the patch sub-domain. In the feed line sub-domain: $dLine = [0, l][-d/2, d/2]$, Eq. 6 is expressed as following:

$$gp_1(x, y) = \begin{cases} N_1(x - (p - 1)\Delta l) & \text{in } dA \\ N_2(-x + (p + 1)\Delta l) & \text{in } dD \end{cases} \tag{6}$$

where: $dA = [(p - 1)\Delta l, p\Delta l][-d/2, d/2]$; $dD = [p\Delta l, (p + 1)\Delta l][-d/2, d/2]$

In patch sub-domain $dPatch = [l, l + L][-W/2, W/2]$, test functions are defined (Eq. 7):

$$gp_2(x, y) = \begin{cases} N_1'(X - (p - 1)\Delta l + l) & \text{in } dA' \\ N_2'(-x + (p + 1)\Delta l + l) & \text{in } dD' \end{cases} \tag{7}$$

where: $dA' = [(p - 1)\Delta l + l, p\Delta l + l][-W/2, W/2]$; $dD' = [p\Delta l + l, (p + 1)\Delta l + l][-W/2, W/2]$

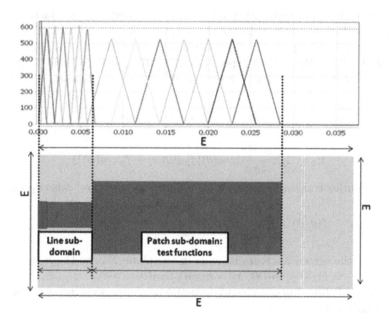

Fig. 3. One-dimensional plot of test functions rooftop type.

Test functions are normalized by factors $N1$, $N2$, $N'1$ and $N'2$. A representation of rooftops plot is given in Fig. 3. According to this formulation, the electric field E is expressed as Eq. (8) in Cartesian coordinates x and y.

$$E(x,y) = \sum_{mn}\sum_{pq} X_p z_{mn} \langle g_{pq}, f_{mn} \rangle f_{mn}(x,y) \tag{8}$$

The expression of the impedance operator is set according to homogeneous mode functions f_{mn} (electric and magnetic transverse TE and TM) of the waveguide mode impedances z_{mn}. MoM-GEC-based implementation leads to a computation of transverse E field. In the second step, we describe the application of aperture theory witch utilizes the computed electric field.

3.3   Aperture Theory Application

Referring to Huygens-Fresnel principle, E field becomes the source of radiation at the aperture. Radiation over aperture theory begins with the expression of Helmholtz solutions of Maxwell equations [9]. Solutions are obtained in terms of respectively electric and magnetic vector potentials. The application of field equivalence principle [9–11] expresses J_s and M_s, respectively electric and magnetic surface current densities, as functions of tangential electric and magnetic fields (Eqs. 9 and 10).

$$J_s = \hat{n} \times H_a \tag{9}$$

$$M_s = -\hat{n} \times E_a \tag{10}$$

We consider the rectangular aperture mounted in perfectly conducting screen at xy-plane. With the help of image theory principle [9], only magnetic current based on electric field prevails (Eq. 10). Consequently, the case of aperture over PEC entails a simplification of expressions describing radiated fields. Over PEC aperture, expressions of radiated field components are written as:

$$E_\theta = 2jk \frac{e^{-jkr}}{4\pi r}(f_x \cos(\phi) + f_y \sin(\phi)) \tag{11}$$

$$E_\phi = 2jk \frac{e^{-jkr}}{4\pi r}(\cos(\theta)(f_x \sin(\phi) + f_y \cos(\phi))) \tag{12}$$

Based on Fourier transform integrals over Cartesian aperture, f is expressed as:

$$f(\theta,\phi) = \int_{Aperture} E_a(x',y')e^{jk_x x' + jk_y y'} dx' dy' \tag{13}$$

In our case, the screen aperture is made in the plane XY, so the k_x and k_y are defined as: $k_x = k\cos(\phi)\sin(\theta)$, $k_y = k\sin(\phi)\sin(\theta)$.
Where $f(\theta,\phi)$ is function of tangential electric field expressed by means of MoM-GEC formulation.

4   Numerical Results

To describe all results related to the above formulation, a computer program Java/Scala-based is written. A convergence study is accomplished in terms of test and mode functions (226000 modes with 89 rooftops). Radiation characteristics are computed within the help of tangential electric field. Figure 4 illustrates electric field distribution calculated by MoM-GEC and CST MWS simulator. Plots show an agreement with physical boundary conditions. Electric field shows discontinuity of its X component at the patch right edge and has zero value on the metal. In our work, we are mainly interested in Fraunhofer-zone. Radiation data are computed in H and E planes: θ samples are set between $-\pi/2$ and $\pi/2$ where ϕ is constant $\phi = 0$, $\phi = \pi/2$, 30 samples are considered for θ and constant ϕ at the working frequency 4.79 GHz. Perpendicularly to the structure plane at $z = 0$, radiated field is computed at Fraunhofer zone ($z = 1$ m) based on Eq. 14.

$$E(\theta, \phi) = |E_\theta|^2 + |E_\phi|^2 \tag{14}$$

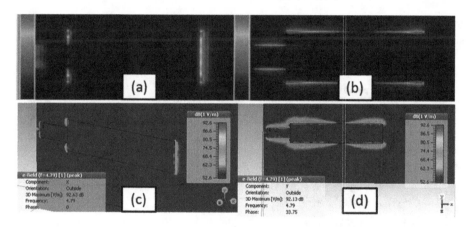

Fig. 4. Tangential E field components computed respectively with MoM-GEC and CST MWS: (a), (b): X and Y components of E field with MoM-GEC. (c), (d): X and Y components of E field with CST MWS.

Figure 5 depicts polar plot of radiated fields computed with MoM-GEC and simulated with CST MWS in H plane. Plots show an angle of aperture of about 67°. The non perfect agreement of the H-plane plots with CST MWS may be attributed to the shielding models in CST and MoM-GEC application. At the observation point r', based on radiated field components, radiation pattern is evaluated according to Eq. 15.

$$Poy(\theta, \phi) = \frac{r'^2}{2z_0}(|E_\theta|^2 + |E_\phi|^2) \tag{15}$$

where z_0 is the intrinsic impedance, r' is the distance of observation point. Figure (Fig. 6) shows polar plots of radiation pattern along the two planes with the two computation tools.

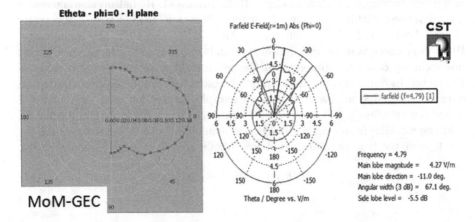

Fig. 5. Radiated Field H-plane polar plots (MoM-GEC computation and CST MWS simulation)

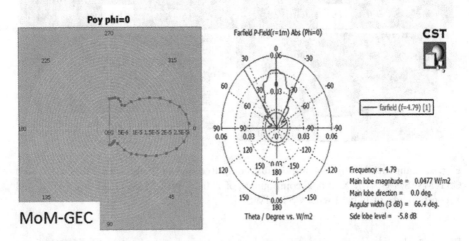

Fig. 6. Radiation pattern along H-plane polar plots (MoM-GEC computation vs CST MWS simulation).

The directivity is calculated by dividing radiation intensity by its average intensity (Eq. 16).

$$Dir = \frac{Poy(\theta, \phi)}{Poy(\theta, \phi)_{avg}} \tag{16}$$

Along the two principle planes, the directivity is computed using polar coordinates (ϕ is constant and θ is variable as mentioned above). Figures 7 and 8 show directivities obtained by both MoM-GEC-based formulation and simulation. By analyzing directivity intensity plots, main lobe value is about 5 dB obtained at the angle 0° producing an acceptable directivity level. Side lobe level is about −5.8 dB.

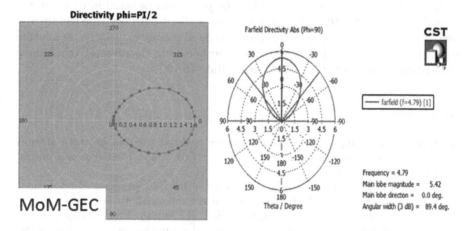

Fig. 7. Directivity along E-plane polar plots (MoM-GEC computation and CST MWS simulation).

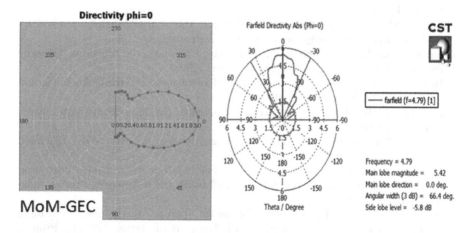

Fig. 8. Directivity along H-plane polar plots (MoM-GEC computation and CST MWS simulation).

5 Conclusion

In this contribution, an investigation of Fraunhofer-zone based on aperture theory is done for planar radiated element contained in open-ended waveguide. The application of aperture antenna theory combined with MoM-GEC analysis is made using Java/Scala computer program. Results described above, show an agreement with both numerical calculation and simulation in terms of radiated field, radiation pattern and directivity. The maximum radiated intensity in the normal direction ($\theta = 0$) to the studied plane is about 5 dB over the rectangular electric aperture. In this paper, we were interested mainly in far-zone, as a future work, our target is to determine radiation properties in the presence of a human body tissue based on Specific Absorption Rate (SAR).

References

1. Zhang, J.H., Wang, J.L.: Maximum power radiated from an aperture antenna before air breakdown in the near-field region. IEEE Trans. Electromagn. Compat. **53**(2), 540–543 (2011)
2. Yaghjian, A.D.: Approximate formulas for the far field and gain of open-ended rectangular waveguide. IEEE Trans. Antennas Propag. **32**(4), 378–384 (1984)
3. Bird, T.S., Lingasamy, V., Selvan, K.T., Sun, H.: Improved finite-range gain formula for openended rectangular waveguides and pyramidal horns. IET Microwaves Antennas Propag. **11**, 2054–2058 (2017)
4. Maheshwari, A., Behera, S., Thiyam, R., Maiti, S., Mukherjee, A.: Near field to Far field Transformation by Asymptotic evaluation of Aperture Radiation field. In: International Conference on Signal Propagation and Computer Technology (ICSPCT) (2014)
5. Lin, Y., Shafai, L.: Moment-method solution of the near field distribution and far field patterns of microstrip antennas. In: IEE Proceedings (1985)
6. Salah, T.B.: Analyse d'une antenne planaire: Utilisation des fonctions d'attache dans la methode des moments. ENIT Tunisia (2003)
7. Harrington, R.F.: Field Computation by Moment-methods. IEEE Antennas and Propagation Society. Wiley (1993)
8. Aubert, H., Baudrand, H.: L'electromagnetisme par les schemas equivalents. Cepadues (2003)
9. Balanis, C.A.: Antenna Theory Analysis and Design, 3rd edn. Wiley-Blackwell (1982)
10. Rengarajan, S.R., Rahmat-Samii, Y.: The field equivalence principle: illustration of the establishment of the non-intuitive null fields. IEEE Antennas Propag. Mag. **42**(4), 122–128 (2000)
11. Sarkar, T.K., Arvas, E.: An integral equation approach to the analysis of finite microstrip antennas: volume/surface formulation. IEEE Trans. Antennas Propag. **38**(3), 305–312 (1990)

Fast Statistical Modelling of Temperature Variation on 28 nm FDSOI Technology

Abdelgader M. Abdalla[1(✉)], Isiaka A. Alimi[1], Manuel González[2],
Issa Elfergani[1], and Jonathan Rodriguez[1]

[1] Instituto de Telecomunicações, Department of Electronics, Telecommunications
and Informatics (DETI), Universidade de Aveiro, 3810-193 Aveiro, Portugal
{a.m.abdalla,i.t.e.elfergani,jonathan}@av.it.pt, iaalimi@ua.pt
[2] Evotel Informatica SL, Madrid, Spain
m.gonzalez@evotel-info.com

Abstract. It is well known that the 28 nm fully depleted Silicon-On Insulator (FDSOI) node has a temperature effect due to the inherent pyroelectric and piezoelectric properties. In this paper, we introduce a spatial interpolation Lookup table (LUT) model considering temperature dependence of nanometer CMOS transistors. The novel methodology is used to build the bias current and capacitance LUTs for MOS transistor circuits under extensive variety of temperature values, evaluated under transient analysis. This innovative LUTs model significantly reduce the simulation runtime with sufficient accuracy using adaptive multivariate precomputed Barycentric relational interpolation for the appraisal temperature effects of 28 nm FDSOI node.

A transient analysis benchmark is employed in order to verify and validate the proposed models according to the well-known simulation models (i.e. the 28 nm FDSOI model and traditional spatial Lagrange model). The proposed model can significantly reduce the size of lookup table, thereby reducing the computational cost. Furthermore, the model outperform the 28 nm FDSOI compact physical model and the traditional spatial Lagrange model due to the reduced simulation runtime by up to eight orders of magnitude considering the temperature effect in 28 nm FDSOI innovation. Moreover, the proposed novel LUT based approaches are able to attain high precision with much reduced computational cost.

Keywords: Statistical modelling · Temperature variation
28 nm FDSOI technology

1 Introduction

The 28 nm FDSOI node is a promising nano-CMOS technology offering several benefits such as reduction in power, space scaling, cost effective platform and performance enhancement. It also enables a lower VDD and acts as an electrostatic

This work was supported by the H2020-ECSEL-2017-1-783127.

V. Sucasas et al. (Eds.): BROADNETS 2018, LNICST 263, pp. 289–298, 2019.
https://doi.org/10.1007/978-3-030-05195-2_28

enhancer to reduce the short channel effects; and provisions for better energy management, thanks to an ultra-thin buried oxide (BOX) and body biasing characteristics over the counterpart conventional Bulk technology [1]. The body biasing feature is vastly efficient for adjusting the transistor channel, tolerating the optimization of dynamic and static power consumption [1]. In spite of its predominant attributes, operation of the 28 nm FDSOI node fluctuates when the temperature changes in relation to the climatic conditions; the materials utilized have inborn pyroelectric and piezoelectric properties that help in influencing its attributes and consequently the circuit performance [2]. The temperature performance of the logic gates and input-output (IO) cells planned depend on FDSOI transistors [3]. A switch in the working temperature causes the mobility to vary and prompts changes in the on-current Ion, threshold voltage VT, and velocity saturation in each device [4]. In this aspect, ordinary compact and physical transistor models, such as Fe-FETs, BSIM, and PSP, comprise a substantial number of parameters and complicated equations in order to characterize the physical mechanisms, beyond the typical characterization for a short-channel device [4–6]. These sort of models have a high level of complexity and offer high precision mirroring the fundamental device physics. All things considered, they together, back-off the evaluation runtime. On the other hand, the empirical behavioral models of the circuit simulation depend on the LUT models. The LUT models comprise of the device input-output qualities and utilize some reasonable numerical interpolation, as well as numerical strategies to get working point values from the LUTs within the simulation process [7–10]. The LUT technique is simple to implement [11,12]. Nevertheless, it requires a high density of data points, which lead to an expansion in the computational cost in the request procedure. In recent times, a novel LUT approach in view of a spatial Lagrange polynomial has been introduced in [13]. The foremost benefit of this approach, is that, numerical model can be obtained from the measured information set. Besides, it has a characteristic ability at the highest order of polynomial for any given arrangement of information. The use of this method (i.e. spatial Lagrange polynomial) to build behavioral transistor model with just a single expression gives an insight into the device behavior over the whole area of biasing and in all areas of operation as well as considering process, voltage and temperature (PVT) variation. Therefore, by exploiting this method, just one equation is required for characterizing the transistor considering all gates-biasing voltages within a high range of temperature, and for both the triode and saturation operation regions of the I-V characteristics [3,13]. However, the principle downside of this technique, is that all work will be tunneled towards recalculating every single degree of the polynomial. This is not compatible with the wide deployment of multi-core architectures. Therefore, researchers have shown an increased interest in sequential optimizations algorithm if and only if it is effective in the perspective of parallel performance. In this paper, we adopt Barycentric rational interpolation because of ease of implementation using adaptive multivariate precomputed method that results in faster simulation and stability [15,16]. Moreover, this method (i.e. Barycentric rational interpolation) has recently attracted an enormous community of both end-users and developers from diverse disciplines. For example, standard optimization software like DAKOTA employs Barycentric rational interpolation for efficient global optimization of stochastic black-box systems [17,18]. This proposed model (i.e. Barycentric rational interpolation) is employed to build LUTs for both current-voltage (I-V) curve and capacitance-voltage (C-V) profile of a transistor as well as transconductance gm over an extensive variety of temperatures. Simulation results are given considering 28 nm FDSOI node. We compare this against legacy methodologies such as conventional Lagrange interpolation, and the compact physical transistor level model portrayed by 28 nm FDSOI in Cadence, exploiting the 5th degree of the polynomial for measuring both the I-V and C-V curve. Such an approach significantly simplifies the transistor model. Additionally, it decreases the computational cost by five orders of magnitude in the transient analysis without loss of fidelity.

This paper is organized as follows: in Sect. 2, mathematical formulas of the DC model for classical Lagrange, and Barycentric rational interpolation are briefly reviewed. Also, novel LUT approaches and their implementation details are discussed; Sect. 3 introduces small signal modeling for the extraction gate -source C_{gs}, drain-source C_{ds}, and gate-drain C_{gd} as well as transconductance g_m; Sect. 4 describes the system analysis; and in section V, model validation and simulation runtime are discussed and verified in transient analysis by comparing simulation results obtained in terms of output current, voltage, and simulation runtime with the measured model and conventional Lagrange.

2   DC Modeling

The dc model needs an appropriate expression to accurately describe and predict the measured current-voltage (I-V) characteristics over a wide temperature range. First we introduce the traditional recursive Lagrange, and Barycentric rational interpolation formulas. Subsequently, the proposed dynamic programming procedure which we developed by both Barycentric rational interpolation is given. The Lagrange interpolating polynomial. Initially, the Lagrange interpolating polynomial, indicated by $P(x)$, is one of a kind polynomial of degree m for which $P(x_i) = f(x_i)$ for $i = 0, 1, \ldots, m$. This can be expressed as [13]:

$$P(x) = \sum_i L_i \cdot f(x_i) \tag{1}$$

where $(x_0, x_1, x_2, x_3, \ldots \ldots)$ and $(x_0, x_1, \ldots, x_m)$ are the nodal points, and the Lagrange coefficient, $L_i(x)$ is given by [9]:

$$L_i = \prod_{j=0, i \neq j}^{m} \frac{(x - x_j)}{(x_i - x_j)} \tag{2}$$

The coefficients have various properties that are suitable to be considered [13]. Lagrange coefficient formed for the $m+1$ points $(x_0, y_0), (x_1, y_1) \ldots (x_m, y_m)$ is a polynomial of degree m which vanishes at $x = x_0 \ldots \ldots x = x_{i-1}, x = x_{i+1}$ however, when $x = x_i$, the value of the multiplier will be 1 (one). The type of the Lagrange coefficient in (refeq2) demonstrates that it depends just on the given x's and is completely free of the y's [14]. We employed the mentioned Lagrange definition of the univariate to elicit the tensor product of the I_{ds} drain current as a function of the gate to source voltage V_{gs} and temperature T, regarding Lagrange polynomial are expressed as follows:

$$I_{ds}(V_{ds}, V_{gs}, T) = \sum_{i=0}^{n} \sum_{j=0}^{m} f(V_{ds}, V_{gs}, T = T_i) \cdot L_{ij}(T_i, V_{gs_i}) \tag{3}$$

where V_{ds}, are the drain to source voltage. For L_{ij} the Lagrange multipliers can be stated as follows:

$$L_{ij}(T, V_{gs}) = L_i(T)L_j(V_{gs}), \ 0 \le i \le n, \ 0 \le j \le m \tag{4}$$

$$L_i(T) = \prod_{\tau=-n, \tau \ne i}^{n} \frac{(T-T_\tau)}{(T_i-T_\tau)} \tag{5}$$

$$L_j(V_{gs_j}) = \prod_{\rho=0, \rho \ne j}^{m} \frac{(V_{gs}-V_{gs_\rho})}{(V_{gs_j}-V_{gs_\rho})} \tag{6}$$

so, we have

$$L_{ij}(T_\tau, V_{gs_\rho}) = \begin{cases} 1 & i = \tau, j = \rho \\ 0 & \text{otherwise} \end{cases} \tag{7}$$

3   Barycentric Rational Interpolation

The traditional Lagrange interpolation has specific limitations in terms of computational cost since each interpolation requires $O(n^2)$ additions and multiplications; increasing accuracy requires addition of a new data pair that results in the calculation of whole new LUTs. This makes the scheme to be numerically unstable, especially for higher order systems. These limitation are compensated by Barycentric rational interpolation [16]. Also, evaluation of each interpolation requires $O(n^2)$ additions and multiplications. We adopt Barycentric Lagrange interpolation because it is fast and stable [16]. This is due to the pre-computed techniques of the Barycentric weights that reduce its computational complexity to $O(n)$ compared to $O(n^2)$ operations of the conventional Lagrange [16,18].

The univariate of the Barycentric rational formula (sometimes called second (true) form of the barycentric recipe) $P(x)$ is stated as follows [16]:

$$P(x) = \frac{\sum_{j=1}^{n+1} \frac{w_j}{x-x_j} f_j}{\sum_{j=1}^{n+1} \frac{w_j}{x-x_j}} \ , j = 1, \ldots, n+1 \tag{8}$$

where w_j is Barycentric weights. The symmetry in Eq. (8) shows that the interpolant $P(x)$ can be computed fast in $O(n)$ operations [16]. This weight is defined as:

$$w_j = \prod_{j=0, j \ne k} (x_j - x_k)^{-1} \tag{9}$$

In order to build the LUT for the proposed model based on Barycentric rational interpolation, we consider multivariate of a continuous function f, i.e. $I_{ds} = f(I_{ds_{ij}}|_{(V_{gs}, V_{ds}, T)})$ for $i = 1, ..., n$ and $j = 0, ..., k$. The drain current I_{ds} for this method is stated as follows [17]:

$$I_{ds}(I_{ds_{ij}}|_{(V_{gs}, V_{ds}, T)}) = \frac{\sum_{\tau=1}^{\alpha+1} \sum_{r=1}^{b+1} f(I_{ds_{ij}}|_{(V_{gs}, V_{ds}, T)})M}{\sum_{\tau=1}^{\alpha+1} \sum_{r=1}^{b+1} M} \tag{10}$$

where $M = \frac{w_{\tau r}(V_{gs_j}, V_{ds}, T=T_i)}{\phi_{\tau r}(V_{gs_j}, V_{ds}, T=T_i)}$

$$\phi_{\tau r}(\cdot) = \phi_\tau(V_{gs} - V_{gs_j})\phi_r(T - T_r) \tag{11}$$

where $w_{\tau r}(\cdot)$ are tensor product of Barycentric weights and can be expressed as:

$$w_{\tau r}(I_{ds_{ij}}|_{(V_{gs}, V_{ds}, T)}) = w_{\tau,\alpha}(I_{ds_c}|_{(V_{gs}, V_{ds})})w_{r,b}(I_{ds_q}|_{(V_{gs}, V_{ds}, T)}), \ 0 \le c \le \alpha, 0 \le q \le r \tag{12}$$

where $w_{\tau,\alpha}(\cdot)$, $w_{r,b}(\cdot)$ are the subsets of the precomputed Barycentric weights for drain current I_{ds} with respect to the temperature variation, and defined as follows:

$$w_{\tau,\alpha} = \prod_{\tau=1,\tau\neq c}^{\alpha+1} (V_{gs_\tau} - V_{gs_c})^{-1} , w_{r,b} = \prod_{r=1,r\neq q}^{b+1} (T_r - T_q)^{-1} \tag{13}$$

4 Small Signal Modeling

The 28 nm FDSOI node small-signal equivalent circuit suitable for low frequency process is depicted Fig. 1. It constitutes the intrinsic and extrinsic components for capacitance gate-source C_{gs}, drain-source C_{ds}, and gate-drain C_{gd}. Also it comprises transconductance g_m, gate, source and drain series resistances R_g, R_s and R_d, respectively [20]. Keeping in mind the end goal to guarantees the charge conservative of 28 nm FDSOI node, the capacitance models are set to be a component of the cross voltage (V_{gs}, V_{ds}) [21]. The previously mentioned capacitances are separated by means of two-port multibias s-parameter estimations at 3 GHz converted into y-parameters as defined [22]:

$$\begin{bmatrix} Y_{11} & Y_{12} \\ Y_{21} & Y_{22} \end{bmatrix} = j\omega \begin{bmatrix} C_{gs} + C_{gd} & -C_{gd} \\ C_{dg} - C_{gd} & C_{ds} - C_{gd} \end{bmatrix} \tag{14}$$

The detailed of the aforementioned equations and all extraction conditions are expressed in [23]. The partner capacitance conditions of (3) and (10) are reformulated and expressed as follows:

$$C_{ts}(V_{ds}, V_{gs}, T) = \sum_{i=0}^{n} \sum_{j=0}^{m} f(V_{ds}, V_{gs}, T = T_i) \cdot L_{ij}(T_i, V_{gs_i}) \ t = g, d \tag{15}$$

$$C_{ts}(I_{ds_{ij}}|_{(V_{gs},V_{ds},T)}) = \frac{\sum_{\tau=1}^{\alpha+1}\sum_{r=1}^{b+1} f(I_{ds_{ij}}|_{(V_{gs},V_{ds},T)})M}{\sum_{\tau=1}^{\alpha+1}\sum_{r=1}^{b+1} M} \quad t = g,d \quad (16)$$

The adaptive univariate precomputed LUT proposed method (i.e. Barycentric rational algorithm) is employed in order to build the multivariate LUTs models for the capacitances C_{gs}, C_{ds}, and C_{gd} as well as transconductance g_m by means of small signal analysis.

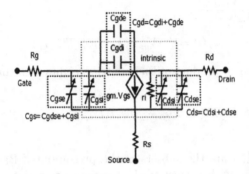

Fig. 1. Comprehensive small-signal equivalent circuit, exploited for the extraction of the extrinsic (represented 'e') and intrinsic (represented 'i') parameters of 28 nm FDSOI node

5   System Analysis

The models have been assessed on 28 nm FDSOI and the same device dimensions as those of in [20] are utilized for simulations. Figure 2 demonstrates the I-V coordinates of the model at the 28 nm FDSOI node with zero body bias and 1.5 V supply voltage, for both PMOS and NMOS devices. At −50 °C, the drain current (I_{on}) is 4.8 mA, though it ascends to 6.2 mA at 120 °C for a gate voltage $V_{gs} = 1.5$ V. This is because of the temperature reliance of the drain current having impact via the threshold voltage and channel mobility as $I_{ds}(T) - \mu(T)[V_{gs} - V_T]$. The $[V_{gs} - V_T]$ term is the set-off drain current that increases with rise in temperature due to the threshold voltage reducing with temperature, as a result of significant errors in the 4th degree of the proposed models as stated in the previous work [14]. This error is reduced with the 5th degree estimate which demonstrates great concurrence with the measured information as appeared in Fig. 2(c–d).

Figure 3 (a–d) shows intrinsic capacitances and transconductance extracted from measurements (black), transitional Lagrange model and the proposed model (i.e. Barycentric rational algorithm). The entire results show excellent match between the proposed approaches and the measured model, as well as the conventional Lagrange model.

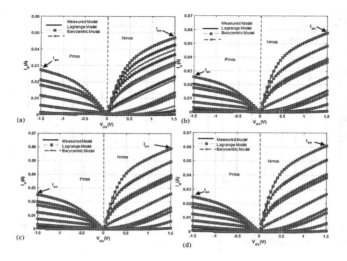

Fig. 2. $I_{ds} - V_{ds}$ characteristics of 28 nm FD SOI: for 5 order (a) -50 °C(b) 60 °C(c) 80°C (d)120 °C

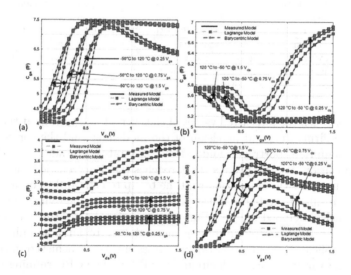

Fig. 3. Intrinsic capacitances and transconductance extracted from measurements (black) , Lagrange model and proposed models matching evaluation for 28 nm FDSOI node: (a) C_{gs} (b) C_{gd}, (c) C_{ds}, (d) g_m

6   Model Validation and Simulation Runtimes

A transient analysis benchmark is used in the inverter circuit in order to verify and validate the proposed models over the BSIM SOI model and traditional spatial Lagrange model as shown in Fig. 4(a) and (b) . The results indicate a great

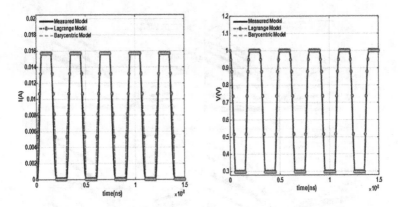

Fig. 4. Precision comparison: verify and validate the proposed models over the 28 nm FD SOI model and traditional.

Table 1. Model simulation runtime compared with 28 nm FDSOI model and the lagrange model in transient simulation

	28 nm FDSOI			Lagrange			Barycentric rational algorithm		
	Step	Time(s)		Step	Time(s)		Step	Time(s)	
		T = −50 °C	T = 120 °C		T = −50 °C	T = 120 °C		T = −50 °C	T = 120 °C
4-bit static Adder	6500	200	245	6505	195	240	6505	20.5	26.7
8 stage NAND	7505	216	260	7506	210	256	7506	22.3	26.1
Inverter	4501	125	165	4507	120	161	4507	12.4	12.4

agreement between the forecasted values of the current and voltage at the output port, which affirms the good precision of the modelling, and the correctness of the model definition, portrayal, and extraction strategy. In addition, with this adequate precision, the two proposed approaches (i.e. Barycentric rational interpolation) can reduce the simulation runtime by up to eight orders of magnitude. This is as a result of the boost in the setup time due to the dynamic programming approach developed by both Barycentric rational algorithms as indicated in Table 1; the Dynamic programming methodology remarkably enhances the simulation proficiency. Simulation runtime assessments are achieved in transient analysis using various benchmark circuits in SPICE. The CPU running time are compared between the proposed models and the 28 nm FDSOI model, as well as the spatial Lagrange interpolation LUT base model. Table I demonstrates that the proposed models have not less than eight orders increase in simulation runtime in contrast to both the spatial Lagrange interpolation LUT and the 28 nm FDSOI model; this is due to the reduction in computational cost, which is as a consequence of the dynamic programming developed by both Barycentric rational algorithms. This progress of computational cost is significantly vital when the whole number of transistors continue expanding in a VLSI circuit [24]. All these results designate that the proposed model enhances model competence significantly without loss of fidelity.

7 Conclusion

The temperature models of the 28 nm FDSOI is discussed and verified with the measured data of both n- and p-channel devices from $-50\,°C$ to $120\,°C$. Using simple adaptive multivariate precomputed developed by Barycentric rational interpolation to extrapolate I-V and C-V, the models achieves reduced simulation runtime with excellent accuracy in circuit analysis. Furthermore, the proposed models can enhance the simulation runtime by up to eight orders of magnitude and beyond without loss of fidelity.

References

1. Planes, N., et al.: 28nm FDSOI technology platform for high-speed low-voltage digital applications. In: VLSI Technology (VLSIT), 2012 Symposium, pp. 133–134. IEEE, Honolulu, HI (2012)
2. Salvatore, G.A., Lattanzio, L., Bouvet, D., Ionescu, A.M.: Modeling the temperature dependence of Fe-FET static characteristics based on Landau's theory. IEEE Trans. Electron Devices **58**(9), 3162–3169 (2011)
3. Kumar, S.V., Kim, C.H., Sapatnekar, S.S.: Body bias voltage computations for process and temperature compensation. IEEE Trans. Very Large Scale Integr. VLSI Syst. **16**(3), 249–262 (2008)
4. Filanovsky, I.M., Allam, A.: Mutual compensation of mobility and threshold voltage temperature effects with applications in CMOS circuits. IEEE Trans. Circ. Syst. I Fundam. Theor. Appl. **48**(7), 876–884 (2001)
5. Ku, J.C., Ismail, Y.: On the scaling of temperature-dependent effects. IEEE Trans. Comput. Aided Des. Integr. Circ. Syst. **26**(10), 1882–1888 (2007)
6. Gildenblat, G., et al.: PSP: an advanced surface-potential-based MOSFET model for circuit simulation. IEEE Trans. Electron Devices **53**(9), 1979–1993 (2006)
7. Thakker, R.A., Sathe, C., Baghini, M.S., Patil, M.B.: A table-based approach to study the impact of process variations on FinFET circuit performance. IEEE Trans. Comput. Aided Des. Integr. Circ. Syst. **29**(4), 627–631 (2010)
8. Bourenkov, V., McCarthy, K.G., Mathewson, A.: MOS table models for circuit simulation. IEEE Trans. Comput. Aided Des. Integr. Circ. Syst. **24**(3), 352–362 (2005)
9. Li, X., Yang, F., Wu, D., Zhou, Z., Zeng, X.: MOS table models for fast and accurate simulation of analog and mixed-signal circuits using efficient oscillation-diminishing interpolations. IEEE Trans. Comput. Aided Des. Integr. Circ. Syst. **34**(9), 1481–1494 (2015)
10. Graham, M.G., Paulos, J.J.: Interpolation of MOSFET table data in width, length, and temperature. IEEE Trans. Comput. Aided Des. Integr. Circ. Syst. **12**(12), 1880–1884 (1993)
11. Rofougaran, A., Abidi, A.A.: A table lookup FET model for accurate analog circuit simulation. IEEE Trans. Comput. Aided Des. Integr. Circ. Syst. **12**(2), 324–335 (1993)
12. Schrom, G., Stach, A., Selberherr, A.S.: An interpolation based MOSFET model for low-voltage applications. Microelectron. J. **29**(8), 529–534 (1998)
13. Touhidur, R.: Physics Based Modeling of Multiple Gate Transistors on Silicon on-Insulator (SOI). The University of Tennessee, Knoxville (2009)

14. Abdalla, A.M., Elfergani, I.T.E., Rodriguez, J.: Modelling the temperature dependence of 28 nm Fully Depleted Silicon-On Insulator (FDSOI) static characteristics based on parallel computing approach. In: 2016 IEEE Nanotechnology Materials and Devices Conference (NMDC), pp. 1–2. IEEE, Toulouse (2016)

15. Hormann, K., Schaefer, S.: Pyramid algorithms for barycentric rational interpolation. Comput. Aided Geom. D. **42**, 1–6 (2016)

16. Berrut, J.P., Trefethen, L.N.: Barycentric lagrange interpolation. SIAM Rev. **46**, 501–517 (2004)

17. Zhao, A., Wang, B.: Lebesgue constant minimizing bivariate barycentric rational interpolation. Int. J. App. Maths Info. Sci **8**(1), 187–192 (2014)

18. Adams, B.M., et al.: DAKOTA, A Multilevel Parallel Object-Oriented Framework for Design Optimization, Parameter Estimation, Uncertainty Quantification, Technical report SAND2014-4253, Sandia National Laboratory (2014)

19. Goldman, R.: Pyramid algorithms A dynamic programming approach to curves and surfaces for Geometric Modeling. Morgan Kaufmann, San Francisco (2003)

20. Kilchytska, V., Makovejev, S., Md Arshad, M.K., Raskin, J.-P., Flandre, D.: Perspectives of UTBB FD SOI MOSFETs for analog and RF applications. In: Nazarov, A., Balestra, F., Kilchytska, V., Flandre, D. (eds.) Functional Nanomaterials and Devices for Electronics, Sensors and Energy Harvesting. EM, pp. 27–46. Springer, Cham (2014). https://doi.org/10.1007/978-3-319-08804-4_2

21. Snider, A.D.: Charge conservation and the transcapacitance element: an exposition. IEEE Trans. Educ. **38**(4), 376–379 (1995)

22. Lai, S., Fager, C., Kuylenstierna, D., Angelov, A.I.: LDMOS modeling. IEEE Microwave Mag. **14**(1), 108–116 (2013)

23. Jang, J.: Small-signal modeling of RF CMOS. Maters thesis, Dept. Elect. Eng; Stanford Univ.; Stanford, CA, USA (2004)

24. Chen, M., Zhao, W., Liu, F., Cao, Y.: Fast statistical circuit analysis with finite-point based transistor model. In: 2007 Design, Automation Test in Europe Conference Exhibition, Nice, pp. 1–6 (2007)

Design of Compact Printed Monopole Antenna with Enhanced Bandwidth and Controllable Filtering Notch for UWB Applications

Issa Elfergani[1]([⊠]), Mina Alrawi[2], Abdelgader M. Abdalla[1],
Jonathan Rodriguez[1,3], Atta Ullah[4], and Raed Abd-Alhameed[4]

[1] Instituto de Telecomunicações, Aveiro, Portugal
{i.t.e.elfergani,a.m.abdalla,jonathan}@av.it.pt
[2] Universidade de Aveiro, Aveiro, Portugal
mina.alrawi@ua.pt
[3] University of South Wales, Pontypridd CF37 1DL, UK
[4] Faculty of Engineering and Informatics,
Bradford University, Bradford BD7 1DP, UK
{A.Ullah5,R.A.A.Abd}@bradford.ac.uk

Abstract. Compact printed monopole antenna suitable for UWB applications has been studied and analyzed. The design procedure of the proposed antenna has been elaborated into five stages, Firstly, the antenna with full ground plane was built, in which shows a narrow band of around 10 GHz. Secondly, the ground plane was optimally cut in order to enhance the antenna bandwidth, this version demonstrates a wide bandwidth from 3.15 GHz to 7.20 GHz. Thirdly, to cover the whole range of the UWB spectrum, a rectangle slot was generated on the micro strip line, this version shows a broad frequency range from 3.15 GHz up to 11 GHz, in which meet the UWB system. However, an electromagnetic interference (EMI) may exist in the UWB spectrum, thus, a simple and effective approach of U-slot was used. The U-slot was printed over the radiating element, in which created a notched band around 6.5 GHz. However, this fixed filtering notch cannot be tuned, therefore, a lumped capacitor was positioned on the best place over the generated U-slot, this makes the introduced rejected band tuned over a broad frequency range from 6.5 GHz up to 5.2 GHz. The results exhibit that the antenna structure may be deemed as an attractive candidate for todays' smart applications.

Keywords: Printed monopole antenna · Tunable notched-band
Defected ground plane

1 Introduction

There has been a tremendous interest in exploiting the Ultra-Wideband (UWB) technology since the Federal Communication Commission (FCC) released the 3.1–10.6 GHz frequency spectrum for unlicensed usage [1]. A broad attention has been given to UWB systems, in which within the UWB system; the antenna has an indispensable effect in UWB signal quality. Thus, a significant amount of research activity

© ICST Institute for Computer Sciences, Social Informatics and Telecommunications Engineering 2019
Published by Springer Nature Switzerland AG 2019. All Rights Reserved
V. Sucasas et al. (Eds.): BROADNETS 2018, LNICST 263, pp. 299–306, 2019.
https://doi.org/10.1007/978-3-030-05195-2_29

has been carried out in the area of the design and implementation of UWB antennas. The most imperative factors in the design of UWB antenna are good matching over the UWB frequency band and low transient distortion [2]. However, depending on the application, the requirements for UWB antenna design may vary significantly, for example, in the case of the mobile handheld devices, the small size, acceptable gain, high efficiency and the omni-directional radiation pattern are highly demanded.

Therefore, to develop a compact antenna that operates in a broadband or ultrawide-band (UWB) range for contemporary wireless communication devices has become of a great challenge for the antenna designers and engineers. The printed antenna structures have been largely used for the UWB systems due to their low compact volume, reasonable cost, less complexity and easy integration with the device's circuit board. This kind of antennas include, the antenna with probe-fed [3], the antenna with microstrip feeding line [4], the planar inverted-F antennas (PIFAs) [5], and the antenna with coplanar waveguide (CPW)-feeding method [6].

However, on the other hand, the above-mentioned antennas [3–6] suffer from some limitations, for example, the antenna with a probe feeding approach needs to be done through a hole to connect and feed the radiating element, in which may lead size increasing and design complexity. The microstrip feeding line antenna usually comes up with a larger size of ground plane, which may affect the antenna radiation, gain and efficiency. The PIFA has such a great advantages of compact volume, easy fabrication, but it suffers from insufficient impedance bandwidth for use in broadband or multiband operation.

In fact, in short-range UWB communications, the trade-off between size, radiation efficiency, gain, bandwidth, and low cost should be optimized to accomplish a suitable antenna design. To meet these requirements, the printed monopole antenna designs have been rolled out. Several printed monopole antenna structures with different techniques have been recently reported for UWB applications [7–10]. The printed monopole antennas have several advantages such low cost, size reduction, broad bandwidth, improved gain and high efficiency. However, despite all the aforementioned of the printed monopole antennas, these antennas still may face some constraints as they are very sensitive to the electromagnetic interferences with existing narrowband wireless communication systems that work below 10 GHz, such as the wireless local area network (WLAN) for IEEE802.11a operating at 5.15–5.825 GHz band and IEEE 802.16 WiMAX system operating at 3.3–3.7 GHz, which may cause severe interference to the UWB system.

Such envisaged interferences caused by these narrow bands can be mitigated by using spatial filters but this approach will lead to several drawbacks such as complexity increase cost, size and weight of the system. Therefore, it is required to design UWB antennas with band-rejection feature in those narrow bands spectrum in order avoid feasible interference, while still keeping the other performance metrics such as the UWB characteristics of an impedance matching and radiation stability, the size compactness of the antenna geometry, and the low fabrication cost for consumer electronics applications. Numerous UWB antennas with single notched-band were proposed in [11, 12], with dual-notched bands in [13, 14] and with triple rejected bands as in [15, 16]. However, these designs have come up with fixed rejected bands, which cannot be shifted to cover other channels. Thus, this paper documents printed monopole UWB antenna design with controllable notched bands.

2   Antenna Design and Procedure

The layout and the full dimensions of the proposed antennas are depicted in Fig. 1. The radiating element with size of 12 mm^2 × 12 mm^2, is printed over 0.8 mm FR4 sub-strate, dielectric constant εr = 4.4 and loss tangent tan δ = 0.017. The dimensions of the substrate are 30 mm^3 × 30 mm^3 × 0.8 mm^3. The other side of the substrate has a rectangular defected ground plane (DGP) copper ground plane with dimensions 30 mm^2 × 9 mm^2, as illustrated in Fig. 1,b. The proposed structures were feed by using a 50-Ω microstrip line size of 10 mm^2 × 1.5 mm^2. The antenna designs are constructed and assembled with the help of the CST EM simulator [17].

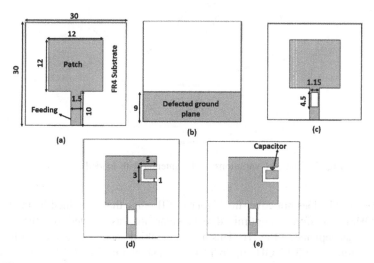

Fig. 1. The proposed antenna designs, (a) top view, (b) bottom view/DGP, (c) with DGP & slotted feed, (d) DGP& slotted feed & U-slot feeding, (e) loaded antenna.

3   Results and Discussions

3.1   The Reflections Coefficients (S$_{11}$)

The reflection coefficients (S$_{11}$) of the proposed antennas are shown in Figs. 2 and 3. As should be noted that the first version of the antenna (full ground plane) exhibits a narrow bandwidth at 10 GHz. However, as the main goal of this work is to develop a compact antenna design for use in UWB applications, thus, the defected ground plane (DGP) approach was employed as seen in Fig. 1b, this antenna version demonstrates a wide bandwidth from 3.15 GHz to 7.20 GHz as illustrated in Fig. 2.

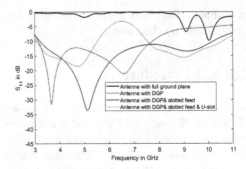

Fig. 2. The S11 variations of the antenna with full ground, with DGP, with DGP & slotted-feed and with DGP & slotted-feed & U-slot

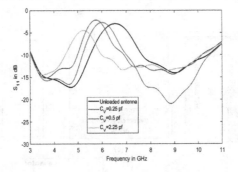

Fig. 3. The S11 variations of the antenna with loaded capacitor

However, this does not cover the higher UWB range that is defined by the FCC (up to 10.3 GHz). Therefore, an optimized rectangular slot was inserted over the microstrip feeding line as depicted in Fig. 1c. This makes the third version able to cover the whole UWB spectrum from 3.15 GHz up to 11 GHz as shown in Fig. 2. The wide spectrum of the UWB system may be subjected to an electromagnetic interference (EMI) with other adjacent narrow systems. Hence it is better to have UWB antenna with built in notch characteristics. Thus, desired notched frequency band at 6.5 GHz is achieved by producing U- shaped slot over the radiating patch as shown in Fig. 1d. By properly selecting the best position of the U-slot, it is feasible to create the desired bandwidth and center frequency of notched band. This forth antenna version design is capable of producing a steeper rise in S11 curve at the notch frequency as indicated in Fig. 2.

Though the forth version of the proposed antennas have advantages of avoiding the interference with the existing systems. However, this is such a fixed rejected band, which is not possible to be tuned to cover several bands of existing systems. Moreover, hence the key issue is the design of a compact volume with good wideband characteristics, including a tunable filtering notched frequency that is able to cover a wide continuous rejected band range, As a result, a lumped capacitor was attached over the proposer location of the U-shaped slot (See Fig. 1e). By varying the capacitance of the capacitor from 0.25pf, 0.5pf and 2.25pf, the created rejected band was smoothly tuned from 6 GHz, 5.7 GHz and 5.2 GHz respectively as shown in Fig. 3. This enables the proposed design to avoid the foreseen interferences such as lower WLAN5.2 GHz, higher WLAN5.8 GHz and band C around 6.5 GHz.

3.2 The Power Gain and Efficiency

The power gains of the proposed antennas are investigated as in Fig. 4. The UWB antenna without notched band shows a smooth gain values vary from 2.2 dBi up to 4.3 dBi over the entire UWB range. The antenna design with fixed rejected band, displays also a smooth gain from 2.1 dBi to around 4 dBi, except at the 6.5 GHz, where the gain was significantly dropped to around −3.9 dBi. In the scenario of the loaded antenna with 0.25pf capacitor, the proposed antenna shows power gains values from 2.1 dBi to 4 dBi, except at the notched band of 6 GHz, where the gain dropped to around −3.1 dBi. When the antenna loaded with 0.5pf capacitor, gain values from 2.2 dBi up to 4.3 dBi were accomplished over the all UWB spectrum, however, a sharp decrease of the 3.6 dBi occurred at the notched band of 5.8 GHz. Also, a smooth gain vary from 2.3 dBi to 4.3 dBi over the frequency range from 3.15 GHz to 11 GHz, with the exception of the lower WLAN5.2 GHz, where the gain was hugely dropped to −2.8 dBi as the rejected band created.

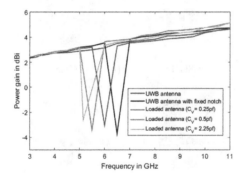

Fig. 4. Power gains of the proposed antennas

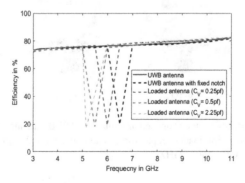

Fig. 5. Radiation efficiency of the proposed antenna

The radiation efficiency of the proposed antennas are analyzed in Fig. 5. The UWB antenna demonstrates flat efficiency values from 78% to 83% over the UWB range from 3.15 GHz up to 11 GHz, while the version of the UWB antenna with fixed rejected band shows efficiency from 77% to 82%, except at the produced notch where the efficiency goes down to 21%. In the paradigm of the loaded antenna, the three loaded versions with 0.25pf, 0.5pf and 2.25pf display smooth efficiency vary from 77.5% to 82.5%, however, the efficiency show significant drop to 21%, 19.5% and 20%, where the filtering notches were generated respectively.

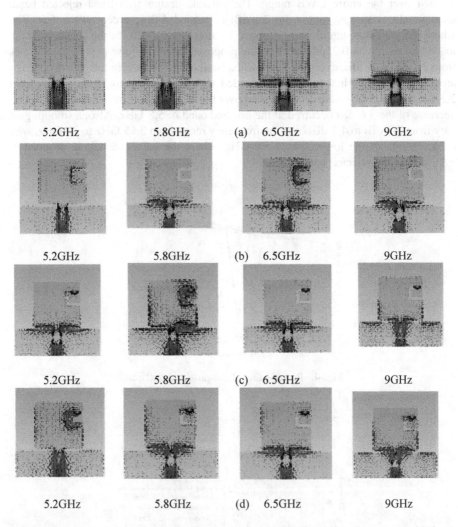

Fig. 6. The current surfaces for the proposed antennas, (a) UWB antenna, (b) antenna with fixed notch, (c) antenna with 0.5pf loaded capacitor, (c) antenna with 2.25pf loaded capacitor, at 5.2 GHz, 5.8 GHz, 6.5 GHz and 9 GHz.

3.3   The Current Surfaces

In order to prove the outcomes in Figs. 2, 3, 4 and 5, the current surfaces of the proposed antenna versions, namely the UWB antenna, antenna with fixed notched band and the antenna with tunable rejected band were studied and analyzed as presented in Fig. 6. Four frequencies were selected, i.e. 5.2 GHz, 5.8 GHz, 6.5 GHz and 9 GHz, which cover the aggregate bandwidth. Most of the currents induce on the feeding line in the case of the UWB antenna over the four targeted frequency bands since there no notched bands created as indicated in Fig. 6a. In the second scenario (antenna with U-slot) most of the currents flow around the feeding line, except at the 6.5 GHz as the current concentrate on both the feeding strip as well as the U-slot as shown in Fig. 6b. This indicates that the U-slot approach acts as an effective stop-band filter and confirms the objective of the U-slot technique in Fig. 2. When the antenna loaded with 0.5pf and 2.25pf, the current mainly concentrate on the feeding line, except at the WLAN5.8 GHz and WLAN5.2 GHz, where the both rejected bands were introduced as depicted in Fig. 6c and d. These findings prove the statement in previous sections for the antenna to simultaneously function as a radiator and stop-band filter within a single system device.

4   Conclusion

A compact volume of UWB printed monopole antenna, including band-notched function for UWB systems has been developed and analysed. Five antenna versions have been designed. The proposed design occupies a compact volume of 30 x 30 x 0.8 mm^3. For bandwidth improvement, a defected ground plane (DGP) was initially used. To further meet the spectrum of the UWB released by the FCC (3.1 GHz to 10.6 GHz), a rectangular slot has been inserted on the proper location over the feeding line. Moreover, a U-shaped slot was added over the radiating patch to obtain the filtering notch feature, while keeping the same UWB spectrum range. Finally, a lumped capacitor has been placed over the U-slot, in which by varying its capacitance values the created rejected band was easily shifted downwards to cover the range from 6.5 GHz up to 5.2 GHz. The proposed antennas indicated stable performances in terms of reflection coefficients, current distributions, gains and efficiency. The proposed final design was able to accomplish the desired band-notched characteristics, making the design as a smart candidate for the UWB applications.

Acknowledgment. This work is carried out under the grant of the Fundacão para a Ciência e a Tecnologia (FCT - Portugal), with the reference number: SFRH/BPD/95110/2013. This work is supported by the European Union's Horizon 2020 Research and Innovation program under grant agreement H2020-MSCA-ITN-2016-SECRET-722424.

References

1. FCC 1st report and order on ultra-wideband technology. FCC, Washington, DC, February 2002
2. Chamaani, S., Mirtaheri, S.A.: Planar UWB monopole antenna optimization to enhance time-domain characteristics using PSO. Int. J. Electron. Commun. **64**, 351–359 (2010)
3. Al-Zoubi, A., Yang, F., Kishk, A.: A broadband center-fed circular patch-ring antenna with a monopole like radiation pattern. IEEE Trans. Antennas Propag. **57**, 789–792 (2009)
4. Sarin, V.P., Deepu, V., Aanandan, C.K., Mohanan, P., Vasudevan, K.: Wideband printed microstrip antenna for wireless communications. IEEE Antennas Wireless Propag. Lett. **8**, 779–781 (2009)
5. Oh, S.K., Yoon, H.S., Park, S.O.: A PIFA-type varactor-tunable slim antenna with a PIL patch feed for multiband applications. IEEE Antennas Wireless Propag. Lett. **6**, 103–105 (2007)
6. Nasimuddin, N., Chen, Z.N.: Wideband multilayered microstrip antennas fed by coplanar waveguide-loop with and without via combinations. IET Microw. Antennas Propag. **3**, 85–91 (2009)
7. Elfergani, I., Hussaini, A.S., Rodriguez, J., Abd-Alhameed, R.A.: Antenna Fundamentals for Legacy Mobile Applications and Beyond. Springer, Cham (2017). https://doi.org/10.1007/978-3-319-63967-3. ISBN 978-3-319-63967-3
8. Ray, K.P., Thakur, S.S., Deshmkh, A.A.: Compact slotted printed monopole UWB antenna. In: International Conference on Communication Technology, pp. 16–18 (2013)
9. Khan, M.K., Khan, M.I., Ahmad, I., Saleem, M.: Design of a printed monopole antenna with ridged ground for ultra wideband applications. In: 2016 Progress In Electromagnetic Research Symposium (PIERS), Shanghai, China, 8–11 August, pp. 4394–4396 (2016)
10. Abid, M., Kazim, J., Owais, O.: Ultra-wideband circular printed monopole antenna for cognitive radio applications. Int. J. Microw. Opt. Technol. **10**(3), 184–189 (2015)
11. Ebadzadeh, S.R., Zehforoosh, Y.: A compact UWB monopole antenna with rejected WLAN band using split-ring resonator and assessed by analytic hierarchy process method. J. Microwaves Optoelectron. Electromagn. Appl. **16**(2), 592–601 (2017)
12. Jangid, K.G., et al.: Circular patch antenna with defected ground for UWB communication with WLAN band rejection. Defence Sci. J. **66**(2), 162–167 (2016). https://doi.org/10.14429/dsj.66.9329
13. Yadav, A., Sethi, D., Khanna, R.K.: Slot loaded UWB antenna: dual band notched characteristics. Int. J. Electron. Commun. (AEÜ) **70**, 331–335 (2016)
14. Elfergani, I., Lopes, P., Rodriguez, J., Lo Hine Tong, D.: Simple and compact planar ultra-wideband antenna with band-notched characteristics. In: Elfergani, I., Hussaini, A.S., Rodriguez, J., Abd-Alhameed, R. (eds.) Antenna Fundamentals for Legacy Mobile Applications and Beyond, pp. 119–134. Springer, Cham (2018). https://doi.org/10.1007/978-3-319-63967-3_6
15. Hamad, E.K.I., Mahmoud, N.: Compact tri-band notched characteristics UWB antenna for WiMAX, WLAN and X-band applications. Adv. Electromagnetics **6**(2), 53–58 (2017)
16. Chen, X., Xu, F., Tan, X.: Design of a compact UWB antenna with triple notched bands using nonuniform width slots. Journal of Sensors **2017**, 1–9 (2017). Article ID 7673168
17. CST-Computer Simulation Technology AG (2014)

On the Performance of Acousto Optical Modulators–Free Space Optical Wireless Communication Systems over Negative Exponential Turbulent Channel

Raed Mesleh$^{(\boxtimes)}$ (iD), Ayat Olaimat, and Ala Khalifeh

Department of Electrical and Communication Engineering,
School of Electrical Engineering and Information Technology,
German Jordanian University, Amman, Jordan
raed.mesleh@gju.edu.jo

Abstract. A novel free space optical (FSO) wireless communication system is proposed very recently utilizing acousto optical modulator (AOM) to externally modulate the laser beam [1]. The idea is to control the diffracted angle of a laser beam incident to an AOM through varying the acoustic frequency propagating inside the AOM. The receiver with multiple photo diodes, spatially distributed and aligned to the preplanned diffracted angles, receive the laser signal and retrieve the transmitted bits. In this paper, we study the performance of AOM–FSO system over negative exponential turbulent channel. A closed-form expression for the average bit error probability is derived and shown to be precise over wide range of channel and system parameters. The performance of the system is compared to the ideal case of no fading and log normal channel.

Keywords: Acousto Optical Modulator (AOM)
Free Space Optics (FSO) · Performance analysis
Wireless communication · Negative exponential channel

1 Introduction

Optical wireless communication (OWC) is an auspicious technology for next generation wireless communication systems due to its multiple inherent advantages. OWC utilizes a huge unlicensed spectrum and predicts a vast increase in the spectral efficiency [2,3]. Free space optical (FSO) is the outdoor technology part of OW communication systems. The market of FSO is expected to grow by 41.4% between 2017 and 2022, according to a recent *Markets and Markets* technical report. Such increase is driven mainly by: *(i)* free and unregulated licensing, *(ii)* enhanced energy efficiency, *(iii)* low carbon emission, and *(iv)* no interference with RF signals.

© ICST Institute for Computer Sciences, Social Informatics and Telecommunications Engineering 2019
Published by Springer Nature Switzerland AG 2019. All Rights Reserved
V. Sucasas et al. (Eds.): BROADNETS 2018, LNICST 263, pp. 307–316, 2019.
https://doi.org/10.1007/978-3-030-05195-2_30

Modulating the intensity of the propagating light is not trivial as the transmitted light has to be positive and real signal [4]. At the receiver, direct detection is generally considered where the variant intensities of the received light are directly converted to current signal. However, weather conditions and scattering severely degrade the performance of FSO system. In particular, weather conditions, such as fog, cause absorption and scattering, which severely degrades the performance [5]. Other issues include deviation of the laser beam, misalignment and angular alterations [6,7]. In particular, misalignment in the link will importantly affect the link performance [8,9].

A novel idea reported recently, called *Acousto optical modulator–FSO (AOM–FSO)*, demonstrated significant performance enhancements over log-normal fading channels [1]. AOM is a device that operates by Bragg diffraction of an incident light beam from an input acoustic signal. The diffracted light intensity and other parameters are controlled through the parameters of the incident acoustic wave. Also, the parameters of the acoustic signal depend on the frequency of the RF signal at the input of the piezoelectric driver at the input of the Bragg cell. For the AOM to function properly, proper design and several conditions must be met simultaneously [1,10,12–14].

In AOM-FSO system, incoming data bits frequency modulate an RF signal, which determines the acoustic wave signal parameters at the output of a piezoelectric transducer [10]. An incident and un-modulated laser beam signal will be diffracted with a frequency that is either decreased or increased by an amount proportional to the acoustic frequency. As such, varying the parameters of the incident acoustic signal control the parameters of the diffracted light beam. In [1], incoming data bits control the resulting acoustic frequency and determine the diffraction angle of the incident laser beam. The receiver considers multiple photo diodes (PD) aligned to the diffracted angles to estimate the modulated angle and retrieve original information bits.

The performance of AOM–FSO system has been analyzed over log–normal channels only in [1]. In this paper, we analyze and discuss the performance of AOM-FSO system over negative exponential (NE) turbulent channel. An accurate formula for the average bit error rate (BER) performance is derived and shown to be accurate over wide range of parameters. Monte Carlo simulation results are presented and discussed to highlight the accuracy of the derived formulas and to study the impact of different channel parameters on the performance.

The remaining of this article is ordered as follows. A revised system model is presented in Sect. 2 along with the considered channel model. Analytical derivation of the average BER is conducted in Sect. 3. Discussion and illustrative results are presented in Sect. 4 and conclusions are drawn in Sect. 5.

2 System and Channel Models

2.1 AOM-FSO System Model

In AOM-FSO system, incoming data bits enter a frequency shift keying (FSK) modulator that is connected to a piezoelectric transducer at the input of the

AOM. In particular, each m bits modulate a specific carrier frequency, f_i, $i = 1, 2, \cdots, M$, with $M = 2^m$ being the number of modulated RF signals. The generated RF frequencies control the piezoelectric transducer output acoustic frequency and an acoustic wave with velocity v_s and $\Lambda = v_s/f_s$ wavelength, propagates through the Bragg cell [11]. AOM-FSO system assumes that an un-modulated laser beam with λ_0 wavelength and P_i power hits the Bragg cell at the Bragg angle, θ_B. The incident optical beam and the acoustic wave interacts and is the cause behind the term *acousto optical modulator (AOM)*. Entering the laser beam at the Bragg angle guarantees the maximum diffraction of the laser beam as given by [11, p. 805, (20.0-1)]

$$\sin(\theta_B) = \frac{\lambda_0}{2n\Lambda}. \tag{1}$$

It is important to note that there exist a unique Bragg angle for each Λ assuming fixed λ_0. Hence, [1] proposes a small changes in the acoustic frequency leading to variant diffraction angles of the incident laser beam around the Bragg angle. Considering a propagating acoustic inside the Bragg cell with v_s velocity, f_s frequency and $q = \frac{2\pi}{\Lambda}$ wave number, results in an acoustic wave intensity given as [11, p. 802, (20.1-2)]

$$I_s = 0.5\varphi v_s^3 S_0, \quad (W/m^2), \tag{2}$$

with φ being the medium mass density in (Kg/m^3) and S_0 denoting the strain amplitude. The variation of the refractive index due to the presence of an acoustic wave is calculated as [11, p. 803, (20.1-6)]

$$\Delta n = (0.5\mathcal{M}I_s)^{1/2}, \tag{3}$$

where Δn denotes the changes in the refractive index and $\mathcal{M}$ is a parameter capturing the effectiveness of varying the refractive index of the medium through the acoustic wave.

The AOM-FSO leads to diffracted laser beam by an angle θ_r and optical power P_r given as [11, p. 803, (20.1-6)]

$$P_r = 2\pi^2 n_0^2 \frac{L^2 \Lambda^2}{\lambda_0^4} \mathcal{M} I_s P_i, \tag{4}$$

with acoustic cell length being L and the refractive index of the medium in the absence of acoustic wave is n_0. The idea of AOM-FSO is to place M receiver PDs at d distance from the Bragg cell. The considered PDs should have a peak responsivity matching the reflected beam frequency. Each considered PD should be properly aligned to one of the pre-designed diffracted angles. Hence, the power at the input of the PD is written as

$$P_{\text{rx}} = \frac{A_{\text{rx}} T 10^{-\alpha \frac{d}{10}} P_r}{\pi (0.5\delta_\theta d)^2} + P_g, \tag{5}$$

where the area of the PD is denoted by $A_{\mathrm{rx}} = \pi(0.5D)^2$, the overall optical efficiency is T, the laser beam-divergence is given by δ_θ and the undesired environment dependent background noise is P_g. The idea behind AOM–FSO system is to let the incoming m bits to modulate frequency signal that will results in unique acoustic signal. Accordingly, each sequence of bits will diffract the laser beam by a certain diffraction angle, θ_i, $i = 1, 2, \cdots, M$. Having M PDs with d_r spacing each properly aligned to one angle facilitate the receiver detection process.

At the output of the Bragg cell, the light is propagated in free space and the signal at the input of the the the ith PD is given by

$$P_{r_i} = \eta\beta P_{\mathrm{rx}}^i h_i + n_i, \quad i = 1, 2, \cdots, M, \tag{6}$$

with η being conversion efficiency, h_i is the channel irradiance between the ith receiver and the Bragg cell and the thermal noise and the shot noise radiations are denoted by n_i which is assumed to white Gaussian process with zero mean and σ_n^2 variance. The normalized path-loss term, β, is

$$\beta = \frac{\beta_k}{\beta_{d_i}(d)}, \tag{7}$$

where $\beta_{d_i}(d)$ is the path loss in clear weather conditions and β_k is the path loss in the presence of weather attenuations given by [5]

$$\beta_k = \frac{D_R 10^{\frac{-\alpha d}{10}}}{(D_T + \delta_\theta d)^2}, \tag{8}$$

where D_R being the PD diameter, D_T the transmitting laser diameter and α denotes the weather-dependent attenuation coefficient (in dB/km), obtained as [5]

$$\alpha = \frac{3.91}{v}\left(\frac{\lambda}{550\,(nm)}\right)^P, \tag{9}$$

with v being the visibility parameter and P is the size distribution coefficient of scattering, which can be obtained according to Kim model as [16]

$$P = \begin{cases} 1.6 & v > 50 \\ 1.3 & 6 < v < 50 \\ 0.16v + 0.34 & 1 < v < 6 \\ v - 0.5 & 0.5 < v < 1 \\ 0 & v < 0.5 \end{cases} \tag{10}$$

The normalized path loss values at different weather conditions are tabulated in Table 1. To estimate the diffracted angle of the laser been, the following formula is considered [1]

$$\hat{\theta}_r = \arg\max_{i\in\{1:M\}} (\mathbf{r}), \tag{11}$$

Table 1. Normalized path loss values at different weather conditions and at $\lambda = $ 690 nm.

Weather condition	Visibility	Path loss (dB/Km)	Normalized path loss (β)
Clear	19	1.58	0.98
Thin fog/Heavy rain	1.9	7.72	0.1939
Moderate fog	0.5	33.96	0.00046
Thick fog	0.2	84.9	0.000000003712

where $\mathbf{r} = \begin{bmatrix} r_1 & r_2 & \cdots & r_m \end{bmatrix}^T$ contains all possible received signal powers at each instant of transmission time. The source bits, which results in the estimated diffracted angle can be retrieved by inverse mapping process.

The received signal to noise ratio (SNR) is given by

$$\bar{\gamma} = \frac{\eta P_{\text{rx}}}{\sigma_n^2}. \tag{12}$$

2.2 Negative Exponential Channel (NE)

The probability distribution function (PDF) of the NE channel is given by

$$f_h\left(h_i\right) = \frac{1}{h_i} \exp\left(-h_i\right), \tag{13}$$

and the PDF of the instantaneous SNR at the ith PD is

$$f_\gamma\left(\gamma\right) = \frac{1}{2\sqrt{\gamma\bar{\gamma}}} \exp\left(\sqrt{\frac{\bar{\gamma}}{\gamma}}\right). \tag{14}$$

3   Performance Analysis

In what follows, the average BER of AOM-FSO system is derived over NE fading channel and in the presence of atmospheric attenuations. The derivation follows similar procedure as proposed in [1] and using the receiver presented in previous section. Initially, the special case of $M = 2$ is assumed and then generalized for arbitrary values of M. Considering (11) and $M = 2$, the BER can be written as

$$P_b = \Pr\left[r_2 > r_1 \left| \theta_1 \right.\right]. \tag{15}$$

(15) states that an error occurs if the received power at the second PD, r_2, was larger than the received power at the first PD, r_1, given that the input bits modulate θ_1. Hence, the detection process is obtained by finding the index of PD the received the maximum power among all received signals, $\mathbf{r} = \begin{bmatrix} r_1 & r_2 & \cdots & r_M \end{bmatrix}^T$, with $(\cdot)^T$ being the vector/matrix transpose operation. Analytically, this is the

same as computing the PDFs of a sorted M random variables each with a unique mean value. This can be roughly estimated as an order statistics formula [15].

Let the order statistics of a random continuous population sample be $X_1, X_2, \cdots, X_M$ with $X_M > X_{(M-1)} > \cdots > X_1$, each with a cumulative distribution function (CDF) $F_X\left(x\,|\mu_x, \sigma_x^2\right)$ and a PDF of $f_X\left(x\,|\mu_x, \sigma_x^2\right)$. Thereby, the PDF of X_i is

$$f_{x_i}(x\,|\mu_i, \sigma_x^2) = \frac{M!}{(i-1)!\,(M-i)!}\left[F_X\left(x\,|\mu_x, \sigma_x^2\right)\right]^{i-1}$$
$$\times \left[1 - F_X\left(x\,|\mu_x, \sigma_x^2\right)\right]^{M-i} f_X\left(x\,|\mu_x, \sigma_x^2\right). \tag{16}$$

For the considered AOM-FSO system over NE channel and in the presence of AWGN, the PDF of the ordered random variables is

$$f_\gamma\left(X|\,\mu_h, \sigma_h^2\right) = \frac{1}{2\sqrt{\gamma\bar{\gamma}}}\exp\left(\sqrt{\frac{\bar{\gamma}}{\gamma}}\right) \times \frac{1}{2}\left(1 + \exp\left(\sqrt{\frac{\bar{\gamma}}{\gamma}}\right)\right). \tag{17}$$

Assuming $M = 2$, the error probability is calculated as

$$P_b = \frac{1}{M}\left(\Pr\left[f_{r_1}\left(\gamma\,|\mu_h, \sigma_h^2\right) < f_{r_2}\left(\gamma\,|\mu_h, \sigma_h^2\right)|\theta_1\right]\right.$$
$$\left. + \Pr\left[f_{r_2}\left(\gamma\,|\mu_h, \sigma_h^2\right) < f_{r_1}\left(\gamma\,|\mu_h, \sigma_h^2\right)|\theta_2\right]\right). \tag{18}$$

The probability of error in (18) can be computed as

$$P_b = \frac{1}{M}\left\{\int_0^{\varepsilon_1} f_{r_1}\left(\gamma\,|\mu_h, \sigma_h^2\right)d\gamma + \int_0^{\varepsilon_2} f_{r_2}\left(\gamma\,|\mu_h, \sigma_h^2\right)d\gamma\right\}, \tag{19}$$

where ε_1 indicates the intersection point between the two PDFs, which are computed numerically.

A list of intersection points for different values of d and d_r are respectively provided in Tables 2 and 3.

For arbitrary values of M, the BER can be calculated as

$$P_b = \frac{1}{M}\sum_{i=1}^{M}\int_0^{\varepsilon_i} f_{r_i}\left(\gamma\,|\mu_h, \sigma_h^2\right)d\gamma. \tag{20}$$

Table 2. Intersection points for different values of d assuming $d_r = 1.25\,\text{cm}$ over NE turbulent channels.

d (Km)	ε for $M = 2$	ε for $M = 4$
1.1	5.8	5.5
2	3.3	3.3
2.5	5	5

Table 3. Intersection points for different values of d_r cm assuming $d = 1$ Km over NE turbulent channels.

d_r (cm)	ε for $M = 2$	ε for $M = 4$
1	3.5	3.5
1.75	7.5	6.4

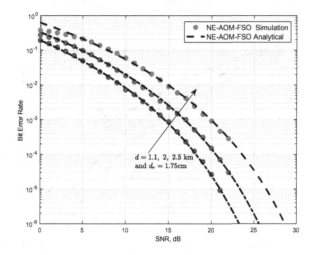

Fig. 1. Analytical and simulation BER results of AOM-FSO system over NE channel for different values of d and $M = 2$.

4 Results

The considered simulation parameters in this paper are listed in Table 4. Also, the pre-designed diffraction angles along with the corresponding acoustic frequencies and the amount of diffracted power are tabulated in Table 5.

Table 4. Simulation Parameters

Laser parameters		Acoustic parameters	
λ_0	1318 nm	L	25.4×10^{-3} m
P_i	10 dB	v_s	3.63×10^{-3} m/s
δ_θ	3.5×10^{-5} rad	$\mathcal{M}$	1.67×10^{-14} m^2/W
θ_B	0.0213 rad	I_s	35 W/m^2
T	1	A_{rx}	4.9×10^{-4} m^2

Table 5. Diffraction angles, powers and acoustic frequencies assuming $P_i = 10$ W.

Acoustic frequency f_s	Diffraction angles θ_r	Diffracted power P_r
224.09 MHz	0.0213 rad	9.9925 W
224.35 MHz	0.021325	9.9915 W
224.622 MHz	0.02135	9.9904 W
224.88 MHz	0.021375	9.9892 W

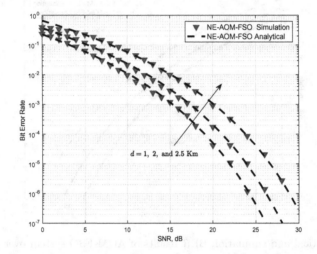

Fig. 2. Analytical and simulation BER results of AOM-FSO system over NE channel for different values of d and $M = 4$.

In the first results depicted in Fig. 1, analytical and simulation BER results for AOM-FSO system over NE channel assuming $\sigma_h = 0.1$, $d_r = 1.75$ cm, $M = 2$ and different values of d are illustrated. Increasing d is shown to deteriorate the performance. This degradation is not due to higher path losses at higher distances, since SNR values are assumed to be the same. The error is rather due to the increase in beam divergence at higher distances, which results in higher BER values. Similar results are reported in Fig. 2 but for $M = 4$. Similar conclusion as made on the previous figure can be stated here as well.

A comparison between the performance of AOM-FSO system over log normal and NE channels is studied and results are shown in Fig. 3. NE channels model high turbulent distribution and degrades the performance of AOM-FSO system as compared to log normal channels. Besides, the lower visibility weather conditions is shown to degrade the performance where the presence of thin-fog is shown to degrade the performance by about 13 dB.

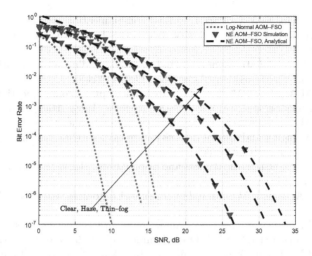

Fig. 3. AOM-FSO performance comparison results over log normal and NE channels in the presence of different weather conditions assuming $d = 1$ Km, $d_r = 1.25$ cm, $\sigma_h = 0.1$ and $M = 4$.

5 Conclusions

This paper studies and analyzes the performance of the recently proposed AOM-FSO system over NE fading channels. Reported results validate the accuracy of the conducted analysis for a wide range of system and channel parameters. The impact of variant weather conditions is also studied and lack of visibility is shown to severely degrade the performance.

Acknowledgment. The work in this paper was supported from the Scientific Research Foundation at the Ministry of Higher Education in Amman, Jordan under grant number ICT/1/9/2016.

References

1. Mesleh, R., Al-Oleimat, A.: Acousto-optical modulators for free space optical wireless communication systems. J. Opt. Commun. Netw. **10**(5), 515–522 (2018)
2. Ghassemlooy, Z., Popoola, W., Rajbhandari, S.: Optical Wireless Communications: System and Channel Modelling with MATLAB. CRC Press, Boca Raton (2017)
3. CISCO, Cisco visual networking index: Global mobile data traffic forecast update, 2015–2020. CISCO, White paper, February 2016
4. Elgala, H., Mesleh, R., Haas, H.: Indoor optical wireless communication: potential and state-of-the-art. IEEE Commun. Mag. **49**(9), 56–62 (2011). ISSN 0163–6804
5. Abaza, M., Mesleh, R., Mansour, A., el Hadi Aggoune: Performance analysis of miso multi-hop FSO links over log-normal channels with fog and beam divergence attenuations. Optics Commun. **334**, 247–252 (2015). http://www.sciencedirect.com/science/article/pii/S0030401814008116

6. Lee, E.J., Chan, V.W.S.: Part 1: optical communication over the clear turbulent atmospheric channel using diversity. IEEE J. Sel. Areas Commun. **22**(9), 1896–1906 (2004)
7. Arnon, S.: Effects of atmospheric turbulence and building sway on optical wireless-communication systems. Opt. Lett. **28**, 129–131 (2003)
8. Khalighi, M.A., Uysal, M.: Survey on free space optical communication: a communication theory perspective. IEEE Commun. Surv. Tutor. **16**(4), 2231–2258 (2014)
9. Khalighi, M.-A., Schwartz, N., Aitamer, N., Bourennane, S.: Fading reduction by aperture averaging and spatial diversity in optical wireless systems. J. Opt. Commun. Netw. **1**(6), 580–593 (2009)
10. Chang, I.C.: Acousto optic devices and applications. IEEE Trans. Sonics Ultrason. **23**(1), 2–21 (1976)
11. Saleh, B.E.A., Teich, M.C.: Fundamentals of Photonics. Wiley, New York (1991). chapter 12
12. Eghbal, M., Abouei, J.: Security enhancement in free-space optics using acousto-optic deflectors. IEEE/OSA J. Opt. Commun. Netw. **6**(8), 684–694 (2014)
13. Nikulin, V.V., Khandekar, R., Sofka, J., Tartakovsky, G.: Acousto-optic pointing and tracking systems for free-space laser communications. In: Proceedings of SPIE, vol. 5892, no. 589216, August 2005
14. Ghosh, A.K., Verma, P., Cheng, S., Huck, R.C., Chatterjee, M.R., Al-Saedi, M.: Design of acousto-optic chaos based secure free-space optical communication links. In: Proceedings of SPIE, vol. 7464, no. 746401 (2009)
15. Casella, G., Berger, R.L.: Statistical Inference, 2nd edn. Duxbury, Pacific Grove (2002)
16. Kadhim, et al.: Characterization study and simulation of MIMO FSO communication under different atmospheric channel. Int. J. Innov. Sci. Eng. Technol. **3**(8) (2016). ISSN (Online) 2348 – 7968

Implementation of Turbo Code Based Xilinx System Generator

Mahmood F. Mosleh[1(✉)], Mais F. Abid[1],
and Mohammed Al-Sadoon[2]

[1] Electrical Engineering Technical College, Middle Technical University,
Baghdad, Iraq
drmahmoodfarhan@gmail.com, maisfalah70@gmail.com
[2] School of Engineering and Informatics, Bradford University, Bradford, UK
M.A.G.Al-Sadoon@bradford.ac.uk

Abstract. The turbo code (TC) is one of the most type of Forward error correction (FEC) code that used in Third Generation Partnership Project (3GPP) which standardization works by the Long Term Evolution (LTE). In this paper an integrated system based TC by LTE standard is implemented. A Simulink model is designed using Xilinx System Generator (XSG) applied by MATLAB version R2012a, ISE design suite version 14.5 and applied by Xilinx Spartan 6 xc6slx45t-fgg484 board using FPGA clock period 10 ns. The system is tested in two steps, in the first one, the Spartan kit is connected within loop of transmitter and receiver. In the second step the Spartan kit is connected to execute the whole system and display the output signal using real scope device. The results confirm that the proposed system is decoded the original signal without any errors.

Keywords: Turbo code · Xilinx system generator · Spartan

1 Introduction

The FEC is active tools that used to increase the reliability of data transmitted in digital communication. Iterative Decoder (ID) is one of attractive channel code which is used in modern communication. TC is the better one of FEC, it is an efficient tool which approaches the limit of Shannon through the use of a convolution codes with a largest constraints length or a block code with the largest blocks length, by the use of iterative and recursive coder TC beat to this limitation [1].

TC used in 3GPP which standardization works by LTE. One of the major task of 3GPP LTE is to increase the speed of radio access in mobile communications. The nature iterative of TC raised their complexity compared to other decoding algorithms, there is two main types of ID algorithms, Soft-Output-Viterbi Algorithm (SOVA) and Maximum A posteriori Probability (MAP) Algorithm which required intricate decoding operations through many of the iterations cycles. So, for FPGA implementation of turbo codes, decrease the complication of the ID while Maintain the performance of bit error rate (BER) is an important in the consideration of the design [2].

For several hardware operations the XSG supplies a group of Simulink blocks that can be implement on different Xilinx FPGAs kits, it is possible to use these blocks to

© ICST Institute for Computer Sciences, Social Informatics and Telecommunications Engineering 2019
Published by Springer Nature Switzerland AG 2019. All Rights Reserved
V. Sucasas et al. (Eds.): BROADNETS 2018, LNICST 263, pp. 317–324, 2019.
https://doi.org/10.1007/978-3-030-05195-2_31

simulate the operation of the hardware system by using XSG Simulink environment. Most Digital signal processing (DSP) needs floating point format for representing data, although it is easy to build this on many of the computers that executing the software of high level such as Simulink, but this is very difficult in the world of the hardware because of the complexity of the floating point arithmetic implementation. That's XSG is used fixed point format to represent all its values in the system.

This paper is divided into two main sections. XSG simulation results where the proposed system is implemented using Simulink MATLAB program and System Generator results with hardware tests are represented where the proposed system is implemented using XSG tools and downloaded to Xilinx Spartan 6 kit for real time by using hardware Co-simulation. Hardware co-simulation merges the ability of MATLAB simulation with a hardware implementation to confirm the ability of the system. The design uses the MATLAB version R2012a and ISE design suite version 14.5.

A contribution of this paper is to implement an integrated communication system included a TC with an encoder and decoder in the transmitter and receiver respectively and to use a co-simulation program interface with MATLAB in order to implement a Simulink model in to the Hdl code without need to write the program in VHDL specially with high complexity circuit like MAP decoder.

Many researchers have been implemented Turbo Decoder (TD) in FPGA blocks in various method. In [3], the authors discussed the implementation of MAP TD with Software Radio Modem. In [4], the authors discussed the efficient power implementation of the Log MAP TD. In [5], the authors discussed the speed improvement and the TD implementation on Central Processing Unit (CPU) based on software defined radio (SDR). The implementation of 3GPP and 3GPP2 turbo encoder on FPGA Xilinx Virtex- IV is reported in [6]. In [7], the authors discussed the implementation of the 3GPP TD on Graphic Processing Unit (GPU).

2 Turbo Code for LTE

2.1 Encoder

TC are a type of the high performance FEC codes, and that was the first operation codes to approach closely to the capacity of the channel. Turbo codes are used in 3GPP LTE mobile communication. In this research, it has been used a turbo encoder according to LTE standard which consists of a two parallel convolution code with two 8-state constituent encoders and one convolutional interleaver as shown in Fig. 1. The task of the convolution interleaver is to take the block of the M-bit data and perform a permutation of this block. The performance of TC depends on the structure of the interleaver and the permutation sequences [8]. The basic rate of Turbo coding according to LTE specifications is 1/3. A block of M-bit data is encoded into a code word with 3 M + 12 data bits, where the 12 tail bits are used for the trellis termination. When begin to encode the input bits of the information, the first value of the shift registers of the 8-state constituent encoders shall be all zero. The convolution encoder may be represented as the follows [9]:

$$G_0 = G1 = 1 + D + D2 + D3 + D6 \tag{1}$$

Then convolution encoder basically multiplies the generated polynomials by the input bit, as the follows

$$A1(k) = G_0 * U(k) = abc...g \tag{2}$$

$$A2(k) = G_1 * U(k) = ABC....G \tag{3}$$

Then interleaving the outputs from the convolution encoder

$$E(k) = aAbBcC...g \tag{4}$$

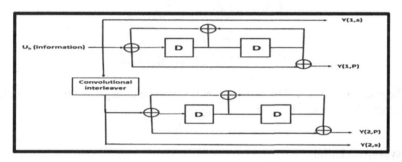

Fig. 1. Structure of the 1/3 CR Turbo encoder in LTE

2.2   The Iterative Decoder

In this research, the algorithm of ID for TD based MAP decoder is shown in Fig. 2. The ID structure is composed of two MAP decoders and interleaver which installed between these two MAP decoders to make permutations to the sequence of the input. The decoding is an iterative operation which exchanges the extrinsic information also called (L-posteriori) between MAP decoders. MAP decoder consisted of forward metric α, backward metric β and extrinsic information L-posteriori. The L-posteriori is calculated by dividing all values for positive states with corresponding values for negative states, and then take the log for such result [10, 11]:

$$log \frac{\sum_{b+} \alpha_{t-1}(s').\beta(s).Z_{et}(s',s)}{\sum_{b-} \alpha_{t-1}(s').\beta(s).Z_{et}(s',s)} \tag{5}$$

Where Z is the branch metric, s' is the previous state and s is the current state.

The α and β are forward metric and backward metric respectively. Each one are calculated using the following equations

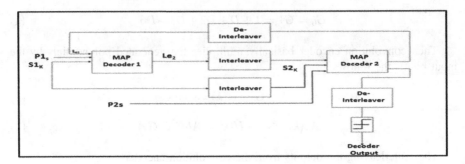

Fig. 2. The ID block diagram

$$\alpha_t(s) = \frac{\sum_{s'} \alpha_{t-1}(s')Z_t(s',s)}{\sum_s \sum_{s'} \alpha_{t-1}(s')Z_t(s',s)} \qquad (6)$$

$$\beta_t(s) = \frac{\sum_{s'} \beta_{t-1}(s')Z_t(s',s)}{\sum_s \sum_{s'} \beta_{t-1}(s')Z_t(s',s)} \qquad (7)$$

The results of Eq. 1 will be two states either positive or negative one which indicate the decoded bit is either 1 or 0 respectively

3 System Model

The system model used in this research is show in Fig. 3. In this section it will explain the function of each block of such system as follows

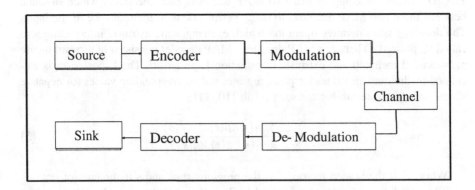

Fig. 3. System model

The source is generating a bit streams. The probability of 1's is 0.5. This stream bit is fed to encoder to apply the encoding process. The encoder block will encode the input data with a CR of 1/3 so that each input bit will be represented by 3 bits. First one is the same input bit called systematic bit, the second and third is the adaptive parity bit. Then the encoder output will be multiplexing the 3 parallel bits into one series row.

The Modulation block will map the input bits into one symbol. The number of bits in each symbol depended on the level of modulation of BPSK which maps one bit in each symbol. The channel used is AWGN type for the purpose of experimentally testing. The parameters of this channel are Eb/No, number of bits per symbol, power of the input signal and the period of symbol. The rest blocks is form the receiver end which apply the inverse function of the corresponding transmitted end.

4 Simulation

The implementation of proposed TD in XSG is show in Fig. 4. The simulation is done by using MATLAB Simulink model and XSG tools. The outputs from the implemented and simulated design have been checked to make sure that the implemented circuit work well as the simulated design and there is not much difference between the MATLAB and ISE designs. The design has used MATLAB version R2012a and ISE design suite version 14.5.

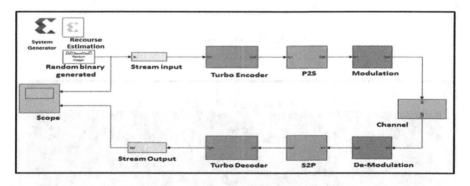

Fig. 4. The proposed system

5 Results

Two cases of hardware proposed Tc implementation has been done using Xilinx spartan6 board.

5.1 The Simulation of SG Result

In this case the input bit stream has been generated using random binary signal generated block as show in Fig. 4. Also, to confirm the result other source using LFSR has been used to generate the signal with 8 numbers of bits, 15 feedback polynomial and 3F initial value in hexadecimal as shown in (Fig. 5), for the above two signals the generated bit file is loaded into Xilinx Spartan 6 xc6sIx45t-fgg484 board using FPGA clock period 10 ns with Simulink system period of 1/3 s. The output signal for random binary signal generated is displaying using the scope of Fig. 4. Figure 6 the transmitted and received signal of random binary signal generated. It is show that the decoder is deconstructing the transmitted signal without error. For LFSR the signal is displayed using scope of Fig. 5. Also, the transmitted and received signal show in Fig. 7 confirm that the decoder can be decoded any signal regardless of source type.

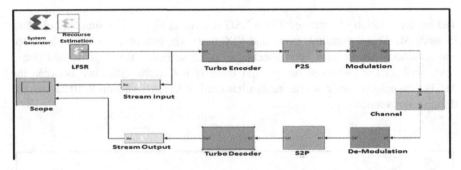

Fig. 5. The proposed system

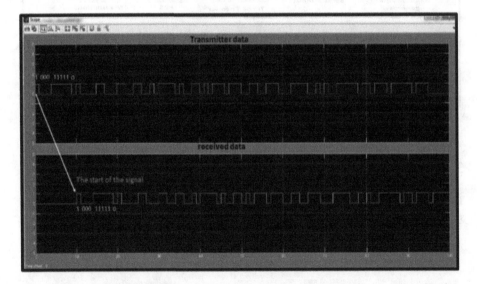

Fig. 6. The XSG results with random integer input block

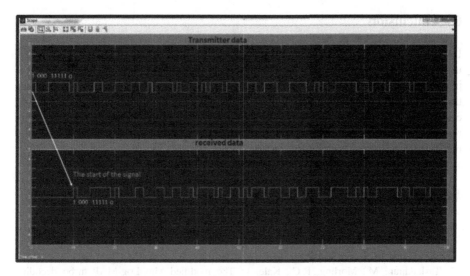

Fig. 7. The XSG results with LFSR input block

5.2 The FPGA Implementation

For the purpose of FPGA implementation it has been used Spartan 6 xc6sIx45t-fgg484 board used for hardware processing. The Spartan 6 kit is connected to the PC through Parallel/USB Programming cable for Joint Test Action Group (JTAG) configuration/ communication. Figure 8 illustrates the hardware implementation which consists of two scopes, one is virtual in PC screen to display the transmitted signal and the second is real device to shows the decode signal. As it is clear in Fig. 8 the system is decode the signal without any error, note that the signal in real scope is a part of virtual scope due to different in scale.

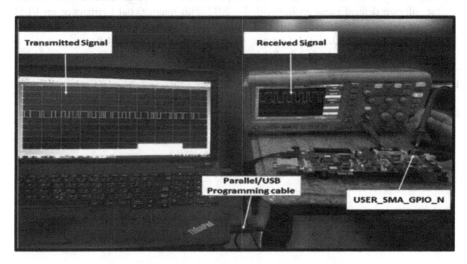

Fig. 8. The XSG results with LFSR input block

6 Conclusion

In this paper it has been building an integrated system consists of an encoder and ID using in addition to modulation and demodulation with AWGN channel. The system is implemented in two cases, the first on is to connect the Spartan 6 in the loop of the transmitter and the receiver and shows the results in two virtual scopes. The second case connect the Spartan to execute the whole system and shows the decoded signal in real device scope. The results confirm that the system is applied in real time and reconstruct the signal without any error.

References

1. Spanos, A., et al.: Reduced complexity rate-matching/de-matching architecture for the LTE turbo code. In: 2014 21st IEEE International Conference on Electronics, Circuits and Systems (ICECS), pp. 411–414. IEEE (2014)
2. Taskaldiran, M., Morling, R.C., Kale, I.: The modified Max-Log-MAP turbo decoding algorithm by extrinsic information scaling for wireless applications. In: Powell, S., Shim, J. (eds.) Wireless Technology. Lecture Notes in Electrical Engineering, vol. 44, pp. 203–213. Springer, Boston (2009). https://doi.org/10.1007/978-0-387-71787-6_13
3. Lin, S., Costello, D.J.: Error Control Coding. Prentice Hall, Englewood Cliffs (2004)
4. Kang, B., et al.: Power-efficient implementation of turbo decoder in SDR system. In: IEEE International SOC Conference, Proceedings, pp. 119–122. IEEE (2004)
5. Huang, L., et al.: A high speed turbo decoder implementation for CPU-based SDR system. In: Proceeding of IET International Conference on Communication Technology and Application, pp. 19–23 (2011)
6. Tripathi, S., Mathur, R., Arya, J.: Unified 3GPP and 3GPP2 turbo encoder FPGA implementation using run-time partial reconfiguration. In: Wireless Telecommunications Symposium (WTS), pp. 1–8. IEEE (2010)
7. Yoge, D.R.N., Chandrachoodan, N.: GPU implementation of a programmable turbo decoder for software defined radio applications. In: 2012 25th International Conference on VLSI Design (VLSID), pp. 149–154. IEEE (2012)
8. Raut, R.D., Kulat, K.D.: Int. J. Comput. Appl. (0975-8887) 1(24) (2010)
9. Sadjadpour, H.R., Sloane, N.J.A., Salehi, M., Nebe, G.: Interleaver design for turbo codes. IEEE J. Sel. Areas Commun. 19(5), 831–837 (2001)
10. Yoo, I., Kim, B., Park, I.-C.: Reverse rate matching for low-power LTE-advanced turbo decoders. IEEE Trans. Circuits Syst. I Regul. Pap. 62(12), 2920–2928 (2015)
11. Nithya, B., Pandiaraj, P., Thenkumari, K.: Development of error correction mechanism based on RCIC turbo codes. LTE Network, Elysium Journal (2015)

SECRET Workshop

Key Management for Secure Network Coding-Enabled Mobile Small Cells

Marcus de Ree[1,2(✉)], Georgios Mantas[1,3], Ayman Radwan[1],
Jonathan Rodriguez[1,2], and Ifiok Otung[2]

[1] Instituto de Telecomunicações, Aveiro, Portugal
{mderee,gimantas,aradwan,jonathan}@av.it.pt
[2] University of South Wales, Pontypridd, UK
ifiok.otung@southwales.ac.uk
[3] Faculty of Engineering and Science, University of Greenwich, London, UK

Abstract. The continuous growth in wireless devices connected to the Internet and the increasing demand for higher data rates put ever increasing pressure on the 4G cellular network. The EU funded H2020-MSCA project "SECRET" investigates a scenario architecture to cover the urban landscape for the upcoming 5G cellular network. The studied scenario architecture combines multi-hop device-to-device (D2D) communication with network coding-enabled mobile small cells. In this scenario architecture, mobile nodes benefit from high transmission speeds, low latency and increased energy efficiency, while the cellular network benefits from a reduced workload of its base stations. However, this scenario architecture faces various security and privacy challenges. These challenges can be addressed using cryptographic techniques and protocols, assuming that a key management scheme is able to provide mobile nodes with secret keys in a secure manner. Unfortunately, existing key management schemes are unable to cover all security and privacy challenges of the studied scenario architecture. Certificateless key management schemes seem promising, although many proposed schemes of this category of key management schemes require a secure channel or lack key update and key revocation procedures. We therefore suggest further research in key management schemes which include secret key sharing among mobile nodes, key revocation, key update and mobile node authentication to fit with our scenario architecture.

Keywords: 5G · Security · Privacy · Key management · Mobile small cells
Network coding · D2D communications

1 Introduction

It has been almost a decade since the 4G mobile network was first introduced. Since that time, many more users and devices joined the network. Not only are our smartphones using the 4G network, but also the rapidly increasing number of devices within the Internet of Things (IoT) concept [1, 2]. Furthermore, since the introduction of the 4G mobile network, the mobile data volume has risen immensely. It is expected that by 2021 the number of wireless devices connected to the network is 100 to 10,000 [3] times higher, and the volume of mobile data is 1,000 times higher [3, 4]. This surge

© ICST Institute for Computer Sciences, Social Informatics and Telecommunications Engineering 2019
Published by Springer Nature Switzerland AG 2019. All Rights Reserved
V. Sucasas et al. (Eds.): BROADNETS 2018, LNICST 263, pp. 327–336, 2019.
https://doi.org/10.1007/978-3-030-05195-2_32

puts a lot of pressure on the current 4G network, which has to share its resources among the growing number of devices. This also causes a reduction in data rates and increases latency.

To address these challenges, new technologies are emerging to create the next generation 5G network [5–9]. These new technologies will deliver higher network capacity, allow the support of more users, lower the cost per bit, enhance energy efficiency, and provide the adaptability to introduce future services and devices. It is envisioned that this new 5G network will be deployed by 2020 and beyond [3, 5, 6, 10], with data rates reaching speeds going up to 10 Gb/s, and reduces the latency to delays as low as 1 ms end-to-end [10].

One approach of increasing throughput inside the 5G network is by utilizing network coding. Network coding is an emerging network technology, which no longer treats data, moving through the network from sender to receiver, as commodities. Traditional routers inside a network can duplicate and forward incoming data packets, but network coding allows multiple packets at a router to be encoded together, before being forwarded. The concept of network coding was first introduced in [11]. It is an emerging communication paradigm that has the potential to provide significant benefits to networks in terms of bandwidth, energy consumption, delay and robustness to packet losses [12–14].

Another emerging technology for the 5G network is small cells. The small cell technology is the most effective solution to deliver ubiquitous 5G services in a cost-effective and energy efficient manner to its users. In particular, mobile small cells are proposed to cover the urban landscape and can be set up on-the-fly, based on demand, using mobile devices (i.e., user equipment) or Remote Radio Units (RRUs) [15]. Moreover, mobile small cells are networks consisting of mobile devices which are within relative close proximity to one another and thus, it allows device-to-device (D2D) communications that enable high data rate services such as video sharing, gaming and proximity-aware social networking. Consequently, end-users are provided with this plethora of 5G broadband services while the D2D communications improves throughput, energy efficiency, latency and fairness [16, 17].

This paper investigates, in terms of security and privacy challenges, a scenario architecture of the EU funded H2020-MSCA project "SECRET" [18] focused on secure network coding-enabled mobile small cells, and explores how existing key management schemes can provide security and privacy in a similar architecture. This will form the basis for designing novel key management schemes that can support efficiently and effectively existing and new integrity schemes against pollution attacks in network coding-enabled mobile small cells. The proposed schemes are expected to provide robust and low complexity key management including secret key sharing among mobile nodes, key revocation, key update, and mobile node authentication.

2   Scenario Architecture

We present a scenario architecture of the EU funded H2020-MSCA project "SECRET" [18] focused on secure network coding-enabled mobile small cells. In this scenario architecture, the technologies of mobile small cells, network coding and D2D communications are combined, as illustrated in Fig. 1. The cellular network, consisting of macro cells, is broken down into mobile small cells. Each mobile small cell is controlled by a hotspot (or cluster-head). This is a mobile node (device) within the cluster of mobile nodes that is selected to become the local radio manager to control and maintain the cluster. In addition, the hotspots of the different clusters are controlled by a centralized software-defined controller. Through cooperation these hotspots form a wireless network of mobile small cells that have several gateways/entry points to the mobile network using intelligent high-speed connections [19, 20]. Data traffic between mobile nodes is established through D2D communications, and optimized by utilizing network coding.

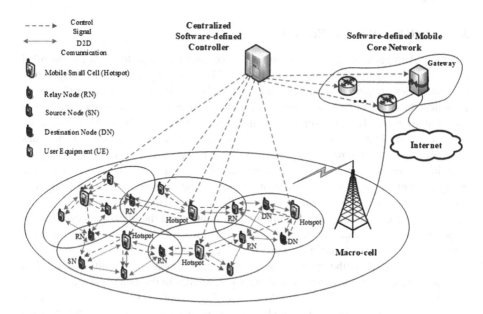

Fig. 1. Scenario architecture

Suppose that a mobile node wishes to share a multimedia file with two other mobile nodes. The mobile node in possession of the multimedia file, the source node (SN), sends this file to the mobile nodes requesting the file, the destination nodes (DNs). Note that these mobile nodes are not required to be in the same mobile small cell, as illustrated in Fig. 1. Through D2D communications, the multimedia file – using multiple hops – is being routed by mobile nodes, through the network of mobile small cells from the SN to the DNs.

This architecture has multiple advantages, compared to the currently employed architecture. By allowing multi-hop D2D communications through a network of mobile small cells, data traffic within this scenario is no longer required to be routed through the base station (BS). This means that the data is no longer required to travel the long distances to and from the BS, but has a more direct route. This significantly reduces latency. Since the transmissions travel shorter distances, the transmissions require less power to reach its destination. This means that this architecture also allows data transmission to be more energy efficient. This architecture also reduces the workload of the BS, which relieves stress on the cellular network.

3 Security and Privacy Challenges

The proposed architecture brings a set of new technologies together, and with that it also comes with a number of security and privacy challenges. This section will explore this kind of challenges that every individual technology poses in our proposed architecture.

3.1 Multi-hop Wireless Network

Allowing data packets in transmission to traverse multiple hops to reach the intended receiver, brings a spectrum of privacy threats. These privacy threats can be split into two categories, data privacy and identity privacy. Data privacy threats cover all attacks in which the attacker tries to uncover information about the data transmitted to the intended receiver. The attacker uses techniques such as eavesdropping and identity impersonation. These attacks are well studied and various cryptographic techniques have been developed to prevent these attacks from being effective. These cryptographic techniques are able to provide data confidentiality using data encryption schemes, entity authentication using identification schemes, and data authentication using signature schemes. These techniques counter all the aforementioned challenges. However, many of these countermeasures require both the sender and the intended receiver to be in possession of a shared cryptographic key. Thus, it is obvious that key management plays a critical role to achieve data privacy [21, 22].

Identity privacy is the other category of privacy threats in a multi-hop wireless network. The challenge of providing identity privacy lies in the establishment of secure communication between two mobile nodes. To establish secure communication between two mobile nodes, both nodes are required to prove their identity to each other. This requirement prevents any attacker from using an impersonation attack. However, both mobile nodes wish to remain anonymous to the intermediate nodes routing the identifying information. This challenge can be solved with anonymous mutual authentication. With anonymous mutual authentication, both mobile nodes participate in an interactive zero-knowledge proof of identity protocol. This protocol involves exchanging challenges to prove their identity to each other, without actually sending any private identifying information. However, all zero-knowledge proof of identity protocols either require both mobile nodes to have a pre-established secret, or depends on a Trusted Third Party (TTP). This TTP is a central control point that every node in the network trusts, but does not fit in our proposed architecture due to the lack of infrastructure. Both mobile nodes are therefore required to have a pre-established secret (such as a shared cryptographic key) in order to communicate [22, 23].

3.2   Network Coding-Enabled Network

A network coding-enabled network allows the encoding of data packets at routers inside the network, and decoding at the receiver's end. This provides significant benefits to networks in terms of bandwidth, energy consumption, delay and robustness to packet losses. Despite these tremendous advantages, networks utilizing network coding technology are vulnerable to the so-called pollution attack. In this attack, a malicious adversary controls a router such that it can mutate data packets by introducing pollution in the original data packet. Network coding causes this pollution to spread downstream by encoding proper data packets with polluted data packets. This leads to the inability to properly decode and retrieve the information at the intended receivers. A successful pollution attack wastes a lot of costly network resources. The challenge posed by this attack is similar to the vulnerability of data modification in any wireless network. Data integrity is required to prevent any polluted data packets from being transmitted further through the network. The research community proposed various integrity schemes [24–34] to solve this problem. However, the efficiency and effectiveness of the integrity schemes are closely related to the key management schemes which are responsible for the generation, distribution, use and update of the cryptographic keys used by the integrity schemes. In the literature, there are various proposed schemes for key distribution which are used in network coding-enabled networks, but they suffer from drawbacks that limit their effectiveness and reliability [28, 29]. Therefore, it is of utmost importance the design of novel key management schemes that can overcome the limitations and drawbacks of the existing key management schemes in order to support efficiently and effectively existing and new integrity schemes against pollution attacks in network coding-enabled mobile small cells.

3.3   Device-to-Device Communications

Device-to-Device (D2D) communications bring into the studied scenario architecture a number of security and privacy challenges. The sole introduction of D2D communications poses challenges when it comes to location privacy. Location privacy is a challenge, since data transmissions between mobile nodes requires close proximity. This allows colluding users to perform a boundary attack to locate nearby mobile nodes. One promising work [35] applied homomorphic encryption to privately identify whether friends are within a nearby distance without revealing the actual user identities. To find out the overall perception when it comes to location privacy, the Princeton Survey Research Associates International held a survey in 2013 and found that 46% of teen users and 35% of adults turn off location tracking features due to privacy concerns [36]. These privacy concerns need to be addressed so that users will allow their devices to be discoverable and participate in content delivery through D2D communications. Fortunately, location privacy can be protected by using identity preserving techniques such as anonymous mutual authentication [22].

Furthermore, in combination with a multi-hop wireless network, D2D communications also brings data privacy challenges (e.g. eavesdropping) along with identity privacy (e.g. identity impersonation) and free-riding issues in the studied scenario architecture [22]. As previously discussed in Sect. 3.1, data privacy can be protected with the use of cryptographic techniques, where the role of key management is of utmost importance, whereas identity privacy can be protected by using techniques such as anonymous mutual authentication. In addition, free-riding means that a selfish mobile device is unwilling to send content to others, while it is still receiving demanded data, for the purpose of saving energy. Free-riding reduces fairness and transmission availability within the network. Thus, a stimulating cooperation mechanism is necessary to prevent free-riding within the network, and several solutions have been proposed to solve this problem [37–41].

3.4 Mobile Small Cells

The introduction of mobile small cells in the studied scenario architecture makes the network dynamic. Every mobile node inside the network is allowed to constantly be on the move. Certain mobile nodes could leave the macro cell, and other mobile nodes could join the macro cell. This network therefore has a constantly changing topology and thus, it poses a problem when it comes to key management. Traditional certificate-based public key cryptography (CB-PKC) relies on a trusted third party called a certifying authority (CA). The CA issues certificates to users inside the network. These certificates are used to verify the identity and provide a cryptographic key at the same time. This CA can be interpreted as the key manager, and it is a central control point that every node in the network trusts. However, a CA does not fit in the studied scenario architecture due to the lack of infrastructure [42, 43]. On the other hand, identity-based public key cryptography (IB-PKC) removes the requirement of certificates, since public keys in IB-PKC are equal to the identity of the mobile nodes. However, private keys are obtained from the Key Generation Center (KGC). KGC holds a master key from which it generates private keys. Consequently, a compromised KGC means that the entire system is compromised. This means that IB-PKC suffers from a single point of failure, along with the key escrow problem [44]. Finally, certificateless public key cryptography (CL-PKC) is introduced to solve these issues. With CL-PKC, private keys are constructed by both the KGC and the mobile user requesting the private key. The KGC generates the first part of the private key, and the mobile user completes the private key by combining it with his own private key. The tasks of the KGC can be distributed among mobile nodes using verifiable secret sharing [45]. A compromised KGC using CL-PKC only provides the attacker with partial private keys. CL-PKC not only solves the single point of failure and the key escrow problem, but it can also satisfy the dynamic topology of the network. Certificateless key management schemes therefore seem a good candidate for the studied scenario architecture, however many proposed schemes still suffer from the private key distribution problem, or they lack key update or key revocation procedures.

4   Cryptographic Security Solutions

Having explored the challenges which are brought forth by the studied scenario architecture, this section discusses how these challenges can be solved. By allowing our scenario architecture to perform multi-hop D2D communication, a spectrum of security and privacy challenges arise. However, cryptographic techniques and anonymous mutual authentication are able to provide secrecy and anonymity. Parties wishing to communicate securely require a shared cryptographic key to take advantage of the cryptographic techniques and anonymous mutual authentication. Key management schemes are responsible for the generation, distribution, storage, use, revocation, and update of these cryptographic keys. It is therefore important to investigate the design of novel key management schemes that fit with our scenario architecture and provide all these functionalities in an efficient and effective manner.

Moreover, to fully exploit the advantages of network coding in our scenario architecture, novel key management schemes are required as most of the existing ones are not able to fully support the data integrity schemes proposed in the literature to prevent pollution attacks in network coding–enabled networks.

In addition, the security of mobile small cells is also affected by key management. The dynamic topology that mobile small cells bring to our scenario architecture poses the challenge of a suitable family of key management schemes. As discussed, CB-PKC and IB-PKC, and their respective key management schemes are not suitable. On the other hand, CL-PKC and certificateless key management schemes seem to be a good candidate. However, existing certificateless key management schemes either lack key update or key revocation procedures, or they require a safe channel for (partial) key distribution which is difficult to realize in our scenario architecture [43].

Therefore, it is of the utmost importance to design novel (certificateless) key management schemes for our scenario architecture. These schemes should provide robust and low complexity key management including secret key sharing among mobile nodes, key revocation, key update and mobile node authentication. Finally, they should also support existing and new integrity schemes against pollution attacks in network coding-enabled mobile small cells in an efficient and effective manner.

5   Conclusion

The studied scenario architecture is suitable to cover the urban landscape of high speed 5G mobile communication. This new scenario architecture exploits the advantages of D2D multi-hop communication and network coding-enabled mobile small cells. However, combining these technologies come with security and privacy challenges. For each technology, we explored their respective security and privacy challenges. We found that there are solutions against the identified security and privacy challenges assuming that there exists a key management scheme able to support cryptographic techniques and protocols in an efficient and effective manner. However, no key management schemes seem to exist which satisfy all the requirements necessary to support all cryptographic techniques and protocols to ensure security and privacy in our scenario architecture. It is therefore of the utmost importance the design of novel key management schemes that can provide robust and low complexity key management including secret key sharing among mobile nodes, key revocation, key update, and mobile node authentication.

Acknowledgments. This research work leading to this publication has received funding from the European Union's Horizon 2020 Research and Innovation programme under grant agreement H2020-MSCA-ITN-2016-SECRET-722424.

References

1. Ericsson: More than 50 Billion Connected Devices (white paper) (2011)
2. Cisco: Cisco Visual Networking Index: Global Mobile Data Traffic Forecast Update, 2016–2021 (white paper) (2017)
3. Hossain, E., Hasan, M.: 5G cellular: key enabling technologies and research challenges. IEEE Instrum. Meas. Mag. **18**(3), 11–21 (2015)
4. Nokia Siemens Networks: 2020: Beyond 4G Radio Evolution for the Gigabit Experience (white paper) (2011)
5. Wang, C., et al.: Cellular architecture and key technologies for 5G wireless communication networks. IEEE Commun. Mag. **52**(2), 122–130 (2014)
6. Chih-Lin, I., Rowell, C., Han, S., Xu, Z., Li, G., Pan, Z.: Toward green and soft: a 5G perspective. IEEE Commun. Mag. **52**(2), 66–73 (2014)
7. Bangerter, B., Talwar, S., Arefi, R., Stewart, K.: Networks and devices for the 5G era. IEEE Commun. Mag. **52**(2), 90–96 (2014)
8. Sucasas, V., Mantas, G., Rodriguez, J.: Security challenges for cloud radio access networks. In: Backhauling/Fronthauling for Future Wireless Systems, pp. 195–211. Wiley, Chichester (2016)
9. Mantas, G., Komninos, N., Rodriguez, J., Logota, E., Marques, H.: Security for 5G communications. In: Fundamentals of 5G Mobile Networks, pp. 207–220. Wiley, Chichester (2015)
10. Andrews, J., et al.: What will 5G be? IEEE J. Sel. Areas Commun. **32**(6), 1065–1082 (2014)
11. Ahlswede, R., Cai, N., Li, R., Yeung, R.: Network information flow. IEEE Trans. Inf. Theory **46**(4), 1204–1216 (2000)
12. Esfahani, A., Mantas, G., Rodriguez, J., Neves, J.: An efficient homomorphic MAC-based scheme against data and tag pollution attacks in network coding-enabled wireless networks. Int. J. Inf. Secur. **16**(6), 627–639 (2017)
13. Iqbal, M., Dai, B., Huang, B., Hassan, A., Yu, S.: Survey of network coding-aware routing protocols in wireless networks. J. Netw. Comput. Appl. **34**(6), 1956–1970 (2011)
14. Chachulski, S., Jennings, M., Katti, S., Katabi, D.: Trading structure for randomness in wireless opportunistic routing. SIGCOMM Comput. Commun. Rev. **37**(4), 169–180 (2007)
15. Radwan, A., Rodriguez, J.: Cloud of mobile small-cells for higher data-rates and better energy-efficiency. In: 23th European Wireless Conference on European Wireless 2017, pp. 105–109. VDE, Dresden, Germany (2017)
16. Asadi, A., Wang, Q., Mancuso, V.: A survey on device-to-device communication in cellular networks. IEEE Commun. Surv. Tutor. **16**(4), 1801–1819 (2014)
17. Zhang, Y., Pan, E., Song, L., Saad, W., Dawy, Z., Han, Z.: Social network aware device-to-device communication in wireless networks. IEEE Trans. Wirel. Commun. **14**(1), 177–190 (2015)
18. SECRET. http://h2020-secret.eu/index.html. Last Accessed 05 May 2018

19. Gupta, A., Jha, R.: A survey of 5G network: architecture and emerging technologies. IEEE Access **3**, 1206–1232 (2015)
20. Chou, S., Chiu, T., Yu, Y., Pang, A.: Mobile small cell deployment for next generation cellular networks. In: Global Communications Conference (GLOBECOM), pp. 4852–4857. IEEE, Austin (2014)
21. Haus, M., Waqas, M., Ding, A., Li, Y., Tarkoma, S., Ott, J.: Security and privacy in device-to-device (D2D) communication: a review. IEEE Commun. Surv. Tutor. **19**(2), 1054–1079 (2017)
22. Zhang, A., Lin, X.: Security-aware and privacy-preserving D2D communications in 5G. IEEE Netw. **31**(4), 70–77 (2017)
23. Lu, L., et al.: Pseudo trust: zero-knowledge authentication in anonymous P2Ps. IEEE Trans. Parallel Distrib. Syst. **19**(10), 1325–1337 (2008)
24. Kim, M., et al.: On counteracting byzantine attacks in network coded peer-to-peer networks. IEEE J. Sel. Areas Commun. **28**(5), 692–702 (2010)
25. Esfahani, A., Mantas, G., Yang, D., Nascimento, A., Rodriguez, J., Neves, J.: Towards secure network coding-enabled wireless sensor networks in cyber-physical systems. In: Cyber Physical Systems: From Theory to Practice, pp. 395–414. CRC Press, Boca Raton (2015)
26. Esfahani, A., Yang, D., Mantas, G., Nascimento, A., Rodriguez, J.: Dual-homomorphic message authentication code scheme for network coding-enabled wireless sensor networks. Int. J. Distrib. Sens. Netw. **11**(7), 1–10 (2015)
27. Esfahani, A., Mantas, G., Rodriguez, J., Nascimento, A., Neves, J.: A null space-based MAC scheme against pollution attacks to random linear network coding. In: International Conference on Communication Workshop (ICCW), pp. 1521–1526. IEEE, London (2015)
28. Wu, X., Xu, Y., Yuen, C., Xiang, L.: A tag encoding scheme against pollution attack to linear network coding. IEEE Trans. Parallel Distrib. Syst. **25**(1), 33–42 (2014)
29. Zhang, P., Jiang, Y., Lin, C., Yao, H., Wasef, A., Shen, X.: Padding for orthogonality: efficient subspace authentication for network coding. In: 2011 Proceedings IEEE INFOCOM, pp. 1026–1034. IEEE, Shanghai, China (2011)
30. Esfahani, A., Mantas, G., Rodriguez, J.: An efficient null space-based homomorphic MAC scheme against tag pollution attacks in RLNC. IEEE Commun. Lett. **20**(5), 918–921 (2016)
31. Esfahani, A., Mantas, G., Silva, H., Rodriguez, J., Neves, J.: An efficient MAC-based scheme against pollution attacks in XOR network coding-enabled WBANs for remote patient monitoring systems. EURASIP J. Wirel. Commun. Netw. **2016**(113), 1–10 (2016)
32. Yang, D., Esfahani, A., Mantas, G., Rodriguez, J.: Jointly padding for subspace orthogonality against tag pollution. In: 19th International Workshop on Computer Aided Modeling and Design of Communication Links and Networks (CAMAD), pp. 85–89. IEEE, Athens, Greece (2014)
33. Esfahani, A., Yang, D., Mantas, G., Nascimento, A., Rodriguez, J.: An improved homomorphic message authentication code scheme for RLNC-enabled wireless networks. In: 19th International Workshop on Computer Aided Modeling and Design of Communication Links and Networks (CAMAD), pp. 80–84. IEEE, Athens, Greece (2014)
34. Esfahani, A., Mantas, G., Monteiro, V., Ramantas, K., Datsika, E., Rodriguez, J.: Analysis of a homomorphic MAC-based scheme against tag pollution in RLNC-enabled wireless networks. In: 20th International Workshop on Computer Aided Modeling and Design of Communication Links and Networks (CAMAD), pp. 156–160. IEEE, Guildford (2015)
35. Mu, B., Bakiras, S.: Private proximity detection for convex polygons. Tsinghua Sci. Technol. **21**(3), 270–280 (2016)
36. Zickuhr, K.: Location-based services. http://www.pewinternet.org/2013/09/12/location-based-services/. Last Accessed 13 Mar 2018

37. Li, Z., Shen, H.: Game theoretic analysis of cooperation incentive strategies in mobile ad hoc networks. IEEE Trans. Mob. Comput. **11**(8), 1287–1303 (2012)
38. Chen, T., Zhu, L., Wu, F., Zhong, S.: Stimulating cooperation in vehicular ad hoc networks: a coalitional game theoretic approach. IEEE Trans. Veh. Technol. **60**(2), 566–579 (2011)
39. Sun, J., Chen, X., Zhang, J., Zhang, Y., Zhang, J.: SYNERGY: a game-theoretical approach for cooperative key generation in wireless networks. In: 2014 Proceedings IEEE INFOCOM, pp. 997–1005. IEEE, Toronto (2014)
40. Chen, X., Proulx, B., Gong, X., Zhang, J.: Exploiting social ties for cooperative D2D communications: a mobile social networking case. IEEE/ACM Trans. Netw. **23**(5), 1471–1484 (2015)
41. Jiang, L., Tian, H.: Secure beamforming in cooperative D2D communications with simultaneous wireless information and power transfer. In: 2016 IEEE/CIC International Conference on Communications in China (ICCC), pp. 1–6. IEEE, Chengdu, China (2016)
42. Zheng, J., Xu, S., Zhao, F., Wang, D., Li, Y.: A novel detective and self-organized certificateless key management in mobile ad hoc networks. In: 2013 IEEE International Conference on Granular Computing (GrC), pp. 443–448. IEEE, Beijing, China (2013)
43. Liu, Q., Bai, X.: Survey on certificateless key management schemes in mobile ad hoc networks. In: 2017 7th IEEE International Conference on Electronics Information and Emergency Communication (ICEIEC), pp. 334–339. IEEE, Macau, China (2017)
44. Anand, D., Khemchandani, V., Sharma, R.: Identity-based cryptography techniques and applications (a review). In: 5th International Conference on Computational Intelligence and Communication Networks (CICN), pp. 343–348. IEEE, Mathura, India (2013)
45. Gharib, M., Moradlou, Z., Doostari, M., Movaghar, A.: Fully distributed ECC-based key management for mobile ad hoc networks. Comput. Netw. **113**, 269–283 (2017)

Security Threats in Network Coding-Enabled Mobile Small Cells

Reza Parsamehr[1,2(✉)], Georgios Mantas[1], Ayman Radwan[1],
Jonathan Rodriguez[1], and José-Fernán Martínez[2]

[1] Instituto de Telecomunicações, Aveiro, Portugal
{parsamehr.r,gimantas,aradwan,jonathan}@av.it.pt
[2] Universidad Politécnica de Madrid, Madrid, Spain
jf.martinez@upm.es

Abstract. The recent explosive growth of mobile data traffic, the continuously growing demand for higher data rates, and the steadily increasing pressure for higher mobility have led to the fifth-generation mobile networks. To this end, network-coding (NC)-enabled mobile small cells are considered as a promising 5G technology to cover the urban landscape by being set up on-demand at any place, and at any time on any device. In particular, this emerging paradigm has the potential to provide significant benefits to mobile networks as it can decrease packet transmission in wireless multicast, provide network capacity improvement, and achieve robustness to packet losses with low energy consumption. However, despite these significant advantages, NC-enabled mobile small cells are vulnerable to various types of attacks due to the inherent vulnerabilities of NC. Therefore, in this paper, we provide a categorization of potential security attacks in NC-enabled mobile small cells. Particularly, our focus is on the identification and categorization of the main potential security attacks on a scenario architecture of the ongoing EU funded H2020-MSCA project "SECRET" being focused on secure network coding-enabled mobile small cells.

Keywords: Mobile small cells · 5G communications · Security
Network Coding · D2D communications

1 Introduction

The recent explosive growth of mobile data traffic, the continuously growing demand for higher data rates, and the steadily increasing pressure for higher mobility have led to the fifth-generation (5G) of mobile communications. 5G communications target to achieve big data bandwidth, infinite capability of networking and extensive signal coverage to support a plethora of high-quality personalised services to subscribers, while at the same time the capital and operating expenditures (i.e., CAPEX and OPEX) of mobile operators are being reduced. Towards this direction, 5G communications systems will integrate a wide spectrum of enabling technologies [1–5].

Small cells technology is considered as a major 5G enabling technology, as it can enable effective delivery of ubiquitous 5G services in a cost-effective and energy efficient manner. Indeed, mobile small cells can cover the urban landscape by being set

© ICST Institute for Computer Sciences, Social Informatics and Telecommunications Engineering 2019
Published by Springer Nature Switzerland AG 2019. All Rights Reserved
V. Sucasas et al. (Eds.): BROADNETS 2018, LNICST 263, pp. 337–346, 2019.
https://doi.org/10.1007/978-3-030-05195-2_33

up on-demand at any place, and at any time on any device. The mobile small cell hotspots are the vehicle for experiencing a plethora of 5G broadband services at low cost with reduced impact on mobile battery lifetime [6–8].

In addition, Network Coding (NC) technology can be foreseen as a promising solution for the wireless network of mobile small cells to increase its throughput and improve its performance. In fact, NC technology is an emerging communication paradigm that has the potential to provide significant benefits to networks as it can decrease packet transmission in wireless multicast [9, 10], provide network capacity improvement [11], and achieve robustness to packet losses [12] and low energy consumption [13]. However, despite the significant advantages of NC technology, network coding-enabled wireless networks are vulnerable to various types of attacks [12, 14–18]. Based on that and the fact that the security is critical factor for the success of upcoming 5G communication networks, such as the network coding-enabled mobile small cells, novel security mechanisms against these types of attacks are required [19–22]. Towards this direction, the first step is the identification of the security threats in such networks.

Therefore, in this paper, we provide a categorization of potential security attacks in network coding-enabled mobile small cells due to the inherent vulnerabilities of NC. In particular, our focus is on the identification and categorization of the main potential security attacks on a scenario architecture of the EU funded H2020-MSCA project "SECRET" [23] focused on secure network coding-enabled mobile small cells.

Following the introduction, this paper is organized as follows. In Sect. 2, we provide an overview of the studied scenario architecture which is focused on secure network coding-enabled mobile small cells. In Sect. 3, a brief overview of the two types of network coding protocols is given. In Sect. 4, the main categories of potential security attacks in network coding-enabled mobile small cells due to the inherent vulnerabilities of NC are presented. Finally, Sect. 5 concludes this paper.

2   Scenario Architecture

In this section, we provide the scenario architecture of the EU funded H2020-MSCA project "SECRET" (See Fig. 1) which is focused on secure network coding-enabled mobile small cells [23] This scenario architecture consists of a macro cell which is splitted into a number of mobile small cells. Each mobile small cell is controlled by a cluster-head (i.e., hotspot), a mobile device (i.e., mobile node) within the identified cluster of mobile devices that is nominated to play the role of the local radio manager in order to control and maintain the cluster. Moreover, the cluster-heads (i.e., hotspots) of the different clusters cooperate to form a wireless network of mobile small cells that have several gateways/entry points to the mobile network using intelligent high-speed connections. It is worthwhile to mention that the cluster-heads (i.e., hotspots) of the different clusters are controlled by a centralized software-defined controller. Finally, the data communication between the mobile devices (i.e., mobile nodes) is established through Device-to-Device (D2D) communications and optimized by network coding technology. In particular, in the studied scenario, it is assumed that a source mobile node (SN), locating at a mobile small cell, wants to multicast packets to two destination mobile nodes (DNs), locating at another mobile small cell. Thus, packets from the SN are coded (i.e., Random Linear Network Coding) and traverse multiple devices, over a multi-hop D2D network, before arriving to the DNs, locating at another mobile small cell, where they are decoded. The multi-hop D2D network consists of a number of User Equipments (UEs), such as legitimate mobile nodes, and relay mobile nodes (RNs), as depicted in Fig. 1.

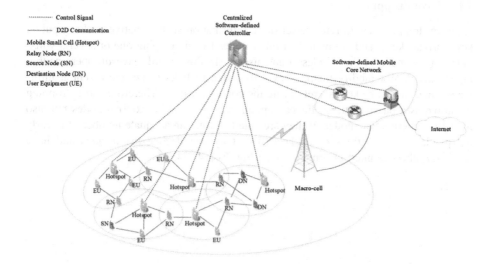

Fig. 1. Scenario architecture

3 Network Coding

Due to low communication bandwidth, packet loss and power consumption constraints, network coding can be a good solution for wireless networks [6, 7]. Network coding methods are generally classified into state-aware network coding protocols and stateless network coding protocols.

In state-aware network coding protocols, each node has partial or full network state information, such as network topology and the packets in the buffer of its neighbours Based on this information, a network code is generated that is decodable by the neighboring nodes. However, the state-aware network coding protocols confront several security issues due to the available knowledge of the network sate information.

On the other hand, the stateless network coding protocols do not rely on the network state information in order to decide when and how to mix the packets at each intermediate node. Thus, the stateless network coding protocols are not affected by dynamically changing topologies. Finally, this kind of network coding protocols are more immune to security threats compared to the state-aware network coding protocols due to their independence of the network state information [11, 12].

4 Security Threats in Network Coding-Enabled Mobile Small Cells

In this section, we present the main categories of potential security attacks in network coding-enabled mobile small cells due to the inherent vulnerabilities of NC.

4.1 Eavesdropping

An eavesdropper aims to retrieve sensitive information such as native packets, public keys, private keys, and passwords of other nodes by wiretapping one or several wired links, or overhearing the wireless transmission. In this regard, eavesdroppers neither inject packets nor modify them. They only listen to links to get the essential information that should be kept secret during the communication. Therefore, eavesdropping is known as a passive attack. Eavesdroppers can not only be external nodes but also malicious intermediate nodes. If they are able to access an adequate number of linearly independent combinations of packets, then they can decode the packets and have access to all transmitted information (see Fig. 2) [14, 24, 25].

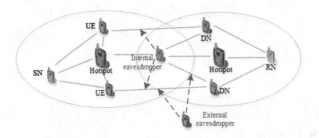

Fig. 2. Internal and external eavesdropping attacker

Eavesdropping attacks are generally classified based on two different views. The first view is based on the level that a node has access to the packets crossing the network and classifies the eavesdropper nodes into three types: (i) nice but curious, (ii) wiretapping, and (iii) worst-case eavesdroppers [25, 26]. Nice but curious nodes are also called non-malicious nodes because they are well behaved in the sense of communication protocols, but they want to obtain some information from the data flows that pass through them. The curious nodes cannot get significant information, because in random linear network coding (RLNC), packets are coded and none of them has access to sufficient number of coded packets. On the other hand, the wiretapping nodes (usually external eavesdroppers) are more capable of accessing the secret information due to their access to subset of communication links (i.e., they have access to more coded packets). Finally, the eavesdropper nodes of the third type are classified as the worst-case node since they have access to all of the transmitted packets. Therefore, in this case, ensuring information confidentiality is not only harder, but also more critical.

The second view is based on the type of the NC protocols (i.e., stateless NC protocols or state-aware NC protocols) [24, 25]. In the case of stateless NC protocols, due to the RLNC properties, eavesdropping attack is less crucial. This is because the eavesdropper is not able to decode the coded packets and obtain native packets until he/she has access to a sufficient number of coded packets. In contrast, in the case of state-aware NC protocols, eavesdropping attack is crucial since the coding is local and each intermediate node decodes packets before recoding them. Thus, the eavesdropper can access native packets.

4.2 Traffic Analysis

Traffic analysis is one of the most common attacks in wireless networks. In traffic analysis attack, the attackers monitor the transmissions in the network in order to extract information about the source and destination of the packets as well as the network topology. In other words, adversaries threat the confidentially of the networks with traffic analysis and monitoring [25, 27]. This threat is crucial in both the state-aware and stateless network coding protocols [24].

4.3 Impersonation

An impersonation attacker sends queries to the victim nodes by using other legitimate node's identity (e.g., MAC or IP address [28]) in order to gain information. State-aware network coding protocols can be affected by this type of attacks due to the fact that these protocols rely on network nodes [14]. In other words, the goal of impersonation attack is to degrade the authenticity property in NC-enabled networks. This attack is a kind of active eavesdropping and sometimes it is the basis for launching further more sophisticated attacks [24].

4.4 Man-in-the-Middle

In the Man-in-the-middle attack, the attacker (i.e., a malicious node) lies on a communication link between the sender and the receiver in order to impersonate other nodes and relays received messages by exploiting link spoofing techniques, such as advertising fake links and sending routing control packets, including wrong information (see Fig. 3) [24, 29, 30].

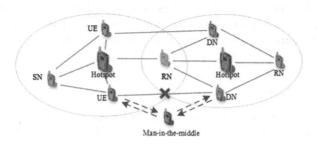

Fig. 3. Man-in-the-middle attack.

4.5 Byzantine Fabrication

Byzantine fabrication attack (Pollution) is a severe security threat where an adversary node injects corrupted packets into the network to corrupt other packets based on the nature of packet mixing in network coding schemes [25]. Additionally, this attack can disrupt the routing operation of network in different ways such as forwarding data packets through non-optimal or even invalid routes and generating routing loops (see Fig. 4) [14, 24]. This attack is a threat to both stateless and state-aware network coding protocols. In state-aware network coding protocols, packet headers normally include topology states and routing information, and thus the attackers can send wrong information to nodes about the state and neighbors' information. Besides, in stateless network coding protocols, headers normally include needed decoding vectors that attackers can change [25].

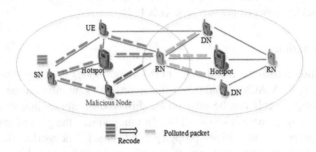

Fig. 4. Byzantine fabrication attack.

4.6 Byzantine Modification

In a byzantine modification attack (Pollution), adversary aims to make some changes (i.e., invalid coding operations) to data in transit and threat the integrity of the packets in the networks [29]. They inject corrupted packets or modify them. There are a lot of attacks which use this technique to threat the networks, such as wormhole, black hole, selective forwarding and dropping attack, man-in-the-middle, link spoofing, routing attacks and repudiation [24]. These attacks can be considered as special types of Byzantine modification attacks. In stateless network coding, the adversary injects or modifies packets in transit, whereas in state-aware network coding the adversary injects or modifies not only packets in transit but also state information such as topology information and buffer state [14, 26].

4.7 Byzantine Replay

In Byzantine replay attack the malicious nodes or SN can reuse coded packets with the same logical identifier that were authenticated previously (e.g., old coded packets that were previously stored on compromised nodes and had successfully passed the integrity verification. Due to sending these old messages, the network resources are wasted and eventually throughput rate is degraded [31, 32]. If a malicious or compromise node is able to find and reuse old coded packets, the data decoding condition could be broken, because they are linearly dependent with other coded blocks that are currently stored (see Fig. 5). Replay attack can reduce network coding throughput, wasting resources and processing time in both stateless and state-aware network coding protocols by injection packets which are repeated into the information flow [14].

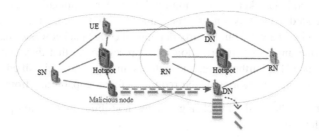

Fig. 5. Byzantine reply attack.

4.8   Wormhole

In this attack two or more malicious nodes collaborate and create a tunnel between two nodes (see Fig. 6). Then, they persuade the neighbor nodes that two side of tunnel are in the same range. Afterwards, these wormhole attackers can record packets and retransmit them through the tunnel. Wormhole attack can have more severe impact on state-aware NC protocols (e.g., disruption of the route discovery process) compared to its impact on stateless protocols [14, 33].

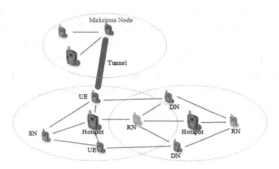

Fig. 6. Wormhole attack.

4.9   Black Hole

The attacker exploits routing protocols to advertise itself as a valid and the shortest path to a destination. In this regard, the nodes are convinced to use this path to send data packets towards that destination. Hence, data packets can be intercepted/eavesdropped or the routing operations simply can be denied (i.e., black-hole attack) that decrease the network performance. This attack can reduce performance of the network in both state-aware and stateless protocols [24, 34].

4.10   Entropy Attack

In entropy attacks, the attacker creates packets containing information already known by the systems (i.e., non-innovative packets). In particular, the adversary node creates a non-innovative coded packet that is a non-random linear combination of coded packets so that the coded packet is linearly dependent with the coded packets stored at downstream node. The valid but linearly dependent coded packet wastes resources as it does not provide any useful information to the receivers so that they can decode the original packets [31]. Furthermore, the authors in [31] have classified the entropy attacks into two main categories which require deferent capabilities from an attacker:

- Local entropy attack: the attacker generates non-innovative coded packets to the local neighboring nodes.
- Global entropy attack: the attacker generates coded packets that are seemingly innovative to local neighboring nodes but are non-innovative to at least one distant downstream node.

4.11   Denial of Service (DOS)

In Denial of Service (DoS) attack, the attacker attempts to make the resources of a system unavailable to the legitimate users, Actually, the attacker targets the availability of the system [14]. For example, in a network coding-enabled network, the adversary can send a lot of requests, such as packet processing and forwarding, to the victim in order to deplete its resources [24]. Moreover, it is worthwhile to mention that there are different types of DoS attacks at different layers that affect differently the network. Thus, DoS attacks include the following main types of attacks: jamming and tempering at the physical layer, collision and exhaustion at the link layer, black holes and routing table overflow at the network layer, SYN flooding and de-synchronization at the transport layer, and finally failure in the web services at the application layer [34, 35]. Finally, in NC state-aware schemes, a malicious node can easily perform a DoS attack by flooding its neighbours with a high volume of corrupted packets or even legitimate packets but old and repetitive packets [14].

5   Conclusion

In this paper, we provided a categorization of potential security attacks in network coding-enabled mobile small cells due to the inherent vulnerabilities of NC. More precisely, we focused on the identification and categorization of the main potential security attacks on a scenario architecture of the EU funded H2020-MSCA project "SECRET" which is based on secure network coding-enabled mobile small cells.

Acknowledgments. This research work leading to this publication has received funding from the European Union's Horizon 2020 Research and Innovation programme under grant agreement H2020-MSCA-ITN-2016-SECRET-722424.

References

1. Wang, C.-X., et al.: Cellular architecture and key technologies for 5G wireless communication networks. IEEE Commun. Mag. **52**(2), 122–130 (2014)
2. Chih-Lin, I., et al.: Toward green and soft: a 5G perspective. IEEE Commun. Mag. **52**(2), 66–73 (2014)
3. Bangerter, B., et al.: Networks and devices for the 5G era. IEEE Commun. Mag. **52**(2), 90–96 (2014)
4. Sucasas, V., Mantas, G., Rodriguez, J.: Security challenges for cloud radio access networks. In: Backhauling/Fronthauling for Future Wireless Systems, pp. 195–211 (2016)
5. Mantas, G., et al.: Security for 5G Communications (2015)
6. Gupta, A., Jha, R.K.: A survey of 5G network: architecture and emerging technologies. IEEE Access **3**, 1206–1232 (2015)
7. Chou, S.-F., et al.: Mobile small cell deployment for next generation cellular networks. In: Global Communications Conference (GLOBECOM), 2014 IEEE. IEEE (2014)
8. Saghezchi, F.B., et al.: Drivers for 5G. Fundamentals of 5G Mobile Networks, pp. 1–27 (2015)
9. Katti, S., et al.: XORs in the air: practical wireless network coding. In: ACM SIGCOMM Computer Communication Review. ACM (2006)
10. Chen, Y.-J., et al.: Topology-aware network coding for wireless multicast. IEEE Syst. J. **12**(4), 3683–3692 (2018)
11. Ahlswede, R., et al.: Network information flow. IEEE Trans. Inf. Theor. **46**(4), 1204–1216 (2000)
12. Ho, T., Lun, D.: Network Coding: An Introduction. Cambridge University Press, New York (2008)
13. Wu, Y., Chou, P.A., Kung, S.-Y.: Minimum-energy multicast in mobile ad hoc networks using network coding. IEEE Trans. Commun. **53**(11), 1906–1918 (2005)
14. Esfahani, A., et al.: Towards secure network coding-enabled wireless sensor networks in cyber-physical systems. In: Cyber-Physical Systems from Theory to Practice, ch. 16, pp. 395–415 (2015)
15. Esfahani, A., et al.: A null space-based MAC scheme against pollution attacks to Random linear Network Coding. In: 2015 IEEE International Conference on Communication Workshop (ICCW). IEEE (2015)
16. Esfahani, A., et al.: An improved homomorphic message authentication code scheme for RLNC-enabled wireless networks. In: 2014 IEEE 19th International Workshop on Computer Aided Modeling and Design of Communication Links and Networks (CAMAD). IEEE (2014)
17. Esfahani, A., et al.: Analysis of a homomorphic MAC-based scheme against tag pollution in RLNC-enabled wireless networks. In: 2015 IEEE 20th International Workshop on Computer Aided Modelling and Design of Communication Links and Networks (CAMAD). IEEE (2015)
18. Yang, D., et al.: Jointly padding for subspace orthogonality against tag pollution. In: 2014 IEEE 19th International Workshop on Computer Aided Modeling and Design of Communication Links and Networks (CAMAD). IEEE (2014)

19. Esfahani, A., et al.: Dual-homomorphic message authentication code scheme for network coding-enabled wireless sensor networks. Int. J. Distrib. Sens. Netw. 11(7), 510251 (2015)

20. Esfahani, A., et al.: An efficient homomorphic MAC-based scheme against data and tag pollution attacks in network coding-enabled wireless networks. Int. J. Inf. Secur. 16(6), 627–639 (2017)

21. Esfahani, A., Mantas, G., Rodriguez, J.: An efficient null space-based homomorphic MAC scheme against tag pollution attacks in RLNC. IEEE Commun. Lett. 20(5), 918–921 (2016)

22. Esfahani, A., et al.: An efficient MAC-based scheme against pollution attacks in XOR network coding-enabled WBANs for remote patient monitoring systems. EURASIP J. Wirel. Commun. Netw. 2016(1), 113 (2016)

23. SEcure Network Coding for Reduced Energy nexT generation Mobile Small cells. H2020-MSCA-ITN-2016-722424 01 January 2017–31 December 2020. http://h2020-secret.eu/index.html

24. Talooki, V.N., et al.: Security concerns and countermeasures in network coding based communication systems: a survey. Comput. Netw. 83, 422–445 (2015)

25. Ostovari, P., Wu, J.: Towards Network Coding for Cyber-Physical Systems: Security Challenges and Applications. Wiley (2017)

26. Lima, L., et al.: Network coding security: Attacks and countermeasures. arXiv preprint arXiv:0809.1366 (2008)

27. Fan, Y., et al.: An efficient privacy-preserving scheme against traffic analysis attacks in network coding. In: INFOCOM 2009 IEEE. IEEE (2009)

28. Wu, B., Chen, J., Wu, J., Cardei, M.: A survey of attacks and countermeasures in mobile ad hoc networks. In: Xiao, Y., Shen, X.S., Du, D.Z. (eds.) Wireless Network Security. Signals and Communication Technology. Springer, Boston (2007). https://doi.org/10.1007/978-0-387-33112-6_5

29. Jawandhiya, P.M., et al.: A survey of mobile ad hoc network attacks. Int. J. Eng. Sci. Technol. 2(9), 4063–4071 (2010)

30. Dong, J., et al.: Pollution attacks and defenses in wireless interflow network coding systems. IEEE Trans. Depend. Secure Comput. 9(5), 741–755 (2012)

31. Newell, A.J., Curtmola, R., Nita-Rotaru, C.: Entropy attacks and countermeasures in wireless network coding. In: Proceedings of the Fifth ACM Conference on Security and Privacy in Wireless and Mobile Networks. ACM (2012)

32. Chen, B., et al.: Remote data checking for network coding-based distributed storage systems. In: Proceedings of the 2010 ACM Workshop on Cloud Computing Security Workshop. ACM (2010)

33. Chiu, H.S., Lui, K.-S.: DelPHI: wormhole detection mechanism for ad hoc wireless networks. In: 2006 1st International Symposium on Wireless Pervasive Computing. IEEE (2006)

34. Mishra, A., Nadkarni, K.M.: Security in wireless ad hoc networks. In: The Handbook of Ad Hoc Wireless Networks. CRC Press, Inc (2003)

35. Padmavathi, D.G., Shanmugapriya, M.: A survey of attacks, security mechanisms and challenges in wireless sensor networks. arXiv preprint arXiv:0909.0576 (2009)

Secure Network Coding for SDN-Based Mobile Small Cells

Vipindev Adat, Ilias Politis$^{(\boxtimes)}$, Christos Tselios, and Stavros Kotsopoulos

Wireless Telecommunications Laboratory, University of Patras, Patras, Greece
{vipindev,ipolitis,tselios,kotsop}@ece.upatras.gr

Abstract. The future wireless networks including the fifth generation of mobile networks have to serve a very dense heterogeneous network of devices with high resiliency and reliability. Network coding is also emerging as a potential key enabler for optimizing bandwidth requirements and energy consumption in highly dense mobile network environments. However, network coding deployments still need to consider security vulnerabilities and their countermeasures, before they can be adapted as part of the emerging mobile network deployments. On the other hand the software defined networking can be employed in the mobile small cell environment to achieve highly efficient and easily configurable network architecture. This paper studies the scope of utilizing the SDN based mobile small cells to implement secure network coded mobile small cells minimizing the overheads and delays.

Keywords: Random linear network coding · Pollution attacks
5G small cells

1 Introduction

The fifth generation (5G) network paradigm has already emerged with stringent throughput and energy requirements [1,2] for accommodating all recently introduced verticals [3,4]. As the future wireless environment is conceptualized it is expected to include different types of cells such as macro, pico and small cells. The concept of cooperated small cells as the basis for the new mobile cell architecture is proposed on this front and network coding schemes can be a key enabler in such a network model to achieve high throughput and resilience [5]. The network coded cooperated small cell environment can provide high data rates at a low energy for the dense population of devices in the 5G era. However, implementing network coding in the mobile environment of small cells can lead to security threats including denial of service, intrusion, byzantine fabrication and false identity etc. This paper addresses the problem of pollution attacks in network coded mobile small cell environment and performance of security schemes

This project has received funding from the European Union's Horizon 2020 research and innovation programme under grant agreement H2020-MSCA-ITN-2016 SECRET-722424.

V. Sucasas et al. (Eds.): BROADNETS 2018, LNICST 263, pp. 347–356, 2019.
https://doi.org/10.1007/978-3-030-05195-2_34

in terms of communication and computational overhead. We consider the homomorphic message authentication codes and signatures to ensure the security of the network. Further, we consider the possibility of the software defined architecture to achieve easily configurable cooperated mobile small cells in an efficient way. The availability of the central controller will also add to ensuring the security of the whole network.

2   Network Coding for Mobile Small Cells

The problem of secure network coding was first studied in [6] which proposed a scheme of admissible linear network codes which will protect the message from eavesdropping. As the possibilities of network coding was explored as a strong energy efficient high throughput communication scheme, more specific threats related to network coding also popped up. The mixing of packets which forms the base of network coding schemes increases the effect of a byzantine fabrication attack since a single corrupted packet can widely spread into the network and corrupt the whole message resulting in devastating effects on throughput and network utilization. This, widely known as pollution attack, is addressed as one of the major security threat in network coded environment. As the network coding schemes varies from interflow to intraflow networks, state aware to stateless protocols, the security schemes against pollution attacks also differs [7–9]. However, for the mobile wireless environment, random linear network coding (RLNC) has been considered as the best suited [10] option due to the frequently changing network situation and we focus more into preventing pollution attacks in a RLNC based mobile small cell environment.

2.1   Random Linear Network Coding and Pollution Attacks

As per the widely used principles of random linear network coding, a message is considered as a number of generations where each generation consists of various packets. Each native packet P_i is considered as a vector of n elements such as P_{i1}, $P_{i2}, \ldots, P_{in}$ over finite field F_q^n where q defines the finite field size. A generation consisting of m such packets will be a $m \times n$ matrix which can be considered as the native generation. However, to enable proper encoding and decoding, the native packets will be augmented with a unit vector of size m which will have all zeros but a 1 at the corresponding position of the native packet in the generation. These augmented packets are encoded with locally generated random coefficients and transmitted by the source node to its neighbouring nodes. The intermediate nodes, on the reception of an innovative generation of packets, re encode it with it's own locally generated random coefficients before transmission. This procedure is followed till the receiving nodes. However, a malicious intermediate node can pollute the whole system by introducing a polluted packet. Due to the mixing of packets at the intermediate nodes, the pollution attacks in network coded environment, if unchecked, can spread over the transmission infecting all the communication involving the initial polluted packet and its parts. The homomorphic MAC scheme proposed by Agrawal et al. [11] was successful in preventing this pollution attacks with a probability of $1/q^L$, where q is the field size and L is the number of tags. However it suffers from the tag pollution attacks in which the adversary tries to pollute the tags attached to the packets to verify it's integrity. In tag pollution attacks, malicious nodes pollute tags of genuine packets resulting in such packets being discarded when incorrect tags are detected, which leads to poor network performance. MacSig [12] proposes the usage of a homomorphic signature over the MAC scheme to certify that the tags attached to the packets are corresponding to the packet itself. Dual HMAC and HMAC [13, 14] try to reduce the computational and communicational overhead of MacSig using a novel key distribution model based on c cover free family. This also provide security against a situation in which a number of compromised nodes act together to pollute the network at a lower key storage overhead at intermediate nodes.

Further, in this study, we consider software defined mobile small cell network for highly configurable efficient deployment as shown in Fig. 1. This will help the system to ensure better efficiency in terms of network utilization. Further if network coding is deployed over this SDN based mobile small cells, the throughput and resiliency of the whole environment can be improved to match the requirements in the 5G era. In this paper, we also propose how the availability of a centralized software defined controller connected to the nodes in the network can be better utilized for ensuring the security of the network. In our proposal, along with the control message some secure information needs to be communicated with the central unit and it reduces the overhead in the communication lines between the nodes and prevents pollution attacks with a high probability.

3   Secure Network Coding in SDN Based Mobile Small Cells

This security scheme is a modification of some existing approaches like Dual HMAC and Homomac [11, 13] by utilizing this central unit to ensure the security. In this approach, the centralized controller is also considered as a trusted party which is connected to all the nodes. We consider the homomorphic hashing schemes discussed in [11, 12] for the integrity of messages and a signature for the authenticity of messages. We further utilize the centralized controller to ensure the security of the scheme with higher efficiency and reduce the computational cost at the intermediate nodes.

3.1   Proposed Security Scheme

Our scheme follows similar message authentication schemes, but utilizes the availability of centralized controller to reduce the computational and communication cost over the channels. The proposed scheme can be explained in the following four steps:

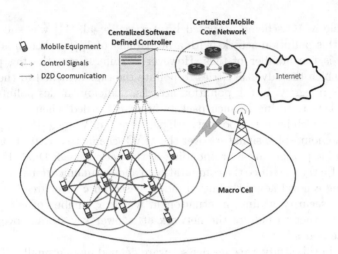

Fig. 1. SDN based mobile small cell architecture.

1. Setup: This first phase of scheme includes the key distribution. A Key distribution centre (KDC) is responsible for this. Since the MAC scheme uses symmetric keys for creating and verifying the tags, KDC distributes a set of L keys to each node in the network. This procedure can be done prior to the actual communication starts. Thus each node will have a set of keys K_i where each key have $n + 1$ symbols in it. The size of a key in our scheme is comparatively less than the other comparable schemes like HMAC and MacSig because we define the tags over the native packets only, excluding the augmented vector part. This is more clearly explained in the tag generation section. Further, each source node will have it's own private key to create the signature over the tags. All the intermediate and receiving nodes will need the corresponding public key to verify the signature. KDC take care of this public key private key generation and distribution as well.

2. Tag generation: In our proposed scheme, tags are generated only at the source nodes, reducing the computational cost at the intermediate nodes considerably. Further only the native packets are considered so that the size of a key is also smaller. The integrity of the packets are ensured by tags created using the key set provided by the KDC. A tag will be generated as

$$Tag_l = \frac{\left(\sum_{j=1}^{n} P_{i,j} \times K_{l,j} \right)}{K_{l,j+1}}, \quad l \in (1, L) \tag{1}$$

Since a generation of m packets are considered in one transmission, there will be $L \times m$ number of tags associated with a particular generation, attached to it. Further, our scheme introduces a novel tag communication scheme including the centralized controller to prevent pollution attacks. For this, each source compute a signature over the tags for a particular generation and communicate this set of tags along with the signature and generation number to the central controller.

Algorithm 1. Verification Algorithm

Data: Received packet $\mathbf{C}_i$, **L** tags corresponding to $\mathbf{C}_i$ retrieved
from the central unit, Key set $\mathbf{K}_s$

Result: 1 if verification is successful and **0** if verification is failed.
In case of a failed verification, the type of the attack is
also reported.

1 **Step 1:**
2 Retrieve the coefficient matrix from the received packet
3 **Step 2:**
4 Multiply the tags retrieved from the central unit with the
   corresponding coefficients
5 **Step 3:**
6 Compare the tags with those appear in the received codeword.
7 **if** *they dont match* **then**
8 | Report Warning and Proceed
9 **else**
10 | Proceed

11 **Step 4:**
12 Create tags for the received packet using MAC algorithm
   (without considering the coefficient part)
13 **Step 5:**
14 **if** *MAC algorithm output matches with the tags retrieved from
   central unit* **then**
15 | 1 ⟵ Return
16 **else**
17 | 0 ⟵ Return

---

3. Verification: The verification process happens at each receiving node. It
   ensures that the tags attached to the received packets are genuine and created at the source. The centralized controller along with the tags attached
   to the received packets enables this verification. On receiving a coded generation, the receiving node will check for the corresponding entry of tags in
   the central controller from the source. The authenticity of this entry in the
   centralized unit can be verified by the public key corresponding to the private key used to sign the entry. Once the right entry is retrieved from the
   centralized unit, then the integrity of the received message can be verified by
   comparing the tags in the entry retrieved from the centralized unit and the
   tags in the received packet. The verification algorithm shown above gives a
   step by step explanation of the verification procedure. Once a generation of
   packets completes the verification process successfully, they are re-encoded
   by the intermediate nodes or decoded to retrieve the original message at the
   destination nodes.

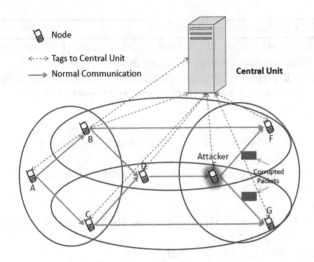

Fig. 2. Architecture for security scheme

4. Re-encoding: The intermediate nodes will re-encode the verified messages before forwarding them further. However, in our scheme no more tag generation is performed at the intermediate nodes. The tags are generated only at the source nodes and after the tag generation all the elements in the packet are considered as the same. This reduces the computational requirements at the intermediate nodes considerably. Thus re-encoding process is very much similar to normal RLNC scheme. The verified generations are multiplied by the locally generated random coefficients.

3.2   Security Analysis

This section analyses how the proposed scheme ensures protection against pollution attacks using the central controller. The security scheme is analyzed over a butterfly network in the SDN based small cell environment as shown in Fig. 2. Before proceeding to the security analysis, it is necessary to define the capabilities of the adversary node. In the scenario described in this paper, only the intermediate nodes are considered susceptible to attacks. The source nodes are considered as trusted and secure. Also the key distribution scheme is considered as secure, especially the asymmetric keys used for signing the entries to the central unit is kept secure and not shared by the source nodes. However, when an attacker compromises an intermediate node, it can have full control over the resources available to the compromised node. Thus if the attacker compromises an intermediate node, it can access the whole key set available to the node as well as decode and analyze the original packets and tags attached to them. Thus the adversary has strong knowledge over the messaging scheme. Further, we consider a situation in which the attacker could compromise more than one node in a neighbourhood and perform a coordinated attack. However, the direct connection from central unit to each node in the network nullify any additional advantages achieved by such mass compromising of nodes since the security systems at the immediate benign node will be able to detect and discard polluted packets.

Data Pollution Attacks: The adversary try to modify the content of the packet and forward the message to the neighbouring nodes. This pollutes the corrupted packet instantly and with further alterations pollutes more and more genuine packets. This points to the necessity of finding out the corrupted packet at the earliest possible instant and prevent it from mixing with other benign packets. In our scheme, a two level verification of tags ensures that the data pollution attacks are detected efficiently at the immediate genuine node receiving a polluted packet. Since the receiving node already have the key set used to create the tags, it can check whether the tags are genuine to the corresponding message part in the received code word. However, since the adversary also have the keyset available from the compromised node, it may have forged the tag for the corrupted message and attach it to the packet. Thus a strong adversary can pass the first verification. However the second level of verification is matching the tags received in the code word with the corresponding tags retrieved from the central controller. If the adversary has to pass this verification, it needs to forge a corrupted packet which will give exactly the same tag as the original packet. That is same as finding another symbol in the symbol space of the original packet such that the MAC generation will result in the same tag for both the corrupted and original packets. This can be considered as a probability of $1/q$, where q is the field size. Further, if there are L tags that will be checked, then it needs to satisfy all these tags and then the probability of creating a corrupted packet that will pass the verification test is $1/q^L$. In practical cases $q = 28$ and $L = 8$ gives a very satisfactory level of protection against the data pollution attacks.

Tag Pollution Attacks: Tag Pollution attacks are a serious problem faced by the homomorphic MAC based security schemes in network coded environment. In such cases, the tags created and attached to the original benign packets are altered by the adversary intermediate nodes. Then these packets will travel till it will detect an altered tag and discarded. Such attacks create two serious issues; network resource under utilization and dropping of genuine packets. Thus it is necessary to detect the tag pollution attack at the immediate neighbouring benign node and further process the transaction of genuine packets. This is ensured in our scheme using the secure communication of tags to the central unit and it's comparison. The authenticity of the entries in the central unit is verified using the signature attached to it. Comparing the corresponding tags in the received packet with those retrieved from the central unit results in the detection of tag pollution attack. In case of the detection of a tag pollution attack, that node can check whether the content is still the same by creating tags for the packet and comparing with the tags retrieved from the central unit and

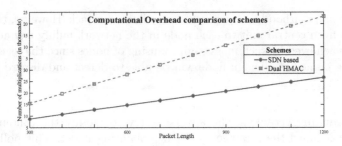

Fig. 3. Computational overhead for different schemes

proceed with the communication after marking a warning against the malicious node. By this way, the network resource wastage and unnecessary dropping of genuine packets can be tackled. It is ensured that this detection of pollution attacks happen at the immediate benign node in the system after adversary.

4   Performance Evaluation

4.1   Computational Overhead

This secure RLNC scheme for SDN based mobile small cell environment requires some extra computations to be performed at each node. A source node has to create the tags and a signature over the tags and all other nodes need to verify the tags and signature. For each tag creation as per the scheme $n + 1$ multiplications are required and for creating a signature over L number of tags, $L + 1$ multiplications will be performed. Thus, a scheme having L tags will have an extra overhead of $L \times (n + 2) + 1$ multiplications over each packet generated at the source node. For the receiving nodes, the verification of MAC requires the same $L \times (n + 1)$ multiplications to verify the L tags. However, the verification of signature over the tags retrieved from the central unit requires $L + 1$ exponentiation. Each exponentiation corresponds to $\frac{3}{2}|q|$ multiplications [12]. This shows a significant advantage over the computational cost caused by the security scheme compared to other similar schemes. For example, HMAC scheme proposed by Esfahani et al. [13], which is proved to be secure against both data and tag pollution attack suffers from a computational overhead in the second order of L. Figure 3 shows a comparison of computational cost of both the schemes when the same number of tags are used ($L = 8$).

4.2   Communication Overhead

The communication overhead results from the extra bits associated to each packet for security purpose. In our scheme, similar to any other MAC based scheme, this corresponding to the tags associated to each packet. Each tag created as per Eq. (1) provide a security level of $1/q$ probability to be broken by

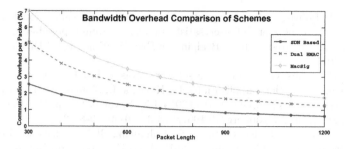

Fig. 4. Communication overhead for different schemes

the adversary. In the general case of L number of tags attached to each packet, where each tag is a symbol, an $L/(m + n)$ communication overhead is suffered per packet, same as the overhead in [11]. Additionally, the tags will be sent to the central unit via control channel which is independent from the communication channel between the devices. Comparing this scheme with other schemes secure against tag pollution attacks, we understand that for the same number of tags, our scheme produces a much lesser communication overhead compared to Dual HMAC [14] and MacSig [12]. Figure 4 shows the comparison of communication overhead induced by each security scheme (for $L = 8$).

5   Conclusion

Since the 5G paradigm is yet to be finalized [15], network coding is being considered for harnessing the bandwidth available for wireless communication. Further, the network coded architecture can be considered to meet the high throughput requirements of heterogeneous mobile small cells with low energy requirements. Since the security challenges needs to be addressed beforehand, an SDN based mobile small cell environment supported by network coding is studied in this work, with specific focus on the security issues. More specifically, the paper discusses a message authentication code based security scheme against pollution attacks in the SDN based small cell environment. The performance analysis and it's comparison with other well known security schemes points out that the computational and communication overheads of security scheme can be considerably reduced at the expense of a secure communication channel between the central controller and other nodes.

References

1. Tselios, C., Tsolis, G.: On QoE-awareness through virtualized probes in 5G networks. In: 2016 IEEE 21st International Workshop on Computer Aided Modelling and Design of Communication Links and Networks (CAMAD), pp. 159–164, October 2016

2. Tselios, C., Politis, I., Tsagkaropoulos, M., Dagiuklas, T.: Valuing quality of experience: a brave new era of user satisfaction and revenue possibilities. In: 2011 50th FITCE Congress - "ICT: Bridging an Ever Shifting Digital Divide", pp. 1–6, August 2011

3. Tselios, C., Tsolis, G.: A survey on software tools and architectures for deploying multimedia-aware cloud applications. In: Karydis, I., Sioutas, S., Triantafillou, P., Tsoumakos, D. (eds.) ALGOCLOUD 2015. LNCS, vol. 9511, pp. 168–180. Springer, Cham (2016). https://doi.org/10.1007/978-3-319-29919-8_13

4. Tselios, C., Politis, I., Kotsopoulos, S.: Enhancing SDN security for IoT-related deployments through blockchain. In: 2017 IEEE Conference on Network Function Virtualization and Software Defined Networks (NFV-SDN), pp. 303–308, November 2017

5. Rodriguez, J., et al.: SECRET - secure network coding for reduced energy next generation mobile small cells: a European Training Network in wireless communications and networking for 5G. In: 2017 Internet Technologies and Applications (ITA), pp. 329–333, September 2017

6. Cai, N., Yeung, R.W.: Secure network coding. In: Proceedings IEEE International Symposium on Information Theory, p. 323 (2002)

7. Dong, J., Curtmola, R., Nita-Rotaru, C.: Practical defenses against pollution attacks in wireless network coding. ACM Trans. Inf. Syst. Secur. (TISSEC) 14(1), 7 (2011)

8. Dong, J., Curtmola, R., Nita-Rotaru, C., Yau, D.K.Y.: Pollution attacks and defenses in wireless interflow network coding systems. IEEE Trans. Dependable Secur. Comput. 9(5), 741–755 (2012)

9. Jaggi, S., et al.: Resilient network coding in the presence of byzantine adversaries. IEEE Trans. Inf. Theory 54(6), 2596–2603 (2008)

10. Ho, T., et al.: A random linear network coding approach to multicast. IEEE Trans. Inf. Theory 52(10), 4413–4430 (2006)

11. Agrawal, S., Boneh, D.: Homomorphic MACs: MAC-based integrity for network coding. In: Abdalla, M., Pointcheval, D., Fouque, P.-A., Vergnaud, D. (eds.) ACNS 2009. LNCS, vol. 5536, pp. 292–305. Springer, Heidelberg (2009). https://doi.org/10.1007/978-3-642-01957-9_18

12. Zhang, P., Jiang, Y., Lin, C., Yao, H., Wasef, A., Shenz, X.: Padding for orthogonality: efficient subspace authentication for network coding. In: 2011 Proceedings IEEE INFOCOM, pp. 1026–1034, April 2011

13. Esfahani, A., Mantas, G., Rodriguez, J., Neves, J.C.: An efficient homomorphic mac-based scheme against data and tag pollution attacks in network coding-enabled wireless networks. Int. J. Inf. Secur. 16(6), 627–639 (2017)

14. Esfahani, A., Yang, D., Mantas, G., Nascimento, A., Rodriguez, J.: Dual-homomorphic message authentication code scheme for network coding-enabled wireless sensor networks. Int. J. Distrib. Sens. Netw. 11(7), 510251 (2015)

15. Bolivar, L.T., Tselios, C., Area, D.M., Tsolis, G.: On the deployment of an open-source, 5G-aware evaluation testbed. In: 2018 6th IEEE International Conference on Mobile Cloud Computing, Services, and Engineering (MobileCloud), pp. 51–58, March 2018

Network-Coded Multigeneration Protocols in Heterogeneous Cellular Networks

Roberto Torre$^{(\boxtimes)}$ (ID), Sreekrishna Pandi (ID), and Frank H. P. Fitzek (ID)

Deutsche Telekom Chair of Communication Networks, Dresden, Germany
{roberto.torre,sreekrishna.pandi,frank.fitzek}@tu-dresden.de
https://cn.ifn.et.tu-dresden.de/

Abstract. In the upcoming era of 5G, the number of devices will increase massively, defining a heterogeneous wireless network. Nodes will be gathered in Mobile Clouds, and communicate between peers to achieve a general benefit. To provide packet resilience, error correction codes will be used. In particular, Random Linear Network Coding is standing out as one of the most successful ones. The interplay between Network Coding and Mobile Clouds creates a mesh network where nodes may receive information from multiple sources. However, RLNC was optimized to provide in-order-delay in D2D communications. RLNC need to adapt to a new heterogeneous mesh network where nodes receive packets from multiple paths. In this paper, we propose a method to improve conventional RLNC protocols by making them be able to manage multiple generations simultaneously. We also identify possible trade-offs between conventional RLNC protocols and our new approach. We conclude that multigeneration protocols have better behavior in terms of throughput and resilience, but the average latency per packet decoded is higher.

Keywords: Random linear network coding · RLNC
Multipath · Multigeneration · Heterogeneous · Cellular networks
Mobile clouds

1 Introduction

Cisco Technical Report of 2017 [1] reported that the number of devices will massively increase up to three times the global population in 2021. New infrastructure elements, such as femto/pico base stations, fixed/mobile relays, cognitive radios, and distributed antennae are being massively deployed, thus making future 5G cellular systems and networks more heterogeneous [2].

The increase in mobile traffic reported by Cisco made companies look for solutions in order to decrease data traffic. One of the most successful ones is Mobile Clouds [3], a cooperative arrangement of dynamically connected nodes sharing opportunistically resources. These nodes need to be co-located to be able

© ICST Institute for Computer Sciences, Social Informatics and Telecommunications Engineering 2019
Published by Springer Nature Switzerland AG 2019. All Rights Reserved
V. Sucasas et al. (Eds.): BROADNETS 2018, LNICST 263, pp. 357–366, 2019.
https://doi.org/10.1007/978-3-030-05195-2_35

to communicate among themselves. If the number of nodes cooperating is higher than 3, clients might expect data from multiple paths, leading to a new paradigm of multipath communication among multiple users. Apart from Mobile Clouds, Wireless Mesh [4] or Platoon Communication [5] will benefit from this system.

New error correction techniques such as Random Linear Network Coding (RLNC) [6] are stepping up in the last years due to its good performance in terms of throughput and packet resilience. Furthermore, it has been studied in [7] that the combination of RLNC and Mobile Clouds can lead to high increases in terms of network throughput, packet resilience, and substantially decrease the energy consumption. RLNC protocols are however not optimized for heterogeneous networks and multipath communications [8], but for providing in-order-delay packets in D2D communications. Hence, packets that arrive out of order might be discarded instantly. Conventional RLNC protocols rely on their redundancies not only to recover from packet erasures but also from the jitter of the network. However, in scenarios where jitter is non negligible such as cellular communications [9], mobile clouds or wireless mesh communications, being able to utilize the packets that arrive out of order may increase the decoding probability, and as a consequence, throughput, and packet resilience.

In this paper, we propose a new algorithm to make RLNC protocols be able to manage multiple generations simultaneously. The destination, where the packets should be decoded, will now be organized in standalone **subdecoders**, a packet buffer that is created every time a packet with new generation arrives. We compare our multigeneration approach with the conventional one, identify possible trade-offs, and perform simulations in order to study how our approach is behaving. We confirm that conventional RLNC protocols are abusing of the coding redundancies to cope with packet arrival fluctuations and this would diminish with a multigeneration approach. However, if a packet is lost, the average latency per packet will increase. RLNC protocols will benefit from this because their redundancy algorithms will no longer require focussing on jitter, but only on packet errors.

The remainder of the paper is organized as follows. In Sect. 2 we give a detailed information about the state of the art. In Sect. 3 we introduce the problem RLNC protocols are currently dealing with. Section 4 gathers our solution proposed. In Sect. 5 we compare the conventional mode with our proposed solution by running software simulations. In Sect. 6 the conclusion of our work is presented.

2   Related Work

Heterogeneous Cellular Networks. Cellular networks have suffered massive changes in the last years. New elements such as smartphones, smart cars, sensors, and IoT have recently appeared making the environment inside the cell more heterogeneous [2]. The amount of traffic is also increasing year by year, making the network ideal for short-range communications, platoon communication, wireless mesh, and cooperative networks [10,11].

Cooperative Mobile Wireless Systems. Cooperative communications are nowadays taking the lead in video streaming and data dissemination. Nodes tend to group into Mobile Clouds [12,13] to increase user energy performance [14] or network throughput. All those technologies exploit the idea of a fully mesh cooperative network [8], where packets can be received from several paths. Hence, the next generation of mobile networks is moving forward a multipath cooperative network.

Random Linear Network Coding. In this emerging heterogeneous networking environment where cellular networks are continuously adapting to new user requirements, it was demonstrated that the use of Network Coding can increase wireless network throughput [15]. A high-performance improvement used to overcome those errors is Random Linear Network Coding (RLNC), which was first introduced in [6]. Some studies also stated that the interplay of Random Linear Network Coding along with different technologies such as Cooperative Networking [16] can substantially increase network throughput and packet resilience in comparison with its predecessors [17], and have created an innovative communication paradigm known as Network-Coded Cooperative (NCC) networks [7,18,19]. However, RLNC has been optimized to provide in-order-delay packets in D2D communications. Regarding future multipath communications, RLNC needs to adapt by using tools like the ones proposed in this paper.

3   Problem Description

RLNC protocols are optimized for providing in-order-delay in D2D communications. However, when the jitter of the network is high, the performance of RLNC decreases significantly. This increase in jitter can happen due to the topology in

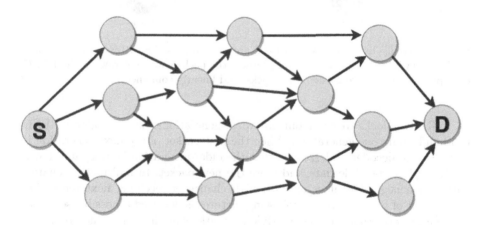

Fig. 1. Example of a mesh network topology with multiple paths. Packets are generated in the Source (S) and must arrive at the destination (D). Multiple paths can be selected for the communication so the propagation delay may vary significantly.

a multipath environment since the packet can arrive from different paths of the network. An example of a multipath mesh network can be observed in Fig. 1. In [20], the authors study the jitter in Ad Hoc networks using different protocols. They obtain average jitters up to 0.1 ms. In this paper, we will use these values to see how RLNC would react to this jitter.

RLNC is a linear block code, like Reed-Solomon or Hamming codes. This means that the transmitted packets are grouped into blocks, then, new coded packets are generated by creating a linear combination of the packets in the block, and later transmitted through the network. The decoder needs to receive as many linearly independent packets as the size of the block in order to be able to decode the information of the whole block. In Fig. 2 the difference between RLNC and a conventional protocol is depicted, and how packets inside a block are linearly combined.

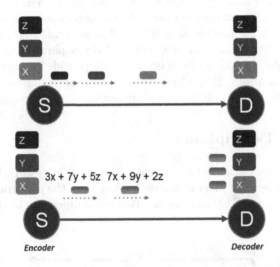

Fig. 2. Difference between a conventional protocol (top) and an RLNC protocol (bottom). Meanwhile in the conventional protocol the packets are sent raw, in the RLNC example the packets are gathered in blocks, and linearly combined.

In RLNC, blocks are commonly known as generations. Each decoder in RLNC can handle only one generation. When the first packet of the next generation is received, the decoder understands that the older generation is over, and it will try to flush all possible data and store the new packet. In multipath scenarios with a non negligible jitter exists a high chance of receiving next-generation packets out of position. In the following pictures is depicted a possible scenario, where a protocol that handles multiple generations at the same time provides a better decoding ratio.

Step 1. As an example, an idle system with one decoder is presented. The decoder has no starting generation. We are assuming a wireless input where multiple sources can be delivering packets.

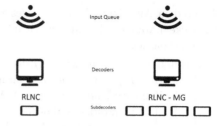

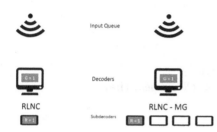

Step 2. The first packet arrives. After receiving it, the systems obtain the generation of the packet, and adjust their internal parameters (Generation, Rank, etc).

Step 3. A second packets arrives with a new generation number. In this case, the left system flushes its memory decoding all posible packets. The right system saves the second packet in a second subdecoder, adjusts its internal parameters, and awaits new incoming packets.

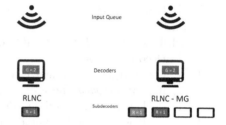

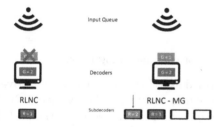

Step 4. A third packet arrives with an old generation number. The system on the left considers this is an old generation packet and discards it. The system on the right keeps it and updates the parameters of the corresponding subdecoder.

4   Multiple Generations in One Coder

The solution we propose in this paper for the problem explained in Sect. 3 consists in making the recoders and decoders be able to handle multiple generations simultaneously. Thus, we add a new concept, the **subdecoder**, a standalone generation buffer which is created every time a packet with a subsequent generation arrives, then this subdecoder is attached to that generation, and when the generation is completed or the system needs to be flushed, the entity is destroyed. The subdecoders are not aware of the rest, and they will not communicate among themselves. There will be a central logic that will create, destroy, and give orders to each of the subdecoders. The logic of this central brain can be observed in Algorithm 1. This represents the workflow when an event (incoming packet) appears. In this algorithm, *Gen* refers to Generation and *In* to the incoming packet.

> **foreach** *incoming packet (In)* **do**
> > **if** *Gen(In) > Current gen.* **then**
> > > **if** *current subdecoders = MAX_SUBDECODERS* **then**
> > > > Flush oldest subdecoder;
> > > > Destroy oldest subdecoder;
> > > > Update decoder metadata;
> > >
> > > **end**
> > > Create new subdecoder;
> > > Increase decoder max. generation;
> >
> > **else if** *Current gen. <= Gen(In) < Oldest gen.* **then**
> > > Find *Gen(In)* subdecoder ;
> > > Update *Gen(In)* subdecoder ;
> >
> > **else**
> > > Discard packet;
> >
> > **end**
> > **while** *source packet to decode* **do**
> > > Decode last packet;
> > > Forward packet to next layer;
> > > **if** *Gen. decoded* **then**
> > > > Destroy oldest subdecoder;
> > > > Update decoder metadata;
> > >
> > > **end**
> >
> > **end**
>
> **end**

end

Algorithm 1. Decoder workflow for each incoming packet

The workflow of the algorithm is described as follows. When a packet arrives at the decoder, the generation of the incoming packet will be extracted. If it belongs to a previous generation than the oldest one in the decoder, the packet will be dropped. If it belongs to a generation between the oldest and the newest generation of the decoder, it will forward the packet to the corresponding subdecoder. This subdecoder will extract the information, update the subdecoder metadata, and forward the packet in case it needs to be recoded. If the generation of the incoming packet belongs to a later generation than the newest one in the decoder, it will first check it another subdecoder can be created. If not, the subdecoder attached to the oldest generation will be flushed and destroyed, leaving an empty spot to the new generation subdecoder. The metadata information of the decoder will be updated as well. When there is an empty spot, a new subdecoder will be created and attached to the new generation, the incoming packet will be forwarded to the subdecoder created and the decoder metadata will be updated.

With the incorporation of subdecoders inside a decoder, the probability of decoding will increase. However, there are some drawbacks that must be considered. The more subdecoders there are on the decoder, the longer the decoder would have to wait until it flushes the oldest subdecoder when a generation is not filled in time. This trade-off will be studied in the following section.

5   Simulations

We consider a simulator of an LTE network, where a base station is encoding and sending data to a user equipment that acts as a decoder. The values of the simulator are gathered in Table 1. We send a total number of $N = 10.000$ packets, the number of packets each generation will have is $G = 100$. The amount of subdecoders the RLNC multigeneration protocol has is 4. The MTU is 1500 bytes, and the propagation time, data rate, and jitter are taken from [9, 20].

Table 1. Parameter settings of the simulator

Parameter	Symbol	Settings
Packets sent	N	10.000 packets
Generation size	G	100 packets
Maximum subdecoders	C	4 subdecoders
Propagation time	T_p	1 ms
Packet length	ℓ	1500 bytes
Data rate	R	11.76 Mbps
Jitter	j	0..0.128 ms

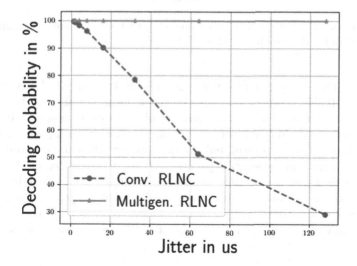

Fig. 3. Decoding probability of the conventional RLNC protocols and multigeneration protocols for the parameters in Table 1

We are assuming the system is aware and adaptive to packet erasures in the channel. Hence, packet losses will only happen due to next generation early packet arrivals. By doing so, we are limiting error losses only to jitter and we can isolate the losses related to network jitter. In Fig. 3 the decoding probability of both systems is shown. It can be observed that when the jitter is minimal, the conventional RLNC protocols start to have problems decoding the whole message, which would lead to an increase of the redundancies and a more inefficient transmission in the network. On the other hand, the multigenaration protocol does not suffer the jitter fluctuations. If the jitter keeps being increased, the multigeneration approach would start losing packets, but the decoding probability of the conventional RLNC would decrease down to almost zero.

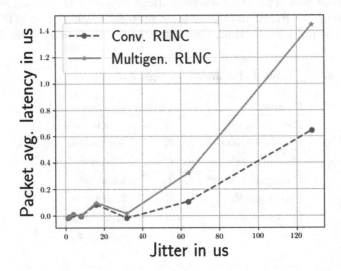

Fig. 4. Extra latency per packet of the conventional RLNC protocols and multigeneration protocols for the parameters in Table 1

In Fig. 4 the average extra latency per packet is depicted. As expected, a conventional RLNC protocol has here a better performance, since all the packets that arrive do not have to wait for packets of previous generations. It can be observed that with a higher jitter, the average latency on each packet increases with a multigeneration protocol, but, on the contrary, there are no losses due to the early arrival of new generation packets. We can conclude that exists a tradeoff between these two parameters, and further studies must be done in order to model the advantages and disadvantages of using multiple generation protocols with different parameters, like the number of subdecoders used, the conditions of the network, the coding ratio, the generation size or the packet size.

6   Conclusion

RLNC has taken the lead of error correction codes in heterogeneous cellular networks in the last years. Nevertheless, RLNC protocols are optimized for D2D communications, but not for multipath, because they can only handle one generation at the same time.

In this paper we propose a novel way of adapting RLNC protocols, so the decoder is able to handle multiple generations simultaneously, making them more suitable for multipath communications. This is done by organizing the decoder in standalone subdecoders, buffers attached to each generation which are destroyed after the generation is decoded. We identify and study a trade-off between the packets decoded and the average latency per packet depending on the network jitter. We confirm that the conventional RLNC protocols have better performance in terms of latency, but the multigeneration approach provides better decoding ratio.

This paper opens up a new approach for RLNC protocols, however, further studies must be done. Studies with a higher complexity must be developed, varying different parameters such as the number of subdecoders used, the conditions of the network, the coding ratio, the generation size or the packet size. Moreover, the possibility of adapting the optimal amount of subdecoders on the fly should also be studied.

Acknowledgements. This project has received funding from the European Union's H2020 research and innovation program under grant agreement H2020-MCSA-ITN-2016-SECRET 722424 [21].

References

1. Cisco: Cisco visual networking index: forecast and methodology, 2016 to 2021. Technical report, Cisco Technologies, 28 March 2017
2. Heath, R.W., Kountouris, M.: Modeling heterogeneous network interference. In: IEEE Information Theory and Applications Workshop, February 2012
3. Fitzek, F.H., Katz, M.D.: Mobile Clouds. Exploiting Distributed Resources in Wireless, Mobile and Social Network. Wiley, UK (2014)
4. Pandi, S., Wunderlich, S., Fitzek, F.H.P.: Reliable low latency wireless mesh networks - from myth to reality. In: 2018 15th IEEE Annual Consumer Communications Networking Conference (CCNC), January 2018
5. Jia, D., Lu, K., Wang, J., Zhang, X., Shen, X.: A survey on platoon-based vehicular cyber-physical systems. IEEE Commun. Surv. Tutorials 18(1), 263–284 (2016)
6. Ho, T., Medard, M., Shi, J., Efiros, M., Karger, D.R.: On randomized network coding. In: Proceedings of 41st Annual Allerton Conference on Communication, Control, and Computing (2003)
7. Renzo, M.D., Iezzi, M., Graziosi, F.: On diversity order and coding gain of multisource multirelay cooperative wireless networks with binary network coding. IEEE Trans. Veh. Technol. 62(3), 1138–1157 (2013)
8. Gheorghiu, S., Toledo, A.L., Rodriguez, P.: Multipath TCP with network coding for wireless mesh networks. In: 2010 IEEE International Conference on Communications, May 2010

9. 3GPP: Physical channels and modulation, September 2015
10. Pedersen, M.V., Fitzek, F.H.P.: Mobile clouds: the new content distribution platform. In: Proceedings of the IEEE (2012)
11. Laneman, J.N., Tse, D.N.C., Wornell, G.W.: Cooperative diversity in wireless networks: efficient protocols and outage behavior. IEEE Trans. Inf. Theory **50**(12), 3062–3080 (2004)
12. Fitzek, F., Katz, M., Zhang, Q.: Cellular controlled short-range communication for cooperative P2P networking. Wirel. World Res. Forum (WWRF) **17** (2006)
13. Albiero, F., Katz, M., Fitzek, F.H.P.: Energy-efficient cooperative techniques for multimedia services over future wireless networks. In: 2008 IEEE International Conference on Communications, pp. 2006–2011, May 2008
14. Albiero, F., Fitzek, F., Katz, M.: Cooperative power saving strategies in wireless networks: an agent-based model. In: Symposium on Wireless Communication Systems, October 2007
15. Ahlswede, R., Cai, N., Li, S.Y.R., Yeung, R.W.: Network information flow. IEEE Trans. Inf. Theory **46**(4), 1204–1216 (2000)
16. Rossetto, F., Zorzi, M.: Mixing network coding and cooperation for reliable wireless communications. IEEE Wireless Commun. (2011)
17. Militano, L., Condoluci, M., Araniti, G., Molinaro, A., Iera, A., Fitzek, F.H.P.: Wi-Fi cooperation or D2D-based multicast content distribution in LTE-A: a comparative analysis. In: 2014 IEEE International Conference on Communications Workshops (ICC), pp. 296–301, June 2014
18. Pandi, S., Arranz, R.T., Nguyen, G.T., Fitzek, F.H.P.: Massive video multicasting in cellular networks using network coded cooperative communication. In: 2018 15th IEEE Annual Consumer Communications Networking Conference (CCNC), January 2018
19. Fitzek, F.H.P., Heide, J., Pedersen, M.V., Katz, M.: Implementation of network coding for social mobile clouds [applications corner]. IEEE Signal Process. Mag. **30**(1), 159–164 (2013)
20. Talooki, V.N., Rodriguez, J.: Jitter based comparisons for routing protocols in mobile ad hoc networks. In: 2009 International Conference on Ultra Modern Telecommunications Workshops, October 2009
21. Rodriguez, J., et al.: Secret-secure network coding for reduced energy next generation mobile small cells. In: ITA Conference (2017)

Multi-tenant Isolation in Software Defined Networks

Sarah Irum[(✉)], Patrick Luedke, Klaus Warnke, and Gerrit Schulte

Acticom Gmbh, Am Borsigturm 48, 13507 Berlin, Germany
{sarah.irum,patrick.luedke,klaus.warnke,gerrit.schulte}@acticom.de
http://www.acticom.de

Abstract. Software Defined Networking (SDN) provides a flexible and programmable infrastructure for future networks. SDN supports multi-domain networks where customers, called tenants, can share network resources on the large data centers. In the multi-tenant environment, tenants can share the network elements while keeping them isolated from each other. In this paper, we describe an isolated multi-tenant solution where the tenants can have control over their assigned network resources. The described approach provides isolation through VxLAN and configuration of flow tables in the OpenFlow switch. VxLAN tunnels are used to isolate packets transmitted by different tenants. Virtual Network Identifiers (VNIs) are assigned to the flow table for identification of the tenant.

Keywords: Software defined network · VxLAN
Network function virtualization · OpenFlow

1 Introduction

Software Defined Networking (SDN) has emerged as an architecture to develop and deploy fast-growing applications over the past few years. SDN provides a dynamic, manageable, cost-effective approach that simplifies today's network capabilities and management. It helps to resolve the issues with the conventional network infrastructure such as large-scale integration of end systems and virtual networks. SDN gained considerable recognition from the researchers because of its benefits for the future Internet architectures such as information-centric networking [1]. SDN separates the control plane and forwarding paths to reduce network energy, provide security mechanisms [2] and data center network management [3]. A centralized network controller is used in SDNs to manage the entire network resulting in faster service provisioning, automation, and efficiency gains. The OpenFlow protocol is used for the communication of SDN controllers and switches.

Traditional network infrastructures manage servers, storage, and networking manually by highly skilled system administrators. This hardware-centric management approach is replaced by the multi-tenant services which offer virtualization and abstraction technologies. SDN technology allows the customers to have

© ICST Institute for Computer Sciences, Social Informatics and Telecommunications Engineering 2019
Published by Springer Nature Switzerland AG 2019. All Rights Reserved
V. Sucasas et al. (Eds.): BROADNETS 2018, LNICST 263, pp. 367–376, 2019.
https://doi.org/10.1007/978-3-030-05195-2_36

a higher level of control over their virtualized network resources in the multi-tenant environment. However, the isolation between tenant domains becomes important in the design of multi-tenant architectures as some of the network resources are shared between the multiple tenants. Virtual Network Function (VNF) architectures together with SDN virtualize the traditional network functions and replace the dedicated network hardware with software applications, which helps in accurate monitoring and manipulation of network traffic [4].

In this paper, we propose a testbed to isolate multi-tenant traffic in SDNs. In the testbed, multiple tenants are connected to multiple OpenFlow switches through one centralized SDN controller. The traffic is isolated using VxLAN overlay networks and flow tables. Virtual Extensible Lan (VxLAN) is the encapsulation protocol for the overlay network on existing Layer 3 infrastructure. It provides scalability to the system, while providing isolation to the tenants [5]. Flow tables are used in the OpenFlow protocol and they match incoming packets to specific flows and specify the functions that are to be performed on the frames.

The rest of the paper is organized as follows. Section 2 will present a brief description of Software Defined Networking and NFV. Section 3 will address the details of the testbed. Finally, Sect. 4 will present our conclusion and future work.

2 Concepts

In this section, we briefly explain the basic concepts and terminologies that are used in this paper.

2.1 Software Defined Networks

The traditional network paradigm focuses on hardware-centric networking, where switches have their own data and control planes, and adding new protocols or updating the existing protocols is a challenge. However, in SDN, switches have become simpler by taking out the control plane from the forwarding devices and managing the switches using the centralized controller devices. SDN introduces the softwarized programmable network, where data and control planes are separated and forwarding decisions are made on centralized SDN controllers. In the data plane, packets are transported through switches towards the destination. Whereas, in the control plane, the SDN controller decides about the packet flow through the network in the data plane. Control plane functionalities include system configuration, management, and exchange of routing table information. The SDN controller sends packet rules to the SDN switches and configures them with the information about the traffic they are handling using the OpenFlow protocol.

2.2 OpenFlow

The OpenFlow protocol is the communication protocol between a SDN controller and one or multiple SDN switches. The controller manipulates the flow entries in the switch such as adding, updating or deleting the flow entries of a flowtable. The OpenFlow switch supports flow-based forwarding using the flow tables. Flow tables contain information about packet flows and their end points. Each packet flow entry contains information of packets such as Ethernet addresses and IP addresses of source and destination, output actions that are to be performed on the received packet, and the total number of transmitted bytes etc. When the switch receives a packet, it matches the flow entry with the flow table. In case a table miss entry, the switch forwards the packet back to the controller, and the controller gives the direction to the switch to manage the packet in the future or it just drops the packet [6].

2.3   SDN Controllers

The SDN controller manages the flows, application and business logic to enable intelligent networking. Tasks of the controller are monitoring of SDN network traffic, providing network statistics, and adding new rules throughout the network. Most popular SDN controllers are Ryu [7], Open Day Light (ODL) [8], POX [9], NOX [10], Floodlight [11] controller. Some of the controllers are configured using Python scripts such as Ryu, POX, NOX, while others are developed in C++ or Java.

2.4   VxLAN

There have been several approaches for the development of OpenFlow standards. Virtual Extensible LAN (VxLAN) was developed to address the scalability problem in the large computing environments. It is a virtual encapsulation technology for operating an overlay network on existing Layer 3 infrastructure [12]. The devices' which support VxLAN' are called virtual tunnel endpoints (VTEPs). The devices that can act as a VTEP are host endpoints, switches, and routers. VTEPs encapsulate VxLAN traffic by adding the number of fields such as the outer media access control (MAC) destination address, the outer MAC source address, the outer IP destination address, the outer IP source address, the outer UDP header, and the VxLAN network identifier (VNI), which is used to uniquely identify the VxLAN traffic. It also de-encapsulates the traffic leaving the VxLAN tunnel.

2.5   Network Function Virtualization - NFV

Network Virtualization (NV) [13] allows executing multiple instances of a network on a shared physical infrastructure. SDN enables NV by distinguishing and forwarding flows to different networks. In Network Function Virtualization (NFV) [14], specific in-network functions are virtualized such as firewalls, load balances, and VPN gateways etc. NFV focuses on data plane programmability and can be used to extend SDN because SDN mainly focuses on the control plane programmability.

3   Implementation

In our testbed, we developed our SDN environment using computer nodes as the hosts using Ubuntu Linux as an operating system. These hosts use the KVM hypervisor to spawn virtual machines. We used OVS switches on each host, which supports the OpenFlow protocol for communication inside SDN. The Ryu controller has been used as SDN controller which provides the control plane capability. In order to achieve isolation in the setup, we modified the flow tables in the OVS switch, and added the entries manually for the traffic control between VxLAN tunnels.

3.1   Creating Virtual Machines Using Hypervisors

There are several existing solutions for the isolation of multi-tenant network in SDNs. In our testbed, multiple tenants are isolated using VxLANs overlays and designing policies for flow tables. Isolation is achieved by assigning the end hosts and tagging the initial flows using tunnel ids. An OpenFlow switch is responsible to enforce policies and it inserts the label into the packet headers. We implemented our solution on the Ryu Controller to evaluate the traffic and isolation of multi-tenants setups.

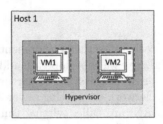

Fig. 1. Two Virtual vachines running on a hypervisor.

For the testbed we exclusively use hosts with KVM (Kernel Based Virtualization) as a hypervisor running on Ubuntu Server 16.04 LTS. For managing KVM, the virsh tool is used because it is scriptable, well documented and capable of communicating with KVM (see Fig. 1).

The host acts as a spawn point for the virtual machines that can be used at a later stage to serve as SDN. In Fig. 2, it is shown that the system consists of multiple hosts containing multiple guest virtual machines according to the requirements of the setup.

3.2   Connecting Virtual Machines with OVS Switch

In the setup, OVS is used as OpenFlow switch. OVS is the multilayer virtual switch that supports OpenFlow enabling network automation through programming. In Fig. 3, a simple topology is depicted in which two virtual machines are

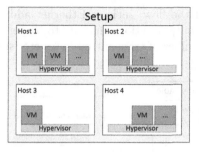

Fig. 2. Four hosts with hypervisors that act as spawnpoints for virtual machines.

connected to the OVS switch and the switch is controlled by the Ryu Controller. The OpenFlow table is configured in the OVS switch by the controller. In this topology, if VM1 transmits a packet to VM2, the packets are first received by the OVS switch connected to VM1, and depending on the flow table entries, the received packet would be forwarded to VM2. The controller is managing all the flow entries in the switch.

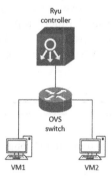

Fig. 3. VM1, VM2 and Ryu controller are connected through OVS switch.

3.3   Configuration of OVS Switch Using OpenFlow

An OVS switch has a flow table with flow entries that can be managed by the SDN controller. The flow entries can control the forwarding of the packets. The decision of forwarding or dropping the packets is made by the controller. Each flow entry specifies a matching pattern and defines the action that can be performed on the packet. When the switch receives the packet, it matches it with the forwarding matching pattern and if the flow entry is not found in the flow table, i.e. with a table miss entry, it forwards the packet to the controller. The controller then adds the flow entry to the switch or just drops it. A flow entry contains information of the flow, such as Ethernet address and IP address of source and destination, output actions that are to be performed on the received packet, and the total number of transmitted bytes etc (see Fig. 4).

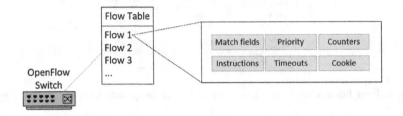

Fig. 4. Flow table and basic composition of a flow entry.

3.4   Connecting Switches Through VxLAN

A Virtual Extensible Local Area Network (VxLAN) supports a large number of tenants in comparison to previous solution VLAN. It encapsulates the network traffic in to the tunnel, and creates overlay networks that are isolated from the providers physical network. Virtual Tunnel endpoints (VTeps) are the devices to perform encapsulation and de-encapsulation on the VxLAN traffic. Each traffic segment is identified by a unique Virtual Network Identifier (VNI) (see Fig. 5).

Fig. 5. OVS switches connected through a VxLAN tunnel.

In real world scenarios, multiple switches are connected to each other for the transmission of the network packets. The testbed is extended by adding more switches. As shown in Fig. 6, three virtual machines are added to the second switch and their virtual ports are defined as well. The Ryu controller manages the communication between the two switches. For the transmission of VxLAN encapsulated packets between the switches VxLAN tunnels are used in the setup.

The Fig. 7 explains the basic topology of a multi-tenant SDN network in which tenant A and tenant B have different virtual networks and their traffic is isolated using VxLAN tunnels. The tunnel is created on both VTEPs (switches) for the transmission of packets. VNIs are assigned on the VTEPs to separate the traffic of both tenants. The VTEP adds headers to the original packet sent by the VM such as VNI, and IP and MAC addresses of source and destination etc. and forwards the packet into the tunnel. Vtep2 receives the packet and removes the UDP headers assigned by the VTEP and sends the packet to the actual destination.

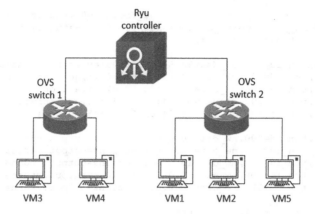

Fig. 6. Five Virtual Machines and two OVS switches that are controlled by a Ryu controller.

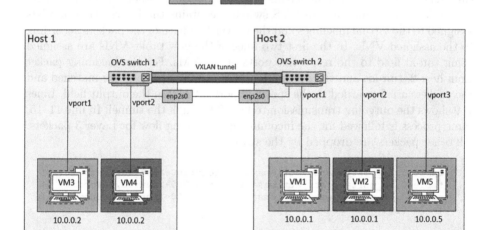

Fig. 7. Setup with five virtual machines distributed among two hosts. Both OVS switches are connected by a VxLAN tunnel with two isolated overlay networks (VNI 100- orange and VNI 200 - light blue). (Color figure online)

3.5   Isolation of Multi-tenants Using Flow Table

In the testbed scenario, two overlay networks are shown that are isolated from each other. The two networks are assigned different VNIs. The first network has VNI 100 and contains VM1, VM3, and VM5. The second network has VNI 200 and contains VM2 and VM4 as shown in Fig. 7. The virtual machines in a single host can have equal IP configuration and same MAC addresses as they

```
1   table=0,in_port=vport1,actions=set_field:100->tun_id,resubmit(,1)
2   table=0,in_port=vport2,actions=set_field:200->tun_id,resubmit(,1)
3   table=0,actions=resubmit(,1)
4
5   table=1,tun_id=100,dl_dst=52:54:00:73:9a:e9,actions=output:vport1
6   table=1,tun_id=200,dl_dst=52:54:00:bc:e0:1a,actions=output:vport2
7   table=1,tun_id=200,dl_dst=52:54:00:53:c2:0f,actions=output:vtunnel
8   table=1,tun_id=100,dl_dst=52:54:00:72:5c:8c,actions=output:vtunnel
9   table=1,tun_id=100,dl_dst=52:54:00:58:6f:45,actions=output:vtunnel
10
11  table=1,tun_id=200,nw_dst=10.0.0.2,actions=output:vport1
12  table=1,tun_id=100,nw_dst=10.0.0.2,actions=output:vport2
13  table=1,tun_id=100,nw_dst=10.0.0.1,actions=output:vtunnel
14  table=1,tun_id=100,nw_dst=10.0.0.5,actions=output:vtunnel
15  table=1,tun_id=200,nw_dst=10.0.0.1,actions=output:vtunnel
16
17  table=1,priority=100,actions=drop
```

Fig. 8. OVS switch 1 flow table.

are separated using the VNI. This prevents IP address collision and any tenant can create a network without having the information of other tenant networks.

In Fig. 8, the flow table of OVS switch 1 contains the information of VNIs assigned to the virtual machines and the forwarding path of the packets according to the assigned VNIs. In the first two lines of the flow table, VNIs are assigned using tun-id field to the respective ports of the VMs. For the incoming packet from host 2, tun-ids and the destination MAC address (dl-dst) are matched and the packets are forwarded to the specified ports (VMs) in the output field. Lines 7–9 shows the outgoing transmission to host 2 through the tunnel. In line 11–15, same process is followed for the incoming and outgoing flow for Layer 3 packets. All other packets are dropped by the switch.

```
1   table=0,in_port=vport1,actions=set_field:100->tun_id,resubmit(,1)
2   table=0,in_port=vport2,actions=set_field:200->tun_id,resubmit(,1)
3   table=0,in_port=vport3,actions=set_field:100->tun_id,resubmit(,1)
4   table=0,actions=resubmit(,1)
5
6   table=1,tun_id=100,dl_dst=52:54:00:72:5c:8c,actions=output:vport1
7   table=1,tun_id=200,dl_dst=52:54:00:53:c2:0f,actions=output:vport2
8   table=1,tun_id=100,dl_dst=52:54:00:73:9a:e9,actions=output:vtunnel
9   table=1,tun_id=200,dl_dst=52:54:00:bc:e0:1a,actions=output:vtunnel
10  table=1,tun_id=100,dl_dst=52:54:00:58:6f:45,actions=output:vport3
11
12  table=1,tun_id=100,nw_dst=10.0.0.5,actions=output:vport3
13  table=1,tun_id=100,nw_dst=10.0.0.1,actions=output:vport1
14  table=1,tun_id=200,nw_dst=10.0.0.1,actions=output:vport2
15  table=1,tun_id=100,nw_dst=10.0.0.2,actions=output:vtunnel
16  table=1,tun_id=200,nw_dst=10.0.0.2,actions=output:vtunnel
17
18  table=1,priority=100,actions=drop
```

Fig. 9. OVS switch 2 flow table.

Figure 9 shows the flow table of OVS switch 2 which contains two VMs of same network VM1 and VM5 respectively and one VM of different network. VM1, VM3, and VM5 are reachable, because they share the same network, while VM2 can't reach the VM1 and VM5 in host 2 because of network isolation. In the first three lines of the flow table VNIs are assigned to all the VMs in host 2. The matching of incoming and outgoing transmission in flow table in host 2 is similar to the matching done in flow table of host 1. However, in host 2 packets from VM2 can be forwarded to VM5 and vice versa as they share the same VNI as shown in line 12–13.

4   Conclusion and Future Work

In this paper, we discuss the main concepts of SDN and the techniques which are used to develop a testbed in a SDN environment. We also describe our testbed for isolation of multi-tenants in SDN. In the testbed, isolation is achieved using VxLAN and the configuration of flows in the flow table of the switch. Ryu controller is used as SDN controller to manage all the communication between switches and hosts. Two OVS switches are created in the testbed and multiple virtual machines are attached to the switches. VxLAN tunnels are created on the switches and VNIs are assigned for the identification of different networks in the tunnel. The flow table is configured for the isolated communication of packets between the switches. With the configured OpenFlow table in the OVS switches and specified VNIs for the VxLAN tunnels, we are now able to create multi-tenant SDNs in the testbed.

In the future, we will focus on the implementation of our testbed in the OpenStack environment [15]. OpenStack is a cloud operating system that allows us to create multi-tenant SDNs in a much faster and scalable way. This will improve the efficiency, and it will allow a more sophisticated SDN setup. We will also develop an outlook to integrate OpenFlow based authentication using IEEE standard mechanisms.

Acknowledgment. This project has received funding from the European Unions H2020 research and innovation program under grant agreement H2020-MCSA-ITN-2016-SECRET 722424

References

1. Ahlgren, B., Dannewitz, C., Imbrenda, C., Kutscher, D., Ohlman, B.: A survey of information-centric networking. IEEE Commun. Mag. **50**(7), 26–36 (2012)
2. S. Shin, P. Porras, V. Yegneswaran, M. Fong, G. Gu, M. Tyson, Fresco: modular composable security services for software-defined networks. In: Proceedings of Network and Distributed Security Symposium (2013)
3. Yu, M., Jose, L., Miao, R.: Software defined traffic measurement with opensketch. USENIX NSDI **vol**, 31 (2013)

4. Fayazbakhsh, S.K., Chiang, L., Sekar, V., Yu, M., Mogul, J.C.: Enforcing network-wide policies in the presence of dynamic middlebox actions using flowtags. In: USENIX NSDI, Seattle, WA, USA, pp. 1–13, 533–546 (2014)
5. Kapadia, S., Subagio, P.H., Yang, Y., Shah, N., Jain, V., Agrawal, A.: Implementation of virtual extensible local area network (VXLAN) in top-of-rack switches in a network environment, Google Patents, US Patent 9,565,105 (2017)
6. OpenFlow Switch Specification. http://goo.gl/1DYxw6. Accessed 14 Oct 2013
7. Ryu: An Operating System for Software Defined Network. http://osrg.github.com/ryu/
8. OpenDayLight. https://www.opendaylight.org/
9. POX: A Python-Based OpenFlow Controller. http://www.noxrepo.org/pox/about-pox/
10. Gude, N., et al.: NOX: towards an operating system for networks. ACM SIGCOMM CCR **38**(3), 105–110 (2008)
11. Floodlight. http://floodlight.openflowhub.org/
12. Mahalingam, M., et al.: Virtual eXtensible Local Area Network (VXLAN): a framework for overlaying virtualized layer 2 networks over layer 3 networks. In: RFC7348 (2014). https://doi.org/10.17487/RFC7348
13. Chowdhury, N., Boutaba, R.: A survey of network virtualization. In: Elsevier Computer Networks (2010)
14. European Telecommunications Standards Institute, Network Functions Virtualisation (2012). http://portal.etsi.org/NFV/NFVWhitePaper.pdf
15. OpenStack. https://www.openstack.org/

Perspectives for 5G Network Sharing for Mobile Small Cells

Fatma Marzouk[1]([⊠]), Rui Alheiro[1], Jonathan Rodriguez[2], and Ayman Radwan[2]

[1] Proef, Porto, Portugal
{fatma.marzouk,Rui.Alheiro}@proef.com
[2] Instituto de Telecomunicações, Aveiro, Portugal
{jonathan,aradwan}@av.it.pt
http://www.proefgroup.com/pt/
https://www.it.pt/ITSites/Index/3/

Abstract. Ensuring enough network resources for all emerging 5G mobile services, with the advent of 5G will be vital. Network sharing is seen as one of the adopted technologies of 5G, to enhance resource utilization by optimizing resource usage among different operators. A key enabler for network sharing is virtualization. While virtualization of the core network has already been implemented in nowadays mobile networks, the virtualization of the Radio Access Network (RAN) is still an emerging research topic that is currently investigated with the aim of exploiting a fully virtualized mobile network. In this paper, we examine a 5G RAN perspective architecture that has the merit of being a Multi-RAT, Multi band V-RAN and using end user equipment as mobile small cells. We highlight its advantages, and identify how virtualization of RAN can lead to efficient RAN resource sharing. Finally, we anticipate how some virtualization functionalities should be extended to manage the particularity of the perspective RAN architecture.

Keywords: 5G · C-RAN · V-RAN · Multi-RAT

1 Introduction

5G represents the next major phase of mobile communication, which is expected to take over the world starting 2020. 5G radio access network (RAN) system is envisioned to be a true worldwide wireless web (WWWW) [1]. This is because such system will seamlessly and ubiquitously connect everything. Besides addressing IoT deployment on a massive scale, 5G is also expected to satisfy the requirement of applications previously not possible that depend on ultra-reliable and low-latency communications.

In order to meet those requirement, 5G research community along with the main stakeholders and players in the field have collectively agreed on the use of certain technologies in the 5G paradigm. Those technologies include, among

© ICST Institute for Computer Sciences, Social Informatics and Telecommunications Engineering 2019
Published by Springer Nature Switzerland AG 2019. All Rights Reserved
V. Sucasas et al. (Eds.): BROADNETS 2018, LNICST 263, pp. 377–386, 2019.
https://doi.org/10.1007/978-3-030-05195-2_37

others: The exploitation of the Multi-Rat technology by integrating the evolved existing mobile-broadband RATs (2G, 3G, WLAN, 4G, etc.) and efficiently use the spectrum; the densification of the network with small cells deployment to increase the spectral efficiency and meeting the 1000x challenge. Another potential technology that has existed for decades and need to be revisited for the design of new concepts suitable for the 5G use cases is Network virtualization for RAN and spectrum sharing.

Virtualization used to be related to sharing network resources among different Operating Systems to allow the creation of virtual machines; operators to allow a mobile operator that does not have its own core network resources to share the one available with other operators; or generally speaking among users [2]. A more recent use case of virtualization is Network Function Virtualization (NFV). This use case has emerged in the mobile packet core network as a practical approach to boost the network flexibility along with Software-Defined Networking (SDN). It is expected that 5G push the network virtualization from the core network towards the RAN. In this context, a Cloud RAN architecture exploiting a combination of virtualization (of software), centralization (of hardware) and coordination techniques (between cells and bands) is introduced in order to achieve many benefits, such as: reducing Capital Expenditure (CAPEX) and Operational Expenditure (OPEX).

In this paper, we analyze why each of the three stated above technologies need to be evolved, revisited with new design approaches, after performing a positioning com-pared to the state of the art research works.

2   Densification in 5G

Densifying the network with much big number of small cells is crucial for enhancing the spectral efficiency and meeting the 1000x challenge [3]. Several studies con-firmed that network capacity doubles by doubling the number of small cells. Unlike the deployment of additional macro base station that involves high costs, small cells are low-power nodes that may be installed everywhere indoors and outdoors, operating in licensed band spectrum and referring to an umbrella term for operator-controlled [4]. Small cells can be used to offload the explosive growth of wireless data traffic from macrocells and improve the macro cell's edge data capacity, speed and overall network efficiency. However, the exponentially growing demand for capacity already requires operators to overlay the macro cell large coverage with smaller and smaller cells in the dense areas to achieve more capacity and use spectrum resources more efficiently. Furthermore, the current solution of using Picocells requires radio infrastructure and planning representing significant costs for operators. Most visions [5–8], agree that 5G networks will be an ultra-dense populated by a hybrid combination of heterogeneous cells, including different generations 3G, 4G and 5G, as well as different types of cells such as macro, Pico, and small cells. For instance, in [9] 5G small cells optimized radio design envisioned as a TDD-based system is proposed. In [10], a network architecture where small cells use the same unlicensed spectrum as Wi-Fi has been introduced along with an interference avoidance scheme based on small cells estimating the density of nearby Wi-Fi access points. Multi-antenna systems such as massive MIMO [11,12] and/or Distributed Antenna Systems (DAS), can also be considered as other method to achieve densification. DAS is functionally similar to picocells from a capacity and coverage standpoint, but is composed of a set of radios deployed in remote locations. Cells in that case are called remote radio heads (RRHs) that have all their baseband processing at a central site and share cell IDs. On a network-wide scale, the cloud-RAN approach extends this as it will be detailed further.

As for 5G with mmWave smalls cells, it is also widely expected that they would be extremely dense in 5G networks to compensate their propagation challenges. In [13] a comprehensive tutorial on the use of millimeter-wave frequencies, notably the 60 GHz band and an analysis of the effect of such cells in coping with the expected growth of this solution is provided.

3   Mobile Small Cells

Several research efforts have been devoted to study the optimal static small cell deployment mainly for urban and hot zone environment with respect to different metrics. While authors, in [14], targeted the maximization of the spectral efficiency of the network, maximization of the throughput was the target of [15] to find optimal locations for placing static small cells. These research efforts assumed that the user or traffic distribution is invariant and did not consider that deploying a static small cell in a given hotspot that usually tends to be dynamic will lead to high operational cost.

In order to do so, other recent works have proposed the use of mobile small cells. Most of the research works [16–22] considered deployment scenarios in outdoor hot-spots and public transit vehicles. For instance, in [17,21] mobile small cell deployment in vehicles is investigated. A demonstration of the performance of its gains is given analytically and through simulation considering the outage probability and the error probability as metrics in [17]. Similarly, the authors of [20] studied the deployment problem of mobile small cells, targeting the maximization of the service time provided by mobile small cells for all users. In [21], studies have been performed for small cells environment to understand the gains of proactive cache. The study addressed the wireless backhaul, side-haul and spectrum allocation, but not the impact of spectrum management and mobility in a virtualized network. In [19], the efficiency of deploying moving small cells on the top of buses to offload traffic in the congested macro cell was shown as a beneficial solution, when the small cell is moving near the traffic hotspot and covers a significant proportion of it.

Although several algorithms for the hotspot localization were proposed in the literature [23,24], using moving smalls cells leads to either sporadic gain or to a performance degradation due to the resulting interference, when the mobile small cell is moving away from the hotspot. In addition, resource management schemes for small cells still need more research efforts. A more fresh and efficient way to tackle this problem, is using on-demand mobile small cells that can be dedicated radio remote heads/units (RRHs/RRUs) or user mobile devices existing in the required location as recently suggested in [25].

Although mobile small cells can potentially provide many advantages, the hyper-densification can pose several challenges. The main challenges for successful UDNs are the management of complexity and inter-cell interference (ICI) coordination, mitigation or management among the macro-cell BSs and the small cells as well as the optimization of network operations, of multi-layer, heterogeneous dense net-works. The emergence of the software-defined networks (SDN), wireless network virtualization (WNV) cloud radio access network (C-RAN) and Self Organizing Networks (SON) provides a promising technological solution for these challenges.

In the following sections we give an overview about the standardization activities related to virtualization for network sharing. Afterwards, we build on this vision of Multi-RAT mobile small cells that take advantages of the Virtualized RAN, describe the overall architecture, the different use case of virtualization for the enablement of the proposed architecture, its benefits and the challenges that it would trigger.

4   Virtualization and Network Sharing

Virtualization concept refers to using an abstraction layers to allow different operating Systems; mobile operators or users to share common underlying physical re-sources and have their own isolated virtual resource. For decades, virtualization of wired resources has been practiced through the creation of Virtual Local network (VLAN) and Virtual Private Network (VPNs). Such virtualization is relatively limited as it involves only few OSI model layers. Recent research efforts have been per-formed with the aim of achieving a service level virtualization applied for mobile networks. Network operators are one of the main key players behind such incentives, as network sharing would allow an operator that does not have infrastructure nor spectrum resources to dynamically share the physical networks operated with other mobile network operators (MNOs). Given this definition, virtualization presents a major enabler for resources sharing among different virtual operators. Recently, some incentives for a fuller RAN virtualization for efficient wireless network sharing are currently gaining strong operator support as a feasible way to accommodate the foreseen increase in mobile traffic, whilst reducing their CAPEX and OPEX.

Lots of attention have also been drawn towards network function Virtualization (NFV), as it would facilitate the creation /management/extension of new services without having to care much about the complexity of the implementation on the physical infrastructure.

The importance of network sharing has been recognized by the 3GPP starting from release 6. In ref. [26], 3GPP defined two architectures of active sharing. In both architectures, the radio access network is shared.

- The Multiple-operator CN (MOCN): In this configuration, each operator has its own CN. And the multiple CN nodes belonging to different operators are connected to the same RNC.
- The Gateway CN (GWCN): In this configuration, the core network is shared in addition to the RAN nodes between multiples operators.

In the following section, we build on the concept promoted in [31] and describe the architecture of the Heterogeneous Cloud RAN based mobile cells, the benefits that it would gain, as well as the main use cases of virtualization, in the context of this architecture.

5 Architecture of Heterogeneous Cloud-RAN Based Mobile Small Cells

5.1 Architecture

The combination of multi-tier HetNet and Cloud architecture is referred to as Heterogeneous Cloud Radio Access Network (H-CRAN). This concept was driven by greater needs for coordination, as well as techniques to increase resource efficiency and advances in network visualization. Cloud RAN appeared as a disruptive concept in cellular network aiming to exploit a combination of centralization, virtualization, and coordination techniques. Traditionally, radio and baseband processing functionality (responsible of coding, modulation, fast Fourier transform, etc.) are integrated inside the BS, while the inter-BS coordination performed over X2 interface. RAN used also to be connected to the rest of the network with backhauling segments. With C-RAN the new concept of front hauling is adopted. As shown in Fig. 1, and in contrast to the traditional approach, with front hauling, the baseband resources are pooled at baseband processing units (BBUs) situated at remote central office. A BBU pool serves a particular area with a number of remote radio heads (RRHs) of macro and small cells for a centralized signal processing and management.

5.2 Benefits

As can be seen from the architecture, the envisioned scenario refers to a Multi-RAT, Multi-band C-RAN based mobile small cells, provides multiple potential ad-vantages, for instance, in terms of providing high-speed services, with dense deployment of mobile small cells, allowing the service of increased number of connected wireless devices. The flexibility provided by the C-RAN based architecture also helps with the adaptation of the network to the highly variable environment envisioned in future networking, especially with the vast adopting of Internet of Things (IoT).

The flexibility of the reference scenarios also enables the network to address the different use-cases envisioned for 5G paradigm. The proposed network structure can provide high speed service (high data rates) to use-case 1 of 5G, namely

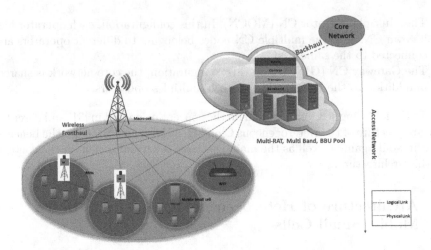

Fig. 1. Perspective Architecture: Multi-RAT, Multi-band C-RAN based mobile small cells with wireless front-haul

Enhanced Mobile Broadband (eMBB). In this case, the wireless fronthaul has to be high-speed link, providing the required high data rate broadband. On the other hand, the second use-case of 5G, the Massive Machine-Type Communications (mMTC), which re-quires a high number of connected devices, can be supported, but with lower data rates. The envisioned scenario can address such use-case through the dense deployment of mobile small cells, which can be easily achieved through the multiple-RAT multiple-band C-RAN, especially that the wireless fronthaul probably does not re-quire high capacity nor high speed. In the next subsection, we analyze the use cases of virtualization that can be fulfilled within this prospective architecture.

5.3   Use Cases of Virtualization within the Proposed Architecture

– *USE CASE 1: Virtualization for Computational Ressource Sharing(V-RAN)*
  This virtualization is embodied through the BBU pool definition within the C-RAN. Based on [27,28], pooling or statistical multiplexing, allows an execution platform to perform the same tasks with less hardware or capacity as the C-RAN capitalizes on the diversity of traffic peaks, hence, improves the utilization efficiency of the infrastructure. That also leads to fewer handover failures and less network control signaling in complicated heterogeneous radio network environments, as well as energy efficient operations and resource savings. Virtualization can also be used to simplify the management and deployment of the RAN nodes, provide isolation, scalability and elasticity, among other things, for the Radio Resource Control (RRC) protocol layer. It has also the potential of providing greater flexibility to the mobile network operator and reducing the network costs. Virtualized BBU Pool can be shared

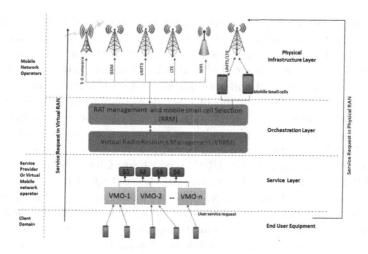

Fig. 2. Virtualization for radio resources efficient sharing

by different network operators, allowing them to rent Radio Access Network (RAN) as a cloud service (RAAS).

- *USE CASE 2: Virtualization for radio resources efficient sharing*

The requirement in this use case is of a network with virtualized RAN supporting the Multi-RAT, Multi Band technologies. The first aim of using the Multi-RAT HetNet approach is to efficiently exploit the unlicensed spectrum by having a 5G RAN system integrating the evolved existing mobile-broadband RATs (2G, 3G, WLAN, 4G, etc) and operating in different configurations. Virtualization will play here a major role to provide abstraction, convergence and sharing of the available multi-RAT re-sources between several service providers. The efficiency of the network can be maximized through the choice of the optimal access technology to be used at given time for each service request/operator, for the communication between end users and mobile cells, as well as for the front-haul between small cells and the backhaul. Given this requirement, the virtualization functionalities need to be further extended with the feature of eventually assigning an optimal mobile small cell/ RAT and technology to be used between to relay the communication to and from an end user equipment.

Figure 2 illustrates the different physical and virtual components involved in this use-case. As it can be shown from the figure, end users equipment solicits the network with different service requests. In the virtual RAN, these service requests are passed to the service layer. At this layer, the virtual mobile operator, also referred to as service provider, operates. Depending on the request, the offered service is classified into one of the offered differentiated services and then relayed to the orchestration layer. This layer, as well as the infrastructure layer, are governed by the traditional mobile opera-tors who owns the physical infrastructure. The orchestration layer is divided into two functionalities: The virtual radio remote management (VRRM) and the RAT management and mobile small cell selection. The VRRM is a functionality that appeared within the concept of virtual-RAN (V-RAN), which is in charge of the creation management and optimization of a set of virtual radio resources, for each of the MVNO, on top of a set of available physical resources. In other words, through the VRRM task, the virtual resources required by the MNOs are mapped onto physical ones, optimized, and monitored. On Top of the VRRM, the traditional entities in the heterogeneous common network for radio remote management (RRM), which are CRRM for common RRM and LRRM for local RRM, operates. In the context of the use-case stipulated by the detailed architecture, these two management schemes have to be extended by the mobile small cell selection schemes. Within this functionality, the decision about whether a multi-hop communication is needed through one or more optimum existent mobile small cells, before being passed to the end physical radio station is made. It is worth noting that mobile small cells are considered here as one of the underlying physical resources.

5.4   Open Research Challenges

The advantages discussed in the previously detailed architecture can be achieved but with some arising research challenges. Some of the identified research challenges, related to the general discussed architecture, are listed below:

- Meeting the requirement of very low latency (1 ms end-to-end) for the 5G Ultra Reliable and Low Latency Communications (URLLC) or critical Machine-Type Communications (cMTC) Use Case is one of the main challenges in the presented architecture. The challenge could be addressed according to the particular use-case, by paying attention to the particular design of front-haul link.
- Managing and controlling the interference induced in the architecture would also be a challenge with the adoption of the multi-RAT multi-band and mobile small cells set-up on demand concept. The question would be determining the optimal set of mobile cells that can offload the traffic and which set of the available RAT would be chosen for the communications, based on some attributes such as (number of devices, used applications and mobility, etc.).
- A third important challenge would be determining the optimal operating point of the network considering the context of highly mobile users/devices. This should be done continuously and automatically which drives the need for the investigation of self-organizing networking (SON) algorithms for the optimization of the multi-RAT, multi-band V-RAN based mobile small cells.

6   Conclusion

In this paper, we analyzed the architecture of Multi-RAT, Multi-band V-RAN based mobile small cells with wireless front-haul. We highlighted two main uses cases of the virtualization within the architecture, and concluded that the virtualization functionality in the V-RAN should be evolved to meet the architecture particularity.

Our future work will concentrate on proposing a set of new algorithms for the identification of the optimal set of mobile small cells and RAT selection for a given hotspot zone.

Acknowledgment. The research leading to these results has received funding from the European Union's Horizon 2020 research and innovation program under grant agreement H2020-MSCA-ITN-2016 SECRET-722424.

References

1. Olwal, T.O., Djouani, K., Kurien, A.M.: A survey of resource management toward 5G radio access networks. IEEE Commun. Surv. Tutor. **18**(3), 1656–1686 (2016)
2. Liang, C., Yu, F.R.: Wireless network virtualization: a survey, some research issues and challenges. IEEE Commun. Surv. Tutor. **17**(1), 358–380 (2015)
3. Bhushan, N., et al.: Network densification: the dominant theme for wireless evolution into 5G. IEEE Commun. Mag. **52**(2), 82–89 (2014)
4. Small cell definition - small cell forum. http://www.smallcellforum.org/about/about-small-cells/small-cell-definition/
5. Series, M.: IMT vision-framework and overall objectives of the future development of IMT for 2020 and beyond (2015)
6. Demestichas, P., et al.: 5G on the horizon: key challenges for the radio-access network. IEEE Veh. Technol. Mag. **8**(3), 47–53 (2013)
7. Chen, S., Zhao, J.: The requirements, challenges, and technologies for 5G of terrestrial mobile telecommunication. IEEE Commun. Mag. **52**(5), 36–43 (2014)
8. Andrews, J.G., et al.: What will 5G be? IEEE J. Select. Areas Commun. **32**(6), 1065–1082 (2014)
9. Mogensen, P., et al.: 5G small cell optimized radio design. In: 2013 IEEE Globecom Workshops (GC Wkshps), pp. 111–116. IEEE (2013)
10. Zhang, H., Chu, X., Guo, W., Wang, S.: Coexistence of WI-FI and heterogeneous small cell networks sharing unlicensed spectrum. IEEE Commun. Mag. **53**(3), 158–164 (2015)
11. Hoydis, J., Ten Brink, S., Debbah, M.: Massive mimo in the UL/DL of cellular networks: How many antennas do we need? IEEE J. Select. Areas Commun. **31**(2), 160–171 (2013)
12. Larsson, E.G., Edfors, O., Tufvesson, F., Marzetta, T.L.: Massive mimo for next generation wireless systems. IEEE communications Mag. **52**(2), 186–195 (2014)
13. Dehos, C., González, J.L., De Domenico, A., Ktenas, D., Dussopt, L.: Millimeter-wave access and backhauling: the solution to the exponential data traffic increase in 5G mobile communications systems? IEEE Commun. Mag. **52**(9), 88–95 (2014)
14. Guo, W., Wang, S., Chu, X., Zhang, J., Chen, J., Song, H.: Automated small-cell deployment for heterogeneous cellular networks. IEEE Commun. Mag. **51**(5), 46–53 (2013)

15. Cheng, H.T., Callard, A., Senarath, G., Zhang, H., Zhu, P.: Step-wise optimal low power node deployment in LTE heterogeneous networks. In: 2012 IEEE Vehicular Technology Conference (VTC Fall), pp. 1–4. IEEE (2012)

16. Sui, Y., Vihriala, J., Papadogiannis, A., Sternad, M., Yang, W., Svensson, T.: Moving cells: a promising solution to boost performance for vehicular users. IEEE Commun. Mag. **51**(6), 62–68 (2013)

17. Feteiha, M.F., Qutqut, M.H., Hassanein, H.S.: Outage probability analysis of mobile small cells over LTE-a networks. In: 2014 International Wireless Communications and Mobile Computing Conference (IWCMC), pp. 1045–1050. IEEE (2014)

18. Feteiha, M.F., Qutqut, M.H., Hassanein, H.S.: Pairwise error probability evaluation of cooperative mobile femtocells. In: 2013 IEEE Globecom Workshops (GC Wkshps), pp. 4705–4710. IEEE (2013)

19. Jaziri, A., Nasri, R., Chahed, T.: Offloading traffic hotspots using moving small cells. In: 2016 IEEE International Conference on Communications (ICC), pp. 1–6. IEEE (2016)

20. Chou, S.F., Chiu, T.C., Yu, Y.J., Pang, A.C.: Mobile small cell deployment for next generation cellular networks. In: Global Communications Conference (GLOBECOM), pp. 4852–4857. IEEE (2014)

21. Kwon, Y.M., Shah, S.T., Shin, J., Park, A.S., Chung, M.Y.: Performance evaluation of moving small-cell network with proactive cache. Mobile Information Systems 2016 (2016)

22. Jangsher, S., Li, V.O.: Resource allocation in cellular networks with moving small cells with probabilistic mobility. In: 2014 IEEE 25th Annual International Symposium on Personal, Indoor, and Mobile Radio Communication (PIMRC), pp. 1701–1705. IEEE (2014)

23. Jaziri, A., Nasri, R., Chahed, T.: Traffic hotspot localization in 3G and 4G wireless networks using OMC metrics. In: 2014 IEEE 25th Annual International Symposium on Personal, Indoor, and Mobile Radio Communication (PIMRC), pp. 270–274. IEEE (2014)

24. Yassin, A., Awad, M., Nasser, Y.: On the hybrid localization in heterogeneous networks with lack of hearability. In: 2013 20th International Conference on Telecommunications (ICT), pp. 1–5. IEEE (2013)

25. Radwan, A., Huq, K.M.S., Mumtaz, S., Tsang, K.F., Rodriguez, J.: Low-cost on-demand C-RAN based mobile small-cells. IEEE Access **4**, 2331–2339 (2016)

26. 3GPP: TR 22.852, 3GPP System Architecture Working Group 1 (SA1) RAN Sharing Enhancements Study Item Overall Description

27. Checko, A., et al.: Cloud RAN for mobile networks–a technology overview. IEEE Commun. Surv. Tutor. **17**(1), 405–426 (2015)

28. Carvalho, M.A., Vieira, P.: Simulating long term evolution self-optimizing based networks. i-ETC: ISEL Acad. J. Electron. Telecommun. Comput. **2**(1), 8 (2013)

Wireless Channel Characterisation over Simulations for an Indoors Environment at 2.4 GHz

Tafseer Akhtar, Ilias Politis[(✉)], and Stavros Kotsopoulos

Wireless Telecommunications Lab, University of Patras, 26500 Rio, Greece
{takhtar,ipolits,kotsop}@ece.upatras.gr

Abstract. Mobile communication is on the brink of another transformation as fifth generation networks and their architectures are already mature for deployment. As the volume and intensity of data flow drastically increases, the technologies that fuel such changes need to be evolved. Mobile small cells are going to play a key role in the deployment of these new communication infrastructures, extending the reach of wireless access. In this paper a number of path loss models for and indoors office environment are simulated using Mininet-WiFi. The channel characterization is based on a set of parameters including RSSI, SINR, latency, throughput, etc. The preliminary results indicate that ITU and multi walls multi floors models are accurate enough to be used as a basis for an intelligent, cloud based radio resource management of heterogeneous wireless mobile small cells.

Keywords: Path loss · SINR · Transmit power · Mininet-WiFi

1 Introduction

It is already clear that fifth generation (5G) networks and services are defined through a set of strict requirements such as throughput gain and consumed energy. The driving force for such dramatic evolution towards a mobile networking paradigm of higher data rates and capacity, ultra-low latency and increased resilience, is the immersive, high quality of experience and ubiquitous smart mobile applications. 5G is also rotating around the notion of multitudes of connected devices over small areas resulting in ultra-dense device-to-device communication networks that will generate and consume huge data volumes [1,2]. The 5G paradigm as it emerges in recent studies [3] and early pilots [4], adopts a number of technological solutions to form the building blocks of the next generation wireless mobile network architecture and address all these challenges [5].

This project has received funding from the European Union's Horizon 2020 research and innovation programme under the Marie Sklodowska-Curie grant agreement No 722424.

V. Sucasas et al. (Eds.): BROADNETS 2018, LNICST 263, pp. 387–397, 2019.
https://doi.org/10.1007/978-3-030-05195-2_38

Specifically, the future networking environment will be characterized by highly dense heterogeneous cells. This heterogeneity is extended not only to the diverse radio access technologies that 5G networks will incorporate (i.e., 3G, 4G, 5G, etc.) but also to the different type of cells that future wireless networks will consider, including macro, pico and small cells [6]. Cloud is already anticipated to be the cornerstone of 5G deployments and as such, Cloud-RAN is considered as a key enabler for efficient base band processing in the cloud [7]. As the future networking environment begins to materialize, it seems that the concept of cooperated small cells may provide a basis for the mobile cell architecture. SECRET project [8] aims to narrow the gap between current networking technologies and the foreseen requirements of 5G for higher networking capacity, ability to support more users, lower cost per bit, enhanced energy efficiency. SECRET project builds on current technology trends, widely accepted to form part of 5G, by aiming to a new deployment of small cells based on the notion of mobile small cells. Another dimension of innovation of SECRET is the provision of wireless fronthaul to provide high-speed reduced-cost energy-efficient connectivity to mobile small cells.

The research in the area of 5G wireless connectivity and communication follows in the steps of 4G and LTE. Evidently, the importance of channel modelling and particularly for indoors environments is still undimmed and offers opportunities for further investigation of the effect that environmental conditions (i.e., building materials, wall and floor surfaces, etc.) can have on the channel behaviour. One of the pillars of 5G networking paradigm is highly dense wireless networks, which may well be deployed indoors. Such communication system need to be developed with a specific focus on indoors propagation modelling, accounting for obstacles of various sizes, multiple walls and floors that intervene in the path of the propagated signals. Therefore, study of path loss models for indoors environments remain interesting. The recent research output has significantly contributed to novel wireless channel characterization through simulations and measurements. A keen interest has been aimed at the 2.4 GHz frequency, which concerns the 802.11b/g/n protocols. Many works have provided empirical data derived from measurements based on actual operating systems at 2.4 GHz [9,10]. Another frequency of interest is the 3.5 GHz channel. Internationally acclaimed as a WiMax frequency, the 3.5 GHz channel has also been featured in scientific works [11], which investigate the variations of the signal amplitude and phase in both indoor and outdoor scenarios. There are, however, many open issues regarding the relation of the large scale fluctuations of the received signal to the intrinsic channel characteristics and site-specific irregularities.

This paper focuses on channel characterization of an office environment through simulations using the Mininet tool with wifi extensions [12]. The simulations aims to study the fluctuation of SINR (Signal to Interference Noise Ratio) over different distances from the transmitting nodes and also measure the required energy for achieving equal SINR for all receiving wireless nodes. The results and conclusions concerning validation of already known path loss models for 2.4 GHz frequency in an indoor environment will provide the basic setup for further studies and development of more intelligent radio resource management functionalities.

The rest of the paper is organised as follows.

2   Simulation Scenario

2.1   Simulation Setup

The experiment scenario contains small cells and nodes, where small cell are acting as access point and nodes (user interface) are connected with these small cells. All the nodes are having similar features (i.e., mode, channel, working frequency, antenna height, antenna gain, etc.) and the two small cells are also similar except the transmission power capability which is varying to observe and analyse the behaviour of nodes. The varying power is used for calculating RSSI (Received Signal Strength Indicator), SINR, path loss and throughput of the whole network.

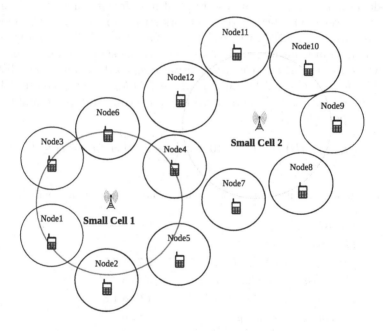

Fig. 1. Experimental network with nodes (UI) and small cells.

Mininet-WiFi tool is used for creating our experimental scenarios, in Fig. 1 the experimental network is described with all its components. There are twelve nodes and two small cells. Both the small cells are connected via a physical LAN (Local Area Network), all the nodes are only receiving the signal from small cells, and not transmitting any signal (downlink only). The distance between small cells is fixed and they are continuously transmitting the signal to the connected nodes. Every node is connected to only one small cell depending on the attributes of small cell in the range. There is no interference effect between any nodes as they are acting as receiver only. Mininet-WiFi is a SDN based emulator which uses mac80211_hwsim Linux kernel module for simulating the IEEE 802.11 radio device, which enables it for more accurate results and close real device behaviour.

2.2 Configurations of Path Loss Models

In Mininet-WiFi there are several path loss models which can be used for analysing the behaviour of experimental network, some of them are for open space and few are for the indoor environment. These are the path loss model we have considered for analysing the behaviour of our experimental network.

Log Distance Path Loss Model. Log distance path loss model is an extension of Frills free space path loss model and it is a generic model that can be used for outdoor environment. It can also be used in different kinds of environment where obstacles can also be a part of network structure. For far field region the transmitter distance $PL(d_0)$, where $d \geq d_f$, is path loss calculated in dB. At the distance (d_0) from transmitter, path loss (loss in the signal power is calculated in dB where movement happens from distance d_0 to d) at any given distance where $d > d_0$, is measured by Eq. (1), where $PL(d_0)$ is Path Loss in dB at a distance d_0, $PL_{d_0 \to d}$ is Path Loss in dB at an arbitrary distance d and n is the Path Loss exponent.

$$PL_{d_0 \to d}(dB) = PL_{d_0} + 10n \log\left(\frac{d}{d_0}\right), \text{ where } d_f \leq d_0 \leq d \qquad (1)$$

Table 1. Path loss exponent for various environments for log distance path loss model.

Environment	Path loss exponent (n)
Free space	2
Urban area cellular radio	2.7 to 3.5
Shadowed urban cellular radio	3 to 5
Inside a building-Line of Sight (LOS)	1.6 to 1.8
Obstructed in building	4 to 6
Obstructed in factory	2 to 3

Table 1 describes the values of path loss exponent that we can used for designing the network, in various kind of environment using Log distance path loss model. Path Loss Exponent (PLE) value depends upon the actual environment that we are modelling. PLE estimation needs empirical values which are collected over different time instants and the values provided here are for reference purpose.

Log Normal Shadowing Model. Log normal shadowing model is similar to the log distance model but in here we also consider the shadowing effect which makes it more practical and accurate compare to log distance model. It is an extension to log distance model where a new variable χ will come into play and added to the Eq. (1) of Log distance path loss calculation. In the real environment scenario the shadowing effect always exists, the path loss is calculated as in Eq. (2).

$$PL_{d_0 \to d}(dB) = PL_{d_0} + 10n \log\left(\frac{d}{d_0}\right) + \chi, \text{ where } d_f \leq d_0 \leq d \qquad (2)$$

In (2) χ is zero-mean Gaussian distributed random variable (in dB) with standard deviation (σ), the variable came into picture when shadowing effect exists. When there is no shadowing effect, the value of this variable is 0. The exponent and deviation of the random variable must be precisely known for modelling the network.

ITU Indoor Propagation Model. The International Telecommunication Union (ITU) path loss model is developed for the indoor environment. It is a radio propagation path loss model that estimates losses inside any closed area in a building surrounded by the walls, which is very appropriate for designing the appliances for indoor environment. The path loss depends upon many different parameters and it is calculated by using Eq. (3) in which L is the total path loss in dB, f is the frequency of transmission in MHz, d is the distance in meters, N is the distance power loss coefficient, n is the number of floors between the transmitter and receiver and $P_f(n)$ is the floor loss penetration factor.

$$PL_{d_0 \to d}(dB) = 20 \log(f) + N \log(d) + P_f(n) - 28 \qquad (3)$$

The calculation of the distance power loss coefficient (N) is based on the frequency range depicted in Table 2.

Table 2. Distance power loss coefficient (N) for ITU path loss model.

Frequency band	Residential area	Office area	Commercial area
900 MHz	N/A	33	20
1.2–1.3 GHz	N/A	32	22
1.8–2.0 GHz	28	30	22
4 GHz	N/A	28	22
5.2 GHz	30 (Apartment), 28 (House)	31	N/A
5.8 GHz	N/A	24	N/A
60 GHz	N/A	22	17

Floor loss penetration factor is also a crucial element for calculating the path loss the calculation of which is summarised in Table 3.

Table 3. Floor loss penetration factor (Pf) for ITU path loss model

Frequency band	No of floors	Residential area	Office area	Commercial area
900 MHz	1	N/A	9	N/A
1.2–1.3 GHz	2	N/A	19	N/A
1.8–2.0 GHz	3	N/A	24	N/A
4 GHz	N	4n	$15 + 4(n-1)$	$6 + 3(n-1)$
5.2 GHz	1	N/A	16	N/A
5.8 GHz	1	N/A	22(1 floor), 28(2 floor)	N/A

ITU path loss model is used mostly for indoor environments. Appliances that use the lower bands (2.4 GHz) are preferred for this model, however it is applicable to a much wider frequency range.

Multi Wall and Floor Propagation Model. For multi wall and multi floor environment the WINNER II channel model is used for calculating path loss. It is based on the stochastic geometry approach which has double direction radio channel model. It has both line of sight (LOS) and non LOS (NLOS) models parameters for various environments, in our experimental setup we are using NLOS model for calculating path loss. For calculating the path loss, the Eq. (4) is used. In (4), d is the distance between transmitter and receiver in meters, f is the channel frequency in GHz, A is the path-loss exponent, B is the intercept, C is the path loss frequency dependence, X is the environment-specific value (i.e., wall attenuation, etc.), FL is the floor loss, n_w is the number of walls between source and destination and n_f is the number of floors between source and destination.

$$PL(dB) = A \log (d) + B + C \log \left(\frac{f}{5}\right) + X + FL \qquad (4)$$

$$X = 12 n_w$$
$$FL = 17 + 4 (n_f - 1)$$
$$n_f > 0$$

For the specific experiment scenario the values for various parameters are fixed and displayed in Table 4.

Table 4. Various fixed parameters for multi walls and floors propagation path loss model

Parameter	Value
Path loss exponent (A)	20
Intercept value (B)	46.4
Frequency dependence (C)	20
Number of walls (nw)	2
Number of floors (nf)	1

All these four path loss model are consider for the analysing the experimental network where our objective is to find the best path loss model which is suitable for small cell environment where the energy loss is minimum and the results closely emulate the real network environments.

3 Results and Discussion

In Mininet-WiFi for developing the experimental scenario, many parameters of nodes (UI) and small cell (Access point) are fixed and same values are used throughout the network. Table 5 showcases these parameters.

Table 5. Various fixed parameters of experimental setup

Simulation parameter	Value
Total small cells	2
Total nodes (UIs)	12
Working frequency (GHz)	2.41
Channel mode	a
Antenna height (m)	1
Antenna gain	5
Channel used	36
Fading coefficient	6
Path loss exponent	3.5
Noise threshold (dB)	−91

3.1 Transmission Power for Achieving Minimum Acceptable SINR

In the experiment, all four path loss models are considered, where transmission power is changed from low to high with respect of distance between node and connected small cell to achieve minimum acceptable SINR (20 dB). The minimum acceptable SINR is needed between source and destination for efficient communication. As the distance between small cell (source) and destination (node) increases the need of transmission power also increase.

In Fig. 3, transmission power of small cell varies from low value to its highest value (which is 20 dBm) to achieve minimum SINR with respect to distance between small cell and connected node. In Log distance and Log normal shadowing the behaviour is almost similar with little variation where with the low value of transmission power, 10 m distance or less is receiving minimum SINR value and they progress almost linearly. The maximum distance they can reach with the maximum transmission power (20 dBm) is around 40 m in both the cases. ITU model shows different behaviour from Log distance and Log normal shadowing path loss model, which is designed for indoor environments, and is suitable for our experimental lab setup. ITU model requires very less power to cover the distance around 15 m for minimum SINR but after that it moves very slowly to cover more distance for minimum SINR. For covering 20 m distance it requires around 15 dBm and it barely reaches 30 m distance when maximum transmission power is applied to achieve minimum SINR. Multi walls and floors model from WINNER II model shows more acceptable behaviour and it is also suitable path loss model for indoor environment and effective for our experimental setup. Here for the coverage of 10 m distance to achieve minimum SINR, it needs around 10 dBm and from that point, it varies almost linearly. The maximum distance coverage is just above 30 m when maximum transmission power is applied. Evidently, after comparing and analysing these four path loss model, we can observe that Multi walls and floors model is most suitable for our experimental scenario as it closely emulated the real network environment.

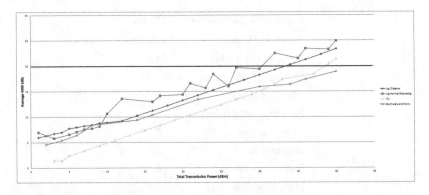

Fig. 2. Comparison of propagation models when combined power of small cell varies to change average SINR

3.2 Total Transmission Power and Average SINR

All the path loss models are compared for analysing the average SINR when the nodes are stationary and only transmission power is varying to control the network. The result of various path loss model is shown in Fig. 2, all four path loss models are compared on the basis of total transmission power and respective average SINR received by the network. The plot includes the total transmission power of both small cells, average SINRand the minimum acceptable SINR (20 dB).

It can be seen that the Log distance model varies linearly after the total power reaches the point around 15 dBm and it achieve maximum 23 dB average SINR when maximum power is applied (40 dBm). The behaviour of Log normal shadowing is irregular and it progresses with the increase in total power non-uniformly, although it achieve highest level of average SINR (25 dB) when maximum power is applied. The behaviour of the ITU model is uniform and it varies linearly from the start and barely reaches above acceptable SINR value when maximum transmission power is applied. Multi walls and floors model performs almost linearly with the increase of transmission power. Although the progress is very slow and it never achieves the average minimum SINR threshold even after applying the maximum transmission power. The comparison of these results leads to the conclusion that the ITU and Multi walls and floors models are more accurate than Log distance and Log normal shadowing models when used in the specific conditions. Hence, these results indicate that the ITU and Multi walls and floors models could be potentially be applied for realizing the network for further analysis and development of intelligent resource management techniques in an effort to maximise quality of experience for wireless users while minimising the energy consumption.

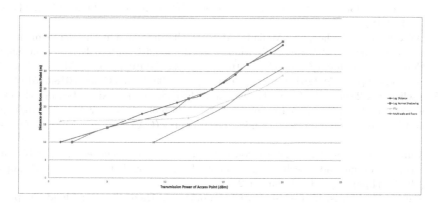

Fig. 3. Comparison of propagation models when combined power of small cell varies to change average SINR

4   Conclusions

The 5G era imposes a set of strict requirements for achieving ultra-low latency, high reliability and high throughputs across wireless mobile devices. Such requirements are more difficult to achieve in densely connected networks. The research studies of path loss models in indoors environments will need to be revisited in an effort to produce more accurate models. Accurate channel characterisation models would pave the road for precise and efficient resource management. Towards this end SECRET project aims to develop efficient radio resource management schemes based on accurate channel characterization in indoors and outdoors environments for provind mobile small cells with maximum quality of experience levels with the minimum energy consumption. This paper proposed Mininet-WiFi as a tool for simulating channel conditions and to this end, it compares a number of native to Mininet-WiFi and newly configured path loss models. The comparison indicates that both the ITU and the Multi walls and multi floors models are accurate enough to form the basis for the future developments.

References

1. Politis, I., Tselios, C., Lykourgiotis, A., Kotsopoulos, S.: On optimizing scalable video delivery over media aware mobile clouds. In: 2017 IEEE International Conference on Communications (ICC), pp. 1–6, May 2017
2. Vlachos, E., Lalos, A.S., Berberidis, K., Tselios, C.: Autonomous driving in 5G: mitigating interference in OFDM-based vehicular communications. In: 2017 IEEE 22nd International Workshop on Computer Aided Modeling and Design of Communication Links and Networks (CAMAD), Lund, pp. 1–6 (2017). https://doi.org/10.1109/CAMAD.2017.8031619
3. Bianchi, G., Biton, E., Blefari-Melazzi, N., et al.: Superfluidity: a flexible functional architecture for 5G networks. Trans. Emerg. Telecommun. Technol. **27**(9), 1178–1186 (2016)
4. Bolivar, L.T., Tselios, C., Mellado Area, D., Tsolis, G.: On the deployment of an open-source, 5G-aware evaluation testbed. In: 2018 6th IEEE International Conference on Mobile Cloud Computing, Services, and Engineering (MobileCloud), Bamberg, pp. 51–58 (2018). https://doi.org/10.1109/MobileCloud.2018.00016
5. Tselios, C., Tsolis, G.: On QoE-awareness through virtualized probes in 5G networks. In: 2016 IEEE 21st International Workshop on Computer Aided Modelling and Design of Communication Links and Networks (CAMAD), pp. 159–164, October 2016
6. Mumtaz, S., et al.: Self-organization towards reduced cost and energy per bit for future emerging radio technologies-sonnet. In: 2017 IEEE Globecom Workshops (GC Wkshps), pp. 1–6, December 2017
7. Tselios, C., Politis, I., Tselios, V., Kotsopoulos, S., Dagiuklas, T.: Cloud computing: a great revenue opportunity for telecommunication industry. In: 51st FITCE Congress (FITCE), vol. 6, Poznan, Poland
8. Rodriguez, J., et al.: SECRET - Secure network coding for reduced energy next generation mobile small cells: a European Training Network in wireless communications and networking for 5G. In: 2017 Internet Technologies and Applications (ITA), pp. 329–333, September 2017
9. Oestges, C., Castiglione, P., Czink, N.: Empirical modeling of nomadic peer-to-peer networks in office environment. In: IEEE Vehicular Technology Conference (VTC 2011-Spring), Budapest, Hungary, 15–18 May 2011
10. Quitin, F., Oestges, C., Horlin, F., De Doncker, P.: Polarization measurements and modeling in indoor NLOS environments. IEEE Trans. Wirel. Commun. **9**(1), 21–25 (2010)

11. Milanovic, J., Rimac-Drlje, S., Bejuk, K.: Comparison of Propagation Models Accuracy for WiMAX on 3.5 GHz. In: 14th IEEE International Conference on Electronics, Circuits and Systems (ICECS 2007), Marrakech, Morocco, 11–14 December 2007
12. Fontes, R.R., Afzal, S., Brito, S.H.B., Santos, M., Rothenberg, C.E.: Mininet-WiFi: emulating software-defined wireless networks. In: 2nd International Workshop on Management of SDN and NFV Systems 2015, Barcelona, Spain, November 2015

A Simulation Study on LTE Handover and the Impact of Cell Size

Muhammad Tayyab[1](⊠), George P. Koudouridis[2], and Xavier Gelabert[2]

[1] Huawei Technologies Finland Oy, Itämerenkatu 9, 00180 Helsinki, Finland
muhammad.tayyab5@huawei.com
[2] Huawei Technologies Sweden AB, Skalholtsgatan 9, 16494 Kista, Sweden

Abstract. In this paper we address the impact of cell size on the handover procedure in a Long Term Evolution (LTE) network. In particular, we highlight the potential problems that may occur when small cell densification is applied. In addition, the impact of the User Equipment (UE) speed is also analyzed. System level simulations are provided using a detailed LTE network simulator accounting for multiple points-of-failure and channel modeling compliant with LTE standards. We conclude that a certain cell size can be found around which any increase or decrease of the cell size brings performance degradations due to different limitations in the uplink. The performance is also degraded as UE speed increases, especially for small cell sizes. And for large cell sizes, we note that low speed UEs handover failures may rise due to the inability to "escape" from a poor radio condition area.

Keywords: LTE · Handover · Performance evaluation · Simulation

1 Introduction

While the development of future cellular networks is often driven by the need for increased bit rates to support data-hungry applications, of equal importance is to provide reliable handover (HO) mechanisms as this directly impacts on the perceived quality of experience (QoE) for the end user. This is particularly true when, in order to provide such increased bit rates, we resort to the deployment of small cell networks in order to boost the capacity in a given area [1]. Cell densification has proven to be a spectral efficient method to increase capacity and has received large attention in recent years (see [2] and references therein). In addition to high data rate demands, networks will need to provide their services to users on the move, probably more so and at higher speeds with the appearance of new transport paradigms such as self-driving vehicles where the user, no longer at the steering wheel, may use that time for digital content consumption. With this in mind, in this paper we will address the impact of cell density and UE speed on the handover procedure in a Long Term Evolution (LTE) network.

While the study of the impact of cell size on the handover procedure is not new, the vast majority of the existing works are devoted to analyze the impact of small cell densification as opposed to a wider analysis covering a range of inter site distances (ISD). Moreover, a large number of works adopt a theoretical approach and, while interesting

© ICST Institute for Computer Sciences, Social Informatics and Telecommunications Engineering 2019
Published by Springer Nature Switzerland AG 2019. All Rights Reserved
V. Sucasas et al. (Eds.): BROADNETS 2018, LNICST 263, pp. 398–408, 2019.
https://doi.org/10.1007/978-3-030-05195-2_39

insights can be provided, there is sometimes a lack of fidelity with respect to the standard which causes that some effects are not appropriately captured. In particular the field of Stochastic Geometry has been in recent years used to model the impact of handover in dense small cell networks see for example [3–6]. Such works lack on capturing effects such as handover failures, and consequent re-establishment and cell-reselection procedures, Radio Link Control (RLC) failures and corresponding retransmissions, etc. In addition, a simulation-based approach is more appropriate to capture the details of the LTE standard. In [7], the performance of handover in dense small HetNets is discussed, i.e. considering an overlapping deployment of both macro and pico cells. In [8], authors examine and evaluate the impact of small cell deployments on mobility performance in LTE-systems. Analysis is done through system level simulations in various scenarios with macro and small cell overlaid deployments. In this paper we focus not only on the problems caused by higher densification but also the problems faced when the cell size increases. Detailed system level simulations considering a wide range of potential failure points are provided.

The rest of the paper is organized as follows: Sect. 2 provides an overview of the handover mechanism in LTE. Section 3 discusses the simulator implementation and modelling aspects. In Sect. 4, numerical results and discussion are given on the performance of LTE handover. Section 5 provides some concluding remarks.

2 Handover Mechanism in LTE

Handover (HO) management is a relevant research point in cellular networks. The overall HO decision procedure in LTE is illustrated in Fig. 1 [9], and consists of four major steps. Firstly, the UE performs downlink (DL) signal strength measurements from both the serving eNBs and other neighboring eNBs. Within the context of HO the serving eNB is referred to as the source eNB or serving cell, while the neighboring eNBs are referred to as the target eNBs or target cell. In the second step these measurements are processed at the UE, and in the third step a measurement reports (measReport) is transferred to the serving eNB. In the fourth and final step, based on the measReport, the serving eNB makes the HO decision and sends a HO request message to the target eNB.

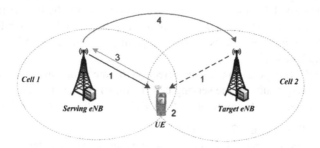

Fig. 1. HO process in 3GPP LTE [9].

The UE and eNB actions related to Radio Resource Management (RRM) procedures for the HO execution constitute the mechanisms for mobility control. In general, mobility control is divided into two stages, mobility control in RRC_IDLE state, which is referred to as cell reselection, and mobility control in RRC_CONNECTED state, which is referred to as handover. In this paper, we are focusing on mobility in RRC_CONNECTED state.

2.1 Mobility Control in RRC_CONNECTED (Handover)

There are two different types of actions that a UE has to perform in RRC_CONNECTED according to the requirements. The first type is, upon measuring and identifying a better neighboring cell than the serving cell, UE reports to the serving eNB and access the target cell on reception of HO command (from serving eNB). The UE performs signal strength measurements over specific reference signal received power (RSRP) from the serving cell as well as the neighboring cells. After processing the measurements, including filtering at layers L1 and L3, if an entry condition is fulfilled, a measurement report (measReport) is triggered to the serving cell. A3 event is used as entry condition to see if the filtered RSRP of the target cell is better than that of the serving cell plus a hysteresis margin (called A3 offset). The entry condition has to be maintained during a time defined by the Time to Trigger (TTT) timer. Once the measReport is correctly received at the serving cell, the HO preparation phase between target and serving cell starts which also includes admission control procedures. Upon successful admission, the target cell acknowledges the HO request sent by the serving cell and prepares for HO. Data forwarding starts between the serving and target cell and a HO command (HOcmd) is sent from the serving cell to the UE. Upon successful reception of the HOcmd, the HO execution phase starts in which the UE accesses the target cell, by means of a random Access Channel (RACH) procedure, and delivers a HO confirmation (HOconf) message. Random access procedure takes two different forms, contention-based and contention-free RACH. In contention based RACH procedure, UE selects a random preamble and start transmission to the target eNB. But there is a chance of preamble collision due to the same preamble from multiple UEs. So, the network has to go through an additional process called contention resolution which is time consuming. In contention-free RACH procedure, the network informs each UE regarding when and which preamble it has to use. To initiate the contention-free RACH process, UE should be in connected mode before the RACH process as in HO case. In order to achieve a good compromise between HO reliability and HO frequency, HO optimization deals with the adjustment of the TTT, A3 offset, and the L3 filter coefficient K [7].

The second type of action is the detection of the radio link failure (RLF) by monitoring the DL quality of the serving cell. Upon RLF detection, the UE selects the best target cell and gets its information for RRC connection re-establishment.

Evaluation of Radio Link Failure (RLF)

In RRC connected state, radio link monitoring enables the UE to determine whether it is in-sync or out-of-sync with respect to its serving cell. On getting consecutive number of out-of-sync indications, UE starts an RLF timer `T310´ as shown in Fig. 2. Both in-sync and out-of-sync (N311 and N310) counters are configured by the network based on the associated in-sync threshold Q_{in} and out-of-sync threshold Q_{out} corresponding to 2% and 10% Block Error Rate (BLER), respectively. The timer stops when a number of consecutive in-sync (N311) indications are reported (case 2 in Fig. 2). If T310 expires, RLF occurs and UE turns off its transmission to avoid interference and try to re-establish a connection within a UE connection re-establishment delay (case 1 in Fig. 2). If the DL radio link quality becomes worse than Q_{out} within a 200 ms period, then out-of-sync occurs. Whilst, in-sync occurs when the DL radio link quality becomes better than Q_{in} within a 100 ms period. These occurrences are reported by the UE to the physical layer and higher layers which may apply L3 filtering for evaluation of RLF [10].

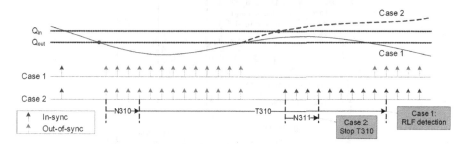

Fig. 2. RLF detection

An overall view of the HO procedure is shown in Fig. 3 [11], which can be divided into 3 phases: HO preparation (0–6), HO execution (7–11) and HO completion (12–14).

3 System Simulation Models

The used LTE simulator considers a hexagonal grid of 16 tri-sectored eNBs. Cell wrap-around feature is included in order to ensure fair interference conditions across the scenario. UEs are randomly placed over the scenario and the mobility model is such that UEs move at fixed speed in straight lines with random directions [0°, 360°].

As for traffic loading, UEs with UL full-buffer traffic are assumed, thus contributing to UL interference towards other UEs. DL interference is artificially generated by setting the transmission power on a number of randomly selected Physical Resource Blocks (PRBs) given a specific load level (in our case a fully loaded case is assumed).

The simulator implements the main features of the Packet Data Convergence Protocol (PDCP), Radio Link Control (RLC), Medium Access Control (MAC) and physical (PHY) layers including, inter alia, segmentation, Automatic Repeat Request (ARQ) at RLC level, and MAC scheduling with chase combined Hybrid-ARQ (HARQ). For the PHY layer, look-up tables are used which map bit error rate (BER) values to measured subcarrier Signal-to-Interference-and-noise-ratio (SINR) values (via the EESM, Effective Exponential SNR Mapping) in order to account for errors over the wireless link.

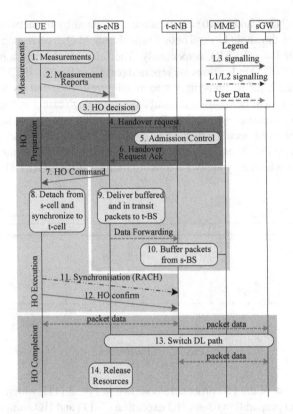

Fig. 3. Intra MME/SG HO procedure (adapted from [11]).

The HO model considers the modelling of L3 RRC signaling over the radio access, including measurement reports, handover command and handover confirmation. L2 signaling (UL and DL allocation) is also captured by modelling the PDCCH. Both L2 and L3 signaling are subject to channel impairments and thus prone to RLC failures.

Moreover, see Sect. 2.1, RLFs are also considered in the simulator with full modeling of the in-sync/out-of-sync states via counters N310, N311 and timer T310.

Summarizing, handover failures (HOF) are captured in the simulator falling into the following categories, with failure points being defined in Table 1.

1. RLF declared by L1 at the UE after timer T310 expiry [12, Sect. 7.3].
2. RLC is unable to deliver a Radio Resource Control (RRC) message after a (max.) number of transmission attempts. Applies to measReport and HOconf messages.
3. RACH failure after timer T304 expiry [12, Sect. 7.3].

The main simulation assumptions are summarized in Table 2.

Table 1. Simulated failure points.

Failure point	Description
F0	T310 expiry before measReport triggered
F1	T310 expiry before measReport received
F2	RLC measReport transmission error
F3	T310 expiry before HOcmd transmission
F4	T310 expiry before HOcmd reception
F5	RACH failure after T304 expiry
F6	T310 expiry before HOconf received
F7	RLC HOconf transmission error

Table 2. Simulation parameters and assumptions.

Feature	Implementation
Network topology	Hexagonal grid of $16 \times 3 = 48$ cells (wrap-around included)
Inter-site distance	From the set {125, 250, 375, 500, 625, 750, 1000, 1250} m
Bandwidth	5 MHz FDD at 2.6 GHz
eNB DL power	43 dBm
Antenna patterns	3D model specified in [13], Table A.2.1.1.2-2
Channel model	6 tap model, Typical Urban (TU)
Shadowing	Log-normal Shadowing Mean 0 dB, Standard deviation: 8 dB
Propagation model	$L = 130.5 + 37.6 \log_{10}(R)$, R in km
UE speed	From the set {3, 30, 60, 120} km/h
RLF detection by L1 of UE	T310 = 1 s, N310 = 1, N311 = 1 as specified in [12] $Q_{in} = -4.8$ dB; $Q_{out} = -7.2$ dB as specified in [14]
HO parameters	TTT = 64 ms, A3 offset = 3 dB, L3 filter coefficient K = 4

4 Performance Evaluation

In this section we provide a numerical evaluation of the HO procedure under different conditions of cell density and UE speed. First, we start with some metric definitions.

4.1 Metrics

HO performance metric definition follows the guidelines in [15, Sect. 5.4.2]. The HO rate (HOR), measured in HO events/s, is defined as the total number of triggered HO events divided by the simulation time (60 s). Similarly, the HO failure ratio (HOFR), measured in %, is defined as the total number of HO failure events divided by the total number of triggered HO events. The ping pong rate (PPR) is defined as the number of ping pong events during a given period of time. In turn, we define a ping pong event as the occurrence of a HO between a source cell and a target cell, followed by another HO to the original source cell, all this happening under a predefined time set to 3 s. Finally, we define the mean time between handovers (MTBH) as the ratio between the total simulation time and the number of triggered HO events.

4.2   Numerical Evaluation

Figure 4 illustrates the handover rate (measured in number of HOs per second) against the ISD and for different UE speeds. As expected, increasing the density of eNBs (lower ISD) results in an increase of HOs due to the increased number of cell borders. This rate notably increases when the ISD falls below 250 m. Also expected is the increase of the HO rate with UE speed. In addition, an increase of the HO rate is also noted for increased ISD values, see ISD = {750, 1000, 1250}. The reason for this will become apparent when analyzing the different channel conditions impacting these deployments.

Next we drive our attention to the handover failure ratio (HFR), i.e. the percentage of those handovers which for one reason or another experienced problems and could not be completed seamlessly. Figure 5 illustrates the HFR against the ISD for different UE speeds. Both lowering and increasing the ISD have negative effects, i.e. increased HFR. For low ISD, failure arises due to adverse channel conditions due to excessive interference from neighbor UEs. Further insights on this will be provided later on. In addition, increasing UE speed contributes to HFR for lower ISDs (125 m, 250 m and 375 m). We can argue that for small cells, higher UE speeds will cause moving away from the source cell which may cause problems during handover. For larger ISDs, 1 km and above, HFR also increases. This is again due to channel adversity as it will become apparent later on. In this case however, we note how the UE speed impact is reversed as compared to the low ISD case. For larger cells, "higher UE speed helps to escape from the cell border". Noteworthy, despite suffering handover failure, LTE implements re-establishment/cell-reselection mechanisms so as to recover the connection with the UE. However, this re-establishment comes at the cost of increased delay and interruption time.

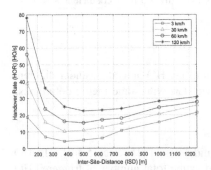

Fig. 4. Handover Rate (HOs/s) against the ISD for different speed values.

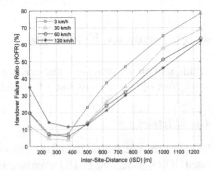

Fig. 5. Handover Failure Ratio (HOFR) in % against the ISD for different speed values.

Figure 6 shows the HO failure breakdown per type F0 to F7. An overall trend is that failures seem to concentrate on UL transmission errors (RLC timer/max. retransmissions expires). For high ISDs, a common failure is that of RACH failure which is due to the poor UL radio conditions for UEs close to cell borders in large cells. Notably at medium to high ISDs, higher failures are noted for lower speeds, indicating that the low speed is not enough to "escape" from these areas with poor conditions. F4 (T310 expiry before HOcmd reception) is very frequent when ISD is small and low when the ISD increases, whereas F5 (RACH failure after T304 expiry) is very frequent for large ISD and very low for small ISDs. The motivation is that, for small cell sizes, the UEs that are able to transmit the measurement report subsequently move out of the serving cell coverage and thus the HO command, sent by the serving cell, cannot reach the UE. For the RACH failures due to T304 expiry for large cells, the UEs transmitted power at the border of the cell compromises the success of the handover.

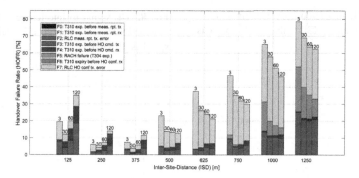

Fig. 6. Handover Failure Ratio (HOFR) in % against the ISD for different speed values. HO failure type breakdown: F0...F7.

To find an explanation to the different HO failure cases we resort to the uplink interference and uplink signal-to-noise plus interference ratio. Below the uplink interference-over-thermal noise ratio and the uplink SINR are plotted in Figs. 7 and 8 respectively. As we see, low ISD (i.e. 125 m) suffer from sever interference in the uplink since UEs are more likely to be closer to each other. However, these same UEs at lower ISDs suffer from better UL SINR conditions (see Fig. 8), since UEs are closer to the eNBs and thus the received power at those can partially compensate for the interference. On the contrary, deployments with larger ISD suffer less interference.

The ping pong rate is presented in Fig. 9. Ping pong events reflect the channel variability conditions, which cause HOs between two neighboring cells given successive A3 events being triggered. Ping pong events can also appear as the consequence of failed HOs to neighboring cells, and the subsequent efforts to reconnect the UE to neighboring cells even if not the most adequate at that time. Accordingly, both low and high ISDs seem to be prone to ping pong events due to channel quality impairments and subsequent HO failures (as already noted in Figs. 6, 7 and 8). An equivalent metric to the ping pong rate is that of the mean elapsed time between handovers (MTBH) which is illustrated in Fig. 10. More frequent handovers (i.e. lower MTBH) is noted for both low and high ISD values for the same reasons explained above. As expected, increasing UE speed results in both increased ping pong events and lower MTBH.

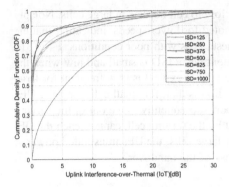

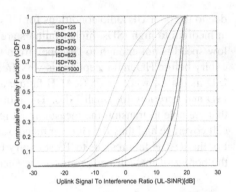

Fig. 7. UL interference-over-thermal noise ratio for different ISD values. UE speed is 30 km/h.

Fig. 8. UL signal to interference plus noise ratio (SINR) for different ISD values. UE speed is 30 km/h.

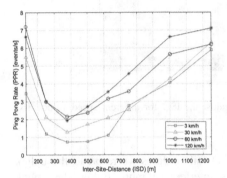

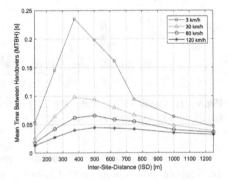

Fig. 9. Ping pong rate against ISD for different speed values.

Fig. 10. Mean time between HOs (MTBH) against ISD for different speed values.

In the above, we have addressed the HO performance in terms of HOF and its causes. Noteworthy, LTE implements reestablishment and cell reselection mechanisms so as to recover from the suffered failures in the shortest time possible. Hence, noting that during part of the HO process, including the reestablishment procedure, the data plane will be unable to deliver packets to and from the UE, it seems reasonable to measure the elapsed time of this event. To this end, we define the HO interruption time (HOIT) as the time whereby the user plane is unable to deliver packets to and from the UE.

Figure 11 shows the empirical cumulative density function (CDF) for the HOIT for different UE speeds and fixed ISD of 250 m. We observe how lower UE speeds benefit from lower HO interruption times, since fewer failures during the handover process are noted in this case (see e.g. Fig. 6). Note also how the HO interruption time is lower bounded thus preventing the curves to reach the 0 ms mark.

Next in Fig. 12 we show the empirical CDF of the HOIT for different ISDs and for a fixed UE speed of 30 km/h. Not surprisingly, HOIT increases both when the ISD is

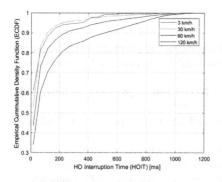

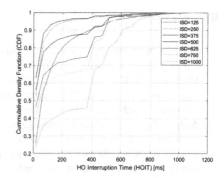

Fig. 11. Empirical cumulative density function (CDF) of the HO interruption time for different UE speeds. ISD = 250 m.

Fig. 12. Empirical cumulative density function (CDF) of the HO interruption time for different ISDs. UE speed = 30 km/h.

small (ISD = 125 m) and when it is larger (ISD = 1000). As mentioned earlier, both low and high ISDs involve different types of handover failures which in turn drive the MTBH to larger values in order to recover from such failures.

5 Conclusions

In this paper we have presented an in-depth simulation analysis on the causes for handover failure in an LTE network when different cell sizes are considered. In addition, the impact of the UE speed has also been assessed. Results show that a certain cell size can be found around which any increase or decrease of the cell size brings performance degradations due to different limitations in the uplink. For small cells, both the increased UL interference due to the proximity of neighboring UE and the higher rate of cell border crossings produce a severe handover degradation. For larger cells, the received power from the UE at the cell border is weak thus UL transmissions are impaired due to poor SINR. In addition, we also note a general degradation of the performance as UE speed increases, especially for small cell sizes. However, for large cell sizes we note that very low UE speeds handover failures may rise due to the inability to "escape" from a poor radio condition area. Future work will be devoted to analyzing the possible improvements via the optimization of the main handover parameters and by also reducing some failure points such as the measurement report transmission by having the network perform UE measurements and decide based on those whether or not to perform a handover.

Acknowledgments. This project has received funding from the European Union's H2020 research and innovation program under grant agreement H2020-MCSA-ITN- 2016-SECRET 722424.

References

1. Gelabert, X., Legg, P., Qvarfordt, C.: Small cell densification requirements in high capacity future cellular networks. In: 2013 IEEE International Conference on Communications Workshops (ICC), pp. 1112–1116 (2013)
2. Anpalagan, A., Bennis, M., Vannithamby, R.: Design and Deployment of Small Cell Networks. Cambridge University Press, Cambridge (2015)
3. Arshad, R., et al.: Handover management in 5G and beyond: a topology aware skipping approach. IEEE Access **4**, 9073 (2016)
4. Arshad, R., et al.: Handover management in dense cellular networks: a stochastic geometry approach. In: 2016 IEEE International Conference on Communications (ICC) (2016)
5. Lin, X., Ganti, R.K., Fleming, P.J., Andrews, J.G.: Towards understanding the fundamentals of mobility in cellular networks. IEEE Trans. Wirel. Commun. **12**(4), 1686–1698 (2013)
6. Bao, W., Liang, B.: Stochastic geometric analysis of user mobility in heterogeneous wireless networks. IEEE J. Sel. Areas Commun. **33**(10), 2212–2225 (2015)
7. Gelabert, X., Zhou, G., Legg, P.: Mobility performance and suitability of macro cell power-off in LTE dense small cell HetNets. In: IEEE 18th International Workshop on Computer Aided Modeling and Design of Communication Links and Networks (CAMAD), pp. 99–103 (2013)
8. Yamamoto, T., Konishi, S.: Impact of small cell deployments on mobility performance in LTE-advanced systems. In: 2013 IEEE 24th International Symposium on Personal, Indoor and Mobile Radio Communications (PIMRC Workshops), pp. 189–193 (2013)
9. Ulvan, A., Bestak, R., Ulvan, M.: The study of handover procedure in LTE-based femtocell network. In: Third Joint IFIP IEEE Wireless and Mobile Networking Conference (WMNC), October 2010
10. Sesia, S., Toufik, I., Baker, M.: LTE the UMTS Long Term Evolution: From Theory to Practice, 2nd edn., pp. 503–529. Wiley, Chichester (2011)
11. 3GPP TS 36.300. (E-UTRA) and (E-UTRAN); Overall description; Stage 2 (Release 15), V15.0.0, Section 10, pp. 93–143, December 2017
12. 3GPP TS 36.331. E-UTRA Radio Resource Control (RRC); Protocol specification (Release 9), v9.2.0, March 2010
13. 3GPP TR 36.814. Further advancements for E-UTRA physical layer aspects (Release 9), V9.0.0, March 2011
14. 3GPP TS 36.133. Requirements for support of radio resource management (Release 9), v9.15.0, March 2013
15. 3GPP TR 36.839 V11.1.0. Mobility enhancements in heterogeneous networks (Release 11), December 2012

The Performance of SLNR Beamformers in Multi-user MIMO Systems

Khalid W. Hameed[1,2], Ahmed M. Abdulkhaleq[1,2], Yasir Al-Yasir[1],
Naser Ojaroudi Parchin[1], Ashwain Rayit[3], Majid Al Khambashi[4],
Raed A. Abd-Alhameed[1(✉)], and James M. Noras[1]

[1] Bradford University, Bradford BD7 1DP, UK
r.a.a.abd@bradford.ac.uk
[2] Al-Nahrain University, Baghdad, Iraq
[3] SARAS Technology Limited, Leeds LS12 4NQ, UK
[4] Al-Zahra College for Women, Muscat, Oman

Abstract. Beamforming in multi-user MIMO (MU-MIMO) systems is a vital part of modern wireless communication systems. Researchers looking for best operational performance normally optimize the problem and then solve for best weight solutions. The weight optimization problem contains variables in numerator and dominator: this leads to so-called variable coupling, making the problem hard to solve. Formulating the optimization in terms of the signal to leakage and noise ratio (SLNR) helps in decoupling the problem variables. In this paper we study the performance of the SLNR with variable numbers of users and handset antennas. The results show that there is an optimum and the capacity curve is a concave over these two parameters. The performances of two further variations of this method are also considered.

Keywords: Beamforming · Generalized eigenvalue decomposition
MU-MIMO · Optimal point · SLNR

1 Introduction

There are steadily increasing demands for higher data rates and channel capacity, with MIMO systems a strong possible solution for higher capacity without increased power transmission. MIMO includes SISO, MISO and SIMO configurations, with variations such as point-to-point [1], multi-user (MU-MIMO) [2] and network or multi-cell MIMO [3].

Though MU-MIMO resembles point-to-point transmission in depending on the state of the channel to transmit signals, it differs in the decoding procedure, with users usually assumed to be non-cooperating. MU-MIMO also depends on the diversity between users to achieve multiplexing between transmissions to users sharing the same time-frequency resource. This is achieved by precoding, also called beamforming.

The simplest beamforming strategy is the zero forcing (ZF) or channel inversion method [4]. This basic method suffers from poor performance at high noise figures, and can be enhanced using regularized ZF [5], sometimes called MMSE [6]; however, some dimensional constraints need to be satisfied, such that the total number of receiving

© ICST Institute for Computer Sciences, Social Informatics and Telecommunications Engineering 2019
Published by Springer Nature Switzerland AG 2019. All Rights Reserved
V. Sucasas et al. (Eds.): BROADNETS 2018, LNICST 263, pp. 409–418, 2019.
https://doi.org/10.1007/978-3-030-05195-2_40

antennas should be less than or equal to the number of antennas at the base station. This condition limits the system geometry. Another approach is to optimize the weights of the beamformer to improve performance. The optimization is either to reduce the total transmitted power [7], the power per antenna [8] or to increase the capacity [9], while keeping other parameters constant. This is done by framing the solving optimization problem in terms of the signal to interference and noise ratio (SINR). This approach has the drawback of coupled variables between different users: an increase in signal power level for one user will increase the leakage (interference) for other users. Another promising optimization technique proposed in [10] and later developed in [11, 12] uses the signal to leakage and noise ratio (SLNR).

This paper examines the performance of the SLNR ratio under variation of SNR, the relation between base station antenna, number of users and antenna per user, developing previous work [13, 14] where the system model in [15] was adopted. Results show that there are some limitations to be considered during the design of a system. The performance of the system is not necessarily monotonic; it can exhibit a peak depending on the number of base station antennas, number of users and number of antennas per user. The results in [13] and [16] were found comparable to the current results of this work.

2   System Mathematical Model

Consider a cell that contains a single base station with M antennas, transmitting signals to K users each with N antennas as shown in Fig. 1.

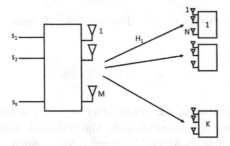

Fig. 1. The system model for MU-MIMO.

The base station uses the same time-frequency resource to send data to these users. The channel from the base station to user i is given by:

$$H_i = \begin{bmatrix} h_{1,1,i} & \cdots & h_{1,M,i} \\ \vdots & \ddots & \vdots \\ h_{N,1,i} & \cdots & h_{N,M,i} \end{bmatrix} \tag{1}$$

The elements of H_i are assumed to be single tap channel (i.e. no inter-symbol interference exists) and they contain two Gaussian parts, real and imaginary. The total channel is then:

$$H = [H_1^T H_2^T \cdots H_K^T]^T \tag{2}$$

and the leakage channel is given by:

$$\hat{H} = [H_1^T \cdots H_{i-1}^T H_{i+1}^T \cdots H_K^T]^T \tag{3}$$

The transmitted vector from the base station X is the sum of the transmitted vector for all of the users:

$$X = \sum_{i=1}^{K} w_i s_i \tag{4}$$

where $w_i \in C^{N \times M}$ is the beamforming vector for user i and s_i is the data symbol for that user. The received signal for user i is:

$$y_i = H_i X + n_i \tag{5}$$

where n_i is the noise vector at user i with variance equal to σ^2.

The system capacity is given by the equation (in units of $b/s/Hz$):

$$C = \log_2(1 + SINR) \tag{6}$$

$$C = \log_2\left(1 + \frac{S}{I + N_0}\right) \tag{7}$$

The signal power received by the user is $|H_i w_i|$, with interfering signal $\sum_{\substack{k=1 \\ k \neq i}}^{K} |H_i w_k|$, so that Eq. (7) can be written:

$$C = \log_2\left(1 + \frac{|H_i w_i|}{\sum_{\substack{k=1 \\ k \neq i}}^{K} |H_i w_k| + N\sigma_i^2}\right) \tag{8}$$

3 SLNR Optimization

The aim is to find a precoder which maximizes the signal to leakage and noise ratio (SLNR): in other words which increases the power through the channel to the intended user while simultaneously minimizing the interference to other users.

As stated in Sect. 1 above, the SINR leads to a coupled optimization problem which is solved by extending the SLNR as in [10–12]. The SLNR is given by:

$$SLNR_i = \frac{S}{L + N_0} \tag{9}$$

where the leakage term is:

$$L = \sum_{\substack{k = 1 \\ k \neq i}}^{K} |H_k w_i| \tag{10}$$

The problem may be formulated in two ways. The first ignores the noise term and maximizes the signal to leakage ratio:

$$\frac{S}{L} = \frac{|H_i w_i|}{\sum_{\substack{k = 1 \\ k \neq i}}^{K} |H_i w_k|} \tag{11}$$

This equation can be rewritten thus:

$$\frac{S}{L} = \frac{w_i^H H_i^H H_i w_i}{w_i^H \hat{H}_i^H \hat{H}_i w_i} \tag{12}$$

with solution [9]:

$$\frac{w_i^H H_i^H H_i w_i}{w_i^H \hat{H}_i^H \hat{H}_i w_i} \leq \lambda_{\max}\left(H_i^H H_i, \hat{H}_i^H \hat{H}_i\right) \tag{13}$$

where $\lambda_{\max}$ is the largest eigenvalue. The optimal beamformer is:

$$w_i^o \propto \max.GEV\left(H_i^H H_i, \hat{H}_i^H \hat{H}_i\right) \tag{14}$$

and if $\hat{H}_i^H$ is invertible then (14) will be:

$$w_i^o \propto \max.EV\left(\left(\hat{H}_i^H \hat{H}_i\right)^{-1} H_i^H H_i\right) \tag{15}$$

The method is extended to include the effect of noise [11], so (11) becomes:

$$\frac{S}{L+N_0} = \frac{|H_i w_i|}{\sum\limits_{\substack{k=1 \\ k \neq i}}^{K} |H_i w_k| + N\sigma_i^2} \tag{16}$$

The corresponding equations for (14) and (15) are:

$$w_i^o \propto \max.GEV\left(H_i^H H_i, \hat{H}_i^H \hat{H}_i + N\sigma_i^2 I\right) \tag{17}$$

$$w_i^o \propto \max.EV\left(\left(\hat{H}_i^H \hat{H}_i + N\sigma_i^2 I\right)^{-1} H_i^H H_i\right) \tag{18}$$

4 Performance of Eigenvalue Decomposition and Generalized Eigenvalue Decomposition: EVD and GEVD

The SLR and SLNR approach has been proposed previously [10–12], but a new viewpoint is obtained here by applying the method over a wider range and analyzing the effects on the behavior of the EVD and GEVD, permitting one to understand the overall benefits for the total system resulting from SLNR maximization. The GEVD for two matrices A and B is given by

$$Av = B\lambda v \tag{19}$$

If B is not singular (i.e. B^{-1} exists) then we can say

$$B^{-1}Av = \lambda v \tag{20}$$

which is the same as $Dv = \lambda v$ for $D = B^{-1}A$. In general if we have a matrix $c \in \mathbb{C}^{N \times M}$ where $N = N_1 + N_2$, we can say it is composed from two matrices a and b:

$$c = \begin{bmatrix} a^T & b^T \end{bmatrix}^T \tag{21}$$

The GEVD for the two matrices $A = a^H \times a$ and $B = b^H \times b$ gives two matrices λ and v. The columns of matrix v contain candidates to be in the null space of matrix b, i.e. give zeros when multiplied by the matrix b. If a is the user channel, b is the leakage channel and c is the aggregated channel, then v is expected to have at least one vector that gives a zero and a non-zero result when multiplied by b and a respectively. However, that can be misleading as this assumption depends on the dimension of c. Table 1 compares the GEVD for different cases of M, N, N_1 and N_2.

Table 1. Performance of GEVD Precoder

Case	Sub case	Solution(s) exist?	Number of solutions
$N < M$		Yes	$> N_1$
$N = M$	$N_1 = N_2$	Yes	$= N_1$
$N > M$	$N_2 \geq M$	No	
	$N_2 < M$	Yes	$(M - N_2)$

Note that the solution vector is associated with the largest eigenvalue for this case. If the equation is flipped to be $GEVD(B, A)$ then the eigenvector associated with the lowest absolute value should be selected.

5 Results

In this section a set of carefully selected representative results is presented to give a clear understanding of the behavior of the system in terms of the SLNR criterion.

Figure 2 below shows performance versus increasing SNR for different numbers of users. As can be seen, the increase in number of users per system increases the capacity due to the increment in total data transferred through the wireless channel.

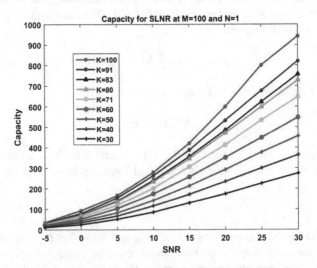

Fig. 2. System performance in terms of capacity versus SNR for different numbers of single antenna users.

The monotonicity of the curve does not hold in all cases; as seen in Fig. 3 the number of antennas per user affects the performance. For low numbers of users, the curves retain the same behavior, but with increasing numbers of users the curves take another shape. Although the shapes are different and there are two sets of curves, the behavior at each SNR is the same. The capacity starts at a certain level and increases to a maximum after which it decreases. At 5 dB SNR the peak is for 60 users while for 10 dB the peak falls to 50 users. At higher SNR the higher capacity relation still holds.

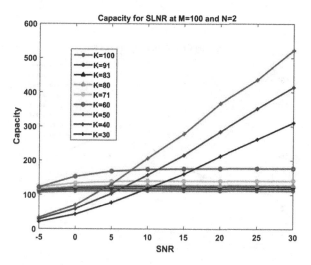

Fig. 3. System performance in terms of capacity versus SNR for different numbers of two antenna users

As can be seen from the figures above, the capacity due to the increment in number of users served by the system can be affected by the number of antennas per user. To give more clarification, Fig. 4 illustrates the effect of varying numbers of user antennas per scenario. There are two types of curves. The first set, for fewer user antennas,

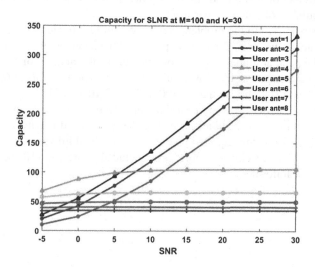

Fig. 4. System performance in terms of capacity versus SNR for different numbers of antennas per users.

resembles the performance shown in Fig. 3, also showing increasing capacity with increasing antenna numbers. The second set has a different shape, tending to saturate at lower SNR values. Below 5 dB SNR the peak is at 4 antennas per user while after 10 dB SNR the peak moves to 3 antennas per user for 30 users served by a 100 antenna base station.

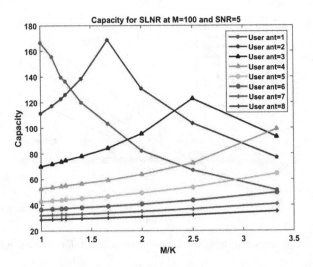

Fig. 5. System performance in terms of capacity versus base station antennas to users ratio.

Another perspective can be got by combining two criteria (the number of users and the number of antennas at the base station) as in Fig. 5. This figure shows that the curves have peaks, at different positions and different values. The position of the peak (in terms of number of users) tends to move down with increase of the ratio M/K as we increase the number of antennas per user.

Another perspective to the problem can be seen in Fig. 6. Here we see a peak also in terms of antenna users: at 2 antennas per user for higher number of users (60 and more), with the peak at higher numbers of antennas as the number of users decreases. The capacity has a concave shape over number of users and it occurs at 60 users when the number of base station antennas is 100 and the SNR is 0 dB.

Finally, Fig. 7 shows a comparison three approaches. The first variation uses the eigenvalue decomposition (in blue) instead of the generalized eigenvalue decomposition (orange line), i.e. using Eq. (15) instead of (14). The third variation (yellow line), shows results where the effect of noise was included using Eq. (18) to evaluate the weights of the beamformer.

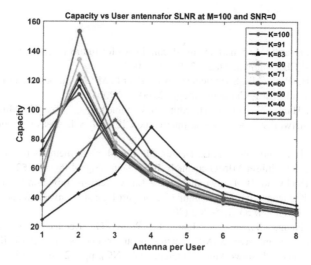

Fig. 6. System performance in terms of capacity versus antenna per user for different numbers of users per cell.

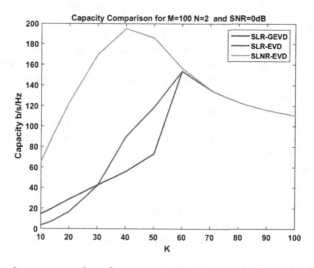

Fig. 7. Capacity versus number of users, comparing three methods. (Color figure online)

6 Conclusion

The performance of SLR based on beamforming with MU-MIMO is presented. The resulting system is not monotonic in all of the four dimensions of interest, namely numbers of base station antenna, SNR, numbers of user antennas and the number of users served by the base station. It is shown that there are peak in performance, and that the capacity variation follows concave curves with variation of number of users and number of handset antennas.

References

1. Alexiou, A., Haardt, M.: Smart antenna technologies for future wireless systems: trends and challenges. IEEE Commun. Mag. **42**, 90–97 (2004)
2. Spencer, Q.H., Peel, C.B., Swindlehurst, A.L., Haardt, M.: An introduction to the multi-user MIMO downlink. IEEE Commun. Mag. **42**, 60–67 (2004)
3. Gesbert, D., Hanly, S., Huang, H., Shitz, S.S., Simeone, O., Yu, W.: Multi-cell MIMO cooperative networks: a new look at interference. IEEE J. Sel. Areas Commun. **28**, 1380–1408 (2010)
4. Spencer, Q.H., Swindlehurst, A.L., Haardt, M.: Zero-forcing methods for downlink spatial multiplexing in multiuser MIMO channels. IEEE Trans. Signal Process. **52**, 461–471 (2004)
5. Peel, C.B., Hochwald, B.M., Swindlehurst, A.L.: A vector-perturbation technique for near-capacity multiantenna multiuser communication-part I: channel inversion and regularization. IEEE Trans. Commun. **53**, 195–202 (2005)
6. Zhang, F., Huang, Y., Jin, S., Jiang, L., Wang, G.: Reduced-backhaul coordinated beamforming for massive MIMO heterogeneous networks. In: 2015 IEEE Wireless Communications and Networking Conference (WCNC), pp. 129–134 (2015)
7. Rashid-Farrokhi, F., Liu, K.R., Tassiulas, L.: Transmit beamforming and power control for cellular wireless systems. IEEE J. Sel. Areas Commun. **16**, 1437–1450 (1998)
8. Yu, W., Lan, T.: Transmitter optimization for the multi-antenna downlink with per-antenna power constraints. IEEE Trans. Signal Process. **55**, 2646–2660 (2007)
9. Shi, S., Schubert, M., Boche, H.: Rate optimization for multiuser MIMO systems with linear processing. IEEE Trans. Signal Process. **56**, 4020–4030 (2008)
10. Tarighat, A., Sadek, M., Sayed, A.H.: A multi user beamforming scheme for downlink MIMO channels based on maximizing signal-to-leakage ratios. In: IEEE International Conference on Acoustics, Speech, and Signal Processing, Proceedings (ICASSP 2005), vol. 3, pp. iii/1129–iii/1132 (2005)
11. Sadek, M., Tarighat, A., Sayed, A.H.: Active antenna selection in multiuser MIMO communications. IEEE Trans. Signal Process. **55**, 1498–1510 (2007)
12. Sadek, M., Tarighat, A., Sayed, A.H.: A leakage-based precoding scheme for downlink multi-user MIMO channels. IEEE Trans. Wirel. Commun. **6**, 1711–1721 (2007)
13. Jung, M., Kim, Y., Lee, J., Choi, S.: Optimal number of users in zero-forcing based multiuser MIMO systems with large number of antennas. J. Commun. Netw. **15**, 362–369 (2013)
14. Hameed, K.W., Abd-Alhameed, R.A., Radwan, A.: Optimal array size for multiuser MIMO. In: IWCMC-SICM, Cyprus (2018)
15. Van Chien, T., Björnson, E.: Massive MIMO communications. In: Xiang, W., Zheng, K., Shen, X. (eds.) 5G Mobile Communications, pp. 77–116. Springer, Cham (2017). https://doi.org/10.1007/978-3-319-34208-5_4
16. Hameed, K.W., Al-Yasir, Y., Parchin, N.O., Abd-Alhameed, R.A., Excell, P.S.: On the equivalence between Eigen and channel inversion based precoders. In: Miraz, M., Excell, P., Ware, A., Soomro, S., Ali, M. (eds.) iCETiC 2018. LNICST, vol. 200, pp. 161–172. Springer, Cham (2018). https://doi.org/10.1007/978-3-319-95450-9_13

A More Efficient AOA Method for 2D and 3D Direction Estimation with Arbitrary Antenna Array Geometry

M. A. G. Al-Sadoon[1,2(✉)], N. A. Abduljabbar[1], N. T. Ali[3], R. Asif[1],
A. Zweid[2], H. Alhassan[1], J. M. Noras[1], and R. A. Abd-Alhameed[1,2]

[1] Faculty of Engineering and Informatics, University of Bradford,
Bradford BD7 1DP, UK
m.a.g.al-sadoon@bradford.ac.uk
[2] Basra University College of Science and Technology, Basra 61004, Iraq
[3] Khalifa University, Abu Dhabi, UAE

Abstract. Direction of arrival (DOA) estimation is currently an active research topic in array signal processing applications. Thus, a more efficient method with better accuracy than the current subspace angle of arrival (AOA) methods is proposed in this paper. The proposed method is called subtracting signal subspace (SSS), which exploits the orthogonality between the signal subspace (SS) and the array manifold vector (AMV). A novel approach applied to the pseudospectrum extracts the correct peaks and removes the sidelobes perfectly. The principle working of the proposed algorithm is given and mathematical model derived. The computational burden of the new method is also presented and compared with other methods. The SSS algorithm is implemented with both linear and planar antenna arrays. An intensive Monte Carlo simulation is conducted and compared with other popular AOA methods to verify the effectiveness of the SSS algorithm.

Keywords: Direction of Arrival · Signal Subspace · Computational burden
Signal processing · Sensor array · Wireless communication

1 Introduction

Localization-based techniques are growing in importance for applications such as mobile communications [1], radar applications [2] and medical services [3]. Estimating directions of arrival (DOA) of signals incoming from different directions on an array of spatially distributed antennas or sensors is one of the most important factors in array signal processing. Capon [4], Multiple signal classification (MUSIC) [5], Estimation of Signal Parameters via Rotational Invariance Technique (ESPRIT) [6] and Propagator [7] are well-known AOA estimation techniques. Massive multiple input multiple output (MIMO) technology is a promising physical layer candidate for the fifth generation (5G) due to its probable advantages such as high energy efficiency, high spectral efficiency and high spatial resolution. An efficient and accurate AOA method is desirable when integrated with massive MIMO in order to minimize the required computational burden in addition to improving the quality of service (QoS) provided

© ICST Institute for Computer Sciences, Social Informatics and Telecommunications Engineering 2019
Published by Springer Nature Switzerland AG 2019. All Rights Reserved
V. Sucasas et al. (Eds.): BROADNETS 2018, LNICST 263, pp. 419–430, 2019.
https://doi.org/10.1007/978-3-030-05195-2_41

by mobile communication operators [8]. It also emphasizes the performance of the beamforming technology, for instance, when the directions of the desired signals and interference signals are estimated accurately, a suitable beamforming algorithm can be applied to enhance the gain of the useful signals and suppress the noise and interference [9]. Generally, obtaining limited hardware cost with large array aperture cause serious challenges for real-time signal processing and parameter estimation.

Thus, several efforts have been made towards reducing the complexity through avoiding the high computational demanding spectra search array. Root-MUSIC technique [10] was proposed to reduce the computational complexity of the MUSIC method by finding the roots of an involved polynomial, which are associated with directional signals. This method is a less computational burden and faster than MUSIC since it does not need an extensive searching through the manifold vector. The main limitation of this method is applicable only to uniform linear arrays. Other attempts have been achieved using specific shapes of the array geometry in order to minimize the degrees of freedom (FOM) in the spectral search process [11, 12]. An efficient-computational subspace method was developed for 2D DOA estimation utilizing an L-shaped array [13]. This method obtains the noise subspace by rearranging the elements of the covariance matrix into three vectors to decrease the computational complexity. An efficient AOA method called Maximum Signal Subspace (MSS) was suggested in [14] to estimate DOAs; it is based on the orthogonality between the antenna array steering vector and the eigenvector which corresponding to the largest eigenvalue. However, it is also applicable only for uniform linear antenna arrays. Recently, a low complexity angle of arrival method called Propagator Direct Data Acquisition (PDDA) [15] has been proposed to estimate the direction of the received signals directly from the received data without the need to construct the covariance matrix, compute the inverse of a matrix, or apply the EVD approach. This, in turn, reduces the computational complexity significantly. The PDDA method is dependent on calculating the propagator vector which represents the cross-correlation between the measurement data from the first element and the other antenna elements.

In this work, we propose a more computational efficient AOA method to compute the directions of arrival signals with any type of antenna array geometry. The proposed method could be a good alternative to the MUSIC method specifically in massive MIMO technology. The SSS method based on the orthogonality between signal subspace and the manifold array vector. A wide range of scenarios with intensive Monte Carlo simulation is performed and the results verified the effectiveness of the SSS method in both 2D and 3D estimation applications. It is also compared with some of the well-known AOA methods and the obtained results show that its superiority. The remainder of this paper is organized as follows. The signal model for DOA estimation with arbitrarily configured arrays is presented in Sect. 2. Section 3 gives the principle working of the proposed approach in addition to the complexity analysis. Section 4 presents numerical simulations with wide scenarios to demonstrate the effectiveness of the proposed method as well as to verify the theoretical analysis. The results are discussed and compared with other AOA methods. In Sect. 5, the conclusions of this work are summarized.

Throughout this paper, lowercase letters are used for scalar quantities whereas boldface lowercase and uppercase letters denote vectors and matrixes respectively.

Superscripts, $(\cdot)^T$, $(\cdot)^H$ and $E\{.\}$ refer to transpose, conjugate transpose and the expected value respectively. The operator $(\bar{a})$ is a unit vector, I_M is the $M \times M$ identity matrix and $\|\cdot\|$ is a matrix or vector norm.

2 DOA Signal Model

Consider P signals arriving from different directions impinging on an M element antenna array, as depicted in Fig. 1. Then, the total received signal, $X(t)$, that includes directions both of elevation angle (θ_k) and azimuth angle (ϕ_k), corrupted by AWGN, is given as described below:

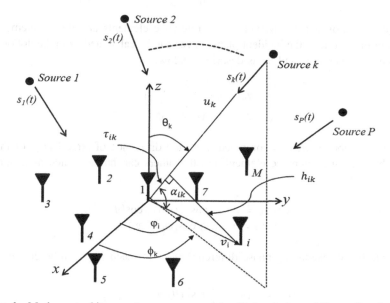

Fig. 1. M-element arbitrary antenna array receiving P signals from different directions.

$$X(t) = A(\theta, \phi)\, S(t) + N(t) \tag{1}$$

where $S(t) = [s_1(t), s_2(t), \ldots, s_P(t)]^T$ is the $(P \times L)$ incident signals, L is the number of snapshots, $N(t) = [n_1(t), n_2(t), \ldots, n_M(t)]$ is an array of AWGN for each channel and $A(\theta, \phi)$ is the steering matrix for P vectors it is defined as follows:

$$A(\theta, \phi) = [a(\theta_1, \phi_1)a(\theta_2, \phi_2)\ldots\ldots a(\theta_P, \phi_P)] \tag{2}$$

From Fig. 1, the unit vector, u_k, that includes the directions of θ_k and ϕ_k for any arrival signal is given as follows:

$$u_k = \cos \phi_k \sin \theta_k \bar{a}_x + \sin \phi_k \sin \theta_k \bar{a}_y + \cos \theta_k \bar{a}_z \tag{3}$$

where $\bar{a}_x, \bar{a}_y$ and $\bar{a}_z$ are unit vectors for Cartesian co-ordinates. The unit vector v_i is the distance from a reference antenna element to the ith element and it is given as follows:

$$v_i = r_i \cos \varphi_i \bar{a}_x + r_i \sin \varphi_i \bar{a}_y, i = 1, 2, \ldots, M. \tag{4}$$

The phase angle (φ_i) between a reference element and the others is defined as follows:

$$\varphi_i = \frac{2\pi}{M}(i - 1) \tag{5}$$

The projection angle (α_{ik}) between a reference elements and the ith elements as shown in Fig. 1 due to the incident plane waves can be calculated from the dot product between unit vectors v_i and u_k as described below:

$$\alpha_{ik} = \cos^{-1}\left(\frac{v_i.u_k}{\|v_i\|.\|u_k\|}\right)$$
$$\alpha_{ik} = \cos^{-1}(\sin \theta_k \cos(\phi_k - \varphi_i)) \tag{6}$$

Once the above angle is computed, the time difference of arrival (τ_{ik}) of the kth signal between the reference element and the others can be calculated as in the following equation:

$$\tau_{ik} = r \cos \alpha_{ik} = r \cos(\cos^{-1}(\sin \theta_k \cos(\phi_k - \varphi_i)))$$
$$\tau_{ik} = r \sin \theta_k \cos(\phi_k - \varphi_i) \tag{7}$$

Next, the corresponding phase difference (ψ_{ik}) for each (τ_{ik}) can be determined:

$$\psi_{ik} = \beta.\tau_{ik} = \frac{2\pi}{\lambda} r \sin \theta_k \cos(\phi_k - \varphi_i) \tag{8}$$

$\beta = \frac{2\pi}{\lambda}$ is the spatial frequency, r is the distance between the reference element and ith element, d is the separation between adjacent elements. Then, the steering vector for an arbitrary geometry can be calculated:

$$a(\theta_k, \phi_k) = \begin{bmatrix} e^{-j\psi_{1k}} & e^{-j\psi_{2k}} & \cdots & \cdots & e^{-j\psi_{Mk}} \end{bmatrix} \tag{9}$$

The array covariance matrix (CM) is given by:

$$\mathcal{R}_{xx} = E[X(t) X^H(t)] = A\mathcal{R}_{ss} A^H + \sigma_n^2 I_N \tag{10}$$

Complete knowledge of covariance matrix, R_{xx}, may not be supposed; instead, the sample-average estimated array input matrix can be used to construct CM as follows:

$$\hat{\mathcal{R}}_{xx} \approx \frac{1}{L} \sum_{n=1}^{L} X(t) X^H(t) \tag{11}$$

3   The Proposed AOA Method

The fundamental idea of this algorithm is applying the EVD approach to the CM or SVD to the received signal data and then sorting the eigenvalues in ascending way. Due to the orthogonal complementarity of the signal subspace (SS) and noise subspace (NS), DOAs can be estimated either from NS such as MUSIC or from SS such as ESPRIT. For computational reasons, SS is preferred since its dimension usually is much smaller than NS. This means the computational burden of the SSS method in the pseudo-spectrum construction stage using SS is much less compared to MUSIC. Further, SS is more efficient to use than NS. The SSS method is based on the orthogonality between the SS and the AMV as shown in Fig. 2.

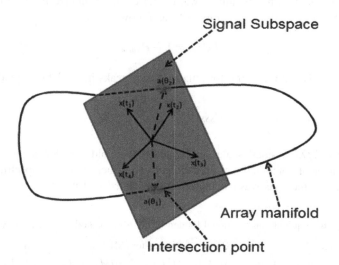

Fig. 2. The orthogonality between SS and AMV.

Applying Eigenvalue decomposition (EVD) approach to $\mathcal{R}_{xx}$ and then sorting the eigenvalues in a descending way yields:

$$\mathcal{R}_{xx} = Q \, \Sigma Q^H = [\, Q_{SS} \ Q_{NS}\,] \begin{bmatrix} \Sigma_{SS} & 0 \\ 0 & \Sigma_{NS} \end{bmatrix} \begin{bmatrix} Q_{SS}^H \\ Q_{NS}^H \end{bmatrix} \tag{12}$$

Where $\Sigma_{SS} = [\lambda_1, \ \lambda_2, \ \ldots\ldots, \ \lambda_P]$ is a vector with dimension $(1 \times P)$ and it represents the largest P eigenvalues; the corresponding eigenvectors of Σ_{SS} are:

$$Q_{SS} = [q_1, \quad q_2, \quad \cdots \quad \cdots, \quad q_P] \tag{13}$$

Whereas $\Sigma_{NS} = [\lambda_{P+1}, \quad \lambda_{P+2}, \quad \ldots \ldots, \quad \lambda_M]$ is a vector with $(1 \times M–P)$ size and represents the lowest P eigenvalues; the coresponging eigenvectors of Σ_{NS} are:

$$Q_{NS} = [q_{P+1} \quad q_{P+1}, \cdots \cdots, \quad q_M] \tag{14}$$

Then, the spatial spectrum of the SSS method can be constructed below formula;

$$P_{ss}(\theta) = \|a(\theta) Q_{SS}\|^2 \tag{15}$$

In order to extract the actual peaks and remove the sidelobe efficiently, we propose the following novel approach; firstly, normalise the pseudospectrum of the above equation using the maximum value:

$$P_{Norm}(\theta) = P_{ss}(\theta)/max(P_{ss}(\theta)) \tag{16}$$

Next, to obtain narrower nulls towards DOAs and minimize the side-lobe levels significantly, subtract $P_{Norm}(\theta)$ from unity as follows:

$$P_S(\theta) = 1 - P_{Norm} \tag{17}$$

Finally, apply the following formula to obtain peaks in the DOA signals,

$$P_{SSS}(\theta) = \frac{1}{P_S(\theta) + \varepsilon} \tag{18}$$

where is $\varepsilon = 1/\lambda_1$ a small scalar value added to avoid possible singularities. The needed number of computational operations to construct the pseudospectrum for SSS and other AOA methods was calculated and presented in Table 1.

Table 1. The required computational burden of the SSS method vs. other AOA methods.

Algorithm	Capon	Propagator	MUSIC	SSS
Computational burden	$M^2 J_\theta J_\varnothing$	$M^2 J_\theta J_\varnothing$	$M(M-P)J_\theta J_\varnothing$	$MP J_\theta J_\varnothing$

where J_θ and $J_\varnothing$ denote the iteration numbers for elevation and azimuth planes respectively. Based on the above arguments, the proposed method gives lower computational burden than the other AOA methods in the spatial spectrum construction stage. Thus, the SSS method will be more efficient to implement with the massive MIMO technology compared to the above-presented AOA algorithms. This, in turn, will minimize the execution time and the required memory storage significantly.

4   Simulation Results and Discussion

A computer simulation is performed with many scenarios to validate the theoretical claims of the proposed method.

4.1   The 2D Estimation of the SSS Method Using Linear Arrays

Firstly, the performance estimation of the proposed method is studied with the variation of the SNR at the antenna array output. Five different values of SNR is set namely: SNR = −20 dB, −10 dB, 0 dB, 10 dB, 20 dB and each SNR three plane waves are assumed arriving from 0^0, 30^0, and -50^0. A uniform linear array (ULA) consisting of ten elements (M = 10) with spacing d = 0.5 λ between each adjacent elements is used; the number of snapshots is taken L = 100. The performance estimation of the proposed method under these conditions is illustrated Fig. 3, it can be seen from this graph that the SSS method produces sharp peaks towards the directions of arrival signals with high resolution through the whole tested SNR range. However, the SNR effect on the performance estimation is clear where the produced peaks became narrow and accurate with increase in SNR and vice versa.

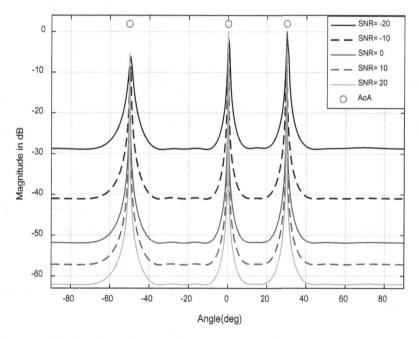

Fig. 3. The performance of the SSS algorithm with different SNR.

Secondly, the performance estimation of the SSS method is examined under various angular separations between AOAs. Seven signals are assumed incident on ULA with these directions $[(\theta_1, \theta_2 = \theta_1 + \Delta\theta_j), (\theta_3, \theta_4 = \theta_3 + \Delta\theta_j, \theta_5 = \theta_3 - \Delta\theta_j), (\theta_6, \theta_7$

$= \theta_6 + \Delta\theta_j)]$, where $\theta_1 = -50°$, $\theta_2 = 0°$, $\theta_3 = 30°$ and $\Delta\theta_j$ is the angular separation between each pair of AOAs. Three $\Delta\theta_j$ are considered namely: $\Delta\theta = [1°, 2°, 3°]$, M = 20, SNR = 10 dB, L = 100 and d = 0.5 λ. 100 Monte Carlo trials for each $\Delta\theta_j$ are conducted and a cumulative distribution function (CDF) is plotted for five steps of $\Delta\theta_j$. The performance separation of SSS is shown in Fig. 4 and the percentage of detection of the AOAs at each step of $\Delta\theta = [1°, 1.5°, 2°, 2.5°]$ is 0.60, 0.76, 0.98 and 100 respectively. These results reflect the strength and effectiveness of the new method.

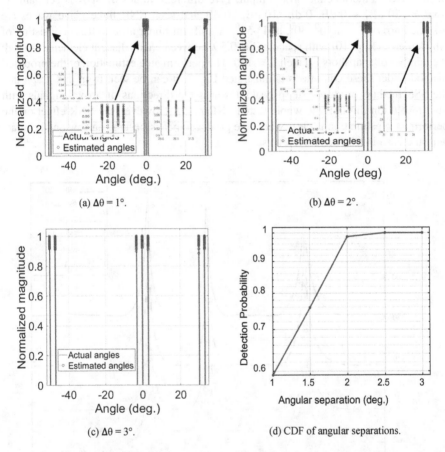

(a) $\Delta\theta = 1°$.

(b) $\Delta\theta = 2°$.

(c) $\Delta\theta = 3°$.

(d) CDF of angular separations.

Fig. 4. The performance estimation and detection of the SSS method with different angular separations.

4.2 The 3D Estimation of the SSS Method Using Planar Arrays

The second scenario presents two simulation examples: the former assumes ten signals are incident from different θ and ϕ angles on a uniform rectangular array (URA) with (10 × 10) antenna elements. The other simulation parameters are L = 2048 and SNR is set to 20 dB and d = 0.5 λ. The latter emulates 25 signals impinging on URA with

(16 × 16) antenna elements. The actual directions of received signals are generated randomly and indicated by red lines. The performance estimation of the SSS algorithm for the first and second scenario is depicted in Fig. 5 and Fig. 6 respectively. As can be seen from these graphs, the SSS method estimated DOAs accurately with less computation complexity in the scanning process stage compared to the MUSIC and other AOA methods as shown in Table 2.

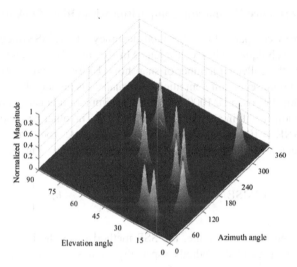

Fig. 5. The 3D performance estimation of the SSS method with P = 10, M = [10 × 10].

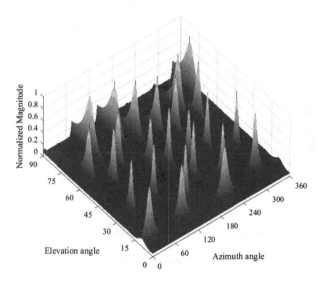

Fig. 6. The 3D performance estimation of the SSS method with P = 25, M = [16 × 16].

Table 2. The required computational operations comparison between the SSS method and other AOA methods.

Algorithm	Capon	Propagator	MUSIC	SSS
M = 100, P = 10	O (1.3×10^9)	O (1.3×10^9)	O (1.17×10^9)	O (1.3×10^8)
M = 256, P = 25	O (8.55×10^9)	O (8.55×10^9)	O (8.02×10^9)	O (5.34×10^8)

4.3   The Performance Estimation Comparison with Other AOA Methods

The final scenario compares the estimation accuracy of the SSS method with four common AOA techniques namely: Capon, Min-Norm, MUSIC and ESPRIT. The comparison tests the collected number of snapshots (L) for received signals and thus a simulation is run with seven different number of snapshots namely: L = [1, 3, 5, 10, 20, 50, 100, and 200]. For each L, 1000 Monte Carlo simulation is carried out to generate three AOAs randomly within angular space [90°–90°]. The other simulation parameters are M = 10, SNR = 10 dB, and d = 0.5λ. The average root mean square error (ARMSE) is calculated and then plotted as given in the below Fig. 7.

$$\text{ARMSE} = \frac{1}{K}\sum\nolimits_{j=1}^{K}\sqrt{\frac{1}{P}\sum\nolimits_{k=1}^{P}\left[\left(\theta_k - \widehat{\theta}_k\right)^2\right]} \tag{19}$$

As can be seen from this figure, the SSS method gives the best estimation resolution among the presented methods especially at a single and fewer number of snapshots.

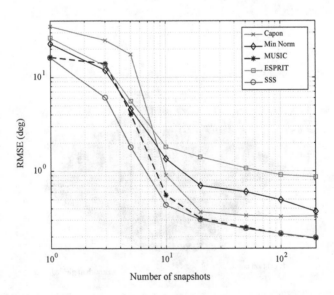

Fig. 7. The SSS performance estimation comparison with other methods.

5   Conclusion

A new high precision technique based on the orthogonality between SS and AMV has been proposed in this paper to estimates the directions of incident signals. The DOA model has been presented and the antenna array steering vector derived for an arbitrary array geometry. The principle and the mathematical model of the SSS method have been also given and demonstrated with many numerical examples for both 2D and 3D estimation applications. The performance estimation of the SSS method was compared with popular AOA algorithms using extensive Monte Carlo simulation and the results verified it has the highest resolution among them. The SSS method is applicable for any type of array configuration and gives less computational burden in the scanning process stage than MUSIC and other well-known AOA algorithms.

References

1. Godara, L.C.: Application of antenna arrays to mobile communications. II. Beam-forming and direction-of-arrival considerations. Proc. IEEE **85**, 1195–1245 (1997)
2. Bencheikh, M.L., Wang, Y.: Joint DOD-DOA estimation using combined ESPRIT-MUSIC approach in MIMO radar. Electron. Lett. **46**, 1081–1083 (2010)
3. Khan, M.A., Saeed, N., Ahmad, A.W., Lee, C.: Location awareness in 5G networks using RSS measurements for public safety applications. IEEE Access **5**, 21753–21762 (2017)
4. Capon, J.: High-resolution frequency-wavenumber spectrum analysis. Proc. IEEE **57**, 1408–1418 (1969)
5. Schmidt, R.: Multiple emitter location and signal parameter estimation. IEEE Trans. Antennas Propag. **34**, 276–280 (1986)
6. Roy, R., Kailath, T.: ESPRIT-estimation of signal parameters via rotational invariance techniques. IEEE Trans. ASSP **37**, 984–995 (1989)
7. Marcos, S., Marsal, A., Benidir, M.: The propagator method for source bearing estimation. Signal Process. **42**, 121–138 (1995)
8. Hameed, K.W., Al-Sadoon, M., Jones, S.M.R., Noras, J.M., Dama, Y.A.S., Masri, A., et al.: Low complexity single snapshot DoA method. In: 2017 Internet Technologies and Applications (ITA), pp. 244–248 (2017)
9. Al-Sadoon, M., Abd-Alhameed, R.A., Elfergani, I., Noras, J., Rodriguez, J., Jones, S.: Weight optimization for adaptive antenna arrays using LMS and SMI algorithms. WSEAS Trans. Commun. **15**, 206–214 (2016)
10. Rao, B.D., Hari, K.V.S.: Performance analysis of Root-Music. IEEE Trans. Acoust. Speech Signal Process. **37**, 1939–1949 (1989)
11. Yan, F.-G., Cao, B., Rong, J.-J., Shen, Y., Jin, M.: Spatial aliasing for efficient direction-of-arrival estimation based on steering vector reconstruction. EURASIP J. Adv. Signal Process. **2016**, 121 (2016)
12. Hao, C., Orlando, D., Foglia, G., Ma, X., Yan, S., Hou, C.: Persymmetric adaptive detection of distributed targets in partially-homogeneous environment. Digit. Signal Process. **24**, 42–51 (2014)
13. Xi, N., Liping, L.: A computationally efficient subspace algorithm for 2-D DOA estimation with L-shaped array. IEEE Signal Process. Lett. **21**, 971–974 (2014)

14. Al-Sadoon, M.A.G., et al.: New and less complex approach to estimate angles of arrival. In: Otung, I., Pillai, P., Eleftherakis, G., Giambene, G. (eds.) WiSATS 2016. LNICST, vol. 186, pp. 18–27. Springer, Cham (2017). https://doi.org/10.1007/978-3-319-53850-1_3
15. Al-Sadoon, M.A., Ali, N.T., Dama, Y., Zuid, A., Jones, S.M.R., Abd-Alhameed, R.A., et al.: A new low complexity angle of arrival algorithm for 1D and 2D direction estimation in MIMO smart antenna systems. Sensors 17, 2631 (2017)

A New Polarization-Reconfigurable Antenna for 5G Wireless Communications

Yasir I. A. Al-Yasir[1,2(✉)], Naser Ojaroudi Parchin[1], Issa Elfergani[3],
Raed A. Abd-Alhameed[1], James M. Noras[1], Jonathan Rodriguez[3],
Amar Al-jzari[2], and Waleed I. Hammed[2]

[1] Bradford University, Bradford BD7 1DP, UK
y.i.a.al-yasir@bradford.ac.uk
[2] Basra Oil Training Institute, Basra, Iraq
[3] Instituto de Telecomunicações, Aveiro, Portugal

Abstract. This paper presents a circular polarization reconfigurable antenna for 5G applications, which is compact in size and has good axial ratio and frequency response. The proposed microstrip antenna is designed on a FR-4 substrate with a relative dielectric constant of 4.3 and has a maximum size of 30×30 mm^2 with 50 Ω coaxial probe feeding. This design has two PIN diode switches controlling reconfiguration between right hand circular polarization (RHCP) and left hand circular polarization (LHCP). To achieve reconfigurability, a C-slot rectangular patch antenna with truncated corner techniques is employed by cutting off two corners on the radiating patch. The proposed antenna has been simulated using CST microwave studio software: it has 3.35–3.77 GHz and 3.4–3.72 GHz bands for both states of reconfiguration, and each is suitable for 5G applications with a good axial ratio of less than 1.8 dB and good gain of 4.8 dB for both modes of operation.

Keywords: Microstrip antennas · Reconfigurable · 5G · Circular polarization

1 Introduction

Many recent books and articles have discussed the use of reconfigurable antennas for "green" flexible RF in 5G applications [1–3]. This topic is of increasing interest for industry because of the requirement for antennas which offer additional functionality and have flexible properties, with the same or smaller physical sizes than previously [4–6]. The 3.4–3.8 GHz frequency band has been identified as a good candidate for 5G applications because of the availability of spectrum [7].

Polarization reconfigurable antennas can help to provide protection from interfering signals in variable environments, offering an additional degree of freedom to increase link quality in the form of altered antenna diversity. In addition, they can be used in active read, write tracking and tagging applications and to enhance channel capacity [8]. Several antennas have been developed to deliver reconfigurable polarization characteristics using switches. Su et al. proposed and fabricated polarization reconfigurable circular-polarized antenna for GPS systems using four photoconductive diodes [9]: by controlling the switching state for each of four diode switches on a

© ICST Institute for Computer Sciences, Social Informatics and Telecommunications Engineering 2019
Published by Springer Nature Switzerland AG 2019. All Rights Reserved
V. Sucasas et al. (Eds.): BROADNETS 2018, LNICST 263, pp. 431–437, 2019.
https://doi.org/10.1007/978-3-030-05195-2_42

microstrip antenna, the radiation polarization can be altered from linear to circular, either left hand or right hand circular polarization (LHCP or RHCP). Khidre et al. [10] designed a single-aperture-fed dual-band reconfigurable antenna for polarization diversity for WLAN applications. The antenna operates at both 2.4 and 5.8 GHz bandwidth using four shorting posts. The impedance bandwidths for the two bands were 3.6% and 4.3%, respectively, and each band radiates horizontal, vertical and linear polarization, controlled by PIN diode switches. Constant radiation patterns are achieved for different states of polarization with a maximum cross-polarization of −13 dB and −9 dB for the two bands, respectively. Boonying et al. proposed a polarization reconfigurable antenna for WLAN applications at 2.4–2.484 GHz controlled by six PIN diode switches [11]. Other researchers have also presented designs for 5G applications – for example in [12], an antenna is designed with circular polarization reconfigurability between LHCP and RHCP, applicable in mobile systems.

In this paper, the diversity of a polarization-reconfigurable microstrip antenna with semicircle slot is investigated, based on an antenna with two PIN diode switches giving rise to orthogonal RHCP and LHCP. The orthogonality should occur at least in the direction normal to the antenna, since it is hard to achieve orthogonal polarizations over the whole sphere.

2 Antenna Design

In the proposed design, the radiator is fed by a 50 Ω standard probe. An FR-4 substrate is used with h = 3.2 mm, ε_r = 4.3 and loss tangent = 0.02. The frequency 3.6 GHz is chosen as the resonance frequency because this frequency is suitable for 5G. A coaxial probe type feed is used. The center of the patch is taken as the origin and the feed point location is given by the co-ordinates (x_f, y_f) from the origin. The location of the feed point is found using CST software, whose parametric optimizer identifies where the input impedance is 50 Ω at the resonant frequency. At 3.6 GHz, the optimized feed point location is (x_f = 14.3 mm, y_f = 14.6 mm). The antenna is designed with two PIN diodes switches, modeled with a lumped element network which gives 0.9 Ω as the resistance value of a diode in the ON state and 0.3 pF as its capacitance value in the OFF state. The optimized dimensions are achieved by using the built-in optimizer embedded with the CST software. CST time domain solver has been used with 10 lines per wavelength as mesh density control properties. The dimensions of this antenna are optimized to ensure good matching at resonance. The geometry of the antenna and its optimized dimensions are shown in Fig. 1 and Table 1, respectively.

3 Simulation Results

In this section, the polarization diversity antenna is studied in terms of return loss, radiation pattern, gain and polarization. The simulation results are generated using CST software.

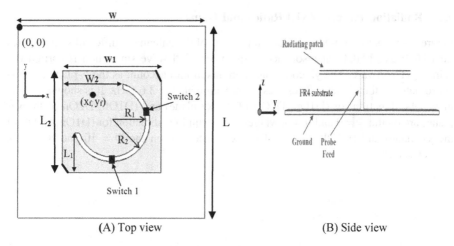

(A) Top view   (B) Side view

Fig. 1. Proposed polarization-reconfigurable microstrip antenna

Table 1. The optimized dimensions of the antenna (Units in mm)

W	L	L_2	W_1	W_2	L_1	R_1	R_2
30	30	17	17	9	8	6	7

3.1 Impedance Bandwidth

The simulation results for the return loss of proposed antenna in Fig. 2 show that, by altering the state of the two PIN diodes, the reflection coefficient |S11| is maintained, which is an advantage of this design. At the resonance frequency, the measured effective bandwidths (S11 < −10 dB) for (D1ON, D2OFF) and (D1OFF, D2ON) are 11% and 8%, respectively, for both states.

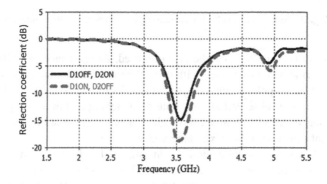

Fig. 2. Return loss for microstrip antenna with two switch modes

3.2   Radiation Pattern, Axial Ratios and Gains

Figure 3 shows the simulated radiation patterns of the antenna in different switch states (in RHCP and LHCP) at resonance frequencies. Full wave simulation is carried out using CST software. The yz-coordinates are taken into account as the E-plane and xz-coordinates as the H-plane. These results are simulated at 3.6 GHz. It is shown that the main lobe direction for (D1On, D2Off of the xz-plane) and (D1Off, D2On of the yz-plane) are on the $\Phi = 0$ and $\theta = 0$, whereas the main lobe direction for (D1On, D2Off of the yz-plane) and (D1Off, D2On of the xz-plane) are on the $\Phi = 10$ and $\theta = -10$, respectively.

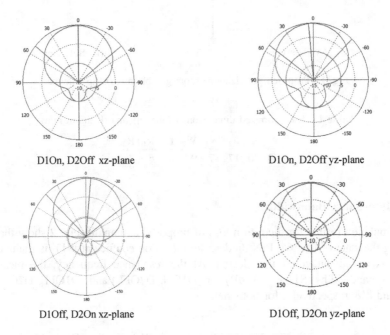

D1On, D2Off xz-plane   D1On, D2Off yz-plane

D1Off, D2On xz-plane   D1Off, D2On yz-plane

Fig. 3. Simulated results for radiation pattern for microstrip antenna

From Fig. 4, the axial ratio can be also observed. At resonance (3.6 GHz), a value of less than 2 dB axial ratio resulted with the difference between the cross-polarization component and the co-polarization component also less than 2 dB. In simulated results, circular polarization is observed at each state of switching and in the xz-plane and yz-plane. However, the results obtained show circular polarization at broadside and at the most important direction in both xz-plane and yz-plane.

Figure 5 shows the captured view of an animated field explaining the sense of rotation of circular polarization for the antenna. It shows that the filed distribution of the proposed antenna is rotating in the left-hand circular polarization in the D1Off, D2On state, whereas the field is rotating in the right-hand circular polarization in the D1on, D2off state.

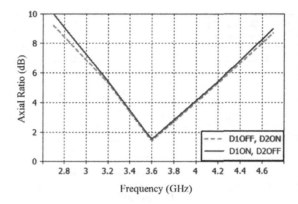

Fig. 4. Simulated axial ratio for the antenna.

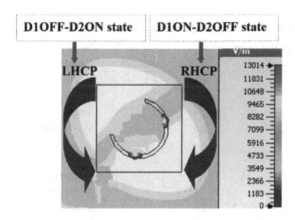

Fig. 5. Captured view of animated field shows the sense of rotation of CP for the antenna.

Figure 6 shows the simulation results for the maximum realized gain of the proposed antenna. The maximum value for simulated gain is 4.8 dB for both switching states for the diodes at the resonance frequency.

4   Comparison with Some Other Existing Structures

Table 2 compares the proposed polarization-reconfigurable antenna with other antennas with similar configurations and performance. It is noticeable that the proposed antenna is better than others with respect to size, number of switches and also the polarization states obtained compared with the design complexity.

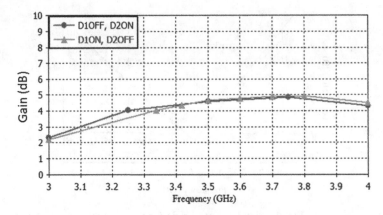

Fig. 6. Simulation results for the realized gain of the proposed antenna

Table 2. Comparison between the proposed structure with some other existing structures.

Ref.	Antenna size (mm^3)	f_0 (GHz)	No. of switches	Design complexity	Achieved polarization
[9]	70 × 70 × 1.6	1.5	4	Simple	LP-RHCP-LHCP
[10]	140 × 80 × 10	2.4	2	Simple	RHCP-LHCP
[11]	80 × 80 × 3.2	2.4	6	Very complex	VP-HP-SP-RHCP-LHCP
[13]	70 × 70 × 10.8	2.4	2	Simple	RHCP-LHCP
[14]	100 × 100 × 3.2	1.5	2	Consists of two layers	HP-VP-RHCP
[15]	67.5 × 39.3 × 1.52	2.4	2	Simple	LP-CP
This work	30 × 30 × 3.2	3.6	2	Simple	RHCP-LHCP

5 Conclusions

A proposed design for a 5G circular polarization reconfigurable-microstrip antenna is presented in this paper. The antenna is reconfigurable for circular polarization to cover RHCP and LHCP under the control of PIN diode switches. The proposed design exhibits 11%–8% effective bandwidth with maximum realized gain around 4.8 dB at 3.6 GHz. Only two switches are used for switching the mode of polarization. The antenna characteristics are kept the same at each polarization mode due to symmetry through switching. The antenna covers the 5G frequency band for potential use in stationary terminals of various wireless applications and it is suitable for WiMax applications and MIMO systems as well.

Acknowledgment. This work is partially supported by innovation programme under grant agreement H2020-MSCA-ITN-2016 SECRET-722424 and the financial support from the UK Engineering and Physical Sciences Research Council (EPSRC) under grant EP/E022936/1.

References

1. Elfergani, I., Hussaini, A.S., Rodriguez, J., Abd-Alhameed, R. (eds.): Antenna Fundamentals for Legacy Mobile Applications and Beyond, 1st edn. Springer, Cham (2018). https://doi.org/10.1007/978-3-319-63967-3

2. Hussaini, A., et al.: Green flexible RF for 5G. In: Fundamentals of 5G Mobile Networks, p. 241–272. Wiley, Hoboken (2015)

3. Al-Yasir, Y., Abdullah, A., Mohammed, H., Mohammedand, B., Abd-Alhameed, R., Beebe, J.: Design of radiation pattern-reconfigurable 60-GHz antenna for 5G applications. J. Telecommun. **27**(2), 1–6 (2014)

4. Bernhard, J.: Reconfigurable Antennas. Morgan and Claypool Publishers, San Rafael (2007)

5. Al-Yasir, Y., Abdullah, A., Mohammed, H., Abd-Alhameed, R., Noras, J.: Design of frequency-reconfigurable multiband compact antenna using two PIN diodes for WLAN/WiMAX applications. IET Microw. Antennas Propag. **11**(8), 1098–1105 (2017)

6. Al-Yasir, Y., Abdullah, A.: Compact frequency-reconfigurable antenna for multi-band wireless applications. In: Progress in Electromagnetics Research Symposium, Guangzhou, China, pp. 2036–2037 (2014)

7. Ofcom Homepage. https://www.ofcom.org.uk/

8. Boti, M., Dussopt, L., Laheurte, J.: Circularly polarized antenna with switchable polarization sense. Electron. Lett. **36**(18), 1518–1519 (2000)

9. Su, H., Shoaib, I., Chen, X.: Optically tuned polarisation reconfigurable antenna. In: Proceedings of IEEE Asia-Pacific Conference on Antennas and Propagation, Singapore, pp. 265–266 (2012)

10. Khidre, A., Lee, K.-F., Yang, F., Elsherbeni, A.Z.: Circular polarization reconfigurable wideband e-shaped patch antenna for wireless applications. IEEE Trans. Antennas Propag. **61**(2), 960–964 (2013)

11. Boonying, K., Phongcharoenpanich, C., Kosulvit, S.: Polarization reconfigurable suspended antenna using RF switches and P-I-N diodes. In: The Fourth Joint International Conference on Information and Communication Technology, Thailand, pp. 1–4 (2014)

12. Abbas, E., Mobashsher, A.: Polarization reconfigurable antenna for 5G cellular networks operating at millimeter waves. In: Proceeding of 2017 Asia Pacific Conference, Malaysia, pp. 772–774 (2017)

13. Khaleghi, A., Kamyab, M.: Reconfigurable single port antenna with circular polarization diversity. IEEE Trans. Antennas Propag. **57**(2), 555–559 (2009)

14. Nishamol, M., Sarin, V., Tony, D., Aanandan, C., Mohanan, P., Vasudevan, K.: An electronically reconfigurable microstrip antenna with switchable slots for polarization diversity. IEEE Trans. Antennas Propag. **59**(9), 3424–3427 (2011)

15. Panahi, A., Bao, X.L., Yang, K., O'Conchubhair, O., Ammann, M.J.: A simple polarization reconfigurable printed monopole antenna. IEEE Trans. Antennas Propag. **63**(11), 5129–5134 (2015)

Frequency Reconfigurable Antenna Array for MM-Wave 5G Mobile Handsets

Naser Ojaroudi Parchin[1(✉)], Yasir Al-Yasir[1],
Ahmed M. Abdulkhaleq[2], Issa Elfergani[3], Ashwain Rayit[2],
James M. Noras[1], Jonathan Rodriguez[3], and Raed A. Abd-Alhameed[1]

[1] Faculty of Engineering and Informatics,
Bradford University, Bradford BD7 1DP, UK
{n.ojaroudiparchin,r.a.a.abd}@bradford.ac.uk
[2] SARAS Technology Limited, Leeds LS12 4NQ, UK
[3] Instituto de Telecomunicações, Aveiro, Portugal

Abstract. This study proposes a compact design of frequency-reconfigurable antenna array for fifth generation (5G) cellular networks. Eight compact discrete-fed slot antennas are placed on the top portion of a mobile phone printed-circuit-board (PCB) to form a beam-steerable array. The frequency response of the antenna can be reconfigured to operate at either 28 GHz or 38 GHz, two of the candidate frequency bands for millimeter-wave (MM-Wave) 5G communications. The reconfigurability function of the proposed design can be achieved by implementing and biasing a pair of diodes across each T-shaped slot antenna element. Rogers RT 5880 with thickness of 0.508 mm and properties of $\varepsilon = 2.2$ and $\delta = 0.0009$ has been used as the antenna substrate. The antenna element is very compact in size with a good end-fire radiation pattern in the frequency bands of interest. The proposed beam-steerable array provides very good 3D coverage. The simulation results show that the proposed design provides some good characteristics fitting the need of the 5G cellular communications.

Keywords: 5G antenna · Cellular communications · Future networks
Reconfigurable antenna · Slot antenna

1 Introduction

The evolution from the current generation of cellular communications to the future generation (5G) is mainly driven by the growing need for higher data rate communications in different applications [1, 2]. Different from the design of antennas for the fourth generation (4G) cellular networks, antenna designs for the future wireless systems at higher frequencies (beyond 10 GHz) would face more challenges and needs more requirements [3, 4]. One example of the requirements for the 5G antennas is the reconfigurability function, where the same antenna is used for different modes such as diversity or cognitive radio (CR) communications. Many antenna designs with reconfigurability function are available for radar or space applications [5–7]. However, those designs cannot be directly adopted for mobile communications, which has

© ICST Institute for Computer Sciences, Social Informatics and Telecommunications Engineering 2019
Published by Springer Nature Switzerland AG 2019. All Rights Reserved
V. Sucasas et al. (Eds.): BROADNETS 2018, LNICST 263, pp. 438–445, 2019.
https://doi.org/10.1007/978-3-030-05195-2_43

different requirements. To address this need, this paper presents a frequency-reconfigurable antenna array that can operate at both 28 and 38 GHz (promising 5G candidate bands) for cellular communications.

The proposed array contains eight slot antenna elements placed on the top of a mobile-phone PCB. The array is compact in size and provides good beam steering characteristics suitable for future mobile terminals. The overall size of the antenna is 60×120 mm^2. Simulations have been done using CST software [8] to validate the feasibility of the proposed frequency reconfigurable-phased array antenna for MM-Wave 5G handset applications. This paper is structured as follows: The configuration of the proposed reconfigurable 5G mobile phone antenna is described in Sect. 2. Section 3 discusses the S-parameters and radiation performances of both the single element and the final design. The final section presents the conclusions of this study.

2 The Proposed Design Configuration

The configuration of the proposed frequency-reconfigurable 5G handset antenna is shown in Fig. 1. As illustrated, eight low-profile T-shaped slot antenna elements are employed on the top portion of the mobile phone PCB. Another set of the proposed beam steerable array could be used at the other side of the PCB to cover the other 3D half-space. It can be seen that the proposed 5G array is compact in size with dimensions 39.8×3.25 mm^2. Furthermore, there is enough space in the proposed mobile phone antenna to include 3G and 4G MIMO antennas. The antenna is designed on a Rogers RT5880 substrate with thickness (h), dielectric constant (ε_r), and loss tangent (δ) of 0.508 mm, 2.2, and 0.0009, respectively.

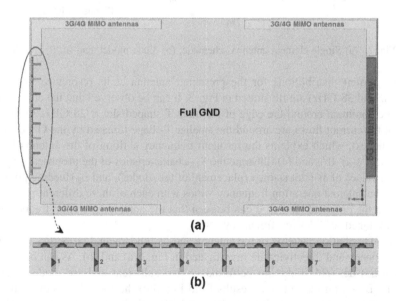

Fig. 1. (a) Configuration of the proposed reconfigurable 5G antenna and (b) its array schematic.

3 Results

3.1 Single Element Reconfigurable 5G Antenna

The configuration of the single element frequency-reconfigurable antenna is illustrated in Fig. 2(a). The antenna element is compact, with size of 3.25×4.8 mm^2. The optimal dimensions of the designed antenna are as follows: $W = 4.8$ mm, $L = 2.75$ mm, $W_1 = 0.45$ mm, $L_1 = 0.5$ mm, $W_2 = 0.4$ mm, $L_2 = 1$ mm, and $x = 0.675$ mm. As illustrated in Fig. 2(a), a pair of active elements (diode switches) across the T-shaped slot can be used to effectively change the dimension of the radiator. As a result, a reconfigurable dual band operation can be achieved. Figure 2(b) depicts the model of the diode. The parameters of an AlGaAs beam-lead PIN Diode (MA4AGBL912) including $R = 4$–4.9 Ω, $C = 26$–30 fF, $L = 0.5$ H (suitable for use up to 40 GHz) have been employed in the simulation of the active element [9]. S_{11} results of the antenna for different switching conditions are shown in Fig. 2(c). It can be seen that the -10 dB impedance bandwidth of the antenna is switchable to operate in frequency bands of 28 GHz and 38 GHz.

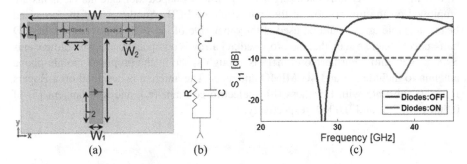

Fig. 2. (a) Single element antenna schematic, (b) diode model, and (c) S_{11} results.

The current distributions for the presented antenna at its resonance frequencies (28 GHz and 38 GHz) are illustrated in Fig. 3. It can be observed that the current flows are more dominant around the edge of the main T-shaped slot at 28 GHz. At 38 GHz, most of the current flows are around the smaller T-shape (created by the ON condition of the diodes), which explains the resonant frequency shifting of the antenna [10].

Figures 4(a), (b), and (c) illustrate the S_{11} characteristics of the proposed design for different values of W (slot size), x (placement of the diodes), and L_2 (feeding point). As shown, the antenna operation frequency varies with each of these different parameters. Based on the obtained results, it can be seen that the antenna operation frequency can be easily tuned to a desired frequency.

The 3D radiation patterns of the antenna and its fundamental properties in terms of total efficiency and directivity are investigated in Fig. 5(a) and (b). As can be seen, the antenna has desirable radiation performance and sufficient end-fire mode at 28 and 38 GHz. Based on the obtained results from Fig. 5(c) the total efficiency of the proposed reconfigurable antenna is more than -0.1 dB with good maximum gain values in the bands of interest.

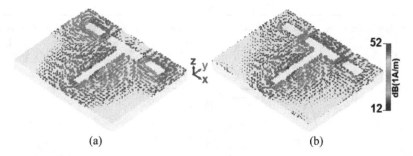

Fig. 3. Current distribution of the proposed antenna at, (a) 28 GHz and (b) 38 GHz.

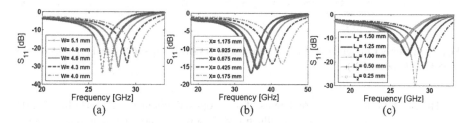

Fig. 4. S_{11} characteristics of the antenna for different values of (a) W, (b) x, and (c) L_2.

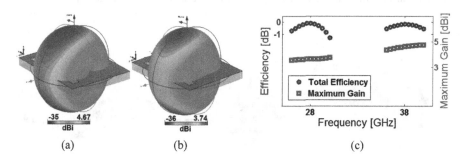

Fig. 5. (a) Radiation pattern at 28 GHz and (b) at 38 GHz, (c) fundamental properties.

3.2   Radiation Properties of the Proposed Design

The proposed array antenna is designed using eight T-shaped reconfigurable antennas. Figure 6(a) illustrates the configuration of the linear array. The array is compact, with size $W_a \times L_a = 39.8 \times 3.25$ mm^2. The antenna element are arranged with a separation of d = 5 mm. It should be notice that in order to achieve the higher scanning angles, the distance between adjacent sources is less than $\lambda/2$ of 28 GHz. Figures 6(b) and (c) show the S parameters (S_{11} to S_{81}) of the array for different conditions of the employed active elements (ON/OFF conditions) at 28 and 38 GHz. It can be seen that the array has good impedance matching with more than 2 GHz bandwidth at 28 GHz, and 4 GHz at 38 GHz. Furthermore, as illustrated, mutual coupling characteristics of less than −13 dB are obtained for the bands of interest.

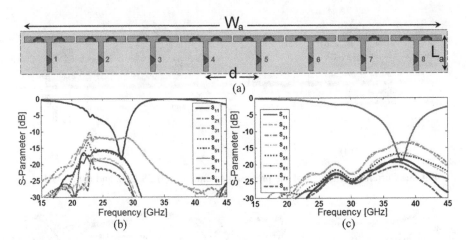

Fig. 6. (a) Array Configuration, (a) S-parameters at 28 GHz (diodes: OFF) and (c) S-parameters at 38 GHz (diodes: ON).

The 3D directional radiation beams of the proposed antenna at 28 GHz for 0°, 30°, 60°, and 80° scanning angle are illustrated in Fig. 7, showing that the proposed reconfigurable antenna array provides wide-angle scanning characteristics with a symmetrical end-fire mode. It has also sufficient values of realized gain [11].

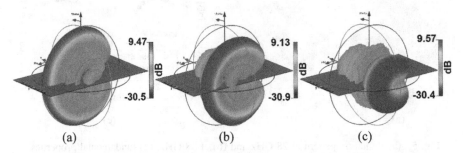

Fig. 7. 3D directional radiation beams for 28 GHz at (a) 0°, (b) 30°, and (c) 60°.

The analysis and performance of the antenna beams are obtained using CST software. The shape and direction of the array beams are determined by relative phases amplitudes applied to each radiating element as below:

$$\varphi = 2\pi(d/\lambda)\sin\theta \tag{1}$$

Where d is the distance between elements, λ is the wavelength of the desired frequency, and θ is the scanning angle. In order to see the radiation beams at different scanning angles, the phase shift between adjacent sources must be calculated according to Eq. (1). The next step is applying the calculated Phased-Shifting with same values of amplitude = 1 for each element. In order to understand the phenomenon behind this process, the phases shifting for different angles are listed in Table 1. The calculated φ for 0°, 30°, and 60° are about 0, 85, and 145, respectively.

Table 1. Required phase shifting for different scanning angles

φ	Port 1	Port 2	Port 3	Port 4	Port 5	Port 6	Port 7	Port 8
0	0	0	0×2	0×3	0×4	0×5	0×6	0×7
30	0	85	85×2	85×3	85×4	85×5	85×6	85×7
60	0	145	145×2	145×3	145×4	145×5	145×6	145×7

2D radiation patterns of the proposed antenna array with realized gain values over wide scanning angles are illustrated in Fig. 8. As can be seen, the antenna provide a very good beam steering with acceptable realized gain values for minus/plus scanning angles.

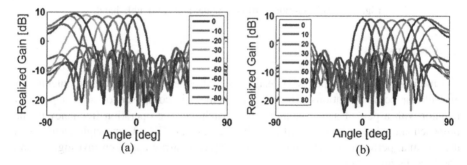

Fig. 8. Beam-steering characteristics of the design for (a) minus and (b) plus scanning angles.

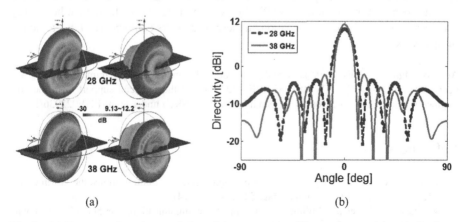

Fig. 9. (a) Beam-steering characteristics of the antenna at different frequencies and (b) directivities of the proposed antenna at 0°.

Figure 9 represents the 3D radiation beams of the proposed reconfigurable array (with directivity values) at 28 and 38 GHz: the antenna has good radiation behaviour in both of the 5G candidate bands. As mentioned above, the employed array has very similar performance with sufficient gain values at different frequencies. The simulated 2D directivity characteristics of the proposed frequency reconfigurable antenna at 0° are illustrated in Fig. 9(b). As can be seen, for the proposed design at 28/38 GHz, more than 10 dBi directivities with low side lobes have been obtained.

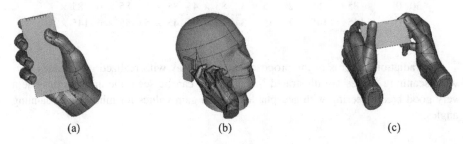

(a)   (b)   (c)

Fig. 10. (a) Data-mode, (b) talk-mode, and (c) double-hand.

4 Conclusion

The motivation of this paper is to design a new frequency reconfigurable antenna for 5G cellular communications. The antenna element is composed of a T-shaped slot radiator with a pair of active elements for switching. The operation frequency of the proposed antenna can be switched to work at 28 and 38 GHz. Using eight elements of the antenna, performance of a mobile-phone antenna array has been investigated and good results are obtained.

The employed array antenna has a compact size and is suitable for handset applications. Due to the importance of the user effect on the antenna performance and also the specific absorption rate (SAR) effects of the antenna on the human body [12] (as illustrated in Fig. 10), investigation on these parameters could be a suitable topic for further work.

Acknowledgment. This work is partially supported by innovation programme under grant agreement H2020-MSCA-ITN-2016 SECRET-722424 and the financial support from the UK Engineering and Physical Sciences Research Council (EPSRC) under grant EP/E022936/1.

References

1. Osseiran, A., et al.: Scenarios for 5G mobile and wireless communications: the vision of the METIS project. IEEE Commun. Mag. **52**, 26–35 (2014)
2. Rappaport, T.S., et al.: Millimeter wave mobile communications for 5G cellular: it will work! IEEE Access **1**, 335–349 (2013)

3. Ojaroudiparchin, N., Shen, M., Zhang, S., Pedersen, G.F.: A switchable 3D-coverage phased array antenna package for 5G mobile terminals. IEEE Antennas Wirel. Propag. Lett. **2**(15), 1747–1750 (2016)
4. Lin, H.-S., Lin, Y.-C.: Millimeter-wave MIMO antenna with polarization and pattern diversity for 5G mobile communications: the corner design. In: IEEE International Symposium on Antennas and Propagation & USNC/URSI National Radio Science Meeting, 9–14 July 2017, San Diego, CA, USA, pp. 2277–2578 (2017)
5. Ghanem, F., Hall, P.S.: A two-port frequency reconfigurable antenna for cognitive radios. Electron. Lett. **45**, 534–536 (2009)
6. Ojaroudi, N., Amiri, S., Geran, F.: A novel design of reconfigurable monopole antenna for UWB applications. Appl. Comput. Electromagn. Soc. (ACES) J. **6**(28), 633–639 (2013)
7. Da Costa, I.F., et al.: Optically controlled reconfigurable antenna array for mm-Wave applications. IEEE Antennas Wirel. Propag. Lett. **15**, 2142–2145 (2017)
8. CST Microwave Studio. ver. 2017, CST, Framingham, MA, USA (2017)
9. MA-COM Technol. Solutions Holding, Inc., AlGaAs beam-lead PIN diode. MA4AGBL912
10. Parchin, N.O., Abd-Alhameed, R.A., Elfergani, I.T.: A compact Vivaldi antenna array for 5G channel sounding applications. In: EuCAP 2018, 3–9 April 2018, London, pp. 1–3 (2018)
11. Parchin, N.O., Shen, M., Pedersen, G.F.: Wide-scan phased array antenna fed by coax-to-microstriplines for 5G cell phones. In: 21st International Conference on Microwaves, Radar and Wireless Communications, MIKON 2016, 3–9 May 2016, Krakow, Poland, pp. 1–4 (2016)
12. Parchin, N.O., Shen, M., Pedersen, G.F.: Small-size tapered slot antenna (TSA) design for use in 5G phased array applications. Appl. Comput. Electromagn. Soc. (ACES) J. **3**(32), 193–202 (2017). ISSN 1054-4887

A 70-W Asymmetrical Doherty Power Amplifier for 5G Base Stations

Ahmed M. Abdulkhaleq[1,2(✉)], Yasir Al-Yasir[2],
Naser Ojaroudi Parchin[2], Jack Brunning[1], Neil McEwan[1],
Ashwain Rayit[1], Raed A. Abd-Alhameed[2], James Noras[2],
and Nabeel Abduljabbar[2]

[1] SARAS Technology Limited, Leeds LS12 4NQ, UK
a.abd@sarastech.co.uk
[2] Faculty of Engineering and Informatics,
Bradford University, Bradford BD7 1DP, UK
r.a.a.abd@bradford.ac.uk

Abstract. Much attention has been paid to making 5G developments more energy efficient, especially in view of the need for using high data rates with more complex modulation schemes within a limited bandwidth. The concept of the Doherty power amplifier for improving amplifier efficiency is explained in addition to a case study of a 70 W asymmetrical Doherty power Amplifier using two GaN HEMTs transistors with peak power ratings of 45 W and 25 W. The rationale for this choice of power ratio is discussed. The designed circuit works in the 3.4 GHz frequency band with 200 MHz bandwidth. Rogers RO4350B substrate with dielectric constant $\varepsilon r = 4.66$ and thickness 0.035 mm is used. The performance analysis of the Doherty power amplifier is simulated using AWR MWO software. The simulated results showed that 54–64% drain efficiency has been achieved at 8 dB back-off within the specified bandwidth with an average gain of 10.7 dB.

Keywords: Asymmetrical Doherty Power amplifier · Drain efficiency
GaN HEMTs · Wireless communications · LTE-Advanced

1 Introduction

The requirement for increasing the amount of transmitted data within a limited bandwidth using mobile communications systems is growing rapidly and this is expected to continue, especially with the developments of the LTE-Advanced system, where the user is being attracted by the video streaming and multimedia data in addition to the Internet of Things technology revolution [1–3]. Hence the 5G mobile generation will include several technologies that can help to achieve the promised goals of the 5G. Some of these are the use of massive MIMO, carrier aggregation, beam forming and more complex modulation schemes which produce a high peak to average power ratio (PAPR). The high PAPR requires the power amplifier to be backed off from the most efficient point into a region where the efficiency drops sharply. As a result, a large amount of supply power will be dissipated as a heat [1]. In particular, a high efficiency performance produces a low linearity of the power amplifier and vice versa. The power

© ICST Institute for Computer Sciences, Social Informatics and Telecommunications Engineering 2019
Published by Springer Nature Switzerland AG 2019. All Rights Reserved
V. Sucasas et al. (Eds.): BROADNETS 2018, LNICST 263, pp. 446–454, 2019.
https://doi.org/10.1007/978-3-030-05195-2_44

amplifier should be designed to produce high efficiency at a large Output power Back-off (OBO). There are several techniques which are used for efficiency enhancements, and these include Envelope Tracking (ET), Envelope Elimination and Restoration (EER), LInear amplification using nonlinear Component (LINC), Chireix outphasing, and the Doherty Power amplifier. However, the simplest technique is the Doherty amplifier, where neither additional controlling circuits nor signal processing blocks are required [3].

The present paper has four sections, starting with the Doherty concept, then a Doherty design example appropriate to 5G, followed by the simulation results and finally the work's conclusions.

2 Doherty Concept

The Doherty combiner was introduced by its inventor W.H. Doherty in 1936 [4] in relation to high power tube amplifiers for broadcasting station. Nearly linear output power can be achieved using two or more power amplifiers by combining their outputs with λ/4 transmission lines. The Classical Doherty power amplifier consists of two separate amplifiers known as the carrier amplifier and the peaking amplifier (Fig. 1). The carrier amplifier is designed to operate as a class AB amplifier whereas the peaking amplifier is designed to operate as class C amplifier. The input signal is split between the two amplifiers, where the carrier amplifier should be saturated at the back-off input power; at the same power level, the peaking amplifier starts feeding current to the output till it becomes saturated at the peak region, where the two power amplifiers give their maximum designed output power [5–7].

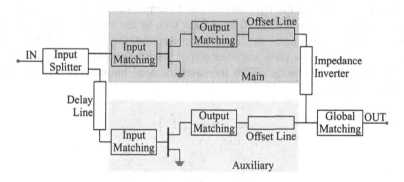

Fig. 1. Doherty Power amplifier structure [2]

The idea of the Doherty depends on the so-called active load-pull technique [1]. Where the operation of the Doherty power amplifier can be divided into three main regions [5–9]:

The low power region, where the input signal level is not sufficient to turn the peaking amplifier on so that the peaking amplifier can (ideally) be represented as an open circuit. On the other hand, the main amplifier is amplifying the input signal as an ordinary power amplifier, however the load is seen by the main amplifier through the λ/4 transmission line (Impedance Inverter), which makes the main amplifier saturate because it sees a high load impedance at this phase, as shown in Fig. 2(a). The impedance seen by the main amplifier depends on the following equation,

$$Z_1 = \frac{Z_T^2}{R_L} \tag{1}$$

where:

Z_1: the impedance seen by the main amplifier
Z_T: the impedance of the λ/4 transmission line
R_L: the load impedance

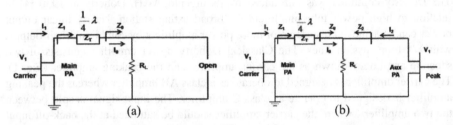

Fig. 2. Doherty operation region [2] (a) Low power region, (b) Medium and high-power region

The second region (medium power region) where the peaking amplifier starts injecting the current into the load and acts as a current source. As the current in the peaking amplifier increases, the load impedance seen by the impedance inverter will be increased, at the same time, the impedance seen by the main amplifier will be decreased. As a result, the main amplifier output voltage remains roughly constant and the total current is increasing which increases the total output power as shown the following equations:

$$Z_2 = R_L \left(1 + \frac{I_o}{I_2}\right) \tag{2}$$

$$Z_1 = \frac{Z_T^2}{R_L \left(1 + \frac{I_2}{I_o}\right)} \tag{3}$$

where:

Z_2: the impedance seen by the Peaking amplifier
I_o: the current after the λ/4 transmission line
I_2: the peaking Amplifier current

Finally, the high-power region, where both amplifiers work at their maximum output current, where the impedance seen by each amplifier is controlled by Eqs. (2) and (3).

The current and voltage behaviour of both the main and the peaking amplifiers is shown in Fig. 3. It can be observed that the peaking amplifier starts injecting the current near the OBO point, whereas the voltage of the main amplifier remains roughly constant after the OBO point but its current increases.

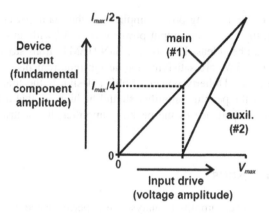

Fig. 3. Main and peaking current amplitude [1]

3 Doherty Design

As mentioned above, the main amplifier should be designed as class AB, whereas the peaking amplifier should be biased as a class C power amplifier. The first issue in designing any power amplifier is to take into account the stability of the transistor to make sure it does not oscillate. Then the input and output matching networks have to be designed for the optimum load and source impedances that achieve the best transistor performance.

Since the peaking amplifier is not behaving as a current source when it is off, but it is still subject to the output capacitance of the intrinsic device and the parasitic elements of its package, the offset line should be inserted at the output of the peaking amplifier to ensure that a high impedance will be seen when the peaking transistor is off below the back-off region, as this is one of the main conditions to satisfy the Doherty concept. After adding the offset line in the output of the peaking amplifier, the phase difference should be compensated by inserting an offset line at the output of the main amplifier.

An important issue in designing the Doherty power is the transistor choosing, which is govern by the following parameters

1. The average power
2. The PAPR

The summation of both parameters determines the maximum output power of the Doherty power Amplifier i.e. the sum of the main and peaking output power, whereas the PAPR represents the same amount of the back-off power that can define the ratio between the peaking amplifier to the main amplifier according to the following equation

$$B = -20\log(1+\delta) \tag{4}$$

where
  δ: is the ratio of the peaking power amplifier to the main power amplifier.

For this paper, the maximum output power was 70 W with an −8 dB back off, so that the ratio δ should be at least 1.5. So that, GaN HEMTs transistors with peak power ratings of 45 W and 25 W are satisfying the design requirements.

Another issue in the Doherty power amplifier design is the line offset, where the output impedance of the peaking amplifier should be high, so that a line offset will be added to the output impedance of the peaking amplifier, its electrical length for this deign case is 29.2°.

4   Simulation Results

A 70 W Doherty power amplifier analysis and performance are simulated using AWR MWO software. Rogers RO4350B material was used as a substrate. The full circuit schematic is shown in Fig. 4 whereas the layout of input and output matching circuits for both main and peaking amplifiers are shown in Fig. 5.

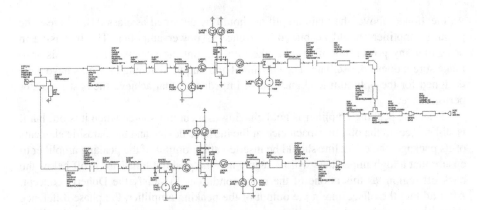

Fig. 4. Full circuit schematic

The performance of the main and peaking amplifiers separately in terms of output power, gain, drain efficiency and Power added efficiency (PAE) are shown in Fig. 6 and Fig. 7 respectively. As illustrated in Fig. 6, about 80% drain efficiency is obtained from the main amplifier with an average gain of 10 dB. Nevertheless, the performance of the peaking amplifier shown in Fig. 7, represents a class C power amplifier where it can be noticed that the peaking amplifier starts injecting the power after the input back-off point.

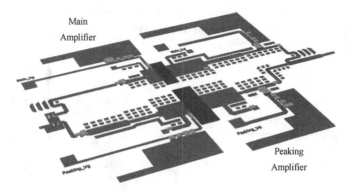

Fig. 5. Input and output matching circuit for Doherty Power amplifier

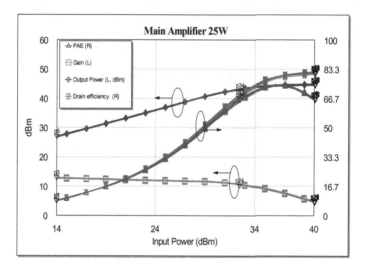

Fig. 6. Main amplifier performance

Furthermore, it can be notice from Fig. 8, the line offset is needed to produce a high impedance seen from the combiner toward the output of the peaking amplifier when the transistor is off in order to satisfy one of the Doherty conditions. It can be noticed that a high impedance can be gotten by adding a line offset.

In addition, it can be noticed from Fig. 9 that the designed Doherty power amplifier has about 63% drain efficiency at 8 dB OBO for 3.4 GHz; however, the efficiency level for other frequencies is less due to the effect of the off-set lines. At the same time, the gain obtained is 10.8 dB. In addition, the total output power of the designed Doherty power amplifier is 48 dBm where both amplifiers participate with their full power.

The achieved simulation results are compared with other works over the same frequency band, as shown on Table 1.

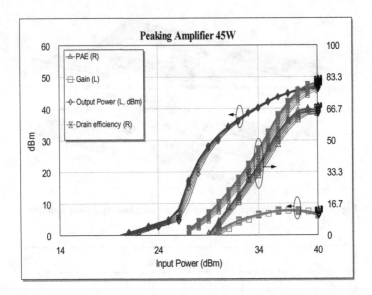

Fig. 7. Peaking amplifier performance

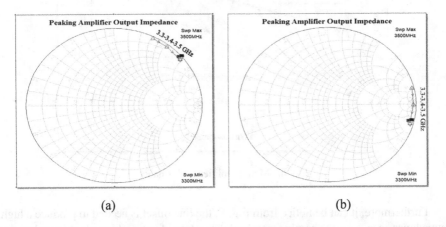

Fig. 8. Peaking output impedance seen from the far end when the transistor is off (a) without line offset (b) with line offset

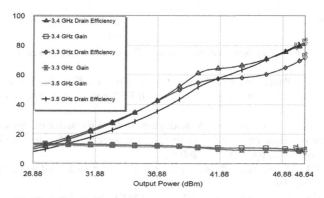

Fig. 9. Doherty power amplifier efficiency

Table 1. Previous work achievements

	Frequency (GHz)	P_{sat} (dBm)	P_{av} (dBm)	OBO (dB)	DE @OBO	Gain dB
[6]	3.3–3.6	43	37	6	38–56[a]	10
[7]	3.4–3.6	43	35	8	63	12.5
[8]	3.35–3.5	49.3	41	8	50.2–55.1	14.75
[9]	3.4–3.6	44.5	36.5	8	40–42[a, b]	25
This work	3.3–3.5	48	40	8	54–64	10

[a]Practical measurements
[b]Power added efficiency @ OBO

5   Conclusions

The Doherty power amplifier provides the simplest way of combining two amplifiers to provide a good efficiency performance around the back off region. The performance of A 70 W Asymmetrical Doherty power amplifier was simulated using AWR MWO; the overall Doherty power amplifier showed, as per design, an 8.3 dB OBO, with 40 dBm average power. The Drain efficiency at the back off point was 63%, whereas the average gain was 10.7 dB.

Acknowledgment. This project has received funding from the European Union's Horizon 2020 research and innovation programme under grant agreement H2020-MSCA-ITN-2016 SECRET-722424 [10].

References

1. Cripps, S.C.: RF Power Amplifier for Wireless Communications. Artech House, Norwood (1999)
2. Camarchia, V., Pirola, M., Quaglia, R., Jee, S., Cho, Y., Kim, B.: The Doherty power amplifier: review of recent solutions and trends. IEEE Trans. Microw. Theor. Tech. **63**, 559–571 (2015)
3. Hussaini, A.S., Abd-Alhameed, R.A, Rodriguez, J.: Implementation of efficiency enhancement techniques in the linear region of operations of power amplifier. In: 7th Conference on Telecommunications, pp. 105–108 (2009)
4. Doherty, W.H.: A new high efficiency power amplifier for modulated waves. Proc. IRE **24** (9), 1163–1182 (1936)
5. Kato, K., Miwa, S., et al.: A 83-W, 51% GaN HEMT Doherty Power amplifier for 3.5-GHz-Band LTE base stations. In: 46th European Microwave Conference (EuMC), pp. 572–575 (2016)
6. Rubio, J.M., Fang, J., et al.: 3–3.6 GHz Wideband GaN Doherty Power amplifier exploiting output compensation stages. IEEE Trans. Microw. Theor. Tech. **60**(8), 2543–2548 (2012)
7. Kosaka, N., Fujiwara, S., et al.: A high-efficiency and high-gain, plastic packaged GaN HEMT for 3.5-GHz-Band LTE base stations. In: IEEE International Symposium on Radio-Frequency Integration Technology (RFIT) (2016)
8. Huang, C., He, S., Dai, Z., Pang J., Hu, Z.: 80 W high gain and broadband Doherty Power amplifier for 4/5G wireless communication systems. In: IEEE MTT-S International Microwave Symposium (IMS) (2016)
9. Hue, X., Baroudi, F., Bollinger, L., Szymanowski, M., Nanan, J.: 12/25 W wideband LDMOS Power Amplifier IC (3400–3800 MHz) for 5G base station applications. In: 47th European Microwave Conference (EuMC) (2017)
10. Rodriguez, J., Radwan A., et al.: SECRET secure network coding for reduced energy next generation mobile small cells: a European Training Network in wireless communications and networking for 5G. In: Internet Technologies and Applications (ITA) (2017)

Design of Asymmetrical Doherty GaN HEMT Power Amplifiers for 4G Applications

Maryam Sajedin[1], Issa Elfergani[1(✉)], Abubakar Sadiq Hussaini[1,2], Jonathan Rodriguez[1], Ayman Radwan[1], and Raed Abd-Alhameed[3]

[1] Instituto de Telecomunicações, Aveiro, Portugal
{Maryam.sajedin,i.t.e.elfergani,
jonathan,aradwan}@av.it.pt
[2] School of Information Technology and Computing,
American University of Nigeria, Yola, Nigeria
[3] Faculty of Engineering and Informatics, Bradford University,
Bradford BD7 1DP, UK

Abstract. In this paper, a 2-stage Doherty power amplifier and a single class B at 3.800 GHz, based on a 10 W GaN-HEMT technology using the bandwidth up to 6 GHz have been designed. The Doherty structure employs a class B bias condition for the main and a class C configuration for the auxiliary devices in the Agilent's ADS design platform. An uneven Wilkinson power divider is applied to deliver more power to the auxiliary device in order to achieve proper load modulation. The RF performances of the Doherty amplifier have been compared with those of a class B amplifier alone. The simulation results exhibit that the Doherty architecture can be considered as an ideal candidate for maximizing average efficiency while simultaneously maintaining amplifier linearity.

Keywords: Doherty amplifier · Power amplifier · High efficiency

1 Introduction

Mobile telecommunication systems typically use complex modulation standards to send more information in a very dense constellation. It is common to have high data rate signals with large envelope fluctuation in the time domain resulting in high peak-to-average (PAR) ratio. In order to prevent in-band distortion and out-of-band emission as well as to satisfy the stringent linearity requirements imposed by the wireless communication standards, the Power Amplifier (PA) are usually operated at the back-off region leading to thermal problems, high energy consumption and/or shorter battery life. Therefore, the key issue in modern PA design is to develop techniques that are capable of improving the average efficiency and to reduce the power wastage. Several architectures have been proposed to enhance the average efficiency of the PA when excited with modulated signals [1]. Among them, the Doherty power amplifier using gallium–nitride (GaN) transistor, has been extensively investigated and widely deployed in modern digital transmitters [2].

© ICST Institute for Computer Sciences, Social Informatics and Telecommunications Engineering 2019
Published by Springer Nature Switzerland AG 2019. All Rights Reserved
V. Sucasas et al. (Eds.): BROADNETS 2018, LNICST 263, pp. 455–465, 2019.
https://doi.org/10.1007/978-3-030-05195-2_45

The basic idea behind the Doherty amplifier is to employ an impedance inverting network to modulate the load presented to the carrier amplifier according to the current supplied by the Auxiliary device, leading to efficient operation [3].

The basic structure of the two stages DPA is depicted in Fig. 1. The modern DPAs are usually implemented by a proper combination of two active devices that operate as Carrier and Peaking power stages. It consists of a power splitter to properly divide the input signal to the device gates, and an output power combining network including an impedance inverter, to sum in phase the signals arising from the two active devices, and impedance transformer connected to the output load. Finally, a phase compensation network connected at the input of the peaking device compensates the phase variation introduced by the impedance inverter.

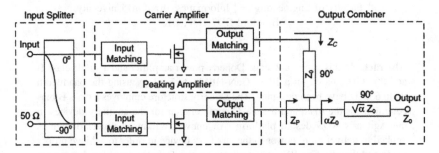

Fig. 1. Doherty power amplifier scheme [4]

Replacing the main and peaking transistors with two equivalent current sources in Fig. 2, the impedance seen by the Main amplifier can be changed by varying the current supplied of the peaking device, while the voltage swing across the Main has to be constant to maximize the efficiency. Therefore, it is necessary to impose an Impedance Inverting Network between the load and the main source. It is assumed that each current source is linearly proportional to the input voltage signal, in such a way, that the constant voltage value at the main terminals will be transformed into a constant current at the other terminals, without considering the value of the load [5].

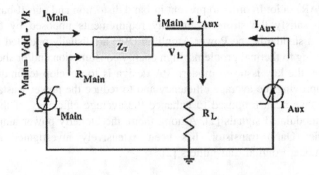

Fig. 2. Structure of equivalent circuit of Doherty amplifier

The organization of this paper is as follows: the working principle of the Doherty Power Amplifier is presented in Sect. 2; a single power amplifier and a Doherty power amplifier are designed in Sect. 3 by using the Cree's CGH40010 transistor in the 3.800 GHz band frequency available in the Agilent's ADS2016.01, whilst the DPA's input uneven power driving used to drive both the Main and the Auxiliary devices, and power combiner are discussed in this section. Then the DPA power gain behavior is discussed and compared with that of single PA according to simulation results; and finally in Sect. 4 the conclusion is given.

2 Doherty Amplifier Operation

The Doherty power amplifier has two distinct operating regions. The simplified output section of a DPA in the two operating regions is shown in Fig. 3. The first region known as the low power region, the power amplifier operates in the class of operation chosen for the main amplifier (in this work Class-B with short circuit harmonics). In this stage, there is not enough input power to turn on the auxiliary PA, which typically is biased in Class C condition. The requirement for this region is to maximize the efficiency by finding the optimum impedance whereby maximum voltage swing can be achieved at back-off [6]. In such a way, when the input power increases, the output power and efficiency increases at twice the normal growth rate.

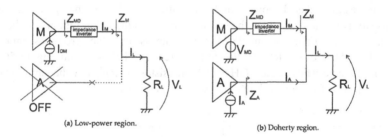

(a) Low-power region.   (b) Doherty region.

Fig. 3. Simplified equivalent output section of a Doherty Power Amplifier (DPA).

The second region is known as the Doherty power region, when the Main device drain voltage reaches its maximum swing at the desired back-off point, and cannot be increased any further; the Auxiliary amplifier is conducting current into the output load, as can be seen in Fig. 3. Since the Main PA preserves a constant output, voltage with increasing output current, the perceived impedance decreases towards the value of the characteristic impedance due to the quarter-wave impedance transformer [6]. The Main PA now acts as a controlled voltage source, operating at peak efficiency and delivers an increasing amount of power, while the Auxiliary device acts as a controlled current source where increasing the current and voltage swings, in proportion to the input voltage, leads to a reduction in the output impedance. At the end, for the peak envelope value, both devices achieve their saturation and observe an optimum resistance equal to the characteristic impedance of quarter-wave line.

Figure 4 shows the ideal behavior of the Main and Auxiliary PA efficiency. For the low power region, the efficiency of a Doherty amplifier is very similar to the efficiency of Class-B amplifier, however, it reaches the maximum value at the back-off point as a result of using twice the optimum load value. At the Doherty region, the efficiency of the Main device remains constant, due to the constant level of saturation, while the efficiency of the Auxiliary device starts to increase. The Doherty architecture is capable of providing the same maximum efficiency over the 6 dB power range.

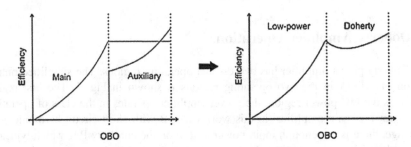

Fig. 4. Class-B/C Doherty power amplifier efficiency.

3   Design of Doherty Power Amplifier

In order to design a class B power amplifier as the Main device, the operating point of the transistor is located exactly at the boundary between the cutoff region and the active region (at −3.1 V) at the gate and 28 V at the drain, is set at the zero quiescent current so it conducts 50% of the RF and the drain current is a half-sinusoid. Figure 5(a) and (b) are the characteristics of the CGH40010F transistor, which show the variation of the drain current as a function of VDS and VGS respectively.

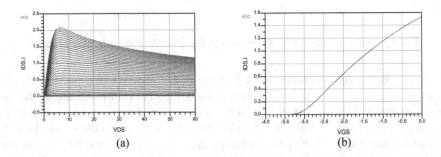

Fig. 5. (a) Plot of IDS vs VDS curvatures for different values of VGS and (b) Plot of IDS vs VGS for VDS = 28 V (The datasheet recommend 28 V at the drain.)

To find the optimal output impedances of the transistor operating in the linear region, the load pull simulation is performed using the non-linear model of the transistor. An optimum impedance for maximum efficiency at the low power region for the main branch, and the optimum impedance for maximum power on the high power regime for both the main and peaking in the DPA must be selected. In order to determine the optimum load that device should see, the efficiency and output power in operating frequency are tracked through varying load impedances and proper impedances deliver maximum efficiency and maximum power should be selected.

In Fig. 6, the single load impedance in the center point of the PAE contours that gives the maximum efficiency of 68.27% - is selected for the output matching network. The output matching network imposes an optimum load for the fundamental frequency, and zero to second and third harmonics in class B (class B exploits the harmonics to increase efficiency). In order to minimize the signal reflection at the input of power amplifier, the input impedance of the PA should be matched with the characteristic impedance of the input source. The input matching circuits implements the conjugate matching between complex impedance of the power amplifier and the signal source impedance.

indep(PAE_contours_p) (0.000 to 17.000)
indep(Pdel_contours_p) (0.000 to 19.000)

Fig. 6. Load-Pull contours at 3.8 GHz (Blue - Power output; Red - PAE). (Color figure online)

As shown in Fig. 7, the output matching network of the DPA is composed by offset transmission lines with characteristic impedance of 50 Ω, connected after the matching circuits of the carrier and peaking amplifiers. The peaking transistor should be able to deliver sufficient output power to ensure proper load modulation for the main amplifier; therefore, an uneven power divider is designed and optimized in order to provide more power to the peaking amplifier than to the carrier PA from the source. The asymmetric powers are combined by the Doherty operation through a quarter-wave impedance converter. Consequently, a second quarter-wave transmission line should be added at the input of the Auxiliary PA to properly compensate the phase shifting introduced by the output λ/4 transformer.

3.1   Offset Line

The offset lines are very important components following the Main and Auxiliary amplifiers for proper load modulation. As shown in Fig. 8, in the low-power region, the load impedance seen by the Main amplifier become double and the output matching network of the main PA is designed to match the optimum impedance determined in

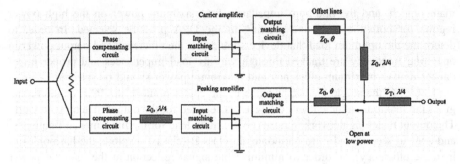

Fig. 7. Two-way Doherty amplifier block diagram

load pull for maximum efficiency and $2Z_{opt}$ to maximize the efficiency and gain; whilst at the output of the peaking amplifier, the offset line is adjusted to high impedance, as close as possible to an open circuit to prevent power leakage to the Main amplifier. The offset lines do not affect the overall matching condition and load modulation [7]. In the high power region, the main and peak currents sum in-phase and decreases. The load impedance of the carrier amplifier varies from $2Z_{opt}$ to Z_{opt}, and the peaking amplifier during the load modulation operation varies from infinite to Z_{opt}. The efficiency of the Doherty amplifier at the maximum input voltage is equal to the maximum efficiency of the amplifiers.

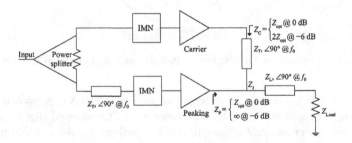

Fig. 8. Load-network schematic for each amplifier at the low and high power regions.

3.2 Power Splitter Design

In order to obtain high efficiency, an uneven Wilkinson power divider presented in Fig. 9 that is applied at the input circuit of the Doherty PA. In this work, the ratio between the input power of the carrier amplifier and peaking amplifier is 2:1. In fact, the peaking amplifier should be approximately double-sized of main amplifier to receive more power. As can be seen in Fig. 9, that unequal-split Wilkinson divider consist of four transmission lines with characteristic impedances of Z0, joined at their outputs with a resistor [8], which is located between the pads at the outputs.

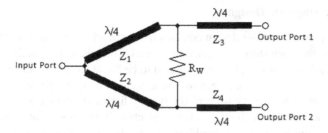

Fig. 9. Topology of unequal Wilkinson power splitter [9]

The asymmetrical input power splitting ensures a very good isolation between the main and peaking ports, and it also causes the saturation delay of the peaking amplifier to maintain high efficiency in the DPA over a wide dynamic range of the back-off power region. The amplifiers with uneven power drive show more efficient operation, with approximately 10–13% increase in ranges of drain efficiency and produce more power than even drive [10]. However, an uneven Doherty amplifier provides less linear gain in the low power region due to the smaller input power delivered to the main amplifier.

3.3   Output Combining Network Design

The Doherty output combining circuit consists of a quarter-wave transmission line with characteristic impedance of 50 Ω, which provides required phase delay and a quarter-wave transmission line of 35.35 Ω impedance that transforms the common load impedance to the final load impedance of 50 as shown in Fig. 10. In the low-power region, where the peak amplifier is turned off, the combining circuit acts as a 1:2 impedance transformer, providing the required load pulling for the main amplifier. In the case of the high power region, particularly at the maximum power point when the main and peak amplifiers deliver equal amounts of output power, the combining circuit functions as a 1:1 combiner.

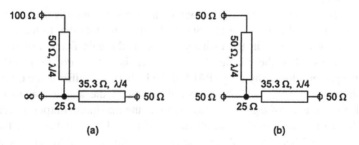

Fig. 10. Output combining network (a) in the low-power region and (b) at maximum power point where the output currents of the main and peaking amplifiers are combined [11].

3.4 Single Amplifier Design

The Class B power amplifier design contains bias networks, input-output AC matching networks, and the open stubs connected in parallel. The schematic simulation results in Fig. 11 indicate a small signal transducer gain to be flat at around 15 dB, and when the gain compression starts the gain decreases with increasing output power. The efficiency of the PA is an important measure of the battery life of the wireless transceivers. At 3.800 GHz the maximum drain efficiency of class B is 60.30% at input power of 35 dBm. This implies that the amplifier enters saturation after it reaches an output power of 40.58 dBm. The Power amplifier class B indicates a PAE of 54.71% at the output power of 40.12 dBm, and input power of 29 dBm.

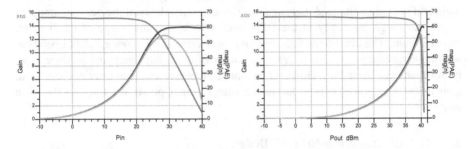

Fig. 11. Simulation results of gain, PAE and efficiency.

3.5 Doherty Amplifier Design

In the proposed design, the single designed class B amplifier is used as the main amplifier. Hence, to complete the Doherty design, a class C amplifier is necessary as a peak amplifier with a supply voltage of 28 V. In order to maintain maximum power transfer, matching circuits are designed at the input and the output of the transistor realized by micro-strip transmission lines as well as bias networks. The used substrate within this work is Rogers4350B substrate with dielectric constant $\varepsilon r = 3.66$ and thickness h = 0.762 mm.

The results of power sweep for harmonic balance simulation is shown in Fig. 12. When the input signal is working at 3.800 GHz, it shows that due to the class C bias state of the peak transistor in the Doherty amplifier, the gain flatness of the Doherty amplifier is worse than the Single class B, which is flat at around 12 dB. On the contrary the power-added efficiency (PAE) of the Doherty amplifier at the output power of 35 dBm point is 52.2%, 10.2% higher than that of the single amplifier and the power-added efficiency of the Doherty amplifier at the maximum output power reaches 60.42%. It clearly indicates that the efficiency of the DPA is higher than that of the class B power amplifier. This is due to the Doherty principle and the electrical lengths of the delay and impedance inverter transmission line previously mentioned.

Figure 13 shows the appropriate impedance transformations on a Smith chart to determine the offset line length of each amplifier.

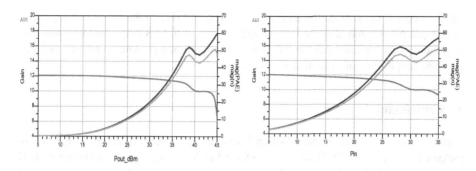

Fig. 12. Simulation results of Gain, PAE and efficiency.

Fig. 13. Impedance transformations on the Smith chart. Red curve: the main amplifier, blue curve: peaking amplifier. (Color figure online)

Figure 14 shows the main and auxiliary device RF current and voltage amplitudes over the whole power range. It is clear that the peaking amplifier dose not consume any current at the low power region. Their voltage and current are close to 0 until 6 dBm.

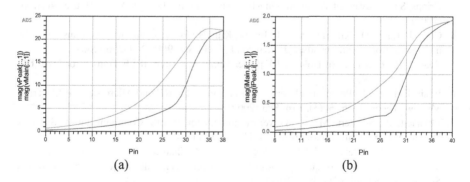

(a)   (b)

Fig. 14. (a) The output voltages of the carrier and the peaking amplifiers, (b) The output currents of the carrier and the peaking amplifiers.

For the upper 6 dB region, the peaking amplifier, and due to the Class-C bias, draws more input power, and also the current and voltage of the peaking amplifier increases very rapidly. At the maximum power point, the carrier and peaking amplifiers achieve the same amplitudes of current and voltage.

4   Conclusion

A class B power amplifier and a Doherty structure have been designed using a 10-W packaged GaN device (CGH40010) from Cree Inc. The single power amplifier class B is biased at threshold voltage. In order to drive the amplifier into the compression point, a 35 dBm of input power is required. At 3.800 GHz, the maximum drain efficiency of the PA is 60.30% at output power of 40.58 dBm. Also, the design procedure and final performance of a Doherty PA have been presented. The carrier amplifier and peaking amplifier were biased in Class-B and Class-C conditions, respectively, with a drain voltage of 28 V. In this design, the matching networks of the carrier and peaking amplifiers were designed to maximize the delivered power to the output. An offset line has been added at the output of the peaking amplifier in order to ensure the open circuit condition at the low power drive levels. This DPA attained an efficiency of 60.42% at 45.13 dBm output power. Thus, the DPA increases the power efficiency, especially at high power levels, in comparison with class B when they operate at their saturation level.

Acknowledgment. This work is supported by the European Union's Horizon 2020 Research and Innovation program under grant agreement H2020-MSCA-ITN-2016-SECRET-722424.

References

1. Franco, M.: Mobile handset power amplifier. IEEE Microw. Mag. **10**(7), 16–19 (2009)
2. Cripps, S.C.: RF Power Amplifier for Wireless Communications. Artech House, Norwood (1999)
3. Cripps, S.C.: Advanced Techniques in RF Power Amplifier Design. Artech House, Norwood (2002)
4. Choi, J., Kang, D., Kim, D., Park, J., Jin, B., Kim, B.: Power, amplifiers and transmitters for next generation mobile handset. J. Semicond. Tech. Sci. **9**(4), 249–256 (2009)
5. Raab, F.H.: Efficiency of Doherty RF power amplifier system. IEEE Trans. Broadcast. **BC-33**(3), 77–83 (1987)
6. Raab, F.H., et al.: Power amplifiers and transmitters for RF and Microwave. IEEE Trans. Microw. Theor. Tech. **50**(3), 814–826 (2002)
7. Reynaert, P., Steyaert, M.: RF Power Amplifiers for Mobile Communications. Springer, Dordrecht (2006). https://doi.org/10.1007/1-4020-5117-4
8. Hussaini, A.S., Elfergani, I.T.E., Rodriguez, J., Abd-Alhameed, R.A.: Efficient multi-stage load modulation radio frequency power amplifier for green radio frequency front end. IET Sci. Meas. Technol. **6**(3), 1–8 (2012)
9. Pozar, D.: Microwave Engineering, 4th edn. (2005)

10. Kim, B., Yang, Y., Yi, J., Nam, J., Woo, Y.Y., Cha, J.: Efficiency enhancement of linear power amplifier using load modulation technique. In: International Symposium on Microwave and Optical Technology Digest, pp. 505–508 (2001)
11. Hussaini, A.S., Abd-Alhameed, R., Rodriguez, J.: Design of energy efficient power amplifier for 4G user terminals. In: Seventeenth IEEE International Conference on Electronics, Circuits, and Systems (ICECS 2010), Athens, No. 533, pp. 617–620 (2010)

Improvement of Indoor Receive Signal Code Power (RSCP) and Signal-to-Interference Ratio (Ec/Io) and QoS Evaluation in Operational Wireless Network Using Distributed Antenna System (DAS)

Haru Alhassan[1,2], Raed Abdulhamid[1(✉)], Umar G. Danbatta[2],
Chidi Digwu[2], Ali Abdullah[1], Mohammed A. G. Al-Sadoon[1],
and Mohammad J. Ngala[3]

[1] Faculty of Engineering and Informatics, University of Bradford, Bradford, UK
harualhassan@yahoo.com, r.a.a.abd@bradford.ac.uk
[2] Nigerian Communications Commission, Abuja, Nigeria
[3] Heaton Education, Bradford, UK

Abstract. All Service Providers (SP) offering many services that needs to regularly measure the values of RSCP and Ec/Io. These two important Key Performance Indicators (KPIs) may assess their network performance and deliver Quality of Service (QoS) to meet both the end user perception and regulatory obligations. In this paper, a well-established real radio network performance evaluation is presented on the basis of Receive Signal Code Power (RSCP) and Signal-to-Interference Ratio (Ec/Io). The focus is to analyze live indoor network performance of the proposed network within the confines of Distributed Antenna Systems (DAS) irrespective of discussions and modelling in the literature. The Tests was carried out by TEMS Investigation, one of the most powerful tools for measuring the mobile wireless network Performance. Results and Analysis section summarizes findings and improvement on the two KPIs.

Keywords: 3G · WCDMA · CPICH · RSCP · RSSI · Ec/Io · QoS
BTS · NodeB · DAS · UE · CSSR · SDCCH

1 Introduction

The Wireless Mobile Technology, is aimed to provide and handling high throughput Internet and multimedia traffic. As example it is based on Wideband Code Division Multiple Access (WCDMA) radio platform for 3G and Orthogonal Frequency multiple Access (OFDM) for 4G and 5G. Generally speaking the Access Technology has sophisticated radio interface with great flexibility in carrying and multiplexing a large set of voice traffic and data services with constant as well as variable throughput ranging from low to very high data rates with efficient support for carrying IP traffic [1]. NodeB coverage is designed for multiple services with largely different bit rates and QoS requirements. This necessitates the need for traffic classification based on QoS

V. Sucasas et al. (Eds.): BROADNETS 2018, LNICST 263, pp. 466–472, 2019.
https://doi.org/10.1007/978-3-030-05195-2_46

targets for different types of services. A large set of features and well-designed radio link layer modes to ensure very high spectral efficiency in a very wide range of operating environments from large macro outdoor cells to indoor cells is incorporated in the current and future network standards.

RSCP denotes the receive power of the primary CPICH (Pilot channel) as measured by the User Equipment [2]. In the RF front systems a physical channel corresponds to a particular multiple accesses through spreading codes. RSCP can be measured in principle on downlink as well as on uplink; it is only defined for the downlink and thus presumed to be measured by the User Equipment (UE) and reported to NodeB through an uplink channel. RSCP is very important parameter in WCDMA and it serves as an indication of signal strength, a handover criterion, in downlink power control, and also helps to calculate path loss. The relationship between RSSI and RSCP is given in Eq. 1 below:

$$RSSI[dBm] = RSCP[dBm] - \frac{Ec}{Io}[dB] \qquad (1)$$

Where, RSSI is the Received Signal Strength Indicator and Ec/Io is the ratio of the received energy per chip (code bit) to the interference level in dB. Ec/Io is most important UE measurement for network planning purposes as it is the basic coverage indicator. In case no true interference (No) is present, the interference level (Io) is equal to the noise level. Ec/Io is also very important for handover decision. The value of Ec/Io varies such that if the value starts to get too low, the user start to have dropped calls, or cannot connect to the network. The value of network Ec/Io of −10 dB to −9 dB is considered to be good by network engineers.

2 Distributed Antenna System (DAS)

Providing uniformly very good Quality of Service (QoS) in a cellular system is challenging due to fading, path loss, and interferences [3]. One of the solution to this problem is to deploy a Distributed Antenna Systems (DAS) where the transmission points are distributed throughout the indoor environment following some type of network topology. The antennas may be connected directly to a nearby BTS or the signal from the BTS may be received off the air. The antennas are networked in the indoor environment using coaxial cable or Optic fiber Cable. DAS are wireless communications architecture where multiple transmission and reception points are connected to single processing unit normally called an equipment hotel. The antennas are spatially distributed in the indoor environment where the QoS improvement is expected as shown in Fig. 1 below.

The distributed antennas are connected to a home base station or equipment hotel using a high bandwidth low latency dedicated connection for distributing the signal to the splitters and then to individual antennas.

In future DAS is expected to dominate the indoor solutions due to the fact that DAS solution is inexpensive and easy to deploy as compared to competing technologies like Femtocells and Picocells [4]. DAS do not use wireless spectrum for transmission between the remote antenna and BTS. Compared to femtocells [5], the distributed

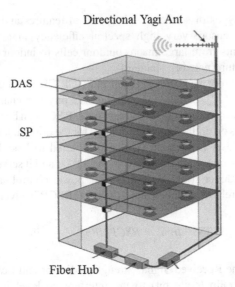

Fig. 1. Indoor DAS system topology

antenna are fully coordinated by a central processing unit normally connected in the site by the operator. Femtocells are a promising solution for improving coverage in residential areas where normally a Drive Test conducted by the Service Provider indicated very low RSSI or dead RF signal zones which resulted in drops calls and call blocking to be very high.

DAS are large scale solution for an entire building and public places while consumers can purchase Femtocells based on their requirements. DAS are also deployed targeting coverage first and then capacity as compared to Service Provider deployed Picocells that are hot spots targeting capacity improvement.

3   Test Configuration

The test was conducted in a sixteen floor Commercial Tower building where the traffic is very high during the normal working hours.

The Distributed Antenna Systems were networked using a network topology as shown in Fig. 1. The Distributed Antennas were installed in the ceiling of the building indoor, and connected using coaxial cable to a NodeB site on the rooftop of the tower building through splitters as shown in Figs. 2 and 3.

RF Measurements were conducted for the RSCP and Ec/Io in the building before and after the DASs installation. The RF measurement was done using TEMS (Test Mobile System) Investigation. The measurement platform is as shown in Fig. 4. TEMS is one of the state of art mobile testing solution that is universally used by telecoms operators to measure, analyze and optimize their mobile networks. It is considered as the basic tool to perform wireless network drive testing, benchmarking, monitoring and analysis. The TEMS Products business was divested to Ascom, Switzerland, on June 2, 2009 [6].

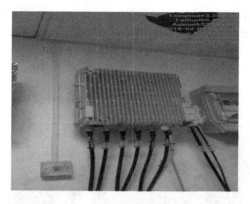

Fig. 2. Splitter connected to DASs and NodeB site on Tower Roof using coax cable.

Fig. 3. DASs installed in the ceiling of the building indoors connected to the splitter.

Fig. 4. Measurement Platform set-up.

Several locations were tested indoor for the RSCP and Ec/Io during the measurement. The tests were conducted before and after DAS installation in the building for comparison. The RF output plots for the Pre- and Post-DAS installation for the RSCP and Ec/Io are shown in Figs. 5(a), (b) and 6(a), (b).

(a)   **(b)**

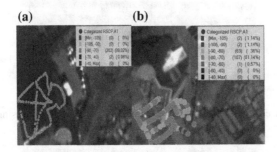

Fig. 5. RSCP RF Plot for Pre-DAS (a) and Post-DAS (b).

(a)   **(b)**

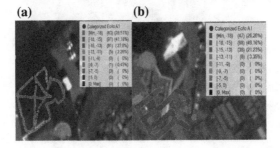

Fig. 6. Ec/Io RF Plot for Pre-DAS (a) and Post-DAS (b).

4   Result and Analysis

1. Call Setup Success Rate (CSSR)

Figure 7 shows the chart for Pre- and Post DAS Call Setup Success Rate (CSSR) for the network. The CSSR is the measure of blocking probability of a network. The lower the CSSR value the higher the blocking probability and vice versa. CSSR is the number of successful seizure of SDCCH channel by the total number of requests for seizure of the channel [7]. It can be seen that the Post-DAS measurement is much better as high as 98% as against Pre-DAS which was 40%.

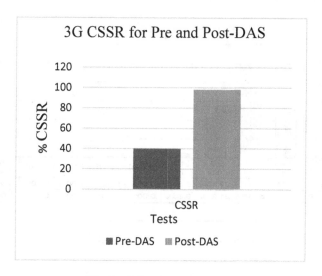

Fig. 7. Call setup success rate

2. Receive Signal Code Power (RSCP)

Figure 8 shows the chart for the RSCP. It can be seen that out of the total number of RF samples measured for the Pre-DAS case, 99.02% of the RF samples were greater than −90 dBm while 99.71% for the Post-DAS case. This indicated that Post-DAS RSCP is better.

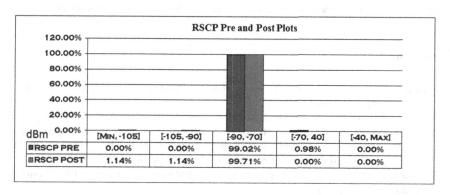

dBm	[MIN, -105]	[-105, -90]	[-90, -70]	[-70, 40]	[-40, MAX]
RSCP PRE	0.00%	0.00%	99.02%	0.98%	0.00%
RSCP POST	1.14%	1.14%	99.71%	0.00%	0.00%

Fig. 8. RSCP chart for Pre and Post DAS

3. Signal-to-Interference Ratio (Ec/Io)

Figure 9 shows the Ec/Io chart in dB. It can be seen that the plot area between -15 dB to Max, the % of the post-DAS RF samples is higher by 2.7%, that is, (49.16% + 21.23 + 3.35 = 73.74% to 41.18 + 27.60 + 2.26 = 71.04%).

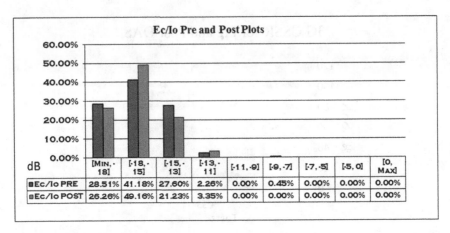

Fig. 9. Ec/Io chart for Pre and Post DAS

5   Conclusion

Practical deployment/ demonstration has proved that Distributed Antenna System is a promising technology for improving indoor coverage and capacity in 3G mobile wireless technology. Installation of DAS in high traffic areas like hotels, malls, railways, public buildings can improve QoS by minimizing call blocking probability and Bit Error Rate (BER). The study shows how DAS can improve both RSCP and Ec/Io which are two important Key Performance Indicators in delivering quality services that leads to better user Quality of Experience (QoE). Further study is needed to investigate effect of interference when multiple DASs are installed in a particular location.

References

1. Laiho, J., Wacker, A., Novosad, T.: Radio Network Planning and Optimization for UMTS, pp. 1–3. Wiley, Chichester (2002)
2. Larroca Solutions. https://www.laroccasolutions.com/141-rscp-rssi/. Accessed 10 July 2018
3. Heath, R., Peters, S., Wang, Y., Zhang, J.: A current perspective on distributed antenna system for the downlink of cellular system. IEEE Commun. Mag. 51(4), 161–167 (2013)
4. Pabst, R.: Relay-based deployment concept. IEEE Commun. Mag. 42(9), 80–89 (2004)
5. Chandrasekar, V., Andrews, J., Gatherer, A.: Femtocell networks: a survey. IEEE Commun. Mag. 46(9), 59–67 (2008)
6. Wikipedia. www.wikipedia.org. Accessed 15 July 2018
7. Kumar, V.S.P., Anuradha, D.B., Vivek, N.: Improvement of key performance indicators and QoS evaluation in operational GSM network. Int. J. Eng. 1(3), 411–417 (2002)

Author Index

Printed in the United States
By Bookmasters